THE POLITICS OF ENERGY DEPENDENCY

Ukraine, Belarus, and Lithuania between Domestic
Oligarchs and Russian Pressure

Studies in Comparative Political Economy and Public Policy

Editors: MICHAEL HOWLETT, DAVID LAYCOCK (Simon Fraser University), and STEPHEN MCBRIDE (McMaster University)

Studies in Comparative Political Economy and Public Policy is designed to showcase innovative approaches to political economy and public policy from a comparative perspective. While originating in Canada, the series will provide attractive offerings to a wide international audience, featuring studies with local, subnational, cross-national, and international empirical bases and theoretical frameworks.

Editorial Advisory Board

For a list of books published in the series, see page 445.

MARGARITA M. BALMACEDA

The Politics of Energy Dependency

Ukraine, Belarus, and Lithuania between Domestic Oligarchs and Russian Pressure

UNIVERSITY OF TORONTO PRESS
Toronto Buffalo London

ISBN 978-1-4426-4533-2

Printed on acid-free, 100% post-consumer recycled paper with vegetable-based inks.

Library and Archives Canada Cataloguing in Publication

Balmaceda, Margarita Mercedes, 1965–, author
The politics of energy dependency : Ukraine, Belarus, and Lithuania
between domestic oligarchs and Russian pressure /
Margarita M. Balmaceda.

(Studies in comparative political economy and public policy)
Includes bibliographical references and index.
ISBN 978-1-4426-4533-2 (bound)

1. Energy policy – Ukraine.   2. Energy policy – Belarus.   3. Energy
policy – Lithuania.   4. Energy policy – Russia (Federation).   I. Title.
II. Series: Studies in comparative political economy and public policy

HD9502.E832B34 2013   333.790947   C2013-903491-9

 This publication was made possible by the financial support of the
Shevchenko Scientific Society, USA, from the Natalia Danylchenko
Fund.

 Canada Council   Conseil des Arts
for the Arts   du Canada

University of Toronto Press acknowledges the financial assistance to its
publishing program of the Canada Council for the Arts and the Ontario
Arts Council.

University of Toronto Press acknowledges the financial support of the Government of Canada through the Canada Book Fund for its publishing activities.

Contents

Acknowledgments

"Following the pipeline" – that is, following the complex web of inter-connections that accompany the energy relationship between Russian producers, post-Soviet transit states, and European consumers – has taken me to many more places than I ever imagined possible. And, indeed, the successful completion of this project would have been impossible without the generous help of many colleagues and institutions in the United States, Germany, Finland, Belarus, Lithuania, Ukraine, and Russia.

In am privileged to enjoy the longstanding support of two home academic communities in the United States. The support and trust of the School of Diplomacy and International Relations at Seton Hall University has given me the long-term support and time horizon without which a project of this magnitude would have been impossible to accomplish. I thank Dean John Menzies, Associate Dean Courtney Smith, and Chair Assefaw Bariagaber for believing I would indeed return after each research trip, and my students for giving me a great reason to do so. Both award-winning researchers in international relations and refugee issues, respectively, Professors Smith and Bariagaber have sacrificed much of their research time in the last years in order to support the growth of our School and its faculty, and their efforts are highly appreciated. School secretary Susan Malcolm solved or soothed every hurdle, kept things operating smoothly, and is crucial to each of our teaching and research successes.

At Harvard, the Davis Center for Russian and Eurasian Studies and the Ukrainian Research Institute have been central to my work, and I thank their directors Timothy Colton, Terry Martin (Davis Center), Roman Szporluk, and Michael Flier (HURI) for their warm welcome throughout my years as Associate at both institutes. Lubomyr Hajda of HURI and Lisbeth Tarlow of the Davis Center deserve special thanks for their friendship, long-term support, and crucial advice at critical moments. From my arrival at HURI as a young post-doc in 1996, to this day, Lubomyr Hajda has been a constant source of advice and practical help in my academic work. That my case is far from an exception is testimony to his great contribution to new generations of scholars in post-Soviet, Ukrainian, and East European studies.

The participants of the Workshop on Post-Communist Politics and Economics at the Davis Center, and, in particular, Oxana Shevel, Dmitry Goremburg, Jerry Easter, Martin Dimitrov, Peter Rutland, Benjamin Smith, and Ivan Katchanovsky provided insightful comments on several papers related to this book project. Halyna Hryn provided crucial advice and insights from her own experience as scholar and editor of *Harvard Ukrainian Studies*, and, most importantly, the help and hand-holding of a friend at critical moments in the preparation of the manuscript. I thank Scott Walker, Digital Carthographer at the Harvard Map Collection, for his generous work creating the maps for this book, and Mary Ann Szporluk, Vytautas Kuokstis, and Marika Whaley for key proofreading, transliteration, and design advice.

The International Research and Exchanges Board (under Title VIII funding from the US Department of State), the Fulbright-Hays program of the US Department of Education, and the Title VIII Combined Research and Language Training Program, administered by the American Councils for International Education, provided crucial support for field research in Ukraine. The opinions expressed herein are the author's own and do not necessarily express the views of any of the funding organizations. The Ukrainian Center for Economic and Political Studies (Razumkov Center) in Kyiv, where I spent nine months of field research, deserves special recognition. In Kyiv, Volodymyr Dubrovs'kyi, Volodymyr Kulyk, Volodymyr Saprykin, and Olena Viter provided invaluable help and enlightening discussions. I am especially indebted to Volodymyr Saprykin, former Director of the Razumkov Center's Energy Program, who offered very insightful advice throughout my work in Kyiv, and read and commented on a previous version of the Ukrainian case study.

Field research in Lithuania was made possible by the generous support of the Alexander von Humboldt Foundation and the hospitality of the Institute of International Relations and Political Science (TSPMI), and in particular Inga Vinogranaite and Raimundas Lopata, to which I am greatly indebted. I thank Tomas Klepšys for research assistance and

Gediminas Vitkus for important insights. I am especially grateful to Vidmantas Jankauskas, former Chairman of the National Control Commission for Prices and Energy, Vaclovas Miškinis, head of Energy Systems Research at the Lithuanian Energy Institute, and Tomas Janeliūnas of the Lithuanian Foreign Policy Review for their detailed comments on a previous version of the Lithuanian case study.

Visits to Belarus were supported, among others, by the Fulbright Foundation, the German Belarusian Society, and Seton Hall University. I am indebted to my Belarusian colleagues for countless interesting discussions, and to Minsk's Internationale Bildungs- und Begegnungsstätte "Johannes Rau" (IBB) and its director (2006–2011), Astrid Sahm, for their warm welcome over the years, and for being the center of countless discussions reflected in this book. I am especially indebted to Leonid Zlotnikov, whose own work on Belarusian economics – as well as our memorable discussions – has not failed to inspire me, and who read and commented in great detail on a draft of the Belarusian case study. From the pages of *Belorusy i Rynok,* Tatsyana Manenok never ceased to fuel my interest, and greatly helped me gain a more nuanced understanding of Belarusian energy issues.

Work in Russia was made possible by a grant from the International Research and Exchanges Board (IREX), and by the generous welcome of the Carnegie Center Moscow and the Russian Academy of Sciences. Nina Poussenkova of IMEMO provided invaluable insights on the Russian case.

The actual writing of this book was made possible by a Humboldt Fellowship at Giessen University in Germany (where Kirsten Westphal excelled as my host), a Shklar Fellowship at the Harvard Ukrainian Research Institute, and a sabbatical stay at the Aleksanteri Institute at the University of Helsinki. Crucial work was made possible by a Marie Curie Fellowship from the European Commission also at Aleksanteri; I am especially indebted to Anna Korhonen for countless hours of work devoted to making this fellowship a reality, and to Anna-Maria Salmi, Markku Kivinen, Pami Aalto, Mikko Palonkorpi, and the Eurasian Energy Group for making my stay a productive and interesting one. Gulsana Koomanova and Inka Leppänen provided valuable technical assistance. A Senior Fellowship at the Alfried Krupp Wissenschaftskolleg in Greifswald, Germany offered an inspiring environment for completing the manuscript, a location made especially poignant by the inauguration of the Nord Stream pipeline from Russia to Greifswald two days after my arrival in October 2011.

I am also indebted to the many research centers which gave me the opportunity to present parts of this research, and where I received invaluable comments. Among them, the Slavic Research Center at Hokkaido University, the Stiftung Wissenschaft und Politik and the German Foreign Policy Association in Berlin, the Aleksanteri Institute at the University of Helsinki, the University of Toronto, the University of Ottawa's Danyliw Seminar, and Mannheim and Giessen Universities in Germany, deserve special recognition. Michael Bradshaw, Ulrich Best, Sabine Fischer, Andreas Heinrich, Juliet Johnson, Valery Kryukov, Vitaly Merkushev, Arild Moe, László Póti, Heiko Pleines, Andrzej Szeptycki, Lucan Way, as well as many other commentators, provided crucial insights and advice on various versions of the individual chapters. I am also indebted to Stacy Closson of the Patterson School of Diplomacy and International Commerce at the University of Kentucky, who kindly agreed to read and comment on the whole manuscript under a tight schedule, and whose own work on another energy-poor state, Georgia, has provided invaluable insights. Daniel Quinlan, editor at the University of Toronto Press, deserves my heartfelt thanks for the highest level of professionalism and helpfulness he exhibited at all stages of our interaction on this book. The comments from two anonymous reviewers were crucial to sharpening the argument of the book and furthering the connections with broader issues of economic reform in transition conditions. Publication support from the Natalia Danylchenko Fund of the Shevchenko Scientific Society is gratefully acknowledged.

My family and loved ones kept me grounded and belonging no matter how far and wide research for this project took me. I thank my parents, Eudoro Balmaceda and Margarita Sastre de Balmaceda, for their steadfast support. Marianne Sághy accompanied and energized my work from multiple locations in the world. Maren Jochimsen was relentless in her hands-on help, encouragement, and demand that I stay on track. She has been a constant source of support and practical advice and, from her own field of work in gender studies, constantly challenged me to rethink my assumptions about the relationship between structures, actors, and culture – and reminded me never to forget how fortunate I am for being able to go on the journey of which this book is but a small keepsake. These loved ones are both the basis and the reason for my hard work on this book.

A Note on Sources, Translations, and Transliteration

Energy research in the former USSR presents serious data and statistical challenges. In particular, preparing time series and comparative tables is not an easy endeavour – most Ukrainian and Belarusian publications give only current snapshot information, while international sources (the most exhaustive being the International Energy Agency (IEA), World Bank, and US Department of Energy) often use different base years, employ different measuring units, and most often have a three-year delay. While conversions to common units have been carefully performed, there is a small margin of error possible, as some of the original units may have been themselves arrived at through conversion from other measuring units. Mapping the development of gas prices presents unique challenges, as price data, often considered a commercial secret, needs to be cobbled from a variety of sources. For coherence and comparability purposes, international (mainly IEA) sources have been used whenever possible. However, IEA data, itself derived from local data, is not immune to the above problems and may not be fully coherent from one IEA publication or table to another.

Although every effort has been made to provide current URL's for electronic materials cited, the nature of the media environment in the countries covered by this book presents unique challenges. This is especially so in the case of Belarus, where censorship and other repressive measures often force media outlets to frequently change websites. In cases where the sites are no longer active, the URL for the original site is provided, as well as the original access date.

Transliteration of Russian-, Ukrainian-, and Belarusian-language materials was done using a simplified US Library of Congress transliteration system. For the few words for which there is a standard English-language usage (such as Yeltsyn and Chernobyl), this has been used instead. As personal names are spelled differently in Russian, Ukrainian, and Belarusian, for authors cited whose names appear in both Ukrainian and Russian, or Belarusian and Russian, in the book, after the first use of the name, any other name associated with that person is added in parenthesis. Unless otherwise noted, all translations from Lithuanian are by Tomas Klepšys, and all translations from Russian, Ukrainian, Belarusian, and German are by the author.

Abbreviations

b	billion
bbl/d	barrels per day
bcm	billion cubic meters (gas)
BLR	Belarusian rubles
m	million
Mt	million tons (oil)
tcm	thousand cubic meters (gas)
toe	tons of oil equivalent
US$	US dollars (in Tables)
$	US dollars (in main text)

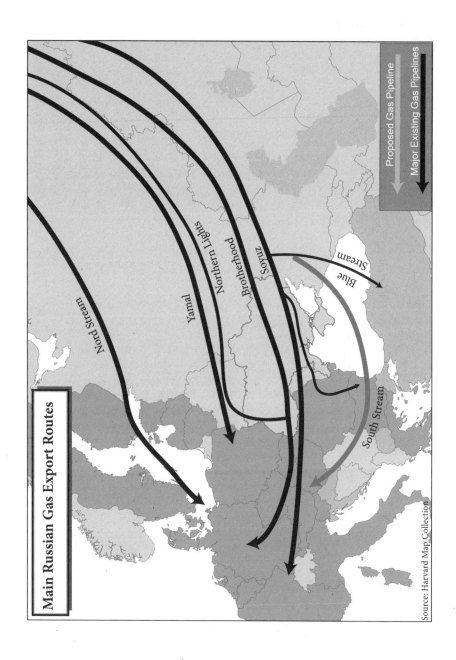

Main Russian Gas Export Routes

Nord Stream

Yamal

Northern Lights

Brotherhood

Soyuz

Blue Stream

South Stream

Proposed Gas Pipeline

Major Existing Gas Pipelines

Source: Harvard Map Collection

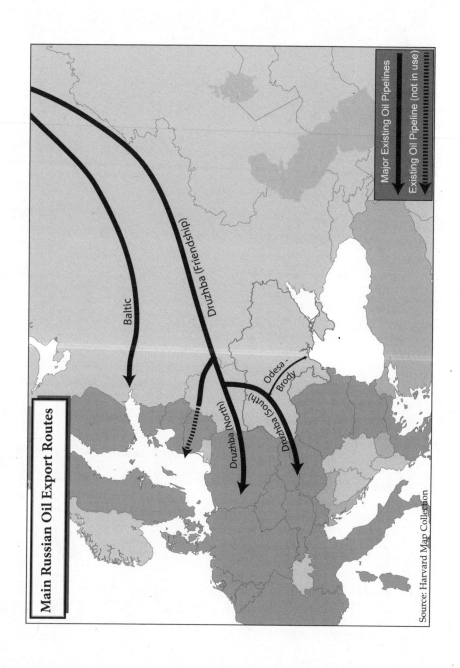

Main Russian Oil Export Routes

Baltic

Druzhba (Friendship)

Druzhba (North)

Druzhba (South)

Odesa - Brody

Major Existing Oil Pipelines

Existing Oil Pipeline (not in use)

Source: Harvard Map Collection

PART ONE

Larger Influencing Factors

1 Introduction: Domestic Politics and the Management of Energy Dependency in the Former Soviet Union

How is national interest developed under conditions of political transition, how does it affect policy, and how is it constructed politically? This book looks at these questions through the prism of three post-Soviet states' responses to one of the most central policy challenges facing them during the first two decades of their independent statehood: how to deal with their overwhelming energy dependency on Russia. As this book goes to press in 2013, the unconventional gas revolution and the expected increase in non-Russian gas supplies holds open the promise of a future free of energy dependency on Russia. As we ponder this hope, we should not lose sight of the social and political factors that helped shape energy policy in the first twenty years of the former Soviet states' independent statehood. In the final analysis, the ability of the shale gas technological breakthrough to live up to its promise will depended on these conditions even more than on technological advances. To understand this bright promise as well as its dark shadows, we need to go back to 1991.

On achieving independence in 1991, Ukraine, Belarus, and Lithuania changed, virtually overnight, from constituents of a single energy-rich state to separate energy-poor entities heavily dependent on Russia and lacking strong national-level institutions to deal with their new energy challenges. They also became politically independent transit states. Energy ties that until then had been endogenous to the centralized Soviet system suddenly became crucial international relations issues. For each of these states, energy supply problems and energy dependency on Russia became crucial factors complicating post-independence statebuilding. In each of the three cases, these problems have been key in terms of effects on the economy, political instability, and relations with

Russia, the European Union (EU), and international financial institutions. In addition to multiple smaller crises, each of these countries had to deal with two main external energy shocks: the sudden transformation into an energy-dependent state following the Soviet dissolution and the sharply increased costs for Russian imports after 2006. In many ways, the story of their first two decades of independence has been the story of the transformation of their economies from reliance on virtually free energy during the Soviet period to (near) world prices in 2012.[1]

Yet the factual record up to the late 2000s reveals surprisingly modest attempts to overcome this dependency – in none of the cases did we see a clear-cut, proactive, and sustained attempt at diversification away from Russia during this period (see Table 1.1). Rather, the energy sector – although in different ways in each of the three cases – and energy dependency became a crucial feeding ground for domestic economic groups. In order to understand these dynamics, this book focuses on, among a number of other factors, rents of energy dependency – the significant windfall profits that, under some circumstances, can be made out of a situation of energy dependency by economic groups within a country. Thus the energy-poor states found themselves between powerful domestic economic actors ("oligarchs") and Russian power.

What domestic factors are enablers of specific types of dependency relationships? How have important energy-related groups affected post-independence political development? The goal of this book is not to develop a comprehensive theory explaining all policy making in post-Soviet states, but to show how an appreciation for domestic factors may help us understand the Former Soviet Union (FSU) states' management of one of their key dependencies on Russia – energy. Doing so can help us gain important insights into the role played by energy groups in these countries' own post-independence political development.

The ways these countries have responded to this dependency present two interesting puzzles.

The first has to do with their inability to take action against their overwhelming dependency on Russia. Why were these states largely unable to adopt policies to reduce their energy dependency on Russia and move towards energy diversification until the external price shock of 2007–2008?

The second concerns variation among the cases. While no state was able to radically reduce dependency on Russian energy, there were interesting variations in the states' responses to this dependency. Belarus did not make diversification an official goal until 2006. Ukraine and

Table 1.1 The Cases and Their Outcomes: An Overview, 1991–2013

Case	General features	Outcomes concerning levels of energy dependency on Russia	Outcomes concerning diversification
Ukraine	Subsidies and the easy accessibility of energy rents led to reduced interest by major actors on breaking energy dependency on Russia, at least until 2006.	Little change in levels of energy dependency on Russia until sharp price increases (2006) and recession (2008) led to reduced demand.	Some geographical diversification through imports. Key instances of post-2006 geographic diversification were based on limited contractual diversification, with all gas imports controlled by a single intermediary company.
Belarus	Little official discussion of national (separate from Russia) energy interests and few moves towards diversification until 2006. New energy rents accessed through the politicization of energy relations with Russia.	Little change in overall dependency. Some increased dependency on Russian gas.	As of 2009, no geographical diversification. Small purchases of Venezuelan oil starting mid-2010 after sharp deterioration of relations with Russia.
Lithuania	Early energy shock with little buffering from the state contributed to a significant decrease in energy consumption. However, energy dependency on Russia continued.	Energy consumption fell sharply 1991– 1993, reducing dependency on Russia as well. Dependency on Russian gas increased in the 2000s due to the EU-ordered closing of the Ignalina nuclear power plant (2004–2009).	No actual diversification until forced by Russia's 2006 suspension of oil supplies via Druzhba pipeline. However, there was a decrease in vulnerability, as dependency on Russian energy imports per unit of GDP diminished. Key attempts (2011 and on) to change contractual relationship with main supplier.

Lithuania, on the contrary, adopted an energy-diversification rhetoric, in both cases complicated by domestic dynamics. In Ukraine, energy policy was often used not for the pursuit of national-level energy goals, but for the distribution of rents among the main economic-political players. In Lithuania, whatever actual gains were made in reducing energy dependency were not so much the result of focused diversification policies, but of broader economic restructuring that resulted in a reduction in the energy intensity of its economy.

Transit policy outcomes also varied, ranging from frequent threats to transit security due to a lack of national-level control and elite scrambling for transit rents (Ukraine), to centralized control (Belarus). These are not simply domestic issues – to reach EU markets, oil and gas from Russia must transit through countries such as Ukraine and Belarus, whose unstable relationships with Russia have created risks for Europe's security of supply. As seen in the gas and oil transit wars between Ukraine and Russia (2006, 2009) and Belarus and Russia (2007), conflict between Russia and the transit states can mean energy supply havoc for energy importers in the EU. Russia's January 2007 stoppage of oil shipments via Belarus in the wake of a rent-sharing confrontation led to a three-day interruption of Russian supplies to Hungary, the Czech Republic, Slovakia, and parts of Germany. And in the winter of 2008–2009, a new energy war between Ukraine and Russia led, for the first time in memory, to a total stoppage of Russian gas supplies to several EU states. Despite the fact that Russian gas started to flow again after two weeks, continuing tensions in Russia's energy relationship with Ukraine and Belarus (where a new gas crisis was narrowly avoided in June 2010) tell us that energy trade issues in the region are much more complicated than we may have previously believed. Although we often designate post-Soviet transit states such as Ukraine as unstable countries, we lack detailed knowledge about the ways in which domestic political factors affect their energy policies and energy transit relationships with Russia. This book aims to look inside this black box by focusing on these until now understudied domestic elements.

A Common Dependency, Different Answers: Alternative Explanations

What explains differences in the energy policies of the energy-dependent post-Soviet states? Our current knowledge can only provide partial answers, if only because the question has received little explicit attention.

Despite the existence of a growing literature on energy issues in Russia,[2] Central Asia (CA), and the Caspian,[3] much less has been written on energy issues in the energy-dependent FSU states and on the role of energy in their relationships with Russia.[4] Even less has been written on the relationship between domestic and foreign energy interest groups in relations with Russia.[5] Recent research on Ukraine has started a debate on the role of domestic factors, especially corruption, in energy relations with Russia, but little has been done in terms of a comparative analysis of the question.[6]

Most problematically, most research on energy dependency in the former Soviet world has looked at the question from a Russian-centred perspective.[7] Almost without exception, the literature available is based on Russian (and Western) sources, neglecting local actors' narratives and insights on these crucial issues. Despite the growing policy attention paid to transit issues, in-depth analysis of domestic issues also remains largely absent from the literatures on energy geopolitics and energy security, as conceptions of energy security continue to focus mainly on security of production, prices, and physical availability of energy.[8]

Conventional Explanations: Russia's Energy Aggression

Much of the literature on post-Soviet energy issues has focused on Russia's new-found energy power and use of energy supplies as a soft power weapon in its relationship with energy-poor post-Soviet states to pursue certain foreign or commercial policy goals.[9] Yet this literature, seeing the energy-dependent states as mostly passive recipients of Russian designs, has largely written off the question of how to explain domestic responses to energy dependency. This conventional narrative is contradicted by the reality of differentiated responses to energy dependency on Russia, and of the crucial role of domestic energy policy-relevant behaviour. While Russia's use of energy for foreign policy goals is an undeniable reality, to look at the question solely in terms of Russia's expansion is only one part of the question.[10]

Economic Modelling and Contractual Approaches
to Post-Soviet Energy Relations

The most direct response to the conventional narrative on Russia's use of energy as a weapon comes from economic approaches, which argue for economic, not political, explanations of this relationship.

The story of Russia's relationship with its energy-poor neighbours is, indeed, an economic story, and economic approaches provide important clues for understanding it. Theories of monopoly supply, of transit monopoly versus supply monopoly (i.e., bilateral monopoly), and models of monopolistic pricing, monopsony, and bargaining provide important insights.[11] While most easily applied to Russian-Ukrainian gas relations as an example of a monopoly supplier (Russia) and a nearly monopolistic transit provider (Ukraine), in general terms such models can be used to understand energy, especially gas trade, between Russia and consumer states in the EU and FSU.[12] Similarly, it is possible to study post-Soviet energy relations (and, indirectly, the management of energy dependency) from the perspective of official relations and contracts between Russian gas and oil companies and those in the energy-poor states.[13] Such perspectives also help us place our cases in the larger perspective of energy-dependent transit states worldwide, and can help guard us against the temptation of considering them exceptionally unique.

However, economic and contractual approaches are not sufficient, in and of themselves, to explain energy policies in the post-Soviet area. There is a political reality above and beyond the economic story, players reacting to these realities and also shaping economic interactions through subjective interpretations of self-interested behaviour. Even if Russian energy policies vis-á-vis the FSU states would have been totally de-politicized, the legacies of the past would affect the way these policies are received and interpreted: throughout the post-Soviet world, energy issues remain highly politicized as foreign policy issues.[14] For the former Soviet states, energy is the most sensitive part of trade with Russia, and trade with Russia is not just trade: it is unavoidably perceived as politically significant trade with the former hegemon. The fact that some Russian politicians have at times openly called for the use of energy as a political weapon in Russia's relationships with various former republics has not contributed to creating a more trustful atmosphere. As a result, trade in this part of the world cannot be explained by profit motives only. These realities require us to go above and beyond an economic analysis and examine the political and even cultural context of their actions and reactions.

In addition, important agreements were at times not formalized on paper, but were made at the level of political agreements between leaders, or as agreements of principle; moreover, in some cases contracts changed so often as to perforce affect actors' expectations of their validity.[15] This relativizes the importance of contracts as a basis for analysis.

At a more theoretical level, how can energy dependency management policy choices in the energy-poor FSU states be explained? The dominance of the conventional explanation has been so strong, and research on the actual energy policies of these states so limited, that few explicitly developed alternative explanations to the variety of responses to energy dependency on Russia can be found in the literature. Thus, it may make sense to look for clues in the literature on broader aspects of policy choice in the post-Soviet states and beyond.[16] Realist, constructivist, public demand, international political economy, and resource-rent approaches can be used to answer the questions of policy choices – such as those related to dealing with energy dependency – with mixed results.

Realist Approaches

Another alternative approach can be found in realism-based explanations. While little specific work has been done in applying realist theory to analyse the energy policies of former Soviet states, some conclusions can be inferred from the larger literature.[17] Realist approaches see the state as the main decision-maker, emphasizing its role above that of domestic actors. Such approaches emphasize states choosing their trade policies on the basis of the strategic opportunities open to them (opportunities that are, in turn, based on the state's capabilities and existing international power configurations).[18] From this perspective, achieving and maintaining energy independence would be part of a state's desire to increase its power and maintain independence more generally. In terms of trade, this would mean that countries will try to "create conditions which make the interruption of trade of much graver concern to its trading partners than to itself."[19]

Yet realist explanations are insufficient to explain why various post-Soviet states have managed their energy dependencies differently. From a strict realist perspective, it should be assumed that the newly independent FSU states would want to increase their independence from Russia, and, thus, would seek to minimize their energy dependency on Russia at almost any cost. In reality, this has been the exception rather than the rule. Realist approaches cannot fully explain why it has been so difficult for these states to adopt policies leading to increased energy diversification, despite the obvious importance of doing so for geopolitical reasons. The reason a realist approach cannot explain these issues satisfactorily is because attention to domestic considerations is missing from this perspective.

Constructivist Approaches

Although not dealing specifically with energy policy, constructivist approaches provide another possible explanation. Looking at the dynamics of post-Soviet foreign trade (re)integration or lack thereof, constructivist-inspired authors have stressed the role of national identity (and its degree of contestation) in the making of foreign economic policy, and have argued that national identity issues have significantly affected the way post-Soviet states have developed economic and trade relations with Russia.[20] Applied to energy policy, the implication is that differences in energy policy can be ascribed to differences in cultural and foreign policy orientations, with those states that are more pro-Russian having a more pro-Russian (and, one could imply, less pro-diversification) energy policy, and those with a pro-Western foreign policy doing more to foster energy diversification. The three cases analysed in this book had different official foreign policy orientations, and, at first glance, it would be tempting to ascribe differences in energy policies to differences in foreign policy and even civilizational orientation. Yet a closer look at the evidence does not support such a view – in many ways the energy policies of officially wavering or anti-integration-leaning Ukraine were more pro-Russian than those of official Russian ally Belarus. (See chapters 4 and 5.) One reason why constructivist approaches cannot account for these outcomes is because they often overlook the real differences in economic interests existing within a single state.

In fact, a problem common to the Russian energy aggression, economic, realist, and constructivist approaches is the limited role played by domestic factors and interests in their analyses.

Public Demand Approaches

Public demand approaches offer a way to bring domestic factors into the analysis by looking at policy questions through the prism of public choices and electoral politics. Public demand theory poses that policies tend to reflect the wishes of the electorate as reflected in elections because, to remain in office, incumbent politicians need to adopt policies that appeal to a majority of voters.[21] Public demand approaches look at the effects of partisanship and electoral competition – including the need for policy differentiation between parties – on policy making, and are based on the premise that those linkages (between voters and politicians) should be based on policy accountability.

Some elements of this approach are appealing and useful. A key assumption of this approach, that domestic politicians have a degree of manoeuvrability and are not totally constrained by outside forces, helps us overcome some of the limits present in other approaches to post-Soviet energy policies. More broadly, this approach helps direct our attention to issues related to how electoral preferences and the voice of various political and social groups come – or not – to affect energy policies and to how differences in energy policy preferences may be used instrumentally by various domestic political groups.[22]

Corina Herron Linden's explanation of early post-Soviet energy policies as related to political enfranchisement and disenfranchisement falls into this general perspective.[23] She argues that Estonia, arguably the only post-Soviet state able to radically restructure away from energy dependency on Russia,[24] was able to do so because the main costs of this restructuring fell on those sectors of the population (the Russian-speaking population constituting the largest population group in energy-intensive industrial areas) that, being politically disenfranchised, could not do much to prevent it.[25] One weakness of this approach, however, is its focus on one disenfranchised population, the Russians in Estonia, at the expense of a focused analysis of the specific political and policy making mechanisms involved. Moreover, it fails to consider another essential difference between Estonia and the other cases: the fact that Estonia has significant alternative energy sources available (oil peat) that it could tap into as a means to diversify away from Russian imports.

More generally, an important limitation to public demand approaches as applied to energy dependency management policy has to do with the fact that while the benefits of energy trade policies are highly concentrated, their costs are usually "evenly spread over the entire population,"[26] making it more difficult for the entire population to mobilize (including in terms of electoral preferences) against this situation. This is especially true in situations where – as in the cases of post-Soviet Belarus and Ukraine – electoral politics were only one part of a broader game including important doses of administrative resources and direct political control by the executive, making an elections-centred approach not nuanced enough to capture the types of pressures converging on energy policy making in these states.

Zeroing-in on the Connections between External and Internal Factors: International Political Economy (IPE) and Resource-rent Approaches

If focusing mainly on the external side of the relationship is not sufficient to explain different responses to energy dependency, it is a good idea to look specifically at the connections between external and internal factors. IPE and resource-rent approaches have much to offer to help us understand these connections in the post-Soviet energy context.

INTERNATIONAL POLITICAL ECONOMY OF TRADE
POLICY MAKING APPROACHES

Ukraine, Belarus, and Lithuania, confronted upon independence with the serious external shock of their sudden transformation into energy-dependent states, provide a prime example of the central issue dealt with by the IPE literature: how states cope with changing external economic conditions. Much of this literature has focused on how various domestic economic sectors are affected differently by changes in the international economic environment.[27] In doing so, it has analysed how specific characteristics of various sectors mediate this influence, focusing on factors such as a sector's level of exposure to the international economy, intensity of demand for its products, its resource and labour-intensity, economies of scale, the specificity of its assets, and whether a sector (or concrete firm) is closer to the country's international comparative advantage. However, this literature has not focused on how various groups' functional position in the domestic system of interest articulation (and, thus, their ability to successfully push for policies beneficial to their own sectors) influences the way international changes will affect them. Thus, looking at how different *sectors* react to changes in the international economic environment is not enough. Looking at the nature of the political system/arrangements as a whole is essential for understanding various groups' abilities to successfully push for policies beneficial to their own interests in situations of external pressure.

RESOURCE-RENTS APPROACHES

The resource-rents literature, meanwhile, argues that energy-resource *abundance* (and the resulting rents abundance) weakens a state's ability to conduct a coherent economic policy. In its most general form, this literature argues that, as these rents make it possible for the state to access significant resources without needing to tax its population, it evolves from a production to an allocation state,[28] weakening crucial links with its citizens, governance, and the ability to formulate economic policy effectively.[29]

Taking this argument a step further, it could be assumed that the opposite – a situation of energy-resource *scarcity* – would lead to more effective policy making and, by extension, a more proactive management of energy dependency. Yet the evidence of our cases does not support these expectations: Ukraine, Belarus, and (to a lesser extent) Lithuania were not able to adjust swiftly to their changed position in the international energy economy in a long-term sustainable way.

However, insights from this literature, which explores the effects of resource rents, particularly oil-export rents, on political systems, can be crucial for understanding the way states have dealt with energy dependency. The focus on rents and their distribution is a crucial first step, allowing us to focus on the winners and losers of certain patterns of energy relations with the major suppliers, and on the role of (formal and informal) institutions and governance/rule of law (or lack thereof) in setting in motion certain patterns in this area.

This book makes two contributions to this literature:

First, whereas the literature has focused on external rents generated by energy exports,[30] the evidence from the energy-poor but often rent-rich post-Soviet states discussed in this book challenges us to reconceptualise the very meaning of resource rents. We seek to recast the issues posed by incorporating more explicitly a broader set of external and internal energy-related rents, including the spillover rents of energy export rents on transit states, and the rents gained from a situation of energy dependency by economic groups within a country. While this reassessment of resource rents fits well within a recent trend in the field differentiating various types of resources and their associated rents,[31] the question of internal versus external sources of rent has not been fully explored. The cases analysed in this book, where resource-related rents accrued not only from external sources (first and foremost Russian subsidies) but also from internal ones (from the privatization of energy dependency-related profits while losses were shifted to the state and the society as a whole), bring crucial new information to bear on this question.

Second, this book can contribute to a better understanding of the ways in which resource-related rents interact with domestic political institutions. Much of the early resource-rents literature assumed the direct impact of these rents on governance, suggesting that, in and of itself, an overabundance of external resource rents would lead to increased authoritarianism and poor governance. A new generation of writings has pointed out the need to look further than at the existence of rents itself, and focuses on the ways in which resources interact with domestic political structures and institutions to lead to various outcomes.[32] Through its focus on the impact of domestic political systems on energy policy making, this book makes an important contribution to this debate.

In doing so, we also engage the broader literature on the role of institutions in transition situations.[33] Here, not only are concrete formal institutions (such as foreign trade institutions and formal constitutional/ political arrangements) important, but also more informal institutions having to do with social norms shaping actors' preferences, expectations, and ways of doing business.[34] Such informal institutions may be especially crucial during periods of political transition.

Institutional settings interact with rents in a variety of ways. Institutions can buffer certain actors (or a country as a whole) from the impact of (worsened) external economic conditions (through sector-specific pricing policies, for example). Yet institutions can do even more: not just softening the blow received by some sectors due to worsened conditions, but, by creating additional opportunities for rent-seeking,[35] institutions can actually create situations where specific economic players can benefit from these worsened external conditions such as an increase in energy dependency. For example, institutions may help shift the cost of energy dependency to the state as a whole, while creating rent-seeking opportunities for private actors.[36] This may lead to a vicious circle: the lack of effective formal institutions creates incentives for the development of informal institutions (including corruption[37]), but these, once created, often undermine benefitted actors' demands for formal institutions, such as rule of law, and property rights.[38] Drawing on important insights from this approach, we further focus on the questions: What happens when formal market institutions, including well-developed property rights and corporate governance structures, are not present? What informal institutions, including corruption, may come to replace them in specific circumstances? How does this situation affect a state's management of an important dependency – such as energy dependency – on another state?

Hypotheses and Claims

What factors explain these policies and variety of responses to a similar policy challenge? This book makes two related claims: first, the nature of the political system matters in terms of how energy dependency is dealt with; and second, the way the gains and losses of that dependency are distributed will further affect the political system.

Claim One: Domestic Politics Matter

This book argues that the energy-poor former FSU states' lack of a proactive energy policy, as well as variation between the cases, is best explained by the nature of their political and interest-representation arrangements and their interaction with energy-related rent-seeking.[39] The central hypothesis is that the nature of the political system/ arrangements in various FSU countries will affect the management of energy dependency in general and, more concretely, the management of energy relations with the largest partner (Russia).[40] In other words, the way the system of interest intermediation in each country affects the connection between the interests of specific energy-related groups and actual state policy will be of central importance for the management of this dependency.

Despite their commonalities in other areas, the three cases differed clearly in the nature of their political and interest articulation systems, which, as will be discussed further on, ranged from a centralized system based on a personalistic near-dictatorship in Belarus, to a fragmented parliamentary system in Lithuania. (See Table 1.4.)

The causal pathway connecting these political systems with dependency-management outcomes starts with domestic institutions (both formal and informal) and how they deal with interest intermediation. This in turn affects the ability of domestic players to impose their preferences regarding the organization of energy trade with Russia, including preferences directly or indirectly affecting the continuation of energy dependency. The contents of these preferences have much to do with the distributional consequences of various ways of organizing energy trade and with the rents of energy dependency that may be accrued, which we discuss in detail further on.

The domestic political system can affect the management of energy dependency in a variety of ways, for example through the ways

Figure 1.1 Intervening Factors between Political Systems and Management of Energy Dependency

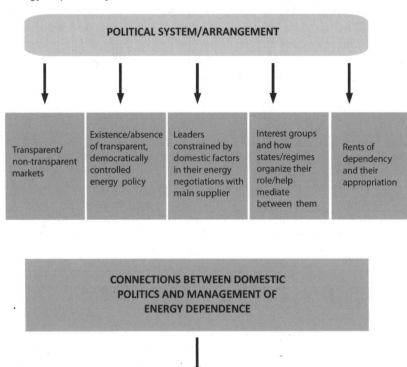

in which it affects (a) the transparency or nontransparency of energy markets; (b) the existence or absence of a transparent, democratically controlled energy policy; (c) leaders' negotiating space or ability vis-à-vis the main foreign partners; (d) the system of interest articulation; and, (e) access to and use of energy rents. These elements are discussed below.

Transparency. Whether the domestic system fosters transparency in energy trade will matter. Lack of transparency privileges certain types of trade (barter for example) that make it more difficult for accurate price signals to be sent to the market. Nontransparent systems also offer fertile ground for corruption and for the appropriation of significant rents at the expense of the state. Nontransparent systems will tend to cooperate with each other and actors benefiting from lack of transparency will also be less willing to work with actors requiring a higher level of transparency.

Democratically controlled energy policies. The management of energy dependency also has to do with the question of *where* are energy policy decisions made: in the open political realm, or in under-the-table deals between politicians and interest articulators?[41] Whether there is a democratically controlled energy policy will matter, as democratically controlled policies have more of a chance to represent national as opposed to particularistic interests. Moreover, only a democratic and generally accepted energy policy can survive contestation and has the chance to be followed de facto. This can have an important impact, as, given the high costs of following an energy diversification policy – compared to the status quo facilitated by the strength of Soviet legacies and of structural factors – such diversification only has a chance if it is part of a long-term, consequent, and generally accepted energy policy.

Leaders' negotiating space. Leaders with little legitimacy at home will have less strength to forcefully pursue the country's energy policies vis-à-vis external actors. At the same time, leaders with few allies in the West may be tempted to seek support from competing powers (Russia for example), restricting the country's policy making sovereignty on energy issues.

Patterns of interest articulation. Broader interest articulation patterns, as reflected in the energy sector, will affect whose groups' interests will gain the upper hand in the policy process and have the capacity to create mechanisms to produce artificial scarcities (discussed further on) that could be turned into corruption possibilities. These interest articulation patterns will also affect whether and to what extent certain groups will be able to benefit from the situation of dependency, privately appropriating related profits while shifting the costs to the state and society as a whole.

Patterns of dealing with rents of energy dependency. A crucial means through which the political system will affect energy policy making is through the distribution of the costs and benefits of energy dependency. Political arrangements will affect who are the winners and losers of certain patterns of energy relations with the main suppliers, which, in turn, will affect whether they will want to prolong this situation of dependency. Large energy-related rents may seem obvious in the case of energy-rich countries such as Russia but counter-intuitive in a situation of energy dependency. Yet, energy can be a very lucrative business for local actors in the dependent country itself (from profits made by intermediaries, to mark ups imposed on monopolized markets, to outright stealing from the state), especially in situations of widespread corruption. In a narrow sense, rents are defined here as profits received without the input of factors of production, in other words, profits received without the creation of value added.[42] For working purposes of this book, however, we adopt a broader definition, understanding as energy rents all energy-related profits.

What has been the relative significance of these rents? While we lack sufficient information to calculate accurately the size of the rents involved, it is possible to, on the basis of information from a variety of sources, gain a sense of the relative importance of various types of rents, to identify their sources of extraction and distribution and reincorporation pathways, the main types of actors benefitting from them,

---

POTENTIAL ENERGY RENT POOLS: SOME EXAMPLES

External

- Energy price differentials between domestic and market prices
- Hidden subsidies through tax and customs preferences
- Potential arbitrage gains to be made from price differentials between import, domestic, and export prices for energy
- Transit revenue
- Payments by external parties for use of gas storage facilities
- Customs and value-added revenue from oil refining and re-export schemes due to preferential tax and duties regimes
- Profits from advantageous barter arrangements

Internal

- Markups imposed on consumers in monopolized markets
- Stealing from the state through provision of unnecessary services that could be provided by state companies themselves
- Profits made by intermediary companies
- Profits from advantageous IOU (*zacheti*) arrangements

---

as well as the associated value-added chains and their effects on the management of energy dependency. On the basis of comparative data, it is also possible to make an estimate of the relative importance of energy-related income and possible rents pools in the three cases.

Calculating the value of such external and domestic rents presents serious methodological problems.[43] As the argument about rents made here concerns their general functioning and not their specific amounts, a detailed calculation of such rents is not necessary. Instead, using the broader term of "potential rent pools" makes sense in terms of conveying the magnitude of these potential rents in each of the cases. For illustration purposes, Table 1.2 presents a rough estimate of potential external rent pools in the gas sector between 2001 and 2006. This table does not intend to be an exhaustive approximation to the issue, as estimating price differentials is especially difficult in situations where, as in Ukraine 1995–2005, despite the existence of an official price, most gas was supplied in exchange (barter) for transit services. In addition, the table does not cover oil-related rents, an important source of external rents in the case of Belarus. Adding external oil rents, a significant element only in the Belarusian case, would only further increase Belarus' per capita pool of potential rent pools, already by far the highest of the three cases.

One useful way to look at the further impact of these rent pools is by focusing on the ways these rents are *extracted*, *distributed*, and *reincorporated* under different systems. Issues related to the *extraction* of rents of energy dependency concern the relative size of these (potential) rents, as well as their source. The *distribution* of energy rents has to do with the type of actors benefitting most actively from their accrual, and with the (formal or informal) mechanisms through which the distribution of these rents is regulated, including mechanisms involved in the transborder distribution (and sharing) of rents, in particular with Russian actors. Finally, looking at the *reincorporation* (or recycling) of these energy rents into the political system is crucial to understand which actors and political patterns are strengthened or weakened in each case.

THE CYCLE OF RENTS MODEL

The first element of the cycle of energy rents concerns their *sources of extraction*. Here the main issues concern the relative size of these (potential) rents, as well as their source (internal or external). External sources may include rents accrued through preferential prices received from the main supplier(s), through preferential tax and duties regimes

Table 1.2 Potential Rent Pools in the Gas Sector, 2001–2006, in US$

External	Ukraine	Belarus	Lithuania
Gas Transit fees	9.73 bn	1.25 bn	0.018 bn
Gas price differentials	20.09 bn	13.79 bn	0.937 bn
Total	29.82 bn	15.04 bn	0.955 bn
Population in 2005	47.1 m	9.8 m	3.4 m
Per-capita value of potential rent pools in the gas area	633	1534	280

Sources: Data for transit income: Belarus (Rakova 2010, 8), Lithuania (Janeliunas and Molis 2006, 22) Ukraine (Pirani 2007, Table 6.5, 83). Price differentials calculated on the basis of the difference between gas prices paid to Gazprom and European prices for 2001–2006. For ease of comparability, for European Prices we use the same prices used in Rakova (2010), which represent average yearly prices and thus differ slightly from prices in Table 1.6. Data for Ukraine from price data in Table 4.3 in this book and import volumes from Russia of assumed 23 billion cubic metres (bcm)/year for 2001–2005 (IEA 2006, 178) and 56.9 for 2006 (cocktail of Russian and CA gas) (Pirani 2007, 28). Data for Belarus from Rakova (2010). Prices for Lithuania calculated on the basis of, for 2001–2004, the average price of $102.25, noted in International Atomic Energy Agency (2004), 78, and the 2005–2006 prices noted in Table 1.6 in this chapter.

also affecting the export of refined products using imported crude oil, through preferential intracorporate arrangements, through transit revenue, and through the arbitrage gains able to be made from the differences between import, domestic, and export prices for energy.[44] By internal rents we mean those accrued mainly from domestic users or the state budget, for example through the shifting of energy losses to the state while appropriating the benefits privately (as when, for example, the state guarantees certain energy loans and ends up taking them over). Understanding the variety of forms these rents may take can help us gain a better understanding of the winners and losers of certain patterns of energy relations with the main suppliers (in our cases, Russia) and of their motivations for maintaining or challenging certain patters of energy dependency.

The sources from which and the means by which these rents are extracted will affect subsequent patterns of rent distribution. Whether internal or external sources of energy rents are being (mainly) accessed at one time or another matters, as it is directly related to the question of who will incur the profits and losses of certain trade and institutional

Figure 1.2 The Cycle of Energy Rents

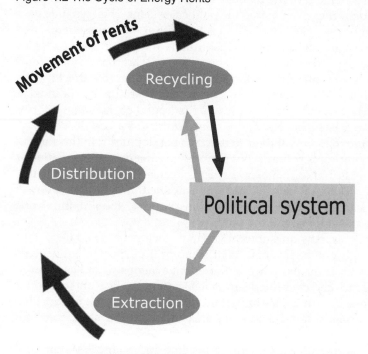

arrangements. In other words, are these profits being made from companies or the budget in the main supplying countries, or from sources within the energy-dependent state itself?

The second element of the model concerns the patterns of energy rents *distribution*. This concerns first and foremost who will accrue these rents. Are these mainly individuals or corporations, or the state budget as a whole? This also concerns the formal or informal mechanisms and institutions by which the distribution of these rents is regulated, including mechanisms involving the transborder distribution (and sharing) of rents, in particular with Russian actors. The transborder sharing of rents also has important implications for the management of energy trade and transit conflict, as in cases such as the Ukrainian-Russian relationship, where conflict often came to be solved through the transborder sharing of rents between elites – using new types of informal institutions such as intermediary companies – rather than through the use of formal governance institutions.[45]

The third element of the model concerns the *reincorporation* (or recycling) of these energy rents into the political system. This dynamic goes above and beyond the issue of *who* is benefitting from these rents, and into issues such as what kinds of institutions and patterns are strengthened or weakened as a result of specific actors' accrual of these rents (and interest in continuing to accrue them). How does this affect further institutional development? The partial-reform literature has pointed to the fact that it is often the winners of a first round of transition reforms that have a vested interest in freezing reforms at a certain point, allowing them to maintain their rent-access possibilities.[46] In this kind of situation, rent-seekers may want not only to safeguard their continued access to rents, but to create mechanisms to create and accrue rents that otherwise would not have existed, for example through the creation of artificial scarcities, embedded in "bad institutions" (Sonin), impacting the future development of the political system.[47]

On this basis, new questions arise: do the actors involved keep alive areas of high potential rents ("rent swamps") purposefully and consciously?[48] Or is the existence of these rent swamps what has allowed the emergence and continued survival of certain political and economic actors? This, in turn, raises important questions about the relationship between structures and actors, an area of long-standing concern for transition scholarship.

The reincorporation of energy rents into the political system also concerns the impact of these rents on incumbent popularity, elections, and on energy policy making. Various rent-seeking schemes associated with the energy sector can have and have had a direct effect on the post-Soviet states' management of their energy dependencies: how various groups will benefit from patterns of managing energy dependency will affect whether they will want to prolong their use, and, more generally, dependency on specific partners.

The way energy rents are reincorporated into the political system will affect not only elections and energy policy making, but also the development of the political system more broadly.

Claim Two: Who Benefits from Patterns of Energy Trade
Will Have Long-term Political Effects

The second major argument of the book is that the domestic distribution of gains and losses from energy relations with the largest suppliers (here, Russia) will, in turn, impact the further development of these states' political systems. This is especially so when the sudden influx of rents coincides with a crucial formative period when new formal and informal political institutions are being set up, such as, for our cases, the first post-independence years.[49] The book looks at this question by analysing the way in which energy rents are further recycled into the political process by helping to create specific political actors, strengthening others, and making resources available for elections and other political contests.

Research Design and Main Variables

Choice of Cases

We focus on three post-Soviet states highly dependent on Russian energy – Ukraine, Belarus, and Lithuania – and on the *management* of their energy dependency relationship with Russia in the period 1991–2013. Our three case studies were chosen from the larger universe of the six former Soviet states that are both energy dependent on Russia and play (or played for most of the period under study) an important role in the transit of Russian oil and gas to further markets: Belarus, Moldova, and Ukraine in the Western part of the former Soviet Union; Latvia and Lithuania in the Baltics; and Georgia in the Caucasus (see Table 1.3).[50] Within this larger grouping Belarus, Lithuania, and Ukraine were chosen because they share a number of important characteristics – largely similar Soviet energy and infrastructure legacies, high levels of energy dependency on Russia, and a role in the direct or indirect transit of Russian energy west; the shared feature of transit specifically to Western markets is important because it implies a similar value-added chain.[51] At the same time, they differ in terms of their domestic political arrangements.[52] We concentrate on oil and gas, as these are the two energy sources where the post-Soviet states are most dependent on Russia;[53] other energy sources, such as nuclear fuel imports, will be discussed as needed for the overall analysis.

The Energy-poor Transit States of the FSU as a Conceptual Category

Our three cases are all energy-dependent states playing a direct or indirect role in energy transit. What makes this grouping significant as a conceptual category is the way the combination between energy poverty and transit role potentiates the effects of each of these factors

Table 1.3 The Case Studies in the Context of Other Post-Soviet Energy-dependent Transit States, 1991–2013*

Case	Level of Energy Dependency on Russia	Orientation towards integration with Russia	Role in Transit of Russian Energy	Main Destination of Transit of Russian Energy	Domestic System
Ukraine	High	Ambiguous	High	WE (EU-15)	President-as-Balancer
Belarus	High	Ambiguous (officially positive)	High	WE (EU-15)	Centralized
Lithuania	High	Negative (EU member since 2004)	Medium	Kaliningrad WE (EU-15)	Fragmented
Latvia	High	Negative (EU member since 2004)	Low (Medium before 2004)	WE (EU-15)	Fragmented
Moldova	High	Ambiguous (Separatist region allied with Russia)	Medium	Bulgaria Romania	Fragmented
Georgia	Medium	Negative (Separatist regions allied with Russia)	Small	Armenia	President-as-Balancer

* Throughout most or all of the period under study

taken individually. Especially under the specific circumstances of the post-Soviet transition (discussed in chapter 2), this combination created a potentially explosive mixture, in turn affecting both rent-seeking opportunities and dependency relations.

Effects on rent-seeking. Energy transit creates special opportunities for rent-seeking that we do not see elsewhere. These opportunities are related to, first, the arbitrage gains able to be made from the price differentials between different markets and, second, to the possibility of accessing these arbitrage gains and other rents through multiple points in both the physical pipelines and value-added chains distinctive of transit states.

Effects on the management of energy dependency. The special combination of energy poverty and a significant transit role also adds some important particularities to the way the dynamics of energy dependency work, in turn affecting policy options. Energy poverty (and the sudden way in which it happened once these states acquired independence) increased the attractiveness of using energy transit in certain ways to deal with the situation – for example, by turning a blind eye to certain actors' stealing of gas from the transit pipelines, and by fostering the barter of transit services for gas supplies, with, as discussed in chapters 2 and 3, a variety of negative consequences.[54]

Each of these two aspects highlights a different side of the issue: domestic and external. Domestically, the combination of energy poverty and role in energy transit means that even in situations where the volume of the energy transited is not so significant for the energy-exporting country, the rents and profits that can be accrued through this transit can be very significant for local players in the transit states. In terms of external relations, the combination of energy poverty and role in energy transit means that these countries have available to them a broader range of bargaining chips vis-á-vis their energy suppliers – for which they are also important partners in their value-added chains – than they would have had otherwise.

Main Variables

THE DEPENDENT VARIABLE: "MANAGEMENT
OF ENERGY DEPENDENCY"
Our dependent variable, type of management of energy dependency, requires some further explanation.

By "management of energy dependency," we mean ways of going about energy issues in a situation of dependency – regardless of whether these are proactive or passive, official policy or unofficial behaviour. This refers in particular to ways of dealing with *diversification, energy trade organization,* and the *general management of energy issues.*

First, management of energy dependency is about ways of going about the direct *management of energy supply diversification issues;* for example, issues related to the establishment and carrying through of a national energy policy and strategy, the development and implementation of energy supply diversification plans, the role of the state in the organization and financing of energy imports, policies concerning the promotion of energy self-sufficiency, the use of alternative energy and energy efficiency programs, and policies about access to energy distribution and transit networks (pipelines).

Diversification can be either domestic or external. Domestic diversification deals with the domestic side of the question by either reducing demand without increasing efficiency (by increasing prices or rationing, for example), or by reducing demand through increasing efficiency, increasing domestic production, and/or changing the energy mix in favour of fuels produced domestically. External diversification, on the other hand, refers to imports from a broader geographical array of suppliers, including reliance on a broader spectrum of contractual forms in order to avoid reliance on a single company or type of contract.

Second, we are referring to ways of going about the *organization of energy trade* with the main current supplier(s) (in the cases considered in this book, Russia, and, to a lesser extent, Turkmenistan), including issues such as (a) what contractual forms this trade will take, (b) how its financing will be organized (barter, credits, etc.), (c) who will guarantee these imports and profit or sustain losses from them, and, (d) whether these imports will take place directly or through intermediary companies, and what will be the role played by these.

Third, we are referring to ways of going about more general energy issues, *in those of their aspects related to and having implications for energy dependency issues:* the structure of policy making in the energy sphere (i.e., how energy policy is made de facto), policies about differential rates and/or subsidies for particular types of users (industrial, residential, or state sector) and how they will be financed, policies about foreign investments in the energy area, and ways of dealing with energy emergencies such as interruptions in supplies.[55] Distinguishing between these various areas in the management of energy dependency allows us to see much more nuance in the variations in outcome than would be the case if we looked only at geographical diversification, and allows for differences in styles of managing energy dependency to emerge more clearly.

Variation in the Dependent Variable: Style of Management of Energy Dependency. By "management of energy dependency," we do not imply a normative stance in the sense of considering only *good* management of energy dependency management at all. Rather than talking only about more or less successful ways of managing an energy dependency relationship, it is more useful to highlight the fact that this relationship can be managed: (a) in more or less *transparent* ways; (b) in ways that predominantly reflect the interests of particularistic interests, or national interests as a whole; (c) in ways that run the spectrum between fostering the continuation of the energy dependency relationship and, conversely, fostering growing energy independence and diversification; and, (d) in ways conducive to a more or less clear, proactive, and consequent energy policy line.

THE INDEPENDENT VARIABLE: DOMESTIC INTEREST
ARTICULATION AND POLITICAL SYSTEM

Our independent variable concerns the nature of the political system/arrangements in various FSU states.

We group the cases in terms of their domestic political arrangements, with emphasis on the de facto system of interest representation: (a) few powerful interest articulators, with most important national-level decisions controlled by the executive itself ("centralized system"[56]); (b) a situation where interest articulators have great power, are unconstrained by clear rules of the game, and have taken over state policies in many areas in exchange for direct and indirect paybacks to those writing the rules; in this situation, the autonomy of the state is limited, and the executive rather acts as balancer between various interest groups, with the purpose of maintaining his own personal power, with democratically controlled state policy limited to a minimum[57] (executive-as-balancer); (c) a situation where interest articulators are active, but function within a fragmented political system, where there is a large number of effective parties, political coordination between parties in the legislature is difficult, and the ability of the president's party to hold a majority in the legislature is severely constrained.[58]

How are these systems related to the question of level of democracy? While analytically independent concepts, among the cases analysed in this book, more centralized control by the executive (Belarus) has been more associated with authoritarianism than balancing or fragmented systems (Ukraine and Lithuania).

Steps in the Analysis

Each of the cases studies is analysed using a similar six-step process, which also constitute the central questions we apply to each case study.

First step. We characterize the political system in terms of level of democratization, transparency and role of the presidency, parliament, and other institutions and the relationship between them. This requires looking not just at the formal domestic political system, but at the

Table 1.4 The Case Studies According to their Domestic Interest Representation Arrangements

Domestic Interest Representation Arrangements	Formal Political System	Number of VetoPlayers[1]	Cases
Centralized: few interest groups, executive as monopolist	Super-presidentialist[2]	One (President)[3]	Belarus 1995–2013
Executive-as-balancer: strong interest groups, unclear rules, executive plays balancing role for own benefit and coalition maintenance.	Presidentialist (Semi-presidentialist, President-parliamentary[4])	Several (clans)	Ukraine 1995–2005 In weaker form, 2005–2013
Fragmented: president not powerful enough to act as balancer	Parliamentary (including features of mixed presidential/ parliamentary systems)	Many (parties)	Lithuania 1992–2013

1 On veto players and corruption see David C. Kang, "Transaction Costs and Crony Capitalism in East Asia," *Comparative Politics* 35, no. 4 (July 2003): 439–58, here 444–45.

2 On superpresidentialism in the former USSR see John T. Ishiyama and Ryan Kennedy, "Superpresidentialism and Political Party Development in Russia, Ukraine, Armenia and Kyrgystan," *Europe-Asia Studies* 53, no. 8 (2001): 1177–91, and M. Steven Fish, "The Executive Deception: Superpresidentialism and the Degradation of Russian Politics," in Valerie Sperling (ed.), *Building the Russian State: Institutional Crisis and the Quest for Democratic Governance* (Boulder, CO, 2000): 177–92. For a comparison of presidential powers in the post-Soviet states, see Elgun A. Taghiyev, "Measuring Presidential Power in Post-Soviet Countries," *CEU Political Science Journal*, no. 3 (2006): 11–21.

3 See also Ronald Wintrobe, "The Tinpot and the Totalitarian: An Economic Theory of Dictatorship," *American Political Science Review*, 84 (September 1990): 849–72.

4 Oleh Protsyk characterizes the Ukrainian system after the 1995 Constitution as "presidential-parliamentary." See his "Troubled Semi-Presidentialism: Stability and the Constitutional System in Ukraine," *Europe-Asia Studies* 55, no. 7 (2003): 1077–95, here 1077. In Protsyk's view of a semi-presidentialist system, the President and Prime Minister effectively constitute a "dual executive" (ibid., 1078).

formal and informal institutional arrangements and the informal distribution of political power and economic resources.

Second step. We ask, what kind of interest articulation system emerges from the given political arrangements?

Third step. We ask, what are the consequences of this system of interest articulation for the relationship between private and national energy policies? What are the implications for the possibility of determining and implementing transparent, broadly supported national energy policies? Here we analyse the role of economic and political actors with strong vested interests in specific ways of organizing the energy relationship with Russia.

Fourth step. We analyse the implications of these systems for the management of energy dependency on *Russia*. The focus is on policy-relevant actions wherever and whenever they may take place, regardless of whether these are official policy or unofficial behaviour. For example, there may be a situation where officially there is an attempt to securitize energy dependency, while, unofficially, the relevant actors are actually doing little to change the situation, and may even be benefitting from the way this energy dependency is being managed. [59]

Fifth step. We ask whether there is a connection between a specific type of system and ways of managing energy dependency. For example, is a system based on the balancing of strong interest groups more prone to the development of particularistic energy policies than a pluralistic one? Is a centralized-by-the-president system more likely to lead to the development of a clear, proactive and consequent energy policy?

Sixth step. We ask, how have the distributive effects of various ways of dealing with energy dependency further affected the development of the political system?

Specificity of the Data Available and Methodological Constraints

Research on post-Soviet energy politics presents some unique challenges. First, the lack of secondary materials makes detailed field research with local sources crucial. Second, while this book uses reliable statistical sources to the full extent available, reliable time-series cross-country statistics on energy and energy policy making in the former Soviet states are available for only a limited number of items; this is especially so concerning Ukraine and Belarus. Third, the complexity and lack of transparency of dominant modes of energy trade in the region, especially in the early and mid-1990s, mean there are some things we will simply never know. For example, given the fact that barter operations were carried out on the basis of special *for barter* discounts and pricing of individual bartered goods, it is virtually impossible to calculate the real (as opposed to nominal) prices paid by Belarus and Ukraine for gas in the early and mid-1990s. Fourth, given the important role played by corruption in the energy story, many powerful energy actors in the countries involved have a vested interest in preventing information on these issues from becoming widely available. Finally, some of the policy outcomes we focus on – *ways* of managing energy dependency rather than changes in percents of energy dependency per se – are not easily quantifiable.

Given these limitations, in-depth, structured case study research, and the triangulation of specific items of information against other sources of reputable information is the best strategy. Moreover, only a case-study approach can help unveil certain dynamics central for the study, such as determining the actors supporting and opposing certain policies. For each of the country case studies, the concrete management of energy dependency was assessed by analysing a number of sub-case studies.

Unique local sources were also tapped, such as limited-circulation trade publications, government documents, and uncensored radio and TV interviews. Between 2003 and 2011, nearly one hundred semi-structured interviews were conducted with energy-related academic experts, journalists, business executives, diplomats, policy-makers, and politicians in Russia, Ukraine, Belarus, and Lithuania, as well as with international experts. Due to the sensitivity of the issue, most of those consulted requested confidentiality, but these consultations provided extremely valuable contextualization for the publicly accessible materials cited in this book.

On the basis of the information available, a model of the ways in which domestic factors may affect the actual management of energy dependency was developed. We expect that, would full information be available, this model would be confirmed.

Key Concepts and Specificities of the Approach

This book proposes to look at energy relationships in the former USSR in a more nuanced way than has been done until now. Four concepts used throughout the book are crucial for developing this more nuanced understanding: asymmetrical interdependence, a differentiated view of energy diversification, rents of energy dependency, and distinct value-added chains.

Asymmetrical Interdependence

When we refer to Ukraine, Belarus, and Lithuania as highly energy dependent[60] and to their energy relationship with Russia as one of dependency, we do not deny the existence of elements of asymmetrical interdependence between both sides. Some of these are the control that can be potentially exerted by transit countries on Russian export routes (pipelines) going through their territories,[61] the influence they have as large and solvent (or potentially solvent) sale markets, and their influence as recipients of important investments by Russian energy companies. In addition, given Russia's limited capacity to process the gas and, especially, oil it produces, oil refineries and gas storage facilities in transit states to Western European (WE) markets became especially important for Russian oil and gas producers as elements in their own value-added chains.[62] These are elements of power these countries can use in formal or informal negotiations with Russia and in the management of their energy dependency more generally. At the same time, the existence of elements of interdependence does not change the basic fact of these states' energy dependency on Russia, only qualifies it and makes it more complex.

A Differentiated View of Energy Diversification: Contractual Diversification

This book looks at energy dependency and energy diversification in ways that go beyond conventional understandings of geographically designated dependency and diversification. While we often concentrate on geographic diversification, energy-source and contractual diversification are crucial, but much less frequently used prisms through which to analyse the situation of the energy-poor transit states. Thus, to fully understand energy dependency and energy diversification, it is important to consider not only the geographical origin of supplies, but also the energy supply mix a country depends on, and the contractual forms these imports take. (Geographical diversification refers to importing energy from several countries and/or geographical areas. Energy-source diversification refers to making a country less dependent on one single energy source in favour of a broader basket of energy sources. Contractual diversification refers to developing a variety of contractual relationships both in terms of companies and of type of contracts even when the energy originates from a single country.)

The last concept, *contractual diversification*, is of special importance for our study. In contrast with geographical diversification, contractual diversification is first and foremost about the *organization* of energy trade and about developing a variety of contractual relationships both in terms of companies and of type of contracts (short-term, long-term, etc.) even when the energy originates from a single country, spreading the risk through a variety of contract types and duration frames. In a broader sense, contractual diversification is also about managing dependency on a single supplier by using contractual means to regulate the relationship. In this sense, contractual diversification can be a means of optimizing trade with the main supplier(s) and, at least in theory, a means of managing the lack of geographical diversification.[63]

Participation in Distinct Value-added Chains

The story of post-Soviet energy links is also one of the reestablishment of value-added chains under new conditions, and of the creation of new chains including old and new actors. Concerning these value-added chains, not only their length and course of flow is important, but also their depth – the various sets of local actors involved, and how various (secondary) networks of actors are incorporated into them. Understanding value-added chains also helps to understand the possible interest of various Russian energy actors in cooperating with specific actors in the energy-poor states with access to important infrastructure (oil refineries, gas storage facilities, etc.) in terms of the completion of particular value chains. Value-added chains help connect rent-seeking schemes at both sides of the border through both formal and informal (including, at times, corrupt) means.

Different types of energy have distinct market and value-added chains, affecting the way participants in these value chains will be involved, both in terms of their interactions with their main supplier, and of the domestic rent-seeking relationships emerging from these. Thus, understanding the differences between oil and gas – the main items of energy trade between the energy-poor states and Russia – is crucial. As shown in Table 1.5, their most crucial differences include: (a) market size (whereas the oil market is largely a global one, gas markets, mainly due to transportation issues, continue to be largely regional ones[64]); one implication is that, whereas there is a quotable world price for oil prices (most often the Brent quotation), there is no such world price for gas;[65] and (b) the fact that, because of the predominance of transportation by pipeline and the higher level of risk, investments, and sunk costs involved, gas contracts need to include specific provisions allocating risk between seller and buyer, especially long-term contracts and take-or-pay provisions committing the buyer to a certain level of yearly purchases for the duration of the contract. Other differences are shown in Table 1.5.

Table 1.5 Oil and Gas: Differences and Their Impact on Market- and Value-added Chains

	Oil	Gas
Type of substance in terms of homogeneity	Not homogeneous. There are different types of oil, differently branded and priced, which are then mixed or not mixed	Relatively more homogeneous by nature (small differences due to level of methane and other substances)
Degree of processing needed before final use	More complex	Less complex
Type of substance in terms of fungibility	More fungible because it can be divided and shipped more easily	Less fungible because it cannot be divided and shipped easily
Transportation options	A variety of options available: tanker, pipeline, rail	Shipped almost exclusively by pipeline User of LNG technology is limited by its high cost
Level of sunk transportation infrastructure costs relative to total costs	Relatively low due to the possibility of shipping by means other than large-sunk-cost pipelines	Relatively large, as transportation mainly limited to pipelines
Upstream and downstream costs as related to total costs	More upstream costs (in relation to total costs)	More midstream and downstream costs (in relation to total costs)
A natural monopoly?	Not a natural monopoly. Relatively lower fixed costs compared to gas allow for multiple firms to share the market profitably.	Usually seen as natural monopoly due to high fixed costs and high economies of scale, which make it unprofitable for additional firms to enter the market.
Importers' ability to respond to blockades/ supply suspensions by switching to other suppliers?	Switch to other suppliers can take place relatively quickly: oil can also be supplied by tanker or rail.	Switch to other suppliers more difficult due to infrastructure issues (fixed pipelines or LNG facilities)
Capacity to be easily substituted by other energy sources?	Relatively low (especially in the transportation sector)	Relatively high
Ease of storage	Relatively easy	Relatively difficult

Broader Contribution

*Contribution to Understanding Russia's Role in the Former
Soviet Region and Beyond*

The issues raised in this book have important implications for the study of the domestic sources of foreign policy, as energy issues are crucial for Ukraine, Belarus, and Lithuania's ongoing relationship with their former hegemon and continuing major partner, Russia, and provide a wealth of evidence for reassessing the impact of domestic factors in this relationship. By doing this, the book also sheds light on the shaping of a new relationship between post-Soviet Russia and former Soviet republics and allies in Central and Eastern Europe above and beyond the cases analysed here. In the last years, much Western attention paid to the international relations of Central East Europe (CEE) has concentrated on strategic and military issues. Yet such emphasis has underestimated the importance of economic relationships, preventing us from fully understanding events in the region. Given their dearth of energy resources, energy supply considerations cannot but affect these countries' international partnerships. If we look only at the question of NATO (North Atlantic Treaty Organization) expansion, it may appear Russia is retreating from the CEE area. Yet from the Baltic ports in the North to Bulgaria in the South, Russian energy supplies and Russian energy companies are making their presence felt in ways that can have a deep impact on local economic and political relationships.

Contribution to Policy Analysis and Policy Making

The questions raised by this book are of direct significance for policy making. First and foremost, as they shed light on the complexity of the post-Soviet energy markets and their link to domestic and foreign policies. Understanding the internal politics of energy policy in the transit states is essential for understanding the real factors affecting energy supply security in the EU states. Confrontations between Russia and the transit states have direct implications for EU energy importers, as made clear by the effects of the gas and oil transit wars between Ukraine and Russia in 2006 and 2009 and Belarus and Russia in 2007. The nature and course of these crises is closely related to the domestic political management of energy dependency in each state.

Looking beyond our case studies and into larger questions of strategic energy supplies to the EU, it has been largely through its relationship with local elites in other transit states that Russia has been able to counter important EU initiatives intended to diversify energy supplies, such as the Nabucco gas pipeline project originally intended to bring Caspian area gas to Europe by 2015. Russia's ability to gain significant support for its own South Stream gas supply project, seen as largely incompatible with Nabucco, had to do largely with its ability to gain the support of domestic players in the countries involved.[66] While these cases go beyond the scope of our book, learning more about the ways in which the interests of local economic elites interact with those of important Russian energy players can provide important clues for understanding the EU-Russian relationship as well.

Contribution to Debates on the Pace of Reform

The issues discussed in this book are crucial to the discussion on the relative advantages and disadvantages of a gradual versus a more radical pace of reform, a central issue in political science debates on the post-Soviet transition.[67] The issue of the connection between pace of reform and emergence of rent-seeking opportunities is crucial to this debate, and an area where this book can provide important insights.

Ever since the 1970s, economists and political scientists have been discussing the connection between governmental restrictions on the economy, rent-seeking, policy making, and institutional development, noting how multiple prices for the same good in different sectors of the same market (wedges between the market value of a good and its controlled price) allow for price manipulations and rent-seeking, with a welfare cost to society.[68] The debate on the relative advantages and disadvantages of gradual versus big-bang reforms is directly related to this discussion, with the pace of reforms directly affecting rent-seeking possibilities. On the one hand, proponents of gradual reform have argued that, in addition to higher social costs, an overemphasis on swift reforms may lead to neglect the building of the necessary economic, property rights, and governance institutions, without which the reform process can be easily captured by rent-seeking interests.[69] On the other hand, those in favour of swifter, more radical reforms earlier on in the transition process have argued that delaying reform creates the conditions for increased rent-seeking and power of rent-seeking groups, as (a) such delay allows certain distortion-creating economic mechanisms (such as barter, multiple prices for the same good in different sectors of the same market, barriers to market entry, and lack of competition) to remain in place, distortions that increase opportunities for rent-seeking; and (b) the more protracted process gives vested interests more time to lobby for the maintenance of such distortions.[70] This situation, in turn, would strengthen the power of those actors benefitting from the very first stages of economic reform and the special rent-seeking opportunities available during this period,[71] but whose rent-seeking would be endangered by further reforms, making it possible for these actors to hinder the further reform process.

Each of the three cases analysed in this book presents rich evidence of the connections between the pace of reform and the rent-seeking opportunities that were created in each case. In the case of Ukraine, delayed reform not only created the room for arbitrage gains and related rents, but also the space for certain actors to emerge, actors that, in a partial reform equilibrium, would hinder the future course of reforms. In the case of Belarus, lack of reforms tied the country to dependency on Russian subsidies; once in place, such subsidies allowed the country to survive economically without engaging in any substantial reforms. In the case of Lithuania, by contrast, early reforms took away from circulation some of the main mechanisms for the accrual of energy rents available in other cases.

Contribution to Debates on Political Development and State Autonomy

Finally, this book helps shed light on a series of questions essential for understanding the nature of transition in the post-socialist world. What is the nature of the political systems taking shape in the post-Soviet states, especially concerning the executive's relationship with interest groups? How do international interest networks created under a previous system collapse, dismantle selectively, or survive and regroup after the collapse of that previous system? How we answer these questions will not only affect the way we look at the link between domestic and foreign policies in the FSU, but also how we conceptualize the role of social actors in post-Soviet societies.

An Overview of Energy Trade Politics in the Former USSR

The larger context shaping the issues addressed in this book is the connection between energy, domestic, and foreign policies in the FSU in the period 1991–2013. Cheap and abundant energy supplies helped keep the Soviet Union together; energy supplies and interdependencies have also been central to both separation and reintegration processes in the area.

These energy links take place in the context of broader dependencies and interdependencies. Above and beyond energy, Russia remains a central economic player in the region, be it through its importance as a market, as supplier of imports and investments, or through the stabilizing role played by remittances by work migrants to Russia. Energy dependency on Russia has been both – depending on the occasion – moderated and/or exacerbated by these larger interdependencies. Among Russia's policies, most crucial for the energy-dependent states have been its ability to create new dependencies after the end of the Soviet Union, and its manipulation of these dependencies for the pursuit of foreign policy goals.

Creating New Energy Dependencies

As will be discussed in chapter 2, the post-Soviet states inherited from the Soviet system a number of legacies that would significantly affect their ability to deal proactively with energy issues after independence – from energy transportation networks to ways of thinking about energy. Despite the dissolution of the Soviet Union, to these dependencies Russia has been able to add new ones since 1991, the most obvious examples of which have to do with market control and control over transit infrastructure.

Russia is not only a monopoly or near-monopoly oil and gas supplier to many of the post-Soviet states, but, for much of the period covered in this book, was able to play the role of monopsonist gas and oil buyer in the region. This is significant for our case studies, as, given the lack of pipelines connecting them to WE suppliers, one of the few diversification options open – at least in theory – to them is buying oil and gas from Central Asian and Caspian producers. Yet Russian actors have been able to hinder these diversification initiatives by buying up or controlling the marketing of much of this energy. In particular, Gazprom has been able to control the marketing of much of the CA states' gas exports, gas that is later sold in the Commonwealth of Independent States (CIS) and Europe. As will be discussed in chapter 3, Russia has largely done this in order to compensate for its own dwindling gas production, and because of the desire to prevent CA gas from competing with Gazprom gas in Europe by marketing this gas on its own;[72] moreover, the desire to prevent the energy-poor states from diversifying away from Russia was likely an important motivation. One of the ways in which Russia has pursued this goal has been by seeking to hinder direct energy trade between the energy-poor states and (potential) CA suppliers, as well as the development of a broader, more institutionalized and more transparent system of regional energy trade. In preventing states such as Ukraine from purchasing oil and gas directly from CA and Caspian suppliers, Russia also sought to prevent the building of new pipelines directly linking Caspian/CA producers to Western markets, such as the Baku-Ceyhan oil pipeline inaugurated in 2005. Moreover, with much of Turkmenistan's and Azerbaijan's production bespoken to Russia,[73] these suppliers simply did not have the volumes of gas and oil available to promise the EU in order to make new pipeline initiatives such as Nabucco economically viable.[74]

A second area where new dependencies have emerged has to do with direct and indirect control over transit infrastructure. Throughout the 1990s and 2000s, Gazprom sought to gain control over important export pipelines and storage facilities through direct purchases and the establishment of joint ventures (JVs).[75] Later on, this strategy was complemented by one focusing on building new oil and gas pipelines that would sidestep the transit countries altogether.[76] At the indirect level of governance over energy transit, Russia has refused to ratify the Energy Charter Treaty providing for negotiated Third Party Access to pipelines crossing its territory, and has not been shy to use this control to prevent diversification away from Russia, as when it refused Ukraine the transit of CA gas in 2000, or refused to transit Kazakh oil to Georgia in 2005.[77]

EXPLOITING INTERDEPENDENCY: MOSCOW'S GROWING
USE OF ENERGY AS A FOREIGN POLICY TOOL

Especially since Vladimir Putin's accession to power in 2000, Russia has not been shy to use these old and new energy dependencies for the pursuit of foreign policy goals. Rapidly rising world oil and gas prices between 2003 and 2008[78] strengthened the Russian government's ability to use energy deliveries as instruments of political pressure both within and outside the FSU. And it became increasingly centralized in doing so. As will be discussed in chapter 3, although by 1996 Russia's energy sector had emerged from the privatization process with the former oil monopolist divided among multiple partially privatized companies, and with the former Ministry of Gas Production, now reshaped as AO Gazprom, only under indirect state control, ten years later the situation had changed drastically. This increased centralization came together with a new will to use energy for domestic and foreign policy goals, a will that was officially enshrined in energy policy documents and became most patently evident with the gas supply cutoffs to Ukraine in 2006 and 2009.[79]

The evidence provided by these events makes it hard to disagree with the interpretation that the Russian state has used – and continues to use – energy dependencies for political purposes, seeking to pressure former Soviet republics into agreeing to Russian-led integration initiatives and otherwise following policies considered desirable by the Russian leadership. The alternative explanation that Gazprom is simply moving to commercially based world market prices in the form of netback pricing in its gas trade with all former Soviet states loses much of its explanatory power against the evidence that, for much of the 2000s, various post-Soviet states were paying widely different prices for Gazprom gas (see Table 1.6).[80] Even keeping in mind the difficulties in comparing these prices given differences in length of transit and other conditions, these differences remain significant.

At the same time, the world economic crisis that erupted in 2008 affected the post-Soviet energy political economy in a variety of ways. Reduced demand for gas in WE markets[81] led to the renegotiation of some of Gazprom's export contracts in these markets, reducing prices, and to growing pressure on Gazprom to seek profitable sales to those markets where it still held an important monopoly position (Ukraine, for example). In oil, the dramatic decrease in world prices (from $138 per barrel of Urals oil in July 2008 to $35 in December[82]), led to a significant decrease in revenues to the Russian state, and also effected relations with the energy-poor transit states by reducing the possible arbitrage gains-related profits that could be accrued by some types of indirect transit operations (through the refining and reexporting of oil in Belarus, for example).

These new dependencies highlight the participation of local partners in the countries involved, who often receive significant profits from the relationship with Russia. In this way, the larger trends in the way

Table 1.6 Pricing of Gazprom's Gas to Selected FSU States, in US$/tcm, 1991 and 2005–2012

	Ukraine	Belarus	Lithuania	Moldova	Georgia	Armenia	Border price in Germany, US$/tcm
1991	0.25	0.25	0.25	0.25	0.25	0.25	108.3
2005	50	55	84	80	65	54.1	212.9
2006	95	55	146	160	110	91.7	295.6
2007	135	118	220	172 (average)	235	110	293.1
2008	179.5	126.8	345	232 (average)	235	110	472.9
2009	232.4*	151	N/A	263 (average)	270	154	318.8
2010	256.7	170	356	252*	280	180	296.0
2011	300	286	400*	361	N/A	180	360.6
2012	432	165	485*	389	235	180	409.8

* Estimated.

Note: Unless noted otherwise, prices are for July 1 of each year.

Sources: Moldova prices: (2005–2009) National Agency for Energy Regulation (ANRE), at www.anre.md (accessed 15 July 2010), (2010) RosBiznesKonsulting (2011) at http://top. rbc.ru/economics/01/01/2011/523960.shtml (accessed 7 May 2011), other sources. Belarus prices: Pirani et al 2010, Table 1, p. 7; Georgia and Armenia, various sources, including the RFE/RL Armenian service, at http://www.azatutyun.am/content/article/2005637. html. Lithuania: (2005–2007) Tomas Janeliunas, "Lithuania's Energy Strategy and Its Implications on Regional Cooperation," in Andris Spruds and Toms Rostoks, eds., *Energy: Pulling the Baltic Region Together or Apart?* (Riga: Zinatne, 2009), 206, (2007–2012) various press reports. Border price in Germany (based on IMF Statistics), available at http://www.econstats.com/commsp/commspaa1.htm (accessed 1 December 2010), IEA, *Ukraine 2012* (2012). Ukraine prices: IEA, *Energy Policies of Ukraine* (1996), IEA, *Ukraine Energy Policy Review* 2006 (2006), IEA, *Ukraine 2012* (2012), other sources. The 1991 prices for Belarus, Moldova, Georgia, and Armenia are estimated from IEA (1996).

Russia has dealt with energy issues in the former Soviet space synergize powerfully with the domestic dynamics that form the core of this book.

Structure and Organization of the Book

This book covers the 1991–2013 period, with small differences in each of the case studies, and with the core of the analysis covering until Viktor Yanukovich's accession to Ukraine's presidency in February 2010 and events in Lithuania and Belarus up to Fall 2010. Events between 2010 and early 2013 are covered in the last section to each case study.

Part I of the book provides the context in which the management of energy dependency in each of the cases takes place. Chapter 2 analyses the legacies of the Soviet system and the path dependencies created by it, and how these legacies helped shape ways of looking at and dealing with energy issues after 1991. Chapter 3 analyses the domestic Russian background affecting relations with the country's energy-dependent neighbours and explores the ways in which its domestic situation may affect Russia's willingness – and ability – to use its role as dominant energy supplier as a foreign policy tool. Part II of the book presents case studies on the management of energy dependency vis-à-vis Russia in each of the countries studied – Ukraine, Belarus, and Lithuania. Part III presents the main empirical-, policy-, and theory-related conclusions and revisits the questions of the impact of domestic political arrangements on energy rent-seeking and the management of energy dependency, and of the further impact of alternative forms of energy rent-seeking on the development of these states' political systems.

2 The Legacy of the Common Soviet Energy Past: Path Dependencies and Energy Networks

"We don't have time to waste talking about history, we only have time to talk about the energy question."

Ukrainian participant in 2000 conference on Ukraine and Its Neighbors[1]

Belarus, Ukraine, and Lithuania's ability to deal with their post-independence energy challenges was significantly affected by their pre-1991 experiences. This chapter analyses the impact of Soviet energy legacies, allowing us to get a better sense of the path dependencies limiting both the energy-dependent states' range of energy options in the post-1991 period, as well as Russia's ability to use energy as a foreign policy tool. In order to do this, the chapter first sketches the Soviet Union's transformation from energy importer to major exporter and its effects on the development of its energy relationship with its immediate Eastern European (EE) transit neighbourhood, before analysing the impact of Soviet legacies for Russia and our case studies, Belarus, Ukraine, and Lithuania.

The Soviet Union's Transformation from Energy Importer to Major Exporter

Impacts, Costs, and Contradictions

Despite having some of the largest oil and gas reserves in the world, the USSR remained a net importer of energy until the early 1970s.[2] The breakthrough came in the late 1970s, when Leonid Brezhnev's gas campaign of massive investments into Siberian gas production (especially newly

Table 2.1 Soviet Gas Exports to Non-CMEA States, 1973–1990

Year	bcm/year	Soviet gas as share of EU-27 consumption, in %
1973	6.8	4
1975	19.3	9
1980	54.8	17
1985	69.4	19
1990	110.0	26

Note: Data on Soviet gas as share of EU-27 consumption is provided for illustration purposes only, as columns 2 and 3 do not necessarily refer to the same countries, as "EU-27" includes a number of countries belonging to CMEA at the time. No composite data on Soviet gas as a share of WE states' consumption during this period was available as of this writing. *Source*: Gazprom's export subsidiary Gazexport, at http://www.gazpromexport.ru/digits/?pkey1=00004 (accessed 25 June 2010). Soviet gas as share of EU-27 consumption: Pierre Noel, ESDS International Case Study, "Reducing the Political Cost of Europe's Dependence on Russian Gas," available at http://www.esds.ac.uk/international/casestudies/russian_gas.asp?print=1 (accessed 25 October 2010).

discovered supergiant fields such as Urengoy, Yamburg, Zapoliarnye, and Yamal) as a response to the fall in productivity of older fields in the European part of the country led to significant increases in production, nearly 50 percent from 1981 to 1987. (A similar process could be observed in the oil sector, with Siberian fields partially replacing production in Azerbaijan, the North Caucasus, and the Volga-Urals region and where production increased more than 20 percent between 1975 and 1980.) The Soviet Union's emergence as a major energy exporter (see Table 2.1) brought with it important changes in its relationship with both its new WE consumers and its Council for Mutual Economic Assistance (CMEA) allies.[3]

The explosive growth of energy exports to WE was accompanied by the development of a massive energy export infrastructure. Despite sanctions imposed by the United States' (US) 1974 Jackson-Vanik amendment, the development of major pipelines to serve these new exports was not to be stopped.[4] The first of these, the Brotherhood (Bratsvo) gas pipeline linking Czechoslovakia and Ukraine, was inaugurated in 1968; followed by, among others, the Oremburg (Soyuz) (1978) and Yamburg (1984) pipelines.[5] (This is in addition to the Druzhba [1964] and other oil pipelines.)

The Soviet-CMEA Energy Relationship: Patterns,
Legacies, and Contradictions

The growth of exports to WE was accompanied by the transformation of the East European CMEA states into the Soviet Union's immediate energy transit neighbourhood and the spectacular growth of their energy dependency on the USSR.[6] Playing an important transit role, the CMEA transit states exhibit important parallels with post-1991 Ukraine, Belarus, and Lithuania, and a brief look at their relationship with the USSR can help us gain a more nuanced historical understanding of the limitations involved in the use of energy supply dependency for political goals.

OVERWHELMINGLY BILATERAL RELATIONSHIPS: USING ENERGY TO
REWARD PRO-SOVIET, PRO-CMEA ALLIANCE BEHAVIOUR

Despite the attempt to turn the CMEA into a model cooperative institution as a way to compensate for the damage in relations brought about by Joseph Stalin's heavy-handed policies vis-á-vis EE, multilateral CMEA energy cooperation remained limited, with members often at odds on how to collaborate or (as in the case of Romania, the only country in the region with significant domestic energy supplies) seeking to maintain a cautious distance from its projects.[7] Given this situation, CMEA energy cooperation became a de facto vehicle for bilateral cooperation between the USSR and individual states, and supplying Warsaw Pact allies with subsidized energy largely a means for Moscow to manage relations with individual states. CMEA pricing rules included a degree of flexibility, allowing the USSR to discriminate bilaterally in its dealings with individual members,[8] and to use energy prices as a tool of alliance management. However, some of the means used, such as the barter of energy supplies for transit, pipeline construction services, and goods not easily available in the USSR, created problems of their own. In particular, the largely nontransparent nature of these mechanisms and of CMEA's pricing procedures created new tensions and a legacy of mistrust in the relationship, as, with widely distorted prices, each side could claim it was being exploited in the trade relationship.[9]

LIMITATIONS TO THE USE OF ENERGY AS A POLITICAL TOOL

Moreover, using energy subsidies to reward alliance loyalty had important limitations. The USSR was limited in its ability to use energy-based negative sanctions as, instead, it was "constrained to use its energy and

other resources to bail out" Eastern European regimes in trouble, regardless of their degree of loyalty, as happened in the case of the Czechoslovakia (1968) and Poland (1970 and 1981).[10] In addition, going too far
in forcing CMEA allies to meet their energy needs in the international
market would have led these countries to become more economically
involved with the West, if only to raise enough hard currency to pay for
these imports.[11] Thus, although the CMEA states' growing energy dependency on the USSR gave it enormous potential influence over them,
supporting these high levels of dependency was costly, making clear
the limits to the use of energy supplies for political goals.[12]

Up to which point do we see a repetition of these patterns in the energy relationship between Russia and the post-Soviet energy-poor transit states? Despite important differences in the political and historical
circumstances surrounding these two sets of relationships, interesting
parallels can be seen in a number of areas.

First, despite the high cost of energy subsidies, in the same way
as the Soviet leadership was apprehensive about pushing the CMEA
states too far into diversifying away from Soviet energy supplies out
of fear this may lead them to develop increasingly close relations with
the West, a possible rationale for continuing low energy prices to Belarus and Ukraine after 1991 was (as will be discussed in chapters 4
and 5) to prevent these states from considering diversification projects,
keeping them bound to Russian oil and gas. By offering low prices in
the short term, Russia helped keep diversification – which, especially
in gas, required significant investments in new infrastructure and
higher prices in the short term – largely out of the game as a realistic
option.

Second, the CMEA experience also tells us much about the limits of
energy as a means to pursue foreign policy goals. Such political use of
energy supplies took place within the context of other key processes,
such as competition between the USSR's three main energy markets
(domestic, Eastern European CMEA, and Western European), already
visible in the early 1970s. Moreover, if, indeed, energy subsidies were
used as a means to reward alliance loyalty, as discussed before, there
were serious limits on the Kremlin's ability to use negative energy sanctions vis-à-vis its CMEA allies. As will be discussed in chapter 5, this
is a situation Russia has encountered once and again in its relationship
with Belarus under President Aleksander Lukashenka, not least because of the political and economic backlash that such sanctions could
create for Russia itself.

*Increasingly Contradictory Role of Energy Exports in Soviet/Russian
Economic Development.*

The contradictions visible in the Soviet Union's costly energy relationship with its CMEA allies were representative of much more fundamental contradictions inherent in the role of energy exports in Soviet political and economic development. On the one hand, the expansion of energy exports to WE brought with it significant economic rewards. By 1985, the USSR was receiving more than 75 percent of all hard-currency revenue from oil and gas exports;[13] it is estimated that, at their peak in 1981, oil and gas profits amounted to more than 40 percent of the Soviet GDP.[14] By the mid-1980s, energy exports had become essential to the functioning of the Soviet system as a whole.[15]

Yet the push for larger exports was not without negative consequences. The shift East of oil and gas production, exemplified by Brezhnev's gas campaign program, increased production and transportation costs significantly, and monopolized such a high share of investment that it virtually paralyzed industrial modernization in other areas.[16] The success of energy exports increased pressure to produce more, which, given prioritization of physical volume-of-production targets over profit, meant oil was often produced even if costs were higher than world market prices.[17] It was estimated that by the late 1980s – with the cost of producing Soviet oil increasing and world oil prices decreasing – the marginal costs of oil extraction and transport may have exceeded export prices.[18]

Finally, income from energy exports may have actually hastened the collapse of the Soviet economic system by allowing the Soviet leadership to deal only with the symptoms of its growing crisis (through the financing of agricultural and consumer goods imports, for example), rather than engaging in much-needed systemic reforms.[19]

Legacies and Path Dependencies for Post-Soviet Russia

The Soviet energy system left important legacies for Russia, affecting the Russian state's ability to use energy as a foreign policy tool, as well as the value-added chains and incentive structures open to various Russian energy players, in turn affecting their interactions with local players in the energy-poor states. These legacies have to do first and foremost with the type of energy development strategies that were pursued, the low levels of energy efficiency built-in into the system, the types of energy mixes it encouraged, infrastructural legacies, and the types of trade arrangements that were privileged.

Soviet Patterns of Energy Resources Development

Soviet energy development emphasized increasing short-term supply at almost any cost. Production techniques focused on quickly extracting gas and oil located in easy-to-reach parts of deposits, but made it much more difficult – and expensive – to get at the remaining parts of these deposits later on. The use of such predatory exploitation (*Rauberwirst- chaft*[20]) methods led to the premature exhaustion of many oil and gas fields from the 1960s on. By the 1990s such methods had made a large number of Russia's oil fields unprofitable, increasing the pressure – and temptation – for many oil companies to rely on state aid.[21]

At the same time, Soviet pricing methods did little in terms of signalling relative scarcities or the relationship between supply and demand.[22] On the contrary, the setting of allowable prices on the basis of expenditures on production (cost-plus pricing), rather than supply and demand provided little incentive for reducing production costs. The fact that costs for energy infrastructure were "managed from a budget entirely separate from revenues generated by energy"[23] further contributed to unrealistically low prices often not covering the full costs of production. In particular, little attention was paid to indirect costs, especially environmental costs, which were kept out of price considerations and policy-planning in general.

Low energy prices also affected the design of pipeline systems. With gas prices low, pipelines were built with an emphasis not so much on efficiency but on saving on expensive, often imported components such as compressor stations, making these pipelines less efficient than similar pipelines elsewhere. This had important implications for the post-Soviet period, as, given the significant amount of gas used to operate the pipelines themselves, reduced pipeline efficiency leads to less gas available for exports.

Lack of Incentives for Increasing Energy Efficiency

The pricing mechanisms discussed above played an important role in hindering gains in energy efficiency. Low energy prices created the illusion of inexpensive energy, discouraging energy-saving measures,[24] and contributing to levels of energy efficiency five or more times lower than in WE states.[25] Moreover, the calculation of energy (especially coal, whose quality varies widely) production in terms of volume rather than caloric value or thermal units encouraged production for production's sake and did little to stimulate improvements in quality.[26]

Systemic factors – in particular distorted price signals and the dominant role of energy-intensive heavy industries – also limited the impact of conservation measures that could be introduced in specific areas of the economy.[27] A supply-oriented energy policy meant that, in situations of crisis, increasing supply at almost any cost was often the default answer, rather than limiting demand. A deeply ingrained over-concentration with fulfilling the plan meant that, if the choice was between not fulfilling output targets and fulfilling them using more energy than stipulated, "plan targets enjoyed priority regardless."[28]

This legacy of inefficiency had important implications for energy relations with the energy-poor states. At first glance, the most obvious implication would be that Russia still has large reserves of energy savings, which, once tapped, could mean more gas and oil available for export. At the same time, as will be discussed in chapter 3, due to the problems in Russia's energy production system, hydrocarbon production stagnated after 1991.

Energy Mixes

The 1970s gas campaign, the widespread use of gas-fired electricity generation, as well as the gasification of towns and cities along export pipeline routes, led. to momentous changes in Russia's energy mix. With the swift move away from coal, other solid fuels and firewood (from 62.5 percent of Total Primary Energy Supply [TPES] in 1960 to 17.9 percent in 1991) and into gas (from 8.2 percent in 1960 to 45 percent in 1991), the increasingly large role of gas in the Russian energy balance (52.2 percent in 1999) is an important legacy of this period.[29] Energy mixes affected the relationship with the energy-poor states, as they affected how much of the gas produced in the USSR would be available for export (and, plausibly, for use for foreign policy purposes), and the behaviour of various Soviet energy actors active in both domestic and international markets.

Trade and Institutional Arrangements Inherited from the Soviet Period

The Soviet period left important trade and institutional legacies. Barter-type trade made energy-related financial flows difficult to verify and made it hard to enforce legal control over the assortment of semi-legal and illegal deals taking place in the sector, from tax evasion to asset-stripping, as became clear in 2001–2002 with the unearthing of serious allegations involving Gazprom's deals for the benefit of gas trading company Itera.

The actual organization of the energy sector would also leave long-lasting legacies. If on the one hand ultimate responsibility for strategic energy decisions was held by the State Planning Committee (GOSPLAN) and the Communist Party of the Soviet Union (CPSU) Politburo, actual production was fragmented among several branch ministries, each controlling the production of a particular fuel; exploration activities were further divided between the Ministry of Geology and the specific energy-producing ministries.[30] In addition to creating serious coordination problems at the time,[31] this fragmentation of the energy policy process would lead to additional policy making difficulties for the post-Soviet states inheriting these structures.

On the other hand, oil and gas exports were centrally controlled by foreign trade organizations specialized in a particular fuel, in the case of gas export monopolist Soyuzgazeksport, whose role was inherited by Gazprom's export division Gazeksport; Gazprom itself is the successor of the Soviet Ministry of Gas Production.[32] Thus Gazprom became the heir to an impressive infrastructure, including not only a vast network of pipelines and production facilities, but also less tangible assets such as profitable long-term contracts with WE, contractual relationships with former CMEA states, and control over Russia's domestic gas transit system (see chapter 3). The growth of export pipelines to WE was accompanied by the development of no less significant institutional and personal relationships with WE national gas monopolists, ties that, inherited by Gazprom, have continued to be significant after 1991; such ties have at times been perceived as compromising the interests of the energy-dependent countries through which Russian oil and gas transit on the way to these markets.

Income from Oil and Gas Exports Traditionally Used to Delay Reform

As discussed previously, high world oil and gas prices – as in the 1970s – allowed the Soviet Union to delay much-needed reforms. This connection proved strong in the post-Soviet period as well, when calls for the reform and de-monopolization of the gas sector were delayed by fears that they may negatively affect the sector's continued ability to produce high foreign-currency revenue. These fears not only helped keep

Russian reform hostage to the ups and downs of the sector, but also helped maintain Gazprom's export monopoly. This situation directly affects the energy-poor states, as they will be greatly hindered in their ability to access lower gas prices until there is a real liberalization of the Russian gas export market; moreover, as will be discussed in the next chapter, without a real reform, few incentives remain for Russian gas production, processing, and distribution to become more efficient.

Legacies and Path Dependencies for the Energy-Poor Transit States

Despite having gained full political sovereignty in 1991, Ukraine, Belarus, and Lithuania continue to be affected by Soviet energy legacies. Although the phrase "Soviet legacies" first brings to mind images of massive pipeline networks, these constituted only one of their elements; other important aspects included energy resource development policies, the patterns of development and dependency relationships built into the system, the types of energy mixes it favoured, infrastructural legacies, policy making, and institutional arrangements, as well as energy-cultural legacies and the mental conceptualization within which these countries would be able to deal with their energy poverty.

Decisions on which Energy Deposits would be Developed in the Non-Russian Republics of the USSR

Moscow kept strong control over the energy development policies of Belarus, Lithuania, and Ukraine, as key decisions took place not at a republican, but at a Union level and were based not so much on bargaining between both sides, but on central planning extended to the various republics.[33] If there was a degree of fragmentation in day-to-day energy production decisions, it was an administrative, not a republic-based division, and republican self-sufficiency was not a consideration. Well-integrated into the CPSU ruling elite, the leadership of pre-independence Belarus, Lithuania, and Ukraine did not seem to have a self-aware republic-centred concept of energy security.[34]

In particular, decisions made in Moscow affected the republics' medium-term energy prospects through the issue of which energy resources would or would not be developed, and how. Ukraine, the only one of our case studies to have ever been an energy exporter, is especially illustrative of how Soviet policies were instrumental in turning a whole republic, in the space of a few decades, from a net energy exporter (and the second most important energy producer in the USSR) in the 1960s to a net importer;[35] by 1988, its energy deficit amounted to 42 percent of consumption.[36] As stated by Dienes, "no other region or republic has seen its energy position change so rapidly for the worse than Ukraine."[37]

The specifics of Ukraine's swift change from virtual self-sufficiency to dependency provide important evidence as to how the system worked in practice. First, many of Ukraine's oil and gas reserves were not exploited, in favour of regions considered more advantageous for exploitation by Moscow, such as Siberia and CA.[38] A second set of reasons had to do with *how* these deposits were developed. Central planning decisions calling for large Ukrainian energy (especially gas) supplies to other Soviet republics and foreign states, together with the use of predatory exploitation methods, led to the heavy over-working and premature peaking of Ukrainian fields in the 1970s,[39] forewarning Ukraine's later energy dependency on Russia. In addition, inefficient policies made the marginal cost of fuel production in Ukraine, especially coal, exceptionally high; by 1991, most of Ukraine's coal production was taking place at a heavy loss. This legacy has continued to affect the industry since then, limiting coal's ability to make a significant contribution to Ukrainian energy production and self-sufficiency.[40]

Patterns of Economic Development: A Legacy of Dependency

Soviet patterns of economic development encouraged the energy-poor republics to adopt a heavy industry-centred, energy-intensive development strategy based on energy abundance, when, considered individually, they were energy poor. With generous cross-subsidization keeping this system alive despite its clear inefficiency, energy consumption grew significantly in the late Soviet period.[41]

These legacies help explain why countries such as Ukraine and Belarus continued to live according to a developmental model based on cheap and easily available energy well after they became dependent on external sources. The social importance of the energy-intensive heavy industrial sector, especially in terms of employment, also helps explain why it was so difficult for these states simply to close inefficient factories and move to a less energy-intensive development model after 1991.

As will be discussed in chapter 6, the Lithuanian case presents a somewhat different situation, as a heavy industry-based model of development never took root there as strongly as it did in Ukraine or Belarus.

As a relative latecomer into the Soviet Union (forcibly incorporated in 1940), Lithuania was not as deeply affected by Soviet industrialization methods as were Ukraine or Belarus. Moreover, there is evidence that the leadership of Soviet Lithuania successfully sought to prevent Moscow-directed heavy industrialization and the concentration of industry in one or two geographical areas from affecting Lithuania as heavily as it did the other Baltic republics.[42]

If this structural element (smaller dependency on heavy industry) made it easier for Lithuania to engage in post-independence economic restructuring, cultural-political considerations, especially the circumstances under which Lithuania acquired independence, also played a role. When Lithuania acquired independence, this did not happen by accident (as some would argue was the case in Belarus), or as a result of an implicit nomenklatura bargain (as some would argue was the case in Ukraine[43]), but as the result of a broad effort to reestablish independence. This fact undoubtedly played an important role in helping the population come to terms with the social costs of economic restructuring, making it possible for the country to embark on a more decisive course of post-independence economic restructuring than did either Belarus or Ukraine.[44]

Energy Mixes

Soviet legacies also affected the dominant types of energy supply mixes in the energy-dependent states. The building of pipelines to service gas exports to WE created incentives for the further domestic gasification of the transit republics, with long-term effects not easily reversible after these pipelines were already in place. The refitting of many power plants and industries from their traditional fuel, coal (and later, heavy oil), to gas, served to solidify these changes. As a result of these factors, by 1991 Ukraine, Belarus, and Lithuania had high levels of gas in their energy mix, in line with the situation in countries possessing large gas reserves (such as Russia or the Netherlands), but not reflecting their situation as gas-poor countries.[45]

Another important legacy of the Soviet period was the building up of a significant – if of questionable safety – nuclear power sector in Lithuania and Ukraine, leading to a continuous growth in the share of domestically produced nuclear energy in their TPES, which by 1990 had reached 7.9 percent in Ukraine and 27.8 percent in Lithuania.[46] While at first glance nuclear power could provide a basis for energy independence by providing an alternative to Russian gas and oil imports, the growing domestic and international campaign against nuclear power, and Russia's monopoly on nuclear fuel supplies, made this possible source of diversification an unrealistic one for the first fifteen post-independence years. (Chapters 5 and 6 discuss the resurgence of interest in nuclear power in Lithuania and Belarus after 2005.)

Development of Strategic Infrastructure

Infrastructural legacies have been crucial for the energy-poor states. Of these legacies, the most important have to do with the development of Russia-centred pipeline systems, refineries, gas and oil storage facilities, and other energy-related industrial infrastructure.

RUSSIA-CENTRED PIPELINE SYSTEMS

The energy transit and distribution system constituted the crown jewel of Soviet energy legacies. Pipelines were built with Union-wide supply goals in mind, not from the perspective of assuring security of supply to each individual republic. This infrastructure was largely centred on Russia, in part due to the fact that most energy consumers were located there. Thus, for example, the gas pipeline connection between Turkmenistan and Ukraine was longer than a possible direct route, as it was not conceived in terms of supplying Turkmen gas to Ukraine at the lowest possible transit cost, but in terms of supplying various Russian cities along the way. This infrastructure was also Russia-centred in the sense that it was controlled by the Union ministries of gas and oil production, located in Moscow. The legacy of hub-and spoke pipelines centred on European Russia greatly limited the energy supply options open to the energy-poor post-Soviet states after 1991, as it provided no usable connections to WE energy networks.

Moreover, there were no direct pipelines in place for these states to be able to import oil and gas directly from emerging producers such as Azerbaijan and Turkmenistan, making those supplies dependent on transit through Russia's pipeline system, and giving Russia the power to manipulate access for political or commercial reasons. Gazprom, seeing CA gas as competition in the WE markets, has at times denied this gas access to its transit grid, imposed punitive transit fees, or has otherwise subjected it to political manipulation.[47] As discussed in chapter 1, Gazprom has also sought to gain ownership over gas pipelines located in the transit states. Lithuania (and, after 2009, Ukraine), with EU help, have taken steps to build connections with existing WE energy networks, but the task is enormous given the overwhelming cost of building new pipelines and the existence of long-term contractual relationships with Russian exporters, which complicate financing issues.[48]

The conceptualization of pipeline systems in Union-wide terms also meant that some infrastructure was not built, as it was simply not deemed necessary. This was often the case with gas metering stations – with the Soviet gas and oil pipeline system administered as a single whole, no metering stations were set up at republican borders – as most notoriously evident in the case of Ukraine.[49] This had important consequences, as the country had to depend on Russia for data on how much gas it had imported, and unequivocal import data was difficult to access. (If pre-1991 legacies and the expense involved in setting up such metering stations partially explains their absence as of 2009, it is likely that their absence was also closely related to lack of interest on the part of important post-1991 actors benefitting from the lack of transparency and additional rent-seeking opportunities facilitated by the lack of such metres.)

SELECTIVE DEVELOPMENT OF GAS AND OIL STORAGE FACILITIES

Following the 1973–1974 oil crisis, most WE countries started to establish systems of oil (and, later, gas) stocks in order to safeguard their energy security, and as a means to gain increased bargaining leverage vis-à-vis suppliers. This was not the case in the Soviet republics. Receiving most of their gas and oil from Russia, the very idea that it would be necessary to maintain gas and oil stocks to bargain for better prices or ward against a possible crisis was foreign to their policy making context; in particular, decisions on whether to build gas storage facilities were made on the basis of the needs of the Soviet gas export system, not of each republic's needs. In those cases where large storage capacities did exist (Ukraine), these were built during the Soviet period in order to "park" gas before further transit to WE. While not originally intended to boost Ukraine's energy security, these facilities remained in place after independence, available for use by Ukraine.[50]

LOCATION OF REFINERIES AND OTHER ENERGY-RELATED
INDUSTRIAL INFRASTRUCTURE

Ukraine, Belarus, and Lithuania also inherited large oil refineries originally built as part of a Union-wide system. Remaining on their territories after the demise of the USSR, they became part of the energy infrastructure of much smaller independent countries. Able to work profitably only as part of a larger network guaranteeing regular crude oil supplies and access to sale markets throughout the former USSR, the virtual dissolution of Union-wide supply and sale markets and the end of stable oil supplies from Russia in the early 1990s led to a virtual paralysis of the sector in Belarus, Ukraine, and Lithuania.[51] By 1999, these effects had made countries such as Ukraine especially receptive to Russian oil companies' offers to take over refineries in debt-for-shares deals; by 2002, most Ukrainian refineries were under the control of Russian oil companies. Existing refining infrastructure also affected the contractual diversification options open to these states after 1991, as individual oil refineries were linked with specific production areas in Russia, in turn controlled by specific oil companies.[52] In addition, the location of industries producing energy-related machinery (such as steel pipes used in pipelines) created long-standing links of interdependency.[53]

Other characteristics of the gas transit infrastructure as it developed during the Soviet period were to have long-term consequences as well. For example, Ukraine's gas transit system is only partially separated from the domestic high pressure system, which means most large Ukrainian gas consumers are connected directly into the transit pipelines.[54] This limits Russia's ability to target a gas supply curtailment – as a means to pressure for payment of gas arrears – to domestic Ukrainian users only, without affecting transit to WE.

SIZE OF ENERGY INFRASTRUCTURE RELATIVE TO REPUBLIC'S SIZE
AND EXCESS GENERATING CAPACITY

Belarus, Lithuania, and Ukraine inherited energy structures intended to work as part of a Soviet-sized whole, not for individual republics. Indeed, for each of them a crucial Soviet legacy is the excess of installed energy generation and processing infrastructure relative to actual domestic needs. While this excess capacity manifested itself differently in each case – in the form of excess oil refining capacity (Belarus) or of a largely nuclear-based electricity-generation capacity (Ukraine and Lithuania) – it also created common challenges after 1991.

Having a large electricity surplus did not necessarily benefit these energy-dependent states, as they lacked the means to store much of the generated electricity and their ability to export it was limited by the lack of connections with EU electricity grids. This is especially so in the case of nuclear-based electricity generation capacities, which cannot provide for the totality of a system's needs, as, being hard to regulate and turn on and off, need to be combined with other, easier to regulate forms of electricity generation such as gas-based generation. With local consumption only a fraction of what the generating infrastructure was able to produce (an especially big problem during the early-1990s economic slump immediately following the Soviet dissolution), maintaining oversized generating capacities increased per-unit production costs, reducing the competitiveness of these countries' exports and creating a burden on the economy as a whole.[55]

State Capacity and the Role of the State and Other Actors in Energy Policy Making

Soviet legacies affected the possible role of the state in the *management* of the post-independence energy situation. They did so in two main ways. First, through the issue of state capacity in energy policy making and in the control of energy infrastructure located within its territory. Second, through the issue of which actors would emerge as crucial policy making players, challenging or preempting the state from playing a guiding role in energy policy, and affecting energy governance patterns.

Soviet energy legacies affected the (non-Russian) post-Soviets states' capacity to exercise control over energy policy. In contrast with Russia (the centre), Ukraine and other former Soviet republics inherited from the Soviet state mainly nominal institutions, ("little more than mailboxes for orders from Moscow"[56]), with responsibilities often too large for them to handle in the immediate aftermath of independence. In addition, as energy links between the Soviet republics were controlled from Moscow, once formal ties with the centre were abruptly cut, the new states had few horizontal connections with other post-Soviet states, while still not being part of international energy treaties and networks.[57] This limited their energy policy making capacity in the post-Soviet period.

With their energy industries largely managed directly from Moscow by branch-specific Union ministries until 1991, Belarus, Lithuania, and Ukraine inherited not so much complete, ready-to-use energy infrastructures and policy structures, as fragments of structures, in particular "fragments of policy structures."[58] This legacy was exacerbated by the absence, at a republican level, of single dedicated ministries dealing with energy as a whole and that could smoothly and proficiently reassemble these fragmented structures, now with republican-level goals.

The effects of such fragmentation could be seen especially clearly in the nuclear energy sector, where Ukraine and Lithuania, despite inheriting large nuclear facilities, "lost the key Soviet structures which had always managed them," while having no equivalent republican-level structures to replace them.[59]

Soviet legacies also affected the role of specific interest groups in energy governance and their ability to challenge or preempt the state from playing a guiding role in energy policy. In the first place, in the Soviet period links within enterprises were stronger than links between these enterprises and the *republican* governments. Second, the system of Moscow-based branch economic ministries meant that enterprise directors in the various republics, depending directly on Moscow, often had little or no contact with the republican capital.[60] In the third place, the economic and political weight of heavy industry supported the rise and consolidation of elites connected to energy-intensive industries such as petrochemicals, metallurgy, and chemical fertilizers. This powerful industrial lobby would come to have an enormous weight in the policy process, especially during the first years after independence, power it would often use to attempt to bloc economic reforms as a way of maintaining its access to state subsidies, including energy subsidies.

Trade and Institutional Arrangements Inherited from the Soviet Period

The legacies of a trade system not based on real prices and cash payments set the stage for a number of problems in the post-1991 period. Because the nominal price of energy supplies meant little to the buyer, inefficiency was promoted.

Many of the energy trade instruments developed during the CMEA period continued to be used after 1991. Paying for energy by supplying the USSR with soft goods hard to export to Western markets, a practice often used in CMEA energy barter, was also an important feature of post-1991 energy relations between Russia and Belarus, where much of the gas and oil supplied by Russia was bartered for Belarusian goods unable to be placed in other markets, and at strongly inflated prices. The persistence of barter relations – which continued to play a central role in energy trade with Ukraine and Belarus throughout the mid-2000s – had a variety of other important effects. While itself often a response to lack of liquidity in the market, barter led to further demonetization of the energy sector and loss of investments.[61] Most importantly, it helped perpetuate a nontransparent environment prone to rent-seeking and corruption. Barter practices made it more difficult to establish the price paid for gas actually supplied, opening the door to potential misunderstandings.

Another important legacy had to do with the role of monopolistic energy structures, such as centralized electricity suppliers and oil and gas exporters. The persistence of these monopolistic structures created special difficulties for countries such as Lithuania (and, to a lesser extent, Ukraine) seeking to adapt to EU regulations. In particular, the legacies of a single monopolist controlling all aspects of the electricity production and distribution process created important hurdles for the liberalization and unbundling of production, transportation, and distribution in electricity and gas markets. These challenges are compounded by the legacy of high reliance on gas, which raises the political costs of increasing consumer gas prices, in turn making it difficult to open the market for competition, as it is unfeasible to open the gas market without allowing companies to charge market prices for the gas supplied.

In addition, one point in Soviet gas export contracts would come to have significant importance in the post-Soviet period: the fact that export contracts to European countries usually specified delivery points well beyond the *Russian* border. (In the case of exports to WE, usually a point on the Western border of a CMEA state such as Baumgarten on the Czechoslovak-Austrian border; in the case of exports to EE, usually a point on the Western Soviet border, such as Uzhgorod on the Ukrainian-Hungarian border.[62]) This legacy has had significant effects, as it means the cost and burden of transit and possible transit complications continues to fall first and foremost on Russia.

Energy Culture and Conceptualization of Energy Security

Another important set of Soviet legacies concerns cultural and mental frameworks: the geographical scale at which energy issues were conceptualized, and the energy-related expectations of the population.

The first issue concerns the geographical scale at which energy issues where conceptualized. In the cases of Ukraine and Belarush in the first years after independence, most economic elites continued looking at energy in Union-wide terms, not in terms of their own state. Thinking in terms of a Soviet-wide energy balance, they continued to see energy inputs as basically unlimited, and to feel as if they lived in an energy-rich state.[63] The realization of their own country's energy poverty came only gradually.

The second issue concerns what could be called Soviet energy culture. In the same way as cheap and plentiful energy supplies served as a bonding agent that kept the Soviet economy – however inefficiently – together, expectations of cheap and reliable electricity and piped-in residential heating supplies became part of the Soviet population's cultural definition of welfare, and part of a minimal energy-social contract between the regime and its citizens, making household consumers carriers of Soviet energy culture.[64] Such expectations of energy-related welfare, part of general expectations of rising living standards, became part of the very legitimacy of Soviet power, in a context in which ideology was becoming less and less central to this legitimization. Even after the demise of the Soviet system, being able to provide such services has been a central element of the new states' legitimacy vis-à-vis their own citizens.

This contributed to a situation where, for the post-Soviet states (and especially for those such as Belarus lacking strong and widely influential elites articulating more identity-based sources of legitimation), the continuous provision and expansion of residential energy services, especially to the countryside, became an important legitimation element for both the states themselves and for their leaders. Implied in the provision side of this unspoken social contract was the expectation of affordable energy prices, an area where the Soviet legacy of extremely low prices had created enduring expectations.[65] Thus a growing emphasis on the absolute importance of low energy prices starts to take shape; the rise of such expectations to a central value was aided by the economic crisis and high inflation of the early 1990s, which reduced household incomes and would have made hypothetical cost-covering, inflation-indexed energy prices much more difficult to afford for the average household.

This had important effects in the short and medium term: an over-concentration on the short-term continuation of low energy prices served to exclude some policy options from the discussion table, while making others much more attractive.[66] Low residential prices isolated consumers from the worst effects of energy dependency on Russia and "made diversification policies, more expensive in the short term, hard to sell politically."[67]

Conclusion: Soviet Legacies, Rent-Seeking, and Asymmetrical Interdependence

The Soviet legacies discussed in this chapter synergized with other characteristics of the transition period (first and foremost thwarted or partially delayed economic reforms) and of the external environment at the time (in particular Russia's desire for continued influence in the other post-Soviet states, which led to the maintenance of barter and other murky multiple-pricing schemes for energy[68]) to greatly facilitate the development of rent-seeking opportunities after 1991. Taken together, these factors contributed to a situation where energy trade became one of the most corrupt areas of the economy, and set into motion a type of institutional dynamic whereby some powerful economic actors would have little interest in increasing transparency in energy trade, especially vis-à-vis the main supplier, Russia.

At the same time, these legacies are not simply one-sided dependency legacies. For example, the same infrastructure originally built to guarantee security of exports for one actor could eventually come to be used to facilitate security of supplies for another, as was the case with gas storage facilities built on Ukrainian territory that, although originally intended to support Soviet exports to WE and not Ukraine's energy security, later became a significant element of Ukrainian counterpower in its asymmetrical interdependence energy and energy-transit relationship with Russia.

Legacies do not explain everything, however. Important differences between our cases were a result not so much of Soviet legacies but of choices made in the early post-Soviet years, in particular the speed of economic reforms, level of state control of the economy, and the nature of political control, governance, and interest representation. After considering the effect of domestic Russian factors in the energy relationship with the energy-poor states (chapter 3), we turn to these issues in more detail in the case studies of Ukraine, Belarus, and Lithuania.

3 The Domestic Russian Background: Domestic Choices, Foreign Energy Policy Levers, and Trans-border Rent-seeking

Russia remains the main energy supplier, transit gatekeeper, and energy rule-setter in the post-Soviet region, and understanding the Russian side of the energy supply question is essential for making sense of energy policy actions and reactions in the energy-poor states.[1] This chapter focuses on the impact of Russia's political economy of oil and gas on the energy-dependency management landscape faced by the energy-poor states. This impact takes place mainly through three dimensions analysed in this chapter: (a) through Russia's own resource base and changing ability to supply foreign markets, which affect Russian export priorities and transit preferences; (b) through changing patterns of interaction between the Russian state and the country's main energy players; and, (c) through the way domestic energy issues affect value-added chains and Russian actors' participation in transborder rent-seeking arrangements with actors in the energy-poor states, also affecting these actors' preferred types of interactions with Russian actors.

Actors in Russia involved in energy production (Gazprom, other gas and oil producers) or with other means of control over their transportation and distribution (Transneft and other state policy making players, including the Kremlin) face choices about where to use or direct these energy resources and associated profits. These choices occur along two dimensions. In a geographic dimension, main choices revolve around whether these resources will be used domestically or externally. In a modalities of use dimension, energy can be used or traded in a spectrum ranging from sale in open markets to trade under various special deals, to political use in domestic and foreign directions. (As a scarce commodity with great potential for arbitrage gains, of course, energy resources can also be used as a means of personal economic gain.) While in practice the dividing lines between these choices are more blurred than they appear on paper, each of these ways of using energy implies different incentive structures for the players involved. These decisions, in turn, are not made in a vacuum, but are the result of the interplay of factors such as the desire for profit maximization (at a state, company, or personal level), maintenance of markets or political influence in an area, and relationships with the Russian state and actors within it. Given this context, this chapter explores how Russia's domestic political economy affected the choices faced by Russian actors in using energy, and the implications of these choices for Russia's energy-poor neighbours, also in terms of how actors in these states will interact with Russian energy actors.

As discussed in chapter 1, oil and gas differ in terms of their production and transportation processes and associated value-added chains. In the Russian case, they also differ markedly in terms of the domestic organization of the sector with – in simplified form – the state retaining control over a monopolized gas sector, and the oil sector more independent of the state and divided into a number of large competing players. These differences also affect the structure of incentives facing players in these two sectors, and the way they assess the choices discussed previously. In addition, gas plays a more prominent role both in the structure of Russia's energy consumption (53.2 percent of TPES in 2008, as opposed to 20.5 percent for oil) and in its exports to Ukraine, Belarus, and Lithuania, a reality also reflected in this chapter.[2] Because of these differences, this chapter addresses both sectors separately, with somewhat more attention paid to gas than to oil issues. We first analyse Russia's domestic political economy of gas and its impact on Russia's energy poor neighbours, before addressing the issue in the case of oil.

The Political Economy of Russian Gas and Its Impact on the Energy-poor States

Post-Soviet Russia's gas relationships are closely related both to the way the sector developed during the Soviet period, and to its post-Soviet transformation. In 1988, the remnants of the Soviet Ministry of Gas Industry were transformed into a state-controlled *kontsern*, and later (1988) it became a vertically integrated joint-stock company, Gazprom. In contrast with the break-up of the oil industry, Gazprom retained control of the near-totality of gas production and transmission, as well as other perks such as sole ownership over gas storage facilities and export pipelines, and a de facto monopoly on gas processing and exports. Similarly, the top leadership of the sector remained virtually unchanged from the Soviet period until the early 2000s.

Reform of the gas sector progressed during this period, but at a deliberately moderate pace. While in the early 2000s relatively radical changes such as the unbundling of Gazprom into separate companies dealing with production, transmission, and distribution were widely discussed, this was de facto replaced by a much weaker option: financial unbundling and functional specialization of 100 percent Gazprom-owned subsidiaries.[3] Rather than dismantling, Gazprom began expanding beyond gas: its 2005 purchase of a majority stake in Sibneft broke the administrative division between oil and gas, and, together with new ventures in the coal and electricity generation sectors, discussed further on, seemed to open the door for the eventual establishment of a powerful global conglomerate encompassing multiple energy sectors.

Russia's Changing Gas Resource Base

DECLINE IN GAS PRODUCTION AND ABILITY TO EXPLOIT
AND TRANSPORT THESE RESOURCES

Russia is a paradoxical energy power, as seen clearly in the gas sector. On the one hand, its large gas resources (in 2009 it possessed 23.7 percent of the world's proven gas reserves and was, until 2009, the world's largest producer and in 2010 continued to be, by far, the largest exporter[4]) make it a crucial player, giving the country a strong basis for international leverage. On the other hand, Russia's gas production has been stagnant or in decline since the late 1980s,[5] and fell significantly in the 1990s. Yet compared to the much steeper decline in oil production during the 1990s, the gas sector remained a relative island of stability in the energy landscape (see Tables 3.1 and 3.2).

Location, accessibility, and cost of exploitation are also important issues affecting which reserves will actually be exploited and brought to market. As discussed in chapter 2, by the late 1980s Russian gas production had come to rely increasingly on Western Siberian fields. As these fields started to decline, Gazprom came under pressure to move production to more remote areas – by the early 2000s, about 37 percent of its reserves were located in hard-to-reach areas in the Yamal Peninsula and the Barents Sea; accessing and bringing this gas to market required especially large investments.[6] Given this situation, one reason these new resources have been slow to come online had to do with Gazprom's investment strategy since 1991, a strategy that largely neglected

Table 3.1 Gazprom's and Total Russian Gas Production, 1991–2009 (in bcm/yr)

Year	Gazprom Production in bcm	Total Production in bcm	Gazprom's production as % of total production	Exports to Europe	Exports to CIS	Total exports
1991	595	643	92.53	91	156	247
1992	599	640	93.59	89	106	195
1993	578	617	93.67	101	79	180
1994	571	607	94.06	105	76	181
1995	560	595	94.11	121	70	191
1996	561	601	93.34	128	70	198
1997	534	571	93.52	120	79	199
1998	554	591	93.73	125	78	203
1999	546	592	92.22	131	74	205
2000	523	584	89.55	133	60	193
2001	512	581	88.12	131	49	180
2002	526	595	88.40	134	51	185
2003	548	620	88.38	142	47	189
2004	552	633	87.20	145	55	200
2005	555.	641	86.58	159	47	206
2006	556	656	86.28	161	41	202
2007	549	653	84.07	154	37	191
2008	550	664	82.83	158	36	194
2009	462	584	79.10	120	47	167

*Including gas from CA.

Sources: For 1991–1994: IEA, Energy Policies of the Russian Federation (Paris: IEA/ OECD, 1995), 168 (Table 1), and 175 (Table 3). For 1995–2009: Russian Statistics Committee (on Russia's gas production), Gazprom (Gazprom's gas production), Russian State Customs Committee (on gas exports).

reserve replacement (the rate at which exploitation of reserves is compensated by the addition of new reserves) and investments geared to increasing production.[7]

THE END OF CHEAP GAS, GAZPROM'S OPTIONS,
AND THE ENERGY-POOR TRANSIT STATES

In the early 2000s, these production difficulties coincided with rising domestic consumption, severely straining Gazprom's ability to fulfil its contractual obligations.[8] At issue is, as noted by the International Energy Agency (IEA), the end of the era of relatively *cheap* gas based on inherited Soviet production infrastructure, and the beginning, not only of higher-cost gas, but also of difficult dilemmas for Gazprom. Some of the options about how to replace this increasingly hard-to-produce gas involved increasing gas imports from CA, and, domestically, increasing efficiency and changing the domestic energy mix to reduce reliance on gas (both of which would require a relative increase in gas prices), encouraging production by independent gas producers, and increasing investments in new, higher-cost fields. While not necessarily mutually exclusive, each of these options had important implications in terms of the relationship between Gazprom and the state, Gazprom and other energy players in Russia, and energy relations with Ukraine, Belarus, and Lithuania.

Externally, these dilemmas involved how to balance various export markets and what kinds of relationships to build with other producers, first and foremost in CA. (Relations with CA are discussed later in this chapter.) As oil and gas demand in WE continued to stagnate (most starkly, but not only, as a result of the 2008–2009 economic crisis), growing emphasis was put on oil and gas export projects aimed at developing China and Asia-Pacific region markets as a means to balance this stagnation.[9]

In addition to production issues, the new situation also involved the issue of how to bring these resources to market, and important choices concerning what kind of transportation options to pursue (upkeep and repair of existing pipelines, building of new pipeline routes, and liquefaction into liquefied natural gas [LNG] for shipment via tankers).[10] Russia's limited gas storage (as noted in chapter 2, after the USSR collapsed significant Soviet gas storage facilities remained in the other former republics) and LNG liquefaction facilities (the first one, which opened in February 2009, is located in remote Sakhalin, limiting its impact on the marketing of gas produced in other areas[11]) meant limited options for what to do with its gas output. This affects Russia's ability to manage export pricing ("parking" gas in the summer and selling in winter when demand is higher), and even its overall ability to monetize the gas it produces.

Echoing the discussion of asymmetrical interdependence in chapter 1, and of how possession of crucial infrastructure such as underground storage facilities can provide a counter-weight to energy supply dependence, this situation strengthened the role of transit countries and those having significant underground storage facilities, such as Ukraine, in Gazprom's value-added and revenue chains.

*Domestic Gas Issues and Their Effect on Sector Actors' Participation
in Trans-border Rent-seeking Arrangements*

During the period covered by this book, domestic energy issues affected Russian gas-related actors' relationships with actors in the
energy-poor states and affected these actors' preferred types of transborder interactions with Russian actors. Among these domestic issues,
the most prominent were Gazprom's relationship with the state, its
monopolization of the gas market, the importance of personal-within-
the-corporation-interests within the company, the role of intermediary
companies, and Gazprom's investment policies. Like pieces of a single
puzzle, these five elements strongly reinforced each other during the
period under study.

GAZPROM'S RELATIONSHIP WITH THE STATE
The question of Russian state influence over Gazprom or Gazprom's
influence over state policy is a complex and longstanding one, and the
relationship is by no means a unidirectional one. Continuing tension
between Gazprom's dual roles – fulfilling both important domestic and
external, economic and political roles – has been an important driving
force in this relationship. While on the one hand the Russian state has
relied on Gazprom the economic player as an important source of foreign revenue and other budget contributions (between 1995 and 1999,
taxes paid by the oil and gas industry amounted to about 12–24 percent
of Russia's consolidated budget[12]), it has also relied on the company to
fulfil a number of broader political and social tasks. These include both
domestic (helping maintain social stability through low energy prices,
providing social services) and foreign-oriented tasks (helping manage
the relationship with Russia's energy-poor neighbours, among others),
and these two goals have often been at odds.

Gazprom and Domestic Energy Supply Issues

A small excursus on policy dilemmas around the role of gas in Russia's domestic energy supply provides a good illustration of Gazprom's
complex relationship with the state. Crucial to Gazprom's domestic role
has been its large-scale supply of gas to residential users and electricity-
generating plants at subsidized prices, contributing to keeping electricity prices low, and helping fulfil deeply held popular expectations born

of the Soviet energy-social contract discussed in chapter 2. Thus some of the contradictions between Gazprom's roles came to the fore through the issue of how much gas should Gazprom supply domestically at subsidized prices (and, thus, how much would it have available for exports), a question closely related to the question of what would be the preferable domestic energy mix. This was so because for most of the period up to 2013 – and especially during the period of economic upheaval in the early and mid-1990s – pricing policies kept domestic gas prices not only significantly below international ones, but also artificially low compared to other fuels, prompting consumers to move to lower-price gas whenever possible, and leading to an increase in the already high share of gas in the country's energy mix, to about 52 percent in 2000.[13]

Energy mix issues and the structure of relative prices for various energy sources (gas, oil, and heating oil, among others) are not trivial, as they affect not only the domestic consumption of these and what will be available for export, but also how the producers of various fuels will benefit from price differentials between domestic and export markets and prioritize supplies to each. In the late 1990s, for example, as price trends made exports increasingly profitable, Gazprom sought to reduce its domestic supply commitments as a way to maximize exports and related profits. In the early 2000s, after the increase in gas use that accompanied the spur of import-substituting growth following the 1998 crisis,[14] this led to growing tensions between Gazprom and domestic electricity producer United Energy Systems (RAO UES), another major domestic political and economic player.[15] Gazprom's preferred means of reducing its domestic supply commitments was RAO UES's conversion of its electricity generating facilities to heating oil or coal as a way to free more gas for export. This, however, was not desirable from RAO UES's perspective, as using these fuels implied significantly increased costs as compared to gas. Subsequently, Gazprom dealt with the issue by aggressively buying actives in the electricity generating sector, and seeking to develop new coal-fired generation facilities where coal from its new partner the Siberian Coal Energy Company (SUEK) could be burned, allowing Gazprom to maximize gas exports.[16]

This example provides a good illustration of the contradictions discussed previously: despite its benefitting from Gazprom's exports and thus theoretically also from a domestic reorientation away from gas as a way to increase these, the state was lukewarm about allowing significant domestic gas price increases as a way to reduce demand, as low domestic energy prices provided an important tool for mitigating the social costs of economic transformation, and because of the role of low energy prices in the competitive pricing of Russian exports of energy-intensive goods such as metallurgical products.

Another way in which the diversity of interests concerning Gazprom's role interfaced with domestic supply issues concerned the issue of domestic gas price increases. The gap between the energy prices charged to consumers inside Russia and those that could be fetched in international markets had a variety of implications for the interrelationship between various players within Russia, for Russia's relationship with international markets and international organizations, and for the relationship with its energy-poor neighbours. In the previous paragraphs, we discussed how Gazprom's bid for higher domestic prices as a way to moderate demand and secure higher profits through exports affected its relationship with other players within Russia.[17] Gazprom's actions also affected relationships with international organizations, as bringing up Russian domestic energy prices to international ones had long been a demand of the International Monetary Fund (IMF), the World Trade Organization (WTO), and the EU, which had argued that below-cost domestic prices represented a hidden trade subsidy.[18] As can be seen from Table 3.2, differences between domestic vs. export prices also affected the relationship with Russia's energy-poor neighbours by helping shape the incentives for selling domestically or exporting.

In November 2006, the Russian government announced that domestic gas prices would gradually increase so as to reach European netback levels by 2011.[19] The plan stipulated that, between 2007 and 2011, gas prices for industrial and household users would increase 40 percent,[20] and that by 2011 domestic gas prices for industry would be such that would guarantee the equal profitability (*ravnaia dokhodnost*) of foreign and domestic sales.[21] Yet it soon became clear that, in order for the principle to be fully implemented, actual increases would need to be much more significant than the originally envisioned 40 percent, and many voices within Russia – including in the Kremlin (e.g., Minister of Economic Development Elvira Nabiullina) – started to argue that, given the economic and social consequences of larger-than-originally planned increases in domestic prices, the principle of raising domestic prices to European levels should not be implemented fully by 2011.[22] In

Table 3.2 Average Gas Sale Prices by Gazprom to CIS/Baltics and Western European Markets (excluding export taxes and customs duties), 2003–2006, in US$ per tcm

	2003	2004	2005	2006
Average (industrial and household) Russian domestic gas prices	22	28	33	40
– (as percentage of sale price to WE)	22.98	27.55	23.55	20.76
Average sale price for CIS/Baltics	34.40	36.33	50.02	76.37
– (as percentage of sale price to WE)	35.93	35.75	35.70	39.65
Average sale price for WE	95.72	101.61	140.09	192.59

The apparent discrepancy between the "Average Sale Prices for CIS/Baltics" in this figure, and prices in Table 1.6 in chapter 1 of this book is due to the fact that prices in Table 1.6 include taxes and customs duties, while the prices quoted here do not.

Source: Data on sale prices to CIS/Baltic and WE from Stern, "The Russian Gas Balance to 2015," Table 12.1, 396; data for domestic gas prices derived from IEA, *Optimizing Russian Natural Gas* (Paris, IEA, 2006), 42.

March 2010, it was announced that the target price parity date had been moved back to 2014.

Effects on Relations with the Energy-poor States: The Case of Belarus

The first and most general connection with the energy-poor states, especially Belarus (that for much of the 1994–2010 period, as discussed in chapter 6, claimed a right to domestic Russian gas prices stemming from its special relationship with Russia), goes back to the very existence of price differentials between domestic Russian prices and those charged them. If there was no difference between domestic and export prices, then there would simply be no reason for Belarus to insist on paying domestic Russian prices.

Russia's announced move to increase domestic prices to European netback ones also affected relations with Belarus in a more direct way. In the 31 December 2006 gas agreements between Belarus and Russia (that put an end to the gas "war" of late 2006 between both countries) it was agreed that by 2011 Belarus should pay 100 percent of the Polish price (minus the difference in transportation costs). This was interpreted by the Belarusian side as valid as long as Belarus and Russia would be moving simultaneously to netback prices by 2011. But when Russia announced that the timeline would be further drawn out, Belarus considered this sufficient reason for new negotiations on the issue and for demanding a suspension of planned increases applicable to it.

Multiple Interests, Gazprom-state Relations and Convertible Points:
Implications for Gazprom-state Relations

Clearly, Gazprom's interests as a corporation – albeit one with significant state ownership – and those of the state were not always compatible. Why, then, would Gazprom choose to forgo the large, nearly assured profits implied in exports to Western markets as compared to domestic sales, especially when that revenue was crucial to Gazprom as a means to compensate for low domestic gas prices and preferential-price deliveries to former Soviet republics? One possible explanation would be that the company was simply forced to do so by the state. A better way to look at this, however, is through the prism of the tension between Gazprom's various interests and goals, as the company, while losing revenue from the opportunity cost of not exporting to higher-paying WE markets, also benefitted politically from its subsidization of domestic consumers. From a Gazprom corporate perspective, the goal of profit maximization through exports to WE coexisted – and at times collided with – the goal of fostering good relations with the state through the provision of various services; it is exactly the provision of such services that largely explains the state's support for Gazprom's monopoly role.[23]

The concept of "convertible points,"[24] focused on the informal side of the relationship between the state and major energy companies, provides us with a useful tool for understanding this relationship.[25] Although the Russian state may not be able to dictate to Gazprom as a corporation what policies to pursue, the company may find it useful to follow state and/or Kremlin preferences anyway. Gazprom can accrue points with the Russian state through services provided domestically or internationally. Domestically, such services have included the provision of social services to Gazprom's nearly 400,000 employees,[26] maintaining supplies to hospitals and other social objects and residential users despite lack of payments, and providing gas to the population at lower-than-international prices. Especially during the liquidity crisis of the 1990s, such policies helped prevent the social unrest that would likely have come from the large-scale disconnection of non-paying consumers. More generally, they contributed to social stability and the legitimacy of the political regime. Internationally, these services have included helping to manage the relationship with Russia's neighbouring states by supplying gas to energy-poor neighbours at preferential prices, or tolerating repeated non-payment on their part.

The concept of convertible points helps us gain a fuller view of the interrelationship between Gazprom and the state in Russia's neighbouring states. When companies such as Gazprom lost potential profits by selling gas to Belarus or Ukraine at preferential prices, they accrued informal points with the Russian state. These points could be later converted into advantages in other areas. How these virtual points were transferred from the foreign policy realm to a domestic arena and eventually converted into monetary benefits varied from sector to sector and case to case. In the gas sector, the conversion often took place informally through access to credits, the setting of gas prices, and the granting of privileges in privatization contracts and other investment opportunities, such as preferential access to especially strategic gas fields.[27]

Clearly, not all the benefits received by the parties in this relationship could be measured in direct monetary terms: the benefits received by the state were primarily political in nature, such as a continued presence in neighbouring states, or influence on their leadership for strategic gains. Similarly, the benefits received by Gazprom also included non-monetary ones, such as protection against international pressure for breaking up the monopoly and significant administrative resources it could, in turn, use for its own benefit in other areas. These administrative resources were related to the official or unofficial regulatory powers granted by the state to Gazprom over a number of areas (such as access to Russia's domestic and export pipeline grid, and the coordination of the development of eastern Siberian gas resources, among others), and to the company's ability to exert pressure on other players with significant resources of their own, for example the judicial system.[28] These administrative resources have been translated by Gazprom into a number of more tangible economic advantages, including gaining a foothold "into many independent gas projects without making significant investments or paying an adequate market price."[29]

The previous discussion highlights the two-sidedness of the relationship between Gazprom and the state. Repeated instances of the company's successful fending-off of attempts by the Ministry of Finance to make it face its full tax liability also speak of its power vis-à-vis parts of the state apparatus. The easing out of Rem Viakhirev as Chairman of Gazprom's board and his replacement by Aleksei Miller in 2001 strengthened the state's formal role in the company. Such gains were consolidated after October 2004, when a complex operation involving oil company Rosneftegaz allowed the state to come to control more than 50 percent of Gazprom's shares, as well as a majority of seats on its Board of Directors, assuring it a direct say in the company's most important decisions.[30] (The further impact of post-2001 changes in Gazprom is discussed further on.)

GAZPROM'S MONOPOLY ROLE

Gazprom's continued monopoly role is the central defining feature of Russia's political economy of gas, a role, in turn, related to the company's political weight and relationship with the state. As of the late 2000s, Gazprom controlled more than two-thirds of Russia's gas reserves, accounted for more than 80 percent of all of Russia's gas production,[31] and owned the Unified System of Gas Supplies (USGS), which permitted it to dictate terms to independent gas producers and control all gas exports. Gazprom's monopoly refers not only to its export monopoly role inherited from the Soviet period[32] (and enshrined into the Law on Gas Exports in 2006[33]), but also to the company's conscious blocking of new producers from entering the domestic gas market. Two issues were at stake here: gas exports by producers other than Gazprom, and the issue of whether associated gas produced by oil companies would be allowed into the USGS, Gazprom's domestic gas distribution system. Until the mid-2000s, Gazprom officials emphasized that allowing producers other than Gazprom into the exports market would only bring down the price of Russian gas in WE, reducing Russia's associated budget revenues. Later, the company's argument changed: that the issue is a purely technical one, having to do with the pipeline's (lack of) physical capacity to transport gas volumes additional to those produced by Gazprom.

A brief examination of these new producers and Gazprom's relationship to them provides important insights into the connection between Gazprom's monopoly and Russia's role as gas exporter. A first group of new gas producers are non-Gazprom, independent producers such as Novatek and Itera. However, the fact that many of these companies have relied largely on fields left over from Gazprom,[34] and are fully dependent on access to Gazprom's gas processing and transportation facilities, has facilitated Gazprom's attempts to increase its ownership control over them, making many of these companies independent only on paper.[35] A second set of new gas market players are oil companies producing small amounts of natural gas, either as associated gas (see further on) or from their own natural gas deposits; LUKoil and Ros-neft have been the major players.[36] Associated gas generated in the course of oil production has been a particularly problematic issue, with producers facing significant hurdles to transport or market this gas.[37] With the gas transit system controlled directly by Gazprom (in contrast with the oil sector, where there is a pipeline authority, Transneft, sepa-rate from the producers) and Gazprom having the prerogative of not transporting other producers' gas, oil companies have had little choice but to sell this gas at the wellhead to Gazprom (or associated com-panies[38]) at extremely low, regulated prices, seriously limiting the profitability of such production. This situation, in turn, has led up to about 25 percent of the gas produced by oil companies being flared in the open air, a loss of about 2.4 to 9.6 percent of Russia's total gas production.[39] Thus, despite the fact that, as shown in Table 3.1, non-Gazprom producers' share in total gas production increased rapidly since 2000, Gazprom's gatekeeper role already at the wellhead level prevented these new players from contributing fully to Russia's gas production.[40]

Impact of Gazprom's Monopoly on the Energy-poor States

With Gazprom a gas export monopolist, the energy-dependent states found themselves at a great disadvantage, not being able to play dif-ferent producers against each other. In addition, Gazprom's active role in hindering the role of other gas producers prevented them from be-coming not only alternative suppliers, but also alternative voices to be reckoned with in the Russian energy policy making process.

Gazprom's gas exports monopoly also increased the Russian state's potential ability to use these exports for political goals. However, as will be discussed further on, Gazprom's monopoly also had more com-plex effects, especially on energy trade schemes and transborder rent-seeking alliances.

PERSONAL-WITHIN-THE-CORPORATION INTERESTS IN GAZPROM

When discussing the relationship between Gazprom and the state in the previous section, the picture presented was one based on a sim-plified view of the company as pursuing corporate interests, vs. the state pursuing state interests. Looking at the company as an amalgam of three different sets of interests: state, corporate, and personal-within-the-corporation interests, provides a more realistic picture.

In particular, at issue have been personal-within-the-corporation interests, which have often been pursued separately from the company's corporate interests. At the same time, this issue cannot be wholly separated from the relationship with the state or close-to-the-Kremlin political elites, which often benefitted from the murkiness inherent in Gazprom's amalgamation of interests. Thus the maintenance of Gazprom's monopoly privileges is best understood as related, not only to its provision of important domestic services, but also to the way lack of transparency in the company made possible the transformation of Gazprom's economic resources into a little-regulated source of revenue (some would say a kind of parallel state budget) that could later be used by the Russian leadership with little if any independent control.

Some of the ways in which these personal interests within the corporation manifested themselves during the period analysed in this book were through the misuse of corporate property for the pursuit of private profit by individuals holding official positions in the company, and through the company's alleged role in helping set up murky intermediary companies, which we discuss in the next section.

The complex relationship between state, corporate, and personal interests within Gazprom had important effects on the energy-poor states. First, the coexistence of these multiple interests added a variety of not officially acknowledged but de facto actors to negotiations between Russia and each of these states. Second, Gazprom's own lack of transparency, lack of clear corporate governance, and mingling of personal, corporate, and state interests in its management limited the company's ability to act coherently vis-à-vis the energy-poor states.

ROLE OF INTERMEDIARY COMPANIES

The growing role of intermediary companies such as Itera from the mid-1990s on was one manifestation of the increased significance of personal-interests-within-the-corporation in Gazprom during this period.[41] Originally developed as a means to facilitate the barter of Turkmenistan gas for Russian products at a time of severe liquidity constraints in the mid 1990s, intermediary companies quickly expanded and, by the late 1990s, had become a central feature of the post-Soviet political economy of gas.[42] Their growth was facilitated by the intermingling of state, corporate, and personal interests in Gazprom, as well as by the companies' dominant role in CA gas markets. Good relations with Gazprom allowed Itera to produce or buy gas at especially low prices; in particular, Gazprom sold gas to Itera at below-market internal transfer prices (thus minimizing taxes), gas that Itera subsequently exported at a higher price. Itera was able to do this because, in contrast with Gazprom, it operated outside of formal state-to-state agreements, was not subject to price ceilings, and could sell gas to countries such as Ukraine for prices higher than those charged by Gazprom. Indeed, if Itera's role in CIS markets has often been analysed mainly in terms of Gazprom's maximization of profits (the main argument being that the original transfer of CIS markets to Itera was a way to reduce Gazprom's losses resulting from politically motivated prices[43]), a closer look reveals the importance of other factors, in particular the role of personal-within-the-corporation interests in Itera's establishment.

Intermediary companies partially supplied gas from their own fields (in the case of Itera), and partially as intermediaries for the transit and/or sale of CA gas to these countries. Of the cases analysed in this book, intermediary companies were especially active in Ukraine, where from 1999 to 2002 supplies by Itera exceeded supplies by Gazprom; between 2000 and 2002, Itera exported more gas to CIS countries than Gazprom.[44] With the acquiescence of important players in each of the countries involved, Itera and related companies were able to divert significant profits from both Gazprom and the importing countries by charging high prices for services such as arranging transit for the benefit, not only of Itera, but of members of Gazprom's top management itself.[45]

If perhaps the best-known incidents of asset-striping in detriment of Gazprom but in benefit of intermediary companies concern Itera, the case is hardly unique. As we will see throughout the following chapters of this book, our case studies present numerous examples of situations where formally state-owned companies have been used by some of their top managers for the pursuit of personal interests.

Impact on the Energy-poor States

The important role played by intermediary companies had significant effects on Russia's gas relationships with CIS states, especially Ukraine. Looked at from the perspective of the energy-poor states, intermediary companies especially active in the trade of CA gas offered the promise of easing the way to geographical and contractual diversification.

In a purely short-term perspective, the deals put in place by intermediary companies could also help moderate price increases, as the official state companies (for example, Gazprom and NAK Naftohaz Ukraini) could be paid less, leaving a margin that could be used to charge lower prices than those charged by non-insider deals, while still retaining a margin for whatever accommodation money could be needed.[46] In a longer-term perspective, however, intermediary companies had much more detrimental effects. For example, it was not in the interest of Itera (and, arguably, in that of those high Gazprom management members presumably linked to it) that the question of the unsanctioned siphoning (e.g., stealing of gas) from the transit pipelines crossing Ukraine be solved. Indeed, totally closing the Ukrainian "black hole" would not have been in Itera's interest, as the company was suspected of illegally exporting 3-4 bcm of gas yearly to points West, but covering this up by ascribing it to "stealing by Ukraine."[47] As shown especially clearly by the Ukrainian case discussed in chapter 4, intermediary companies were often used for the shared appropriation of rents by Ukrainian and Russian elites, serving as an important mechanism for the short-term harmonization of their interests. Even when intermediary companies such as Itera and RosUkrEnergo officially presented themselves as devoted to coordinating interests in the energy area, it could hardly be expected that, given these interests, such companies could play a long-term positive role in helping reduce long-standing tensions between Ukraine and Russia around the gas stealing issue.

Last but not least, the misuse of corporate property for the pursuit of private profit through companies such as Itera affected the pressures and rent-seeking opportunities experienced by actors in the energy-poor states. Thus, for example, actors in the energy-poor states acquired new incentives to engage in corruption.[48] As will be discussed in more detail in chapters 4 and 6, intermediary companies provided actors in both Russia and the energy-poor states with important rent-seeking opportunities, and cannot be seen as one-sidedly benefitting the Russian side alone. Their important role in trade with the energy-poor states, however, is directly related to Gazprom's internal organization and domestic role. Paradoxical as this may seem at first, it was Gazprom's de facto monopolization of post-Soviet gas trade that set the stage for the important role played by intermediary companies. This is so because it was exactly this monopoly role that gave Gazprom (or, more likely, influential players within it) the ability to sway actors into accepting such intermediary companies.

It could be argued that this very monopolization made it easier for those pursuing personal interests within the corporation to push under-the-table, nontransparent arrangements on their energy-poor partners than if there was no monopolization. This is so because in the absence of a real competitive gas market, it was easier for actors within Gazprom to peddle alternative, poorly regulated deals as the only possible means for diversifying contracts. With Gazprom enjoying access to proprietary information on gas flows, as the sole regulator of the export pipeline, and with a "relatively costless and effortless way of hiding its profits,"[49] managers also involved in other schemes were able to effectively present these as alternatives to the company's monopoly.[50] In other words, the monopoly and gate-keeping powers held by Gazprom as a corporation gave individual actors within it the perfect conditions to create artificial scarcities that could then be turned into rent-seeking opportunities.[51]

The rise of intermediary companies, many of which dealt with CA gas, took place in the context of Gazprom's growing involvement in CA markets. Thus a small excursus on the issue is in order, before we return to issue of changes in Gazprom after 2001.

Gazprom, Central Asia, and the Energy-poor States: A Brief Excursus

One of the options available to Gazprom to compensate for its own decreasing production was to tap CA gas production. By the early 2000s, CA gas had become essential for Gazprom to make up the difference between its domestic production and its total commitments (domestic demand and export contracts to CIS and WE markets).[52]

Yet these increased imports from CA were also the result of a business decision: that it would more advantageous to import gas from CA for re-export to WE markets than to engage in the large-scale development of expensive new fields.[53] (While this model worked more or less efficiently as long as CA leaders could be coaxed into selling gas to Gazprom at prices significantly lower than WE prices, this changed cardinally in 2008 as Gazprom and Turkmenistan signed an agreement providing for, effective 2009, the sale of that gas to Gazprom at European prices, while WE gas prices declined.[54])

What were the implications of Russia's growing reliance on, and growing role in, CA gas markets, for Russia's energy-poor neighbours? First, CA gas was used by Gazprom for something more than simply filling in for domestic production – it was also used to delay the demonopolization of the domestic gas market, as it allowed Gazprom to continue to fulfil its export commitments without opening access to exports to other Russian producers. This affected Ukraine, Belarus, and Lithuania by preventing the emergence of alternatives to Russian supplies from Gazprom. Second, Gazprom's buying up of a significant share of (in some cases the whole) gas production of CA states such as Turkmenistan created obvious problems for the energy-poor states' ability to diversify, as – at least in theory – CA gas was the only realistic alternative to sole dependency on Russian gas open to some energy-poor states such as Ukraine. Third, Gazprom's near-monopolization of CA gas exports and gatekeeper role in their marketing facilitated the involvement of Russian-based intermediaries in energy trade between CA and the energy-poor states.[55] This made it possible for new forms of corruption to emerge, best exemplified by companies such as Eural Trans Gas and RosUkrEnergo that, as discussed in chapter 4, were able to, with the acquiesce of important players in each of the countries involved, divert significant profits from Gazprom and the importing countries by charging high prices for services, such as arranging transit, that could be offered directly by Gazprom at a much lower price.[56]

Last but not least, the actual modalities under which CA gas trade was conducted – under whose control and under what rules of the game – had important effects in terms of the energy poor states' broader energy trade with Russia. How manipulations around CA gas would be part of corrupt rent-seeking arrangements also involving Russian players would come to affect the possibility of this gas becoming a factor of real diversification (as opposed to pseudo-diversification) for these states.

Pre- and Post-2001 Changes in Gazprom and Their Impact on Personal Interests within the Corporation

Impatience with the asset striping and other personal-interest-within-the-corporation deals to the benefit of Itera and other intermediary companies going on at Gazprom – as well as with the company's alliance with Kremlin foe Moscow mayor Yuri Luzhkov – partially explains the government's 2001 initiative not to reappoint Gazprom CEO Viakhirev.[57] Most often, the change has been interpreted as a reassertion of Gazprom's corporate interests, as opposed to personal interests within the corporation. Together with growing state control of the oil sector after 2003 (discussed later in this chapter), Viakhirev's dismissal is most often interpreted as an example of growing state control of the energy sector. An alternative explanation of this change, however, focuses on Putin's need to establish full control over Russia's biggest company after he became president in 2000; thus Viakhirev's replacement by Miller, and that of gas-sector professionals with many years of experience by younger professionals from the close-to-Putin

St. Petersburg group with little gas experience but proven loyalty to the new president.[58]

While these personnel changes signalled a strengthening of Putin's allies within the company, they did not, however, mean an end of divisions within the company, nor an end of personal interests within the corporation.[59] Indeed, rent-seeking through intermediary companies did not end with Viakhirev's removal. As will be discussed in detail in chapters 4, 5, and 6, if around 2002–2003 a trend towards replacing Itera or other suppliers for the benefit of either Gazprom itself (in the case of Belarus) or other Gazprom-related intermediary companies (Ukraine, Lithuania) could be observed, this change seemed to have been more about the names of the companies involved than about a cessation of their often corrupt rent-seeking. In terms of divisions within the company, it is worth noting the emergence of a strong pipeline lobby within Gazprom during this period – a phenomenon with both policy (building of new pipelines sidestepping Ukraine and Belarus) and potential rent-seeking implications.[60] Another example of divisions within Gazprom concerns the tension between *siloviki* (representatives of the security apparatus) and civilians within the company, best exemplified by the conflict between head of the Presidential Administration Igor Sechin and Dimitry Medvedev during the latter's tenure as chairman or vice-Chairman of Gazprom's board (2000–2003).

Despite these caveats, it is clear that after 2001 Gazprom becomes a more consolidated entity, as seen, for example, by the way subsidiaries associated with private-interests-within-the-corporation were bought back by the company after 2001. After 2001, Gazprom is also more protected by the executive, as seen by its success at reducing its tax liabilities and at fending off attempts by reformers (such as the Minister of Economic Development German Gref) to restructure the company.[61]

GAZPROM'S INVESTMENT POLICIES

Gazprom's investment strategies have been blamed by many for the company's declining production after 1991. Even if figuring into the equation the company's difficult economic situation in the early- and mid-1990s, at issue have been fundamental questions of investment preferences given these limited resources. Much of Gazprom's investment policy since 1992 was directed, not so much towards upstream operations (e.g., replacing reserves and increasing production), or core downstream activities (assuring reliability of deliveries and the efficient use of existing pipeline infrastructure), but towards the acquisition of non-core businesses (*neprofilnie aktivy*). Plans to develop high-cost and less immediately crucial midstream infrastructure such as new pipelines largely duplicating already existing ones through Ukraine and Belarus, would also be examples of this tendency. Although serious discussion of building pipeline infrastructure specifically to bypass Ukraine and Belarus – the Nord Stream and White Stream projects – did not start until about 2006, already in the earlier period Gazprom was devoting significant investment resources to major alternative export infrastructure projects, such as the Yamal-Europe pipeline through Belarus and Blue Stream through Turkey. Gazprom's purchase of newspapers and TV stations critical of the Russian government, arguably at the request of the Kremlin and with the aim to limit their critical voice, was an additional area of questionable investments.

Impact on the Relationship with the Energy-poor States

The neglect of investments in production and core transit infrastructure had important consequences for the relationship with the energy-poor states.

First, whereas the state of disrepair of export pipelines crossing Ukraine has received most attention, lack of investments in the upkeep of Russia's own aging pipeline system led to the inefficient operation of the turbines moving gas through the pipeline, and to reduced pressure ratings that in turn limited the amount of gas the system could transport, in addition to increased losses through gas leaks. These are not trivial issues, as gas used in the operation of the gas pipeline system itself is gas that is not available for export.[62] Reduced pipeline throughput capacities led, in turn, to smaller spare transmission capacities (repeatedly cited by Gazprom as the crucial reason for limiting third party access) and hindered the development of domestic competition in the upstream sector.[63] The causality, however, could be looked at differently: in fact, Gazprom has used lack of spare capacity in the system as an excuse for limiting third party access to its pipeline system. Limited investments in the core downstream sector also affected Gazprom's ability to bring to market the gas it produces, strengthening dependency on transit states and neighbouring countries having significant storage facilities.

The Political Economy of Russian Oil

The specificities of the Russian oil industry are closely related to its development in the post-Soviet period. Following a 1992 presidential decree calling for the breakup of the state monopoly on oil, a number of companies were set up either on a geographical (the Eastern Oil Company), republican (Tatarstan's Tatneft, Bashkortostan's Bashneft) or a vertically integrated basis combining production units, refineries, and distribution facilities irrespective of the geographical location of their units (LUKoil, Surgutneftegaz). While a significant portion of shares was sold to company insiders, the state would retain a majority of shares in most of these companies until the 1994–1995 loans for shares program where, cash-strapped, the state put oil and other strategic industries up as collateral for large loans. With the nonrepayment of these loans, some of the country's most strategic assets (including oil companies Sidanko, Yukos, and Sibneft) became the property of emerging private banks. This process was also widely seen as President Boris Yeltsin's capitulation to budding domestic oligarchs, whose economic power grew immensely as a result of the deals. By 1996, Russia's oil sector had emerged from the privatization process with the former oil monopolist divided among eleven vertically integrated, partially privatized companies.[64]

Russia's Changing Oil Resource Base

Similar to the case of gas, the early 2000s signified for Russia the end of cheap oil. As can be seen in Table 3.3, the disarray immediately following the Soviet demise led to sharp declines in oil production, which went from 461 million tons in 1991 to 301 in 1996. Production stabilized between 1996 and 2000, and started to grow again in 1999 – strongly until 2004, and at a much more moderate pace until 2007, after which it started to decline slightly.[65] By the late 1990s, growing export prices relative to production costs led the oil companies to seek to maximize exports as a means to increase liquidity, but their strategy during this period was a short-term one, as they sought to increase production for export largely through the acquisition of smaller companies, and not by investing in substantial exploration that would ensure the long-term sustainability of such level of exports.

Strong increases in production in the early 2000s coincided with the consolidation of private control over oil companies. Undoubtedly, the increase in world oil prices during the 2000s, which made production from previously marginal fields profitable, was an important contributing cause, but there is debate about other causes at play. Some have argued that it was the new companies' Western management style that

Table 3.3 Russian Oil Production and Exports, 1991–2010 (in Million Tons)

Year	Oil Production	Exports to CIS (for 2003–2009 FSU)	Exports to Rest of the World	Total Exports
1991	461	117	57	174
1992	396	76	66	142
1993	344	48	80	128
1994	316	38	89	127
1995	307	31	91	122
1996	301	23	103	126
1997	306	21	106	127
1998	303	25	112	137
1999	305	22	112	135
2000	323	17	126	143
2001	347	23	135	158
2002	361	N/A	N/A	185
2003	421	44	181	225
2004	459	49	205	255
2005	470	46	205	251
2006	481	42	205	248
2007	491	37	217	253
2008	489	35	203	238
2009	494	34	211	246
2010	505	N/A	224	234

Sources: (1991–2000) IEA, *Russian Energy Survey 2002* (Paris, OECD/IEA, 2002), 73, 91 (Tables 4.5 and 4.9), (2001) Catherine Locatelli, "The Russian oil industry between public and private governance: obstacles to international oil companies' investment strategies," *Energy Policy* 34 (2006): 1078 (Table 2), (2002) Shinichiro Tabata, "Observations on the Influence of High Oil Prices on Russia's GDP Growth," *Eurasian Geography and Economics* 47, no.1 (2006), 96 (Fig. 1), (2007–2012), calculated by the author on basis of various press sources. Unit conversions by the author.

was first and foremost responsible for these improvements and that, similarly, post-2005 declines in production are to blame on inefficient management after the increase in state control. Others have argued that it was actually the 1998 economic crisis that helped boost oil production, as the devaluation of the ruble reduced production costs in comparison to export prices, which increased sharply in the 1999–2000 period.[66] Still others argue that these increases in production were mainly the result of easy-to-lift oil left on the ground during the period of decreased production in the mid-1990s.[67] The trend towards increased production continued until 2007.

As in the case of gas, in addition to production volumes, reserve replacement ratios are an important indicator of future production trends. Whereas in the Soviet period yearly additions to reserves typically far exceeded production, exploration of new reserves fell drastically after 1991, reducing reserve replacement, which fell below production for most of the period 1994–2004.[68]

Domestic Oil Issues and Their Effect on Sector Actors' Participation in Transborder Value-added Chains and Rent-seeking Arrangements

Some of the same types of domestic issues that we saw in the case of gas also affected relations with the energy-poor states in the case of oil. However, the specificities of oil production, transportation, and value-added chains also played a role, meriting a separate discussion. Some of the most important issues at stake were issues related to the state of oil-related infrastructure, the state's relationship with major Russian and international oil companies, the role of Transneft as exports gatekeeper, and the impact of taxation modalities in the area. Each of these elements, which we discuss further on, had important implications for Russia's energy-poor neighbours.

EXISTING INFRASTRUCTURE

Two aspects of Russia's oil infrastructure were to have an important effect on relations with energy-poor neighbours: limited export pipeline capacity and limited oil refining capacity. A shortage of oil export pipeline capacity, largely due to poor maintenance, limited oil producers' ability to bring oil to market, and allowed the state to use access to oil export capacity as means to influence private oil companies. Another important infrastructure issue concerned Russia's limited oil refining capacity. During the Soviet period, decisions on the building of refineries were made on the basis of the USSR as a single energy market, with specific oil refineries throughout the USSR linked with specific production areas in Russia.[69] As a result, some of the largest and most advanced refineries were located outside Russia – especially in Belarus and Ukraine – a factor that would increase the attractiveness of refining in these countries as an often more profitable means of supplying

WE markets (and, in some cases, close-to-the border Russian markets as well). With refining capacities far exceeding local production, these refineries came to rely on ties with Russian producers for their survival; Russian producers, in turn, had strong incentives to use these idle refining capacities as a way to maximize their own value-added chain. As noted in chapter 1, at issue was not so much Russia's lack of refining capacity per se, but the lack of modern facilities offering the necessary deepness of refining to maximize the added value of exports to WE.

OIL COMPANIES' RELATIONSHIP WITH THE STATE

In the case of oil, relations between state and private actors developed somewhat differently than in the case of gas due to the different historical trajectories of both sectors since 1991, as well as structural factors, such as Gazprom's ownership of its export pipelines, while oil producers had to rely almost exclusively on export pipelines owned by Transneft.[70]

Earlier in this chapter, we discussed how the use and transfer of "convertible points" from the foreign policy realm to a domestic arena, and eventually converted to monetary benefits, varied from sector to sector and case to case. In contrast with the case of gas, the means available to the Russian state – at least until 2003 with the onset of the confrontation with Yukos – to affect the behaviour of oil companies seem to have been more formal than in the case of gas. The main instruments used for this were export taxes, the ability to regulate the size of exports vis-à-vis domestic supplies, export quotas and, more generally, control of access to the export pipeline by transit pipeline operator Transneft.[71]

The regulation of exports through the Transneft state-owned system of oil export pipelines has been crucial given Russia's oil export pipeline volume deficit relative to production.[72] Although all companies were in theory allowed to export about 30 percent of their production, de facto those with greater lobbying power were able to export a higher percentage of their production.[73] Additional export quotas (*dopqvoty*) were granted for a variety of reasons, for example, as compensation for otherwise unpaid (or paid only subsequently) services to the state.[74] Yet there seemed to be no fully institutionalized system as to the adjudication of additional quotas, leaving the system prone to manipulation on the basis of political or other interests. This added significance to the question of who controls Transneft; given its power, it is not surprising that the company found itself at the centre of repeated battles for its control throughout the 1990s and early 2000s.

The Yukos Case and Its Effects on the Energy-poor States

The years 2003–2004 marked a key a change in the main means of influence used by the state in its interaction with oil companies. If until about 2003 the main means for such influence was control over export infrastructure (through pipeline operator Transneft for oil and Transneftprodukt for oil products), after 2003 we start to see the beginnings of stronger and more direct control. Many ascribe the change in government tactics to the breakdown of the compromise achieved between President Putin and Russian oligarchs upon his coming to power, in the sense of the state respecting their ownership rights – however murkily acquired – over strategic assets such as oil companies, in exchange for some changes in their behaviour (a less speculative approach), and, most crucially, a retreat from politics.

Nothing served as a clearer sign of these changes as the arrest of Yukos' – until then Russia's largest oil company[75] – CEO Mikhail Khodorkovskii in October 2003. By December 2004 Yukos had been largely dismantled, with much of its property passing to state hands.[76] In particular, Yukos' filing for bankruptcy to cover the government's tax claims facilitated the sale of its assets to largely state-owned Rosneft, which became Russia's largest oil producer as a result.

Changes in the relationship between major oil players and the state affected relations with the energy-poor states through the effects of ownership changes on who would control the use – including the use for political purposes – of these companies' assets in the energy-poor states. This was most clear in the case of Lithuania, where Yukos had purchased a controlling package of shares in the Mazeikiu Nafta refinery in 2002 (see chapter 6). In that case, the poor relationship between Yukos and the Russian government made it impossible for the refinery to access necessary crude oil supplies from Russia, dooming the enterprise from its very start. Second, as Mazeiku Nafta came under threat as a result of the Russian state's decision to liquidate the assets of its mother company, Yukos, the company, feeling threatened by the Kremlin and in urgent need for cash to pay its growing tax bill, responded by agreeing to sell the totality of its share package in the refinery. As the battle for control of Yukos' assets continued, Rosneft, which had assumed Yukos' debt, sued to block the sale of Mazeiku Nafta to the new bidder, Poland's Orlen, but was not successful.[77]

State Control or Crony Control?

Yukos' liquidation was followed by other significant changes increasing the state's role in the oil sector. The growing state presence in the energy sector was seen not only through the state reaching ownership of 51 percent of Gazprom's shares in 2005, but through the reversal of policies concerning foreign investment in important gas projects such as the Sakhalin II project – where, in disregard to previous agreements, foreign investors (the Royal Dutch Shell–led consortium) were pressured to retreat from the multi-billion dollar oil and gas development project and a controlling stake in the project was transferred to Gazprom.

In September 2005, Roman Abramovich – one of Russia's wealthiest oligarchs remaining after the forced easing out of Khodorkovskii in 2003 – under pressure from the Kremlin, sold a majority stake in Sibneft, Russia's fifth-largest oil producer, to Gazprom, whose acquisition of Sibneft's assets was especially notable as it made it a significant oil producer, broke the administrative division between oil and gas, and seemed to pave the road for the eventual establishment of a powerful state-controlled *kontsern* encompassing both oil and gas assets, which could become a mighty instrument for the pursuit of foreign policy goals. By 2008, the Russian government had significantly increased its ownership role in the oil sector, holding 75 percent of shares in Rosneft, Russia's largest oil producer, and significant minority stakes in several smaller oil companies.

How should we interpret these events? Is the story of the Russian gas and oil industry after 2003 simply one of increased *state* control? The conventional narrative would argue that the changes in the Russian oil (and gas) sector after 2001, including but not limited to Yukos' takeover, represented an increased level of state control over the sector. Although there was, indeed, increased state ownership in both sectors, two caveats are in order. First, state ownership in and of itself does not tell the whole story, as the means for control of an enterprise may take a variety of forms – from setting the rules of the game to controlling the transportation of its products – above and beyond ownership. Second, despite widespread coverage of Putin bringing the state back in, the actual meaning of this often-used phrase is unclear. First, because of the lack of a consistent policy due to competition between different leadership factions with different agendas.[78] Second, because of the continued lack of clarity as to whether what is being presented as state interests in the battle against anti-Putin oligarchs may actually concern the private interests of Putin's close associates.[79] Moreover, given the lack of democratic control over policy making, Putin's proclaimed drive to free the state from the power of interest groups was, de facto, prone to be accompanied by an increase in opportunities for business capture by new close-to-the-Kremlin elites.[80]

Particularities of Russia's Oil Taxation

Russia's oil taxation system, known for giving companies few incentives to increase production from existing fields or to invest in expanding future production capacity, had important effects on relations with the energy-poor states. This was due not only to the nature of Russian oil taxation (that, despite fine-tuning in the early 2000s, remained generally highly onerous for producers), but also to uncertainty about its application, including the existence of significant and particularly nontransparent informal taxes.[81] More generally, the weakness of both property rights and user rights (such as exploration licenses) for mineral resources, often used as a means for compelling oil companies to share resource rent with the state, created strong disincentives for oil companies to invest, fostering short-term strategies focused on maximizing output instead.[82]

One specificity of post-Soviet Russia's oil regulation system has been the continued use (with a short interruption from 1996 to 1999) of oil export duties (*eksportnye poshlini*, often translated as export taxes), an instrument rarely used by other countries.[83] Officially justified by the state as a way to create institutional incentives or disincentives for oil exports, such duties and taxes were also used to regulate access to scarce export pipeline capacity and, possibly, for more direct political purposes.

Russian companies' interests in the energy-poor neighbours were impacted by such export regulations, which affected incentives to engage in various refining and re-exporting schemes in order to maximize sales to high-profit markets and, thus, profits. This is so because shipments to certain CIS or Customs Union countries, most notably Belarus (as well as, during some periods, Ukraine) did not count as exports during much of the 1991–2013 period.[84] (Indeed, the issue of which countries should be exempted from these export duties was a constant issue of debate, and also used by the Russian side for political purposes.[85])

The impact was especially seen in the case of Belarus, which, for most of the period examined in this book, was not considered a foreign export destination and deliveries to which were not subject to export duties.[86] Exporting crude oil to Belarus for refining and subsequent sale to third markets was an attractive means of circumventing Russian export limitations, and also allowed the Belarusian government to reap very large profits that, as will be discussed in chapter 6, became crucial for its economic and political survival. As export limitations on the part of the Russian government increased, this often led to more oil being shipped to Belarus (and Ukraine) for refining and subsequent indirect export in the form of oil products. Similarly, 2002 changes in the tax code making the size of oil export duties dependent on world prices increased the incentives for Russian companies to avoid these during periods of rising world oil prices by engaging in such refining and re-exporting schemes.[87]

Conclusion

Throughout the period covered by this book, Russian energy actors had to balance a number of different interests vis-à-vis the state and other local and international actors. This helps us explain, among others, their willingness to supply oil and gas to CIS markets despite their very limited profitability until 2008. Lower price levels in most post-Soviet markets were largely compensated by the possibility for large and easily accessible rent-seeking through arbitrage gains from price differentials between different energy markets (in turn related to the way exports to various post-Soviet markets were designated and taxed[88]), by the importance of transit countries as elements in Russian companies' value-added chains, and by the system of virtual "convertible points," which allowed domestic energy producers to convert their losses in an area into advantages in other aspects of their relationship with the state.

These three elements manifested themselves differently in the oil and gas sectors. In the case of oil, through a more institutionalized relationship between the state and oil companies, and, in the case of gas, subsumed, in a much more politicized way, into the general relationship between Gazprom and the state, a relationship complicated by the multiple roles often played by the Gazprom leadership, at times as Gazprom managers and at times as private rent-seekers.

Russia: An Energy Giant with Feet of Clay?

During the period covered by this book, Russia remained a paradoxical energy power. On the one hand, its large gas and oil resources made it a crucial player, giving the country a strong basis for international leverage. On the other hand, significant domestic problems (declining gas production, creeping Dutch disease, an outdated and poorly managed energy infrastructure, and over-dependency on volatile energy revenues) made Russia an energy giant with feet of clay. In particular, the broader disbalances in the Russian economy often referred to in shorthand as "rentier state disease" also affected Russia's ability to project its energy power in neighbouring states.

While there is little doubt that Russia has sought to use energy as a means to exert political power over its energy-poor neighbours, Russia's use of energy for foreign policy goals was itself limited by a number of domestic factors. Some of these factors, as we have discussed in this chapter, had to do with physical limits on the resource itself and the cost involved in bringing supplies to market. Russia's growing commitments to use energy in other geographical directions (including domestically for various policy and political reasons) further limited the energy resources available for political pressure on the neighbouring states. Last but not least, domestic Russian rent-seeking around oil and gas (and the Kremlin's either participating in it or tolerating it for domestic political reasons) also affected Russia's ability to use energy as a means of foreign policy pressure. As will be seen in the following case studies, however, the role of Russian energy actors in the energy-poor states went well beyond Russia's ability to use energy as a foreign policy tool. Rather, energy actors on both sides of the border found themselves tied to each other in a multitude of ways, deeply enmeshed into local value-added and rent-seeking chains and, ultimately, in the domestic cycle of energy rents.

PART TWO

Case Studies

4 Ukraine:
Energy Dependency and the Rise of the Ukrainian Oligarchs

Our first case study is Ukraine, a country whose energy troubles since independence have brought energy-poor post-Soviet states to international attention.

In the winter of 1993–1994, energy supply problems and an energy war with Russia led to freezing home temperatures in Ukraine.[1] As citizens froze, their trust in their leaders and in the wisdom of having chosen Ukrainian sovereignty started to wane. In the winter of 2008–2009, an energy war between Ukraine and Russia led to a cut-off of gas supplies and the prospect of freezing home temperatures in Romania, Bulgaria, Slovakia, and other parts of the EU and the Balkans. As citizens faced the crisis, their trust in Russia as a supplier, Ukraine as a transit state, and in the EU as an institution to which some national sovereignty could be transferred in exchange for a basic level of everyday security, started to wane. What happened in these fifteen years, and in the period after the 2008–2009 crisis? How did Ukraine's domestic conditions affect the country's ability to react proactively to its changing international energy environment?

Ukraine as Case Study

Ukraine's recurring crises in its energy relationship with Russia have brought it repeatedly to the international headlines. Perhaps the best-known case of a post-Soviet energy-dependent state, Ukraine's situation is largely representative of that of the other cases. Although its absolute level of energy dependency (ca. 42 percent in the mid-2000s[2]) is lower than that of Belarus and Lithuania, once nuclear fuel is included in the picture, this level, at about 53 percent, becomes more alarming.[3] As will be discussed further on, however, Ukraine's energy dependency on Russia is also moderated by elements of asymmetrical interdependence.

Ukraine's Transit Role and Asymmetrical Interdependence

Ukraine's importance as a transit route for Russian oil and gas west was highlighted during the gas crises of January 2006 and 2009, when Russian-Ukrainian disputes came to affect WE consumers directly. Despite recurring crises, as of 2010 more than 80 percent of Russia's gas exports to WE went through Ukraine, exports representing about 56 percent of Gazprom's profits.[4] Although Ukraine's role in oil transit is smaller (transiting 14–17 percent of total Russian oil exports in the mid-2000s[5]), it remains the world's "most significant hydrocarbon transit country."[6]

In addition to its transit role, three additional elements increase Ukraine's potential energy bargaining power vis-á-vis Russian energy actors. First, its extensive underground gas storage facilities are important for Gazprom as they allow gas to be parked for later sale in EU markets at peak demand periods for higher prices. Ukraine's thirteen gas storage facilities are unique not only due to their size (equivalent to 21 percent of Europe's total underground gas storage capacity[7]), but also to their location, as most are situated near Ukraine's western borders, in close proximity to EU markets. Second, Ukraine's important oil refining facilities, located near the border with Poland and the Odesa port, were attractive to Russian companies as a convenient means of supplying WE markets.[8] Finally, Ukraine – the fifth largest gas importer and eighth largest gas user in the world as of 2007[9] – was becoming increasingly interesting as a paying market, especially as Ukrainian gas prices continued to grow closer to WE prices starting in 2007.

Despite Russian subsidization of energy supplies to Ukraine in the form of preferential prices and barter arrangements for most of the post-Soviet period, the previous factors highlight Russian energy actors' self-interest in retaining Ukraine as both transit partner and sale market. This partially explains Russian actors, especially Gazprom, offering Ukraine a buffer from and/or gradual transition to world prices for much of the 1991–2005 period, much less likely to create a restructuring of the economy away from Russian supplies than a sudden price increase.[10]

Other Specific Characteristics of the Ukrainian Energy Situation

An important specificity of the Ukrainian case during the period examined in this book concerns its being simultaneously *energy-poor but rent-rich*. Because of its dual role as both an important energy market and energy transit route (being, by volume, the largest gas transit country in the world[11]) several billion US dollars of energy-related real or virtual money changes hands in Ukraine yearly (expenditures on gas imports alone were ca. $14 billion in 2011, up from and ca. $ 8.6 in 2008; gas transit revenue amounted to $2.34 billion in 2008, and $1.88 billion in 2009[12]; see also Table 4.3). Of the cases analysed in this book, it is in Ukraine where we see the largest range of potential domestic rent-acquisition opportunities in the energy trade area, and the largest revenue potential in energy rent-seeking. It is also in this case that domestic struggles for the control of energy-related profits have been most keen, and have had the clearest repercussions throughout state and society.

How did the model of extraction, distribution, and recycling of energy rents manifest itself in the Ukrainian case? The chapter investigates how Ukraine's central role in energy transit, the continuation of preferentially priced supplies by Russia, and the domestic institutional system interacted to create unique opportunities for Ukraine-based actors to access both domestic and external rents. In terms of the distribution of rents, the chapter will analyse how Ukraine's political and interest representation system affected the distribution of these rents between various domestic groups. Concerning the recycling of these rents into the political system, our chapter examines how energy rents contributed to the emergence of important political players and groupings, to their increased power, and to their attempts to steer energy policy making in ways that would allow them to continue accessing these new sources of rents.

The chapter proceeds as follows. After a brief overview of the development of the Ukrainian economy and political system since independence and its impact on energy policy making, the chapter analyses Ukraine's management of its energy dependency between 1992 and the election of Yanukovich as president in February 2010. The last section extends the analysis to 2013, looks at the outcomes of such management, and concludes with an assessment of the effects of such management patterns on Ukraine's domestic politics and foreign relations.

The Ukrainian Economy since Independence: Major Trends

Ukraine's energy policies were influenced by changes in the country's overall economic situation and policies since independence. The early years, largely coinciding with the tenure in office of first Ukrainian President Leonid Kravchuk (1991–1994), were marked by the effects of Soviet disintegration and the collapse of intra-USSR trade, leading to a sharp decrease in exports and associated revenue.

While Kravchuk's tenure was not characterized by as blatant and widespread corruption and rent-seeking as would come to exist during later years, the lack of any serious economic reforms during this period may have been at the root of later problems. Kyiv's policy response to the post-Soviet disintegration crisis was based largely on the generous provision of cheap state credits and other subsidies, leading to growing deficits, inflation (which at its high point in 1993 reached more than ten thousand percent per year) and a severe liquidity crisis. From 1991 to 1998, Ukraine's real Gross Domestic Product (GDP) also declined cumulatively by more than 62 percent, among post-Soviet states second only to Turkmenistan's.

The introduction of the Hryvnia as national currency in September 1996 set into motion a more general stabilization of the economy under Leonid Kuchma's first term as president. However, reforms remained haphazard and contradictory, largely as the result of the lack of a clear reform coalition in the Parliament (Verkhovna Rada, thereafter Rada). The period started around 1999 and continuing until 2001, coinciding with Viktor Yushchenko's brief tenure as Prime Minister (PM), was characterized by a short hiatus of relatively bold reforms, especially the start of large-enterprise privatization and reforms aimed at reducing barter transactions and arrears in the energy sector. However, the privatization campaign, including the sale of major oil refineries to Russian companies, was plagued by problems of lack of transparency and insider dealings.[13] Yuschenko's other reforms were largely stalled after his removal from office.

The early- and mid- 2000s saw the Ukrainian economy growing again, with GDP reaching 12 percent annual growth in 2004. However, this period of growth between Yushchenko's dismissal as PM in 2001 and his return to power as president in 2005 was not accompanied by a renewed commitment to economic reform, and can rather be characterized as a period of "frozen transition"[14] under "competitive oligarchy with high growth."[15] Despite the immediate political watershed of the Orange Revolution of 2004–2005, for much of the period 2006–2008,

Ukraine seemed to continue to be stuck in a no-man's land of limited reforms despite robust levels of economic growth.[16] Much of this growth, however, was based on the increase in the volumes and prices of steel and iron exports; dependence on such exports, together with Ukraine's dependence on imported gas (much of it used, in turn, for metallurgical production), made the country especially vulnerable to terms-of-trade shocks. In the fall of 2008, the world financial crisis led to the collapse of Ukraine's main exports, steel and chemical products, leading to an annualized (y/y) GDP decline of 20 percent and plunging the country into a major financial crisis. With the help of a large standby program from the International Monetary Fund (IMF), the economy started to stabilize in 2010. (The original $16.5 billion program was not fully implemented, however, due to the IMF's concerns about the pace of reform, especially in the energy sector.)

These economic changes had important effects on Ukraine's energy sector and on her energy relationship with Russia, first and foremost by affecting the country's energy demand and its capacity to pay for energy imports. They also affected the power of various interest articulators, the types of energy-related rents available, and limited the range of policy choices available to the Ukrainian leadership.

Ukraine's de facto Political System Since Independence

A central argument of this book is that the nature of their political arrangements has affected the energy-dependent countries' management of their dependencies by affecting the way energy rents will be accessed, distributed, and recycled into the system, as well as by affecting the opportunities available for the articulation of Russian energy actors' interests in each country. How did the specific features of the Ukrainian political system under Presidents Kuchma (1994–2004) and Yushchenko (2005–2010) affect energy policy making? Following, we focus on three important elements of this system – the system of interest articulation, the role of the executive, and the role of the parliament – whose interaction greatly affected the way politics and policy making were de facto conducted in Ukraine.

Politics and Interest Representation under Kuchma

In the early post-independence period (1992–1994), the main cleavages between groups had to do largely with each group's position in the economic structure as well as its sectoral interests[17] (such as those associated with the agrarian sector, the former CPSU nomenklatura, the managers of state enterprises ["red directors"], and new businesses), not so much on regional relationships. By the mid-1990s, however, the main interest articulation cleavages start to change to regional-based ones. Many red directors (many of whom had by now gained ownership or de facto control over state property), Kuchma's original power base, start to merge their interests with new regional economic structures,[18] and various groups within the "party of power,"[19] forming durable regional-based structures, which eventually became known as "clans" or, more accurate for the case of Ukraine, business-administrative groups (BAGs).[20]

While not free of internal conflict, by the late 1990s the Dnipropetrovsk, Donetsk, and Kyiv clans, Ukraine's main in-system (see further on) BAGs, had each developed separate public identities and mighty structures including media outlets, regional leaders and political parties, and representation in the Rada and in more informal policy making arenas.[21] Each of these main BAGs also had important energy-related interests.[22]

President Kuchma played an important role as balancer between these players. This "balancing" system centred on in-system BAGs; that is, those groups participating in the president-centred system of exchange of economic favours for political support; consequently, our discussion of the 1994–2004 period focuses on these groups. Much of the distribution of energy rents during this period would be based on this balancing.

However, it is important to note that during the Kuchma period non-system groups were also active, many of them associated with former members of the main in-system groups that had grown dissatisfied by the system and defected from the Kuchma camp, for example former deputy head of the Social Democratic Party of Ukraine (united) (SDPU[o]) Oleksandr Zinchenko, "sweets baron" Petro Poroshenko, and Kyiv major Oleksandr Omel'chenko. While these non-system elites had a much smaller access to the system of rents in exchange for political favours, they had access to their own sources of income – including some energy-related rents – much of which was deposited or invested abroad, outside the control of the Kuchma regime. Moreover, they had their own party structures (including, after 2002, Yushchenko's Nasha Ukraina) and control over some important media outlets.[23] Such independent access to economic resources by non-system groups, as well as control of some of the necessary structures to transform these resources into political muscle, is one major difference between the Ukrainian and Belarusian cases, affecting the way energy rents would be recycled into the political system.

Role of the Executive

While BAGs competed for control over policies and related economic benefits, they had a common interest in the maintenance of a predictable system of presidential balancing between them, as opposed to the wild and often excessively violent system of economic competition prevalent in the mid-1990s. This balancing was promoted through both divide-and-rule measures intended to play various groups against each other, and more integrative measures to keep the level of conflict under control by adding a measure of predictability to the system of access to governmental positions and state-related rents.[24]

Formally a democracy, the Kuchma regime was characterized by the lack of transparent policy making and by the existence of an informal balance between various BAGs, arbitrated by the president. Further, Kuchma's regime can be described as one based on competitive authoritarianism where, despite the existence of democratic institutions, these are systematically manipulated by the regime through bribery, cooptation, and other informal means that nevertheless fall short of a clear violation of existing laws.[25] Kuchma's role as arbiter came to be reflected in the 1996 constitution, which gave the president significant additional powers and represented recognition by the main interest articulators of their "need of a strong president as a means of [regulating] their influence on each other."[26] The new constitution greatly strengthened presidential powers, creating, in D'Anieri's words, "one of the most powerful presidencies in the world."[27] Despite occasional disagreements with his prime ministers, the president's significant formal and informal powers clearly gave him the upper hand in that relationship, to the point that the Ukrainian system under Kuchma could be characterized as a presidential one.[28]

The president's formal powers – such as the power to appoint the government (subject to approval by the Rada), as well as the authority to appoint regional governors under Ukraine's unitary system – buttressed his institutional position by putting important limits on the potential independence of the Cabinet of Ministers[29] and strengthening presidential party of power clientelistic structures as well as governors' dependence on the president.[30] These formal powers were reinforced by considerable informal ones, especially over law enforcement agencies and the tax administration, constituting mighty administrative resources able to offer both selective rewards (such as preferential access to rents) and selective retribution (such as blackmailing or harassment by the tax service) when necessary[31] to favour allies or disadvantage competitors.

Role of the Verkhovna Rada

The significant presidential powers described above were highlighted by the relative inefficiency of other policy institutions, first and foremost the legislature. During the Kuchma period, the situation in the Rada was such that there was often no natural majority able to draft legislative initiatives proactively and have those passed in a timely and effective way.[32] Together with preexisting regional cleavages, this often led to a situation where the political struggle between parties would become largely reduced to "competition between the various BAGs for the rent."[33] Rada regulations in place until 2005 also contributed to this situation, as they encouraged the structuring of internal groups not along party lines, but on the basis of fluid factions that could be easily manipulated by economic interests.[34] The single mandate district electoral system in full (until 1998) or partial (until 2005) use at the time fostered competition between individual candidates, not parties, and fostered the election of a large number of deputies formally unaffiliated with any party, available to be recruited for membership in these factions – most often in one of the centrist factions close to the president – as part of their participation in the system of potential clientelistic rewards. Parliamentary immunity from criminal prosecution, a perk offered only by Rada membership, made the body especially attractive for businessmen working in the grey zone between legality and illegality, and their large presence in the Rada helped solidify the body's role as a means for furthering their interests.[35]

*Ukraine's Political and Interest-representation System
after the Orange Revolution*

The logic of interest representation changed after the Orange Revolution of late 2004, but only to a limited extent. While the Orange Revolution did not bring with it transparent policy making, the roles of various formal political institutions changed, as well as the main cleavages along which interest differentiation took place. Ukraine's political dynamics during the Yuschenko presidency (2005–2010) were characterized by the protracted impasse between two main interest-political groups (those represented by Yushchenko and on-and-off PM Yuliia Tymoshenko) and the mutual blocking of each other's policy making initiatives.

Interest Articulators and de facto System of Interest Articulation

Three important developments affected interest articulation following the Orange Revolution. One was the entrance into the "big oligarchs" political stage of new names, in particular Orange Revolution supporters such as Petro Poroshenko and Kostyantin Zhevago. In addition, old cleavages gave way to increased fluidity in interest alliances, with some division within the (close-to-the Donetsk BAG) Party of Regions, and some attempts by President Yushchenko to establish close relations with the Donetsk BAG as well. Last but not least, changes in the Ukrainian constitution, effective 1 January 2006 (discussed further on), crucially affected the interaction between president, PM, and the legislature.

Role of the Executive

If a central feature of the formal Ukrainian system under Kuchma was the coexistence of strong interest articulators and a strong president, after 2005 this was transformed in the direction of strong interest articulators and a somewhat weaker president. This was largely the result of the constitutional changes that came into force on 1 January 2006, significantly reducing the power of the president and increasing that of the PM and the Rada, now vested with the power to elect the PM and the Cabinet rather than merely approving presidential appointees. This synergized with informal factors such as President Yushchenko's growing alienation from the country's political life and competition with PM Tymoshenko, reducing his "leverage over resurgent elite struggles."[36]

Indeed, if we associate Kuchma with the role of arbiter between various economic groups, Yushchenko's name was, between 2006 and 2010, much more closely associated – in press reports and many analytical circles – not so much with balancing between BAGs, but with the direct lobbying of commercial interests, especially those of Dmytro Firtash, head of gas intermediary RosUkrEnergo.[37]

Role of the Verkhovna Rada

If during the classic balancing period under Kuchma it was often very difficult to create working coalitions in the Rada, the problem worsened after 2005. In addition to preexisting problems such as the weakness of parties themselves *as parties* (as opposed to vehicles for a single leader or economic interest group) and electoral and Rada regulations reducing parties' incentives for working together,[38] new issues came to affect the Rada's work, such as the fact that by 2008 many deputies in Yushchenko's own party, Nasha Ukraina-Natsionalna Samoborona (NUNS) had stopped supporting his legislative initiatives.[39] The shifting role of the Party of Regions, the ambiguous nature of its opposition, especially because of its intermittent bargaining with President Yushchenko through well-connected economic players such as Rinat Akhmetov and Borys Kolesnikov,[40] and constant speculation on whether it would ally with the Bloc Yuliia Tymoshenko against Yushchenko also contributed to this situation. At the same time, the Rada continued to be a main arena for the lobbying of economic interests; despite much talk and manipulation as a campaign issue in the 2007 Rada elections, parliamentary immunity remained in place throughout the Yushchenko presidency.[41]

Ukraine's Track Record in the Management of its Energy Dependency

How did the nature of these political arrangements affect Ukraine's management of its energy dependency since independence?

Management of Energy Dependency in the Early Post-independence Years

ENERGY AND THE SHOCK OF INDEPENDENCE

Ukraine's energy situation at the time of independence was characterized by high dependency on Russian energy supplies, dependence on Russian pipelines for the transit of CA energy sources, and high levels of energy inefficiency. In 1991, about 55 percent of Ukraine's TPES came from imports,[42] with the overall dependency on energy imports from Russia at about 50 percent.[43] Despite continued preferential pricing as compared with WE prices (see Table 4.3 in page 124 below), energy prices still increased significantly during the first post-independence years.[44]

As Ukraine's economic situation and ability to pay for imports deteriorated rapidly during this period, the burden of energy dependency on Russia worsened as well. From negligible before independence,[45] energy import costs quickly soared to account for about 50 percent of total import expenditures and more than two-thirds of Ukraine's total foreign debt by late 1994.[46] By that time, current-year arrears vis-á-vis Russia had grown to $1.9 billion, equivalent to nearly 20 percent of Ukraine's total exports that year.[47]

How did Ukraine deal with these challenges? Rather than starting with overarching policy declarations, a look at concrete energy policy-relevant actions provides a better starting point for answering this question.

MANAGEMENT OF ENERGY DEPENDENCY DURING THE EARLY
POST-INDEPENDENCE PERIOD

As a response to the growing burden of paying for energy imports, two sets of strategies were pursued, dealing with nuclear power and gas respectively. In the nuclear sector, there was an attempt to maintain and increase generation capacity as a means to reduce dependence on imported energy and increase the percentage of nuclear-generated electricity as a means of replacing gas-fired power plants.[48] There was also a concerted attempt to maintain nuclear infrastructure. When the last functioning reactor of the Chernobyl Nuclear Power Plant (NPP) was forced to close in 2000 due to an agreement with the EU, the lost generation capacity was quickly replaced by increasing production in Ukraine's other three NPPs, and by the commissioning of two new units, Khmelnytsky-2 and Rivne-4, which came on line in 2004.[49] Ukraine's nuclear sector faced some of the same challenges as its Lithuanian counterpart, in particular the change from all-Soviet to republican control of the sector, and EU pressure for the decommissioning of Chernobyl-type reactors. Yet it was relatively easy for Ukraine to regain control of the sector, as it had access to a strong base of local nuclear energy specialists. Moreover, Ukraine possessed its own deposits of nuclear fuel raw materials such as uranium and zirconium, which it sent to Russia to produce nuclear fuel rods.[50]

In the gas area, the main strategies pursued involved cushioning the burden of increased import prices by transferring these costs to the state. This took place either in terms of the actual economic cost, or of the political costs incurred, for example through giving Russia control of most of the Black Sea Fleet in 1997 in exchange for forgiveness

Table 4.1 Ukraine: Gas Prices for Residential and Industrial Users, in US$/tcm, 1991–2008

Consumer group	Import price	Households	District Heating Companies	Budget-financed public organizations	Industrial Users
Year					
1991	0.25	0.45	N/A	N/A	0.98
1992	9.30	0.60	N/A	N/A	7.00
1993	49.80	3.05	N/A	N/A	10.98
1994	22.30	2.53	N/A	N/A	24.26
1995	56.00	41.53	N/A	N/A	80.00
1999	42.00*	43.70	43.5	53.1	61.5**
2006 (1 January)	95.00	38.00	60.9	57.6	N/A
2006 (1 July)	95.00	88.80	137.0	130.0	141.50
2007 (1 January)	135.00	68.30	135.9	171.1	171.10
2008 (1 April)	179.50	66.00	131.2	214.5	214.50

* Estimate

** 2001

Note: Residential prices are for households without metres; from 2007 on, for households consuming less than 2,500 cubic metres per year. Exchange rates as per National Bank of Ukraine.

Sources: IEA, Energy Policies of Ukraine (1996), Table 3, 53, IEA, Ukraine Energy Policy Review 2006, Table 5.7, 183, Pirani, "Ukraine."

of gas-related debt.[51] Such policies made energy dependency bearable to the main economic actors (first and foremost large industrial players, but household consumers as well) by allowing them continued access to relatively low-cost energy, thus subsidizing production and exports (see Table 4.1). The cost was transferred to the state through, among others means, state guarantees, high inflation, a devaluated currency, and growing budget deficits and foreign debt. The political costs should not be neglected either: while the economic roots of recurring Ukrainian-Russian gas supply crises should not be minimized, Ukraine also presents a powerful example of Russia's use of the energy weapon as a means to seek to influence the foreign policy orientation of a post-Soviet state. Already clear with the 1990s attempt to use energy concessions to gain control of important Black Sea naval infrastructure, this was seen repeatedly in the 2000s, as when the Putin government sought to use the threat of rising prices to – among other goals – pressure Ukraine to join a pro-Russian economic, political, and military bloc.

The contractual framework for gas trade in place between 1994 and 2005 also facilitated the sheltering of domestic consumers from the effects of worsening external conditions. One way this took place was through the organization of energy imports from Russia on a barter basis, especially in gas. Whereas Ukraine moved relatively quickly (by late 1994) to largely market prices for oil and oil products, this was not the case with gas, where barter arrangements allowed for low import prices.[52] For most of the period between 1994 and 2005 much of the gas imported from Russia was, although nominally priced in US dollars, paid for mainly through the barter of transit services.[53] In this contractual framework, which remained in place for roughly the same period as Kuchma was in office, the various elements of the Ukrainian-Russian gas relationship (transit, storage fees, and export prices for Russian gas) were "negotiated as a package."[54] Transit and storage fees charged to Russia, extremely low by international comparison,[55] were partially compensated by the low import price of the gas received, nominally at $50 per tcm.[56] Until the early 2000s these prices were generally slightly lower than those charged to other CIS states, but the gap grew increasingly larger in the 2000s (see Table 4.3). In addition, Ukraine imported gas from Turkmenistan, mostly on a barter basis.

As part of this system, the Ukrainian gas importer (NAK Naftohaz Ukraini or its functional predecessors) was obliged to supply the public sector (residential consumers, budget-financed organizations, and the district heating sector) at low, state-regulated prices often not covering import prices.[57] A major difference with both the Belarusian and Lithuanian cases, where for different reasons and to different extents, gas sales to residential and industrial users regularly covered import prices in full.

This contractual basis sheltered both industries and (especially) residential consumers from the full economic pressure of energy scarcity, and helped delay the development of a long-term energy policy based on the reality of energy poverty.[58] After 1994, industrial gas users and oil-product consumers had to face considerable price increases, but gas and (mainly gas-generated) heating prices charged to residential consumers remained stable (and even decreased in real terms if accounting for inflation) afterwards, encouraging energy waste at the household

Figure 4.1 Organization of the Ukranian Gas Market: an Overview, 1994–2005

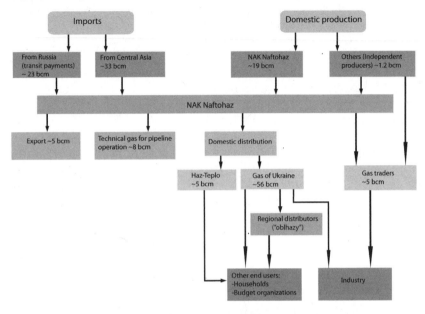

Source: Modified from IEA, IEA, *Ukraine Energy Policy Review* 2006, 178 (Figure 5.1a).

level.[59] This cushioning of the energy shock allowed managers of state-owned enterprises to continue seeing energy inputs as basically un-limited, as they had been perceived during the Soviet period. In other words, they still behaved as if they lived in an energy-rich state.

As a result of these factors, during much of the period from inde-pendence to 2004, many did not see the point of an energy diversifica-tion policy based solely on political and energy independence goals *as a value in itself*, and were ready to support diversification initiatives only if they were also economically advantageous in the short term.

Management of Energy Dependency in the Kuchma Period, 1994–2004:
The Use and Abuse of Rents of Energy Dependency

By the time Kuchma became president in 1994, a new type of player had entered the political and economic scene – the regionally based BAGs, which benefitted systematically from the available energy rents and lack of transparency in the sector. The combination of old ways of looking at energy dependency on the part of the main players, plus new rent-seeking opportunities (discussed further on) would turn out to be decisive for the way Ukraine would deal with its energy dependency in the next ten years. Crucial to this period, in addition to the continued external subsidization and external rents, was the increase in internal rents and subsidization at the expense of the Ukrainian state.

As the Ukrainian political system evolved, so did the ways in which energy rent-seeking was more commonly organized: if in the early 1990s energy rent-seeking took place in a more or less spontaneous way, and during 1996–1997 it became nearly monopolized by the dominant BAG of the time (PM Pavlo Lazarenko's Dnipropetrovsk group, discussed further on), by 1998 it had become more institutionalized as part of the larger balancing system.

Energy rent-seeking activities during the Kuchma period could be further differentiated in terms of whether they worked as part of a balancing system per se where the president would function as arbiter between the main players, or where they were accessed in a more centralized manner.

RENTS EXTRACTED BY BAGS AS PART OF THE BALANCING SYSTEM
Between 1994 and 2004, energy rent-seeking and politics interacted mainly through the balancing system built around President Kuchma. The main participants of this system were regional-based groupings (BAGs), each of which had important energy-related interests, access to their own sources of income and a variety of formal and informal means of projecting their power. This was not simply a top-down relationship dictated by the president, as each of the main BAGs had significant means to exert influence on this area.

A brief look at the main rent-seeking opportunities in the gas and oil sectors can provide useful insights into the ways in which BAGs were able to access energy rents, and into the ways in which Ukraine's energy dependency was de facto managed during this period.

Rents Extracted by BAGs as Part of the Balancing System: The Gas Sector

Rent-seeking possibilities in gas area were especially well-suited for manipulation by BAGs due to the gas supply system's strong dependence on regional gas distribution networks, where the power and influence of regional-based interests could come in especially handy. Among the many gas-related rent-seeking schemes active during this period, the best-known relate to gas reexport, to selective payments to gas companies from the state budget, the selective transfer of liabilities to the state, to price manipulations and to the unsanctioned siphoning of Russian transit gas.

REEXPORT OF RUSSIAN GAS

A first source of rent-seeking involved the (usually illegal) reexport of low-priced Russian gas. Given the large differentials between Ukrainian and WE prices (see Table 4.3), this was an area with evident possibilities for arbitrage gains and rent-seeking, and it quickly became one of the main sources of private rent in the first post-independence years. One of the best-known instances dates from 2000, when Gazprom accused Ukraine of illegally reexporting 10 bcm of its gas, mainly to Poland and Hungary.[60]

The rent-seeking mechanism worked simply: a gas distributor would buy Russian gas at low, special-for-Ukraine prices, to be later reexported to Central and Western Europe at a much higher price. In some, but by no means all cases, the reexported gas had been illegally siphoned from the exports pipeline. In either case, the profits from these operations went to specific individuals, not to the Ukrainian state budget as a whole. Thus, it would be incorrect to characterize reexport operations as Ukraine's means of moderating its energy predicament. On the contrary, illegal reexports as a means of rent-seeking became a major irritant in relations with the main supplier, Gazprom, providing an excuse for harsher measures on its part;[61] in 2001 Gazpron pressured Ukraine to impose punitive export taxes on all gas it exported (including gas produced in Ukraine) as a way of discouraging reexports. This measure prevented Ukraine from exporting its domestically produced gas, reducing incentives for investments in domestic production.

SELECTIVE PAYMENTS AND SELECTIVE TRANSFER
OF LIABILITIES TO THE STATE

A second important means of gas-related rent-seeking involved the selective payment of gas purchases to gas companies from the state budget and the selective transfer of liabilities to the state, a mechanism most widely in use during the mid-1990s. Here rent-seeking had to do with the allocation to well-connected private gas distribution companies of the most profitable industry-supply contracts at the same time as state-owned companies were left with the least able-to-pay residential consumers. When the choice existed, the state most often paid such companies instead of paying state-owned ones. Moreover, until sovereign guarantees were eliminated in 1996, private gas importers were usually able to obtain state guarantees for their gas imports from Russia, often allowing them to transform their private debt into state debt.

Transferring the liability of non-payments to the state meant that the state would take over responsibility for payments to Gazprom should the original firm be unable to do so. In many cases, this meant the original company – after having received at least partial payment from its own industrial customers and most often depositing the received money abroad – would neglect to pay Gazprom, declare bankruptcy (making its debt disappear by being converted into state debt vis-à-vis Gazprom), and resume work shortly afterwards under a new name.[62] Such selfless treatment by the state was most often reserved for companies linked privately to the regulators themselves, a situation facilitated by the frequent absence of a clear division between regulatory organs (such as the National Commission for Regulation of Natural Monopolies in the late 1990s) and the companies they were entrusted to regulate.

Privileging politically connected private companies through taking over their debt had serious long-term implications, as the unpaid debts taken over by the state eventually had to be carried by the budget, contributing to inflation and to the increase of Ukraine's foreign debt. Moreover, domestic gas producers (most of them state-owned) were unable to sell their gas at cost-covering prices, making them nearly insolvent and unable to maintain their gas production infrastructure, reducing Ukraine's chances of becoming more energy self-sufficient. Gas production declined significantly between 1990 and 1995 (see Table 4.5).

The allocation of the most profitable gas supply contracts to well-connected companies opened a whole set of new rent-seeking possibilities, with additional detrimental effects for the Ukrainian economy. Contracts giving the right to supply industries under monopoly conditions gave suppliers the power to force extremely onerous deals – and possibly bankruptcy – on the company buying the energy, in order to subsequently acquire this company at a very low price. Such manipulations were especially popular vis-á-vis gas-intensive industries such as metallurgy, machine-building, and electricity-generating companies. Perhaps the best known example of rent-seeking through the monopolization of gas contracts for a region is that provided by PM Lazarenko (1996–1997), who used his political power to increase market control by his own regional Dnipropetrovsk gas supply company,

Iedyni Enerhetychni Systemy Ukrainy (IESU).[63] After Lazarenko carried out a radical restructuring of the gas sector specifically to benefit IESU, the company's business quickly grew to supply half the natural gas traded in Ukraine and started to acquire power and influence in the traditionally rival Donetsk region, thus threatening the tacit division of rent-seeking opportunities between the major BAGs. An increase in the violent settling of accounts between these two groups let many to believe the free-for-all in the rent-seeking field had simply gone too far.

BARTER AND PRICE MANIPULATIONS

A third area of gas-related rent-seeking involved price manipulations through barter and related operations. While gas-for-transit barter constituted the basis of the gas supply contracts with Russia during the 1994–2005 period, merchandise barter and discounted bills of exchange[64] were also used, especially during the low-liquidity period in the early- and mid-1990s, and in trade with Turkmenistan well after 1995.

Through complex barter deals (trading goods, IOUs, and even tax scrip for gas), gas traders (*hazotreideri*) were not only able to guarantee continued gas supplies to Ukraine despite serious liquidity problems, but to make substantial profits. IOUs were seldom traded at face value, but various levels of discount were applied to them depending on the level of risk. By manipulating differences in the level of discount at various stages in the chain of payments, a significant profit could be made. Because the crucial value of the discount in specific bills of exchange operations was set by state officials,[65] the system was especially amenable to corruption.

While at first sight barter arrangements allowed Ukraine to secure gas supplies at times of chronic liquidity problems, they had negative consequences in the medium term. Such price manipulations benefited gas traders – at times including officials in state energy companies acting, not as representatives of their corporations but as individuals – as they allowed them to charge consumers much higher prices than those paid to Gazprom.[66] Barter-related price manipulations often led to artificially inflated prices, increasing Ukraine's state debt vis-à-vis Gazprom. Doctored and often corrupt barter deals also created inefficiency and tension in trade deals with Turkmenistan, leading to repeatedly suspended or cancelled gas supply agreements,[67] and cut short the possibility of these imports being used as a long-term, dependable means of energy diversification. Thus, although imports from Turkmenistan amounted to up to 42 percent of Ukraine's gas imports (2004), they never were managed in such a way as to create a real basis for energy diversification nor for decreasing energy dependency on Russia.

STEALING OF RUSSIAN GAS

One of the most controversial issues in the Ukrainian-Russian energy relationship has been the repeated stealing (or "unsanctioned siphoning") of Gazprom-owned gas intended for export to WE. Such accusations gave Ukraine much negative public relations attention, the most damaging of which was Gazprom's 2000 suit at the International Commercial Arbitration Court, which ordered NAK Naftohaz to pay for about $88 million of stolen gas. Accusations continued even after Vice PM Tymoshenko's official 2000 acknowledgment that stealing had taken place.[68]

The disappearance of Russian gas, often exploited by Gazprom to present Ukraine as an unreliable transit partner, also helped justify Gazprom's search for new transit routes bypassing the country. This concerns in particular the Yamal pipeline through Belarus and Poland, completed in 2006; the Nord Stream gas pipeline offering a direct link to Germany (first two of four planned lines completed 2011–2012); and the South Stream project that would, when completed (completion announced for 2015), reach, via southeastern Europe, the Baumgardten gas hub in Austria for further transit west.[69]

Yet many indications point to the fact that at least part of the stealing was not carried out unilaterally by the Ukrainian side, and not as a means to deal with rapidly growing prices in the early- to mid-1990s, as argued by some authors.[70] A closer look reveals a more nuanced situation possibly involving the agreed disappearance of gas, not excluding the collusion of private interests-within-the-corporation on both sides of the border.[71] At the same time, such stolen gas – especially given unclear record-keeping on incoming and outgoing gas[72] – also played a further role, as it increased Ukraine's debt to Gazprom, debt that would later dovetail with Gazprom's and the Kremlin's strategy vis-à-vis Ukraine.

Rents Extracted by BAGs as Part of the Balancing System: The Oil Sector

While the potential for large-scale rent-seeking in the oil sector was more modest than in the gas area due to the smaller scale of possible arbitrage gains (since ca. 2002 Ukraine had been largely paying European

Table 4.2 Ukraine's Crude Oil Production, Consumption, and Transit, 2004–2011, in Million Tons (Mt)

Year	Domestic Consumption (incl. refining)	Imports (via pipelines) for Refineries	Domestic Production	Transit
2004	26.44	22.4	4.31	32.4
2005	19.47	15.3	4.43	31.3
2006	15.60	11.7	4.52	33.2
2007	14.70	11.1	4.47	39.8
2008	13.47	8.2	4.34	32.8
2009	N/A	9.4	4.0	29.1
2010	14.5	9.7	3.6	20.1
2011	14.4	N/A	3.3	17.7

Sources: Oil transit and imports for refineries: NAK Naftohaz, http://www.naftogaz.com/www/2/nakweben.nsf/0/B9D8558AE5F6C551C22574090044D7A8/$file/Oil TransmissionE.gif (accessed 12 October 2011), IEA: *Ukraine 2012*, 131, 133, 139. Production: International Energy Agency, *Energy Statistics of Non-OECD Countries* (Paris: IEA/OECD, various years), OECD/ IEA, *Energy Balances of Non-OECD Countries* (Paris: OECD, various years), OECD/IEA, other sources.

prices for oil imported from Russia), abuse-of-influence rent-seeking schemes existed there as well. These revolved mostly around tax evasion and tax preferences.

The best example of such preferences were a number of officially designated Enterprises with Foreign Investment (EFIs), allowed between 1992 and 2002 to import oil products (mainly gasoline) tax-free, which gave them an enormous market advantage, not only vis-á-vis other potential importers, but also vis-á-vis local oil refineries. Official designation as a tax-free EFI was only available to companies supported by politically well-connected patrons.[73]

Such tax preferences had important effects on Ukraine's ability to manage its energy dependency. Flooding of the market with tax-free oil products contributed to the weakness of Ukrainian refineries, a weakness later used by Russian companies to buy-out most Ukrainian refineries at low prices starting in 1999. By 2000, with Ukrainian refineries starting their recovery after large Russian investments, such privileges had strongly counter-productive effects, as they subjected Ukrainian-produced oil products to competition from cheap tax-free imports.

Although less profitable than gas reexport due to the smaller price differentials, oil reexport was also a source of rent-seeking throughout the early-mid 2000s.[74]

RENTS ACCESSED CENTRALLY THROUGH NAK NAFTOHAZ
AND OTHER NAK-TYPE COMPANIES

The rent-seeking arrangements described previously were intrinsically related to the balancing system, as they were based on the provision of preferential access to energy rent-seeking opportunities to specific groups, in exchange for the informal sharing of profits, recycled into regime-maintenance and election-preparation activities and contributions, all while seeking to maintain some balance between the main BAGs.[75] This type of politicized rent-sharing arrangement was most prevalent throughout the early and middle years of the Kuchma presidency. After 1998, however, it started to coexist with Kuchma's attempts to exercise more direct control over energy rents. Kuchma's changed approach could be seen first and foremost as a response to the monopolization of rent-seeking power by PM Lazarenko in 1996–1997 (discussed previously), which led the president to the firm resolution never to allow power to be monopolized by a single clan again.[76]

This desire for more direct control over energy rents was pursued first and foremost through the establishment of NAK Naftohaz in 1998, which acquired control over money transfers related to gas payments, Ukraine's gas purchases from Turkmenistan, the use of Ukraine's transit pipeline system, the licensing process for gas imports, and over the nearly 23–25 bcm of gas supplied yearly by Gazprom up to 2005 as payment for gas transit (see Figure 4.1 for an overview of NAK's role).

Direct access to energy-related rents seemed to be especially important to Kuchma as a way to access resources to finance his electoral bloc's campaigns for Rada (1998) and presidential (1999) elections. Indeed, money from energy rents – domestic or foreign, accessed directly or indirectly, working in favour of the incumbent or not – played a central role in all Ukrainian national elections under Kuchma.[77]

Concrete Mechanisms for Rents of Dependency Extraction through NAK and NAK-like Organizations

Of the various rent-seeking opportunities available through NAK Naftohaz, some of the most lucrative revolved around price manipulations and the adjudication of advantageous transit services contracts to companies presumably associated with the top management.[78] In particular, gas imports from Turkmenistan became a major source of rents thanks to the adjudication of advantageous contracts to preferred companies, as shown by the cases of Itera, Eural Trans Gas, and RosUkrEnergo.

Itera, an important intermediary in the sale of Turkmenistan gas to Ukraine from the late 1990s and up to 2001, was able to skim a significant profit out of the relationship by overcharging Ukraine and underpaying Gazprom (the owner of the Russian segment of the pipelines the gas had to transit through) for transportation and other services. It was able to do so thanks to its special relationship with important actors in both Ukraine and Russia; the active support of at least a part of Gazprom's management proved especially useful, as the company gave it some of its contracts and, later, preferential access to its pipelines for the transit of Turkmenistan gas to Ukraine. In Ukraine, Itera's rise in the mid-1990s was greatly supported by PM Lazarenko.[79]

Although somewhat less significant than gas-related trade, NAK Naftohaz-centred oil trade activities were also an important source of centralized rents President Kuchma could tap into.[80] Among these schemes, the most significant were those that gave companies possibly associated with NAK Naftohaz executives (such as the offshore company Collide) advantageous contracts as operators of the Odesa oil terminal, among others,[81] opening the door to a further privatization of energy policies and to larger deals such as those related to the reversal of the Odesa-Brody pipeline, discussed further on.

The use of NAK Naftohaz as, among other roles, a means to funnel energy rents could not but have a serious negative impact on Ukraine's ability to deal proactively with its energy dependency. The establishment of a national energy company largely with personal rent-seeking aims gave individuals interested in sabotaging from within attempts at a proactive management of energy dependency a strong institutional base, something that would become evident when then-first vice PM Yuliia Tymoshenko sought to reform the sector in 2000–2001 (discussed further on). Moreover, the fact that NAK Naftohaz was intentionally given a special status subordinating it, not to the Fuel and Energy Ministry, but directly to the Cabinet of Ministers, contributed to a significant reduction in the Ministry's policy making competencies, and pushed energy policy farther away from any semblance of clear governance rules. Such lack of clear governance rules made it easier for NAK

Naftohaz to be misused for rent-seeking purposes by interested actors within and outside the company.[82]

Energy Rents under Kuchma: A Wrap-up

While they diverged in terms of the actual mechanisms used and the degree of formal legality or illegality involved, what these various Kuchma-era schemes had in common – and the main way in which they affected the management of energy dependency – was the privatization of energy dependency rents and profits (often by politicians using their administrative power to access energy rents), while shifting the costs to the state and the society as a whole. The central logic bringing these various schemes together was the fact that the accrual (and sharing between politically connected economic groups) of often corruption-related energy profits frequently came at the expense of the state budget, of the population at large, and of a national energy policy.

In this sense, these rents were not necessarily external rents – while many of them may have been related to manipulations around Russian special-for-Ukraine, lower-than-market energy prices and to the stealing of potential tax revenue from the Russian state and of revenue from Gazprom, the majority of them had to do with revenue and potential revenue diverted from the Ukrainian state. (This was in stark contrast with the case of Belarus, discussed in the next chapter, where most of the energy rents accessed came from external sources.)

The previous examples tell a story of the de facto management of energy dependency coming not as a result of a proactive and coordinated policy, but largely as a by-product of various rent-extraction arrangements. One possible exception to this logic are the energy-related reforms of PM Yushchenko and first vice PM Tymoshenko in 2000 and early 2001. Two caveats are needed here, however: First, the reforms were not initiated out of altruistic motives but because of pressure coming from the IMF and Russia (which, under the weight of its 1998 economic crisis, was demanding an increased level of cash payments for energy exports to Ukraine). Second, Tymoshenko was not necessarily reforming the energy sector as an uninterested outsider: before her break with former PM and IESU head Lazarenko, she had played a central role in that company, a company central to energy rent-seeking and corruption in the mid-1990s.[83]

Tymoshenko's reforms pursued three main goals: to increase cash payments and reduce the role of barter in energy transactions, to battle corruption in the domestic oil sector by establishing oil auctions, and to reestablish some degree of state control over gas purchases from Turkmenistan. Two additional goals were to increase transparency in the coal market (also through the establishment of auctions), as well as in the privatization of regional electricity distributors (*oblenerhos*).

These initiatives faced fierce opposition from energy-related players, who, it is estimated, lost up to $1.8 billion in forgone rents, explaining their eagerness to stall these reforms after organizing Tymoshenko's removal from office in January 2001.[84] The attempt to reestablish state control over gas purchases from Turkmenistan was successful (direct sales to a wholesale market controlled by the state were established), but only in the short term; many of Tymoshenko's initiatives to eliminate barter in Ukrainian-Turkmenistan gas trade were vetoed by President Kuchma.[85] After Tymoshenko's dismissal, as will be discussed further on, intermediary companies importing gas from Turkmenistan came back with a vengeance.

A second pillar of the reforms, the attempt to increase transparency in the oil market, had mixed results. The basic aim of these reforms was to end the practice of the sale of domestically produced oil at very low prices ("at a price three times lower than its market price"[86]) through a variety of sweetheart deals, which made domestic production increasingly unprofitable, hindering attempts at increasing oil production and self-sufficiency (see Table 4.2). Tymoshenko sought to change this by making sale by auction compulsory for a certain percentage of domestically produced oil, an initiative that was partly successful at the time. Related attempts to set up the sale of domestically produced coal and gas through auctions, however, were less successful, and, after Tymoshenko's dismissal, subsidies to the coal sector actually increased.[87]

Despite these setbacks, the long-term positive significance of these changes should not be underestimated. Cash payments to NAK Naftohaz, grew from 15.8 percent in 1999 to 87 percent in 2001.[88] The move away from barter, both domestic and vis-á-vis Gazprom, increased transparency, reduced the possibilities for corruption, and, with the increase in cash payments, also helped remove one major element of friction with Gazprom. The reforms had a long-term effect in terms of contributing to changing the structure of opportunities faced by Ukraine's largest economic groups, with important effects for the economy as a whole. For example, with the increase in liquidity in the Ukrainian market, local energy players were no longer finding barter deals as profitable as they had in the 1990s.

At the same time, which of the Yushchenko-Tymoshenko reforms would survive after their departure from office (i.e., the move away from barter) was also a reflection of the ways in which the rent-seeking interests of the most important players were changing after the conclusion of a first stage of rent-accumulation based on energy trade. Indeed, these reforms were taking place as this first stage was giving way to a second generation of rent-seeking, in which steel and other metallurgical exports were becoming the main source of new profits. These two stages are connected in a variety of ways. Much of the initial gas profits were invested by Ukrainian oligarchs in the metallurgical sector,[89] and, as one of Ukraine's most energy-intensive industries, metallurgy was one of the main beneficiaries of low energy prices, often received at the expense of the state.[90] While the 2000–2001 Yushchenko-Tymoshenko reforms did indeed affect rent-seeking, the evidence does not support the enthusiasm of authors such as Aslund in presenting these reforms as largely ending rent-seeking in commodities trade,[91] as the case of RosUkrEnergo's profits later on in the decade, discussed further on, tells us.

Some of the fiercest opposition to Tymoshenko's reforms came from the energy policy making establishment itself. In 2000, for example, in the confrontation between Tymoshenko and NAK Naftohaz's head Ihor Bakai each of them sought support from different actors within Gazprom, a circumstance with clear policy implications, as each of these coalitions argued a totally different valuing of Ukraine's debt vis-á-vis the company, a continued source of tension between the sides. (In 1999–2000, for example, the management of NAK Naftohaz argued Ukraine's debt to Gazprom amounted to about $1 billion, while first vice PM Tymoshenko argued the amount was more than $2 billion.)[92]

AFTER THE REFORMS: ENERGY POLICIES AND THE MANAGEMENT OF ENERGY DEPENDENCY FROM YUSHCHENKO'S DISMISSAL TO THE 2004 ELECTIONS

That energy rent-seeking continued after 2001, and that it had important effects on Ukraine's management of its energy situation is shown by two brief case studies of Ukraine's energy policy during the 2002–2004 period: the Odesa-Brody pipeline, and the organization of gas imports from Turkmenistan.

Inability to Develop a Clear and Consequent Energy Policy: The Case of Diversification Possibilities through the Odesa-Brody Pipeline

Originally envisioned in the early 1990s as a way of fostering Ukraine's energy supply diversification, problems followed the Odesa-Brody project from the very beginning. Completion of the project, originally envisioned for the mid 1990s, was repeatedly delayed, and the pipeline only completed in 2002.

From the very beginning, lack of coordination and policy indecision contributed to these delays. In its initial years, the project was not carried out at the level of national policy (as a project of this magnitude and geopolitical significance would warrant), but at the level of one specific state company, the Druzhba Pipeline System, making the building of the pipeline largely dependent on a single enterprise's financial situation, its relationship with Ukraine's other major pipeline system (the Transdniester Pipeline System), and the political fortunes of Druzhba's head and Odesa-Brody's "father" Liubomyr Buniak, in particular his confrontation with National Security and Defence Council (RNBO) head (2000–2001) Yevhen Marchuk.[93]

In addition, the Odesa-Brody project was poorly coordinated with oil supply policies. Thus, when the pipeline was finally completed in 2002, no Caspian oil was ready to flow through it, which called for Poland's foot-dragging on building the connecting segment to Plotsk, essential for the pipeline's ability to find WE costumers, and, thus, for its economic viability.

The building of the Pivdennyi (Yuzhnyi) oil terminal in Odesa, intended to receive Caspian oil to be transported northwest through the pipeline, was subject to similar fits and starts, largely due to the interference of individuals who, being involved in the resale of Russian oil in Ukraine, wanted to obstruct the project and the importation of Caspian oil.[94]

ROLE OF RUSSIAN AND UKRAINIAN INTEREST GROUPS

Undoubtedly, there was a Russian desire to torpedo the Odesa-Brody project.[95] However, the controversy around the future of the pipeline was much more than an issue of Ukrainian vs. Russian interests. Russian companies did not need to create domestic conflict about the pipeline, but simply to manipulate existing Ukrainian conflicts on the issue taking place at the level of state companies, political elites, and Business-Administrative Groups.

Nothing exposed conflicting Ukrainian interests around Odesa-Brody as clearly as the Tiumenskaia Neftianaia Kompaniia's (TNK)[96] 2003 proposal for a reversal of the pipeline: to transit Russian oil from Brody in the North to Odesa in the South to be shipped further west by tanker, that is, in the opposite direction as originally intended, a proposal made against the background of a lack of available export capacities in the Russian pipeline system at a time when the difference between domestic and export prices was especially large. The TNK proposal exacerbated conflict between those for and against the reversal in the midst of state-owned oil transit monopolist Ukrtransnafta, a conflict taking place in the context of larger battles on the relative role of the company vis-à-vis other energy policy making institutions (such as the Ministry of Fuel and Energy headed by anti-reversal Serhii Yermilov) going on at the time. Yermilov's position in favour of the as-intended use of the pipeline, in turn, reflected that of the Donetsk group and the Industrial'na Spilka Donbasu (ISD), which hoped to build good relations with the EU in order to secure access to WE markets for its metallurgical products and participate in privatization projects in EU states.[97] Yermilov's position put him at odds with NAK Naftohaz, the country's largest energy company, and its head Yurii Boiko, who formally declared support for the project but argued its short-term impossibility due to the lack of available Caspian oil. Similarly, it has been argued that Ukrtransnafta, under the control a pro-reverse faction, did everything it could to torpedo negotiations with possible suppliers of Caspian oil – including a concrete proposal by Kazakhstan's Tengizshevroil – while conducting a sophisticated public relations campaign aimed at convincing the public that no interested suppliers were available, and that it would be more profitable to use the pipeline in reverse direction to transit Russian oil from Brody to Odesa.[98]

As a result of these contradictions, between 2003 and 2004, Ukraine repeatedly changed its policy concerning the pipeline, sending potential partners contradictory signals. After preparing the ground in late 2003 and early 2004 for a possible reversal of the pipeline by removing from office several key anti-reversal players, in July 2004 the Ukrainian government officially accepted TNK's reversal proposal, initially for a three-year period. That then-PM Yanukovych played a role in this decision, as well as the fact that Russian oil companies saw their interests in

Ukraine (including the reverse use of the pipeline) better guaranteed by a Yanukovych than by a Yushchenko presidency was shown by the fact that, of the $300 million in Russian contributions (of a total of $600 million) PM Yanukovych reportedly spent on the 2004 presidential campaign, the largest share is likely to have come from energy companies.[99]

Although the immediate economic benefit of using the Odesa-Brody pipeline in a reverse direction seemed obvious (immediate cash payments and higher transit fees than those Russian companies would pay for transit in the same direction through the Transdniester Pipeline System, which could also transit Russian oil south for further shipment through Odesa), such a decision would also have very serious long-term implications both in terms of Ukraine's energy security, other energy transit commitments, and broader relationships with both Russia and Western institutions.[100] Moreover, if looked at from the perspective of Ukraine's total oil transit revenue (including other transit commitments) and not narrowly Odesa-Brody, reversing the pipeline made little economic sense.[101] The fact that by 2004 short-term interests had won out over longer-term ones tells much not only about the power of interest groups in Ukraine, but about the lack of a strong national policy capable of overcoming these differences.

Gas Supplies from Turkmenistan

A second example illustrating the failure of the 2000–2001 reforms to bring about lasting changes in energy rent-seeking has to do with the organization of gas imports from Turkmenistan. By now tainted by negative publicity, Itera – between 1998 and 2001 the main or sole intermediary in the transit of CA gas to Ukraine – was de facto replaced with new and less-known companies such as Eural Trans Gas. Despite declarations by the new Gazprom leadership installed in 2001 to the effect that the company would avoid middlemen in gas exports, similar rent-seeking patterns continued.[102] Its work in arranging the transit of CA gas to Ukraine via Russian pipelines brought companies such as Itera, Eural Trans Gas, and RosUkrEnergo enormous profits, but led Gazprom to lose between $130 million and $1 billion, money it paid for services it could have provided itself.[103] Intermediary companies' profits were made possible by barter operations, where the favoured companies would be paid for their services in gas, usually between 37.5 percent (RosUkrEnergo) and 41 percent (Itera) of the supplied gas, which they would later export to WE at much higher prices.[104] Such arrangements, while benefitting neither NAK Naftohaz nor Gazprom, created large profits for well-connected individuals not only in Eural Trans Gas, but also in the highest echelons of government and NAK Naftohaz. Often working in coordination with managers on the Russian side,[105] Eural Trans Gas's head, Dmytro Firtash, "had the support of the new Gazprom management."[106] It has been argued that preparing Eural Trans Gas's smooth entrance into the Ukrainian market was one of the tasks specifically entrusted by President Kuchma to Yurii Boiko as he became head of NAK Naftohaz in 2002.[107]

The continuation of rent-seeking and corruption in gas imports from Turkmenistan had serious negative effects on Ukraine's management of its energy dependency, as they cut short the possibility of these imports being used as a long-term, dependable means of energy diversification. Imports from Turkmenistan were also affected by Turkmenistan's other relationships (both with Russia and with Russian-controlled intermediary companies such as Itera), and remained subject to Russian influence, as they had to be transported through Russian pipelines. A new challenge for Ukraine emerged in 2003, when Turkmenistan signed a long-term gas delivery contract with Russia that, from 2007 on, promised to sell to Gazprom almost the entire Turkmenistan gas production, leaving little free capacities for exports to Ukraine.[108]

EFFECTS ON THE POPULATION AND RESIDENTIAL CONSUMERS

Although the arrangements described above had a clearly detrimental effect on Ukraine's ability to manage its energy dependency, their effects were not felt directly by residential consumers in the short run. In fact, before they were raised in 2006, Ukrainian residential gas (and electricity) rates were some of the lowest in the former USSR, at $35.2 per tcm, lower than in energy-rich Russia ($44.3) or highly Russian-subsidized Belarus ($52.8).[109] They had remained unchanged since 1998, and, in fact, had declined significantly in real terms.[110] Low residential prices buffered Ukrainian consumers from the worst effects of energy dependency and made diversification policies, more expensive in the short term, hard to sell politically. But low energy prices were no free lunch either – the higher costs for gas were paid indirectly by the population, in the form of inflation and higher foreign indebtedness.

Interestingly, the issue of low prices was one where the interests of certain economic elites, deeply ingrained popular beliefs, and the interests of populist politicians coincided in the short term. While at times benefitting privately from deals around Ukraine's energy dependency, leading politicians such as President Kuchma continued to pursue the instrumental securitization of the issue, using the rhetoric of the dangers of energy poverty and energy dependency for their own political purposes both at the international (in relations with the EU and other Western partners) and domestic levels (where overconcentration on the catastrophe that could befall the country should energy prices increase served to exclude some policy options from the discussion table, while making others seem much more attractive). While de facto used to justify not investing in expensive alternative energy infrastructure, such rhetoric helped justify other policy options, such as giving a special role and privileges to intermediary companies able to offer lower energy import prices by, de facto, reducing the profit of the state and state companies and distributing the difference between themselves and the importers.

As a result of arrangements such as these, Ukraine's ability to take control of its energy situation during the Kuchma period was limited. Moreover, they increased the already high cost of energy dependency by diverting to intermediary companies and corrupt managers resources that could have been better used in efficiency improvements and in the maintenance and development of Ukraine's energy transit infrastructure.

Management of Energy Dependency in the Post-Orange Revolution Period

UKRAINE'S CYCLE OF RENTS AFTER THE ORANGE REVOLUTION
How did the structure and effects of energy rent-seeking change after the Orange Revolution of 2004? How did it affect Ukraine's management of its energy dependency?

Despite the central role of an anti-corruption rhetoric in Yushchenko's 2003–2004 anti-Kuchma campaign, things did not change as hoped for after the Orange Revolution, and energy rents continued to be a prime area of competition between BAGs during the Yushchenko period. The very first two scandals of the Yushchenko presidency, just weeks after his inauguration – on oil reexports involving the Justice minister, and on the misuse of state police power to help particular players in the battle for the control of oblenerho electricity generating companies[111] – were directly related to the distribution of energy profits. These early scandals are significant because they clearly showed, only a few weeks after Yushchenko's inauguration, the serious differences in economic interests coexisting within the coalition, and also Yuschenko's inability or unwillingness to separate business and politics. Indeed, much of what was to happen in the months following Yushchenko's inauguration can be related to the attempt of newly-in-power economic groups to share into preexisting energy schemes, and to competition for access to energy rents, in particular, between some reincarnation of Itera and relative newcomer RosUkrEnergo networks.

The case of intermediary company RosUkrEnergo and its adaptation to post-Orange revolution conditions tells us much about the ability of the new orange powers-that-be to find a place in existing gas trade rent-seeking schemes. In March 2005, the government led by PM Tymoshenko started to investigate corruption in government monopolies, including NAK Naftohaz, but there was significant opposition, especially within the company itself. Much of the investigation came to a halt in mid-August 2005. The order came from the very top: at some point that summer, President Yushchenko seems to have warned State Security Service (SBU) head and Tymoshenko ally Aleksandr Turchinov to stop the investigation. As the investigation continued despite this warning – with people close to the PM's office insinuating Security Council head Poroshenko was involved in energy wrong-doing – Yushchenko responded by dismissing both Poroshenko and PM Tymoshenko on 8 September; there are strong indications that Tymoshenko's dismissal was related to the desire to put a stop to the investigations.[112]

THE JANUARY CRISIS AND THE 4 JANUARY 2006 AGREEMENTS

The crucial deepening point for post-Orange Revolution energy rent-seeking came with the 4 January 2006 agreements with Russia that brought to an end the three-day stoppage of gas supplies by Gazprom that sent shivers throughout Europe – although for less than three days, supplies to EU members Austria, France, Hungary, Poland, Romania, and Slovakia were reduced by between 14 percent and 40 percent.[113]

Before analysing the actual run-down of the crisis, let us consider the objective factors leading to it. By 2005, the model of gas trade largely based on the barter of gas supplies for transit services, in place since 1995, had undoubtedly gone into crisis.[114] While this model had guaranteed Ukraine stable prices well below European ones, both sides were dissatisfied with the arrangements. For the Yushchenko administration, the low transit fees paid to Ukraine (as of 2005, the lowest in Europe with the exception of Belarus) and the lack of transparency implied in the barter arrangement was a cause for dissatisfaction;[115] already in the Spring of 2005 Ukraine had proposed to Gazprom

Table 4.3 Ukraine: Russian Gas Prices and Transit, 1991–2010, in bcm and US$

Year	Import prices	Transit volumes (to both WE and CIS)	(of which Transit volumes to WE)	Moldova prices (for comparison)	Border price in Germany, US$/tcm
1991	0.25	113.9	99.7	0.25	108.3
1992	9.30	122.9	92.9	N/A	85.1
1993	49.80	125.2	95.2	N/A	93.5
1994	22.30	128.9	99.7	N/A	83.2
1995	56.0	137.7	110.2	58	97.1
1996	42.0*	139.9	116.5	80	99.0
1997	42.0*	133.2	108.4	80	96.1
1998	42.0*	141.1	114.9	80	80.8
1999	42.0*	133.3	118.7	80	65.1
2000	42.0	120.6	109.3	80	124.3
2001	42.0	124.4	105.3	80	139.4
2002	42.0	121.6	106.1	80	96.0
2003	42.0	129.2	112.4	80	125.5
2004	50.0	137.1	120.3	80	135.2
2005	50.0	136.4	121.5	80	212.9
2006	95.0	128.5	113.8	160**	295.6
2007	135.0	115.2	112.1	172 (average)	293.1
2008	179.5	119.6	116.9	232 (average)	472.9
2009	232.4	95.8	92.8	263 (average)	318.8
2010	256.7	98.6	95.4	252**	292.0

* Estimate. Between 1994 and 2005, despite a nominal import price of $50/tcm, Ukraine's gas imports from Gazprom were largely payments in kind for the transit of Russian gas to EU markets, with total transit costs being equal to the total costs of gas imports from the company.

** Effective April 1.

Sources: Transit data from NAK Naftohaz, www.naftogaz.com. Sources for 1991 and 2005–2010 prices as noted in Table 1.6. Ukraine prices 1992–1993 from Krasnov and Brada, "Implicit subsidies," Table 1 (p. 830), 1994–1995 from IEA, *Energy Policies of Ukraine* (1996), 57, 2000–2004 from Institute of Economic Research and Policy Consulting, Kyiv, http://ier.org.ua/papers_en/v12_en.pdf.

moving away from the arrangement. For the Russian side, continued low prices to Ukraine were untenable against the background of growing prices to European and other CIS consumers, a trend visible from Table 4.3.

Despite these mounting tensions, however, Ukraine continued to neglect its main counterweight to energy dependency on Russia, gas imports from Turkmenistan, which continued to suffer from allegations of unpaid debts and unfulfilled barter contracts. Ukraine's mismanagement of this key relationship added to the pressure to transfer such trade to other companies acting as contractual, not just transport inter- mediaries as had been in the pre-2005 period.

Above and beyond these objective factors, a detailed analysis of developments between November 2005 and January 2006 gives some reason to believe that the escalation of the price dispute with Gaz- prom was actually used as a means to create an artificial scarcity as a cover to introduce new rent-seeking schemes by actors on both sides of the border. Events developed as follows: after a series of progres- sively increasing demands for price increases in the fall of 2005,[116] and a possibly Russian-provoked standoff[117] with a price demand that had risen quickly from $95 to $150 to $230 per tcm (in comparison with the then current price of $50), supplies were suspended. Four days later, in the midst of last-minute negotiations in Moscow, a solution suddenly appeared. In the middle of a seemingly escalating conflict with little prospects for agreement between the sides, suddenly, a breakthrough happened once an intermediary company, in the words of Oleksandr Chalii, former First Deputy Minister for European Integration, "ap- pears as if on a white horse" to "save the situation."[118] After the en- trance of the new player (the intermediary company RosUkrEnergo) into the scene, the conflict was solved after the terms of its participation were agreed upon; that is, once a way was found (through carving out a highly profitable role for the company) "to provide important play- ers in both Ukraine and Russia important profits, even at the expense of the Ukrainian and Russian budgets."[119] That the forced escalation of the conflict may have been a means to open the way for rent-seeking is shown by the fact that the bargain prices the intermediary was ul- timately able to offer, and that seemed much lower than those under discussion at the high point in the escalation, were, in reality, the same that had been originally offered by Russia ($95/tcm) when the conflict started. Thus, it may be asked, why was this confrontation needed? The answer may lay in the artificial scarcities and the opportunities for rent-seeking created by the confrontation itself.

Ukrainian behaviour in the run up to the crisis was also highly problematic. As noted by the International Energy Agency, it was unclear why Ukraine did not seek recourse to international arbitration at the time of the price increase ultimatum by Gazprom, given the fact that the 2004 contract between Gazprom and Naftohaz stipulated the sale price of "USD 50 per 1 000 m^3 of gas that Ukraine received as transit payment was not subject to change" from 2005 to 2009.[120]

If at the time of the crisis chaos was the dominant impression, in hindsight a somewhat different perspective emerges, one open to the possibility that premeditated mismanagement was at play. Negotiations were conducted in an atmosphere of secrecy and lack of transparency.[121] Despite President Yushchenko's ambiguous declarations (such as stating that he did not know the specifics of any Ukrainian participation in RosUkrEnergo), it became clear that he very much remained "the country's main gas person"[122] as President Kuchma was before him, and not only probably knew of the real owners behind RosUkrEnergo, but may have received important benefits from them as well, given his apparent connection with Firtash.[123] As would later become clear, Firtash, RosUkrEnergo's main Ukrainian owner, was likely present in the early January 2006 negotiations with Gazprom, with the Ukrainian delegation possibly following "not the instructions of the Ministry of Foreign Affairs and the Ministry of Economics, but those of [RosUkrEnergo representatives] Firtash and Voronin."[124] The conflict of interest (and, thus, the possibility of corruption) was clear – Ihor Voronin would later become, parallel to his position as deputy chairman of NAK Naftohaz, acting head of the company's de facto competitor UkrHazEnergo.[125]

The five-year agreements signed in 4 January 2006 represented a major change from earlier modalities of Russian-Ukrainian gas trade.[126] In addition to clauses relating to the end of direct purchases from Gazprom and the sale of all gas to Ukraine through RosUkrEnergo, and to the establishment of a JV between both companies to market gas inside Ukraine, they established the contractual separation of transit and supply, a separation crucial to establishing transparency in energy trade. Although not specifying a mechanism for gas price increases that would reflect changes in market prices in Europe, the agreements started the process of moving gas prices paid by Ukraine closer to European ones,[127] not a trivial issue given the disincentives for investments in energy-saving technology created by too-low prices.

There are, however, good reasons to believe the January 2006 agreements significantly worsened the country's energy security situation even in comparison with the Kuchma period.[128] There was no transparency on how these new prices were formed. While the agreement locked Ukraine into charging low gas transit fees until 2009, it set up yearly increases in the price of gas supplies. This allowed gas prices to be increased unilaterally, while transit fees could not, increasing uncertainty and the fear that the terms of trade for Ukraine may worsen. They also made Ukraine weaker in its asymmetrical interdependence relationship with Russia, as they significantly lowered the already low gas storage prices charged by Ukraine.[129] Most important, however, was the question of contractual diversification[130] and the fact that, by making RosUkrEnergo the sole operator of the country's gas imports, Ukraine became, de facto, contractually tied to a single supplier that received large profits in exchange for ill-defined and, most likely, unnecessary intermediary services.

Although this is not the first time that intermediaries had played a role in gas supplies to Ukraine, there were important qualitative differences between their role before and after the 4 January 2006 agreements. If in the 1990s and early 2000s intermediary companies (such as Itera and Eural Trans Gas) were paid large sums to organize the transport of Central Asian gas to Ukraine, under the 2006 agreements RosUkrEnergo became not just the transporter, but also the operator of Ukrainian gas imports from CA and Russia, giving the company much more power in the relationship.

At the same time, CA gas also played another, more controversial role. If there was a silver lining in Ukraine's loss of contractual diversification through the 2006 agreements, it was the small element of geographical diversification involved, as – per the agreements – in 2006 Ukraine was supposed to receive more than 50 percent of its gas imports from Turkmenistan;[131] RosUkrEnergo would supply gas produced, not only in Turkmenistan, but also in Kazakhstan and Uzbekistan, countries from which Ukraine had imported very little or no gas in the past. According to statistics compiled by the Ukrainian Fuel and Energy Ministry and cited by Pirani, in 2006 and 2007 Ukraine imported more gas from CA than from Russia.[132] (However, it is impossible to know the origin of the gas imported by Ukraine in the 2006–2008 period. This is so not only because of the physical impossibility of distinguishing Turkmenistan-originated gas from Russian gas once both are mixed in the pipelines, but because the January 2006

contract was specifically for a cocktail of gases assumed to come from
Russian and CA sources, but where the actual origin the gas was not
guaranteed.)

Thus, at first glance, it would seem as if Ukraine was getting geographical diversification at the expense of contractual diversification.[133]
But in reality it was likely getting neither – CA gas was most likely
not imported to Ukraine from CA, but rather virtually transited or
provided on a swap basis (i.e., CA gas went to Russia, and Russian
gas to Ukraine). While in and of themselves such swaps are not unusual in international gas trade, what is most interesting in this case is
that the *idea* of importing CA gas was most likely used as a construct
to justify both the need for RosUkrEnergo's services, and sharply increased prices. It has been repeatedly argued that the gas Ukraine was
importing from Turkmenistan was in reality Russian gas renamed as
CA gas with the express purpose of charging Ukraine higher prices.[134]
All of this, of course, largely neutralized the positive effects of the
geographic diversification component officially found in the 2006
agreements.

Thus despite the change in contractual forms, rent-seeking and the
privatization of the profits of energy trade and the shifting to the state –
and the country as a whole – of the many loses continued as central
elements of the Russian-Ukrainian gas relationship. Thus, for example,
a follow-up agreement in February 2006 gave a newly formed joint venture, UkrHazEnergo (equally owned by RosUkrEnergo and NAK Naftohaz) the right to sell gas directly to industrial users in Ukraine, taking
away a significant part of NAK Naftohaz's most profitable domestic
market. As a result, UkrHazEnergo retained most of the profits, while
official oil-and-gas company NAK Naftohaz not only lost significant
profits, but continued to be contractually obliged to supply gas to residential users and district heating companies at regulated, loss-making
prices. While the loss of these industrial users cannot be seen as the
main reason for NAK Naftohaz's continuing financial weakness in the
following years – the real reason being the company's obligation to subsidize Ukrainian residential and communal customers put on the company by the Ukrainian government – this revenue loss undoubtedly
played a contributing role. This meant not only an increased danger
of bankruptcy for NAK Naftohaz, but also signalled ambivalence on
the part of the NAK Naftohaz management about the well-being of the
company.[135]

CHANGES IN RENT-SEEKING MECHANISMS AFTER THE
JANUARY, 2006 AGREEMENTS

Two elements of the January 2006 agreements – the sharp increase in gas prices, which increased from $95 per tcm in January 2006 to $130 in 2007 to $179.50 in 2008, – and the entrance of UkrHazEnergo into the domestic gas market under preferential conditions – brought with them changes in the structure of incentives for various types of rent-seeking that also came to affect the actual management of energy dependency. In particular, the price increases prodded some metallurgical companies to invest in energy-saving modernization programs, shifing from gas-powered, open-hearth furnaces to electric arc technology.

The entrance of UkrHazEnergo into the domestic gas market and mother company's RosUkrEnergo's de facto control of a growing number of oblhazy regional gas distributors through their shadow privatization also had important implications for the battle over control of Ukraine's gas transit system.[136] In a déjà vu to the mid-1990s, the virtual monopoly on gas supplies to industrial enterprises held by UkrHazEnergo gave it the means, to, if wanted, forcibly bankrupt companies by sharply increasing prices, either as a goal in itself or as means for hostile takeover. This instrument was used repeatedly by the RosUkrEnergo/Firtash group to gain control over *oblhazy* and other industries under the control of rival companies.[137] In addition, the company's de facto growing control over the oblhazy also gave it the means to cut off supplies to residential customers, raising the prospect of politically costly social unrest and increasing its (and Gazprom's) leverage in the relationship with NAK Naftohaz.

Control over regional gas distribution networks also had important implications for the control of Ukraine's gas transit system. Although we normally do not associate regional distribution pipelines with international transit, in Ukraine the distinction between large-diameter transit pipelines and smaller ones is less clear than it may seem at first glance, and some international transit can take place through them.[138] This means that, through gradually taking control over regional gas distribution systems, UkrHazEnergo could also gain an additional foothold in the profitable international gas transit area. This was especially significant considering the fact that the privatization of NAK Naftohaz and its large-diameter gas pipeline network continued to be barred by law; thus, UkrHazEnergo's move to control domestic gas pipelines opened a way of circumventing such prohibitions.

THE YUSHCHENKO-TYMOSHENKO CONFLICT AND THE MANAGEMENT OF
ENERGY DEPENDENCY IN THE RUN UP TO THE JANUARY 2009 CRISIS

As time progressed – and especially after Tymoshenko's December
2007 return to power as PM in the wake of her bloc's victory in the
September Rada elections and a new alliance with Yushchenko – the
negative effects of RosUkrEnergo's role became increasingly clear, with
more and more voices calling for an end to the preferential relationship
and for the reestablishment of direct contracts between Ukraine and
its gas suppliers, first and foremost Gazprom. Not surprisingly, the issue became an increasingly acrimonious bone of contention between
Tymoshenko and Yushchenko, whose relationship had improved only
very temporarily in 2007.

In this confrontation, Tymoshenko made the call for direct contracts with Gazprom and the removal of RosUkrEnergo the centre of
her campaign; President Yushchenko, on the other hand, emphasized
the positive role of the company in making possible relatively low gas
prices for Ukraine. Their differing policy preferences and interests on
oil also came to a head on the issue of the oil company Vanco's right
to prospect for oil in the Black Sea, where a 2006 exploration permit
received by the company was rescinded by PM Tymoshenko in May
2008, arguing corrupt dealings.[139] A third conflict, on the role of the
Privat business group, revolved around control of the Kremenchuk oil
refinery, the Ukrainian-Tatarstan JV Ukrtatnafta and, by implication,
of several other refineries in Western Ukraine.[140] Last but not least, the
president and PM continued to be at odds concerning the Odesa-Brody
oil pipeline. Although both officially supported the goal of moving the
pipeline to its originally intended use to bring Caspian oil to Ukraine,
Tymoshenko had accused structures close to the president of trying to
implement the change through a corrupt plan involving an offshore
company.

In this context, the lack of clearly divided spheres of competence
between president and PM – itself partially a result of the constitutional changes that came into force on 1 January 2006 reducing the
power of the president – greatly contributed to the crisis that would
unfold in January of 2009. Throughout 2008, lack of clarity as to who
was in charge of negotiations with Russia complicated the situation.
In addition, such lack of clarity put in danger agreements of principle
reached by Tymoshenko during visits to Russia in March and October
2008.

Despite the continued political crisis, 2008 had offered some promising prospects that gas relations with Russia could be regulated and a new crisis avoided. After a crisis in late February due to NAK Naftohaz's unpaid debt to RosUkrEnergo that many feared would lead to a cutoff of supplies, and that many saw as an attempt by Gazprom to frighten Ukraine away from seeking to remove intermediary companies,[141] Tymoshenko's 12 March negotiations in Moscow, and the resulting agreement of principle between the sides, brought back the prospect of doing away with both domestic gas distributor UkrHazEnergo (effective March 2008) and RosUkrEnergo (effective some months later). In exchange, prices would increase, an additional 1.4 bcm of Russian gas was acknowledged as debt, and Gazprom was promised the right to sell at least 7.5 bcm of gas directly to Ukrainian industrial users after RosUkrEnergo would leave the market. Despite some uncertainly about the agreements, energy relations with Russia regained a sense of relative calm in the following weeks. Discussions on RosUkrEnergo subsided, until it was quietly announced in mid-April 2008 that, after all, the company would retain its intermediary role.[142] Thus, while the battle against RosUkrEnergo was going on above the surface and for public consumption, at the underground level those (such as RosUkrEnergo) who needed to defend their interests found a way to do so.

A new Tymoshenko-Putin meeting in early October brought the possibility of a change in contracts to a three-year transition to market, netback gas prices to Ukraine in exchange for European-level fees for transit through Ukraine. It also brought renewed hope that Ukraine would start buying gas directly from Gazprom starting 1 January 2009.[143] Such agreements of principle were expected to be firmed up during NAK Naftohaz' head Oleg Dubina's visit to Moscow on 11 November. Yet, as a result of unknown circumstances, the result of the visit was exactly the opposite: no agreement, and a hardening of Gazprom's position vis-á-vis NAK Naftohaz. The situation started to escalate rapidly after that. On 1 January 2009, arguing unpaid debts, Russia cut gas supplies destined to Ukraine. Seven days later, as a means of exerting additional pressure, it cut all gas supplies through Ukraine, stopping all Russian supplies to EU members Bulgaria and Romania, as well as to Moldova, Serbia, Bosnia-Herzegovina, Croatia, and the Former Yugoslav Republic (FYR) of Macedonia.

In order to understand this escalation, it is worthwhile to take a look at the economic background to the January 2009 conflict. Its roots can be found in the long-standing issues left unresolved by the 2006 agreements that, in particular, did not provide a clear mechanism of price formation and did not reflect the netback pricing principles since 2006 officially favoured by Gazprom as the guiding principle of price formation in all exports. As a result, the 2006 agreements failed to deal with the gap between for-Ukraine prices and European ones, a gap that had continued to grow despite price increases set by the agreement for 2006–2008 (see Table 4.3). Thus – especially considering the loss of Gazprom revenue expected from falling oil and gas price trends in Europe – pressure from Gazprom to increase prices to Ukraine was to be expected. On the Ukrainian side, even with a relatively moderate increase in prices, pressure was mounting due to NAK Naftohaz's increased inability to keep up with payments, leading to a debt of, at the lowest estimate, $1.3 billion by November 2008. These problems were made worse by the domestic politization of the issue, in particular the continued conflict between PM Tymoshenko and President Yushchenko, a conflict in which energy issues – and accusations or negligence or corruption between the sides – became the main bone of contention between them, and virtually paralyzed policy making on the issue.

The situation started to escalate quickly after energy minister Dubina's failed November 2008 negotiations in Moscow. Moscow demanded immediate payment of NAK Naftohaz's debt to Gazprom/RosUkrEnergo, amounting to, according to Gazprom, $2.4 billion ($1.3 billion according to NAK Naftohaz.)[144] (Although the debt was technically to RosUkrEnergo, it was to Gazprom indirectly through the intermediary.) As an alternative to immediate payment, Gazprom proposed to Ukraine either repaying the debt in the form of transit services in 2009 (with $2.4 billion equaling 14 months' worth of transit services), or maintaining the current scheme involving RosUkrEnergo.[145] Both schemes were rejected by the Ukrainian side; the proposed barter scheme would have meant a severe blow to NAK Naftohaz, as transit fees provided about 90 percent of the company's hard currency earnings.

The way the crisis escalated, however, tells us that Gazprom's striving for netback pricing of sales to Ukraine was not the sole (or possibly most important) issue at stake in the negotiations, with issues concerning the profitable role of intermediary suppliers an equally if not even more important issue. (RosUkrEnergo's profits from the reexport of Russian gas were calculated at $2.25 billion in 2006 and ca. $2.9 billion in 2007.[146]) Clearly, a serious battle on the future of intermediary companies and energy rents was raging beneath the surface and, less openly, within the Russian leadership as well.

While we do not know with full certainty what transpired during the January 2009 negotiations, the past record alerts us to pay close attention to the ways in which domestic Ukrainian conflicts for control of energy policy interface with divisions within Gazprom. From past instances in 2000, 2007, and 2008, we know there is a track record of parallel groups within Ukraine's energy policy making structures, in alliance with their own set of allies within Gazprom, supporting wholly different assessments of Ukraine's debt vis-á-vis the company, with important effects for Ukraine.[147] This was likely the case in 2009 as well.

During the period from 1 January to 19 January, both sides – and especially Russia – showed little haste to end the dispute, despite the significant monetary and reputational costs involved. On the contrary, new Russian accusations calling into question Ukraine's ability to be an honest or even technically able partner in European gas transit seemed to further escalate the conflict daily.[148] On the Ukrainian side, it is hard to avoid the impression that those in charge purposefully linked the transit-to-Europe conflict with the conflict on prices and supplies, as, had the specifically transit conflict been solved before the conflict on prices, the EU may have lost an important incentive to act as a mediator, and Ukraine would have thus lost a chance to multilateralize the conflict, as opposed to having to face Russia on its own. (In the first days of the conflict, before it came to affect transit to the EU, the EU explicitly referred to the conflict as one between two economic actors in which it would neither arbitrate nor participate in any other way.[149])

The impasse was solved once PM Tymoshenko travelled to Moscow on 18 January for direct negotiations with PM Putin. (Although Tymoshenko and Yushchenko had made a rare show of unity at the beginning of the crisis, it was clear that Tymoshenko held a closely guarded monopoly on negotiations with Putin. In fact, as it later emerged, even Tymoshenko's cabinet and NAK Naftohaz refused to sign the deal, which "was only finally settled on her [Tymoshenko's] own authority";[150] abuse of power was the key accusation in the subsequent trial against Tymoshenko.) Supplies were restored on 20 January. Tymoshenko triumphantly declared that the agreements, based on the elimination of intermediary companies and the move to a European pricing formula (see further on) with a 20 percent discount on the first year, would help prevent another New Year's Eve conflict.

Was Tymoshenko right in praising the agreements as a guarantee of stability? A brief review of the contracts tells us that many of their clauses could be seen as positive for Ukraine in the medium and long-term.[151] First and most importantly, they did away with RosUkrEnergo's intermediary role, establishing a ten-year direct contract between Gazprom and NAK Naftohaz, a significant improvement for Ukraine. Second, they included a clear price formula based, for the first time in Ukrainian-Russian gas relations, on the European netback principle. Third, the contracts guaranteed a minimum transit of 110 bcm per year for the duration of the contract, thus assuaging Ukrainian fears that some of Russia's new pipeline projects would lead to reduced transit through Ukraine. Also for the first time in Russian-Ukrainian gas relations, the contract specifically regulated the issue of so-called technological gas, an area of much misunderstanding in the January 2009 crisis, as Ukraine argued some of the gas Gazprom accused it of stealing was simply technical gas needed for the operation of the pipeline.[152]

Yet the contract also contained a number of worrisome elements. First, the "European" base price of $450 per tcm used in the contracts was in fact higher than the price paid by many WE importers. Second, the contracts led to significant immediate gas price hikes (first quarter prices for 2009 were $360/tcm), likely to have a short-term negative impact (although a likely positive one in the long term) on Ukrainian industry, which in 2008 had been able to adapt to the price increase to $179.50 largely thanks to record high prices for its main exports, a situation that was fully reversed by 2009. Third, the contract included strict take-or-pay clauses and heavy penalties for late payment; should NAK Naftohaz be unable to make those payments on time, it would be automatically moved to 100 percent prepayment for the reminder of the ten-year contract.[153] Fourth, repeating some of the dynamics involved in UkrHazEnergo's role between February 2006 and March 2008, Gazprom was given the right to, through a daughter company, market 25 percent of the imported gas directly to industrial users, strengthening its role in the domestic Ukrainian market and once again reducing one of NAK Naftohaz's few sources of profit.[154] Most importantly, gas transit fees paid Ukraine would remain unchanged (at $1.6/tcm/100 km plus a mechanism for indexation) making them, relative to the price of gas, even lower than their 2008 levels.[155]

These factors compromised NAK Naftohaz's ability to pay on time for gas imports, bringing the danger of a new crisis. Even before the full content of the agreements was known, a new political struggle around them started, a struggle that would play a crucial role in the run up to the February 2010 presidential elections. Observing the situation from the sidelines, the Party of Regions called for the impeachment of the president and dismissal of the PM. President Yushchenko indirectly accused PM Tymoshenko of treason for signing agreements he saw as clearly negative for Ukraine; others hinted she may have signed an agreement clearly negative to Ukraine in exchange for Russia's ignoring of still outstanding cases of corruption against her dating from the 1990s and/or support in a future presidential bid.[156] For her part, Tymoshenko once again accused Yushchenko of an alliance with RosUkrEnergo's Firtash. While politicians in Kyiv were adjudicating blame for the new agreements, NAK Naftohaz was having increasing difficulties paying for gas imports, to the point that an emergency $500 million cash emission by the National Bank in May 2009 was used to help pay the bill to Gazprom. RosUkrEnergo, for its part, while no longer the official intermediary, continued to play an active role through its partial ownership of several regional gas distributors, and through its suit against NAK Naftohaz at the Stockholm Arbitration Court, which it accused of illegally appropriating 11 bcm of gas belonging to RosUkrEnergo from gas underground gas deposits.[157]

Given these tensions, it is not surprising that dissatisfaction with the agreements became a major political issue, a major force propelling Yanukovich's popularity growth in 2009, and his successful bid for the presidency in February 2010.

A Snapshot of the Outcomes

How did the political dynamics discussed previously affect Ukraine's actual energy outcomes? To what extent where the energy diversification slogans proclaimed by every Ukrainian government since 1991 reflected in actual policy? We can look at the track record in terms of three issue areas: the direct management of energy supply diversification, the organization of energy trade, and other aspects of energy policy having implications for energy dependency issues.

Management of Energy Supply Diversification Issues

DOMESTIC DIVERSIFICATION: ENERGY DIVERSIFICATION VIA ENERGY
SAVINGS, ENERGY EFFICIENCY, AND INCREASED PRODUCTION

The first and most obvious way of offsetting external energy dependencies is by dealing with the domestic side of the question: reducing demand through increasing efficiency, reducing consumption without increasing efficiency (by increasing prices or rationing, for example), changing the energy mix in favour of fuels produced domestically, and increasing domestic production. How did Ukraine fare in these areas?

Energy Savings and Energy Efficiency Programs

Largely as a result of pre-1991 legacies, Ukraine's energy efficiency remained very low in international comparison. Because market prices for energy were not introduced in the first years after independence, neither were individual consumers pushed to reduce consumption, nor was the country as a whole forced to abandon an energy-intensive production mix in favour of a more efficient one. In part because of the continued political power of the state-owned heavy industrial sector and its managers, energy-intensive industries shrunk less than industry as a whole during the depressed 1991–1995 period, and their impact on average energy intensity increased as well.[158] As a result of these factors, Ukraine's energy intensity grew significantly from 1991 to 1995, as GDP fell much more rapidly than energy consumption.[159] This difference in the role of large, energy-intensive industries in the Ukrainian and Central European and Baltic states, for example Lithuania (where they were often allowed to go bankrupt or were massively restructured) seems to explain the difference between energy intensity development patterns in Ukraine and the early reformer countries, where decreases in energy intensity were observable since 1991. In the early and mid-2000s, the success of energy-intensive metallurgical exports[160] and the ability of related income to compensate for the costs of the higher energy consumption resulting from this industrial structure contributed to keeping Ukraine tied to an energy-intensive industrial model.[161]

Throughout the mid-1990s and early 2000s, the Ukrainian government launched a number of energy efficiency initiatives.[162] While small-scale projects (for example, programs aimed at increasing energy efficiency in public buildings) produced positive results, there were serious obstacles on the way to improving energy efficiency on a larger scale. By 2005, more than half of households did not have gas meters, and were charged for gas on the basis of flat-rate calculations, discouraging gas conservation. Moreover, many of the energy efficiency measures implemented at the local and regional level were obstaculized by often contradictory legislation, corruption, and the continued influence of large energy-intensive industries and the nuclear lobby. Despite these obstacles, as a result of small-scale developments, energy intensity decreased gradually in the period 1995–2010.[163]

Rapid gas import price increases after 2006 further prodded Ukraine towards lower energy use and more energy efficiency. This was especially so for the industrial sector, where, partially as a result of the increase in gas prices effective 1 January 2006, from 2005 to 2006 industrial gas consumption went down by 16 percent;[164] further changes in industrial gas consumption are discussed at the end of this chapter. (As domestic production decreased, however, this reduction in consumption did not immediately lead to a reduction in energy dependency, which reached 43.6 percent in 2008.)

This development was first and foremost due to changes in the metallurgical sector, where, despite its history as a traditionally highly energy-intensive and energy-inefficient industry, rapid gas price increases prompted companies to engage in energy-saving modernization programs.[165] Helped by rapidly increasing exports profits from growing world prices for steel, industries such as Akhmetov's Systems Capital Management started to invest heavily into energy efficiency improvements even before the 2006 gas price increases, while seeking separate gas import agreements with Moscow to secure lower gas prices. Higher energy prices also created new cleavages between industries able to modernize quickly, and those unable to do so.

Yet even after these improvements, Ukraine retained high levels of energy intensity (see Table 4.4) and remained one of the most inefficient energy users in the world. When calculated on a purchasing power parity (PPP) basis, Ukraine's 2006 energy intensity was tied in the tenth worst place worldwide, surpassed only by low-GDP states, countries at war, and large energy producers. At nominal GDP values, Ukraine occupied the second place in the world, after Congo, and had significantly worse values than all post-Soviet states with the exception of Turkmenistan and Kazakhstan.[166]

Table 4.4 GDP, Energy Use and Energy Intensity in Ukraine, 1990–2011

	1990	1991	1992	1993	1994	1995	1996	1997	1998	1999	2000
GDP in billion US$ at current prices	81.85	77.46	73.94	65.64	52.54	48.21	44.55	50.15	41.88	31.58	31.26
GDP in US$ at 2005 prices (PPP)	418.4	383.2	346	296.8	228.7	200.8	180.7	175.3	172	171.6	181.8
GDP as percentage of 1990 GDP (PPP)	100	91.58	82.69	70/93	54.66	47.99	43.18	41.89	41.1	41.01	43.45
TPES/energy use (in million tons of oil equivalent)	253	250.6	219.9	189	160	160	151	141	134	133.5	132
Energy use as percentage of 1990 use	100	98.81	86.91	74.70	63.24	63.24	59.68	55.73	52.96	52.76	52.17
Energy intensity Kg of oil equivalent per US$ 1,000 GDP at 2005 PPP	602	659	655	725	816	831	819	789	787	736	676

Table 4.4 (Continued)

	2001	2002	2003	2004	2005	2006	2007	2008	2009	2010	2011
GDP in billion US$ at current prices	38.00	42.39	50.13	64.88	86.14	107.75	142.71	180.35	117.23	136.41	165.24
GDP in US$ at 2005 prices (PPP)	198.5	208.8	228.5	256.1	263	282.2	304.5	311.5	265.4	276.5	291
GDP as percentage of 1990 GDP (PPP)	47.44	49.9	54.6	61.2	62.85	67.44	72.77	74.45	63.43	66.08	69.55
TPES/Energy use (in million tons of oil equivalent)	132	135.5	141.5	141	143.24	137.43	137.3	136.14	112.3	130.5	N/A
Energy use as percentage of 1990 use	52.17	53.35	55.92	55.92	56.61	54.32	54.28	53.81	44.38	51.58	N/A
Energy intensity Kg of oil equivalent per US$ 1,000 GDP at 2005 PPP	649	633	562	543	487	451	437	437	423	472	N/A

Sources: World Bank World Development Indicators, available at www.databank.worldbank.org

Energy imports can also be reduced through energy-mix diversification; that is, by switching to fuels more commonly available domestically. At a high point in 2005, 47.1 percent of Ukraine's TPES was covered by gas, one of the highest levels in the world; the share of gas in Ukraine's total energy supply had increased by more than 10 percent since the early 1990s, making the country increasingly gas-dependent on Russia.[168] With the increase in gas prices in 2006, the share was reduced to 40.87 percent in 2007 and 40 percent in 2010.

In Ukraine's 2007 energy mix, gas was followed by coal (29.56 precent of TPES), oil (10.84 percent), and nuclear energy (17.55 percent). Of these, only coal and nuclear energy were real alternatives to imported gas, but political, economic, and environmental issues stood on the way of either becoming a long-term substitute. In the case of coal, the poor quality of local coal sorts, high production costs, manipulation of prices by BAGs, and the de facto bankruptcy situation of most mines were major factors preventing coal from becoming a real alternative.[169]

Diversification through the increased use of nuclear energy was also problematic. Despite the fact that, in a conscious effort to reduce dependency on imports, Ukraine saw the role of nuclear power grow from 7.9 percent of TPES in 1990 to 17.55 percent in 2007, this did not bring a move away from dependency on Russia, as the nuclear fuel needed for the type of reactors in use in Ukraine needs to be imported from Russia, minimizing the geographical diversification effect of an increased use of nuclear power.[170] Moreover, nuclear energy was not a reliable diversification solution for Ukraine given significant opposition from local environmental groups as well European institutions' uneasiness about new nuclear projects given the Chernobyl legacy.[171]

In terms of renewable resources, both the 1996 National Power Energy Program and the 2001 Alternative Energy Resources bill aimed to develop alternative and renewable energy resources (such as hydro-electric, solar, wind, geothermal, biomass, and waste power). The combined share of these sources increased from 0.5 percent of total TPES in 1990, to 1.41 percent in 2007 – hardly impressive neither in absolute terms nor in terms of trends in most European countries, where the use of renewable and biomass resources grew substantially during this period.

Increased Domestic Production

As discussed in chapter 2, Ukraine was, until the 1970s, an important oil and gas producer. After that, energy production started to decline quickly, partly as a result of the shift of energy investments to Western

Siberia and of the use of predatory production methods leading to the premature peaking of Ukrainian reserves in the 1970s (see Table 4.5). Domestic oil production (which in the mid 2000s covered ca. 16–20 percent of Ukraine's domestic needs), already in decline since the late 1970s, was also affected by post-independence policy decisions decreasing the attractiveness of investments in domestic production. Throughout the period covered in this book, despite some attempts to establish an oil exchange to increase transparency in pricing, sweet-heart deals reducing oil prices for certain consumers were common, which often meant the sale price of domestic oil was too low to make domestic production profitable.[172]

The lack of a stable legal framework, as well as of a sound incentive structure also hindered domestic oil production. In particular, this had to do with the taxation of upstream operations, and with an exploration licensing regime that provided few guarantees to prospectors that they would be granted a production license later.[173] Despite the passing of Production Sharing Agreement (1999) and Oil and Gas (2001) laws intended to simplify licensing procedures and thus encourage foreign investments in the oil and gas area, corruption and complicated, investor-unfriendly rules also hindered the entrance of foreign investors (especially Western ones) into oil production areas. In the Yushchenko period, the aforementioned revocation of Vanco's production license in 2008, symptomatic of the lack of a stable legal framework, kept away investments much needed to increase oil and gas production.

In gas production as well, despite the discovery of several gas and oil fields in the mid-2000s, bringing these into actual production was a challenge, as many of these reserves are located at great depth and require expensive technology to be efficiently exploited.[174] The requirement that all gas produced domestically by NAK Naftohaz subsidiaries and independent producers be sold to NAK Naftohaz for further sale to the residential sector at low prices – which often barely cover production costs – reduced the incentives for domestic production. In addition, Ukraine's energy production and distribution system was sorely outdated, both leading to significant energy losses and limiting the growth of domestic production.[175]

External Diversification

GEOGRAPHIC DIVERSIFICATION: THE DECLARATIVE LEVEL
At the declarative level, Ukraine has undoubtedly been a champion of geographic diversification. Already in 1996 a "Concept for the Diversification of Gas and Oil Supplies," including proposals for increased

Table 4.5 Oil and Gas Production in Ukraine, 1940–1977 and 1990–2011, in Mt of Oil and bcm of Gas

Year	Oil* (Mtoe)	Gas (bcm)
1940	0.35	0.5
1945	0.25	0.78
1950	0.29	1.53
1955	0.53	2.93
1960	2.20	14.3
1965	7.60	39.4
1970	13.60	60.9
1975	12.80	68.7
1977	10.50	67.0
1990	5.40	28.1
1995	4.20	18.2
1999	4.80	18.1
2000	4.40	18.01
2001	4.20	18.20
2002	3.97	18.40
2003	4.17	19.51
2004	4.31	19.20
2005	4.43	19.39
2006	4.52	19.51
2007	4.47	19.5
2008	4.34	21.05
2009	4.0	21.10
2010	3.65	20.30
2011	3.30	200

* Oil figures include gas condensate.

Sources: for oil, for 1940–1977 from Dienes and Shabad, *The Soviet Energy System* (New York: V. H. Winston & Sons, 1979), 46–47, for 1989, and 1990 Dienes et. al., *Energy and Economic Reform*, 99. Data for 1990–2000 International Energy Agency, *Energy Statistics of Non-OECD Countries* (Paris: OECD, various years), 2001–2008 from US Energy Information Administration, http://www.eia.doe.gov/pub/international/iealf/tableg2.xls (Oil Production; Table reposted 19 December 2008), IEA *Energy Balances of Non-OECD States*, various issues. 2009–2011 from IEA, *Ukraine* 2012.

For gas: 1940–1977: Dienes and Shabad, *The Soviet Energy System*, 70–71; 1990–1999: Kostiukovskii, "Enerhetichna kriza v Ukraini," *Energetichna Politika Ukraini* 2000, no. 4 (April 2000), 46–50. 2000–2006 data from EIA, converted from trillion cubic feet, 2007 and 2008 data (both est.) from 2007 CIA World Factbook, available at https://www.cia.gov/library/publications/the-world-factbook/geos/up.html#Econ (both accessed 23 April 2009). 2009–2011 from IEA, *Ukraine* 2012.

diversification through imports from Turkmenistan, Iran, Uzbekistan, and the Near and Middle East, was adopted by the Ukrainian government. The concept also supported the building of a pipeline to transit Caspian oil to Ukraine (the Odesa-Brody pipeline). The 1997 National Security Doctrine adopted by the Rada also emphasized the problems created by Ukraine's dependence on Russian oil and gas.

A second wave of diversification proposals came in 2000 during the government of PM Yushchenko, marked by a government declaration calling the import of more than 30 percent of gas from a single source economically unsafe for the state.[176] Ukraine's official support for diversification was reflected in its joining of the EU's Traseca program intended to support the flow of Caspian oil supplies to European markets, and Vice PM Tymoshenko's support of the idea of building a gas pipeline from Turkmenistan to WE via Ukraine bypassing Russia, an idea that was resurrected (as the White Stream project) once she occupied the PM's office in 2005.

GEOGRAPHIC DIVERSIFICATION: THE DE FACTO LEVEL

Despite strong pro-diversification activism at the declarative level, the actual de facto diversification policies followed by both the Kuchma and Yushchenko presidencies were often haphazard and contradictory. In fact, it is impossible to ascertain with certitude up to which point pro-diversification declarations were made sincerely and up to which point they constituted a form of instrumental securitization of energy dependency issues and were simply intended to reassure the West of Ukraine's commitment to strengthen its economic independence from Russia despite little proactive policy making in the area.

Both the case of the Odesa-Brody oil pipeline, and of gas imports from Turkmenistan provide excellent examples of how what started as an official diversification initiative ended, through the impact of rent-seeking actors, de facto working in the opposite direction. As discussed earlier, the gas supply relationship with Turkmenistan was mismanaged to such an extent that, from a possible source of geographical and contractual diversification, it became a magnet for corruption and, in its own way, an incentive for Ukraine to become even more dependent on a single supplier through intermediary companies such as RosUkrEnergo.

Concerning oil diversification, the outcomes as of 2009 were even less encouraging: although, in a reflection of the lower level of monopolization in the Russian oil industry compared to gas, the degree of contractual diversification was higher than in the gas sector, in terms of geographic diversification even the existence of an important pro-diversification infrastructure (the Odesa-Brody pipeline) could not guarantee its use in a pro-diversification direction, with the pipeline switched to a reverse, anti-diversification direction in 2004. Ukraine continued to import oil almost exclusively from Russia, with much smaller amounts imported from Kazakhstan and occasional supplies from Iraq in the 2007–2009 period. In October 2009 Ukraine's largest refinery, Kremenchuk, announced an agreement to import about 240,000 tons of oil per month – about 50 percent of its requirement – from Azerbaijan.[177]

Ukraine's lack of oil diversification was compounded by the fact that, despite policy initiatives to the effect unveiled in 1998, 2001, and 2004 at the time of each major oil supply crisis,[178] by 2012 Ukraine had not taken clear steps to develop a 90-day reserve of oil and oil products in order to help stabilize the market and act as a buffer in case of interruptions in the supply of Russian oil; the country's oil storage amounted to only a minimal portion (a few days' worth of supplies) of its yearly needs.[179] These examples make clear the distance between theory and practice in Ukrainian diversification policy.

Contractual Diversification and Organization of Energy Trade with the Main Current Supplier(s)

In contrast with geographical diversification, contractual diversification is first and foremost about the organization of energy trade and about developing a variety of contractual relationships both in terms of companies and of type of contracts (short-term, long-term, etc.) even when the energy originates from a single country. In this sense, contractual diversification can be a means of, at least in theory, managing the lack of geographical diversification. In this area, Ukraine's track record during both the Kuchma and Yushchenko periods was rather poor. If some aspects of contractual diversification fell beyond the control of the Ukrainian side (the fact that no alternative Russian gas exporter to Gazprom was available, for example), in other areas the Ukrainian side consciously entered into unfavourable contracts with various (mainly Russian and Russian-controlled) companies, contracts that took away income, diversification options, and decision-making power from the Ukrainian state. These contracts, as discussed earlier in this chapter, were most often with offshore companies of dubious precedence and involved the transfer of highly profitable areas of activity to them at the expense of state income and state decision-making power.

If after 2006 some of the means of cushioning Ukrainian users from the shock of worsening external energy conditions used in previous periods (for example, making dependency bearable to the main industrial actors by giving them access to relatively low-cost energy that allowed them to subsidize exports) were no longer viable, or at least not as viable as before because of the price increases,[180] another instrument was used: finding a way of moderating the transition to world prices by sharing the profits with nontransparent actors on the Russian side of the border as well, first and foremost in the form of granting privileged contracts to intermediary companies such as RosUkrEnergo.[181]

Ways of Going about General Energy Policy Issues

Under both the Kuchma and Yushchenko periods, Ukrainian energy policies were only partially democratically controlled, as real policy making was concentrated in the Presidential Administration, NAK Naftohaz, and informal bargaining structures that remained outside the realm of democratic governance. This lack of democratic control was an especially serious problem for Ukraine, considering the fact that given the difficulties involved in pursuing energy diversification (due first and foremost to the strength of structural and mental legacies and the power of interest groups), diversification policies can only have a chance to succeed if they are part of a generally accepted and well-legitimized energy policy. In Ukraine, the opposite was the rule, especially in the 2005–2010 period, with nearly each major energy policy decision or event carrying – in the context of the growing confrontation between President Yushchenko and PM Tymoshenko – in its wake a minor or major government crisis and mutual accusations of working against national interest.

Due to some of the factors discussed previously as well as to the lack of dedicated funding, Ukraine struggled with the drafting and approval of a new energy policy strategy document for years. Preliminary work for the drafting of a new Energy Strategy of Ukraine to 2030 occurred only in piecemeal fashion, without a strong coordinating centre, and with major delays. Completion of the strategy, originally planned for December 2002, was postponed twice, and had not been completed by the December 2004 elections. The Energy Strategy of Ukraine to 2030,[182] finally approved in March 2006 (i.e., in a rather different energy environment than the one in the early 2000s when work on the project started) turned out to be rather weak. The document has been criticized for including contradictory goals, as well as a number of technical inaccuracies and inconsistencies.[183] Many, including the IEA, referred to the document as more a declaration of wishes and intentions than a clear strategic policy plan.[184] As seen throughout this chapter, implementation of adopted energy policies was also a problem, made worse by the power and policy interference of Ukraine's strong economic interest groups. In fact, it can be safely argued that much of Ukrainian energy-related policy throughout the period covered by this book was a by-product of energy rent-seeking activities.

Thus, Ukraine's overall record in the post-independence period has been one of lack of institutionalization of energy policy making, with de facto energy policy often the result of factors and decisions having little to do with the country's energy security. Formal energy policy making mechanisms were only weakly institutionalized. The various formal actors that could play a role in the determination of a coherent energy policy were weak and no match for the mighty informal interests active in the area.[185]

Direction of the Management of the Energy Dependency Relationship

What does the track record in each of these areas tell us about the direction of the management of energy dependency in post-independence Ukraine?

As discussed earlier, energy dependency relationships can be managed in a variety of ways having to do with the following issues: (a) *transparency* of management, running the spectrum from transparent to non-transparent; (b) whether it predominantly reflects the interests of particularistic interests, or national interests as a whole, running the spectrum from particularistic to non-particularistic; and (c) whether it is managed in ways that foster the continuation of the energy dependency relationship or, conversely, foster growing energy independence and diversification.

In terms of the spectrum from transparent to nontransparent, the record has been clearly one of lack of transparency. For example, few details of Ukraine's gas and oil supply negotiations and contracts have been voluntarily made public; most of what has seen the public light has been through information leaked by politicians or journalists. Although this did not change after the Orange Revolution, the marked improvement in terms of increased freedom of the press since then has meant that although the energy actors themselves may continue to prefer working away from the gaze of public scrutiny, an increasingly proactive press made sure many details of such transactions come to light.[186]

In terms of reflecting the interests of particularistic interests or national interests, particularistic interests clearly had the upper hand; with few exceptions, this did not mean a single group, but a number of domestic and transborder groups, sometimes competing and sometimes coalescing, while all trying to make an economic and political profit out of Ukraine's energy dependency situation. This did not change with Yushchenko's coming to power in 2005.

In terms of the spectrum between fostering the continuation of the energy dependency relationship and proactively fostering growing energy independence and diversification, the fact that de facto control over important areas of energy policy was actually exercised by economic actors either with a clear interest in the maintenance of Ukraine's energy dependency status quo (especially in the pre-2005 period) or, in the best of cases, indifferent to it – as long as they could guarantee their own energy-related profits – had important effects on Ukraine's actual energy policies.

Main Developments since 2010

One of the first measures taken by President Yanukovich after taking office in February 2010 was the April signing of new agreements with Russia (the so-called Kharkiv agreements), providing for a nearly 30 percent discount on gas import prices (in volumes up to 40 bcm) in exchange for the extension of the stationing of Russia's Black Sea Fleet in Crimea until 2042 instead of 2017. Soon after the signing of this agreement, however, it became clear that the agreement would do little to control the unprecedented gas price increases stemming from the provisions of the 2009 agreements signed by then PM Tymoshenko, in particular the base price of $450 per tcm set in the contract.[187] Thanks to this, by early 2012 Ukraine was paying $425 per tcm, about $40 more than other Gazprom consumers such as Germany.[188] (By late 2012, the price was $432/tcm.) While the gas bill was increasing quickly, Ukraine's gas transit volumes and revenue declined, by 19.1 percent in 2012 alone.[189]

As a result, energy relations between both sides continued to deteriorate despite general expectations that relations would improve after the coming to power of "pro-Russian" Yanukovich, and, in particular, that the 2009 agreements would be revised to terms more favorable to Ukraine and more in tune with trends in other Gazprom contracts with European consumers (where a weakening of demand after 2008 had led to lowered prices and a relaxation of onerous take-or-pay provisions). From the very beginning, Yanukovich's attempt at a revision of the 2009 contracts was deeply tied to domestic political processes, in particular the criminal process against opposition leader Tymoshenko, convicted in October 2011 for abuse of office in signing the contracts; the claimed illegality of the 2009 contracts was cited as reason for the need for revision. Unstable relations with Russia also affected the oil sector, where the country's decision not to join the Russia-Belarus-Kazakhstan Customs Union despite intense lobbying from Moscow created deeply unfavorable conditions for oil products exports to Russia (as well as a flooding by Russian and Belarusian products), and led – in addition to other preexisting factors – to a steep decline in refining. By mid-2012 only one of Ukraine's major refineries was working. Meanwhile, both illegal imports and illegal refining had made significant inroads, with losses in the hundreds of millions per year to the state.[190] Domestic oil production also went down, increasing relative dependency on imports from Russia; Ukraine also lost significant oil transit volumes (see Table 4.2).

Yet the new economic reality of exposure to gas market prices meant, for the first time in the history of independent Ukraine, a clear economic incentive for a reduction in energy imports from Russia. A number of unprecedented developments followed: In particular, gas consumption went down by nearly 10 percent between 2008 and 2011 (and an even more startling estimated 20 percent between 2008 and 2012[191]). In particular, industrial gas consumption declined sharply with the decline in production resulting from the 2008–2009 crisis. While Ukraine's industrial output went down by 22 percent in 2009, industrial-sector gas consumption during the same period went down even faster, by nearly 40 percent.[192] It must be noted, however, that much of the reduction in gas consumption was due, in addition to modernization efforts in the metallurgical industry, to the effects of the global economic crisis (Ukraine's GDP went down by 15 percent in 2009);[193] after the immediate crisis gas demand partially recovered, going up to 59.3 bcm in 2011. After relatively rapid decreases in energy intensity between 2000 and

2008, that indicator started to stagnate and increase again in 2008–2010. This also had to do with the limited impact of the import price shock on the public/residential sector (ca. 56 percent of total gas use) where, despite much-publicized rate increases, prices, when adjusted for inflation, "more or less remained flat" from 2005 to mid-2012.[194] Moreover, the relative gap between the prices paid by households and import gas prices grew significantly between 2004 and 2012.[195] Thus, despite other changes, one central feature of the Ukrainian energy economy has not changed despite the price shock: the significant difference between the prices of gas supplied to the industrial sector (at full import cost recovery levels) and to the public/residential sector (at prices much below recovery levels), creating incentives for illegal supply schemes involving public sector gas for industrial use.[196]

In November 2012, Ukraine started to import, for the first time in its history, very small amounts of gas (0.06 bcm) from the German company RWE, via reversed flows through Poland, at a lower price than gas imported from Gazprom. Ambitious plans for further development of unconventional gas sources and an LNG terminal were also drawn and embodied in the draft *Updated Energy Strategy of Ukraine for the Period till 2030* presented for discussion in June 2012. A milestone was reached in 2011 when, for the first time, small amounts of oil transited via the Odesa-Brody pipeline in its intended direction; that is, Azeri oil from Odesa to Brody and farther to Belarus (however, such transit stopped in 2012).[197] These developments went together with a trend toward the increased centralization of political power under President Yanukovich, although as of this writing it is still too early to tell whether there is a causal relationship at play and whether this centralizing trend will hold.

Ukraine and the Shale Gas Revolution

Significant reserves of unconventional gas (amounting to 1.2 tcm, the fourth largest in Europe) have been identified in Ukraine, in particular since 2011; in January 2013 Ukraine signed a $10 billion, 50-year production-sharing agreement with Shell to develop these reserves. While the potential of these developments is enormous (the official goal is to produce from 3 to 5 bcm of unconventional gas by 2020, with best-case projections of up to 20 bcm by 2035[198]), it must be kept in mind that, because significant production would take decades to develop, these reserves will not be able to immediately compensate for Ukraine's own domestic gas production declines since 2009, and problems due to instability in regulatory arrangements (as shown by the conflict around Vanco discussed earlier in this chapter) cannot be excluded. This new opportunity also means that Ukraine is at a clear crossroads in its energy situation; how able it will be to seize this opportunity will, to a great degree, depend on whether it is able to develop an effective and transparent energy policy system.

Conclusion

Real and Apparent Power in the Relationship with Main Energy Suppliers

Throughout the period covered by this book the energy relationship between Russia and Ukraine was not so much one of unilateral Ukrainian dependency on Russia as one of asymmetrical interdependence, with each actor bringing to the table a number of power elements. Ukraine's importance in terms of transit, storage, and as market, at least at first glance, should have given it significant power in the relationship with Gazprom and other Russian energy actors. Yet such assets, in principle crucial instruments for the management of energy dependency, can be used either for the purpose of moderating and negotiating this dependency, or of increasing energy rents for private actors. In the case of Ukraine, the prevalent pattern of management of its energy dependency limited the policy impact of these important bargaining elements. For example, Ukraine could use its high level of underground gas storage facilities (equivalent to ca. 41 percent or more of yearly domestic gas use, compared with ca. 3 percent for Belarus and none for Lithuania[199]) to increase its resilience and ability to moderate gas dependency. In reality, however, such facilities were used mainly for the furthering of Gazprom's gas export interests, and for those of intermediary companies such as RosUkrEnergo, to which their use has been provided at prices many times lower than international ones.[200] Ukraine's blatant energy dependency on Russia, its recurring problems in paying for these supplies, together with the government's inability to take a united, strong policy stance on energy issues, made the country especially vulnerable to price fluctuations and unable to respond proactively to changes coming from the outside, for example Russia's new pipeline initiatives, which, by 2015 could sidetrack a significant amount of oil and gas transit volumes away from Ukraine, further reducing its bargaining power. Between 2011 and 2012, Ukraine's transit of gas to Europe and other CIS countries fell by nearly 20 percent, from 104 to 84 bcm.[201]

Ukraine's Cycle of Rents

How did the cycle of extraction, distribution, and recycling of energy rents work in the Ukrainian case? One particularity of the Ukrainian case was the apparent ease with which energy rents, both domestic and external, could be accessed. One important source of external energy rents was the highly preferential gas prices offered to the country until 2005. While this was not unique (Belarus received highly preferential prices for even longer), what was unique in the case of Ukraine was the combination between preferential prices and the existence of a plurality of powerful domestic actors, acting in a setting that not only allowed them to access these rents, but often both to rewrite the rules of the game, and affect energy policy more generally, in order to guarantee their continued access to these rents.

An important feature of the Ukrainian system was the transborder sharing of energy rents, in particular with Russian actors.[202] Indeed, this transborder sharing was, de facto, one of the main mechanisms for the management of energy conflicts between Ukraine and Russia.

In terms of the recycling of energy rents into the political system, the impact of Ukraine's energy magnates went well beyond their ability to dictate the country's energy policies at crucial junctures in its development. In none of our other cases, for example, did we see such a large participation of powerful energy-related actors in the country's parliament. During the Kuchma presidency, through a variety of illegal, semi-legal, and legal schemes, the energy system became a rich feeding ground for those with the right connections. Huge economic – and political – capitals were made as a result, especially by the most successful traders. As famously noted by Ihor Bakai, former head of Ukraine's NAK Naftohaz, who knew from his own experience, "all major political fortunes in post-independence Ukraine were made on the basis of Russian oil and gas."[203]

The phenomenon of well-connected groups reaping generous rents from energy trade and, indeed, from energy dependency (the rents of energy dependency as defined in chapter 1) is by no means unique to Ukraine. What made Ukraine unique was the sheer size of these rents, the ease with which they could be accessed by those with the right political connections, and their huge role in the development of its political system at exactly its most important formative period following independence. The availability of large energy rents exactly during the first, formative years of Ukrainian statehood had an important impact on its development. Considering the vast amount of rents that could be accessed through various energy-related schemes, it is not surprising that both old-school managers of state-owned energy-intensive industries and emerging oligarchs would find a common interest in freezing real economic and energy reforms for the simple reason that it was in their interest to maintain a system that allowed them to amass vast riches – legal and illegal – in record time. Even when gas and oil consumption went down as a result of the increased prices and the economic crisis that started in 2008, the formative impact of energy-dependency rent-seeking in the development of Ukrainian institutions is not diminished – the issue is not only whether dependency on Russia decreased but also how the way energy dependency and rents were dealt with, exactly in the first, formative, years of Ukrainian independence, will affect the political system. This impact is likely to remain for years and decades to come.

Rents of Dependency and Energy Policy

Corporations and private energy actors within corporations on both sides of the Russian-Ukrainian border were able to find common interests exactly through the joint access to and appropriation of rents of dependency, as exemplified by the January 2006 agreements. Indeed, this joint access to rents of dependency has been one of the most important mechanisms bringing together Russian and Ukrainian energy elites. Yet such a means of managing of its energy dependency on Russia hindered a clearer definition (and implementation) of Ukraine's national energy interests. On the Russian, especially Gazprom, side as well, private actors within the corporation were able to accrue profits privately at the cost of revenue for the corporation as a whole, but Ukraine's greater energy vulnerability amplified the effects of such a situation and meant that the private misuse of national companies and national policy had a much more significant effect on its national energy situation than was the case in Russia.

RENTS OF DEPENDENCY AND POLITICAL AND ECONOMIC REFORM
The fact that, in the 1990s, the winners of the first stage of what could with some largesse be called reforms had a vested interest in the

maintenance of an energy-intensive system had everything to do with the survival of such a system despite Ukraine's reality of energy scarcity. So in this case the institutional structure (the system of exchange of access-to-rents privileges for political and economic support) was crucial for the maintenance of energy-rich-country policies in a situation of energy poverty.[204]

Easy to access and able to further the short-term interests of most political and economic actors with a voice in Ukraine's energy policy making system, the country's energy rents proved simply too good to give up. While the benefits of the related mismanagement of Ukraine's energy policy were received by a few actors for whom these rents accrued in concentrated form, the costs of such a management of energy dependency were much more broadly spread out. Even if largely sheltered from external energy shocks until 2006 through artificially low residential energy prices, the population as a whole would ultimately need to pay for the resulting inflation and budget deficits in the form of increased state debt. Future generations were not spared either, forced to pay the direct and indirect price of Ukraine's missed opportunities in the energy and energy transit area.

5 Belarus:
Turning Dependency into Power?

Like Ukraine and Lithuania, Belarus gained political independence while remaining highly dependent on Russia and Russian energy. But it differed sharply in terms of its political dynamics, with, as will be shown in this chapter, important effects on the energy relationship with Russia.

Belarus as Case Study

Belarus and Asymmetrical Interdependence

Depending on foreign sources for about 86 percent of its energy supply, Belarus is the most energy-dependent of our three cases, and one of the most energy-dependent states in all of the former USSR. Annually, it can cover none of its gas needs, and only about 8 percent of its oil needs.[1] Of our three cases, it is the one whose economy is most deeply centered on gas (which comprises about 65 percent of the country's TPES), and one of the most gas-dependent countries of the world.[2] Gas is also crucial as nearly 80 percent of Belarus' exports consist of highly energy-intensive products,[3] making low gas prices and cheap, mainly gas-generated electricity central to the country's export competitiveness even more crucial for Belarus than for the other cases. Belarus' virtual lack of underground gas storage facilities amplifies the effects of this dependence, making the country largely unable to withstand a stoppage of supplies by tapping into such reserves.[4] In contrast with the other two cases, Belarus has never possessed a NPP in its territory – although, as the main area contaminated by the Chernobyl accident of 1986, it suffered the most from the effects of nuclear power.

Although less well-known than Ukraine as a transit country, Belarus is one of the most important countries for Russian gas exports to WE. In 2007, about 20 percent of Russia's total gas exports outside the CIS and Baltics and 36 percent of Russian oil exports to the EU transited through Belarus,[5] which offers the shortest route from Russian oil and gas fields to the main WE markets. This transit potential, however, is limited by the state of disrepair of Belarus' pipeline system, most of which was built in the mid-1960s.

While at first glance Belarus' energy relationship with Russia may seem to be shaped by the same type of asymmetric interdependence as the Ukrainian case (important transit role but high dependence on Russian energy), a number of differences make Belarus' asymmetrical interdependence on Russia more asymmetrical than Ukraine's.

First, while both countries' roles in the transit of Russian oil are largely similar, Belarus' smaller (20 percent) role in gas transit has given it much less bargaining power than Ukraine's 80 percent role. The structure of ownership of the main gas pipelines further diminishes Belarus' bargaining power. While Ukraine owns all gas transit pipelines crossing it, during the period coverd by this book only one of the two main gas pipelines crossing the country (the Beltransgas pipeline) belonged to Belarus, while Gazprom owned the Yamal pipeline (which in 2007 carried 63 percent of all gas transited).[6] Thus, the fact that only slightly more than one-third of Russian gas transiting through Belarus did so through Beltransgas pipelines – themselves since 2006 controlled by a fifty-fifty Russian-Belarussian JV – limited Belarus' technical and legal ability to block gas transit.

These elements highlight Belarus' limited bargaining power vis-á-vis Russia in the economic and energy areas. Yet our picture of these asymmetrical interdependencies would be incomplete without mentioning President Lukashenka's political and psychological power vis-á-vis Moscow that, as we discuss later in this chapter, allowed him to compensate the lack of economic counterpower for much of the 1994–2012 period.

How did the model of extraction, distribution of, and recycling of energy rents manifest itself in the Belarusian case? This chapter looks at this cycle from the perspective of Belarus' unique political situation and relationship with Russia. In terms of rents extraction, the special relationship with Russia (i.e., both states formally being in the process of building a Union State) allowed Belarus access to certain rents not available to the other two cases; at a more informal level, the relationship allowed access to rents above and beyond those specified in formal agreements. In terms of the distribution of rents, our chapter looks at the effects of Lukashenka's style of political control on who would have access to these rents, and how they would be distributed domestically. In terms of these rents recycling into the political system, we investigate how they affected the survival of Lukashenka's political economic model.

Our chapter proceeds as follows. The following section looks at Belarus' political system under Lukashenka and at the ways in which it has affected energy policy making. We then look at Belarus' management of energy dependency during the "high years" of the 1994–2004 period; and during the "low years" after the deterioration in energy trade conditions with Russia starting in 2004, before summarizing the outcomes of Belarus' energy policies since independence.

Belarus – The de facto Political System since Independence

Responding to the Challenges of Independence: Lukashenka's Economic Record

Understanding Belarus' role in the Soviet system is essential for understanding how both masses and elites came to approach the challenges of independence, including its energy challenges. One of the areas most devastated by the World War II, Belarus was rebuilt with the help of citizens from throughout the USSR, many of whom settled there permanently; after the war it rapidly recovered to become one of the most developed Soviet republics. Vastly industrialized and closely integrated into the Soviet division of labour, many referred to Belarus as the most perfectly Soviet republic of the USSR. Despite the existence of a small but highly motivated pro-independence movement, Belarus reached independence without a real commitment by the larger national political elites.[7] Highly dependent on the Soviet Union *as a system*, Belarus was hard hit by the Soviet breakup, with hyper-inflation (at 2220 percent in 1994), a 20 percent drop in GDP from 1993 to 1994, and a more than 50 percent decline in living standards from 1990 to 1994[8] (see Table 5.1). Infighting over language policy, together with popular frustration over growing corruption and income differentiation, led to a strong protest vote against incumbent Premier Viacheslav Kebitch in 1994, and to the election of a populist, Lukashenka, as president in July 1994.[9]

Table 5.1 GDP, Energy Use, and Energy Intensity in Belarus, 1990–2011

	1990	1991	1992	1993	1994	1995	1996	1997	1998	1999	2000	2001	2002	2003	2004	2005	2006	2007	2008	2009	2010	2011
GDP in billion US$ at current prices	17.269	17.833	17.022	16.280	14.931	13.972	14.756	14.128	15.222	12.138	12.736	12.354	14.594	17.825	23.141	30.210	36.961	45.275	60.763	49.037	55.211	55.132
GDP in US$ at 2005 prices (PPP)	66.54	65.74	59.43	54.91	48.49	43.44	44.66	49.75	53.93	55.77	59.00	61.79	64.91	69.48	77.43	83.49	92.25	101.34	112.79	114.18	118.67	124.96
GDP as percentage of 1990 GDP (PPP)	100	98.79	89.31	82.53	72.87	65.28	67.11	73.00	81.04	83.70	88.66	92.86	97.55	104.43	116.36	125.47	138.63	152.29	169.50	171.59	178.34	87.79
TPES/Energy use (in million tons of oil equivalent)	42.3	40.7	38.3	31.4	26.8	24.7	25.4	25.3	24.8	24.1	24.6	24.7	25.2	26	26.8	26.8	28.6	28	28.1	26.7	27.7	N/A
Energy use as percentage of 1990 use	100	96.2	90.5	74.2	63.3	58.4	60	59.8	58.6	56.9	58.1	58.3	59.6	61.4	63.3	63.3	67.6	66.2	66.4	63.3	65.5	N/A
Energy intensity (Kg of oil equivalent per $1,000 GDP at 2005 PPP)	684	632	582	560	578	578	517	467	440	425	407	395	380	352	322	312	281	256	243	234	N/A	N/A

Source: World Bank World Development Indicators, available at www.databank.worldbank.

Lukashenka's policies sought to counter the effects of the Soviet demise by stopping painful economic reforms, including the privatization process shyly started in 1993, and by promising to build a strong relationship with Russia. The process, however, was not devoid of challenges. A new economic program started in 1996, based on monetary expansion, led to increased GDP growth in 1997–1998, but at the expense of higher inflation. The subsequent tightening of price controls succeeded in lowering inflation, but led to shortages, as some first-necessity consumer products, being priced lower than in neighbouring Russia, quickly disappeared into the other side of the border.[10] The next important challenge would come from Russia's 1998 crisis, which led to a sharp decline in Russian demand for Belarusian goods.

Despite these challenges and the lack of structural reforms, the economy started to grow in the mid-1990s; from 1997 to 2007 it maintained high GDP growth rates averaging 7.2 percent per year.[11] As will be discussed in more detail later on in the chapter, such growth was largely made possible by the special oil trade relationship with Russia, which helped translate the large increase in world oil prices in the mid 2000s into rents and a huge economic boom for Belarus. This contributed to steadily rising wages (which grew from an average of $100 per month in 1997 to $420 in June 2008) and living standards.[12] Such increase in living standards is especially significant considering the longstanding connection between rising living standards and state legitimacy in Soviet and post-Soviet Belarus.[13] It is perhaps this increase in living standards since 1994 that explains – together with repression, discussed further on – why Lukashenka remained popular for much of this period, and why there was little popular uproar over his growing authoritarianism.

How do these results compare with those of other post-Soviet states? In comparison to most post-Soviet states, Belarus' immediate post-dissolution crisis was shorter and milder; it was also the first to regain pre-1992 GDP levels. In contrast with them, where the mid-1990s were characterized by large wage arrears, in Belarus wages and pensions remained modest but promptly paid. All of this, however, was not the result of the successful completion of an economic reform process, but rather of the fact that such process– with all of its painful side-effects – had not really started. Indeed, throughout the 1994–2013 period, the Belarusian economy continued to be dominated by large, energy-inefficient, and often near-bankrupt state-owned enterprises.[14] Any real economic restructuring would have led, in the short term, to the closing of many of these inefficient factories, increasing unemployment and popular dissatisfaction. Thus, a constant flow of inexpensive energy was needed to keep these enterprises alive, unemployment low, and popular satisfaction with Lukashenka high.[15] This reality would inevitably have a major impact on energy policy.

This period also saw the development of a official relationship between Belarus and Russia, intended to lead to the establishment of a single Union State. This included a Commonwealth Agreement (April 1996), a Treaty on the Union of Belarus and Russia (April 1997) and, a Union Agreement (December 1999). While much in these agreements (such as the plan for monetary union by 2005) remained vague or was never implemented, they still held important symbolic value. They also set the basis for closer cooperation in the military and strategic areas, which proceeded much more successfully, including the installation in Belarus of Russia's western airspace air-defence warning radar system (October 2003) and the deployment of S-300 anti-aircraft missile systems (2005–2006), as well as the signing of a treaty integrating both countries' air defence systems (2009).[16]

Formal Political System and Institutions

Lukashenka's authoritarian tendencies quickly strengthened after his coming to power. Compared with his peers in Ukraine and, especially, Lithuania, the Belarusian president had much larger formal and informal powers; the power of representative institutions was negligible compared with the other two cases.

Belarus' formal political system has been shaped by its 1994 constitution and by the results of the November 1996 and 2004 referenda, which, among others, allowed the establishment of an undisclosed budget for the Presidential Administration outside the control of parliament or other representative bodies. These trends were highlighted by the increasing presidential takeover of judicial and legislative powers starting in 2005.[17]

Informal Institutions and de facto Political System

Lukashenka's presidential style has also been characterized by a disregard for formal institutions, even highly compliant ones such as individual ministries and the government-controlled parliament, the National Assembly. Three informal practices have been especially relevant in this process: Lukashenka's vertical system of control, his direct appeal to the masses, and his control of factions and clans within the system.

Lukashenka's system of top-down control ("presidential vertical") based largely on the intimidation, surveillance, and blackmailing of his own associates, has been a central feature of Belarus' political system since 1994. Such measures fit in well with Lukashenka's broader system of political control, a system characterized by moderate levels of open repression, but a type of repression taking place not only, or not even most importantly, through the imprisonment and killing of political opponents, but through less spectacular lower-key preemptive measures, such as restrictions on freedom of the press and administrative harassment of those with opposing views.[18]

Lukashenka's populist appeal to the masses provided a counterpart to his intimidation tactics. In fact, there is a connection between both – Lukashenka's periodically cleaning up of corruption in the upper ranks of government strengthened his image as a benevolent czar, prevented from carrying out virtuous policies only by the interference of self-interested officials. Lukashenka thus created the perception of a direct, unmediated link between himself and the population, which explains why he has not created his own political party. In fact, despite the fact that Lukashenka's officially-proclaimed large margin victories in the September 2001 (with 75.4 percent of the votes according to official sources) and March 2006 presidential elections (with 82.6 percent) were most likely the result of manipulation, for much of the 1994–2004 period he was able to maintain a degree of popular support, hovering around 35 percent in the early-to-mid 2000s – not an overwhelming figure but far ahead of any opposition figure.[19]

A third element of Belarus' de facto political system has to do with clan politics and informal power networks. While some have looked at these clans as based mainly on geographical connections and emphasized the power of the Mogilev group from Lukashenka's home region, others have emphasized a more administrative-unit based division (focusing on the role of distinct administrative groups, especially the security forces [*siloviki*] associated with long-term Lukashenka right-hand Viktor Sheiman). Confrontations between these groups, complicated by the entrance into the scene of Lukashenka's son and presumed heir-in-grooming Viktor in 2006, brought into the open the conflict between powerful groups for control over profitable state-supported rent-seeking, which we discuss further on in the chapter.

Despite the undeniable fact of the existence of these informal networks, possible similarities with powerful BAGs in Ukraine are limited by Lukashenka's playing of a much more central role than Kuchma ever did in Ukraine. Belarusian analysts see much of the struggle between clans as a struggle for closeness to Lukashenka, with access to serious money-making possibilities available "only on the basis of one's closeness to the President [*sic*]."[20]

Similarly, Belarusian oligarchs had very limited access to sources of income independent of the president, giving them significantly less freedom of action than in the Ukrainian case.[21] This had to do, first of all, with continued state control of the economy (up to 75 percent in the 2000s, one of the highest levels in the world), and with bureaucratic and tax disincentives for the establishment of new businesses. Both means were used actively to prevent the emergence of autonomous sources of economic power, ensuring that all major administrative and economic players remained dependent on Lukashenka's personal favour.

While in Kuchma's Ukraine money made by various clans was mightily and openly streamed into the financing of various political groups, in the case of Belarus the rents accrued by clans close to Lukashenka did not find their way into such variety of politically active recipients, clearly affecting the further recycling of energy rents into the political system. If such moneys made it into politics, it was to back the president through support of various projects associated directltly with him and for which he regulartly sought business contributions. The weakness and lack of unity of the Belarusian opposition – already debilitated by Lukashenka's repression and virtual monopolization of the media – made it nearly impossible for these dynamics to be effectively challenged.

Implications of the de facto Political System for Energy Policy

Lukashenka's system of vertical control crucially affected the energy policy making system, as well as relations with Russian energy actors. This took place in four main ways. First, through cadre policy: starting around 1997, experienced top managers, including those at the largest energy companies, gas operator Beltransgas and petrochemical concern Belneftekhim, start to be replaced by cadre with no experience in the area but having strong connections with the president. Second, the system of vertical control deprived energy-sector managers of any substantial say in policy making, in particular in negotiations with Russia, as Lukashenka kept close personal control over such issues. The requirement of presidential approval for privatization deals over

$80,000, further limited enterprises' freedom of action.[22] Presidential control over important energy policies and the use of energy companies (such as Beltransgas) for the pursuit of political goals outside the companies' profile was also aided by the general lack of transparency in the sector.[23] Third, any real energy policy debate was nipped in the bud. Dissent within the energy establishment was dealt with harshly, as when head of national petrochemicals giant Belneftekhim Aleksandr Borovskii criticized – at a low-profile plant meeting – the way negotiations with Russia had been conducted in late 2006. After his declarations mysteriously appeared in a website, he was arrested and accused of corruption.[24]

Finally and most importantly, during this period there was no democratic control over energy policy making – or over policy making in general. Belarus lacked an independent energy regulatory organ such as existed in most European countries, including Ukraine and Lithuania. Representative institutions such as the National Assembly had very little real policy making power, in contrast with, in particular, the Lithuanian case, where the Seimas was particularly active and fractionalism within it was a major element in energy policy making. These factors opened the door for an energy policy based largely on one-man decisions and the politization of energy relationships.

The High Years: Belarus' Track Record in the Management of its Energy Dependency, 1994–2004

Given its political system, how did Lukashenka's Belarus actually manage its energy dependency on Russia? This section discusses this management during the high years of relatively good relations and high Russian energy subsidies to Belarus, 1994–2004.

The Starting Point: Belarus at the Time of Independence

Belarus attained independence in 1992 in a state of deep dependence on Russia, a by-product of its high level of integration into Russia-centred USSR-wide economic processes. It depended on imports (almost exclusively from Russia) for about 87 percent of its energy (1990). In 1992, its first year of independence, it had to spend 25 percent of its GDP on energy imports.[25]

The large role of energy in relations with Russia makes an analysis of Belarus' energy situation since independence difficult to disentangle from the ups and downs of the relationship. Such connection was seen clearly in the "zero option" 1996 agreement reached in the wake of a particularly difficult economic period for Belarus, where the country accumulated a $1.27 billion gas debt vis-á-vis Gazprom.[26] As per the agreement, Belarus' gas debt to Russia up to that date was pardoned, in exchange for leasing to Russia, free of charge, two military telecommunications facilities.[27]

Despite the fact that already in 2001 Belarus' Concept of National Security noted as a problem the fact that Belarus received 99.9 percent of its energy imports from a single supplier, the document did not mention Russia specifically,[28] and apprehension about excessive reliance specifically on Russia was not reflected in policy proposals until the mid-2000s. In fact, few conscious, official moves towards energy self-sufficiency or towards an independent conceptualization of energy security were seen before 2004. Until 2004, the country explicitly advocated a joint energy balance with Russia, and energy dependency was not seen as a problem.

Crucial to Belarus' management its energy dependence in the 1994–2004 period was, externally, the attempt to deal with energy relations with Russia at an almost exclusively political level, in order to extract as much rent as possible. Internally, the approach concentrated on gearing the economy to extract maximum advantage of these rents as well. We discuss these two aspects in the following sections.

External Management

POLITIZATION: GENERAL

While Belarus' direct economic bargaining power was quite limited, Lukashenka was able to manipulate the relationship with Russia so as to make his country significantly more crucial to the Russian leadership than would be warranted by purely economic factors. The key had to do with Belarus' military-strategic importance for Russia, and with Lukashenka's ability to politicize the relationship. This strategy capitalized on the trauma of loss of empire by manipulating the Russian elites' psychological insecurities, offering an ego boost in the form of an alliance with Belarus, an alliance presented as a promise of a revived (post-Soviet) Union. In doing so, he was selling, not only Belarus as an ally and last defender of the USSR, but the *idea* of a strong and successful Soviet Union, deeply longed after by many Russian citizens. As fittingly stated by Vadim Dubnov, editor of the Russian journal

Novoe Vremia, "Lukashenka turned the status of being 'Russia's only real brother' into a natural monopoly, no less significant than Gazprom's monopoly on Belarus."[29]

The message of Belarus as Russia's last ally was craftily aimed at both the grassroots Russian electorate, especially in the provinces, and at the Russian leadership; Lukashenka used his popularity with the Russian masses to put pressure on the leadership. The underlying logic here is that many Russian leaders in the late 1990s, uneasy about a potential Lukashenka run for a possible joint Union State presidency, but even more afraid of eliciting the wrath of their own voting publics should they let Belarus down, were eager to neutralize Lukashenka's role in domestic Russian politics, and found it was safer to do so by – at least outwardly – embracing him and his goals than by opposing him openly.

ENERGY IN THE CONTEXT OF THE RUSSIAN-BELARUSIAN RELATIONSHIP: VIRTUAL INTEGRATION, REAL DETERIORATION

Lukashenka's presenting of Belarus as flagship supporter of a reborn Union masked growing contradictions in the relationship, in particular concerning the Belarusian government's deep suspicion towards Russian energy investments and Russian irritation over Belarus-supported smuggling and related abuse of its open border with Russia, which created large losses to the latter.[30] Agreements on a single currency also remained unimplemented, mainly due to Belarusian insistence on retaining significant control over emission decisions, and to the reticence of the Russian Central Bank to tie the Russian economy to that of a country that remained largely unreformed. The pattern was clear: constant talk of unification, especially from the Belarusian side, but little in terms of real economic integration. Thus, little real economic integration took place after the signing of the Union Agreement in 1999.

These realities have led a number of authors to describe the Belarusian-Russian relationship as a game of "virtual integration," where both sides had much to gain from constant declarations, posturing, and outdoing each other as to the desirability of a union, but much less to gain from real integration.[31] In contrast with breaking with Lukashenka, which would carry with it high political costs, virtual integration was cheap, and yielded high short-term political dividends. It also allowed Lukashenka to keep extracting energy rents and subsidies from Russia to a degree unlikely under a situation of full integration. Under full integration, Belarus would have been unable to, for example, maintain different oil export tariffs from Russia (discussed further on), allowing billions of dollars in potential income to be redirected from Russia to Belarus in the process.

GAS: EXTERNAL MANAGEMENT DURING THE HIGH YEARS, 1994–2004

In the gas sector, the politization of energy negotiations was used for two concrete goals: first, maintaining *and increasing* the volume of low-price gas supplies from Russia (indeed, such supplies increased significantly during this period: if in 1990 Belarus imported 14.1 bcm of gas, by 2006 this had increased to 21 bcm[32]). Second, limiting the real impact of any actual gas price increases by extracting concessions from Russia. These goals were pursued by presenting Belarus as an unavoidable transit gatekeeper, by politicizing negotiations over gas prices and volumes, and by selling the promise of joint Russian-Belarusian control over the country's gas transit system.

Gas Transit: The Yamal Pipeline and the Gatekeeper Myth

A first crucial element in Belarus' management of its gas dependency on Russia during this period was the attempt to present the country as both gatekeeper and most reliable route for the transit of Russian gas to Western markets. This strategy was especially visible in negotiations around the Yamal pipeline, Belarus' most important gas transit project to date. The pipeline, started in 1991, was conceived as part of a much larger, $36 billion project involving the development of the Yamal gas fields in Siberia and the transport of this gas to WE via a 6,670 kilometer pipeline passing through Belarus, Poland, and Germany.

Building and maintaining control over the Yamal pipeline was central for Gazprom's value-added chain in the mid-1990s: lacking the resources to develop cost-intensive new gas fields, the company sought to increase revenue by increasing its stake in the WE domestic gas distribution market. This strategy required a reliable gas transit system, and, given worsening relations with Ukraine and repeated instances of gas stealing from the transit pipeline in the second half of the 1990s, the company became keen on using a possible Belarusian-Polish corridor as an alternative to transit via Ukraine.

Yamal was also very important for Lukashenka's domestic power: it represented an important influx of investments that could be used to modernize Belarus' aging gas transit system, and bolstered his domestic image as an irreplaceable partner to Moscow. Yamal also put a powerful lobbyist, Gazprom, behind the political project of Belarusian-Russian integration; many Belarusian opposition figures saw Gazprom's transit interest as the main motivation for the establishment of the Belarus-Russia Union in 1997. The Yamal project also contributed to increasing Belarus' bargaining power vis-à-vis the Russian government and Gazprom. As we discuss further on in the chapter, this would become especially evident in the post-2004 period.

Politization of Gas Price Negotiations

A second element of Belarus' gas strategy during this period had to do with the politization of negotiations on gas supplies. Even after a hard-won 2002 agreement ("About the creation of equal conditions in the field of price policy"[33]) made available to Belarus similar gas prices as those available to nearby areas of Russia (an average of $22–$25/tcm in 2002) for the expected period of five years, plenty of space for negotiation and disagreement remained, as the agreement applied only to the limited quantities established in the yearly agreements between Gazprom and Belarus, which were a constant source of disagreement. The story repeated itself yearly: the amounts set in the yearly agreement usually ran out by November, and discussions on how much additional gas would be provided, and at what prices, started shortly afterwards.

Such politization was also made clear through the Belarusian reaction to the November 2002 reduction in supplies, the first open signal of trouble in Belarusian-Russian energy relations (Gazprom, claiming unpaid debts and delays in the privatization of Beltransgas, reduced gas supplies to Belarus by 50 percent and demanded an increased price of $150/tcm instead of the domestic Russian price of ca. $22–$25/tcm). Belarus' immediate response was decisively angry, with the Foreign Ministry calling the reduction in supplies "a premeditated attempt to exert economic pressure"[34] and President Lukashenka seeking to politicize the issue by tying it to broader issues in the relationship, presenting a bill for services rendered by Belarus in the context of the Belarusian-Russian Union. Yet the crisis was surmounted in less than two weeks, as Belarus agreed to pay an outstanding debt of $250 million, the Russian Central Bank agreed to provide a $40 million export credit to Belarus to compensate for higher gas prices,[35] and the Belarusian government promised to introduce legislation to eliminate a 1998 ban on privatizing Beltransgas.[36] This set into place a pattern that would become increasingly visible after 2004.

Beltransgas: Fighting for Control, Selling the Dream

The third element of Belarus' gas strategy during the 1994–2004 period centred around selling the promise of joint Russian-Belarusian control over the country's gas transit system, Beltransgas, while actually seeking to retain control over it.

Beltransgas, with its 7,377 kilometer network of low- and high-volume pipelines and two underground gas storage facilities,[37] was crucial to Gazprom's export value-added chain and had been on its wish list since the early 1990s. Repeated attempts to gain control over Beltransgas in the 1990s failed to come to fruition due to disagreements on how the company would be valued, with Gazprom estimates regularly being much lower than those offered by the Belarusian side.

A new burst of activity preceded Belarus' September 2001 presidential elections; Gazprom's significant informal help in Lukashenka's campaign was predicated on the expectation that, after the elections, negotiations on the creation of a Beltransgas JV would go forward successfully. The April 2002 agreements on the sale of gas to Belarus at domestic Russian prices was predicated on the same expectation.

However, little real progress took place after the 2001 elections; although Gazprom fulfilled its part of the agreement, the Belarusian side did not.[38] Under pressure from the 50 percent reduction in gas supplies by Gazprom in November 2002 discussed previously, Belarus started to move on the process of privatizing Beltransgas; a law lifting existing restrictions on its privatization was passed shortly thereafter.[39] But this also failed as, when the process reached a critical stage in 2003, Lukashenka made new demands, in particular a $5 billion valuation of the company, contrasting sharply with the Russian valuation at $1 billion.[40] Later that summer, as it became clear that Gazprom would not be able to buy Beltransgas, Russia raised the question of canceling domestic Russian gas prices for Belarus. On 1 January 2004 Belarus started to pay $46.68 per tcm of gas, more than twice than before.

Although the future of Beltransgas would not become clear until after 2006, this brief overview of negotiations in the 1994–2004 period provides a good sense of the main tactics favoured by the Belarusian government: delaying the moment of truth – much in the same way as it had been delayed in the process of Belarusian-Russian virtual integration in general – seeking, from the very beginning, to tie negotiations on the future of Beltransgas with discussions on the future of Gazprom's gas supplies to Belarus.

OIL: EXTERNAL MANAGEMENT DURING THE HIGH YEARS, 1994–2004

If a very public politization seemed to be the hallmark of Belarus' management of the gas relationship with Russia, in oil matters there seemed to be much less public positioning. This may have been related to differences in the structure of ownership on the Russian side: with the oil sector still largely under private control for most of this period, there was no single Russian counterpart on which blame could be easily adjudicated for political purposes, such as Gazprom in the case of gas.

Belarus' strategy focused on the attempt to maximize its transit role, and to maximize rents from the oil refining and reexporting business. In these two areas, Belarus was able to reap important benefits from its relationship with Russia, but these were also areas of frequent conflict.

Concerning the strategically crucial transit area, in the mid-2000s about half of Russian oil exports (not including exports to the CIS and Baltics) went through Belarus, most of that through the Druzhba pipeline.[41] While the actual volumes hovered between 52 and 84 million tons between 1994 and 2004, Belarus' role in this transit declined sharply – if they represented about 62 percent of Russian exports in 1994, their role had declined to less than 40 percent in 2004.[42]

Belarus' main source of energy rents turned out not to be transit per se, but the refining and reexporting of Russian oil under especially favourable trade terms. Cooperation in this area was an obvious proposition given the dependencies and synergies created by the single energy infrastructure inherited from the Soviet period. Belarus had some of the largest and most modern oil refining facilities in the USSR. With a refining capacity many times larger than the quantity of oil the country produces, Belarusian refineries could work profitably only as part of a larger, (Soviet) Union-wide system guaranteeing regular crude oil supplies and access to international markets. At the same time, Belarusian refineries provided Russian oil companies important logistical advantages, as it was often more economical to supply the nearby Russian oblasts with oil refined in Belarus than in Siberia or the Volga region, where many Russian refineries are located. A result of these synergies has been the keen interest, already since 1992, of Russian oil companies – and especially LUKoil and Slavneft – in acquiring full or partial ownership in Belarus' two refining complexes, Mozyr and Novopolotsk.

As in the case of Ukraine, Belarusian refineries had gone into a deep crisis in the mid-1990s due to a lack of stable oil supplies. Yet by the late 1990s the crisis had not only been surmounted, but the sector had been so revitalized as to become one of Belarus' most important sources of foreign revenue. This was due, first of all, to the abolition of customs barriers, which made it possible for Russian companies to enter into advantageous schemes involving oil refining in Belarus for the purposes of avoiding taxes and export duties levied by Russia, making Belarus an important part of these companies' value-added chains. The Belarusian government further helped Russian oil companies maximize profits through special arrangements such as tolling operations (where oil is transferred to a refinery for processing, but without changing ownership), which made the importation, refining and reexportation of crude oil especially profitable to Russian suppliers. Such arrangements also allowed Russian oil companies to overcome some of the export limitations related to pipeline capacity set by Russia's Transneft.[43] By refining in Belarus, Russian companies not only overcame these restrictions, but were able to increase profits by increasing exports of oil products – considerably more profitable than crude oil – to WE markets.

Second, the political unification process provided certain guarantees, both to Belarus (that the Russian oil companies would keep their supply commitments) and to Russian oil companies (that it was safe to invest in Belarusian refineries). Last but not least, in the mid-1990s the Belarusian government launched an aggressive refinery modernization program, aimed at increasing the production of highly refined oil products and gasolines that could fulfill EU standards and thus fetch higher prices in WE markets, a policy all the more remarkable when looked at in the context of trends in the rest of the Belarusian economy, where factories remained outdated and extremely inefficient.

Central to Lukashenka's management of oil issues was his desire to attract Russian capital for modernization, while at the same time preventing Russian companies from taking control of these refineries. This tension was reflected in the struggles for the control of Belarus' two refineries, Mozyr and Naftan, which we discuss briefly below and retake in the next section of the chapter in our discussion of the post-2004 period.

MOZYR REFINERY

Mozyr's strategic location (at 200 kilometers from the Polish border, the CIS's westernmost refinery) and being one of its most modern refineries made it especially attractive to Russian companies. Established in 1975, Mozyr was privatized in 1994, with 42.7 percent of its shares belonging to the Belarusian state, 42.6 percent to Slavneft (until 2002 a Belarusian-Russian JV), 12.2 percent to a company owned by the company's workers and former workers (MNPZ Plus), and 2.4 percent to other investors. Despite the common interests discussed previously, relations between the Belarusian government and the Mozyr management in the second half of the 1990s were far from smooth due to, among other reasons, the Belarusian leadership's desire to keep the refinery under tight governmental control despite its lack of a controlling package of shares. The Belarusian government sought to do this through a variety of means, such as by attempting to gain control of minority shareholder MNPZ Plus and to exercise control through the imposition of a state controlling share (itself established in a legally questionable way).[44]

NAFTAN (NOVOPOLOTSK)

In contrast with Mozyr, 99.8 percent of Naftan's shares remained in state hands even after the company's corporatization in 2002. Naftan (also known as the Novopolotsk refinery after its home city), was also highly coveted by Russian investors, and in the mid-1990s, LUKoil and Yukos had made several proposals for the creation of a joint venture. Although an agreement was reached in 1995, the deal did not go through, as neither Yukos nor LUKoil were granted special conditions as originally agreed.[45]

In 1999, Naftan embarked on an ambitious modernization program allowing it to increase exports of higher-priced light oil products, in turn rekindling the interest of Russian companies. In a pattern similar to that followed by Gazprom, LUKoil and Slavneft supported Lukashenka's 2001 reelection campaign in exchange for promises that Naftan would be privatized. The promise, however, was not kept by the Belarusian president, leading to a cooling of relations.[46]

In both the Mozyr and Naftan cases, a pattern repeated itself in Belarusian responses to Russian privatization proposals: going ahead with the project in its planning stages when maximum concessions from the Russian side could be accrued (for example, support for Lukashenka's 2001 presidential bid), only to later create a number of obstacles to the actual implementation of the agreement. Yet, despite the fact that the privatizations sought by LUKoil and other Russian companies did not go through, refining in Belarus continued to be highly profitable for Russian companies due to the preferential tax and duty regime provided by the Belarusian and Russian sides.

Domestic Management

The rent-maximization strategy observed in Belarus' external management of its energy situation was also pursued domestically, with a shift to less expensive fuels – even if this increased the country's dependency on foreign sources – and average domestic prices usually covering the full cost of imports.

Gas: Domestic Management during the High Years[47]

GAS AND MORE GAS

Increasing the role of gas in the country's energy supply mix was an important element of Belarus' energy management during this period, a conscious policy aimed at keeping domestic costs of production under check through increasing the role of low-price Russian gas.[48] Thus, from 1990 to 2007 the role of gas in the country's TPES grew from 43 percent to 65 percent, a very significant increase in international comparison.[49] In particular, the role of gas in electricity generation grew from about 48 percent in 1992 to about 95 percent in 2005, as many electricity generation stations were refitted to work on gas when gas prices for Belarus became especially competitive starting in the late 1990s.[50]

A second particularity of Belarus' domestic gas management during this period was the fact that, in overall terms, payments by end-consumers covered – and often provided a significant premium over – the gas prices Belarus was charged by Gazprom (see Table 5.2).[51] While this is a common practice internationally, it was unusual in a post-Soviet context where countries such as Ukraine routinely charged consumers and industries prices lower than those charged by Russia and other gas suppliers, creating chronic losses.

At the same time, the burden of cost-covering gas prices was not distributed equally across all users. As seen in Table 5.2, while the agricultural sector and residential consumers enjoyed low prices, much of the cost was borne by the bulk of industrial enterprises, which were charged higher prices than residential users. (In addition, a few industrial enterprises were charged preferential gas prices of about 50 percent–80 percent of the official price, but neither the list of these companies nor the official criteria for inclusion have been made public.[52]) Such policies bring to the fore the role of populism in Lukashenka's way of conducting and marketing energy policies. [53]

Table 5.2 Belarus: Gas Import Prices and Prices Paid by Final Users, in US$/tcm, 2000–2011

	2000	2001	2002	2003	2004	2005	2006	2007	2008	2009	2010	2011
Gas imports from Russia, in bcm	17.1	17.3	17.6	18.1	19.6	20.1	20.8	20.6	21.1	17.6	21.7	20
Import price paid by Beltransgas*	30	30	17-22	30	46.7	55	55	118	127	151	170	265
Price paid by industrial users	40-55	40-55	40-55	60-65	70	72.3**	75.6**	141.7***	171.3***	205.5***	261.3***	275.9
Price paid by residential consumers	N/A	N/A	N/A	N/A	N/A	82.7	84.4	101.7	214.9	174	159	143.8

* Average price of imported gas including both the basic amounts purchased from Gazprom at fixed prices, plus additional supplies purchased from Gazprom or other suppliers at higher prices.

** Data from IPM, "Rost tsen na gas," 12.

*** Data from Simon Pirani, Jonathan Stern, and Katja Yafimava, "The April 2010 Russo-Ukrainian Gas Agreement," 7 (Table 1).

Other sources: Yafimava, *Post-Soviet Russian-Belarussian Relationships*, 58; Dashkevich, *Energeticheskaia Zavisimost' Belarusi* 20 (Table 3), and IPM, *Monitorng Infrastrukturi Belarusi 2010* (Minsk: IPM, 2010) 39, other press sources.

Oil: Domestic Management during the High Years

Domestic oil management concentrated in three areas: seeking state control of refineries (discussed previously), maintaining profit margins from the domestic sale of oil and oil products, and extracting concessions from refineries and Russian oil companies, concessions that would allow the government to subsidize some domestic users, especially the agricultural sector.

Concerning prices charged to domestic users, the same type of dynamics observable in the gas sector also seemed to be at play in the oil sector, where the price of oil products in (such as gasoline) was higher than in neighbouring states, despite the fact that Belarus paid lower import prices.[54] (Oil products supplied to the agricultural sector, however, were subsidized.)

A third aspect of domestic oil dependency management concerned the attempt to extract significant benefits from Russian oil companies, in particular the obligation to sell 50 percent of their oil to Belarusian companies, guaranteeing them high profits.[55] Russian oil companies were also forced to subsidize the agricultural sector.[56]

Belarus and Energy Rents during the High Years, 1994–2004

Both micro-level and macro-level energy rents were accrued by Belarus during its high years of energy relations with Russia, 1994–2004.

MACRO-LEVEL RENTS
The main ways in which enery rents accrued to Belarus during this period were through the indirect subsidization of its economy through lower-than-international gas and oil prices and barter arrangements, through the extra income generated by transit fees, direct and indirect reexport of energy, taxes paid by energy companies, and through semi-legal and illegal energy transactions.

Lower Than International Gas and Oil Prices

As seen in Tables 5.2 and 5.4, the first and most obvious way in which Belarus benefited financially from the energy relationship with Russia during the 1994–2004 period was through gas and oil prices much lower than those charged WE importers or – since the early 2000s – other former Soviet states (see Table 1.1 in chapter 1). According to IMF estimates, the subsidy effect of selling Belarus gas and oil at preferential

Table 5.3 Hidden Russian Subsidization of the Belarusian Economy, 2004–2006, in billion US$, 2004–2006

	Gas price differentials	Oil price differentials and preferential taxation	Total
2004	1.80	1.52	3.32
2005	2.89	2.83	5.72
2006	4.28	3.56	7.84

Note: "price differentials" defined as reference price for Western European markets minus Belarus price times volume.
Source: Tables 3.1 and 3.2 in Rakova "Energeticheskii sektor," 10–11.

prices amounted, by 2004, to 10 percent of the country's GDP, with 6–7 percent being the result of subsidized gas prices and 3 percent of oil prices.[57] Adding into the equation preferential tax treatment in the oil area, Rakova calculated hidden subsidies in the amount of about $3.3 billion to $7.84 billion per year in 2004–2006 (see Table 5.3).

While for most of the 1999–2004 period Belarus purchased gas from Russia at commercial prices, these were de facto very advantageous for Belarus as barter arrangements and the existence of multiple exchange rates significantly reduced the effective price.[58] Prices were further reduced by the 2002 agreement establishing that Russia would sell gas to Belarus at the same (domestic) price as to industrial consumers in Russia's fifth region, Smolensk. Thus, the basic price of gas charged by Gazprom was reduced to about $22 per tcm – one of very few examples of gas price reductions in the post-Soviet era. This arrangement remained in place until 2004.

Although not as heavily subsidized as gas, thanks to corporate arrangements and special tax and customs arrangements oil prices charged to Belarus during this period were about 40 percent lower than world market ones; the per-ton difference between the prices charged to Belarus and non-CIS (mainly WE) markets grew significantly in the mid-2000s (see Table 5.4).

Barter

Preferential energy prices to Belarus had to do not only with low prices in and of themselves, but with the widespread use of barter, in the mid-to-late 1990s accounting for 74 percent of Belarus' energy imports from Russia (before starting to decline rapidly around 2002).[59] Barter

Table 5.4 Belarus: Foreign Trade of Oil and Oil Products, 2001–2010, in Million Tons (Mt) and billion US$

	2001		2003		2004		2005		2006		2007	
	Mt	$	Mt	$	Mt	$	Mt	$	Mt	$	Mt	$
Export of oil products	7.66	1.21	10.56	1.96	12.96	3.3	13.46	4.84	14.8	6.7	15.1	7.6
Export of oil	–	–	0.8	0.144	1.55	0.31	1.75	0.6	1.72	0.73	1.25	0.68
Total export of oil and its products	7.66	1.21	11.36	2.104	14.51	3.61	15.21	5.44	16.52	7.43	16.35	8.28
Imports of oil from Russia	11.91	1.38	14.89	1.988	17.81	3.232	19.24	4.193	20.9	5.66	20.02	7.4
Imports of oil products from Russia	0.167	0.02	1	0.148	1.18	0.16	0.973	0.153	1.233	0.485	0.9	0.49
Total import of oil and its products	12.077	1.4	15.89	2.136	18.99	3.392	20.213	4.346	22.133	6.145	20.92	7.89
Import price of oil to Belarus from Russia US$/ton	115.8		133.1		181.5		218		270		366	
Price of Russian oil exports to non-CIS, US$/ton	156.4		181.2		233		350		470		485	
Income from oil and oil products' exports after paying for imports of oil and oil products	–0.19		–0.032		0.218		1.094		1.285		0.39	

Table 5.4 (Continued)

	2008		2009		2010	
	Mt	$	Mt	$	Mt	$
Export of oil products	15.52	10.73	15.83	7.1	11.3	6.75
Export of oil	1.46	0.99	1.72	0.788	0	0
Total export of oil and its products	16.98	11.73	17.548	7.89	11.3	6.75
Imports of oil from Russia	21.5	9.49	21.5	7.065	14.7	6.76
Imports of oil products from Russia	2.5	1.47	3.78	1.276	1.58	0.9
Total import of oil and its products	24	11.96	25.98	8.341	16.28	7.66
Import price of oil to Belarus from Russia US$/ton		441		329		460
Price of Russian oil exports to non-CIS, US$/ton		626		420		801 (est)
Income from oil and oil products' exports after paying for imports of oil and oil products		−0.23		−0.45		−0.91

Sources: Calculated on the basis of Ministry of Statistics and Analysis of the Republic of Belarus, *Foreign Trade of the Republic of Belarus. Statistical abstracts.* (Minsk, yearly), *Rossiia v tsifrakh 2008. Ofitsialnoe izdanie Federalnoi sluzhby gosudasrtvennoi statistiki* (Moscow, 2008) and (for data on the first half of 2008) the statistical compendium *Sotsialno-ekonomicheskoe polozhenie Rossii* Nos. 1–7 (2008). Special thanks to Leonid Zlotnikov for his help in the preparation of this table.

arrangements during this period included a chronic overvaluation of Belarusian products, automatically reducing the real price of the purchases.[60] The existence of multiple exchange rates for much of this period often amplified the subsidy- effects often associated with barter, and opened new possibilities for price manipulation, arbitrage gains, and rent-seeking.

Income from Transit Fees

Although during this period there were set dollar prices for Belarus' transit services, these services were de facto provided in exchange for lower prices charged for Russian gas and oil. Oil transit fees remained low, at about 30 percent–50 percent of the fees charged by neighbouring states such as Poland and Ukraine. As a result, the income accrued by Belarus from strictly oil transit activities was not significant. Yet low transit fees played an important indirect role: they made it especially attractive for Russian oil companies to use transit through Belarus (as opposed to Ukraine) for their oil exports west, and, thus, to supply oil to Belarusian refineries. Thus, low transit fees were a crucial factor in assuring access to high profits through oil refining and reexport.[61]

Oil Refining and Reexports

Of all the sources of income related to Russian energy, none proved more profitable to Belarus than the export of refined oil products (in addition to gasoline, mainly heavy oil products such as diesel fuel, heavy heating oil, and lubricants) to Western markets. Here, the essential mechanism of rent creation had to do with the importation of crude oil from Russia at low prices and free of any Russian export duties, its refining, and subsequent reexport at world prices, a process through which Belarus would not only accrue profits from the added-value process and the price differentials, but would receive the related export duties as well. Between 1994 and 2004, the combination of lower-than-market and only slowly rising prices for oil paid by Belarus, and much faster-growing prices for oil products in WE markets generated substantial profits for Belarus. Accordingly, the weight of oil products' exports in Belarus' overall exports grew massively in the 2000s – from 8 percent in 2000 to 38.8 percent in 2006.[62] In the mid-2000s, export duties on oil products provided about 10 percent of the total income of the Belarusian budget.[63]

A central element of the oil refining and reexports story concerns the fact that the practice that was actually followed concerning the division of oil export duties between Russia and Belarus seemed to be in clear violation of agreements signed between both countries. Point 3, section B of the 1995 Agreement on a Customs Union prescribed that both states would apply the same customs duties towards third countries;[64] proceeds from export duties would be divided on a 85–15 basis, with the largest share going to Russia.[65] Yet, until January 2007, the totality of those export duties remained in Belarus. A related and equally contested issue concerned the level of export duties applied by Belarus and Russia. Both the 1995 Agreement on a Customs Union and a 2001 agreement on the unification of customs regulations within the Union of Russia and Belarus made clear Belarus was to apply export tariffs on oil products similar to those in place in Russia. However, Belarus failed to implement the agreement. (In 2005, for example, while Russia's oil export duty for light oil products was $133.5 per ton, Belarus' was only $68.2.[66])

How can Russia's allowing Belarus' noncompliance with signed agreements be explained? Perhaps one reason for Russia's lack of zeal in applying the agreements had to do with the fact that in the mid-1990s world oil prices remained low, meaning low total export duties as well, reducing Russia's incentives to fully apply the agreements. Yet undoubtedly part of the story also had to do with, as discussed previously, Lukashenka's ability to apply political pressure on Russia.

When oil prices (and also revenues from Belarusian oil products exports) start to increase rapidly around 2004, Russia acquired a much stronger impetus to claim its half of the export duties. Changes in the structure of the Russian oil sector also help us understand changes in Russian attitudes after 2006. Until 2005, the lopsided application of the agreements benefitted Russian oil companies very concretely, as they were able to gain additional profits at the expense of reduced revenue for the Russian budget. With increased central control over the oil business in the wake of virtual destruction of Yukos, it could be expected that those central structures also wanted to acquire greater control over oil export duties as well.

In the gas area as well, nonnormative behaviour by the Belarusian side was overlooked by Russia. As noted by Belarus' most respected energy journalist, Tatiana Manenok (Tatsiana Manenak), already since the late 1990s Belarus was engaging in the unsanctioned taking of gas from the pipeline, in the amount of 5–6 percent of the volumes contracted from Gazprom, but until a real crisis with Gazprom took place in late 2002, Gazprom ignored the issue, not bringing it up in its discussions with Belarus.[67] After that, Gazprom started to take the issue more seriously, and by 2004, had diametrically changed its assessment of the Belarusian transit routes from realiable to unreliable.

Tax Income from Energy Companies

Tax income from oil and gas companies provided an additional source of macro-level rents. In the mid 2000s, oil and gas companies were the largest contributors to the budget, with the Mozyr and Naftan refineries and Beltransgas occupying the first three places and accounting for about 8–14 percent of Belarus' total tax revenue between 2004 and 2007.

MICRO-LEVEL RENTS AND CORRUPTION

To what extent has corruption been part of the Belarusian energy rent-seeking experience? While we currently have only very limited evidence on energy corruption in Belarus, there is indirect evidence of illegal or semi-legal activities. Two mechanisms were the illegal re-export of Russian oil and diesel initially supplied to Belarus at lower-than-world prices, which created losses for Russian oil exporters (which lost part of their expected exports to more profitable markets)[68] and the purchase of oil from Russian companies for refining in Belarus at somewhat higher than usual-for-Belarus prices, also in exchange for kickbacks.

What was Lukashenka's personal role in these operations? Belarusian analysts disagree on this issue. Some see him as making a significant personal profit from corrupt deals organized by the Presidential Administration.[69] Other commentators, such as Feduta, give less importance to the question of personal profit, and emphasize Lukashenka's weak understanding of the dividing line between Presidential Administration funds and his own, and his using all moneys in the Administration as if they were his own, not necessarily or not only for his own enrichment, but for pursuing chosen policies.[70]

Concerning one important rent-seeking area, rents accessed through the importation of oil from Russia to be refined in Belarus and subsequently exported, some interesting patterns could be observed. There are good reasons to believe, for example, that some significant oil-import quotas were given to specific businessmen in exchange for providing financial support to some projects especially favoured by the president.[71]

Russian Actors and Belarusian Rent-seeking

Up to which point were Russian actors involved in these deals? First, from the few oil-related corruption cases that became public, we know that they often involved kickbacks from foreign partners. While private Russian actors benefitted, the Russian budget suffered important losses from the two mechanisms discussed above. Second, we should not exclude the possibility of Russian involvement in more indirect forms of corruption, such as those related to Russian energy companies' (such as LUKoil, Slavneft and Gazprom) direct or indirect contributions to Lukashenka's electoral campaigns, most clearly seen in the run up to the September 2001 presidential elections. Although none of these companies was able to cash in on Lukashenka's promises, at least one side of the exchange of favours took place – it has been reported that, in the election year, Slavneft made more than $5 million worth of donations, including in-kind contributions to collective farms, and additional donations to state-supported social projects, thus providing free political advertisements for Lukashenka.[72]

ENERGY RENTS AND THE SURVIVAL OF THE LUKASHENKA REGIME

The rents accrued in exchange for Belarus' unique political relationship with Russia were crucial for the survival of the Lukashenka regime. First, they helped keep the unreformed Belarusian economy alive by keeping afloat the less productive areas of the economy. Second, these rents guaranteed GDP growth and rising living standards; high hard-currency revenues from the export of oil products to Western markets also allowed the Belarusian government to maintain a high (some would say artificially high) value of the Belarusian ruble vis-à-vis the dollar, crucial for the government's social policy as it made imported consumer goods increasingly accessible to the Belarusian population. Third, these accrued rents had the potential to bring additional resources into the nontransparent budget of the Presidential Administration. Fourth, the recycling of energy rents, both in the form of preferential energy tariffs and of outright payments, made possible the more targeted support of core groups within the Lukashenka electorate,[73] first and foremost the countryside and police and security forces. As stated by Zaiko and Romanchuk, "Russian petrodollars allowed all of us to live beyond our means . . . from the director to the doorman."[74]

On the other hand, the economic benefits accruing from the relationship with Russia allowed Belarus to keep in place an outdated and ultimately unsustainable economic model. While barter arrangements brought quick profits and allowed Belarus to sell much of its industrial production, there was an important downside, as it stimulated the production of outdated, uncompetitive goods for which there was limited demand outside that created by barter with Russia,[75] and that could hardly support Belarus' entrance into more competitive markets.

Despite these warning signals, due to good fortune or good design, during this period the Belarusian government was able to manage its energy situation in a way that seemed to satisfy most actors involved: Belarusian energy users were receiving relatively inexpensive energy. Russian oil suppliers were avoiding (Russian) taxes and increasing profits. The Belarusian budget was reaping record revenue, and Gazprom was on the way to making the Belarusian economy fully dependent on Russian gas.

The Low Years, 2004–2010

The Gas Stoppage of February 2004 as Watershed?

On 18 February 2004, Gazprom, citing broken agreements on the privatization of Beltransgas and the stealing of its gas from the transit pipeline, suspended gas shipments to Belarus. Although the cutoff lasted less than twenty-four hours and supplies were resumed after Beltransgas signed a ten-day supply agreement with independent gas suppliers,[76] the event was unprecedented: not even during the worst accusations of gas stealing against Ukraine had Gazprom fully stopped gas supplies, affecting not only domestic consumers but also third countries.[77] This event marks a dividing line in Russian-Belarusian energy relations. After this incident the tone of their interactions changes: regular threats of increasing gas prices to world levels start to be heard ever more frequently, as well as dire predictions by Belarusian, Russian, and Western observers that Belarus would not be able to withstand these increases and that, as a result, the regime would collapse or, subject to energy blackmail, would be forced to join a Russian-led Union on Russian terms (or even the Russian Federation itself), with a significant loss of sovereignty.

Much of the changed energy dynamics and rhetoric we start to see around 2004 was a delayed reflection of the new tone in Belarusian-Russian relations following Putin's election as president in 2000. It is around this time that Russia begins to harden its position concerning a possible Belarusian-Russian Union, making it clear that, in order for crucial agreements such as that on monetary union to move forward, Belarus would have to give up a significant degree of sovereignty.

Broader changes were also taking place in the economic relationship between both countries. In contrast to the late 1990s and early 2000s, Russia was slowly losing its position as main market for Belarusian exports.[78] This had to do both with the rapid increase in oil products exported to the EU and with declining Russian demand for traditional Belarusian exports such as tractors and TVs, laying bare Belarus' rapidly declining competitiveness in the non-oil refining sectors. Indeed, Belarus' oil refining and exports strategy, while creating massive profits, also brought with it serious sectoral disbalances, of which small signs were already visible as early as 2004. With 25.4 percent of its export earnings coming from oil products in 2004 (growing to 38.8 percent in 2006, see Table 5.5), energy-poor Belarus was slowly catching its own Dutch disease, as domestic manufacturing was becoming more expensive due to the strengthening of the local currency vis-á-vis the dollar.[79] Hostage to an economic strategy based on oil refining and reexporting, the Belarusian government had only limited incentives to deal with this situation.[80] In terms of an energy dependency management strategy, the role of refining centre was hard to give up, not only because of the high profits it provided, but also because of its role in guaranteeing stable supplies of low-priced Russian oil.[81]

Belarus' Overall Management of its Energy Dependency, 2004–2010

THE LAST ALLY REVISITED

These changed political and economic conditions forced Lukashenka to revisit some aspects of his strategy. While he continued to play the nostalgia-for-the-Soviet-empire card, by 2004 neither President Putin nor the Russian public were as receptive – at least openly – to such discourses as they had been before 2004. Putin, a relative newcomer to the political stage, shared none of the "Belavezh complex" (perceived guilt for the demise of the USSR) of his predecessor Yeltsyn.[82] With the Russian economy flush with new energy export revenues, presenting Belarus to the Russian public as an oasis of stability and prosperity was becoming increasingly difficult, especially given Lukashenka's sharply reduced access to the Russian media after Putin's accession to the presidency. Despite these limitations, Lukashenka continued to use politization as a strategy after 2004, but now with an increased emphasis on the military and strategic value of Belarus as Russia's last ally.

In this, Lukashenka had luck on his side: virtually every time the relationship with Russia threatened to go sour, a new international crisis would reaffirm Belarus' continued value as an ally. Thus, for example, as Russian-US relations started to worsen around March 2003 in the run up to the invasion of Iraq, Lukashenka was able to pressure Moscow to reassess his value and to support his bid to lift term limits in the 2004 referendum.[83] Similarly, several other events in 2003–2004 helped boost Lukashenka's value as an ally: the coming to power of strongly anti-Russian Mikheil Saakashvili in the wake of Georgia's Rose Revolution, the expansion of NATO to Russia's borders with the accession of Estonia, Latvia, and Lithuania to the alliance in 2004, and the Orange Revolution in Ukraine. Similarly, Poland's 2008 announcement of its intention to set up a NATO radar station in its territory contributed to renewed Russian fears of Western encroachment in Russia's immediate neighbourhood, which was used by Lukashenka as an important bargaining chip in the relationship.

Indeed, a certain regularity could be observed: every time relations between Russia and the West worsened, the relative value of Belarus as an ally increased, and relations between Minsk and Moscow improved, at least in the short term. This was especially evident in the strategic and military areas, where Belarus' military modernization and increased cooperation with Russia dovetailed well with Putin's increasingly anti-Western rhetoric. At the same time, during the few periods when relations with the West showed a positive tendency, Lukashenka also used this as a bargaining chip in the relationship with Russia.

GAS: EXTERNAL MANAGEMENT, 2004–2010

During this period, Belarus sought – with varied success – to continue its previous strategy around Yamal, Beltransgas, and price negotiations.

Yamal and Belarus as a Gatekeeper: Negotiations on Yamal as a Means to Exert Pressure on Prices and on Beltransgas Negotiations

If during the 1994–2004 period its role in the building of the Yamal pipeline had allowed Belarus to present itself as an indispensable transit gatekeeper, now that the project was near completion, Lukashenka used his power to block its final stages (four compressor stations, as well as a long-term lease guaranteeing Gazprom's rights to the land under the pipeline) from being completed, as a means to pressure Russia to move negotiations on Beltransgas and on gas prices in a manner agreeable to the Belarusian side.[84] Indeed, it is hard to avoid the impression that Lukashenka deliberately created these hurdles as a way to retain leverage over Gazprom on the price issue. Eager to complete construction of Yamal's Belarus segment, Gazprom was willing, for the time being, to maintain low prices for Belarus. In April 2005, Gazprom and Beltransgas agreed informally that gas prices for Belarus ($46.68/tcm) would remain unchanged throughout 2006 if work on Yamal proceeded as planned.

Although using Yamal as a means of pressure was successful in the short term, Lukashenka's belief that having control over the pipeline would give him some real, long-term leverage over Russia was clearly overstated. Lukashenka's unpredictability started to become more and more of a liability to a Russia that was becoming less romantic in the relationship with Belarus. Thus, it was only natural that, once the first line of Yamal was completed in 2006, Gazprom's attitude would change. Despite the fact that the original 1999 agreement envisioned the building of two parallel Yamal lines by 2008, this started to seem more and more unlikely. Russia officially backed away from the second Yamal line project in November 2007, a problem for Belarus as transit income from a second line could potentially have covered, at prices current then, a third of Belarus' gas import costs.[85]

This came in the wake of another defeat for Lukashenka: Gazprom's September 2005 agreement with Germany on the building of the Nord Stream gas pipeline from Russia to Germany by-passing Poland, Ukraine, and Belarus. Clearly, Gazprom's decision to build Nord Stream and transit future gas volumes through it as opposed to a second Yamal line had to do with the desire to have alternatives to its current transit partners, especially Belarus, no longer seen as reliable as in 1999. Gazprom's frustration about the slow pace of negotiations on the creation of a gas transit JV on the basis of Beltransgas undoubtedly also played a role in the decision.

*Beltransgas and Russian Energy Investments: Delaying
the Moment of Effective Russian Control*

Belarus sought to use negotiations on the future of Beltransgas as a means of managing the overall gas relationship with Russia, continuing to use the same central tactic used from 1994 to 2004: promising to create a JV with Gazprom, but delaying the actual sale of shares. As in the pre-2004 period, the question of how Beltransgas would be valued continued to be a crucial hurdle. It was only in July of 2004 that both sides agreed on naming an independent auditor to assess the value of the company, but little happened until 2006.

What changed, however, was the attitude on the Russian side. Growing frustration with Lukashenka meant that, not only did Gazprom feel justified to seek additional transit routes bypassing Belarus, but that, to the extent that interest in transit through Belarus continued, the desirable forms of cooperation changed – from one based on informal agreements to one based on the desirability of contractually grounded control of Beltransgas.

Throughout 2005, Lukashenka faced strong pressure from the Kremlin, with Moscow making the continuation of preferential gas prices conditional on gaining control over at least 50 percent of Beltransgas.

Belarus found itself under new pressure in 2006, when Gazprom renewed the threat of sharply increased prices should Belarus continue to delay the establishment of a JV.[86] Lukashenka's increasing isolation from Western institutions was leaving him one-on-one with Russia, making it hard to avoid Gazprom's pressure and giving Russia increased power in the relationship. In December 2006 an agreement of principle was reached (signed only in May 2007) covering both gas price increases and ownership of Beltransgas. On the basis of this agreement, from 2007 to 2010 Gazprom would acquire 12.5 percent of Beltransgas' shares each year, up to 2010, when it would reach ownership of 50 percent of shares in the company, for a total price of $2.5 billion.

Although the 2007 agreement could be seen as a defeat for Lukashenka, and it included certain provisions protecting Gazprom's property rights,[87] it also contained elements favourable to Belarus, as it was tied to a gradual timeline for gas price increases, and 50 percent of the purchase price would be paid in cash, as opposed to gas supplies.[88] However, it soon became clear that the Belarusian side had no intention of relinquishing real control of the company, or allowing Gazprom to reap significant profits from it. Beltransgas was included in the list of profitable companies required to make contributions to the Energy Ministry's Innovation Fund, to which it was made to contribute $70 million in 2007 (at 19 percent of the yearly value of its products and services, a significant burden on the company).[89] In addition, the mark-ups (*nadtsenki*) usually added to the price paid by end-consumers were significantly reduced, thus reducing Beltransgas' profitability, which fell to an estimated 1 percent in 2007.[90] Instead, potential profits were either skimmed directly from the top and transferred to separate non-tax budget funds (the Energy Ministry's Innovation Fund), or shared with end-consumers in the form of lower prices. This last point is especially significant, as until then Beltransgas had mainly passed on price increases to end-consumers. As shown in Table 5.2, 2007, a year where residential gas prices were lower than import prices paid by Belarus, was an exception to the trend set in the previous years.

Politization of the Relationship and Price Negotiations

Lukashenka's politization of the energy relationship with Russia only increased after 2004. His basic strategy here was to make sure that any gas price increases would create high costs for the Russian leadership – both high political costs vis-á-vis its own domestic electorate, and high reputational costs vis-á-vis WE partners.

An example of this manipulation was Lukashenka's response to the February 2004 gas cutoff, which he called "terrorist." Stating that Belarusian-Russian relations "will be poisoned by gas for a long time to come,"[91] he also threatened to cut-off military cooperation. This strong reaction helped Lukashenka lobby concessions from the Russian leadership, in particular the provision of a $150 million credit (plus an additional $25 million to support trade) on favourable terms, extended as compensation for the gas price increases.

Yet no less important than these economic concessions was the political and public relations victory Lukashenka was able to score in the aftermath of the February 2004 cutoff. Although by now no longer able to reach the Russian electorate directly, Lukashenka was able to appeal to the population's old Soviet pride, allegedly affronted by Putin, through his passionate declarations that Belarus was being forced to raise the money to pay for Russian gas "from the Chernobyl victims, from those who were rotting in the trenches," defending the Soviet Union in the Second World War.[92] Vis-á-vis the EU, Lukashenka was able to present the cutoff as a Russian threat to European energy security. Vis-á-vis the Belarusian electorate – even including the opposition – he was able to present himself as a defender of Belarusian national interests in the face of Russia's encroachment and insult.

The outcome of this first gas war of 2004 exemplifies Lukashenka's ability to turn his country's very weakness vis-á-vis Russia into a comparative advantage. Following the gas cutoff, as noted previously, a pattern was established where Russia would increase prices but, at the same time, offer Belarus a number of other advantages. Thus the pattern seen in the 1994–2004 period continued; after the Rose Revolution in Georgia, Belarus found it easy to present itself as Russia's last ally in the post-Soviet area.

Similar concessions took place after subsequent gas price increases: after Belarus' complaints that changes in Value Added Tax (VAT) legislation that entered into effect in January 2005 would affect it negatively, in June 2005 Russia agreed to provide Belarus an additional $146 million credit as compensation.[93] For 2006, Belarus was offered gas prices of $46.80/tcm in exchange for expected political loyalty and moving towards shared control over the country's gas pipeline system.

A similar politization took place following Russia's October 2006 announcement of its intention to significantly increase gas prices to Belarus, to up to $200 per tcm. Lukashenka once again reacted by taking the offensive: "Such a price increase, in that amount, that is, unequivocally, the break-off of all relations."[94] Yet this politization was not simply something that happened after the fact, as a reaction to Russian gas supply reductions, but a preemptive behaviour that actually helped shape the conflict itself and could thus be seen as a form of preventive management of the relationship. As noted by Yaroslav Romanchuk concerning the rapid escalation of the conflict in December 2006: "The Belarusian side is not planning to sign the contract before New Year, because, . . . [it] needs a big scandal, a very big scandal. A scandal just about negotiations, that is not a scandal. But a scandal with a suspension of gas supplies, that is the kind of scandal that the Belarusian side is seeking to direct, among others, against Russia, presenting it as an unreliable partner . . ." before new negotiations would start. "After that, an agreement will be signed in January." In this interpretation, the Belarusian side was in fact provoking a scandal in order to receive some concessions to soften the increase in gas prices.[95]

Crisis Management: Gas Shock Delayed after the January 2007 Gas and Oil War

The 2004 crisis could be seen as a dress rehearsal for the much more serious crisis that took place nearly three years later – the so-called gas and oil war of December 2006–January 2007.

THE DECEMBER 2006–JANUARY 2007 GAS CRISIS

In the gas area, the real shock came at the end of 2006, when, in the negotiation of prices for 2007, Gazprom started to propose prices as high as $200 per tcm, an almost fourfold increase. (This was accompanied by an even more dire confrontation in the oil trade area, discussed further on.) After tense negotiations ending a few minutes before midnight on 31 December 2006, prices for 2007 were increased more than 100 percent to $100 per tcm, with further increases planned.

GAS SHOCK DELAYED

Even after the shock of the January 2007 gas price increases, preferential treatment of Belarus continued. Despite the prediction of some analysts,[96] Belarus, at least in the short term, survived the increase in Russian gas prices started in 2007. The December 2006 agreement offered a gradual, set in advance, transition to European gas prices.[97] According to the December 2006 agreement, in 2008 gas prices paid by Belarus would be equivalent of 67 percent of European prices (i.e., prices to Poland, not counting additional transit costs), in 2009 80 percent, and in 2010 90 percent, before moving fully to European prices in 2011.[98] In reality, however, prices charged to Belarus throughout October 2008 remained well below the values that would come up from such a price formula, reaching $127.9 per tcm in the second quarter of 2008, when European (Polish) prices had reached $340 and thus a 67 percent share would amount to about $220.[99]

Second, the shock value of the increase in gas prices can itself be qualified, since the faster rise in European prices than those charged to Belarus meant gas subsidies actually increased in 2007.[100] Third, Belarus found ways to delay and soften the effects of these price increases – for the first half of 2007, for example, it succeeded in reaching an agreement by virtue of which, for the first half of 2007, it would only pay 55 percent of the new price of $100, with the rest put on credit.[101] Thus, the additional nearly $1.3 billion in gas importation costs represented by the January 2007 agreements was to be paid in the second half of 2007, aided by a new stabilization credit in the amount of $1.5 billion extended on favourable conditions by Russia in December 2007. In November 2008, Belarus and Russia reached an agreement for a new, $1 billion stabilization loan from Russia, also provided on favourable terms.[102]

GAS: DOMESTIC MANAGEMENT, 2004–2010

In terms of domestic management, pre-2004 policies continued after 2004 with the attempt to recover import costs by passing them in full to most end users. However, the cross-subsidization of key constituencies (mainly agricultural users, but also selected industrial users) continued, at the expense of higher prices charged to most industrial consumers. For most of the period between 2004 and 2007 (the last year for which full data is available) the one group that consistently paid the lowest prices for electricity – from 14 percent to 34 percent less than its production cost – was the agricultural sector.[103] In contrast, during that same period, industrial users consistently paid significantly higher prices – 52.27 percent to 87.5 percent higher – than production costs.[104]

Nascent Attempts at Diversification: Energy Source Diversification and the Decision for Nuclear Power

The post-2004 period saw the beginnings of an interest in diversification, although this interest played itself out differently in the gas and oil areas. Whereas in the case of oil (discussed separately further on) there was a renewed interest in geographic diversification, in the case of gas geographical diversification (or, for that matter, contractual diversification) was not discussed until 2009, in part because of the more onerous infrastructural hurdles involved. However, after 2004, a number of policy documents started to pay increased attention to the risks associated with dependence on a single supplier and to diversification – especially energy source diversification – and increased energy efficiency as possible answers.

Analysis of an exhaustive database of energy-related legislation (including ministerial and presidential decrees and resolutions) covering the years 2002–2008[105] reveals that although already in 2004 official documents were calling for the use, by 2012, of 25 percent of local and alternative sources of energy for heat and electricity generation,[106] geographical energy diversification as a national goal was not mentioned widely until 2007.[107] The year 2007, immediately following the gas and oil confrontation with Russia, was especially rich with policy declarations in support of energy savings and energy diversification. Presidential Directive No. 3 of June 2007 set concrete goals concerning geographic diversification: by 2020, dependency on a single supplier was to be no more than 65 percent of the country's energy use, down from 87 percent in 2007.[108] The Concept of Energy Security approved by the president in September 2007 set the ambitious goal of increasing energy consumption by "only" 130 percent between 2005 and 2020, while increasing GDP by 320 percent during the same period.[109] The main means for reaching this goal are presented as increasing investments in the energy sector, reducing dependency on gas by developing coal-fired and nuclear electricity power plants, and increasing the use of renewable and local energy sources (peat, wood, and coal). The Energy Modernization Program[110] approved in November of that year also spelled out the goal of reducing energy intensity by 25 percent from 2007 to 2010.[111] Additional policy initiatives were launched aimed at domestic conservation and, in the fall of 2008, the Belarusian government introduced additional regulations intended to reduce energy use by the largest industrial enterprises, doubling the price for electricity use above a certain limit.[112] And in August 2010, the Council of Ministers approved a new energy policy document ("Strategy for the Development of Belarus' Energy Potential") calling for a reduction in dependency on energy imports from Russia from 82 percent (2009) to 64 percent–57 percent in 2020. It also called for collaboration with Lithuania and Poland in the building of LNG terminals on their territories in order for Belarus to import up to 10 bcm of LNG per year.[113]

Yet there was a major limitation to all the energy source diversification and energy efficiency programs announced since 2004: not based on market principles, they were unlikely to be effective given the continued state monopolization and lack of institutional reform in the energy sector, and were hindered by the general lack of policy making transparency characteristic of Belarus during this period. These macro-level factors seriously limited the positive effects of any targerted energy efficiency initiatives.

Moreover, with prices enterprises were allowed to charge for their products still calculated on the basis of cost-plus principles (*zatratnoi printsip*), a reduction in energy use and energy expenditures would mean a reduction in the sale price of the final product, providing no incentive for managers to increase efficiency.

Thus very soon these conservation-based policy initiatives were de facto (although not at the declarative level) largely replaced by one energy source diversification initiative much more compatible with continued top-down, state-controlled, and nontransparent policies: the building of a NPP,[114] a decision confirmed by the Security

Council in January 2008.[115] A well-known independent Belarusian journalist considered the decision to build a NPPt "practically taken by
Lukashenka alone."[116]

The course itself of the debate and decision-making process around
the NPP tells us much about the nature of enery policy making in
Belarus. While at the start of the process there was a small degree of
public discussion, with some state organizations shyly expressing safety
concerns,[117] after the Security Council took the political decision to support the project, all discussion officially stopped. At this point, Lukashenka began to take a much harsher approach towards anyone expressing
reservations on the project, effectively accusing them of treason.[118]

According to the decision approved in January 2008, an NPP with a
2,000-megawatt capacity would be built in Astravets, twenty kilometers
from the Lithuanian border, by 2016. Although forcefully presented by
the state-controlled media as the only viable solution to Belarus' energy
dependency, several factors made it unlikely that the NPP, as planned,
could help reduce this dependency. Instead, it was likely to create four
additional types of dependencies on Russia: equipment and spare parts
dependency, as Belarus would most likely buy the equipment for the
plant from Russia; fuel dependency, as it would need to buy the nuclear
fuel from Russia; waste disposal dependency, as it would need to turn
to Russia for storage of its nuclear waste; and increased financial dependency, since with few means of its own to finance the $9 billion project,
Belarus would need to obtain credits, most likely from Russia. Given
the rapid deterioration of relations with Russia in mid-2010, however,
it was not clear whether an agreement would be found between both
sides allowing for an as-planned start to construction.[119]

Much of the argument for the building of the NPP was based on
the expectation that electricity consumption in Belarus would double
between 2007 and 2017, something not yet proven. At the same time,
the expectation itself of a large generation capacity coming online would reduce the incentives to making Belarus' economy more
energy-efficient.

OIL: EXTERNAL AND DOMESTIC MANAGEMENT, 2004–2010

Due to intention or simply good fortune, the interrelationship between
oil and gas markets during the first part of this period (2004 to mid-
2008) worked to Belarus' advantage. Indeed, the first years of energy
pressure from Russia (until 2007, mainly gas pressure) coincided with

years of growing world oil prices, which allowed Belarus to greatly increase profits from the oil refining and reexport business, revenues it could use to compensate for tightened conditions in other areas. As seen from Table 5.4, between 2004 and 2006, Belarus' income from oil and oil products exports allowed it not only to pay for Russian oil imports, but to make a significant additional profit as well. This, as put in the words of a Russian analyst, allowed Belarus to "pay for Russian gas with Russian oil."[120] As acknowledged by the Belarusian opposition itself, 2006, the best (and near-last) year of the oil refining and reexport rents boom, was, or at least was largely perceived as being, "the best year ever for the Belarusian economy."[121]

Oil Refining

As world oil prices started to increase after 2004, the Belarusian state strengthened its presence in the refining sector. This was especially clear in the case of the Mozyr oil refinery. As pressure from Slavneft (owner of 42.5 percent of Mozyr's shares) to increase control over the company grew, the Belarusian state counterattacked by, among other measures, attempting to increase its share in the refinery by seeking to force the minority (12.2 percent) shareholder MNPZ Plus to turn over its shares to the state and by forcedly introducing a state controlling share in it.[122] Mozyr was also forced to make a $100 million non-tax contribution to the Belarusian budget.[123] Thus, despite Mozyr continuing formally as a private corporation, the state was able to establish de facto control over it.

This renewed interest in gaining control of nominally private Mozyr was related to the growing role of oil products exports in Belarus' budgets by 2004. By then, despite being highly dependent on imported oil (producing less than 20 percent of its oil needs in the mid-2000s), in per capita terms Belarus was exporting as much in oil products as oil-rich Russia.[124] The fact that Belarus received Russian oil at lower-than-market prices, while exporting oil products at world market prices, brought a veritable rents windfall to the country as international oil and oil products prices increased sharply in the mid 2000s, while prices charged to Belarus increased more gradually; the IMF estimated this additional yearly benefit as representing about 2 percent–3 percent of GDP in the mid-2000s.[125] As seen from Table 5.4, the actual value of these exports grew exceptionally fast: from $3.3 billion in 2004 to $7.6 billion in 2007 and $10.7 billion in 2008, accompanied by a similar

Table 5.5 Belarus': Trade Balances in Oil and Oil Products, 2000–2010, in Million Tons (Mt)

Year	Domestic production	Import of oil and oil products	Supplies (production + imports)	Export of oil and oil products	Domestic use	Percentage of domestic oil use covered by domestic production (domestic production/ domestic use)	Oil and oil products' exports as % of overall exports
2000	1.85	12.1	13.95	8.10	5.85	31.6	20.2
2001	1.85	12.0	13.85	8.10	5.75	32.1	18.2
2002	1.85	14.5	16.35	10.50	5.85	31.6	20.9
2003	1.82	15.8	17.62	11.36	6.25	29.1	22.7
2004	1.80	18.0	20.70	14.10	6.60	27.2	27.4
2005	1.79	20.2	22.01	15.20	6.80	26.3	35.4
2006	1.78	22.1	23.88	16.52	7.38	24.1	38.8
2007	1.76	21.1	22.86	16.35	7.55	23.2	35.6
2008	1.74	24.0	25.74	16.98	8.76	19.8	37.5
2009	1.72	25.3	27.02	17.55	9.47	18.2	38.0
2010	1.70	16.3	18.00	11.30	6.68	28.0	37.9

Sources: Ministry of statistics and analysis of the Republic of Belarus, *Foreign trade of the Republic of Belarus. Statistical abstracts.* (Minsk, various years)

increase in the role of oil and oil products products exports in Belarus' overall exports.[126]

Oil Crisis Management: The January 2007 Gas and Oil War

THE JANUARY 2007 OIL CRISIS

Before the gas war was even temporarily settled in late December 2006, a serious confrontation started to brew in the oil area. Its start could be dated to late 2006, when – effective 1 January 2007 – Russia decided to eliminate oil export tax preferences for Belarus. This was preceded, in the fall of 2006, by the Russian proposal that the export duties charged on Russian oil refined in Belarus go 85 percent to Russia, and 15 percent to Belarus, instead of 100 percent to Belarus (as had been *de facto* the case since at least 1995), and the threat (made true on 1 January 2007) to introduce export duties (*poshlina*) on oil exports to Belarus should Belarus refuse to comply with the arrangement. Effective 1 January 2007, supplies would have to pay the full $180/ton duties, instead of none, as has been the case since 1995. As a response, on 4 January (retroactive to 1 January) Belarus introduced a special transit tax of $45/ton on the transit of Russian oil through Belarus (in addition to the previously agreed-to transit fee) intended to partly compensate for the new Russian duties. Russia declared Belarus' new special duty illegal, refusing to pay it. After Belarus began siphoning Russian oil headed for Europe, allegedly in lieu of the payment owed by Russia, on 8 January Russia's pipeline monopoly Transneft shut supplies to the Druzhba oil pipeline entirely, briefly interrupting oil supplies to Poland and other points west – the first time ever that Russian (or Soviet) oil supplies to EU consumer countries had been interrupted. After a battle of wills lasting until 10 January, the two countries agreed to transition gradually into a new division of oil export duties (see further on), and supplies via Druzhba were resumed a day later; Belarus also agreed to impose the same level of export duties on oil products as imposed by Russia.

OIL SHOCK DELAYED

Despite the shock of these confrontations, Belarus and Russia found ways to soften and delay the shock until the 2009–2010 period. We discuss these briefly below.

Without any cushioning measures, the change in oil trade modalities represented by the new division of export revenue effective 1 January 2007 would have meant a yearly loss of $2 billion to the Belarusian budget. Belarus first responded to the new situation with a series of measures that, while compensating for some of the lost revenue, also put a significant burden on refineries (whose profits plummeted from 20 percent to 1 percent after a 37.6 percent reduction in oil products exports in January 2007 as compared with January 2006[127]). As a result, a number of corrective measures were introduced effective 1 March 2007, intended to make oil refining in Belarus more attractive to Russian producers, providing compensation equivalent to (or, in some cases, exceeding) the Russian export duty paid.[128] Thus, income to the Belarusian budget grew as a result of the newly imposed export duty, but there were also significant new net expenses due to the compensations paid to oil products exporters.[129] In addition, oil transit fees through Belarus were increased – about 50 percent in dollar terms – for the first time since 1995, nevertheless remaining about 50 percent lower than fees charged by Poland and Ukraine.[130]

Yet Russia also took a more conciliatory position after the initial crisis. After originally insisting on accruing 100 percent of the oil export duties, on 10 January, Russia agreed to a gradual transition on the sharing of export duties: in 2007, 70 percent for Russia and 30 percent for Belarus, in 2008 80 percent and 20 percent, and in 2009 85 percent and 15 percent, and 100 percent to Russia starting in 2010. In addition, although special treatment to Belarus was supposed to be phased out gradually, duties on oil supplied to Belarus continued to be lower than those charged neighbouring states: in 2007, 29 percent of the regular level, to be gradually increased to 33.5 percent in 2008 and 35.6 percent in 2009.[131] This reduced Belarus' additional expenses stemming from Russia's newly imposed oil export duties from about $3 billion to about $ 1 billion. There was also an agreement limiting oil price increases;[132] in 2007, Belarus was still receiving oil at prices at least $100–$130 lower than world ones. Oil products continued to be Belarus' largest export, contributing 37.5 percent of foreign earnings in 2008 and 38 percent in 2009 (see Table 5.5). Belarusian economists calculated that, even under the harder trade conditions in force after January 2007, the Russian subsidization of the Belarusian economy through lower gas prices, sharing of export duties for refined oil products, and not charging of export duties on a significant portion of crude oil amounted to $6.4 billion (2007), $9.95 billion (2008), and $4.15 billion (2009).[133]

The question thus inevitably arises: why did Russia continue to support Belarus at this moment, given Lukashenka's aggressive declarations against it, when it seemed to have in its hands the key to force

Belarus into much more direct compliance with Moscow's policies? In addition to Belarus' continued value to Russia as "last" ally, a sudden and total collapse of the Belarusian economy and a sudden stream of migrants out of the country could bring significant destabilization to Russia as well. But there may have been another motivation for the Russian side: Russia's desire to use such softening measures to delay the moment of truth for Belarus and keep the country dependent on the Russian economy. With the building of the Nord Stream pipeline looming in the horizon, Belarus' room for manoeuvre was narrowing, and maintaining Belarus' dependency on Russia could be used instrumentally to prevent Belarus from finding alternative energy sources before a changed correlation of forces. Such changed correlation of forces, set to take place after the pipeline would be completed and Russia would be able to transport most of its gas to WE without depending on Belarus, would mean a dramatic reduction in Belarus' transit counterpower vis-a-vis Russia, and Russia's increased ability to pressure Belarus, especially on military, strategic, and integration issues.[134]

Such moment of truth seemed to be approaching by 2010. Despite Lukashenka's further politization of the issue and attempt to make Belarus' joining of a previously agreed Russia-Belarus-Kazakhstan Customs Union (inaugurated in July 2010) conditional on Russia cancelling export duties on oil for participant states, Russia's position did not change. Russia's intransigency on the issue seemed to be related to Lukashenka's perceived unreliability as an ally, manifested in his wavering concerning recognition of Abkhazia and South Ossetia after the August 2008 military conflict with Georgia. After a further worsening of relations in mid-2010, exemplified by a new threat of suspension of gas supplies and transit due to unpaid gas debt by Belarus and transit services by Gazprom, a meeting between Lukashenka and Moscow-foe Georgian President Saakashvili and a Kremlin-supported anti-Lukashenka discreditation campaign in the Russian TV, relations seemed to have reached a point of no return.[135]

Although Belarus was able to soften the impact of these changes in the very short term (the important months leading to the December 2010 presidential elections), especially through increased exports of commodities such as potash fertilizers, the writing on the wall was clear: the country's model of incorporation into the international economy based on the large-scale subsidization of its backward economy through heavily subsidized gas, and on the sharing of oil rents from Russia, was coming to an end.

Shy Attempts at Oil Diversification

The Belarusian side responded to this new situation by, first and foremost, seeking out new partners. In contrast with gas, where the transit infrastructure is much less flexible, oil presented Belarus with some real geographic diversification possibilities once the decision to diversify was taken. One such opportunity came from Venezuela, where Hugo Chávez's regime appeared as a sympathetic partner of convenience for Lukashenka, and where an oil-producing JV was already established in 2007. Between April and August 2010, four shipments of Venezuelan oil had been received, routed via terminals in Odesa and Muuga (Estonia), and more were planned through Lithuanian ports.[136] Although these first shipments, about 0.32 million tons in total, represented less than 1.6 percent of Belarus' yearly oil imports, the March 2010 agreement between Presidents Lukashenka and Chávez spoke of yearly supplies of 4 million tons, about 20 percent of Belarus' yearly imports. Although the prices reportedly paid were nearly 20 percent higher than those paid to Russia at the time (ca. $550/T including duties),[137] the technical qualities of the lighter Venezuelan oil allowed for easier processing into higher-profitability light oil products, partially compensating for the higher price.

In addition, beginning in 2006, Belarus started to show increased interest in new oil transportation options such as participation in the Odesa-Brody oil transit system and its possible extension to Gdansk.[138] The Belarusian energy security blueprint up to 2020,[139] approved by the president in November 2004, envisaged that, by the end of 2010, 20 percent of Belarus' oil imports should come from non-Russian sources, shipped through ports in the Baltic and Black Seas. In addition, Belarusian government delegations visited the United Arab Emirates and Azerbaijan in 2007–2008, and agreements were reached with Azerbaijan on small-scale oil supplies to Belarusian refineries and on Belarusneft gaining permission to produce oil there.[140] Such a proactive search for new sources of oil imports was in sharp contrast with Belarusian policies and initiatives of the previous period, 1994 to 2004.

Changed External Conditions and Rent-Seeking Possibilities

ENERGY RENTS, CORRUPTION, AND THE LOW YEARS
As oil trade rules and the structure of profit-sharing with Russia changed starting in January 2007, the possibilities for access to rents through oil

operations started to diminish. With the pie becoming smaller, groups benefitting from these rents became more protective of them, wanting to limit other players' access to this business. In addition, other players informally involved in the oil business (such as, reportedly, Vladimir Konoplev, until September 2007 head of the National Assembly) found it hard to continue to do business as usual given Lukashenka's son Viktor's entrance into the scene and interest in controlling oil-related financial flows as well.[141] Konoplev's September 2007 resignation as head of the National Assembly was repeatedly understood in this context.[142]

An additional response to the crisis was the decision to move forward on a proposal discussed intermittently since the late 1990s: the creation of a centralized, state-controlled oil company that would replace the multitude of tolling operators (*neftetreideri*) still working in the market with a single state company controlling revenue flows in the oil sector. Under the name Belarusian Oil Company, (Belorusskaia Neftenaia Kompania [BNK]) and established on the model of the Belarusian Potash Company, controlling exports of Belarus' other significant commodity, potash fertilizers, BNK sought to increase state control of the oil sector and ease out remaining neftetreideri. The aim was to keep in state hands the money spent by the state in subsidies to tolling oil suppliers, subsidies that in 2007 amounted to more than 50 percent of budget revenues from export duties on oil products.[143] As of early 2008, however, the company had achieved only modest success. While it was exporting 80 percent of the oil products produced directly by its parent companies (Naftan, Mozyr, Belarusneft, and Beloruskii Neftianoi Torgovii Dom), it had had very limited success in controlling the export of oil products produced by tolling operators.[144]

PRESSURE ON THE REGIME DUE TO CHANGING OIL
AND GAS TRADE CONDITIONS

Although Belarus was able to largely soften the short-term shock of new oil trade rules with Russia, and despite GDP and consumer spending growth in 2007, signs of trouble were visible already that year. Some of these signs were worsening trade balances (Belarus' trade deficit increased from 3.9 percent of GDP in 2006 to 6.9 percent in 2007[145]), lack of investment capital, and the fact that many domestic companies had to take large credits to compensate for the higher energy prices.[146] Despite official reluctance to acknowledge the growing crisis, the government felt compelled to take some belt-tightening measures in 2008, such as the elimination of many social subsidies. Although some of the price increases were passed on to final users, reserves especially earmarked in the 2008 budget to cushion the energy price increases helped the Belarusian government gain some breathing space before more drastic measures would need to be taken.[147] Because of the softening measures discussed below, however, the effects of the changed gas trade conditions came to be felt gradually and in milder form than originally expected by most Western and Belarusian analysts.

In addition, the Belarusian government responded with a number of mild liberalization policies intended to bring more capital into the system (through new loans for the major Belarusian banks and the shy beginnings of privatization[148]), to attract new foreign (especially Western[149]) investors (the elimination of the state's right to a controlling share in enterprises, for example), to reduce government expenses (the elimination of a number of social programs), and to simplify the registration of new businesses.[150] The tax burden on enterprises was also reduced (2008), presumably to help them cope with the burden of increased energy prices.

Despite the changes in energy trade conditions with Russia starting in 2007, Russia's subsidization of the Belarusian economy through preferential energy trade conditions continued, in 2007 amounting to 12 percent–20 percent of Belarus' GDP.[151] Thus Russian assurances that the relationship with Belarus has been moved to an exclusively commercial basis are not supported by the actual record. When the relationship did deteriorate significantly in mid-2010 it was, again, on the basis of a political dispute more than an economic one.

Belarus' Energy Situation and Trajectory Since Independence – A Snapshot of the Outcomes

What were the actual results of Belarus' particular way of dealing with its energy dependency? Let us review briefly the main results in terms of energy diversification and in terms of the direction in which the energy dependency relationship was managed.

Management of Energy Supply Diversification Issues

DOMESTIC DIVERSIFICATION: ENERGY DIVERSIFICATION VIA ENERGY SAVINGS, ENERGY EFFICIENCY, AND INCREASED PRODUCTION

How well did Belarus fare in terms of domestic diversification, especially energy efficiency? As shown in Table 5.1, although by the mid-late 2000s Belarus' energy efficiency levels remained well below Western levels, there were very important developments since 1996 as GDP grew strongly during this period but energy use only moderately.

Based on official statistics, Belarus' progress in terms of reducing energy intensity was one of the fastest in the world.[152] Highly respected Belarusian economists such as Leonid Zlotnikov and Elena Rakova, have questioned these assessments, however, pointing to possibly inflated GDP figures and to the disconnect between official energy intensity trends and the lack of any significant modernization outside the oil refining sector.[153] Moreover, despite the ambitious new goals set in the 2007 initiatives, the first results were not encouraging: from early 2007 to early 2008 energy intensity did not go down 7 percent–8 percent as planned, but increased 3.9 percent.[154] Interestingly, the government did not introduce energy intensity (the amount of energy required to produce a given amount of GDP) as an official indicator of energy security until 2007.[155]

Domestic Diversification: Energy Mix Diversification

Energy imports can also be reduced through energy-mix diversification, i.e., by switching to fuels more commonly available domestically.

The post-independence period witnessed a massive change in Belarus' energy mix, with a significant decrease in the use of oil, and an increased use of gas. While some of this could be attributed to the weight of Soviet legacies, it was more likely the result of conscious policies aimed at moving away from higher-priced oil to more heavily subsidized gas. As noted before, the role of gas in the country's TPES increased massively from 43 percent in 1990 to about 65 percent in 2007.[156] At the same time, the role of oil declined from 62.6 percent in 1990 to 26.5 percent in 2005, [157] mainly as a result of the conscious move to gas-fired electricity generation once the price of Russian gas for Belarus became more advantageous than that of oil.

Yet this massive shift did not amount to .diversification – while energy-source diversification is based on the idea of replacing fuels not available domestically by those that are, or at least on the idea of spreading dependency risks among various energy sources, Belarus' energy mix reorientation towards gas made the country significantly more dependent on the one energy source it does not possess at all, the one energy source most difficult to diversify due to structural transportation constraints (as in gas there is little alternative to transportation via pipeline), and the one that would make the country even more dependent on its monopolist supplier, Russia.

Despite the fact that already in 1997 the Belarusian Academy of Sciences had recommended that reliance on gas be reduced and that local energy sources be developed, the generalized euphoria at the time "that Russia will supply us with cheap gas and only cheap gas" made the government unwilling to listen to these recommendations.[158] Finally, Belarusian polices during this period were based on an ecologically unsustainable dependency on highly energy-intensive industries.

EXTERNAL DIVERSIFICATION

External diversification involves receiving imports from a broader geographical array of suppliers, including reliance on a broader spectrum of contractual forms in order to avoid reliance on a single company or type of contract.

Even at the purely declarative level, Belarus did very little in terms of geographic diversification until 2006. During the period between 1994 and 2005, energy diversification was not an issue; the emphasis was on a common energy balance with Russia. As noted previously, even considering the importance given to reducing energy use presented in a number of official policy documents starting in 2004, and the general discussion of the need to reduce dependency on the de facto sole external supplier (Russia), there was little discussion of concrete goals concerning energy diversification until 2007.

At the *de facto* level, until 2006, there were also very few changes in terms of geographical diversification. On the contrary, the country moved away from some of its few non-Russian alternative sources of imported energy, which gave Russia increased possibilities to play one country against another (i.e., Belarus and Ukraine) in its search for cheaper energy transit possibilities. If in 1993 Belarus imported a small amount of electricity from Lithuania, Latvia, and Ukraine, and that provided Belarus' sole non-Russian source of imported energy, by 2005 the country was importing all of its electricity from Russia. By 2007, the country's level of energy dependency of foreign (overwhelmingly Russian) supplies was 87 percent.[159]

ALTERNATIVE SYSTEMS FOR THE SUPPLY AND TRANSIT OF GAS AND OIL

Belarus has been so identified with – and has benefited from – a Russian-centred system of energy supply that it is difficult to imagine the country playing a role in an alternative system of energy supplies. Rather, throughout much of the 1990s and early 2000s it played an opposite role – as a kind of wedge dividing a possible Baltic-Black sea alternative energy transit corridor.

However, some of these possibilities were quietly discussed even during the high years of Lukashenka's energy relationship with Russia. Already in 1995, Belarus researched the possibility of using Ukraine's Odesa-Brody pipeline to supply Belarusian refineries. In May 2004, the highly respected independent Belarusian economic weekly *Beloruskii Rynok* reported discussions between Belneftekhim, Latvian oil transit operator LatRosTrans, Ukrtransnafta, and the Ukrainian Institute of Oil Transit on a possible oil transit route that would join the Odesa-Brody pipeline with Belarusian pipelines, and later go on to the Ventspils port in Latvia, through the route Odesa-Brody-Mozyr-Polotsk-Ventspils; a memorandum of intent was also signed in 2004.[160] While official Belarusian comments on the issue were rather muted until 2005, with the growing deterioration of relations with Russia, increased importance was given to these possibilities. Since 2006, in the aftermath of Russia's indefinite suspension of oil supplies to the Latvian port of Ventspils, as the Belarusian leadership became more sober about the possibility of an oil supply cutoff by Russia, joining a Caspian-Black Sea-Baltic energy transport community became an increasingly realistic option.[161]

Similarly, new Russian attempts starting in 2004 to sideline Belarus as a transit route for its gas and oil, made clear by plans to build the Nord Stream (gas) and Baltic Pipeline System-2 (oil) pipelines making possible the avoiding of Belarus as a transit route[162] gave the country an incentive to become more proactive in the development of oil and gas transit routes and supply options independent of Russia.

Contractual Diversification and Organization of Energy Trade with the Main Current Supplier(s)

In contrast with geographical diversification, contractual diversification is first and foremost about developing a variety of contractual relationships both in terms of companies and of type of contracts (short-term, long-term, etc.) even when the energy originates from a single country. In this area, Belarus' record has been poor. Russia has been the only supplier contracted, and – with the exception of early 2000s purchases from a number of Gazprom-related independent firms – there has not been a diversification into a variety of contractual forms.

In contrast with Ukraine, Belarus has never consciously imported gas or oil from CA, not even through Russian-centred intermediaries. So in the case of Belarus, not only was there no contractual diversification, but no geographical diversification either. At the same time, the country seemed to avoid some of the perils associated with giving up control of large areas of energy policy to intermediary companies, as happened in the case of Ukraine with RosUkrEnergo.

Direction of the Management of the Energy Dependency Relationship

What does the track record in each of these areas tell us about the direction of the management of energy dependency since independence? In the spectrum between transparent and nontransparent, the Belarusian case was even less transparent than the Ukrainian one, with even basic information concerning electricity and gas prices for some users not publicly available.

Where particularistic interests more often reflected in policy, or nonparticularistic ones? We lack sufficient evidence to fully assess the role of particular interests (and, related to it, corruption) in Belarus' energy policy. However, we can safely hypothesize that President Lukashenka's greater degree of direct control over energy policy prevented some of the runaway capture of the field by particularistic interests – as happened in Ukraine – from happening in Belarus. However, this was far from a situation of clear democratically-based governance in energy policy making.

Main Developments since 2010

If Belarus had managed to soften the impact of the 2007–2009 changes in its energy relationship with Russia, and to avoid the "moment of truth" in the relationship, such a moment seemed to be approaching by 2010, related to Russian dissatisfaction with Lukashenka's continued refusal to recognize Abkhazia and South Ossetia and his foot-dragging concerning the privatization of Belarusian refineries to Russian capital. In January, Russia doubled the effective amount of duties on oil exports to Belarus, leading to reduced oil products exports.[163] Yet, aided by increased income from Belarus' other main export, potash fertilizers, Lukashenka was able to provide major wage increases in the runoff to the 19 December 2010 presidential elections. (The elections, won by Lukashenka under far from transparent circumstances, were followed by harsh repression against the opposition.) A week before the elections, the Kremlin promised new oil concessions, and in January 2011 abolished export duties on all oil exported to Belarus. Although this advantage was partially cancelled by a near month-long suspension of oil deliveries in January while Russian and Russian oil actors discussed prices,[164] the year as a whole showed strong increases in oil products exports.

Yet the bill for 2010's expansionist policies came soon after the elections, in 2011, when an unprecedented inflation and decline in real wages hit Belarus. The situation was made worse by the rapid increase in gas import costs as a result of the 2007 agreements: from 2.8 percent of GDP in 2006 to about 9 percent in 2011.[165] By April, the prospect of mass unemployment became a real threat. Desperate to reduce expenditures on gas, and for an influx of foreign currency, Lukashenka finally gave in on an issue he had considered anathema for a decade and a half: the sale of the remaining 50 percent of Beltransgaz in exchange for Russian approval of a $3 billion loan from the Stabilization Fund of the Eurasian Economic Community (EurAsEC), a reduction in the 2012 price of gas from about $286 to $165 per thousand cubic meters (a yearly saving of $3 billion compared to the 2011 gas bill),[166] and promises of domestic Russian prices from 2014 on. Similar concessions were seen on the oil front, where effective oil prices were reduced for 2012, lowering Belarus' oil bill and increasing revenues from refining and (re) exporting by at least $2 billion.[167] Costums Union provisions also made the export of Belarusian products to markets such as Ukraine extremely competitive.

This new influx of money allowed the Belarusian economy to survive in the short term, but meant a further delay in the reform of Belarus' economy. These concessions also meant that many of the diversification measures that began to be implemented in 2010 – such as the import of Venezuelan oil (ca. 1.3 million tons in 2011)[168] through a swap with Azerbaijan via the Odesa-Brody pipeline – lost their economic incentive. In June 2012, imports from Venezuela stopped.

Tensions with Russia, however, returned in mid 2012, as Russia made public its dissatisfaction with Belarus' presumed violation of export-duty sharing arrangements by illegally exporting oil products as solvents and lubricants as a way to avoid sharing oil export duties with Russia, with Russian budget loses calculated at over $1.5 billion.[169]

Between 2010 and 2013, Belarus behaved in the same manner as it had in the previous sixteen years: seeking to extract concessions from Russia that would allow the unreformed Belarusian economy to stay afloat and President Lukashenka to finance the populist measures that allowed him a modicum of popular support. In relations with Russia, the pattern of cyclical highs and lows also continued. Yet now both the highs and the lows were becoming lower, and Belarus' bargaining position was quickly worsening, not only because of the sale of Beltransgas, but also because of some of the policy making limitations brought about by Belarus joining the Customs Union and Russia's increased development of oil transit capacities that could replace Belarus' role in transit; despite the commitment to maintain gas transit volumes up to 2014 attached to the Beltransgaz purchase agreement, the future looked uncertain.[170]

Conclusion

Rents of Dependency and Belarus' Management of its Energy Dependency

This chapter has provided numerous examples of the types of *external rents* the Belarusian government was able to extract from its energy relationship with Russia. In fact, it was first and foremost through the privileged energy relationship with Russia – and the attendant external rents that came from it – that the Belarusian government sought to manage its extreme energy dependency.

At least until 2008, the distribution of the macro-level energy rents accrued by the country as a whole resulted in a rent-extraction and redistribution cycle that allowed Lukashenka to secure substantial levels of popular support through large subsidies to the countryside, the maintenance of full employment, and the steady improvement of salaries and living standards, while still being able to finance the modernization of the oil-refining sector, and possibly add to the budget of the Presidential Administration as well.

Belarus' Cycle of Rents

How did the cycle of extraction, distribution, and recycling of energy rents work in the Belarusian case? As seen in this chapter, the particularities of Belarus' political system affected each element of the process. In terms of rents extraction, Belarus' special relationship with Russia allowed the country access to certain rents – those related to the refining and reexport of Russian oil under special tax conditions – not available to the other two cases. Moreover, President Lukashenka's ability to politicize the relationship made possible access to sources of rents above and beyond those specified in formal agreements, and allowed the country to continue to do so for some time after relations had taken a turn for the worse. Lukashenka's ability to politicize the relationship, in turn, was related to his domestic monopolization of power, i.e., to the absence of other viable independent actors in the country that could offer Russian energy players their own, parallel games, as was the case in Ukraine for example.[171]

In terms of the distribution of rents, Lukashenka's signature political style played an important role in terms of who would have access to these rents, and how they would be distributed domestically. His gatekeeper role and strong control over governmental policy meant no other actors could access energy-related rents without the direct approval and participation of the president. At the same time, redistributive policies in the form of the subsidization of energy for important sectors of the electorate, such as the rural population, constituted an important element of Lukashenka's populist appeal.

In terms of the recycling of these rents into the political system, whatever players that could accrue rents at an individual level – with President Lukashenka's previous approval – found it very difficult to turn these rents into a source of independent political power, as a clear precondition to any access to rents was that this access should take place quietly and in a low-key manner. Thus, whatever energy-related rents made it into politics was through their support of various projects associated with President Lukashenka, contributing to his popularity and the further consolidation of his power.

What Have We Learned about Russian Energy Behaviour in the Region?

If we look at the Belarusian-Russian energy relationship between 1992 and 2013, a cyclical pattern can be seen where Gazprom (and the Russian government) put pressure on Belarus, pressed for higher gas prices with the implicit threat of reducing supplies, and on some occasions has carried these threats through, but this was followed by other concessions on Russia's part that de facto compensated for the higher prices.

It would seem as if the logic of self-interest on the part of Russian companies (for example, Gazprom's reaction to Belarus' foot-dragging on the sale of Beltransgas shares) worked only up to a certain point. When that point was about to be reached and Belarusian-Russian relations were just about to go truly sour, the Russian government seemed to find sufficient strategic arguments to step in, provide continued support, and keep the game of virtual integration going. Thus, for example, after an unprecedentdly acrimonious Kremlin media campaign against President Lukashenka in the summer of 2010, in December of that year, barely a week before the presidential elections in Belarus, Moscow seemed to provide a renewed blessing to Lukashenka's electoral bid, by promising renewed concessions in the oil trade area in the form of duty-free crude oil supplies.[172]

Especially puzzling in this context is the fact that Russia's highly preferential treatment of Belarus continued well after the core of the relationship – and trust – between President Lukashenka and the Russian leadership had been seriously damaged. While Lukashenka's ability to politicize the relationship and even blackmail his Russian partners played an important role, it would be inaccurate to believe the Russian side did not politicize the relationship as well. Rather, the contrary seemed true: as of 2005, most gas export prices to CIS and WE costumers were decided by Gazprom itself – with the exception of sales to Belarus.[173] At least until December 2006, the case of Belarus was a clear exception to Gazprom's declared policy of moving towards market (netback) pricing in its sales to post-Soviet states.[174]

Information about how Belarus dealt with its energy dependency on Russia, and on its success in maintaining energy subsidies well after the core relationship between both countries had been damaged also forces us to reassess our views about the Belarusian-Russian relationship. Given our widely held assumptions about Belarus as a Russian client state, the Belarusian energy relationship with Russia turned out to be highly paradoxical. In the short term at least, President Lukashenka seemed to be able to push his interests – and perhaps the short term interests of Belarus as well – more forcefully than less officially pro-Russian states such as Ukraine. Yet benefitting from Russian energy rents was not self-sustainable, as it depended on high world oil prices, low oil import prices, and a tricky political game with Russia. This was a game Lukashenka would play craftily until at least 2006, one that, however, could not offer a viable longer-term basis for the country's economic development. Belarus failed to adopt a sustainable energy strategy able to serve it after the privileged relationship with Russia would be gone.

6 Lithuania: Energy Policy between Domestic Interests, Russia, and the EU

Lithuania as Case Study

Part of the EU since 2004 but isolated from its energy networks, Lithuania presents an interesting counterpart to the Ukrainian and Belarusian cases. It shares with them common Soviet legacies, high levels of energy dependency on Russia, and a lack of structural links with Western energy suppliers. Yet despite these commonalities, Lithuania is unique in a number of ways. First, it is a much smaller country, with a much smaller population. Second, its role in direct and indirect energy transit is smaller than in the other two cases. Third, while for all three cases one of the most important legacies of Soviet energy policies was the excess of installed energy infrastructure compared to actual domestic needs, this factor was uniquely significant in the Lithuanian case.

Important differences also come to the fore within the foreign policy and domestic politics areas. Of the three cases, only Lithuania is a member of the EU and NATO. In contrast with Ukraine and Belarus, each of which has led its own brand of deeply ambiguous relationship with Russia and toyed with at least some aspects of Russian-led post-Soviet reintegration, Lithuania's policy towards Russia has been much clearer: one of avoiding conflict but also ruling out any possibility of integration.[1]

As discussed in chapter 1, energy dependency is never a one-way street, but is both moderated and complicated by important elements of (asymmetrical) interdependence. Lithuania brings both strengths and weakness to its energy relationship with Russia. On the weakness side is not only Lithuania's lack of significant domestic energy resources – producing only very modest amounts of oil, which never covered more than 2 percent of domestic consumption – but also its virtual lack of gas and oil storage facilities to cushion demand fluctuations and guarantee supplies in case of a cut-off. In addition, throughout the period covered in this book, the Baltic states, including Lithuania, were – and have been recognized as such in official EU documents – an "energy island" due to their lack of energy connections to the rest of the EU.[2] While this isolation makes Lithuania's situation similar to that of its Baltic neighbours Latvia and Estonia, compared to them, it is the largest energy actor – the largest in population, the largest gas importer,[3] and the one playing the largest role in energy transit, including the transit of Russian gas, as well as (until 2009) electricity (from the Ignalina NPP, the Baltic States' sole nuclear power plant) and oil products exports from the Mazeikiu Nafta oil refinery (the Baltics' sole refinery), making the energy rents potentially available through and in Lithuania larger than in the Latvian or Estonian cases. The rents potentially available in Lithuania during this period were, however, significantly smaller than those available in Ukraine or Belarus.

What elements of strength does Lithuania bring to the energy relationship with Russia? Although in a more limited way than in the Ukrainian or Belarusian cases, the relationship is moderated by the country's energy transit role for Russian gas supplies (to Kaliningrad). In addition, until mid-2006 – when Russia stopped oil shipments via the Druzhba pipeline – Lithuania also played an important role in the indirect transit of Russian oil through refining at the Mazeikiu Nafta refinery and subsequent reexport to Western markets.

Lithuania's membership in NATO and the EU since 2004 gives it an element of power in the relationship. Membership in these organizations, especially the EU, gives Lithuania the possibility to multilateralize its energy relationship with Russia, bringing it out of the purely bilateral context and into that of the EU's larger energy policy and relationship with Russia. At the same time, as will be discussed in the conclusion to this chapter, membership in these organizations did not bring Lithuania the degree of energy security it hoped for.

How did the cycle of extraction, distribution, and recycling of energy rents manifest itself in the case of Lithuania? This chapter looks at this cycle from the perspective of Lithuania's unique situation as an EU member but still largely isolated from its energy networks, and analyses how Lithuania's political and economic trajectory since independence, as well as the development of its relationship with Russia, affected the types and magnitude of energy rents available. It will also investigate how the nature of Lithuania's main economic groups and the constraints and opportunities placed on them by the system of interest articulation affected the domestic distribution of these rents, the possibilities for the sharing of these with actors in Russia, and their recycling into the political system.

Our chapter proceeds as follows. After a brief overview of the development of the Lithuanian economy since independence, we discuss the evolution of the Lithuanian political system since 1991 and its impacts on energy policy making. We then analyse Lithuania's actual management of its energy dependency since 1991, before assessing the outcomes of such management.

Lithuania's Transformation Process: A Brief Overview

Lithuania was the first Soviet republic to declare its independence from the USSR and the first to form a coalition government, that led by the broad-based popular movement Sajudis in March 1990, where moderates within the Lithuanian Communist Party (LCP) "cooperated with the opposition to sustain the drive for independence."[4] The USSR recognized Lithuania's independence in September 1991. Throughout the following year, under Sajudis control of both parliament (Seimas) and government, rapid economic reforms were pursued, including the beginnings of energy price liberalization. But as the social costs of reform started to pile up, many reformers lost support, leading to a return to power of the former communists led by Algirdas Brazauskas of the Lithuanian Democratic Labour Party (LDLP), which controlled the Seimas from 1992 to 1996. While this period saw important reforms, such as the establishment of a stable currency, the *Litas* (1993), privatization could not get off the ground fully. State subsidies kept many unprofitable enterprises alive, and reforms began to lag behind those in Latvia and Estonia.[5] Yet while Lithuanian reforms could be considered slow in comparison with Latvian or Estonian ones, they could not but be considered fast in comparison with Ukraine or Belarus.

This relatively slow pace of economic reforms continued until 1996, when the Conservative Party/Homeland Union gained control of both the Seimas and the government. Starting in 1996 but especially 1998, a number of more proactive policies were introduced, such as a more

Table 6.1 GDP, Energy Use and Energy Intensity in Lithuania, 1990–2011

	1990	1991	1992	1993	1994	1995	1996	1997	1998	1999	2000	2001	2002	2003	2004	2005	2006	2007	2008	2009	2010	2011
GDP, in billion US$ at current prices	10.50	10.29	8.56	7.42	6.96	7.90	8.42	10.13	11.25	10.97	11.43	12.16	14.16	18.61	22.55	25.96	30.09	39.10	47.25	36.84	36.30	42.73
GDP in US$ at 2005 prices (PPP)	46.22	43.60	34.33	28.76	25.95	26.80	28.19	30.30	32.61	32.26	33.31	35.55	37.99	41.89	44.97	48.48	52.28	57.42	59.10	50.39	51.06	54.06
GDP as percentage of 1990 GDP (PPP)	100	94.3	74.2	62.2	56.1	58.0	60.9	66.1	71.0	70.0	71.2	76.0	81.2	89.5	96.1	103.4	111.1	121.0	124.7	109.0	110.5	117.0
TPES/Energy use (in million tons of oil equivalent)	16.06	17.05	11.02	9.10	8.13	8.77	9.47	8.96	9.40	7.97	7.13	8.26	8.86	9.25	9.39	8.84	8.72	9.45	9.43	8.63	6.93	N/A
Energy use as percentage of 1990 use	100.00	106.16	68.61	56.66	50.62	54.60	58.96	55.79	58.53	49.25	44.39	51.43	55.16	57.59	58.46	55.04	54.29	58.84	58.71	53.73	43.15	N/A
Energy intensity (Kg of oil equivalent per $ 1,000 GDP at 2005 PPP)	348	391	321	317	313	326	336	296	288	247	214	232	233	221	209	182	167	165	160	171	136	N/A

Source: World Bank World Development Indicators, available at www.databank.worldbank.org.

active promotion of foreign investments. The July 2001 alliance be-tween the centre-left New Union Party and LDLP successor the Lithua-nian Social Democratic Party (LSDP)[6] led to the formation of a coalition government under PM Brazauskas, which, in power until May 2006, saw through many of the reforms needed for EU membership, includ-ing a tighter, deficit-control budget, as well as other market-oriented reforms. A period of renewed growth ensued, and between 2001 and 2007 Lithuania maintained, together with the other Baltic states, some of the fastest growth rates of the CEE region, averaging about 8.2 per-cent per year. (See Table 6.1.) This period of rapid growth was cut short by the impact of the 2008–2009 world crisis, which led to a 22 percent contraction in GDP from 2008 to 2009.

Lithuania's de facto Political System since Independence

In this section, we discuss Lithuania's political system as it has emerged since independence, and how its development has affected energy pol-icy making.

Formal Level: A Parliamentary System with a Twist

In contrast with Ukraine (semi-presidentialist) and Belarus (super-presidentialist), where presidents, either formally or informally, have played a central role in policy making, in the case of Lithuania this role has been much more limited. Although not a full parliamentary system as Latvia and Estonia, Lithuania's system can be characterized as par-liamentary with some features of a mixed presidential/parliamentary system.[7] While various Lithuanian presidents have exhibited different levels of engagement, their role has been less central than in other post-Soviet states.[8]

As a result of these factors, the Lithuanian political system can be characterized as being largely decentralized, and having multiple cen-ters of power, whose relative weight is often hard to asses: the presi-dency, the PM and ministerial system, and the Seimas. In addition, due to the nature of its party politics, the Lithuanian system has not been conducive to the development of a stable two-party system.[9] As will be discussed further on, the multi-party system was made more complex by the entrance of new populist parties in the early- and mid-2000s and the subsequent swift disappearance of some of their leaders from the political scene following a series of raucous political scandals.[10]

During the first years of independence this institutional multipolarity was somewhat compensated by a certain balance between two dominant parties representing the post-Communist (mainly the LDLP) and anti-Communist (mainly Sajudis/Homeland Union/Conservative) groupings. Starting in the mid-to-late 1990s, this divide starts to be replaced by one between these established parties (LDLP and Homeland Union) and, on the other hand, populist newcomers with often weakly institutionalized party structures (Rolandas Paksas, Viktor Uspaskich, and to a lesser extent Artūras Paulauskas); a complicated and unstable web of coalitions and divisions between parties ensues.[11]

As a result of these factors, in most or all elections after independence no single party performed well enough as to form a government on its own. Between 2006 and 2008 in particular, a minority ruling coalition was established, led by the LSDP, without participation by the party holding the largest number of seats in the Seimas, the Labour Party.[12]

In addition to differences in the formal political system, one central difference between the Lithuanian case and the others analysed in this book is that while in one of the cases (Belarus) the person at the top of the policy making structure did not change between 1994 and 2010, and in the other (Ukraine), there were only two major political changes (Yushchenko's Orange Revolution of 2004 and Yanukovich's election as president in 2010), in the case of Lithuania there was much more fluidity in terms of both leaders (President and Seimas) and of dominant political parties. Such unstable coalition politics continued, in various shapes and forms, for much of the period under study.

Informal Level: No Party of Power, Less Possibilities for Clientelism

One of the consequences of Lithuania's formal institutional arrangement, with its multiple centers of real power, has been that the monopolization and use of administrative resources by any one dominant political actor, as seen in Ukraine or Belarus, has been much more difficult. As noted by Kimitaka Matsuzato and Liutaras Gudžinskas, the Lithuanian elite's inability to control votes, in contrast to their counterparts in most CIS states,[13] reduced the possibilities for clientelism, and also made the consolidation of a party of power as seen in countries such as Ukraine nearly impossible.[14] While a certain degree of patronage politics has undoubtedly been present in Lithuania, the crucial difference is that no single actor had the power to control large-scale administrative resources.

The policy making effects of Lithuania's fragmented political system could be summarized as follows: longstanding fractious coalition governments increased the danger of continuous delays in policy making. In many ways, this was a similar situation to that seen in Ukraine under Kuchma, but with one crucial difference: whereas in the Ukrainian case the lack of natural majorities in the Rada could be overcome by President Kuchma's strong informal powers and his ability to use them to create situational coalitions, no Lithuanian president or PM had similar powers at his or her disposal. Moreover, in the case of Lithuania the frequent inroads made by populist parties may have created a threat to effective government by the very nature of their orientation. Despite these threats, such instability had limited costs given a "broad policy consensus in favor of an open economy and pro-Western foreign policy."[15]

Political System and the Institutional Setting of Energy Policy Making

Lithuania's constitutional system also affected the institutional setting for energy policy making. On the basis of 1995's Law on Energy, the Seimas is responsible for setting the main outlines of energy policy; it approves the National Energy Strategy and a five-year strategy implementation plan developed by the Cabinet of Ministers.[16] In day-to-day practice, however, the lion's share of energy policy decisions was made at the ministerial level, for most of the period under study the Ministry of Economy. This prominent role of the Ministry helped moderate the instability associated with the fractious dynamics of coalition governments as discussed previously.

The special role of the Ministry of Energy was already noted in 1995's Law on Energy, but by 1996 the Ministry had been dissolved and made into a subdivision within the new Ministry of Economy.[17] In January 2009, following the Conservative/Homeland Union victory in the parliamentary elections, a separate Ministry of Energy was reestablished. This was a result of the higher priority given to the energy question by the Conservative/Homeland Union party as a response to the negative changes in Lithuania's external energy environment since 2006 (discussed further on) and of the perceived need to get a firmer grip on important energy projects that, despite much discussion, had been slow to move to implementation in the previous years.

Lithuania's Management of its Energy Dependency – The Track Record

Four main periods can be distinguished in Lithuania's management of its energy dependency: from independence to 1996, 1996 to 2004, 2004 to 2006, and the period starting in 2006.

Independence to 1996: Goal-oriented Infrastructure Building

Lithuania's energy situation at the time of independence was characterized by four main elements: high reliance on nuclear power, the existence of large excess electricity-producing capacities, low levels of energy efficiency, and high levels of dependency on energy imports from Russia (ca. 70 percent in 1990).[18]

Lithuania got a taste of its energy vulnerability and of the kind of pressure it would have to face as an independent state even while still officially part of the USSR: in April of 1990, after its declaration of independence, it faced a three-month oil blockade from Moscow intended to dissuade Lithuanian leaders from continuing on the path to independence.[19] Although the blockade may have succeeded in the short term (leading to a six-month moratorium of the independence declaration in exchange for the lifting of the blockade), it also strengthened the political elite's understanding of energy policy as a crucial national issue, and its resolve to seek a multi-party consensus on reducing the country's energy vulnerability vis-à-vis Russia – something we do not see in Belarus or Ukraine until much later. Such consensus was also part of a broader consensus on the need to take whatever measures would be necessary in order to rejoin Europe as soon as possible.[20]

1992–1993: DIVERSIFICATION BY SHOCK

Part of the reduction in Lithuania's energy vulnerability came simply as a result of the price and supply shock of 1992–1993: in the space of two years, Lithuania's energy supply and consumption was drastically reduced. (After 1993, however, it remained relatively stable).[21] Such large reductions were not, at this point, the result of increases in energy efficiency, but of steep price increases, of the bankruptcy faced by many industrial enterprises resulting from the general economic contraction during this period,[22] and especially in 1991, of unilateral reductions in Russian supplies. Compared with Ukraine and Belarus, this reduction was much more sudden, with the country's TPES more than halving between 1991 and 1994 (see Table 6.1).

The rise in import prices was felt soon after independence. By 1993, Lithuania was paying an estimated $80–$85 per tcm of gas, not including transit fees.[23] In contrast with Ukraine and Belarus, where gas prices were liberalized, even partially, much later than those of oil and oil products, in Lithuania gas and oil prices started moving towards average European levels at generally the same time, with the implication that in Lithuania a sharp upward price pressure specifically on gas was felt much earlier than in Ukraine or Belarus.[24] The smaller increase in import prices for oil as compared to gas may be explained by the fact that, in the case of oil, Lithuania played a value-added role as provider of services (such as refining in Mazeikiu Nafta) to Russian oil companies in exchange for oil supplies. By 1993 Lithuania – as well the other Baltic States – had lost most of their energy price privileges from Russia.[25]

One of the responses to import price increases was the deregulation, by 1992, of prices for gasoline and most oil products. Soon afterwards, residential gas and electricity prices were increased and equalized with industrial ones, but district heating (mainly gas generated) and heating oil continued to be heavily subsidized.[26] At the same time, some basic energy reforms such as the unbundling of electricity production, transmission, and distribution, were not accomplished during this period.[27]

STRENGTHENING CONTROL OVER NUCLEAR POWER
GENERATION AS AN ENERGY ALTERNATIVE

It was the nuclear energy area that saw the most proactive policy initiatives in the immediate post-independence period. Although the Ignalina NPP, whose two reactors were commissioned in 1983 and 1987, was not intended by Soviet planners as a contribution to *Lithuania's* energy security and independence, but to the electricity supply of the whole northwest region of the USSR, once Lithuania acquired independence it became an important factor in the country's search for increased energy independence. The issue was not so much one of increasing Ignalina's output, but of preserving its existing capacity at an economically difficult time, and making it work for Lithuania's, not Russia's, energy needs – not a trivial question considering the fact that the NPP had long been administered from Moscow, that as of 1991, it was manned by an almost exclusively Russian crew, and that Russia could be expected to use energy as a means of political pressure.[28]

The Lithuanian government made it a priority to retain Ignalina's technical personnel and to prevent it from becoming a pawn of Russian pressure, and measures to the effect were swiftly implemented. Thus in the fall of 1991, Ignalina employees, most of whom came from Russia or where ethnic Russians from other Soviet republics, were offered immediate citizenship and job stability, as well as competitive salaries.[29] Ignalina's director Viktor Shevaldin, an ethnic Russian, was retained in his position and was given a vote of confidence by the Energy Minister when enmeshed in a tax scandal in 1996; he remained director of the NPP until its closing in 2009.

Although Lithuania was unable to break its dependence on Russian nuclear fuel (the fuel used by the RBMK-type Ignalina reactor was produced only in Russia), it was able to significantly diversify Ignalina's technical support structure – especially with Swedish assistance – so that it could continue functioning even without Russian support. This was crucial considering the fact that, as discussed in chapter 2, Ignalina had been built and, until the early 1990s, continued to operate virtually without Lithuanian participation. Ignalina's role must be seen in the context of one of Lithuania's most important inheritances from the Soviet period: the excess of electricity-generation capacity compared to domestic consumption, to which Ignalina made a significant contribution, for most of the 1994–2004 period accounting for about 80 percent of Lithuania's electricity production. To an even greater extent than Ukraine or Belarus, Lithuania's Soviet-era energy infrastructure was heavily oriented towards exports to other Soviet republics, making its situation "in its essence without analogy in any country."[30] So paradoxically, despite its heavy dependence on Russia for primary energy sources, for most of the late-Soviet and post-Soviet period Lithuania was a large electricity exporter.[31] Such a situation provided Lithuania with additional instruments to deal with its energy dependency, but also created additional problems.

In and of itself the existence of a large electricity surplus is not enough as a counterweight to energy dependency. It does not solve the issue of primary fuel supply, as the need for (imported) fuel, in this case nuclear fuel, remains; it is not always possible to substitute electricity easily for other types of energy commonly used in the transport and industrial sector; and, in addition to the difficulty of adjusting NPP electricity outputs to fluctuations in demand, once generated, electricity is very difficult to store. Despite the important step of expanding a pumped storage unit (the Kruonis Pumped Storage Plant) in 1994, storage issues in particular limited the foreign trade benefits of Lithuania's large tradable electricity surplus.[32] Lacking a connection with EU electricity networks, Lithuania's electricity export and import possibilities still depended on transit facilities provided by Russia's largest electricity company, RAO UES, limiting its ability to export this electricity in an economically advantageous way.[33] These conditions continued to largely hold true until Ignalina's full closure in 2009.

Despite these limitations, Lithuania could use Ignalina's large generating capacity indirectly in the management of its energy dependency, especially during the deep decrease in energy supplies from Russia in the 1991–1993 period. By maintaining electricity production levels but reducing exports, Lithuania was able to rely on Ignalina for a significant part of its domestic electricity needs, thus reducing its vulnerability during this period.[34]

Behind the de facto nationalization of the nuclear energy sector, however, was an even more crucial development: the fundamental turn around, both in public opinion and elite-level policy, concerning the desirability of nuclear power. If in the late 1980s and early 1990s the struggle against nuclear power, mainly associated with Soviet control and the Chernobyl accident, was a powerful unifying factor in the national and independence movement, by the time Lithuania gained independence in 1991, these same leaders, many of whom owed the growth of their authority exactly to their leadership in the anti-nuclear campaign, quickly turned around and sought to remove the question from public debate.[35] Thus nuclear power changed from being seen as a personification of Soviet imperial control over Lithuania, to being seen as a guarantee of the country's independence.

OIL INFRASTRUCTURE DIVERSIFICATION

Together with nuclear power, some of the swiftest policy responses aimed at reducing Lithuania's energy vulnerability were seen in the oil sector. The aims were twofold: first, establishing fuel-loading port facilities that could be used in case of an interruption in pipeline oil supplies from Russia, and second, strengthening Lithuania's role in the oil value-added chain for its main supplier, Russia – from mainly an end-consumer to a full participant in refining and transit – in order to increase its bargaining power in the relationship.

The Butinge Oil Terminal, independent Lithuania's first large-scale infrastructure-development project, aimed at pursuing both goals named previously. Started in 1995 and completed in 1999 and complemented by the mid-1990s by the modernization of the Klaipeda Oil Products Terminal, it would allow Lithuania to receive large quantities of crude oil via tanker – most importantly, oil shipped from the West by sea, crucial in case of an oil blockade from Russia – something it was previously unable to do. As the terminal would also be able to handle large-scale oil transhipment for export, Butinge could strengthen Lithuania's role in the Russian oil and oil products exports value-added chain. As loading figures indicate, this strategy was at least partially successful during the period up to 2003.[36]

The relatively swift completion of the Butinge project reflects a level of consensus and governmental proactivity hardly seen in Lithuania after that. Such determination is especially clear considering the significant cost of the project (estimated at between $260 million and $300 million), the fact that it siphoned government resources away from other important areas, and the opposition it faced.[37] The determination to keep Butinge and Klaipeda under national control was also seen in the treatment of possible Russian investments. Although Russian companies (first and foremost LUKoil) attempted to obtain a majority share in both projects, the Lithuanian government rejected this plan, fearing even partial Russian ownership would compromise the terminals' national security role.[38] In hindsight, however, it is clear that Butinge's impact was not so much in terms of Lithuania's day-to-day management of its energy dependency, but in terms of guaranteeing *emergency* oil supplies, as happened during the post-2006 stoppage of oil supplies from Russia via the Druzhba pipeline. Lacking the economic means – or the political will to make this a priority – to buy Western oil shipped by tanker instead of less expensive Russian oil shipped via pipeline, the terminal ended up being largely used in a reverse direction, for the export of Russian oil west. While such reversed use increased Lithuania's role in its main supplier's value-added chain, this, many would argue, actually helped consolidate the presence of Russian capital in the Lithuanian energy sector.[39]

In addition, the Lithuanian government also pursued *contractual diversification* in oil during this period, by securing a diversity of oil supply contracts with Russian suppliers – in addition to main supplier LUKoil, contracts were secured with other suppliers from several regions of Russia, as well as US-owned Mobil, at the time producing in Russia.[40] Although this oil came solely from Russia, it was diversified in a contractual sense.

Of all the geographical and energy-mix diversification options considered during this period, however, by 1996 the only one that had proven economically viable was the purchase of Orimulsion (a bitumen-based fuel able to replace heavy oil in power plants) from Venezuela.[41] This allowed Lithuania to modestly reduce its consumption of heavy oil (*mazut*) used in power-plants; however, given Orimulsion's poor ecological record, it was never a sustainable long-term option.

GAS

At the time of independence, Lithuania's gas supply situation was especially problematic, as it not only received all of its gas from Russia, but through only one pipeline (traversing via Belarus), increasing its vulnerability to interruptions in Russian supplies.[42] Despite the good intentions of the first post-independence years, gas diversification turned out to be a much more difficult challenge than oil diversification. Although the use of LNG technology would become an increasingly realistic option in later years, in the early 1990s its high cost excluded it as an economically competitive alternative. The rather modest results in the gas area as compared to oil had to do with the nature of the good (as gas diversification involves much larger structural investments than oil, which can be transported more competitively through rail and tanker), as well as with the situation in Russia and the different levels of state control over the two areas. While the gas sector was almost totally monopolized by Gazprom at this time, during this same period there were several Russian oil companies Lithuania could negotiate with.

REDUCING AND RESTRUCTURING OF THE ENERGY DEBT VIS-À-VIS RUSSIA

In addition to pursuing a proactive policy in the oil and nuclear areas, Lithuania engaged in a concentrated effort to limit energy indebtedness vis-à-vis Russia. This was pursued by instituting a low-tolerance policy towards domestic energy arrears[43] and by the restructuring of energy debts away from direct debt to Russia and into domestic bonds and international debt obligations. Thus, a 1996 restructuring was able to reduce Lithuania's energy debt from $60 million to about $20 million.[44] Stabilizing the energy debt to Russia was very significant given the experience of other CIS countries, whose indebtedness was used repeatedly as means of pressure for the sale of energy infrastructure as payment for energy debts.

1991–1996: A BALANCE

Despite the stark changes in economic policy throughout this period, there was significant continuity in energy policy, most evident in the commitment to the building up of an oil diversification infrastructure. Many of the energy policies put in place during this period followed – although at a slower pace than originally planned – the original plans for transformation of the sector as laid out by Energy Minister

Algimantas Stasiukynas (1993–1995) at the beginning of his term.[45] Contrary to the expectation that a government led by post-communists would pursue a more pro-Russian energy policy, and the Conservative Party a more Western-oriented one, many pro-diversification measures were actually put into place by the former communists during the first half of Brazauskas' 1993–1998 presidency, when the Seimas was also controlled by his party, the LDLP. These measures, such as the passing of Lithuania's first energy law, the establishment of an energy price regulation agency,[46] and the partial privatization of some government-owned energy enterprises, passed despite the often vocal disagreement of the opposition, were crucial for Lithuania's reestablishment of policy making control over the energy sphere.

1997–2004: Politicized Privatization and the Stalling of Real Diversification

By 1997, Lithuania's original diversification push had waned and new, large-scale diversification initiatives became rarer. While diversification remained official policy, the events of the following seven years would de facto hamper and delay the diversification effort.

Following, we analyse 1997–2004 developments as they took place in four main areas: infrastructure development, measures aimed at strengthening Lithuania's counter-power in the energy trade relationship, measures aimed at complying with EU admission criteria, and measures affecting the contractual side of Lithuania's relationship with its main supplier, Russia.

INFRASTRUCTURE DEVELOPMENT MEASURES

Although few high-profile infrastructure projects were completed during this period, one achievement was crucial: gaining real access to the Incukalns gas storage facility in Latvia, an important emergency-preparedness asset given Lithuania's lack of gas storage facilities in its territory.[47] However, the use of Inculkans as an element of real energy counterweight to buffer seasonal peaks in gas demand was limited by the fact that most of the gas stored there was owned by Gazprom, which had an operating contract on the facility going until 2017.[48]

During this period a number of other major infrastructure projects were discussed, in particular the building of electricity and gas connections with Poland, stated as a goal in the 2002 National Energy

Strategy.[49] However, these projects did not make it to the planning or implementation stage during this period.

MEASURES AIMED AT STRENGTHENING LITHUANIA'S COUNTERPOWER
IN THE ENERGY TRADE RELATIONSHIP

If building a new, diversification-oriented transit infrastructure presented difficult challenges, Lithuania sought to use existing infrastructure to expand its own role in Russia's value-added chain and its associated counterpower in the relationship with its main supplier.

This was especially clear in Lithuania's management of its gatekeeper role in the transit of Russian energy and other goods to the Kaliningrad exclave.[50] Lithuania sought to retain this leverage by seeking to maintain or increase gas transit volumes to the region – despite a fall in gas transit volumes in the early 1990s, these started to recover quickly in the early and mid 2000s.[51] In a related arrangement, Lithuania provided electricity to Kaliningrad and, in exchange, received nuclear fuel from Russia. During this period, Lithuania also sought to link the question of electricity exports to Kaliningrad (which in the early 2000s imported ca. 95 percent of its electricity from Lithuania) to broader issues in the energy relationship with Russia.[52]

Lithuania saw its role in gas transit to the Kaliningrad region as an important element of its own power vis-à-vis Russia, as a virtual guarantee against a possible Russian gas embargo, as any interruption in supplies to Lithuania would also affect Kaliningrad.[53] Yet there were important limitations to Lithuania's ability to use this transit role, as actual control over the pipeline to Kaliningrad was largely held by Gazprom. Thus Lithuania's self-image as gas gatekeeper may have been more a "psychological self-trick" than a reality.[54]

In addition, Lithuania sought to expand its role as a transit country for Russian gas exports by actively promoting the idea of the building of a gas pipeline from Russia to WE going through the Baltic States and Poland (Amber Pipeline). In the early 1990s, during the early stages of negotiations with Gazprom on the privatization of state gas company Lietuvos Dujos (LD), it also sought to include an agreement on the building of an additional gas pipeline to Kaliningrad (part of the Amber Pipeline transiting further into Poland and WE) as part of the agreement.[55] Lithuanian hopes were high, as such a pipeline, if fully used, would have provided Lithuania with additional transit income, increased security of supplies (as it would have added a second gas import pipeline), and additional leverage in its relationship with Gazprom by making it a transit country, not only to Kaliningrad, but also to WE.[56] However, Gazprom refused the request; later on, as Russia's planning of the Nord Stream pipeline (to which the Amber Pipeline would have been an alternative) started to move forward, hopes for the project were dashed.

In the oil area, during this period Lithuania sought to strengthen its counterpower in the relationship by strengthening the role of the Mazeikiu Nafta refinery in the indirect transit of oil products, an issue directly related to the question of the contractual management of the energy dependency relationship, which we discuss later in this section.

MEASURES TO COMPLY WITH EU ADMISSION REQUIREMENTS
ALSO AFFECTING THE MANAGEMENT OF ENERGY DEPENDENCY

The 1997–2004 period was marked by Lithuania's negotiations on EU admission, negotiations that had an important impact on energy policy, especially in terms of regulatory policy and nuclear issues. The year 1997 was a watershed, as the government stopped the large-scale subsidization of most energy prices, including household gas, heating, and electricity prices. An independent National Control Commission for Prices and Energy (NCCPE), established that year, was empowered to set – using technical and economic means but not political principles – prices for those types of energy where, due to lack of competition, free-market prices could not exist (electricity, district heating, hot water, and natural gas).

A Law on Gas (2001) and Law on Electricity (2002) were passed as a way to assure the implementation of the EU's Electricity and Gas Directives, the gist of which concerned the opening of markets and nondiscriminatory Third Party Access to hitherto monopolized systems. As a result of the 2001 Law on Gas and subsequent amendments, from 2000 to 2007 Lithuania saw a gradual opening of its gas market, increasing the type and number of gas consumers that became, at least theoretically (see further on), eligible to choose a supplier freely. The unbundling of the national electricity company Lietuvos Energija (into separate generation, transmission, and distribution companies) also took place in 2002.[57]

The most crucial issue of debate with the EU concerned the future of the Ignalina NPP. With the closing of Ignalina a non-negotiable condition for accession,[58] in 2002 an agreement was reached with the EU as to the closing of its first reactor by 2005 and the second in 2009. This decision was part of Lithuania's National Energy Strategy, approved in 2002, but with accession a priority, little of the needed homework was completed either before the decision was taken, or in terms of preparing Lithuania's energy system for life after Ignalina's full decommissioning in 2009. After the signing of the agreement, the Lithuanian government increasingly started to challenge the EU on this matter, especially on the closing of Ignalina's second block, scheduled for 2009. Some of the reasons for Lithuania's insistence vis-à-vis the EU – issues that had remained largely undiscussed before the agreement was signed – had to do with fear that, after the closing of Ignalina's second block, dependency on Russian gas would increase significantly given Ignalina's large role in Lithuania's energy supply (ca. 27 percent in the 2005–2007 period).[59] As discussed previously, however, despite its important role in power generation, nuclear power did not solve the problem of energy dependency on Russia, as the fuel used in Ignalina's RBMK-type reactor is produced only in Russia. On the contrary, by providing a relatively easy answer to the problem of energy security, Ignalina's large generation capacities sheltered Lithuania from the need to engage in a proactive search for new energy links and sources.[60]

Lithuania's misunderstanding with the EU concerning Ignalina's future is representative of broader problems in the relationship: while accession negotiations prompted steps towards the implementation of EU energy efficiency and other guidelines, the actual policy impact was limited not only by disagreements on the future of nuclear power, but by the very way EU regulations were transposed to the local context. As noted by Tomas Janeliūnas when discussing the 2007 National Energy Strategy, "some strategic objectives ... appear as if copied from official EU documents without specific considerations about the Lithuanian situation."[61]

CONTRACTUAL DIVERSIFICATION AND CONTRACTUAL MANAGEMENT

As discussed in chapter 1 of this book, contractual diversification (and in a broader sense, contractual management) can be an important means of managing energy dependency, in particular dependency on a single supplier, by either spreading risk through a variety of contract types and time frames, and/or by using contractual means to regulate the relationship. In the case of Lithuania, such contractual management played an important role in energy policy in the 1997–2004 period, through the privatization of Lithuania's most important energy companies, the Mazeikiu Nafta (MN) refinery and the national gas company

Lietuvos Dujos; the period 1997–2004 is largely signed by both drawn-out sagas. As the account presented in the next pages will make clear, however well-intended, the way these two privatization processes actually came to pass would as much help set back as further real energy diversification.

The Three Privatizations of Mazeikiu Nafta

Mazeikiu Nafta, the sole oil refinery in the Baltic States, is Lithuania's largest enterprise, providing about 25 percent of the country's tax income for most of the post-independence period. From the time of its commissioning in 1980 to its first privatization in 1999, the refinery's fate was closely tied to LUKoil, the company's operator and main supplier until the early 1990s, contributing to the LUKoil management's belief that it had a certain "historical right" to it.[62]

"DON'T LET IVAN CLOSE TO THE PIPE!"[63]: THE CONSERVATIVE
GOVERNMENT AND THE FIRST MN PRIVATIZATION, 1997–2002
Privatizing MN emerged as the key energy policy priority of the mid-late 1990s as a result of both practical and political considerations. Reflecting the situation faced by all oil-poor post-Soviet states, the end of Soviet-era ties and the resulting erratic crude oil supplies from Russia had plunged MN into a deep crisis. The idea of privatizing it to a Western company was dearly held and supported by the conservative government in the 1997–1998 period. With the normally highly profitable refinery at the brink of bankruptcy in the mid and late 1990s, partially as a result of repeated oil supply interruptions from Russia, and partially as a result of the widespread criminal activity surrounding the company during this period, many believed that the company should not under any circumstances be sold to a Russian company.[64] Instead, the ideal was privatizing to a US company, with the double goals of, first, as famously put by then-Economics Minister Vincas Babilius, "not to let Ivan [get] close to the pipe,"[65] and second, to get the United States more deeply invested in guaranteeing Lithuania's energy security, something many assumed would happen once a large US investment would be in place in the country. The Conservative Party's a priori goal to privatize MN specifically to a US company affected the timing and transparency of the process; direct negotiations with US oil company Williams International were started in July 1998 without seriously pursuing other investors.[66]

MN's privatization to Williams benefitted from little of the national consensus enjoyed by earlier energy projects such as Butinge. The strongest opposition came from Brazauskas' LSDP, which argued repeatedly that Williams could not guarantee the necessary oil supplies. The LSDP's authority on the issue was weakened, however, by widespread rumors of personal connections between Brazauskas and LUKoil; it is widely believed that the LSDP's campaign in the October 2000 parliamentary elections was funded largely by Vaizga, an oil trading company tied to LUKoil.[67] Strong resistance came not only from the opposition, but also from the very top of the government itself, especially from Paksas after his appointment as PM in May 1999.[68] President Valdas Adamkus ultimately turned against the sale, but the process went ahead anyway because it was supported by the Conservative Party, at this time in control of the Seimas, and especially by the economics minister and PM at the start of the process, Vincas Babilius, and Gediminas Vagnorius, respectively. By the time the agreement was signed, a new PM, Paksas, was in office but resigned soon afterwards, together with his whole Cabinet (on 27 October 1999) in disapproval of the agreement. Paksas left the Conservative Party shortly thereafter, first joining the Liberal Union and in 2002 creating a new party, the Liberal Democratic Party.[69]

MN was sold to Williams in 1999; by 2002, it was a failed entity. Although the politicized way in which MN's privatization was conducted contributed seriously to its ultimate failure, a number of other negative circumstances also played a role: the poor economic health of the refinery, the 1998 Russian crisis, and declining oil prices, which reduced the refinery's profits and made some of the guarantees offered by the Lithuanian government kick in. These factors made it difficult for the government to fetch a high price for MN at the time of the sale, forced it to offer generous guarantees to Williams, and contributed to the ultimate failure of the enterprise.

These factors synergized with LUKoil's pressure, which was felt at all stages of the privatization process.[70] Its veiled threat to cut oil supplies should the company be sold to Williams, as well as the recent history of erratic supplies, made Williams more aware of the risks it was incurring and prompted it to raise its minimum requirements for the deal, including generous clauses intended to protect it in case of a worst case scenario. As a result of the factors discussed previously, much of this worst case scenario turned into reality, and the Lithuanian state was left with no choice but to compensate Williams for much of the loss, calculated at about $200 million–$365 million.[71] Unable to work profitably because of the irregular supplies, Williams left in 2002.

If the economic costs of the MN–Williams fiasco were high, perhaps even more so were the political costs it claimed. While the first political effect of the scandal was PM Paksas' October 1999 protest resignation over the deal,[72] it is hard to imagine Paksas as a victim in this issue: his authority and popularity as a populist leader increased significantly as a result of his uncompromising stance on the Williams case. As noted by prominent energy analyst and long-term director of the Lithuanian Energy Institute Jurgis Vilemas, "anyone who fought against Williams' entrance to Lithuania received significant political dividends in the [October 2000] elections. This form of public relations became one of the most effective means of entering big politics."[73] The politicians who most clearly benefited from this wave of public disappointment were the same who would shortly thereafter, as populist leaders, mount a strong challenge to the Lithuanian political system as it had developed since independence; without doubt, their standing grew vastly as a result of the Williams' fiasco. Thus, it could be argued that Williams' failure, while not in itself a direct cause of the rise of populism in Lithuania – the real cause being the high social costs of transition for some social groups – nevertheless contributed to its electoral success at exactly this time. Thus, while Williams' failure provided loses rather than profits that could be recycled into the electoral process, the political capital acquired by anti-Williams politicians, and its impact on the 2000 elections, should not be underestimated.

THE SECOND PRIVATIZATION OF MN (TO YUKOS)

As Williams' failure became increasingly obvious, Williams and the Lithuanian government sought to find a way out of the situation. Despite LUKoil's ability to supply MN and many Lithuanian politicians' longstanding links with LUKoil, given its own sabotaging of the refinery's operations, a sale to that company was not acceptable to large segments of the population and the Seimas. Yukos, at this point Russia's second largest oil company, appeared as a more broadly acceptable alternative. Accounting for nearly 20 percent of total Russian oil production in the early 2000s, the company also brought to the table its presumed independence from the Russian government, especially in contrast with LUKoil.

Paksas reappeared as an important player at this moment, when he returned to the position of PM following the October 2000 parliamentary elections, disapproving of the agreement with Yukos. Yet, politically weakened by his confrontation with Seimas speaker Paulauskas (formally his partner in the New Politics coalition that controlled the Seimas from October 2000 to June 2001), he was unable to prevent the agreement; his second resignation as PM, in June 2001, came shortly before the agreement was to be signed.[74] In July 2002, Yukos bought 26.85 percent of the refinery, and in October, an additional 26.85 percent,[75] committing to supply MN for ten years in exchange for being allowed to export crude oil directly through the Butinge terminal.

LUKoil's defeat vis-á-vis Yukos in the MN bid had important domestic implications. In particular, it further alienated LUKoil's Lithuanian allies, in particular Paksas. The sale also had foreign policy implications, as the Kremlin found it much more difficult to use the company for the pursuit of foreign policy goals than had been the case with Gazprom, Transneft, or LUKoil.

THE THIRD PRIVATIZATION OF MN (TO PKN ORLEN)
The Yukos solution proved short-lived, as the company's very existence came under threat as a result of the Russian state's decision to liquidate its assets in the wake of a major tax and political scandal centred on its CEO Khodorkovskii. Yukos, in urgent need of cash to pay its growing tax bill, responded by agreeing to sell its package of shares (53.7 percent) in MN.[76]

Thus in 2006, a new tender was announced and the third privatization of MN began. The process was highly controversial from the very beginning, with important political groups warning that the refinery should not be sold to either of the two wholly or partially Russian- owned bidders, LUKoil or TNK-BP, leaving only Kazakhstan's KazMunaiGaz and Poland's PKN Orlen as realistic options. In May 2006 a preliminary decision was made to sell to PKN Orlen. Russian pressure could be felt throughout the process: when an accident interrupted oil supplies in July of 2006, Russia's Transneft, in charge of the pipeline, did little to repair it in a timely manner, thus giving Lithuania a taste of what could happen (no oil supplies from Russia via pipeline) should the refinery be sold to the wrong company. A costly fire at the refinery in October 2006 – where many presumed to see Russia's hand – and Russia's excessive foot-dragging on the question of subsequent repairs made many see the Kremlin trying to bully Lithuania into selling to LUKoil.[77] A more accurate understanding would be to see these events as indeed messages, but first and foremost to PKN Orlen as a potential buyer, by trying to scare it into withdrawing from the bid.[78] Although Russian courts, having ordered the liquidation of Yukos' assets, tried to prevent the company from selling its shares to PKN Orlen, the sale became official in December 2006. The refinery continued to work but, given the Druzhba showdown, had to import Russian oil by tanker via Butinge, instead of less expensively by pipeline.[79] As a result, the refinery's profitability declined seriously, from about $319 million in 2005 to a loss of $34.4 million in 2009.[80] Yet what was lost was much more than the refinery's profits: Lithuania's role in the value-added chain of its main supplier, Russia, was significantly reduced.

Lietuvos Dujos: Privatization Without Diversification

A second important element of Lithuania's contractual management during this period concerned the privatization of Lithuania's national gas company LD. Although a governmental goal since 2000, protracted wavering on the form this privatization should take delayed its completion until 2004.

At least three versions of the privatization proposal were discussed. At the start of the process, in 2000, talk was of privatizing only 30–35 percent of LD's shares, with the state keeping the rest, a proposal widely criticized as not going far enough.[81] A year later, a number of politicians and energy-related businessmen proposed earmarking a set percentage of shares for private Lithuanian capital.[82] (Curiously, the argument of Gazprom's local allies was that domestic capital should be included in order to defend Lithuanian interests vis-à-vis the Russian company, a suspicious proposition given their close ties to Gazprom.[83]) A third version of the privatization proposal – and the one ultimately pursued – involved earmarking a set percentage of shares to a Western strategic investor, a gas supplier, and the Lithuanian state.

The decision on the privatization formula to be used was finally approved in October 2001 after Brazauskas became PM following Paksas' resignation. The proposal on domestic investors failed thanks to strong opposition from the centre-right coalition controlling the Seimas at the time, which feared it could be used by Gazprom and its intermediary companies to gain control of the company. Following the pattern used in Estonia, Latvia, and elsewhere in Central and Eastern Europe,[84] it was agreed that 34 percent of the shares would go to a Western strategic investor, 34 percent to a gas supplier and about 24 percent to the Lithuanian state.[85] For each of the parties, special requirements were established; for example, a single foreign company was prohibited from both holding a majority stake in an energy company and simultaneously being its main supplier, a condition evidently composed with Gazprom in mind.[86]

The debate on LD took place at a time of crisis in the Lithuanian political system, reflected in the deep loss of votes of the two major parties, the LSDP and the Homeland Union. In the October 2000 parliamentary elections two new, populist-related parties (the Social Liberals/New Union and the Lithuanian Liberal Union) made the strongest showing.[87] President Adamkus sought to counter the perceived threat by creating a broad centrist coalition (New Politics), of which Paksas (Liberal Union), offered the PM position by the president, became the head. Paulauskas of the Social Liberals/New Union became speaker of the Seimas. Although some saw this coalition as an attempt by President Adamkus to neutralize populist elements by incorporating them into the political elite,[88] the coalition was rather tenuous from the very start, and its ultimate collapse in June 2001 – around disagreements on MN – contributed to the further delay of LD's privatization.

LD's privatization was further complicated by disagreements between the main coalition partners, especially on the possible earmarking of a set of shares for domestic investors, favoured by Paulaskas' Social Liberals and opposed by Paksas' Liberal Union.[89] The path to the final decision on the modality of privatization was fraught with complications, threats to the coalition, and opportunities for outside influence.

RUSSIAN ACTORS AND THE LD PRIVATIZATION: FORMAL AND INFORMAL PRESSURE

From the very beginning of LD's privatization there was, in practice, only one possible contender for the supplier package of shares: Gazprom.[90] This lack of competition undoubtedly reduced the company's sale price. Gazprom clearly took advantage of its power as Lithuania's sole gas supplier, repeatedly stating that, should it not find the privatization conditions acceptable, it would simply not participate. Should this have happened, it would have meant that Gazprom would sidestep LD and sell all of its gas through affiliated intermediary companies (discussed further on) at higher, possibly unregulated, prices, and directly to large buyers, making LD largely irrelevant in Lithuanian gas trade.[91] This in fact is what Gazprom did in 2001, when it directed 75 percent of its gas exports to Lithuania through intermediary companies or direct sales to large consumers, making LD, with only a 25 percent share of the market, largely irrelevant.[92]

LD'S PRIVATIZATION: GAZPROM'S GAINS AND NEW ROLE

Through the tactics discussed previously, Gazprom was able to negotiate an especially low price for its 34 percent package of shares in LD, as well as additional advantages through other clauses of the contract.[93] Central to these additional clauses was the question of gas price formation, and of what part of Gazprom-supplied gas would be subject to which kind of price regulation by the Lithuanian energy price regulatory agency, the NCCPE. One side of the issue had to do with the terms of gas pricing for gas sold to LD; a second and more interesting side of the question concerned gas supplies and price regulation for gas sold outside of LD, an issue closely related to the role of Gazprom-affiliated intermediary companies such as Dujotekana. Gazprom made its acceptance of the privatization agreement conditional on two related conditions: that it should be allowed to sell 30 percent of its gas through structures outside LD, and that there should be, in addition to a regulated market, also a nonregulated market for "free consumers." Gazprom repeatedly insisted on a point not related to its official interests in the deal: that not all its gas exports to Lithuania should go through LD, and that other gas importers (de facto meaning only Dujotekana, as no other similar companies existed) be allowed to charge a much higher markup on gas imports than LD.[94] Gazprom's proactive lobbying for the legal existence and profit-making rights of Dujotekana in the midst of negotiations on the privatization of LD was impressive, especially considering the point was not related to its official interests in the LD privatization deal.

The LD privatization contract reflected Gazprom's requirement that it be contractually bound to sell to LD only 70 percent of its gas sold in Lithuania;[95] this gas could be sold at no more than a 15 percent markup. But volumes above this 70 percent – in practice, mostly gas sold through Dujotekana – were not subject to any limit on the markup applied, creating a large potential source of profits. This also meant that free consumers – that is, those not necessarily supplied by LD – would not pay regulated prices, but unregulated, "free" prices. Considering that the totality of gas supplied to Lithuania came from Gazprom; that is, that there was no real competitive gas market in Lithuania, the idea of free or market prices basically meant Dujotekana's ability to sell gas to these consumers at its chosen, significantly higher price.[96] Despite the pitfalls involved, from a short-term perspective, leading Lithuanian politicians, however, probably found this type of contractual concession to Gazprom more desirable – in public relations terms – than further lowering the price of Gazprom's share package, as a lower price would be much more of a red flag to suspicious voters, than more obscure provisions concerning gas market regulations.

What were the reasons behind Gazprom's lobbying for Dujotekana? At first glance, two: the desire to avoid price controls on gas exported to Lithuania (as Dujotekana would be allowed to charge a much higher markup on gas imports than LD), and the desire to maintain additional levers of influence in the Lithuanian gas market. Not obvious at first glance but nevertheless important, guaranteeing Dujotekana's existence may also have been important in terms of Gazprom – with the support of other Russian actors – being able to use gas supplies for political purposes.

1997–2004: A BALANCE

Instead of a continuation of high-cost diversification infrastructure projects, the 1997–2004 period was characterized by a series of relatively low-key developments that, when taken together, would play a significant role in the management of energy dependency. While the privatization of MN and LD was an essential precondition for the moving forward of economic reforms and for the broader reorientation of the Lithuanian economy towards the West, a look at the actual record makes it hard to avoid the feeling that, in both cases, their extreme politicization got in the way of carrying these processes through proficiently and, thus, of fostering real, sustainable diversification. Diversification as a goal in and of itself was somewhat lost within this larger process, and by the end of the period, achievements in this area were rather limited. Although the price of oil supplied by Russia was only a few percentage points lower than world prices during this period (see further on), the fact that this oil was conveniently supplied by pipeline, and at prices somewhat lower than the international price at the time, gave little incentive for engaging in geographic diversification, which at this point, given the absence of alternative pipelines, would have meant relatively costly large-scale imports by tanker through the Butinge oil terminal.[97] (There was an attempt to secure an oil supply agreement with Kazakhstan in the 1999–2000 period, but it was ultimately unsuccessful, in part due to uncertainty about whether Russia's

Transneft would grant access to its pipelines to transit the oil.[98]) In the gas area, where 1997–2001 import prices averaged \$102.25 per tcm,[99] there was little progress in terms of geographical diversification. In practice, gas diversification measures amounted to contractual diversification, that is diversification away from direct Gazprom supplies by moving a significant percentage of the purchases to other companies. In this case, however, this did not amount to more than contractual pseudo-diversification, as these intermediary companies were fully controlled by Gazprom and its Lithuanian partners, and the process was initiated by Gazprom itself, with very different goals. We discuss this apparent paradox in the next section of this chapter.

How do we explain this retreat? The fact that Lithuania saw itself bogged down in two expensive, politically divisive, and excruciatingly drawn-out privatization processes did little to consolidate support for governmental energy initiatives. By 1997, the most obvious and relatively cheap infrastructure diversification projects had already been carried out, and Lithuanian elites seemed to lack the consensus and/or political will to go to the next stage of much more expensive investments in energy security.

2004–2006: Paksasgate, Uspaskichgate, and the Creeping Power of Intermediary Companies

Lithuania's accession to the EU in May 2004 was a momentous event for the country, but was eclipsed by the impeachment of President Paksas – the first time such an impeachment happened in Europe – just a few weeks earlier. The following two years were marked by a major discussion on the modalities of gas pricing, two major political scandals, and the closing of Ignalina's first bloc. This section discusses the first two issues, while Ignalina's closing is discussed in detail in the next section.

PROTRACTED DISCUSSION ON THE MODALITIES OF GAS PRICING
The years immediately following LD's privatization in 2004 were marked by a protracted discussion on gas pricing that was, at its core, a discussion on the role of Gazprom and related intermediary companies. The opening of the debate in the Seimas in spring 2005 was prompted by the need to pass a new framework gas law by July 2005 in order to implement the EU's 2003 Gas Directive, the essence of which was the need to guarantee an open gas market with free prices.[100] This was a

difficult feat considering Lithuania's dependency on a single supplier, with the implication that, should the market be deregulated before real competition was established, this could actually strengthen the power of the current monopolist, Gazprom.

The rather chaotic political situation at the time, however, made it extremely difficult to pass a law, which was eventually postponed until 2007. No party had reached a definite majority in the October 2004 Seimas elections, leading to an unstable coalition government and a very complicated political situation, which slowed down Seimas negotiations on the issue. In addition, the government itself was divided. If the official government position agreed with Gazprom's argument that delaying price deregulation would contradict the LD privatization agreement, this period was also marked by Uspaskich's (by now Labour Party leader and Economics Minister[101]) crusade-like campaign against the high profits of the major gas intermediary company, Dujotekana.

This unstable political situation in turn took place in the context of a major political crisis in Lithuania, a crisis having to do first and foremost with the growing loss of legitimacy of the major parties that had dominated Lithuanian politics since independence. Among others, the crisis manifested itself in two major political scandals that rocked Lithuania in the 2004–2006 period, the *Paksasgate* and the *Uspaskichgate*, both of which had important implications for the management of energy dependency.

THE PAKSASGATE, ENERGY POLICY, AND THE MANAGEMENT
OF ENERGY DEPENDENCY

The first major scandal was that involving President Paksas, who took office in February 2003, and was impeached in April 2004 for a variety of corruption-related wrong-doing, first and foremost the granting of Lithuanian citizenship to a Russian businessman, Yurii Borisov, in exchange for financial support in the December 2002 presidential elections.[102] Although not often highlighted in press accounts, it is believed that this support may have been a cover for support from Russian energy companies (such as LUKoil and RAO EES), to contribute, through the businessman, an additional $6 million to the Paksas campaign.[103] Moreover, although Borisov was not involved in energy business directly, his area of business, semi-legal trade in weapons and military equipment with close connections with the Kremlin,[104] was likely to include some of the same players as those active in similar types of semi-legal gas and oil trade.

THE USPASKICHGATE, INTERMEDIARY COMPANIES, AND THE MANAGEMENT OF ENERGY DEPENDENCY

The second major scandal of this period is the so-called Uspaskich-gate – the dismissal and flight from Lithuania of Russian-born Economics Minister and leader of the Labour Party Uspaskich in 2005. While seldom discussed in relation to energy issues, a closer look at the incident reveals important energy-related elements and tells much about the intertwining of Russian energy companies' interests and those of local elites.

The Rise and Fall of Uspaskich's Gas Intermediary Business

Uspaskikh's rise from welder for Gazprom to one of Lithuania's ten richest people in 2005[105] was closely related to the Russian company. The connection with Gazprom had been crucial throughout, be it in his early business providing construction services in Russia using Lithuanian workers, or with Gazprom-affiliated gas importation intermediary companies.[106] He enjoyed an exceptionally close relationship with Gazprom, at some point being "the only person in Lithuania with a constant direct access" to the company.[107] Uspaskich's rise took place in the context of Gazprom's successful (re)building of ties with some of the most important local economic players through newly created intermediary gas companies and a system of preferentially priced direct supplies.[108] The main gas intermediary in Lithuania at this time, Stella Vitae, was controlled by the Industrial-Financial Corporation of Western Lithuania (associated with two of Lithuania's strongest businessmen, Antanas Bosas and Rimantas Stonys), Gazprom, and (with 35 percent of the shares) the Russian company Auri reportedly controlled by Tatiana Dedikova, daughter of Gazprom's CEO Viakhirev.[109] Together with Bosas, Uspaskich controlled Vikonda, another important gas intermediary company.

That Uspaskich could make a fortune through a gas intermediary company is hardly surprising. As discussed in chapter 3, intermediary companies had been a part of the post-Soviet energy landscape since the dissolution of the USSR, offering a means of dealing with the liquidity and other transaction problems of the early post-dissolution years; their location between supplier and buyer put them in a choice position to access energy-related rents, both legal and illegal, through nontransparent trade.[110] At the same time, in the 1990s corruption around these companies seemed to have more of a parasitical, opportunistic nature to it, not systematically tied to the pursuit of Kremlin policy in the region. This provides an important point of comparison to the situation as it would develop after the 2001–2003 period.

As discussed in chapter 3, around 2001, with the removal of Viakhirev as head of Gazprom, important changes start to take place in the post-Soviet gas trade landscape. Perhaps best-known is the process by which Itera and its associated companies started to be systematically thrown out of traditional Gazprom markets – in each of our three cases, Ukraine, Belarus, and Lithuania, the role of both Itera, Itera-controlled, and other intermediary companies starts to decline sharply around 2001. However, this did not mean the end of intermediary companies; rather, they came to be replaced by a much smaller number of companies with a closer connection to Gazprom. In the case of Lithuania, where several intermediary companies dealing in Gazprom gas shared the market, they come to be replaced by a single company, Dujotekana, to which Gazprom transfers its supply contracts in 2002.

After a new management took control of Gazprom in 2001, Uspaskich's star with the company starts to fall. In 2001, Stella Vitae's and Vikonda's roles as preferred Gazprom agents in Lithuania were taken over by a new company, Dujotekana. Despite the existence of an agreement between Gazprom and Stella Vitae going up to 2006, the company was suddenly left without gas in late 2001, as all of its quotas were transferred to Dujotekana, which, within eight months, became the largest gas importer in Lithuania, supplying 40.3 percent of gas imports.[111]

After the gas intermediary business was taken away from Stella Vitae and him in the 2001–2002 period, Uspaskich began a virtual crusade against Dujotekana (and indirectly Gazprom) and its high profit margins, using his Labour Party's plurality in the Seimas for this aim. It is exactly at this time that the corruption accusations against Uspaskich come to light – indeed it has been argued that the Lithuanian State Security Department (VSD) specifically brought to public attention materials intended to compromise Uspaskich.[112] Facing serious accusations of corruption in his Russia-related construction business, Uspaskich was asked by President Adamkus to resign as economics minister in May 2005.[113]

The picture that emerges is one where the (perfectly timed) unveiling of the evidence against Uspaskich is likely to have been related to retribution for his anti-Dujotekana campaign but also for his own campaign against Seimas speaker Artūras Paulaskas. (It comes as no surprise that Dujotekana would have been angered by Uspaskich's proposals, as they would have slashed the company's high profit margins, which by 2004 had reached 32 percent.[114])

These confrontations, in turn, seem to be related to the transposition, to Lithuania, of conflicts between two competing groups within Gazprom: a group related to Yeltsin-era networks (represented by Uspaskich), and "the new group, Vladimir Putin's clan, tied to Rimantas Stonys,"[115] head of Dujotekana. Thus, a three-level confrontation took shape concerning Dujotekana and its profits: at the level of the Seimas, at the level of Lithuanian energy-related elites, and at the level of different groups within Gazprom. A similar situation was observed around the battle for control of an important electricity company in Kaunas, which we discuss later in this chapter.

Interestingly, the media's concentration on Uspaskich's – and Paksas' – wrongdoing in the 2004–2005 period allowed a whole set of other wrongdoing – that centred around Dujotekana's activities, discussed in the following sections – to remain largely unnoticed by public opinion at the time. As one of the leaders of the public outcry about Uspaskich's corrupt activities, Dujotekana's head Stonys was not only able to defray attention from lack of transparency in his own company but also, ironically, by fighting Uspaskich, to establish himself "as a Lithuanian patriot and statesman."[116] This is important to keep in mind as we consider Dujotekana's role more generally, and how the group associated with it came to be identified in the media as "the statesmen's group."

The events analysed above tell us that, although superficially uneventful, the period 2004–2006 was actually very rich in important energy policy developments. If the loudest examples of Lithuania's energy negotiations with Russian energy players took place first and foremost through the privatization of MN and LD, a less loud but no less significant process was taking place through the issue of intermediary energy trade companies.

INTERMEDIARY COMPANIES AND THE MANAGEMENT OF ENERGY DEPENDENCY: MATERIALS FROM THE STATE SECURITY DEPARTMENT'S INVESTIGATION OF 2006–2007

In March and April 2007 an unprecedented set of materials was made available to the public – the transcripts of a portion of the Seimas' National Security and Defence Committee's investigatory interviews on the activities of the Valstybės saugumo departamentas (VSD), the country's State Security Department in the 2005–2006 period, in which the name of the gas trade intermediary Dujotekana comes up so often that it becomes a main protagonist of the story.[117] These materials offer a unique perspective into the evolution and functioning of Gazprom's intermediary gas companies in the FSU as a whole, and also provide important clues as to why Lithuania failed to adopt a more proactive energy policy during this period.

The Seimas investigation goes back to August 2006, when VSD officer Vytautas Pociūnas dies after falling from a window in Brest, Belarus. As Pociūnas had until a year earlier been in charge of the VSD's economic security department, public opinion and the Seimas were puzzled not only by the unclear circumstances of his death,[118] but also by the fact that the head of such a high-profile VSD department should have been transferred to the Lithuanian consulate in a provincial Belarusian city exactly at the time of a serious energy security crisis, namely that surrounding the (re)privatization of the MN refinery and related Russian interference. The possibility was discussed that Pociūnas' banishment to Belarus was the result of his having fallen out of grace with VSD head Arvydas Pocius,[119] this in turn being related to Pociūnas' investigation of possible foul play involving Dujotekana.[120] Soon afterwards, the Conservative Party (TS) initiated a Seimas investigation on Pociūnas' death, which would turn into a much broader investigation into the VSD and Dujotekana.

The materials coming out of this investigation provide evidence for a new view of the swift changes in intermediary companies taking place around the 2001–2002 period in most energy-dependent countries in the region: that of a collusion of private plus intelligence interests within Russia, with the participation of a number of local players in the energy-dependent states.

Dismissal of First Intermediary Companies and
Replacement by Dujotekana

As noted earlier, in December 2001 Gazprom embarked on a major reorganization of its intermediary business in Lithuania, with Stella Vitae's role as its preferred agent abruptly transferred to a new company, Dujotekana.[121] Given its timing – shortly after Putin's access to the presidency in 2000 – it is hard to avoid the conclusion that the Russian president himself played some role in the replacement of old intermediary companies with new ones. The changes also took place at the height of Gazprom's confrontation with Itera, and it has been argued that Gazprom decided to suspend supplies specifically to Itera's Lithuanian operations as a test of what could happen in other markets.[122]

Involvement of Local Security Services in the Work of Intermediary Companies: The Case of Dujotekana and the VSD

As discussed in chapter 3, the change in intermediary companies represented not so much a victory of Gazprom's corporate interests against private interests within the corporation, but the replacement of some private interests by others.[123] An argument can be made that, once Putin came to power in 2000, perhaps because of his own security services background, he rediscovered the political and economic potential of energy intermediary companies, and acted to maximize it. This required a change in partners, both in Russia and abroad. In the case of Lithuania, it has been argued this meant the replacement of former Gazprom allies such as Uspaskich by the Dujotekana structure led by Stonys.[124] Some of the "new, better trained personnel"[125] needed for this task seemed to have come from the secret and security services, in the form of indirect supporters of the company. Similarly, control over the Russian side of Lithuanian intermediaries was transferred from Viakhirev's circle to that of close Putin associate Vladimir Yakunin, head of Russian railways.[126]

On the Lithuanian side, as can be deduced from the Seimas investigation documents, some members of the VSD became involved as well.[127] Although no direct evidence is available on this, much indirect evidence was presented in the Seimas inquiry interviews on the use of Dujotekana profits for securing the support of a large number of politicians and public figures. Although the picture presented by several Lithuanian media outlets of the real centre of power located in the VSD and Dujotekana as compared to an inactive and easy-to-influence President Adamkus[128] may have been overly alarmist, the available materials speak of a significant amount of power concentrated in the hands of Dujotekana's chairman Stonys, and of his contacts deep into the state structure.

Dujotekana, the VSD, and Private Interests: The Case of the Kaunas Combined Heat and Power Plant

The transposition of Gazprom-internal conflicts into Lithuanian companies through the work of intermediary companies was also seen in the confrontation between two Russian groups for control of the Kaunas Combined Heat and Power Plant (Kaunas CHP)[129] in 2006. Having privatized the Kaunas CHP in 2003 as part of a consortium where it held 99 percent of the shares, in the 2005–2006 period Gazprom decided to transfer the management of the company to Dujotekana, with 0.5 percent of shares only a very minor partner.[130]

Here the battles between two Russian personal-within-the-corporation interest groupings – those around Yakunin (associated with Dujotekana) and Aleksandr Ryazanov (associated with the Energijos sistemų servisas [Energy system service] company) – seemed to have been transposed onto Lithuanian soil.[131] On the Lithuanian side, the interests of the previous Kaunas CHP management (Algimantas Stasiukynas) fell close to those of Ryazanov, and the emerging Dujotekana group, represented by Stonys, close to those of Yakunin.[132] The confrontation seems to have been prompted by Ryazanov's – until 2001 considered to be "one of the three most powerful people inside Gazprom"[133] – fall from grace within the Gazprom leadership and dismissal as chairman of its management board, thereupon some of the Lithuania-related rent-seeking schemes associated with him come into crisis, as a struggle in Lithuania and Russia begins as to who would inherit them.[134]

Although at first glance there may seem to be nothing special about this situation, upon closer observation two important elements emerge: first, the fact that these are not just private interests or just personal-interests-within-the-corporation, but interests supported by parts of the Russian (and Lithuanian) security services. In addition, once the security service component in the work of these intermediary companies becomes more important, the *means* used for the pursuit of personal interests within such companies change, and the stakes increase as well. On the Lithuanian side, Dujotekana sought to enlist the help of the VSD.[135] This was not an isolated incident: as it subsequently became known, exactly around this time part of the VSD was busy doing other kinds of unauthorized work, such as collecting compromising materials on Uspaskich, before such an inquiry had been authorized by the Seimas.

The Domestic Context to the VSD Scandal

The VSD investigation materials confirm the importance of looking at the domestic context in which Russian influence takes place. What emerges is a picture much richer than one of simply one-sided Russian energy pressure on Lithuania, or of populist politicians Paksas and Uspaskich as the main culprits of Russia-related foul play and corruption, but a more complex picture of nuanced interactions involving ordinary, run-of-the-mill political figures. As noted by the business newspaper *Verslo Zinios*, whereas in the past only high-level political leaders were involved in (Russia-related) corruption, the Dujotekana web reached many people occupying "important, but not senior posts."[136] Dujotekana, using profits generated by its import operations – as it was able to charge a significant markup on this gas – was able to distribute broadly and generously among a large number of politicians, public-opinion makers, and educational institutions.[137]

The question that emerges is: what kind of domestic conditions would allow such developments to take place? At the very least, the evidence that emerged at this time suggested that the government had lost some degree of control over the security services,[138] with Dujotekana able to influence some players within the VSD itself. At the same time the existing evidence does not support allegations about the VSD's wholesale involvement in support of Dujotekana. Rather, it points to a somewhat looser situation, where some individual VSD members had good contacts with Dujotekana, but not with the Russian security services directly.

2004–2006: A BALANCE

The two years following LD's privatization process in 2004, largely taken up by the Paksas and Uspaskich scandals, were characterized by a status-quo in energy policy. Discussion of the most centrally important issues – such as how Lithuania could deal with its energy needs after the closing of the Ignalina NPP – was delayed. Energy dependency on a single source, Russia, did not diminish. Companies such as Dujotekana were allowed to continue making high profits due to special agreements with the state. At the same time, the webs of dependency acquired a more sophisticated form, as exemplified by Dujotekana's growing role in Lithuanian political and economic life. Perhaps this domestic complacency on energy policy was related to unrealistic expectations as to what short-term results the joining of NATO and the EU could bring in terms of guaranteeing Lithuania's energy security. On the contrary, Lithuania's foot-dragging on energy issues and the protracted delay in the passing of a gas law did not help Lithuania's relationship with the EU. It also did not help in terms of discussions with the EU on the future of Lithuania's Ignalina NPP, which we discuss in the next section.

Thus it is not until 2006 that the search for real energy diversification receives new impetus.

2006–2010: A Return to Diversification?

In the 2006–2010 period we see Lithuania turning to a more proactive pro-diversification policy. The reasons for this change can be found in three areas. The first is the coming to light of the VSD/Dujotekana scandal that, largely unflattering for the Lithuanian government and political class, put pressure on the government to reassert Lithuania's control over its energy policy.

The second is the shock of the Ukrainian and Belarusian gas and oil crises of 2006, 2007, and 2009. This element is especially significant given Lithuania's higher vulnerability than either of these two countries to a possible cut-off in Russian gas supplies. Lithuania had neither the limited geographic diversification Ukraine had access to, nor the counter-power provided by Ukraine's and Belarus' strong transit role. Thus it is understandable that the Belarusian and Ukrainian crises moved Lithuanian policy makers and large energy importers such as MN to more proactive positions.[139]

The third is the energy shock experienced by Lithuania in the 2006–2010 period. If the period 2006–2010 represented an external energy shock to Belarus and Ukraine mainly due to sharply increased gas and oil prices and Russia's search for new transit options sidelining these two countries, Lithuania's shock included some additional elements. In addition to significant price increases – gas prices went from about $85 per tcm in 2005 to $345 in 2008[140] – and the possible reduction of Lithuania's bargaining power vis-à-vis Gazprom brought about by the building of the Nord Stream pipeline that would render unnecessary Lithuania's transit services for gas supplies to Kaliningrad,[141] two other elements coincided to worsen Lithuania's energy security situation. First, the suspension of Russian oil supplies through the Druzhba pipeline, which greatly reduced Lithuania's ability to use oil refining and reexports as leverage in the relationship; and, second, the final closing of the Ignalina NPP, which forced Lithuania to seek a replacement for the nearly 27 percent of TPES generated by the facility up to 2009.[142]

The new attitude towards energy security and towards avoiding too large a level of energy vulnerability vis-à-vis Russia was reflected in Lithuania's 2007 National Energy Strategy, which highlighted issues that had been ignored or had received only marginal treatment in previous versions.[143] The Strategy clearly presents Lithuania's dependence on a single supplier of gas and nuclear fuel as a major threat to the country's security,[144] sets out measures to be implemented in order to reduce dependency on that single supplier, and specific dates by which each of these measures needed to be completed. Some of the specific measures mentioned were the building of a new regional NPP by 2015, the reaching of a 90-day oil and oil-products stock reserves by 2010, the building of new high-efficiency heat and power generating facilities, the development of a regional natural gas storage facility, and the increase in the share of renewable resources in the country's TPES to 20 percent by 2025.[145] The coming to power of new centre-right government in October 2008, led by Andrius Kubilius, and a new president, Dalia Grybauskaite, in July 2009, lent new energy and political will to this strategy.

INFRASTRUCTURE DEVELOPMENT
This sense of urgency brought home the need to act together with other Baltic states to deal with the consequences of the new energy environment.[146] Three projects dominated discussions of energy infrastructure during this period: a proposed LNG terminal, electricity links with Poland and Sweden (electricity bridge) and a new NPP to replace Ignalina. While discussions on the building of an LNG terminal that would have added flexibility to Lithuania's gas supply system went relatively smoothly and only lack of funding prevented a move to the feasibility study stage before 2008,[147] discussions on the electricity link[148] and, especially, on the new NPP dragged out, as they involved a complex interaction of domestic and foreign actors. One major new initiative, the building of a new gas pipeline linking Lithuania and Poland, which would make it possible for Lithuania to import almost 50 percent of its gas from Poland, was unveiled in June 2010.

Discussions on a New NPP and the Challenges of Baltic
Regional Cooperation

Discussions on the future of nuclear power were prompted by revised assessments of the future impact of Ignalina's 2009 closing: in contrast with the rather mild picture painted by pre-2005 assessments, the picture unveiled in 2007 and 2008 was one where the price of producing electricity would double, electricity shortages would grow, and gas imports from Russia would need to increase significantly.[149] On this basis, the draft National Energy Strategy discussed by the Seimas in early 2007 stated that Ignalina's closing before appropriate replacement electricity production sources were created may turn out to be an "impossible burden for consumers and the country's economy."[150] Many started calling – despite the EU's statement that the previous agreement was not negotiable – for Lithuania to renegotiate with the EU to keep the reactor open. In May 2007, however, the Seimas failed to pass a law extending Ignalina's operation past 2009; an October 2008 referendum on seeking special dispensation from the EU to operate the NPP after 2009 also failed to attract the 50 percent plus one of voter participation needed to validate its results.[151]

Although the building of the new NPP was generally greeted in Lithuania, there was concern about possible lack of transparency in the financing of the project, given a government-supported investment scheme, the Lithuanian Electricity Organization (LEO Rt.), seen by many as unduly benefitting a private company, NDX Energija/VST.[152] In September of 2009, with a new president and PM in power, the Seimas voted to dissolve LEO Rt.

The high-cost of infrastructural projects also prompted the Baltic States to think about pooling resources. This is significant, as until the 2005–2006 period, Baltic regional energy cooperation was very limited.[153] A number of large cooperative projects involving all the three post-Soviet Baltic States and Poland were considered, first and foremost a jointly financed nuclear power station (the Visaginas NPP) to replace the Ignalina NPP, an agreement reached by Lithuania, Latvia, and Estonia in March 2006 and amended in 2007 to include Poland as well.

Despite the importance of such joint regional infrastructure projects, important challenges emerged. One important hurdle to the building of an electricity bridge to the West was Poland's opposition, as Poland – which largely used coal to generate electricity – feared cheap electricity from a Lithuanian NPP could flood its markets. Other concerns raised by the Polish side included the possibly negative ecological impact of the proposed electricity bridge route through one of its national parks, and the high cost involved. Despite much discussion concerning the joint building of a NPP with Lithuania by Poland, Latvia, and Estonia, by 2010 it was clear that Poland and Estonia were seeking to build their own NPPs. Added to Belarus' plan to build its own NPP and Russia's plan to build a NPP in Kaliningrad – all planned to come online between 2016 and 2020 – this situation opened the prospect of uncoordinated electricity overproduction in the region. More specifically, the planned building of an NPP in Kaliningrad threatened to bring to an end Lithuania's electricity exports to the region, whose continuation was a key assumption for the building of a new NPP in Lithuania. These conditions added new hurdles to the finding of a strategic investor for the new NPP; after a one-year tender process, the winner and only eligible bidder, the Korean company KEPKO revoked its proposal in 2010.[154] Above and beyond these financial and logistical problems, however, stood deeper questions about nuclear power's ability to be a real element of long-term energy diversification for Lithuania or – as discussed previously – mainly a distraction away from the search for sustainable energy alternatives.

CONTRACTUAL DIVERSIFICATION AND CONTRACTUAL MANAGEMENT:
POLITICAL PRESSURE FOR A REVISION OF PREFERENCES GIVEN
INTERMEDIARY COMPANIES

During this period, the issue of contractual diversification and contractual management was manifested first and foremost through the issue of gas price regulation. With Dujotekana's credibility taking a deep plunge as a result of the Seimas investigation, a public opinion shift took place in favour of increased price regulation and against privileges held by intermediary companies, but the government remained divided on the issue. While the Economics Ministry opposed price regulation, a presidential spokesman argued EU regulations allowed the regulation of gas prices in isolated markets where there is no competition, such as Lithuania.[155]

In March 2007, under increased EU pressure, the Seimas passed a law regulating gas prices, replacing the previous law that regulated prices only for "regulated" costumers, and not "eligible" costumers entitled to choose a supplier freely. This, however, was not the end of the story, as the Economics Ministry sought to prevent the new law from entering into force.[156]

The coming to power of a new president, and a new PM in the 2008–2009 period opened the door for important initiatives in the area of contractual diversification and contractual management of Lithuania's energy dependency. In May 2010 the government launched an initiative to restructure LD by unbundling it into separate distribution and transmission companies, with the aim of increasing the state's say in decision making in the company.[157]

MEASURES AIMED AT STRENGTHENING LITHUANIA'S
COUNTERPOWER IN ENERGY TRADE RELATIONSHIPS

During this period Lithuania's longstanding goal of strengthening its negotiation counterpower vis-á-vis its main supplier by safeguarding its role as participant in Russia's energy trade and value-added chains suffered a setback. On the oil front, Lithuania's attempts to resume its role in the refining and reexport of Russian oil via MN and the Butinge terminal were sharply reduced with Russia's indeterminate suspension of supplies following fire damage to the pipeline in August 2006. On the gas front, Lithuania's hopes of maintaining and expanding its role in gas transit in the region were threatened by Russia's decision to build the Nord Stream gas pipeline with a branch to Kaliningrad, which upon completion would render unnecessary Lithuania's nearly 1 bcm per year transit services. Given this situation, Lithuania sought, to no avail, to apply pressure through the EU as a means to persuade Russia to resume oil supplies via the Druzhba pipeline by temporarily blocking negotiations on a new Partnership and Cooperation Agreement between the EU and Russia in 2007 (together with Poland) and 2008.[158]

Lithuania's Energy Situation and Trajectory since Independence – A Snapshot of the Outcomes

This chapter has analysed the ways in which the Lithuanian government and other political and economic actors dealt with the country's main energy challenges. In this section, we ask ourselves: what were the main results of these policies, in terms of diversification, and of the management of energy dependency more generally?

Management of Energy Supply Diversification Issues

DOMESTIC DIVERSIFICATION: ENERGY DIVERSIFICATION
VIA ENERGY SAVINGS, ENERGY EFFICIENCY AND
INCREASED PRODUCTION

As noted in chapter 1, diversification can be either domestic or external (imports from a broader geographical array of suppliers). In the first post-independence years, Lithuania engaged mainly in domestic diversification through reductions in both demand (from declining economic activity) and supply (due to problems with Russian supplies).

Lithuanian energy demand went down dramatically in the years immediately following independence, stabilized, and began to grow moderately after 2001; it more than halved from 1991 to 2007.[159] Much of the 1991–1993 decline, the steepest in Lithuania's post-war history, came as a result of a drastic decline in industrial activities – in 1993, final energy consumption in manufacturing was at only 33 percent of its 1990 level.[160] (Among all the new EU members, Lithuania registered the highest decrease in energy Total Final Consumption between 1991 and 2001.[161]) This reduction and the associated domestic diversification in the years following independence was the result of policies by the main supplier, of the various sectoral effects of the broader economic transformation process, and of Lithuanian state policies intended to promote energy efficiency.

At the same time, for most of the period under study the government's over-concentration on supply-side questions such as the future of nuclear-power driven electricity generation led to the relative neglect of other important, mainly demand-side, issues such as the heating supply sector and energy efficiency issues in general.[162]

At the time of independence, Lithuania had low levels of energy efficiency and high levels of energy intensity. As in the cases of Ukraine and Belarus, as a result of the rapid GDP decline, there was a temporary increase in energy intensity following independence. As shown in Table 6.2, in contrast with Ukraine and Belarus, however, where overall energy intensity reached its peak only by 1996, in the Lithuanian case, with swifter reforms and a much earlier end to cross-subsidization, the increases in energy intensity were much more temporary (1991 and 1995–1996 only). The closing of inefficient industrial plants and (to a lesser extent) conscious energy-saving plans allowed Lithuania to moderately increase its energy efficiency between 1991 and 1996, and more rapidly after that.[163] Yet as of 2006, Lithuania's primary energy intensity (calculated at market prices) was nearly 2.5 times higher than the EU-27 average.[164]

During the first decade of transition, energy intensity developed differently in different branches of the economy, with the construction, agriculture, and trade and services sectors showing the greatest reductions (with energy intensity reaching ca. 28 percent of its 1991 value in 2001), followed by industry (ca. 50 percent). On the other hand, only a marginal reduction in intensity was seen in the household sector.[165] This was mainly due to the fact that, as noted earlier, despite the deregulation of other types of energy, residential heating prices remained regulated and heavily subsidized until 1997, discouraging energy savings.[166] Low household energy prices were an important feature of the first post-independence years; the Seimas, often playing populist politics, refused (until at least 1995) to allow the necessary increases in household prices. From 1991 to 1995, cross-subsidization was used to maintain low heating prices, with the burden of Russia's increased energy prices transferred to the industrial sector, with a variety of negative effects, leading to industries' reduced profitability and, in some cases, bankruptcy. The policy also affected households indirectly, as prices for industrially produced goods increased and as growing industrial unemployment severely reduced many households' incomes.[167] In addition, the payments crisis in the first years after independence contributed to decapitalization of the heating system until 1997, decreasing its efficiency.[168]

When household energy prices were largely liberalized in the 1995–1997 period, energy pricing started to play an opposite, demand-limiting role: as energy prices started to approach WE ones, but disposable incomes remained significantly lower, high energy prices became one important restraining factor on energy use by the poorest sectors of the population.[169] As cross-subsidization ended in 1997, a serious energy-efficiency policy could begin to be implemented. In 2001 and 2006, Lithuania adopted five-year National Energy Efficiency Programs aimed at increasing energy efficiency in the building, commercial, and generation sectors and at increasing the role of renewable energy resources in the country's TPES.

Thus much of the overall reduction in energy intensity since 1991 was due to the end of cross-subsidization, price increases, retooling of enterprises to make them more efficient, and changes in the structure of the economy leading to a smaller role of traditionally energy-intensive sectors (industry) and a larger role for low-intensity sectors of the economy, such as services.[170]

DOMESTIC DIVERSIFICATION: ENERGY MIX DIVERSIFICATION

Energy imports can also be reduced through energy-mix diversification; that is, by switching to fuels more commonly available domestically. The period up to 2009 was characterized by an increase in the role of domestically produced energy (until 2004, nuclear as well as renewable resources) and a decrease in the use of oil and, much more modestly, coal. While the role of oil in the country's energy supply decreased significantly (from 42.4 percent of TPES in 1990 to 29.2 percent in 2007), the share of gas – the area where the structural hurdles for diversifying away from Russian sources are greater – in the TPES declined only slightly in comparison with 1990. Gas saw its role drastically reduced in the post-independence years (from 29 percent in 1990 to 16.7 percent in 1993), but increased again after the closing of the first Ignalina block in 2004, reaching 30.9 percent of TPES in 2007. Russian gas remained crucial for one sector of the Lithuanian energy economy – the heating system, where in 2008 it accounted for 77 percent of heating fuel; following Ignalina's closing in 2009, the role of gas in electricity generation increased dramatically as well. More generally, with the exception of renewable resources and the partial exception of nuclear-generated electricity (where Lithuania continued to depend exclusively on Russia for its nuclear fuel), these energy-mix changes concerned the substitution of some imported sources by others, not a shift to domestically available energy sources.

What energy sources represented alternatives to those traditionally imported from Russia? Of all the sources named previously, only domestically produced oil, wood, and renewable resources were real alternatives to Russian imports. Renewable resources have played a relatively modest but increasing role helped by a number of laws providing price support for electricity produced with renewable resources, and providing tax incentives for the use of biofuels.[171] Lithuania's results in this area were the most impressive of our three cases, with EU programs and incentives undoubtedly playing a role in this. In particular, the EU's 2008 Renewable Resources Initiative aimed at reducing CO_2 emissions by 20 percent and increasing the role of renewable resources to 20 percent of energy supply by 2020 (the so called 20/20/20 initiative), together with the challenges presented by the closing of the Ignalina NPP, provided a strong impulse to the use of renewable resources towards the end of the period covered by this book.[172]

EXTERNAL DIVERSIFICATION

Geographic Diversification: The Declarative Level Lithuania's basic national security documents, approved in 1996 and 2002 (as well as the updated version in 2005) recognized the potential threat to Lithuanian national security stemming from excessive dependency on a single energy supplier that may use strategic assets for political pressure.[173] Yet as noted previously, it is only in the 2007 National Energy Strategy that the issue of diversification becomes a real priority.

Diversification: The de facto Level Not all of the rather limited diversification goals set forth in the 2007 Energy Strategy were carried out to completion. Although significant progress was made in areas such as the building up of oil reserves and the establishment of gas metering stations on the Lithuanian-Latvian border, other stated goals, such as connecting Lithuania's electricity networks to Poland's, were not achieved.[174]

By 2008, Lithuania continued to rely on a single supplier (Russia) for about 60 percent of its primary energy. In the very few cases where diversification occurred – for example through the limited (test) importation of Venezuelan oil to replace Russian oil when Russia stopped supplies through the Druzhba pipeline in 2006 – it was more as a response to Russian actions than as the result of a proactive diversification policy; as of 2008 the Butinge terminal was used almost exclusively to import Russian oil (in 2007 supplying 97.8 percent of Lithuania's oil) shipped by tanker.[175] The only example of continued geographical diversification was the small-scale importation of Orimulsion from Venezuela until 2007, but as noted earlier due to ecological concerns this was never a realistic long-term solution.[176]

A serious difference could also be observed between the oil and gas sectors: if by 2007 Lithuania possessed, at least theoretically, all the technical capabilities needed for diversifying oil supplies, and was technically secured against possible supply disruption from any one country, in the gas sphere it continued to fully depend structurally on Russia.[177]

Contractual Diversification and Organization of Energy Trade with the Main Current Supplier(s)

In contrast to geographical diversification, contractual diversification is first and foremost about developing a variety of contractual relationships both in terms of companies and of types of contracts even when the energy originates from a single country. In this area, Lithuania's record was mixed. In the oil area, it succeeded in achieving a significant degree of contractual diversification, importing from a variety of supplier companies and (to a lesser extent) countries. The actual level of contractual diversification fluctuated during the period under study, depending on the state of deliveries via the Druzhba pipeline and on the level of Russian state control over oil companies. Despite oil purchases from a variety of Russian suppliers, shipments via the pipeline remained under control of Russia's Transneft.

As discussed earlier, the organization of gas trade in Lithuania since independence did not encourage real contractual diversification. In great part because of the special relationship between Gazprom and Dujotekana, actual competition in the gas market was absent.[178]

On the other hand, as a result of factors discussed earlier in this chapter – a sharp reduction in energy consumption due to changes in the economy, reduced affordability of residential energy for several years following 1997 and increased domestic production and declining energy intensity – Lithuania was able to reduce its overall dependency on imported energy from 70 percent 1990 to 42 percent in 2003,[179] but after closure of the first Ignalina NPP unit it increased again to about 62 percent in 2007 and 80 percent after the closing of Ignalina's second unit in December 2009.[180]

The overall picture that emerges is a split one. If Lithuania was indeed able to significantly reduce its level of energy dependency (including energy dependency on Russia), this had more to do with the drastic reduction in energy demand in the first years following independence and increases in energy efficiency after 1996, than with proactive measures to diversify day-to-day sources of gas and oil. A few additional caveats are in order. First, this outcome can be partially explained by Lithuania's considerable reliance on nuclear power, which in 2003 covered 37 percent of the country's TPES.[181] However, the decline in Lithuania's energy dependency from 1991 to 2003 cannot be explained by the existence of nuclear power capacities alone – Lithuania had the same nuclear capacity in 1990, when its energy dependency was more than 70 percent. The difference is explained by reduced overall energy demand, increased energy efficiency, and the use of some nuclear capacities to cover domestic needs instead of exports.[182] More generally, although according to the principles of international statistics, electricity generated by nuclear power plants is considered a local energy source, irrespective of the country from which the nuclear fuel was imported, as acknowledged by official Lithuanian publications, given the fact that about 30 percent or more of the country's TPES was produced on the basis of imported nuclear fuel, the real degree of energy dependency was 86.2 percent in 2006.[183] (Should Lithuania's 1990 energy balance be analysed using the same criteria, the country's real level of energy dependency in 1990 would have been close to 97.3 percent.)[184]

At the same time, the percentage of energy dependency in and of itself may not be enough to provide a full picture. Looking at gas and oil vulnerability – net imports of energy (measured in oil equivalent) per unit of GDP – and intensities (see Table 6.2) may provide an important additional perspective. Looked at from this perspective, Lithuania's energy situation improved significantly since independence.

Direction of the Management of the Energy Dependency Relationship

What does the track record in each of these areas tell us about the direction of the management of energy dependency since independence? In the spectrum between transparent and nontransparent, the Lithuanian

Table 6.2 Lithuania: Oil and Natural Gas Intensities, in toe per million EUR of GDP

	1990	1995	2000	2001	2002	2003	2004	2005	2006	2007
Oil	426.9	325.1	189.9	199.7	189.8	163.5	164.9	162.4	151.0	140.6
Natural gas	291.7	218.2	180.8	166.5	166.6	163.9	152.4	149.4	137.7	149.0

Source: Vlacovas Miškinis, LEI.

case was clearly much more transparent than the Belarusian case, and also significantly more transparent than the Ukrainian one. The existence of an independent energy regulatory authority, the NCCPE, since 1997, with its requirement to make public extensive reports on the energy market and pricing policies, made a significant contribution to transparency.[185] Seimas investigations of several energy-related cases were an additional transparency-fostering element. However, transparency was far from full, and the complexity of the policy making system within the Seimas, together with the perceived problem of corruption in the press[186] made it difficult for the public to fully know what was going on.

Were particularistic interests more reflected in policy, or non-particularistic ones? If one starts from the assumption that it was in Lithuania's national interest to diversify its energy supply and to develop ways to withstand Russian pressure, then we could say that Lithuania was able to develop a largely non-particularistic policy in the oil area, but that particularistic interests were able to significantly influence gas policy. Did the de facto policies followed foster the continuation of the energy dependency relationship with Russia, or growing energy independence and diversification? In this area as well, we see a significant difference between oil and gas, with the oil policy much more directed at diversification than the gas policy.

Main Developments since 2010

Of the major initiatives unveiled in the 2008–2010 period, several had moved forward successfully by early 2013, anchored in a new Energy Policy Strategy (2012) setting out measures to reduce energy dependency on Russia to 35 percent by 2020.[187] Key to this reduction in dependency was the building of the new NPP, but this process faced new hurdles in 2012–2013. After Poland's withdrawal from the project in December 2011, cooperation with Estonia and Latvia continued; a concession agreement with Hitachi was signed and approved by the Seimas in May 2012. However, in an unbinding October 2012 referendum held in parallel with parliamentary elections and pushed by the opposition Social Democratic Party, nearly 63 percent of voters rejected the building of the NPP. With the party's victory in the elections and its leader Algirdas Butkevičius becoming prime minister in December, it seemed unlikely that the project would be realized in the short term, but by January 2013 the final decision was being delayed until a new cost calculation would be available, and the idea of holding a second referendum was being supported by President Grybauskaite and other politicians.

But a key development in Lithuania's energy security front came not from infrastructure measures aimed at geographic diversification, but from bold legal moves that would have an impact well above and beyond Lithuania, with the potential to affect the conditions of Gazprom work throughout all of Europe. Already in mid-2009 the Lithuanian government started discussing plans to carry out the "unbundling" of its gas system in accordance with the EU's Third Energy Package, choosing the full "unbundling" of its system; that is, separating the gas supply company from the control of gas delivery and distribution infrastructure. This was the most radical of the three options allowed by the EU, and Lithuania was the first state to pursue it.[188] In practice, this meant that Gazprom would need to give up its control of Lithuania's pipeline system. Shortly thereafter, Gazprom refused to grant Lithuania the same market-based price discounts (estimated at ca. 15 percent) as it did neighboring Latvia and Estonia, part of a broader set of discounts negotiated with a number of EU consumers as a result of slumping demand in Europe; by early 2013, Lithuania was paying $540 per tcm, the highest rate in Europe. On January 2011, Lithuania logged a formal complaint against Gazprom at the European Commission, accusing the company of abusing its dominant market position to engage in price-fixing behavior as retaliation against its unbundling plan. This helped set into motion a much larger EU investigation into Gazprom, setting off an anti-trust case against the company opened by the EU's Directorate General of Competition in September 2012. It is hard to underestimate the potential impact of this case, as change concerning the main issues named in the case (exploitative pricing, clauses banning the resale of gas, and third-party access to pipelines) could potentially lead to the dismantling of the Gazprom gas supply model in Europe as a whole and open the door to much broader competition and interlinking of European energy markets. That small Lithuania could set into motion such key developments is a testimony not only to the empowerment given to it by its EU membership, but also to the relatively consequent nature of its energy policy since 1991.

Conclusion

Essence of the Management of Energy Dependency

The Lithuanian case is more difficult to characterize than either the Belarusian or the Ukrainian ones, but no less interesting. Official Lithuanian energy policy since 1991 focused on energy diversification. Yet actual reductions in energy dependency on Russia between 1991 and 2004 (when the partial closing of Ignalina makes it increase again) were achieved was not so much as the result of consequent energy policy measures aimed at acquiring a broader geographical set of suppliers, but of economic restructuring (for example, the move to average European prices in oil and gas and the imposition of a strict payments discipline, which promoted energy conservation and prevented Lithuania from acquiring new external energy arrears after 1995), leading to strong decreases in energy use. In other words, instead of geographical diversification per se, what we see is (for most of this period) a decrease in Lithuania's energy vulnerability vis-á-vis Russia resulting mainly from domestically oriented policies. In the case of Lithuania, the external shock of higher energy prices came much sooner and more dramatically than in the case of Ukraine or Belarus, where the external shock was not felt at least until 2007. Because this external shock was mostly *not cushioned* by subsidies to industrial energy users, it translated into higher industrial energy prices, contributing to industrial restructuring and to a significant decrease in energy consumption. Similarly, the doing away with mechanisms such as barter, cross-subsidization, and inexpensive credits took away some of the main instruments for energy rent-seeking seen in the other cases.

Thus while official energy policy goals were not always translated into effective, implemented policies, some of these policy goals were achieved through other means. This did not mean, however, the end of energy dependency on Russia, but it reduced the level of energy vulnerability, net imports of gas or oil per unit of GDP.

One important conclusion of the Lithuanian case has to do with the clear differences in the content and direction of energy policy between the gas and oil sectors. This had to do not only with intended policies, but also with infrastructural limitations that made diversification much more difficult in the case of gas than in the case of oil. Similarly, it is no coincidence that it was in the oil area, where intermediary companies were less active than in the gas area, that a proactive energy policy aimed at a real diversification was most successful. Interestingly, although Ukraine and Belarus also faced the same structural differences between oil and gas as did Lithuania, the differences in policy between both sectors were not so marked. Of the three countries analysed in our study, until 2003 only Lithuania took some clearly proactive measures in terms of oil diversification.

A second conclusion concerns the uniqueness of energy infrastructure-building initiatives as a policy field in the first post-independence years. In a dynamic that may at first seem paradoxical, wide-scale economic reforms greatly slowed down in the period 1992–1996, yet the development of energy diversification infrastructure advanced strongly during this period. How to make sense of this situation?[189] Perhaps this tells us something about the ability of the Lithuanian government at the time, as discussed by Sabonis-Chafee, to "buffer" (isolate) energy infrastructure policy from other policy fields and societal pressures during these early years?[190]

*Kremlin Goals, European Union Diversification, and Lithuania
as an Energy Weak Link*

Lithuania's management of its energy dependency takes place within the context of Lithuania's broader political, economic, and energy relationships, first and foremost with the EU and Russia. In a multitude of ways, this domestic management – in turn the result of the interaction of factors within and outside Lithuania's borders – affected the possibilities and opportunities available to various Russian energy actors in Lithuania, as well as the structure of rents available to them. What did these various Russian actors see in Lithuania?

Despite Lithuania's limited weight as an energy transit player, the Lithuanian case is vital for understanding the interconnection between Gazprom and local actors throughout the CEE region. Despite not being, for example, one of the transit states for the Nabucco gas pipeline diversification project whose elites, as in the case of Bulgaria, Romania, and Hungary, have been consciously targeted by Russia in order to weaken support for the project, in a broader sense Lithuania can be seen as a crucial link to EU policy and, in this capacity, very important for some Russian actors as well.

To understand this role it makes sense to revisit some of the main observed goals of the Russian leadership in Lithuania (ca. 1991–2010). In addition to goals related to corporate interests, such as Gazprom's attempts to control gas imports to Lithuania for profit motives, other interests may include geopolitical goals such as control of port infrastructure in the Baltics, and the Russian leadership's desire to use Lithuania as a bridgehead into the EU through its energy investments in the country, or even as a means to foster divisions within it, as well as within the post-Soviet Baltic states. Paradoxically, Lithuania's accession to the EU, while offering important protections against possible Russian interference, also made the country more attractive to Russian players, especially due to EU-inspired legislation calling for the liberalization of gas markets.[191] Thus, as noted by the Conservative Party: "By joining the EU and NATO, we believed we would be a bridgehead of the West in the East . . ., but at the same time Russia seeks to use us as a bridgehead of the East in the West."[192] Such Russian goals in Lithuania, including using it as an entrance point to the EU, take place in the context of relatively better relations with Lithuania than with Latvia or Estonia.[193]

Impact of EU Membership

What was the impact of EU membership – and, between 1992 and 2004, of Lithuania's striving for it and preparation for accession – in Lithuania's energy policy? Both membership itself and the measures put in place to assure accession had significant effects, especially in terms of implementing energy efficiency guidelines and moving to a greater use of renewable resources. No less important was EU support for European-priority infrastructure development projects such as the electricity link Baltic Energy Ring.[194] Despite the clearly unfulfilled expectations of Lithuanian politicians in this area, EU membership also helped set Lithuania's general relationship with Russia on a new basis, and provided the possibility of putting pressure on Russia through the EU. But the impact on actual policy was limited by, among other factors, differences between EU and Lithuanian preferred policies concerning the closing of Ignalina NPP and Lithuanian dissatisfaction with EU policies perceived as not taking into account the needs of small, energy-dependent and energy-isolated states such as itself.[195]

Rents of Energy Dependency, Political Actors, and Political Development: Lithuania's Cycle of Energy Rents

A number of similarities and differences emerge between the Lithuanian and the other cases analysed in this book, similarities and differences that become especially clear when looked at through the prism of rents of energy dependency. Here comparisons with the case of Ukraine, where intermediary companies played an important role, are especially interesting. At a certain level, the role played by Dujotekana between 2001 and 2004, where it controlled more than 30 percent of Lithuania's gas imports, seems to echo the patterns evident from the Ukrainian case in the wake of the 2006 gas crisis, when a gas trading intermediary of dubious origin (RosUkrEnergo) was given virtual control of all of Ukraine's gas supply decisions and local elites were able to reap substantial profits from the energy dependency relationship. At the same time, there were also important differences. In the case of Lithuania, the possibilities for easily accessed rents were much more limited than in the other two cases. This had to do with a number of different factors: objective conditions (Lithuania's geographical location, which limited its potential transit role), the lukewarm state of bilateral relations with Russia (as a result of which preferential prices and the related arbitrage gains possibilities were much more limited than in the case of Ukraine or Belarus[196]), and domestic factors (changes in the economic system that excluded the use of some of the main means for the accrual of energy rents available in other post-Soviet cases, such as discounted bills of exchange and barter operations).

The smaller size of these available rents also meant differences in terms of their distribution. Lithuanian players also had some access to energy rents, but because of the absence of lower-for-Lithuania prices and domestic cross-subsidization, the kind of hyper-rents that their counterparts in Ukraine could access was simply not available to them.

In the case of Lithuania, the kinds of political actors benefiting from energy rents seemed to be less durable than in the Ukrainian case. In the Lithuanian case, the kind of income and power individual actors acquired through their association with intermediary companies such as Dujotekana did not seem to be transferable to a later period when political conditions may have changed, but seemed to last only as long as the person was actively involved in the business, as the case of Uspaskich would seem to show. Because of its more modest magnitude, the kind of income and power individual actors acquired through their association with intermediary companies such as Dujotekana did not seem to provide enough of a critical mass to guarantee political influence at a later date when political conditions may have changed.[197]

Whereas in the case of Ukraine there seemed to be a relatively narrow circle of actors accruing extremely high rents from the relationship, in the Lithuanian case the indirect fruits of gas intermediary companies

. seemed to have reached a much broader circle, through Dujotekana's small contributions to a wide variety of parties, organizations, and individuals. In terms of the recycling of these rents into the political arena, it is important to note, however, that the number and strength of political actors *created* (as opposed to supported but not created) by intermediary companies such as Dujotekana seems to have been smaller in Lithuania than in Ukraine.

Energy Rents and Policy Making

The effects of this situation on actual energy policy were less marked than in the case of Ukraine. Dujotekana/Gazprom's attempts to keep high profit margins affected energy policy by, for example, supporting preferential treatment for Dujotekana. Yet in the Lithuanian case, a single intermediary company was never given the same level of control over supply decisions as happened in the Ukrainian case. A central difference lies in the fact that, because of the differences in political system, Ukraine's energy corruption situation, although heavily politicized and instrumentalized by all main political forces, never made it to a full parliamentary investigation carried to conclusion.

Despite the existence of corruption and lobby power of important economic groups, it is important to recognize the significance of the Lithuanian political system in terms of self-regulation and, ultimately, keeping these elements under some degree of control; here EU initiatives and the requirements of the accession process undoubtedly played a role. While Lithuanian energy policy did not necessarily become more proactive because of that, the country was able to keep the worst effects of a conflagration of political and energy power under check. Even the results of the scandals surrounding President Paksas and the security services in the mid-2000s – and ending with Paksas' impeachment – are, in the final analysis, testimony of the Lithuanian political system's achievement of significant transparency and limitation of powers nearly twenty years after independence.[198]

PART THREE

Conclusions

7 Conclusion: Managing Dependency, Managing Interests

"[E]ach unhappy family is unhappy in its own way."[1]

Leo Tolstoy

Comparing the Cases: Dealing with Energy Dependency

What have we learned from the cases of Ukraine, Belarus, and Lithuania? How do our three cases compare in terms of the results of their management of energy dependency?

If looked at simply in terms of their dependency on Russian energy supplies, none of the three cases showed significant progress. In the period between 1991 and 2007, the last year for which full official data was available at the time of writing, Belarus' energy dependency (overwhelmingly on Russian energy) went from 89 percent to 85 percent, Ukraine's from 50 percent to 43 percent and Lithuania's from 70 percent to 62 percent.[2] However, a deeper look reveals important differences.

Looking at the results not simply in aggregate terms for the period as a whole, but taking into account the timing of important externally defined events, such as the decommissioning of crucial nuclear infrastructure, provides a more nuanced picture. Thus, for example, between independence and 2003, the last year in which the Ignalina NPP was in full operation, Lithuania was able to reduce its energy dependence by nearly 26 points, whereas Belarus' and Ukraine's situation remained largely unchanged.[3] This result puts Lithuania in a clearly different category than the other two cases.

The areas where we saw the largest variation between the cases had to do with, first, the *management* of the dependency situation, and second, with the way the strategies adopted to deal with this dependency in the 1992–2010 period affected each state's capacity to deal with the challenges of a subsequent period when they would be expected to pay world prices for their oil and gas imports. How did our three cases fare in these two respects?

The Cycle of Rents and the Management of Energy Dependency in Ukraine, Belarus, and Lithuania

Even behind the façade of no changes in levels of energy dependency until 2007, much was actually happening. This is nicely captured by looking at how the cycle of rents worked in each of our three cases. In the face of the apparent status quo in terms of energy dependency levels, the impact energy monies could have through their movement in the domestic system was simply remarkable. The cycle of rents associated with the energy dependency relationship with Russia was characterized by the specificities of their extraction, distribution, and reincorporation into the political system in each of the cases.

ENERGY RENTS: SOURCES OF EXTRACTION
In each of the three cases, internal and external rents were accrued, but at different times and in different proportions. In the case of Lithuania, the period when external rents could be accessed – in the form of lower-than-market energy import prices – was short, as the country moved relatively quickly to (near) world market prices in its gas and (especially) oil trade with Russia. As a result, the possibility for price manipulations and arbitrage gains based on price differentials between Russian, Lithuanian, and WE prices was limited.[4] In this case, domestic sources of rents – in the form of above-the-norm profits that gas supply companies such as Dujotekana could impose on captive markets due to the lack of competition – were relatively more important. More generally, two other factors limited the possibilities for easily accessed rents compared to the other two cases. The first factor has to do with Lithuania's limited transit role.[5] The second factor concerns changes in the economic system, which took away from circulation some of the main mechanisms for the accrual of internal energy rents available in other post-Soviet cases, such as cross-subsidization, selective payments for gas from the state budget, IOU's, and barter operations.

In the case of Belarus, in contrast, the rents extracted were mainly external in nature, accrued through significant price subsidies, especially in gas, and preferential tax treatment, especially in oil. These rents constituted, in the 2000s, about 10 percent of the country's GDP.

In the case of Ukraine, on the other hand, both external and domestic rents were accessed and extracted. In fact, some of the most profitable arrangements involved the simultaneous accessing of both external and internal rents; that is, even when external rents were accessed, they also involved the diversion of revenue and potential revenue from the Ukrainian state and some Ukrainian consumers. In the case of the transit and supply of Central Asian gas to Ukraine, the adjudication of advantageous transit services contracts to well-connected private companies allowed these to simultaneously access internal (in the form of overcharging Ukraine's NAK Naftohaz for the intermediation of transit to Ukraine) as well as external rents (in the form of underpaying Gazprom, owner of the Russian segment of the pipelines the gas had to transit through) for transportation and other services, leading both states to lose hundreds of millions of dollars in revenue. Here the crucial difference between Ukraine and the other cases concerns the fact that energy rents in Ukraine most often involved revenue and potential revenue diverted from the Ukrainian state. This was in stark contrast with the case of Belarus, where most of the energy rents were external rents accruing from lower-than-market oil and gas prices charged by Russia.

ENERGY RENTS: DISTRIBUTION

How these rents would be distributed – accruing to society as a whole, or mainly to specific actors and, if so, which actors – is an important issue with a variety of significant implications. The distribution of energy rents has to do first and foremost with issues such as the type of economic and political actors participating most actively in their accrual, and the formal or informal mechanisms regulating the distribution and, at times, transborder sharing of these rents.

In terms of the domestic distribution of rents, we saw somewhat different patterns in each of the cases. In the case of Ukraine, there was a situation of highly concentrated rents, accessed by small but powerful groups. For most of the period under study these rents were distributed through informal bargaining between the country's main BAGs, often via their balancing through the president. In the case of Lithuania, energy rents were distributed among a larger number of actors benefitting from the sharing (in the form of contributions to a variety of social and educational institutions) of a portion of intermediary companies' profits. In the case of Belarus, with some exceptions (rents accessed directly by the president and the Presidential Administration) energy rents seemed to have been broadly redistributed, mainly through the subsidy effect on the economy as a whole or reinvestment in the profitable oil refining sector.

The patterns of transborder distribution of rents also differed among the cases. The evidence of the 1991–2013 period leads us to believe that there was a higher level of sharing of rents (and also more corruption) in the gas than in the oil sector. Such transborder sharing of gas rents seemed to take place frequently in the cases of Ukraine and (to a lesser extent) Lithuania, but less so in the case of Belarus. In the case of Belarus, until 2007 gas rents seemed to have been extracted almost exclusively by the Belarusian side in the form of special-for-Belarus prices much lower than European ones.[6] If in the Belarusian case there seemed to be little or no transborder sharing of gas-related rents, the most important supplier, Gazprom, benefitted from the indirect rewards it could receive from the Russian government for services provided in Belarus. In the case of Ukraine, the transborder sharing of rents – including those accrued through corrupt means – with actors in the main supplier states (Russia and, to a lesser extent, Turkmenistan) played a significant role. This transborder sharing took place first and foremost through the role of intermediary companies. Indeed, this sharing seemed to be an important mechanism for the management (and "solving") of energy conflicts; corporations and private energy actors within corporations on both sides of the Russian-Ukrainian border were able to find common interests exactly through the joint access to and appropriation of these rents, as exemplified by the January 2006 agreements discussed in chapter 4.[7] Such sharing of (possibly corrupt) rents with Russian actors hindered a clearer definition and implementation of Ukraine's national energy interests.

In the case of Lithuania, the limited size of potential energy rents also meant differences in terms of their further distribution. While Ukraine-related income could be very significant for Gazprom as a whole, the rents possible in the Lithuanian case would be significant at a much more individual level – to specific individuals or groups both in Russia and Lithuania involved in the business of Gazprom-favoured intermediary companies.

An additional element related to the distribution of energy rents has to do with the gatekeeping of access to energy rents and with whether non-system elites associated with opposition political groups could have access to these. Here we could see important differences between the cases: whereas both in the cases of Ukraine and Lithuania it was possible for non-system elites to have access to energy rents without

Table 7.1 Access to Energy Rents by Groups Not Directly Favoured by the Executive
(Alternative Elites/Non-system Groups)

	Ukraine	Belarus	Lithuania
Alternative elites independent of the executive?	Few, but active	Minimal	Yes, plural elites
Open competition between elites?	Yes	No	Yes
Alternative elites having access to own sources of income?	Some	Minimal	Yes
Alternative elites having own parties?	Yes	No – opposition parties were small, heavily persecuted, had minimal economic base, access, and impact	Yes (but parties not so much based on one economic clan or elite as in Ukraine)
Alternative elites having own media?	Yes	No	Yes

the approval or intervention of the executive, this was virtually impossible in the case of Belarus (see Table 7.1).

ENERGY RENTS: REINCORPORATION (RECYCLING)
Energy rents can be reincorporated or recycled into the political system in a variety of ways, including through the creation and strengthening of certain political actors, through their impact on elections, and through their impact on policy making and the establishment and strengthening of certain patterns of policy making.

In terms of the creation or strengthening of certain political actors, one important point concerns whether this potential source of income could be accessed and used – and, if so, how – by a variety of political elites, not only those in close favour of the executive. When discussing the distribution of rents, we noted the importance of their gatekeeping and of whether opposition (non-system) political groups could have access to these rents. One further element has to do with how these rents

sed once accessed. For example, did these alternative elites
ructures and institutions (parties, media outlets) where these
profits could be reinvested and thus transformed into further political
power?

In the case of Ukraine, the energy importation and distribution system not only became an important source of income for those with the
right connections, but also transformed these original connections into
greatly increased political power. Huge economic – and political – capitals
were made in this manner, especially in the first post-independence
years, and those who accrued these capitals found themselves at the
centre of political power.[8]

In the case of Belarus, the effect in terms of the creation of new political actors was much less straightforward than in the other two cases, in
great part due to the tighter restrictions on political activity. In this case,
there were strong limitations on alternative political elites' access to independent sources of income, and much less of a desire (given the high
potential cost of transgressing against Lukashenka's rules of the game)
by any elites with access to these funds to use them openly for political
purposes. At the same time, there were important indirect effects. The
significant increase in real wages – especially in comparison with the
drop in living standards in the years immediately preceding Lukashenka's coming to power in 1994 – as a result of the trickling down of
energy rents can be assumed to have led to increased support for President Lukashenka. Most importantly, Belarus' use of rents to increase
overall income levels took important potential sources of support away
from the opposition and, together with repression, helps explain why
there was so little generalized public uproar over Lukashenka's growing authoritarianism.

In the case of Lithuania, in contrast, the number and strength of specific political actors created (as opposed to supported but not created)
by energy rent-seeking seems to have been smaller than in Ukraine.

New Path Dependencies and Ability to Deal with Future Challenges

The patterns of dealing with energy dependency used in the 1991–2010
period are also significant because of their impact in terms of the options available to each of the cases in the subsequent period.

By 2010, Ukraine, Belarus, and Lithuania were facing gas prices moving increasingly closer to – and often exceeding – European ones.[9] But
which of these states were better prepared to deal with this challenge?

Table 7.2 The Cycle of Rents in Ukraine, Belarus, and Lithuania, 1991–2013

	Extraction: Main sources	Distribution: Main beneficiaries	Recycling: politically-relevant outcomes
Ukraine	External and Domestic	Multiple small and powerful elites	Creation of powerful political elites
Belarus	External	Presidential Administration Economy as a whole	Strengthening of President Lukashenka's power
Lithuania	Pre-2005: internal and external Post-2005: internal	Redistribution to broad sets of elites	Populist politicians challenge of status quo

Although in the case of Lithuania the final closing of the Ignalina NPP in 2009 triggered a significant increase in gas dependency on Russia, the country, which since 2007–2008 was paying European prices for its gas imports from Russia, was better prepared to deal with these challenges than either of the two other cases.

Between 1992 and 2005 both Ukraine and Belarus followed energy policies that, in the short term, seemed to keep most powerful political and economic actors reasonably happy. However, these policies had serious medium-term consequences. In the case of Belarus, although the country had cumulatively gained tens of billions of dollars in hidden energy subsidies from Russia, the way in which the country's economy became systemically geared towards maximum use of cheap energy, in particular gas, as a way to maximize profits from special-for-Belarus prices meant higher adaptation and social costs when this energy became too expensive for the system to continue to be viable. In addition, the general lack of economic reforms made the country less able to adapt to external shocks. Instead of using the rents accumulated in the high years of high energy subsidies from Russia to finance and cushion the social cost of economic reforms, Belarus sought to use these subsidies to keep alive the existing but unviable economic model, and sought to maximize its gains from these subsidies by moving to greater reliance on gas. Although advantageous in the short term, this abnormally high dependence on gas exacerbated structural problems and limited the system's ability to adapt in the long term.

In the case of Ukraine, even when in per-capita terms the level of subsidies and external rents was smaller than in the case of Belarus, low gas prices reduced incentives for energy saving and the use of renewable energy resources. At the same time, price advantages also contributed to the boom in steel and iron exports, in the early-to-mid 2000s composing about 35 percent of Ukraine's exports. Although an important source of revenue in the short term, dependence on such steel and iron exports, together with Ukraine's dependence on imported gas (much of it used, in turn, for metallurgical production), made the country especially vulnerable to terms-of-trade shocks, and limited its ability to respond proactively to changes coming from the outside, for example Russia's new pipeline initiatives, which by 2015 could sidetrack a significant amount of oil and gas transit volumes away from the country.

Revisiting the Hypotheses

Let us return briefly to the main hypotheses presented at the beginning of the book.

Claim 1: Domestic Institutions Matter in the Management of Energy Dependency

In all three cases, the role of the executive and his formal and informal powers in the system of interest articulation emerged as an important factor. In the case of Ukraine, the balancing of various BAGs' interests by the president – or, in the 2005–2009 case, his active lobbying for one group – played an important role in actual energy policy outcomes. In the case of Belarus, Lukashenka's politization of the energy relationship with Russia was only possible thanks to his virtual monopolization of domestic power and the absence of strong independent actors who could offer Russian energy players their own, parallel games, and access to alternative value-added chains and rent-seeking opportunities. In the case of Lithuania, in contrast, the lack of a strong executive, and his inability to wield significant administrative resources reduced the possibilities for clientelism and use of these administrative resources as a means to access energy rents.

The evidence of Ukraine, Belarus, and Lithuania also highlighted the importance of informal structures in the management of energy dependency. This holds true at several levels. First, when considering the nature of the political systems involved. Thus, for example, while on paper both the Ukrainian (especially after the 2005 constitutional changes) and Lithuanian systems could be considered mixed presidential-parliamentary systems, the difference in informal powers available to the president accounted for important differences in the way these systems worked de facto, including in terms of their effects on the domestic distribution of energy rents. Second, through the issue of the informal institutions that emerge when formal ones fail to work effectively. For example, the lack of well-established mechanisms for the discussion of energy issues and the negotiation of new contracts and prices[10] created the space for the functioning of informal institutions such as the sharing of often corrupt rents, as a means to the harmonization of interests between actors in Russia and some of the energy-poor states, for example Ukraine. And, third, the importance of informal structures became clear through the crucial policy role of informal networks and institutions, which on occasion came to undermine national energy policies or the very possibility of developing one.

Energy rent-seeking and corruption is not a monopoly of the post-Soviet states. Many examples exist, especially in energy-rich developing states, as well as developed states (e.g., Enron). The difference, however, lies in the ability of the institutional system to limit the scope of this corruption and to prevent – or not – certain corrupt patterns from substituting permanently for energy policy making. That difference was seen in our cases as well, with Lithuania, for example, being much more successful than Ukraine in terms of bringing to light and limiting energy corruption.

REAL GOALS OF ENERGY POLICY: ENERGY POLICY BY ANY OTHER NAME

Strictly speaking, none of our case studies engaged in a proactive energy policy *specifically as energy policy* until sharply higher prices starting around 2006–2007 forced them to do so. In the case of Ukraine, energy policy seemed to be, rather, a by-product of various means of rents extraction in the energy area, and of bargaining over their distribution. The impact of rent-seeking on Ukraine's energy policy making was so significant as to outweigh any proactive and coordinated policy that might have been in place.

In the case of Lithuania, for most of the period under study a reduction in the country's energy vulnerability vis-à-vis Russia was the result not so much of a proactive diversification policy, as of changes in broader economic policy. In the case of Belarus, more than a proactive energy policy aimed at dealing head-on with the issue of energy dependency and lack of diversification, what we saw for most of this period was an attempt to use the situation of energy dependency to extract a maximum of (mainly short-term, but not only) rents from the relationship with the main energy supplier, Russia.

*Claim 2: Who Benefits from Patterns of Energy Trade
Will Have Long-term Political Effects*

The second major argument of the book was that the domestic distribution of gains and losses from energy relations with the largest suppliers (here, Russia) would impact the further development of these states' political systems. How did our three cases fare concerning this question?

The sudden availability of large energy rents exactly during the first years of statehood is likely to have an important impact on its development. This is especially so when the sudden influx of rents coincides with a crucial formative period when new formal and informal political institutions are being set up. This was the case in Ukraine, Belarus, and (to a much lesser extent) Lithuania.

Thus a cyclical pattern could be observed: on the one hand, the nature of the political system affected how energy rents would be accessed and distributed in the system; at the same time, the way these rents would be reincorporated into the political system would further impact its development.

Implications for Policy

*Tension between Goals: Diversification versus Increased Role in Russian
Energy Value-added Chains*

As seen from our case studies, with the exception of Lithuania, energy diversification was not, de facto, a main policy goal until the late 2000s. Instead, what we often encountered was the instrumental securitization of the energy dependency question, functioning more as a rhetorical device to satisfy external or domestic audiences than as a guide to actual policy. To the extent, however, that there was a sincere desire to do something to moderate the negative effects of energy dependency on Russia, there was often a tension between two goals: establishing infrastructure to diversify supplies (or at least infrastructure that could allow for diversified supplies in the case of an emergency), and strengthening the role of the respective country in the energy value-added chain of its main supplier, Russia – be it through its role as export transit country, or through refining-and reexport schemes – as a way to both maintain a degree of leverage, and as a means of also accessing spill-over profits from Russian oil and gas exports. This explains, for example, the reverse use of infrastructure originally intended to provide access to non-Russian sources of oil and gas, such as the Odesa-Brody pipeline in Ukraine and the Butinge oil terminal in Lithuania. This tension was seen to different degrees in each of the cases. In the case of Lithuania, both goals seemed to have been equally strong until the mid-2000s, with a small preponderance of the first (diversification) after 2006 and, especially, 2010. In the case of Ukraine, both goals seemed to have been equally strong, with the specificity that the often unfettered rent-seeking by individual actors involved the misuse of the country's transit role to such an extent, that it came to threaten the very functioning of that transit role. This situation prompted and/or justified Russia's pursuit of transit options sidestepping Ukraine, which threatened to diminish seriously the source of the transit income altogether. In the third case, Belarus, goals related to participation in Russian value-added chains took absolute precedence over diversification goals.

Pseudo-solutions to the Issue of Energy Dependency:
Low Prices as Trojan Horse[11]

The factual record of the 1991–2013 period also alerts us to the dangers of over-concentration on securing low energy prices as a pseudo-solution to the problem of energy dependency.

As discussed in chapter 2, Soviet energy culture placed great emphasis on the provision of reliable and low-priced electricity and heating services. The economic crisis and high inflation of the early 1990s, which reduced household incomes and would have made hypothetical cost-covering, inflation-indexed energy prices much more difficult to pay for the average household, helped consolidate these views in the post-Soviet period, and provided great impetus for a renewed political emphasis on the absolute primacy of low energy prices. For both Belarus and Ukraine, the maintenance of low end-user (mainly residential, but also industrial) energy prices during the first post-independence years was a double-edged sword. On the one hand, it moderated the rise in unemployment, and made possible the survival of certain industries and the subsidization of energy-intensive exports. Yet looking in hindsight at this period (in its clearest form, roughly 1992–1997), it seems clear that the over-concentration on low prices as an absolute goal (as opposed to, for example, allowing energy prices to rise and providing targeted subsidies to vulnerable groups), and the virtual inability to conceptualize energy security in any other way, was one of the biggest determinants of energy *insecurity* for both Ukraine and Belarus.

Such overconcentration on low prices had consequences at several levels: at the level of prices domestic consumers were expected to pay, at the level of what was paid to domestic energy producers, at the level of prices paid for imports from Russia, and as a justification for not investing in alternative import infrastructure or in large-scale energy saving projects. At each of these levels, unsustainably low energy prices actually helped undermine the energy security of the state. At the level of residential (and, in many cases, industrial) consumers, low energy prices reduced incentives for conservation; prices too low to cover the cost of imports and network maintenance deprived energy companies of the funds needed to maintain and modernize the countries' transit systems, in turn an important source of revenue. At the level of domestic production, as seen in the case of Ukraine, state-determined prices paid to domestic producers were too low as to provide incentives for increased domestic production.[12] The fact that national oil and gas company NAK Naftohaz was forced to supply residential users and budget organizations at prices not able to cover importation or production costs made the company chronically weak, a situation that synergized perfectly with the designs of those set on capturing it for their own personal profit.

At the level of imports from Russia, the overconcentration on low prices provided fertile ground for corruption and nontransparent deals, and helped support the special role and privileges given to intermediary companies,[13] which were often able to offer lower energy import prices by, de facto, siphoning profits off the state and state companies and distributing the difference between themselves and the importers.

Most importantly, overconcentration on the short-term continuation of low energy prices served to exclude important policy options from the discussion table, while making others much more attractive. Low residential prices isolated consumers from the worst effects of energy dependency on Russia and made diversification policies, more expensive in the short term, hard to sell politically. Thus it is not surprising that real energy diversification policies only started to be discussed seriously after the price of imported Russian gas started to approach international levels after 2007.

What Have We Learned about International Relations in the Post-Soviet Region?

PATTERNS OF INTERNATIONAL RELATIONS AND RUSSIAN
BEHAVIOUR AND IN THE POST-SOVIET AREA

The cases of Ukraine, Belarus, and Lithuania provide interesting insight on patterns of international relations and Russian behaviour in the post-Soviet area. First, as shown by the example of energy relations, informal Russian-initiated bilateral ties proved more important as contrasted with formal (CIS) institutions. In the absence of a network of transitional institutions following the demise of the USSR, these newly independent states often had to face Russia one-on-one, without a broader institutional web to help deal with economic and other issues arising from the Soviet dissolution.[14] Moreover, Russia itself had not ratified membership in important organizations and treaties (most notably the Energy Charter Treaty) a fact that, given Russia's role as main supplier, negatively affected the energy-dependent states' ability to use the treaty's dispute-resolution mechanisms to their fullest extent.

Second, Russia exhibited a track record of establishing de facto economic sanctions, without calling them that, as in the case of the closing of the Druzhba pipeline shipping oil to Lithuania alleging technical reasons.[15] Third and most importantly, many of the energy contradictions between Russia and its energy-poor neighbours were de facto managed not through institutionalized negotiation mechanisms, but through the transborder sharing of rents between elites.

In both the Ukrainian and Belarusian cases, we saw repeated instances of the artificial escalation of energy conflicts with Russia – either as a way to create artificial scarcities that opened the door to rent-seeking deals (Ukraine in 2006), or as a means to pressure Russia into concessions by forcing the politization of negotiations (Belarus). One of the clear losers of such games and of the possibly staged escalation of bilateral conflicts were European gas consumers, which say their supplies reduced or suspended as a result. The lack of more institutionalized means of price setting and managing of energy conflicts allowed such games to take place, but at a very high cost for energy users.

THE EUROPEAN UNION, RUSSIA, AND THE MANAGEMENT
OF ENERGY DEPENDENCY

The European Union – as a beacon to aspire to, investor, rule-setter whose regulations members and aspiring members would need to adopt, and as the main importer of the oil and gas directly or indirectly transited through Ukraine, Belarus, and Lithuania – played a complex and at times contradictory role in the way these countries would deal with Russia and energy dependency. On the one hand, the role of the EU in terms of promoting energy diversification and the liberalization of energy markets was significant. At the same time, however, EU initiatives such as those calling for significant investments in Ukraine's gas transit system seemed often to remain in a no-man's-land due to problems raising investments, as well as Russian uneasiness about how these initiatives would affect its own role as an exporter and investor. More generally, the lack of a clear, unified EU energy position vis-à-vis Russia hindered it from playing a more proactive role in the prevention and resolution of disputes between Russia and the transit states. And, paradoxically, it was the shock of these conflicts' direct effects on European consumers that acted as a wake-up call to the Union, leading to unprecedented discussions on the need for a single EU policy on energy, and the first steps towards its implementation.[16]

In the case of Belarus, despite a history of difficult relations with the EU during the mid-2000s, the EU as a market was crucial for the country to be able to cash in on some of the oil trade advantages from Russia, as these EU countries remained – despite ups and downs in political relations – the main importers of oil products refined in Belarus.

*Rents of Energy Dependency, Bargaining Counterpower,
and Asymmetrical Interdependence*

While, as discussed in chapter 2, legacies are important, they do not explain everything. Some of the differences between Belarus, Ukraine, and Lithuania, for example, were a result not so much of Soviet legacies but of choices made in the early post-Soviet years (in particular the speed of economic reforms, continuing level of state control of the economy, and the nature of political control and systems of interest representation in each case). In particular, infrastructure and infrastructural legacies in and of themselves can only go so far in explaining outcomes.

There is a direct connection between energy rents and the de facto use by an energy-dependent country of the elements of counterpower available to it. Let us assume a country has an important means of counterpressure on the main supplier, for example physical control over pipelines through which important energy exports of the supplying country must transit, or control over other important infrastructure for its gas supplier, such as underground storage facilities. To the extent that these domestic facilities become part of rent-seeking games involving the provision of domestic services at lower-than-average prices in exchange for special arrangements facilitating the sharing of rents between local and foreign actors, the more difficult it becomes to use them as a real and effective element of counterpower vis-á-vis the main suppliers.

The case of Ukraine is highly illustrative of this point. Ukraine's importance in terms of transit, storage, and as market, at least at first glance, should have given it significant power in the relationship with Gazprom and other Russian energy actors. Such assets, in principle crucial instruments for the management of energy dependency, can be used either for the purpose of moderating and negotiating this dependency, or of increasing energy rents for particular players. In the case of Ukraine, however, the prevalent pattern of management of its energy dependency limited the policy impact of these important bargaining elements. For example, Ukraine could use its significant gas storage facilities (equivalent to ca. 41 percent or more of yearly domestic gas use, compared with ca. 3 percent for Belarus and none for Lithuania) to increase its resilience and ability to moderate gas dependency. In reality, however, they were used mainly for the furthering of Gazprom's gas export interests, and for the benefit of intermediary companies such as RosUkrEnergo, to which use of these facilities was provided at prices many times lower than international ones. Similarly, transit-related rents could be managed in a variety of ways leading to different revenue levels; for much of the period 1991–2009, gas transit fees were set at a very low level, in exchange for relatively low import prices, in an arrangement that facilitated the sharing of rents between the two sides, but not the proactive use of Ukraine's transit power as an effective means of counterpower vis-á-vis Russia.

This relates to the question of real versus apparent counterpower in a situation of asymmetrical interdependence: some countries, such as Ukraine, seemed to have significant counterpower, but neglected it. The case of Belarus represents an interesting counterpart to that of Ukraine's management of asymmetrical interdependence situations. A number of factors would make us think of Belarus' more limited bargaining power vis-á-vis Russia: the country's smaller role in the transit of Russian gas exports to Western markets, its more limited ownership rights over the main pipelines crossing its territory, higher level of energy dependency, and the 2007–2011 sale of Beltransgas to Gazprom. Yet,

Table 7.3 Apparent and Real Power in Asymmetric Interdependence Energy Relationships with Russia, 1991–2013

Country	Level of Apparent Power	Level of real power vis-á-vis Russia	Possible explanations
Ukraine	Medium	Low	Elite corruption and disunity
Lithuania	Low	Medium	Implicit EU backing
Belarus	Low	Medium-high	• Russia's desire for military cooperation • Lukashenka's centralized power

perhaps due to, among other factors, the more limited nature of domestic rent-seeking compared to Ukraine and to President Lukashenka's political and psychological power vis-á-vis Moscow, the country was largely able to compensate for its lack of economic counterpower vis-á-vis Russia, and it would seem as if Belarus was able – at least until 2008 – to use this limited leverage more effectively than Ukraine was able to. As discussed in chapter 5, after 2008 and especially 2010, the Belarusian-Russian relationship takes a clear turn for the worse. While, as discussed in chapter 5, even during this period President Lukashenka was able to reduce the impact of these new external conditions, it seemed highly improbable that he would be able to return Belarus to the previous high levels of indirect energy subsidization by Russia.

Implications for Our Understanding of Transition and Foreign Policy in the Post-Soviet World

What Have We Learned about National Interests and Their Implementation in the Former Soviet World?

Although the de facto energy dependency management strategies followed by each of our cases differed, one element present in all of them – although of differing importance in each of the cases – was the division, in one way or another, of energy rents between local and Russia-based elites. Although this was most blunt in the case of Ukraine, it also played a role in the case of Belarus – most clearly through the division of oil trade gains between Belarus and Russian exporters – and Lithuania, where Russian-controlled intermediary companies were able to share their profits with local actors. All of this forces us to re-think our assessment of national interests in the post-Soviet area and to pay more attention to the ways in which the interests of various actors interact on the basis of, on the one hand, the path dependencies estab-lished during the Soviet period and, on the other, of the rent-seeking possibilities opened by various post-Soviet arrangements.

Implications for other Energy-poor Transit States

Belarus, Ukraine, and Lithuania form part of a larger group of energy-dependent states also playing a direct or indirect role in energy transit. These include, in addition to our case studies, countries such as Mol-dova and Georgia in the FSU, Austria, Slovakia, Hungary, and Bulgaria in the EU, and Morocco, Tunisia, and Turkey. Despite the growing pol-icy attention paid to transit issues, we know little about these countries as a distinct subgroup, and in-depth analysis of domestic issues as they affect their transit role remains largely absent from the current debate, which has focused mostly on geopolitical perspectives and externally focused understandings of energy security. The conclusions from our case studies can provide important insights for understanding the be-haviour of other energy-poor transit states worldwide.

The evidence presented in this book has shown the importance of domestic issues for understanding the transit policies of energy-poor states. Through these cases, we have also learned that the impact of energy-related rents and profits can be as significant in energy-poor states as it is in the case of energy exporters. Understanding these do-mestic factors can help us gain a better understanding of the multiple layers of domestic and external bargaining affecting negotiations be-tween transit and supplier states worldwide. Further research on the connection between domestic politics, use of transit role, and relation-ship with the main suppliers may help us gain a better understanding of a group of countries whose importance is becoming ever more cru-cial as the EU states seek to diversify their energy supplies.

Limits of a Domestic-focused Perspective

This book has focused on the domestic management of a country's energy dependency. This does not imply, however, that all outcomes will be determined solely by the domestic management of depen-dency, nor that energy dependency and its negative consequences can be surmounted by simply pursuing the "right" style of managing this dependency. No matter what the content of this management will be, other factors – structural legacies and path dependencies created by the Soviet system, cultural factors, international price dynamics, participation in transborder marketing and value-added chains, and international political relationships – will play important roles in the determination of energy outcomes. Having said this, how a country will manage its energy dependency *will* make a difference in terms of what it makes out of this situation of dependency, and will help set the stage for the way the country will deal with challenges of both state building and energy security in the years to come.

Looking Back, Looking Ahead: World Prices, the Shale Gas Revolution, and the Politics of Energy Dependency

For the traditionally energy-dependent states of Central and Eastern Europe, the new decade starting in 2010 brought with both new challenges (in the form of sharply increased energy import prices) and new opportunities (major discoveries in unconventional gas). We should not lose sight, however, of the social and political factors that helped shape energy policy in the first twenty years of these states' independent lives – it is only to the extent that transparency in policy making and a widely agreed-to and supported policy exists that these states will be able to deal proactively with this new situation. The sharp increase in gas prices, by 2010 approaching or exceeding prices paid by WE importers, is as much an opportunity (as seen in the case of Lithuania, an opportunity to eliminate ways of doing business that fostered rent-seeking and corruption) as it may be an economic burden. While it may have been the external shock of heavily increased gas prices that provided the key incentive for new energy initiatives, such as the building of infrastructure to access LNG supplies as a means of diversifying away from exclusive imports of Russian gas, it will be largely the types of domestic factors explored in this book that will determine whether these states will be able to adapt proactively to this new situation and turn this challenge into new opportunities.

The unconventional (often referred to by its best-known component, shale) gas "revolution" presents similar challenges and opportunities. Since 2009, major discoveries have been made in unconventional gas in CEE. By early 2013 several states in the region had signed agreements with major companies to prospect and develop these resources, in particular Ukraine with its 2013 fifty-year, $10 billion agreement with Shell.[17] In addition, the development of Poland's unconventional gas reserves – estimated to be the largest in Europe – could have an impact on the energy situation of the region as a whole, as well as possible shale gas exports from the United States in LNG form. Yet the unconventional gas revolution is not only about technological breakthroughs, but also about the cultural, regulatory, and governance issues that may determine whether these technologies will be successfully implemented.[18] This successful implementation has to do not only with the development of mechanisms facilitating technology transfer and safeguarding the interests of both local parties and major foreign investors, but also with the development of appropriate mechanisms to safeguard the interests – first and foremost ecological – of the local populations affected by these developments.

There are no easy answers to these challenges, but what is important to keep in mind is that *how* these states will deal with this new opportunity, and whether it will help these states move to more sustainable energy futures, will to a great extent depend on the strength of their domestic energy *and* political governance and their ability to develop a strong regulatory framework to deal with this new opportunity, including its environmental challenges. In order for the shale revolution to live up to its promise, it is crucial that the needs and interests of all those affected be taken into account. Here, as in 1991, governance issues, and the issue of how the gains and losses of this new development will be distributed among the population and the elites, will be crucial.

Appendix: Chronologies of Main Energy Events for Ukraine, Belarus, and Lithuania

Ukraine: Main Energy Events, 1991–2013

Winter 1993–1994	Disruption in supplies of Russian gas and oil lead to an energy crisis and freezing home temperatures in Ukraine
July 1994	Kuchma takes office as President
May 1997	Black Sea Fleet agreements give Russia control of most of the Fleet in exchange for forgiveness of gas-related debt
July 1997	PM Lazarenko resigns and flees the country after accusations of massive energy corruption
2000–2001	Reformist team of PM Yushchenko and vice PM Tymoshenko seek to institute energy reforms
Nov.–Dec. 2007	Orange Revolution
January 2005	Yushchenko takes office after winning repeated elections in December 2004
December 2005	Gas supply confrontation with Russia
January 2006	Three-day suspension of gas supplies
January 4, 2006	Gas supply agreement gives control of gas supply to intermediary company RosUkrEnergo
December 2008	Gas supply confrontation with Russia
January 2009	14-day suspension of gas supplies by Russia stops all Russian supplies to Bulgaria, Romania, Macedonia, Serbia, Bosnia-Herzegovina, and Croatia

January 19, 2009	Supplies are restored as an agreement sharply rising prices and eliminating RosUkrEnergo's role is signed
2009	Growing energy policy confrontation between President Yushchenko and PM Tymoshenko
February 2010	Yanukovich elected president
April 2010	Kharkiv agreements provide for a nearly 30 percent discount on gas prices in exchange for extension of stationing of Russia's Black Sea Fleet until 2042
January 2012	Despite the Kharkiv discounts, gas import prices reach $425 per tcm, about $40 more than European reference prices
January 2013	Ukraine and Royal Dutch Shell sign a $10 billion, fifty-year PSA for the development of unconventional gas resources
January 2013	Citing "take-or-pay" clauses in its contract, Gazprom demands Ukraine pay a $7 billion fine for contracted gas not taken in 2012

Belarus: Main Energy Events, 1991–2013

July 1994	Lukashenka elected president
April 1997	Treaty on the Union of Belarus and Russia signed
May 2002	New Russia-Belarus agreement gives Belarus access to domestic Russian gas prices
January 2004	Russian cancelation of domestic gas prices agreement comes into effect
February 2004	Citing broken agreements on the privatization of Beltransgas and the stealing of its gas from the transit pipeline, Gazprom suspends gas supplies to Belarus for 24 hours
December 2006	Gas confrontation with Gazprom
January 2007	Dispute on the division of oil export rents between Belarus and Russia
	Transneft suspends oil shipments to or through Belarus, briefly interrupting oil supplies to Poland and other points west
May 2007	Agreement on a Belarusian-Russian JV on the basis of Beltransgas signed

January 2010	Gazprom reaches 50 percent ownership in Beltransgas
April 2010	First shipments of Venezuelan oil arrive
July 2010	Belarus belatedly joins Russia-Kazakhstan Costums Union after a dispute on taxation of energy trade
July 2010	Russian media campaign against Lukashenka
December 9, 2010	Lukashenka announces a renewal of duty-free oil supplies from Russia after a meeting with Russian President Medvedev
December 19, 2010	Belarus' Central Election Commission declares Lukashenka the winner of presidential elections, while results are not recognized as free by the United States and the EU
January 2011	Russia abolishes export duties on all oil exported to Belarus
January 2011	Three-week suspension of oil supplies to Belarus while a price agreement is negotiated with Russian suppliers
March 14, 2011	Agreement signed with Russia regarding the building of a nuclear power station
September 2011	Agreement with Gazprom on sharp reduction of gas prices effective in 2012
November 2011	Agreement with Gazprom on move to domestic Russian prices effective in 2014
December 3, 2011	Gazprom officially becomes owner of 100 percent of Beltransgas shares
May 2012	New tensions with Russia as Belarus is accused of exporting oil products as solvents and lubricants to avoid paying Russia its due share of export taxes

Lithuania: Main Energy Events, 1990–2013

April–July 1990	Oil blockade from Moscow after Lithuania declares independence
1995	Construction of Butinge Oil Terminal starts
1999	Construction of Butinge Oil Terminal completed
October 1999	Mazeikiu Nafta refinery sold to Williams
August 2002	Williams leaves Mazeikiu Nafta after being unable to secure sufficient supplies

2004	Privatization of national gas company Lietuvos Dujos
April 2004	Lithuania joins NATO
May 2004	President Paksas impeached
June 2004	Lithuania joins EU
December 2004	First Ignalina NPP unit decomissioned
July 2006	Russia stops oil shipments via the Druzhba pipeline
December 2009	Second and last Ignalina NPP unit decomissioned
May 2010	New goverment inititive calls for the unbundling of Lietuvos Dujos and increased state decision making in the company, reducing Gazprom's power in the company
December 2010	Tender process for the building of a new NPP is de-railed as sole eligible bidder revokes its proposal
August 2012	Lithuania sues Gazprom for $1.9 billion at the Stockholm Arbitration Court, claiming it has intentionally distorted prices since 2004
October 2012	In a consultative referendum, a majority of voters reject the building of a new nuclear power plant
January 2013	Lithuania starts paying $540/tcm for gas imported from Gazprom, the highest price in Europe

Notes

1. Introduction

1 As shown in Table 1.6, gas prices charged countries such as Ukraine grew from about $0.25 per tcm in 1991 (nearly 1/450 of the European price) to $432, over 105 percent of that price, in 2012.

2 See, among others, Lesli Dienes, Istvan Dobozi, et al., *Energy and Economic Reform in the Former Soviet Union* (New York: St. Martin's Press, 1994); Pauline Jones Luong and Erika Weinthal, "Prelude to the Resource Curse: Explaining Oil and Gas Development Strategies in the Soviet Successor States and Beyond," *Comparative Political Studies* 34, no. 4 (2001): 367–99; David Lane, ed., *The Political Economy of Russian Oil* (Oxford: Rowman & Littlefield, 1999); Adam N. Stulberg, *Well-Oiled Diplomacy: Strategic Manipulation and Russia's Energy Statecraft in Eurasia* (Albany: State University of New York Press, 2007); Robert E. Ebel and Rajan Menon, *Energy and Conflict in Central Asia and the Caucasus* (Oxford: Rowman & Littlefield, 2001); and Mehdi Parvizi Amineh, *Globalisation, Geopolitics and Energy Security in Central Eurasia and the Caspian* (The Hague: Clingendael International Energy Programme, 2003).

3 See Ebel and Menon, *Energy and Conflict*, and Amineh, *Globalisation*.

4 Most of the available literature focuses on rather narrow and technical topics, such as calculating energy subsidies, structural reform, or future energy demand on the basis of single case studies. See for example Gregory V. Krasnov and Josef C. Brada, "Implicit Subsidies in Russian-Ukrainian Energy Trade," *Europe-Asia Studies* 49, no. 5 (July 1997); Christian von Hirschhausen and H. Engerer, "Post-Soviet Gas Sector Restructuring in the CIS: A Political Economy Approach," *Energy Policy* 26, no. 15 (December 1998); Edilberto Segura, "Energy: Current Problems and Long-term Strategy," in *The EU and Ukraine: Neighbours, Friends, Partners?*, ed. Ann

Lewis (London: Kogan Page, 2002); M. Horn, "Energy Demand until 2010 in Ukraine," *Energy Policy* 27, no. 12 (November 1999); Theresa Sabonis-Chafee, "Power Politics: National Energy Policies and the Nuclear Newly Independent States of Armenia, Lithuania and Ukraine" (Ph.D. dissertation, Political Science, Emory University, 1999); Stacy Closson, "State Weakness in Perspective: Strong Politico-Economic Networks in Georgia's Energy Sector," *Europe-Asia Studies* 61, no. 5 (July 2009): 759–78; and "Networks of Profit in Georgia's Autonomous Regions: Challenges to Statebuilding," *Journal of Intervention and Statebuilding* 4, no. 2 (June 2010): 179–204.

5 Most of the literature on interest groups in CEE and the post-Soviet states has focused on formal trade associations, labour unions, and tripartite agreements between the state, entrepreneurs, and trade unions. See for example Paul Kubicek, *Unbroken Ties: The State, Interest Associations and Corporatism in Post-Soviet Ukraine* (Ann Arbor: University of Michigan Press, 2000).

6 Margarita M. Balmaceda, *Energy Dependency, Politics and Corruption in the Former Soviet Union: Russia's Power, Oligarch's Profits and Ukraine's Missing Energy Policy, 1995–2006* (London: Routledge, 2008).

7 By Russian-centred perspective we do not mean necessarily a pro-Russian perspective, but one where Russia is the central actor and most of the materials used are Russian or refer to Russia.

8 European Commission, Directorate of Energy and Transport, *Towards a European Strategy for the Security of Energy Supply: Green Paper* (Luxemburg, European Communities: 2001) and European Union, Directorate of Energy and Transport, *Second Strategic Energy Review – Securing our Energy Future* (EU, European Commission, 2008).

9 See Anita Orban, *Power, Energy and the New Russian Imperialism* (Westport, CT: Praeger, 2008); Keith Smith, *Russia and European Energy Security: Divide and Dominate* (Washington, DC: CSIS, 2008); Marshall Goldman, *Petro-state: Putin, Power, and the New Russia* (Oxford: Oxford University Press, 2008); Janusz Bugajski, *Cold Peace: Russia's New Imperialism* (Westport, CT: Praeger, 2005); and Edward Lucas, *A New Cold War: Putin's Russia and the Threat to the West* (London: Palgrave Macmillan, 2008).

10 While the main goal of this book is not to explain Russian behaviour towards the energy-poor states, but these states' *responses* to their energy dependency, it is important to note one important limitation in the energy-as-weapon approach in terms of explaining Russia's behaviour in the FSU. If, indeed, energy can be used as a political weapon, it is important to recognize that it can also be used for other purposes, and that these various

ways of using energy are often in competition with each other. As will be discussed in chapter 3, actors in Russia with control over energy resources are constantly making choices about where to use or direct these resources, of which direct external economic pressure on their post-Soviet neighbours is only one among many options.

11 I thank Ivan Katchanovsky for interesting insights on this issue. For examples of such approaches as applied to the gas trade relationship between Russia and its energy-poor neighbours see, for example, Yuri Yegorov and Franz Wirl, "Ukranian Gas Transit Game," *ZfE Zeitschrift für Energiewirschaft*, no. 2 (2009): 147–55, C. von Hirschausen et al., "Transporting Russian Gas to Western Europe – A Simulation Analysis," *The Energy Journal* 26, no. 2 (2005): 49–68; and David Tarr and Peter Thompson, "The Merits of Dual Pricing of Russian Natural Gas," *World Economy* 27, no. 8 (2004): 1173–94. On the obsolescing bargain between transit states and energy suppliers and how the relative bargaining power between both evolves, see Raymond Vernon, *Sovereignty at Bay: The Multinational Spread of US Enterprises* (New York: Basic Books, 1971); and Ekpen J. Omonbude, "The Transit Oil and Gas Pipeline and the Role of Bargaining: A Non-technical Discussion," *Energy Policy* 35, no. 12 (December 2007): 6188–94.

12 In the case of Ukraine, for example, the monopoly model can explain Russia's market power to charge Ukraine any price for its gas – a price that can be set at either very low or very high levels depending on political considerations – while Ukraine has, in theory, a nearly similar market power in terms of setting the price for Russian gas transit. Yet while both Ukraine and Belarus may lose their positions as (near) monopolists for the transit Russian gas and oil to WE due to Russia's transit diversification projects (discussed in chapters 3, 4, and 5), until 2012 Ukraine and Belarus have not been able to break Russia's role as gas supply monopolist.

13 For excellent detailed analyses of Ukrainian-Russian gas contracts, see the work of the Natural Gas Research Program of the Oxford Institute for Energy Studies led by Jonathan Stern and, in particular, Simon Pirani's contributions noted in the bibliography.

14 As discussed further on, some of the constructivist and constructivist-inspired literature (see the references to Wendt, Katzenstein, Abdelal, and D'Anieri in the bibliography) can provide important insights for our project. In addition, the larger IR literature on trade policy making can provide interesting insights. Joanne Gowa, for example, analyses the factors that induce states to trade with their allies rather than with their enemies. Her work is relevant for helping understand some of the particularities of trading with a country that is seen as an adversary, particularities that

go beyond traditional economic calculations. See Joanne Gowa, *Allies, Adversaries, and International Trade* (Princeton, NJ: Princeton University Press, 1994).

15 Ukraine's gas supply contracts are a case in point. In 2004, 2006, and 2009 five- and ten-year contracts were signed, each superseded by a new contract – itself coming into being as the result of a major crisis – well before their expiration date.

16 Much of the literature on policy making in post-Communist states has concentrated on social policy in the new EU member states and is only of limited use for understanding energy policy.

17 Sabonis-Chafee uses an implicitly realist approach in her analysis of Lithuanian, Ukrainian, and Armenian energy policies in the first post-Soviet years. However, her analysis is hindered by an overestimation of both state capacity and unified, consistent political will to move away from energy dependency on Russia. See Sabonis-Chafee, *Power Politics*.

18 See Stephen Krasner, "State Power and the Structure of International Trade," and Stephen Krasner, "Oil Is the Exception," in *International Political Economy: Perspectives on Global Power and Wealth*, eds. Jeffry A. Frieden and David A. Lake (New York: Bedford/St. Martin's Press, 2000).

19 See Albert O. Hirschman, *State Power and the Structure of Foreign Trade* (Berkeley: University of California Press, 1980; originally published in 1945), 16. See also the discussion of Hirschman in Paul D'Anieri, *Economic Interdependence in Ukrainian-Russian Relations* (Albany: SUNY Press, 1999), 13–16; and Jonathan Kirshner, "The Political Economy of Realism," in *Unipolar Politics: Realism and State Strategies after the Cold War*, eds. Ethan B. Kapstein and Michael Mastanduno (New York: Columbia University Press, 1999).

20 See Rawi Abdelal, *National Purpose in the World Economy: Post Soviet States in Comparative Perspective* (Ithaca, NY: Cornell University Press, 2001); and Andrei P. Tsygankov, *Pathways after Empire: National Identity and Foreign Economic Policy in the Post-Soviet World* (Lanham, MD: Rowman & Littlefield, 2001).

21 See Adam Przeworski, Susan Stokes, and Bernard Manin, eds., *Democracy, Accountability and Representation* (Cambridge: Cambridge University Press, 1999), 8; and Andrew Lawrence Roberts, *Politics of Social Policy Reform in Eastern Europe* (PhD dissertation, Princeton University, 2003), 10.

22 See Victoria Murillo, *Political Competition, Partisanship and Policy Making in Latin American Public Utilities* (Cambridge: Cambridge University Press, 2009).

23 Corina Herron Linden, "Power and Uneven Globalization: Coalitions and Energy Trade Dependence in the Newly Independent States of Europe" (PhD dissertation, Political Science, University of Washington, 2000).

24 While this may have seem the case in 1999 (the last year covered by Linden), looked at from a longer-term perpective, Estonia's success in breaking away from dependency on Russian energy seems more modest.

25 The other side of this argument would be that, in places like Ukraine (and, in a somewhat different way, Belarus), the fear of the popular upheaval that could come from the (broadly enfranchised) population if energy prices would be allowed to rise sharply was one of the reasons for the state not wanting to increase energy prices.

26 Fiona McGillivray, *Privileging Industry: The Comparative Politics of Trade and Industrial Policy* (Princeton, NJ: Princeton University Press, 2004), 8.

27 See, for example, A. Frieden and R. Rogowski,, "The Impact of the International Economy on National Policies: An Analytical Overview," in *Internationalization and Domestic Politics*, eds. R.O. Keohane and H.V. Milner (Cambridge: Cambridge University Press, 1996); McGillivray, *Privileging Industry*; and Helen Milner, *Resisting Protectionism: Global Industries and the Politics of International Trade* (Princeton, NJ: Princeton University Press, 1988).

28 Hazem Beblawy and Giacomo Luciani, eds., "The Rentier State," vol. 2, in *Nation State and Integration in the Arab World* (London: Croom Helm, 1987).

29 See Hossein Mahdavy, "The Pattern and Problems of Economic Development in Rentier States: The Case of Iran," in *Studies in the Economic History of the Middle East* (Oxford: Oxford University Press, 1970); and Richard M. Auty and Alan H. Gelb, "Political Economy of Resource-Abundant States," in *Resource Abundance and Economic Development*, ed. R. M. Auty (Oxford: Oxford University Press, 2001). On paths out of the resource curse see Macartan Humphreys, Jeffrey D. Sachs, and Joseph E. Stiglitz, eds., *Escaping the Resource Curse* (New York: Columbia University Press, 2007).

30 Beblawy and Luciani make the existence of rents *from an external source* crucial for a state to be considered a rentier state. Beblawy and Luciani, "The Rentier State." See also Douglas A. Yates, *The Rentier State in Africa: Oil Rent Dependency and Neocolonialism in the Republic of Gabon* (Trenton, NJ: Africa World Press, 1996); and Merrie Gilbert Klapp, *The Sovereign Entrepreneur: Oil Policies in Advanced and Less Developed Capitalist Countries* (Ithaca, NY: Cornell University Press, 1987).

31 See, for example, Michael Ross, *Timber Booms and Institutional Breakdown in Southeast Asia* (Cambridge: Cambridge University Press, 2001); and Richard

Snyder, "Does Lootable Wealth Breed Disorder? A Political Economy of Extraction Framework," *Comparative Political Studies* 39, no. 8 (2006).

32 For example, Pauline Jones Luong and Erika Weinthal, "Rethinking the Resource Curse: Ownership Structure, Institutional Capacity, and Domestic Constraints," *Annual Review of Political Science* 9 (2006); Benjamin Smith, *Hard Times in the Lands of Plenty: Oil Politics in Iran and Indonesia* (Ithaca, NY: Cornell University Press, 2007); and Thad Dunning, *Crude Democracy: Natural Resource Wealth and Political Regimes* (Cambridge: Cambridge University Press, 2008). See also Michael L. Ross, *The Oil Curse: How Petroleum Wealth Shapes the Development of Nations* (Princeton, NJ: Princeton University Press, 2012).

33 The phrase "transition period" is used here as a conventional designation of the post-Soviet economic transformation process, and does not imply a judgment as to where such as transition has or should have led.

34 See, for example, Kimberly Marten Zisk, *Weapons, Culture and Self-Interest: Soviet Defense Managers in the New Russia* (New York: Columbia University Press, 1997); Gerner Grabher and David Stark, "Organizing Diversity: Evolutionary Theory, Network Analysis and Post-socialism," in *Theorising Transition: The Political Economy of Post-communist Transformations*, eds. John Pickles and Adrian Smith (London: Routledge, 1998), 54–75; and G. Helmke and S. Levitsky, "Informal Institutions and Comparative Politics: A Research Agenda," *Perspectives on Politics* 2, no. 4 (2004): 725–40.

35 For example through new types of intermediary companies, such as, most prominently, Itera and RosUkrEnergo, organized around often corrupt rent-seeking.

36 For example, through energy trade arrangements involving barter and a variety of grey market mechanisms such as the mutual offsetting of loans and the resale of discounted IOU's, bills of exchange, and tax arrears scrip. Some of these costs shifted to the state have to do with the additional transaction costs created by factors such as cronyism and corruption. See Douglass North, "A Transaction Cost Theory of Politics," *Journal of Theoretical Politics* 2 (1990): 355–67.

37 Corruption, of course, is only one extreme example; informal institutions, in and of themselves, are not necessarily positive or negative.

38 On this issue, see A. Shleifer and R. Vishny, *The Grabbing Hand: Government Pathologies and Their Cures* (Cambridge, MA: Harvard University Press, 1998); K. Hoff and J. Stiglitz, "After the Big Bang? Obstacles to the Emergence of the Rule of Law in Post-communist Societies," *World Bank Policy Research Working Paper 2934* (December 2002); Karla Hoff and Joseph E. Stiglitz, "The Creation of the Rule of Law and the Legitimacy of Property Rights: Political and Economic Consequences of a Corrupt Privatization,"

NBER Working Paper No. 11772 (November 2005); Anders Aslund, Peter Boone, and Simon Johnson, "Escaping the Under-Reform Trap," *IMF Staff Papers* 48 (2001); and Viktor M. Polterovich, "Institutional Traps," in *The New Russia*, eds. Lawrence R. Klein and Marshall I. Pomer (Stanford, CA: Stanford University Press, 2000).

39 Other factors – expensive-to-replace pipeline systems centred on supplies from Russia inherited from the Soviet period, international price dynamics, and foreign policy commitments – also play important roles in the determination of actual outcomes in terms of levels of energy dependency.

40 Such management of energy relations also affects the opportunities available for the realization of Russian energy interests in each country, although we cannot assume a single Russian energy interest vis-á-vis each country.

41 For working purposes, and when a more precise definition would be out of place, various entities seeking to articulate their interests through state policy will be defined collectively as *interest articulators*. This concept includes lobbies, interest groups, and interest associations, as well as other more informal arrangements.

42 We differentiate "rent-seeking" (the attempt by an individual or entity to obtain unjustifiable high profits, often through the illegal or semi-legal manipulation of the economic environment, including by lobbying, bribing, or using privileged information) from "corruption," which we understand specifically as the use of public office for private gain.

43 For example, calculating the rents accrued in a barter operation in the 1990s would require access to each of the barter coefficients used at the time of the operation, something clearly unfeasible. Similarly, many of the rents at stake were, it is assumed, accrued on the basis of corrupt operations, making research in this area especially complicated. Authors such as Gaddy and Ickes estimate rents in the Russian oil and gas sector on the basis of production figures (see Clifford C. Gaddy and Barry W. Ickes "Resource Rents and the Russian Economy," *Eurasian Geography and Economics* 46, no. 8 [2006]: 559–83). Their approach, however, is not fully applicable to our cases, where the rents involved are much more the result of lower-level transactions than in the Russian oil and gas production case, where they can be calculated on the basis of production figures.

44 Arbitrage refers to the possibility of making a profit out of manipulating price differentials for the same good between various markets or within sectors of the same market. Among other reasons, such arbitrage possibilities existed due to Russia's desire to maintain a special relationship with the post-Soviet states, including through the provision of gas and oil at preferential prices.

45 For a discussion of the trans-border sharing of corrupt rents through intermediary trader RosUkrEnergo as a means to solve the 2006 Russian-Ukrainian gas confrontation, see Balmaceda, *Energy Dependency*.

46 See Joel S. Hellman, "Winners Take All: The Politics of Partial Reform in the Postcommunist Transition," *World Politics* 50, no. 2 (1998): 203–34.

47 See Konstantin Sonin, "Why the Rich May Favor Poor Protection of Property Rights," William Davison Institute (University of Michigan) *Working Papers Series* No. 544, December 2002, available at http://deepblue.lib.umich.edu/bitstream/2027.42/39929/2/wp544.pdf. For examples of the creation of artificial scarcities, see Somboom Siriprachai, "Rent-Seeking Activities in Developing Countries: A Survey of Recent Issues" (available at ftp://econ.tu.ac.th/class/archan/SOMBOON/my%20discussion%20Papers), citing James M. Buchanan, "Rent-seeking and Profit-seeking," in *Toward a General Theory of the Rent-Seeking Society*, eds. J.M. Buchanan, R.D. Tollison, and G. Tullock (Texas: Texas A & M University Press, 1980).

48 We use the term "rent-seeking swamps" to denote areas of economic activity where a significant amount of money is exchanged (relative to the country's GDP, for example), and where opportunities for rent-seeking are easily available. These rent-seeking swamps not only allow rent-seeking to take place, but attract and foster it. Prime, though not sole examples of rent swamps are oil and gas export and transit systems. Other possible cases of rent-seeking swamps found in the literature (although not discussed as part of a single phenomenon) are those of gambling in Macao and, possibly, the case of income from US military bases and from preferential access for Philippine products in American markets in the Philippines and the sudden influx of large and illegal drug trade revenue to Bolivia in the early 1980s. What seems to be common to these situations is the fact that these rents, in a pseudo Dutch Disease dynamic, distort incentives and crowd out value-adding activity. (Olexander Babanin, Vladimir Dubrovskyi, and Olexyi Ivaschenko, *Ukraine: The Lost Decade and the Coming Boom* [Kyiv, 2001], 29 [FN 10]). See S. Lo, "Bureaucratic Corruption and its Control in Macao," *Asian Journal of Public Administration* 15, no. 1 (1993): 32–58; Paul Hutchcroft, "Booty Capitalism: Business-Government Relations in the Philippines," in *Business and Government in Industrializing Asia*, ed. Andrew McIntyre (Ithaca, NY: Cornell University Press, 1994), 225; and Michael Johnston, "The Political Consequences of Corruption: A Reassessment," *Comparative Politics* 18 (July 1986): 456–77.

49 For a discussion of such formative impact in the case of post-revolutionary Iran, see Smith, *Hard Times in the Lands of Plenty*.

50 Armenia is dependent on Russian gas but does not currently play a significant role in the transit of Russian energy. In addition, Tadzhikistan and Kyrgyzstan are largely energy dependent, but mainly on their neighbours and not on Russia.

51 By direct transit we mean transit by pipelines and (in oil) through transfer ports for shipment by tanker. By indirect transit we mean first and foremost the refining and (re)export, as oil products, of crude oil from Russia.

52 Why these three cases and not Latvia, Moldova, Georgia, or Armenia? In addition to their much less significant role in the transit of Russian energy, the Soviet legacies of Georgia and Moldova are somewhat different from those of our three case studies, as they remained less industrialized. Lithuania was chosen over Latvia as representative of Baltic energy-dependent states for two main reasons. First, compared to Latvia, the sharpness of the confrontation with Russia on the issue of Russian minorities was significantly weaker (and the size of this minority much smaller, at about 5 percent in Lithuania versus 27 percent in Latvia), taking away from the equation one additional factor often complicating energy relations, and allowing us to focus more specifically on the energy relationship. Second, Lithuania is a better example of an energy poor *transit* state, as it played a transit role, albeit in a limited way, for the whole period under discussion, while Latvia's transit role ended in 2004 when Russia stopped the trans-shipment of oil through Latvian ports. For a discussion of the role of tensions around Russian minorities as a factor in energy relartions between Russia and the Baltic states, see Agnia Grigas, *The Politics of Energy and Memory Between the Baltic States and Russia* (Aldershot, England: Ashgate, 2013).

53 Focusing on oil and gas is also useful for comparing the implications of their different forms of organization in the main supplier country, Russia, as well as both goods' differing value-added chains.

54 For a detailed discussion of gas stealing, see chapter 4.

55 Energy emergency preparedness involves items such as capacity for import buffering, electrical power plants' capacity to switch between two or more fuels, the availability of unused electricity-generating capacity, diversification of fuel sources, state of import infrastructure such as ports and other facilities, and the availability of emergency fuel stockpiles allowing a country to withstand a certain period without the use of imports. Adapted from Sabonis-Chafee, *Power Politics*, 89.

56 With some modifications, this could be compared with the situation of stationary banditry discussed by Olson. See Mancur Olson, *Power and Prosperity* (New York: Basic Books, 2000).

57 This situation is also analytically close to Hellman's view of a captured state where particularistic actors have gained such great power within the state that they can use its institutions and resources for their own goals as opposed to general interests. See Joel S. Hellman and Mark Schankerman, "Intervention, Corruption and State Capture: The Nexus between Enterprises and the State," in *Economics of Transition* no. 3 (2000): 545–67; and Hellman, "Winners Take All." For the World Bank definition of state capture, see World Bank, *Anticorruption in Transition: A Contribution to the Policy Debate* (Washington, DC: World Bank, 2000).

58 For a discussion of the effects of a fragmented political system in other cases, see Barry Ames, *The Deadlock of Democracy in Brazil* (Ann Arbor: University of Michigan Press, 2001); Scott Mainwaring, *Rethinking Party Systems in the Third Wave of Democratization* (Stanford, CA: Stanford University Press, 1999); and Peter R. Kingstone, "Privatizing Telebrás: Brazilian Political Institutions and Policy Performance," *Comparative Politics* 36, no. 1 (2003): 21–40.

59 On securitization see Barry Buzan, Ole Wæver, and Japp de Wilde, *Security: A New Framework for Analysis* (Boulder, CO: Lynne Rienner Publishers, 1998); and Barry Buzan and Ole Wæver, *Regions and Powers: The Structure of International Security* (Cambridge: Cambridge University Press, 2003). In the energy area, we refer to securitization as the social construction and articulation of energy dependencies as existential security threats. It is important to note, however, that securitization may take place for instrumental purposes; that is, to gain some concrete advantage vis-à-vis domestic publics or foreign actors. Thus, we can talk about the instrumental securitization of energy dependency.

60 For working purposes, we define high energy dependency as a situation where (a) more than one-third of a country's total energy supply comes from foreign sources; (b) more than 50 percent of a country's annual consumption of *a major energy source* (in most of the FSU states, oil or gas) come from foreign sources; or (c) a country depends on *a single external provider* for more than 60 percent of its imports of a major energy source for that country or 45 percent of its consumption of that energy source. Our three case studies fulfill these requirements and are clearly energy-dependent on Russia.

61 See also Paul Stevens, *Transit Troubles: Pipelines as a Source of Conflict* (London: Chatham House, 2009).

62 While for a large part of the post-1991 period much of Russia's refining capacity went unused, this coexisted, especially until 2000, with a deficit of

usable refining capacity, as the existing facilities, often outdated, were not able to deliver the necessary deepness of refining. See IEA, *Russian Energy Survey 2002*, 66.

63 For example, if throughout the period under study long-term contracts with a duration of about 20–30 years were the rule in Gazprom exports to WE, complemented by a small but growing number of short-term arrangements and spot-market sales, the usual arrangement in sales to CIS countries was yearly contracts, often subject to political volatility and negotiated at the very end of the previous year or even (with Belarus) after the start of the new year. For an economic perspective on the contractual management of energy relationships, see D. Finon and C. Locatelli, "Russian and European Gas Interdependence: Could Contractual Trade Channel Geopolitics?" *Energy Policy* 36, no. 1 (2008): 423–42; and C. von Hirschhausen and A. Neumann, "Long-Term Contracts and Asset Specificity Revisited: An Empirical Analysis of Producer-Importer Relations in the Natural Gas Industry," *Review of Industrial Organization* 28, no. 2 (2008): 131–43.

64 While liquefied natural gas (LNG) technology is contributing to the creation of a global gas market independent of pipeline networks, its impact is so far limited by its high relative cost, especially at lower gas prices. However, this is expected to change as gas prices rise and the relative cost of LNG technology decreases.

65 In the absence of such world price, and following International Monetary Fund (IMF) usage, we use as benchmark for European market prices the quoted prices for Russian natural gas at the border with Germany.

66 See Derek Brower, "NE: Gazprom Is Winning its Caucasian Chess Game with EU," *Business New Europe*, 15 December 2006, available at http://derekbrower.wordpress.com/2007/01/06/hello-world/ (accessed 10 January 2007). In 2007–2008, Bulgaria and Serbia signed agreements with Gazprom giving the company preferential access to its energy markets and transit routes. See Judy Dempsey, "Russia Extends Energy Spree, Buying Serbian Oil Monopoly," *New York Times*, 23 January 2008, A6.

67 These debates also involved debates about the sequencing of various reforms. See Oleh Havrylyshyn, *Divergent Paths in Post-Communist Transformation* (Basingstoke, Hampshire: Palgrave Macmillan, 2006), chapter 1.

68 See Anne Krueger, "The Political Economy of Rent-Seeking Society," *The American Economic Review* 64, no. 3 (1974). I thank an anonymous reviewer for the useful image of price wedges.

69 See for example Hoff and Stiglitz, "After the Big Bang?"

70 See for example Hellman, "Winners Take All." For a broader discussion see Havrylyshin, 33.

71 See the conclusion to chapter 2 for a discussion of the new types of rent-seeking opportunities created by the specific confluence of Soviet legacies plus factors specific to the early post-Soviet transition period.

72 This may explain Gazprom's agreement to significantly increase gas purchase prices paid to Turkmenistan starting in 2008. Gazprom's relations with Turkmenistan have seen significant instability since then.

73 In January 2006, Gazprom began purchasing the totality of Turkmenistan's gas exports, much of which was subsequently re-sold to Ukraine. In 2010, the company aggressively pursued gas contracts with Azerbaijan in an attempt to prevent the realization of the Nabucco project by hindering its access to gas supplies. Jürgen Flauger and Klaus Stratmann, "Das Gas-Poker," *Handelsblatt*, 9 September 2010, 1, 4.

74 In July 2009, the EU and Turkey signed an agreement on the building of the Nabucco Gas Pipeline, eventually to extend from gas fields beyond Turkey's eastern border to Austria and further to other Western European markets. However, even at the signing of the document it was not clear where the needed volumes of gas for the pipeline would come from. By early 2013 partners were discussing replacing the original project with a downsized version running from the Bulgarian-Turkish border (rather than the original Georgian-Turkish border) to Austria. In June 2013, the Nabucco West consortium lost a bit to transport Azerbaijani gas to Western Europe.

75 In 1999, in addition to its de facto takeover of the Transdniester separatist region's gas transit system, Gazprom gained control of 50 percent (plus one) of shares in Moldova's gas transit company MoldovaGaz. In December of 2006, Belarus agreed to sell to Gazprom 50 percent of gas transit company Beltransgas over four years; the remaining 50 percent was sold in December 2011. As of 2009, Gazprom owned 37.1 percent of the Lithuanian gas operator Lietuvos Dujos. In addition, Gazprom has been keen to gain control of the gas transit systems in other post-Soviet states: in November 2006, Armenia and Gazprom reached an agreement increasing the latter's share in ArmRosGazprom, the pipeline's operator, to 58 percent. These attempts come in the wake of and dovetail nicely with Russia's majority state-owned electricity near-monopolist RAO-UES's (after 2008, Inter RAO UES) successes in gaining significant ownership in electricity generation and grid infrastructure in Armenia, Georgia, Moldova, Tadzhikistan, Lithuania, and Kazakhstan, also important for transit purposes.

76 Among these initiatives, the most important have been, in oil, the Baltic Pipeline System (BPS-1, commissioned in 2001, and BPS-2, commissioned

in 2012) developing Russia's capacity to ship oil from Russian Baltic Sea ports, thus making unnecessary trans-shipment through Butinge (Lithuania) or Ventspils (Latvia). In gas, the Yamal Pipeline through Belarus and Poland (inaugurated in 2004), the Nord Stream pipeline connecting Russian gas fields with Germany (first branch completed 2011), and the South Stream pipeline (completion planned for 2015) have been the main initiatives.

77 The Energy Charter Treaty was first signed in 1994 as the European Energy Charter and later extended to include a growing number of non-European participants. A basic premise of the Charter is non-discrimination in energy transit, so that "all the signatories must allow the transit of energy from third parties, and must not disrupt this in the event of a conflict with one of the parties." Janne Haaland Matlary, *Energy Policies in the European Union* (New York: St. Martin's Press, 1997), 76.

78 Between 1998 and until they started to decline in 2008, Urals oil prices increased more than thirteen-fold, from about $10 to $138 per barrel, boosting Russia's foreign-currency earnings (source: IEA).

79 See *Ėnergeticheskaia Strategiia Rossii na period do 2002 goda* (Russia's Energy Strategy up to 2020), Moscow, September 2003. Full text in Russian available at http://www.minprom.gov.ru/docs/strateg/1 http://www.gazprom.ru/articles/article4951.shtml (accessed 14 February 2013). See also Bertil Nygren, "Putin's Use of Natural Gas to Reintegrate the CIS Region," *Problems of Post-Communism* 55, no. 4, (July/August 2008): 3–15.

80 Netback pricing refers to prices based on the replacement value of gas (based on the price of competing fuels, in particular fuel oil) at the delivery point. In case of Gazprom contracts with former Soviet states, such netback prices are usually calculated on the basis of the replacement cost of gas in Germany (Gazprom's largest WE export market) minus transportation costs between Germany and the specific country. In theory (as long as European markets are not saturated) such prices should cover the opportunity costs of exporting to that country and not Germany. See Ferdinand Pavel and Inna Yuzefovych, "How to Deal with 'European Prices' in Ukraine," *GAG/IERPC Policy Paper Series* PP/06/2008 (October 2008), available at www.kiev.ier.ua (accessed 15 November 2009). The basic rationale behind netback pricing is the desire to achieve a level of pricing that assures equal levels of financial return on export operations to different markets or countries. For more on netback pricing in the post-Soviet area, see Energy Charter Secretariat, *Putting a Price on Energy: International Pricing Mechanisms for Oil and Gas* (Brussels: Energy Charter Secretariat, 2007).

81 An additional factor affecting expectations of future demand for Russia's gas was the start of shale gas drilling in Poland. This gas could start reaching CEE markets by the mid-2010s, reducing demand for Russian gas.

82 Source: IEA.

2.   The Legacy of the Common Soviet Energy Past

1 Conference on "Ukraine and Its Neighboors," Kennan Institute, Washington, DC, May 2000.

2 This was due to a number of factors, including the virtual paralysation of the industry as a result of World War II damages.

3 CMEA members were the USSR, Bulgaria, Cuba, Czechoslovakia, the GDR, Hungary, Mongolia, Poland, Romania, and Vietnam. In this chapter, the term "CMEA states" is meant in the narrower sense of East European CMEA members, thus excluding Cuba, Mongolia, Vietnam, and the USSR.

4 See also Per Högselius, *Red Gas: Russia and the Origins of European Energy Dependence* (Basingstoke, Hampshire: Palgrave Macmillan, 2013).The debate around these sanctions had significant longer-term effects, however: as the United States argued that the new pipelines would lead to increased WE political dependency on the USSR, the International Energy Agency responded with a statement agreeing to "avoid undue dependence" on a single source of imported gas. (IEA Ministerial Communique, Paris, May 8, 1983, Annex I, 9, quoted in David M. Adamson, "Soviet Gas and European Security," *Energy Policy* 13, no. 1 [1985]: 13–26, here 25). Although never an official policy prescription, the statement was widely interpreted to suggest "Soviet gas should not constitute more than one-third of the consumption of major European countries." (Jonathan P. Stern, "Soviet and Russian Gas: the Origins and Evolution of Gazprom's Export Strategy." In *Gas to Europe: The Strategies of Four Major Suppliers*, ed. Robert Mabro and Ian Wybrew-Bond. Oxford: Oxford University Press/Oxford Institute of Energy Studies, 1999, 152–3). This became a rule of thumb much referred-to since then. As shown in Table 2.1, however, even if making the calculation on the basis of the broader group of EU-27 countries (including Estonia, Hungary, Latvia, Lithuania, Slovakia, the Czech Republic, Poland, Romania, and Bulgaria, much more energy-dependent on Russia than the EU-15 grouping), the share of Soviet gas as percentage of consumption, although significantly increased from 1973 to 1990, never exceeded 26 percent.

5 Very often segments of one and the same pipeline would carry different names, for example in and outside of Soviet territory.

6 From 1950 to 1970 the East European CMEA states went from net exporters of energy (at ca. 13 percent of their energy consumption) to net importers, at ca. 11 percent. Calculated on the basis of John P. Hardt, "Soviet Energy Policy in Eastern Europe," in *Soviet Policy in Eastern Europe*, ed. Sarah M. Terry (New Haven, CT: Yale University Press, 1984), 192, and Vienna Institute of Comparative Economic Studies, *COMECON Data 1989* (New York: Greenwood Press, 1990), 402.

7 See William M. Reisinger, *Energy and the Soviet Bloc: Alliance Politics After Stalin* (Ithaca, NY: Cornell University Press, 1992), 48. On CMEA energy cooperation see also Marie Lavigne, *International Political Economy and Socialism* (Cambridge: Cambridge University Press, 1991), ch. 6, and Margarita M. Balmaceda, "Der Weg in die Abhängigkeit: Ostmitteleuropa am Energietropf der UdSSR." Special issue on *Europa Unter Spannung: Energiepolitik Zwischen Ost und West*, *Osteuropa* 54, no. 9–10 (September-October 2004): 162–79. On the effects of this situation on the actual building of joint pipelines, as in the cases of the Druzhba, Orenburg, and Yamburg pipelines, see John M. Kramer, *The Energy Gap in Eastern Europe* (Lexington, MA: Lexington Books, 1990), 28, and Ulrich Best, "Die anderen Räume des Sozialismus. Internationale Baustelln in der Sowjetunion und ihre Erinnerung," in Kakanien Revisited, http://www.kakanien.ac.at/beitr/emerg/UBest1/ (accessed 21 August 2011).

8 Michael Marrese, "CMEA: Effective but Cumbersome Political Economy," *International Organization* 40 (1986), 298, quoted in Reisinger, *Energy and the Soviet Bloc*, 17.

9 See Kramer, *Energy Gap*, xiii, and Javier Estrada, Arild Moe and Kare Dahl Martinsen, *The Development of European Gas Markets* (Chichester UK: John Wiley & Sons, 1995), 167.

10 Reisinger, *Energy and the Soviet Bloc*, 70, 151.

11 See J.G. Polach, "The Develpoment of Energy in East Europe, in *Economic Development in Countries of Eastern Europe*, ed. John P. Hardt (Washington, DC: US Government Printing Office, 1970) and Hardt, "Soviet Energy Policy," 195.

12 Reisinger, *Energy and the Soviet Bloc*, 20. The opportunity costs involved in subsidized deliveries to CMEA states were especially high at times when the growth of these supplies coincided with a sharp rise in oil prices, as happened in the aftermath if the 1973–1974 oil crisis. (Oil prices charged to the CMEA states remained unchanged up to 1974, while the price charged to the West increased to OPEC levels.) Hardt, "Soviet Energy Policy," 199.

13 Calculated from Stern, "Soviet and Russian Gas," 182. Thus, the 1980's popular phrase "Samotlor fed half the country," referring to Russia's largest oil field.

14 Clifford C. Gaddy and Barry W. Ickes, "Resource Rents and the Russian Economy," *Eurasian Geography and Economics* 46, no.8 (2005): 559–83, here 562. Gaddy and Ickes's original uses the word "rents" instead of "profits." They define rents as "the sale of the resource minus economic, or opportunity costs," and estimate rents in the Soviet/Russian oil and gas sector by looking at the spot price of oil and gas actually produced, minus the cost of production. See also the Appendix to ibid, "Russia after the World Financial Crisis," *Eurasian Geography and Economics* 51, no. 3 (2010): 281–311.

15 See for example Stephen Kotkin, *Armageddon Averted* (New York: Oxford University Press, 2001), and Gaddy and Ickes, "Resource Rents."

16 Thane Gustafson, *Crisis Amid Plenty: The Politics of Soviet Energy under Brezhnev and Gorbachev* (Princeton, NJ: Princeton University Press, 1989), 37–8. According to Gustafson, the gas campaign took as much as 80 percent of total industrial investment and 13–15 percent of the work force in 1980.

17 Sarah Dixon, *Organisational Transformation in the Russian Oil Industry* (Cheltenham, UK: Edward Elgar, 2008), 24.

18 See Gustafson, *Crisis Amid Plenty*, 266.

19 See Dmitry Travin and Otar Marganiya, "Resource curse: rethinking the Soviet experience," in Vladimir Gelman and Otar Marganiya, eds., *Resource Curse and Post-Soviet Eurasia: Oil, Gas, and Modernization* (Lanham, MD: Lexington Books, 2010).

20 Leslie Dienes, Istvan Dobozi, and Marian Radetzki, *Energy and Economic Reform in the Former Soviet Union* (Palgrave: St. Martin Press, 1994), 48, see also 49–55.

21 It has been argued that 40 percent of the oil produced in 1999 came from non-rentable fields. Milana Davydova, "Zavedomo Ubytochnoe Slianie: Ob'edinionui neftianuiu kompaniu zhdiot nesladkaia zhizn za chet dotatsii," *Nezavisimaia Gazeta*, 9 February 1999.

22 Austvik and Tsygankova argue that in the Soviet Union "[n]atural resources were considered unbounded, derived from Marxist labour theory of value that stated that only labour imparts value in a production process. Hence, natural resources were considered free goods as no labour was used in creating them. As the price of the resource was set to zero, extensive resource management and under-pricing of petroleum products was

justified." Ole Gunnar Austvik and Marina Tsygankova, "Petroleum Strategies in Norway and Russia," first draft of article in *Osteuropa* (September 2004), 10. (German version available at *Osteuropa* 54, no. 9–10 [2004].)

23 Gustafson, *Crisis Amid Plenty*, 66.

24 For example, while production and transportation costs were rising steadily, the sale price of oil to Soviet enterprises remained largely constant from 1967 to 1982. Ed Hewett, *Energy, Economics and Foreign Policy* (Washington, DC: Brookings, 1983), 12, footnote 12.

25 In 1998, Russia's level of energy intensity was 1.74 oe (tons of oil equivalent) per 1,000$ 1990 USD GDP compared with the 0.18 for Germany and 0.31 for the United States. IEA, *Key World Energy Statistics 2000*, available at http://www.iea.org/statist/keyworld/keystats.htm. Purchase Power Parity figures are 0.87 for Russia, 0.23 for Germany, and 0.31 for the United States.

26 See Ihor Karp, "Problems of Ukraine's Energy Sector and Ways of Their Resolution," in "Concept of the State Energy Policy of Ukraine through 2020," Ukrainian Centre for Economic and Political Studies, *National Security and Defense*, no. 2 (2001), 70.

27 By the 1980s, such systemic factors (as opposed to more easily changeable technological factors) accounted for almost 75 percent of apparent Soviet energy over-consumption. Dienes et al., *Energy and Economic Reform*, 134–5.

28 Estrada, Moe and Martinsen, *Development of European Gas Markets*, 165.

29 *Sources*: For 1960, Jeremy Russel, *The Energy Factor in Soviet Foreign Policy* (Lexington, MA: Saxon House/Lexington Books, 1976), 22; for 1991 and 1999, IEA, *Russian Energy Survey 2002* (Paris: IEA, 2002), 49 (Table 3.1).

30 Hewett, *Energy, Economics*, 10.

31 See Hewett, *Energy, Economics*, 20, footnote 24, also 42–3.

32 On Gazprom's transformation from Soviet ministry to joint-stock company, see Yakov Pappe, "Otraslevie lobby v pravitelstve Rossii (1992–1996)," *Pro et Contra* (Fall 1996): 61–78.

33 While such bargaining may have indeed taken place behind closed doors, we lack sufficient information to make an accurate assessment on this.

34 Lithuania presented some particularities in this respect, with a republican-centred view of ecological security evident in official documents as early as 1986. See Leonardas Rinkevičius, "Shaping of the Public Policy Culture in Lithuania: Sociological Exploration of Change in Environmental Policy and Public Participation," *Sociologija. Mintis ir Veiksmas*, no. 1 (2006), 113–27, here 119.

35 See Dienes et al., *Energy and Economic Reform*, 98. Despite lacking significant oil reserves, this was compensated for by large coal and gas production.

36 Dienes, "Energy, Minerals," 129.

37 Ibid. There are some parallels between this situation and that the Eastern European CMEA states, a region that, as a whole, changed quickly from net energy exporter to net importer of energy from the USSR in the 1960s. See Russel, *Energy Factor*, 89.

38 Despite having important estimated gas reserves, much of the Black Sea Shelf remained unexplored until the 1990s. See *Russian Petroleum Investor* (November 1996), 56, and IEA, *Ukraine Energy Policy Review 2006* (Paris: OECD/IEA, 2006), 175–6.

39 Dienes et al., *Energy and Economic*, 98. See also Dienes, "Energy, Minerals," 129. Between the 1960s and 1980s Ukraine exported "a significant part" of its natural gas production. Dienes, "Energy, Minerals," 140–1.

40 As noted by Babanin et al., in the early 2000s, the average production cost of Ukrainian coal was "150 percent of the selling price. That is, the profitability is negative 50 percent." Olexander Babanin, Volodymyr Dubrovskyi, and Oleksii Ivashchenko, *Ukraine: The Lost Decade . . . and the Coming Boom?* (Kyiv: CASE Ukraine, 2002). In the mid-2000s, Ukrainian coal was reportedly priced "20–40% below costs at the mines." IEA, *Ukraine Energy Policy Review 2006*, 46.

41 In the case of Ukraine, for example, energy consumption grew significantly in the last Soviet years: from a TPES of 200.59 Mtoe in 1987, to 252.63 in 1990. IEA, *Energy Policies of Ukraine* (1996), 183.

42 While the main rationale was to prevent the massive migration of Russian-speaking industrial workers and their compact settlement in industrial areas (as happened in Latvia and Estonia), the general nature of industrial development was affected as well. See Rinkievičius, "Shaping of the Public Policy," 116–17. See also Leonardas Rinkievičius, "Lithuania: Environmental Awareness and National Independence," in *Public Participation and Sustainable Development: Comparing European Experiences*, eds. A. Jamison and P. Ostby, Pesto Papers 1 (Aalborg: Aalborg Universitetsforlag, 1997).

43 See Taras Kuzio and Andrew Wilson, *Ukraine: Perestroika to Independence* (London: Macmillan, 1997).

44 While Lithuania's economic reform progressed more slowly than that of its Baltic neighbours Latvia and (especially) Estonia, it moved significantly faster than in Ukraine or Belarus.

45 In 1990, gas comprised about 30 percent of Lithuania's and Belarus' TPES, and 36.5 percent of Ukraine's. Data for Lithuania from http://hdrstats.

undp.org/en/countries/data_sheets/cty_ds_LTU.html. Data for Ukraine from http://hdrstats.undp.org/countries/data_sheets/cty_ds_UKR.html.

46 The 1990 data for Lithuania are from http://hdrstats.undp.org/en/countries/data_sheets/cty_ds_LTU.html; data for Ukraine are from http://hdrstats.undp.org/countries/data_sheets/cty_ds_UKR.html.

47 In the fall of 2000, in the midst of Ukrainian-Russian negotiations on the gas debt, Russian Vice-Premier Viktor Khristenko made the following veiled threat: Ukraine should choose either Turkmen gas or Russian gas, but not both. While the threat was later not enforced, Russia pressured Ukraine into imposing punitively high gas export duties (formally intended to discourage the re-export of Russian gas), on all gas exports, also affecting its capacity to export domestically produced oil. See Viktor Yadukha, "Bolshoi gazovyi secret," *Segodnia*, 20 November 2000, and Aleksandr Bekker, "Polufinal. Rossiia i Ukraina pochti dogovorilis," *Vedomosti*, 20 November 2000.

48 Many of the contracts with Russia include take-or-pay clauses, which reduce a state's ability to enter into new contractual relationships with alternative suppliers.

49 As of 2012 there were no gas metering stations on the Ukrainian side of the border with Russia, with all measurement of import flows taking place on the Russia side and "at a far distance from border crossing points." *Energy Policies Beyond IEA Countries: Ukraine Energy Policy Review 2012* (Paris: OECD Publishing 2012), 104. During the January 2009 Ukrainian-Russian gas crisis, the lack of such metering stations on Ukrainian territory was one of the main arguments used by Russia to call for a group of international observers to monitor cross-border gas flows and possible gas stealing.

50 In 1999, Ukraine had gas storage facilities of 35 bcm of gas, equivalent to 164 days of consumption, a high level in international comparison.

51 The reasons for such unstable supplies were somewhat different in each case. In addition to political reasons, while in Belarus and Ukraine the main reason for unstable supplies were payment arrears, in the case of Lithuania it was mainly LUKoil's desire to gain control of Lithuania's sole refinery, Mazeikiu Nafta.

52 For example, Belarus' two oil refineries were established during the 1960s and 1970s to complete the technological chain of oil produced in Siberia and the Volga region. In the case of Ukraine, some of the main links were with the Tyumen area. Valerii F. Dashkevich, *Energeticheskaia Zavisimost' Belarusi: posledstvia dlia ekonomiki i obshestva* (Minsk: Izdatel I. P. Lovginov, 2005), 10, and David Wilson, *The Demand for Energy in the Soviet Union* (London: Croom Helm; Totowa, NJ: Rowman and Allanheld, 1983), 185.

53 For example, much of the metallurgical industry supplying the pipeline sector was located in Ukraine (Dienes et al., *Energy and Economic Reform*, 98). Thus, it should come as no surprise that, in the fall of 2000, Russian companies importing Ukrainian pipe pressured the Russian government to drop some sanctions against Ukraine so that this pipe could continue to be supplied.

54 Petra Opitz and Christian von Hirschhausen, "Ukraine as a Gas Bridge to Europe," working paper no. 3, Institute for Economic Research and Policy Consulting, October 2000, 4.

55 See Saulius Kutas and Jurgis Vilemas, "Legacy of the Past and Future Energy Policy in Lithuania," paper prepared for the World Energy Council, 2005, available at http://www.worldenergy.org/wec-geis/publications/default/tech_papers/17th_congress/1_4_31.asp?mode=print&x=59&y=5 (accessed 20 February 2007), 4.

56 Volodymir Pokokhalo, *The Political Analysis of Post-Communism* (Kyiv, 1995), 166.

57 Although this situation has largely changed since 1991, with all of our three cases integrated into the Energy Charter process and the International Atomic Energy Agency, and Lithuania and Ukraine into the WTO as well, this initial institutional isolation seriously limited the range of policy instruments available to the energy-dependent states. Moreover, Russia itself has not ratified membership in the Energy Charter Treaty, which, given Russia's role as main supplier, cannot but affect the energy-dependent states ability to use the treaty's dispute-resolution mechanisms to their fullest extent.

58 Sabonis-Chafee, *Power Politics*, 16.

59 Lithuania and Ukraine had to face serious technical issues, including the fact that, as noted by Sabonis-Chafee, in some of these cases they did not even have blueprints to the nuclear power plants on their territories, and faced an almost immediate wave of emigration of ethnic Russian power plant operators. Sabonis-Chafee, *Power Politics*, 21, 77.

60 An excellent example of this situation and its impact on energy policy has to do with the administration of pipeline systems. The Ukrainian SSR, for example, had no single pipeline system, but two ("Druzhba" and "Transdniester"), both of which belonged directly to the Soviet Transneft system. As a result, their day-to-day operation and strategy depended, in a very clear and practical way, on Moscow. Until 2001 (i.e., almost ten years after the dissolution of the USSR), they continued to function as independent companies. See Oleksandr Todiichuk, interview in *Oil Market Weekly* (*Nefterynok*), 30 October 2001. Accessed through the by-suscription-only

ISI Emerging Markets portal, available at www.securities.com (thereafter noted as "via ISI").

61 See Christian von Hirschhausen and Volkhart Vincentz, "Energy Policy and Structural Reform," *Eastern European Economics* 38, no. 1 (2000), 68.

62 Matthew J. Sagers, "Comments on the Flow and Taxation of Oil-Gas Export Revenues in Russia," *Eurasian Geography and Economics* 43, no. 8 (2002): 628–31, here 630, footnote 6.

63 Balmaceda, *Energy Dependency*, 46.

64 By 1991 "more than 75% of the total Soviet population (including rural population) was connected to the gas system, the majority via district heating," an indirect result of the building of pipelines to service the export of Soviet gas to WE. Stern, "Soviet and Russian Gas," 146 and 195, footnote 16.

65 Even after multiple-fold increases in dollar terms between 1991 and 1995, by that year Russian households were spending "less than 1% of the family budget on energy, while the share for Western households is between 5% and 6%." IEA, *Energy Policies of the Russian Federation* (Paris: OECD/ IEA, 1995), 30 (footnote 10); see also 25 (Table 1) and 26 (Table 2). See Costa Esping-Anderson, *Politics against Markets: the Social Democratic Road to Power* (Princeton, NJ: Princeton University Press, 1985) on how previous welfare structures may affect the later expectations of various social actors.

66 This was especially true in the case of Ukraine, where, before they were raised in 2006, residential gas and electricity prices, unchanged since 1998, were some of the lowest in the former USSR, at $35.2 per tcm lower than in energy-rich Russia ($44.3 in 2004–2005). See Balmaceda, *Energy Dependency*, 66.

67 Ibid., 68.

68 For example, by late 2005, the domestic price for Russian natural gas was about $37/tcm, while it was being sold to Belarus for $46.68 and to Western European markets such as Germany for $230, allowing for plentiful rent-seeking opportunities along the arbitrage gains chain. This remains true even considering the accounting inaccuracies inherent to barter-based transactions.

3.   The Domestic Russian Background

1 On Russia's role as absolute leader in gas sector institutional changes in the region, see Tatiana Mitrova, "Natural Gas in Transition: Systemic Reform Issues," in *Russian and CIS Gas Markets and their Impact on Europe,*

ed. Simon Pirani (Oxford: Oxford University Press for the Oxford Energy Institute, 2009), 21.

2 Data on Russia's gas TPES from International Energy Agency Energy Statistics, at http://www.iea.org/stats/pdf_graphs/RUTPESPI.pdf (accessed September 5, 2011).

3 See Mitrova, "Natural Gas in Transition," 23.

4 In 2009, the boom in shale gas production in the United States made it the largest gas producer in the world, overcoming Russia. Data on gas reserves from Statistical Review of World Energy, June 2010, 22.

5 As discussed in chapter 2, there are several reasons for this decline, having to do with the legacies of predatory production methods, taxation, pricing, and investment policies. Heinrich, however, cautions against using actual gas production data as evidence of production problems or future production capacity, as, given storage difficulties, "gas is produced only after supply contracts have been signed." Andreas Heinrich, "Under the Kremlin's Thumb: Does Increased State Control of the Russian Gas Sector Endanger European Energy Security?" *Europe-Asia Studies* 60, no. 9 (2008): 1539–74, here 1556.

6 Sakhalin oil and gas, produced in close proximity to key Asian markets, is a partial exception. See Michael Bradshaw, "A New Energy Age in Pacific Russia: Lessons from the Sakhalin Oil and Gas Projects," *Eurasian Geography and Economics* 51, no. 3 (2010): 330–59, here 332–5.

7 Gazprom's reserve replacement ratio went from about 450 percent in 1991 to less than 50 percent between 1994 and 2001, with a return to about 100 percent between 2002 and 2005. IEA, *Optimizing Russian Natural Gas* (Paris: OECD/IEA, 2006), 28 (Figure 1).

8 Fears were repeatedly voiced about a possible shortfall in Gazprom's supplies to WE. Various estimates exist as to the size of this shortfall and when it would kick in. See Table 5 in Heinrich, "Under the Kremlin's Thumb," 1559, and Jonathan P. Stern, "The Russian Gas Balance to 2015: Difficult Years Ahead," in *Russian and CIS Gas Markets and their Impact on Europe*, ed. S. Pirani (Oxford: Oxford University Press for the Oxford Institute of Energy Studies, 2009). EU gas demand fell, presumably temporarily, following the 2008 global crisis.

9 See Bradshaw, "A New Energy Age," 333.

10 Each of these options, in turn, implied different value chains and patterns both in Russia and in the transit and importing countries.

11 Despite high expectations about LNG processing and shipment by tanker as means of helping solve energy transit security challenges, the technology still faces important limitations having to do with its high cost, limited

use for landlocked countries or for those without appropriate port facilities, and the fact that under current technology up to 20 percent of gas is lost in the process of liquidification, making LNG as problematic as coal from a sustainability point of view. I thank Michael Bradshaw for this insight. Further development of LNG plants in Russia is in doubt following the discovery of unconventional (shale) gas in the United States, which reduced the prospects of the United States as a market for LNG gas from Russia's Shtokman field. Bradshaw, "A New Energy Age in Pacific Russia," 333.

12 See Table 7 in S. Tabata, "Russian Revenues from Oil and Gas Exports: Flow and Taxation," *Eurasian Geography and Economics* 43, no. 8 (2002): 610–27, here 616. For most of the late 1990s and early 2000s period, gas amounted to about 15 percent–20 percent of all exports to non-CIS states; the figure rises to 38 percent–58 percent when oil exports are included. Table 3.5 in Jonathan Stern, *The Future of Russian Gas* (Oxford: Oxford University Press, 2005), 129.

13 Migration from coal to gas was especially notable. Russia's coal market was liberalized through the use of an exchange in the early 2000s, with the result that by 2005 its (per calorie) price was nearly 1.5 times higher than that of gas, leading to increased demand for gas. Dashkevich, *Energeticheskaia Zavisimost' Belarusi*, 37.

14 See IEA/OECD, *Energeticheskaia Politika Rossii. Obzor 2002* (Paris: OECD, 2002), 41.

15 Many independent observers saw the debate on Gazprom supplies to RAO UES not only as one of domestic supplies vs. exports, but also as a political issue related to a possible desire to curtail the power of Anatolii Chubais' (head of RAO UES). See Lyudmila Romanova, "Budet' li Gazprom renatsionalizirovan?" *Nezavisimaia Gazeta*, 6 November 1999.

16 State monopoly RAO UES was dissolved in 2008; our discussion here refers first and foremost to the pre-2008 period. As part of RAO UES' reorganization, its generation, transmission and sales units were separated to create separate companies, which would be subsequently privatized. RAO UES's electricity generation network was also broken up into a number of smaller producers, which have been sold individually to foreign and domestic investors, most notably Gazprom.

17 It must be noted, however, that Russia's domestic gas demand has been relatively inelastic, and we simply do not know how demand would react to sharply increased prices. See Stern, "The Russian Gas Balance to 2015," 75–6.

18 IEA, *Optimising*, 43. After protracted negotiations, Russia joined the WTO in August 2012.

19 This goal was enshrined in the May 2004 agreements between Russia and the WTO. See Heinrich, "Under the Kremlin's Thumb," 1567. European netback prices refer to the replacement value of gas at an European delivery point (usually the German border), minus transportation costs, in practice understood to mean the equal profitability of European and domestic sales.

20 It must be noted, however, that this initiative was not so much about a deregulation of gas prices, but about a "regulated transition to higher prices." Mitrova, "Natural Gas in Transition," 36.

21 On the significant methodological difficulties of calculating equal profitability gas prices, see Stern, "The Russian Gas Balance to 2015," 73–4.

22 "Gazpromu pridiotsia podozhdat'," *Vedomosti*, May 28, 2008.

23 As stated by the International Energy Agency, "it is the system of subsidized prices to Russian gas consumers principally that maintains Gazprom's dominant position." IEA, *Energeticheskaia Politika Rossii* (2002), 145. For a firm-focused perspective on Gazprom's relationship with the Russian state, see Rawi Abdelal, "The Profits of Power: Commercial *Realpolitik* in Europe and Eurasia," *Harvard Business School Working Papers* 11-028, available at http://hbswk.hbs.edu/item/6505.html (accessed 1 December 2010).

24 For a detailed discussion of "convertible points," see Margarita M. Balmaceda, "Russian Energy Companies in the New Eastern Europe: the Cases of Ukraine and Belarus," in *Russian Business Power: The Role of Russian Business in Foreign and Security Policy*, eds. Andreas Wenger, Jeronim Perovic, and Robert W. Orttung (London: Routledge Curzon, 2006), 67–87.

25 The relationship between Gazprom and the Russian state plays itself out at several levels simultaneously: a direct relationship, and a more complex, indirect relationship. The first relationship plays itself out through the dynamics of corporate governance and membership in Gazprom's board of directors, and other overseeing bodies, and the relative influence of the state in these organs. The second game refers to a more complex, informal set of relationships.

26 Data are for the mid-2000s.

27 Bruce, citing Russia's *Kommersant*, discusses the possibility of Gazprom being compensated (by Russia's Ministry of Finance) for some of the debt forgiven Belarus by means of a complicated tax credit system. See Chloë Bruce, "Friction or fiction? The gas factor in Russian-Belarusian relations," *Chatham House Briefing Paper* REP BP 05/01 (May 2005), available at

http://www.chathamhouse.org/sites/default/files/public/Research/
Russia%20and%20Eurasia/bp0501gas.pdf, 10 (accessed 15 February 2013).

28 Heinrich, "Under the Kremlin's Thumb," 1549.
29 Ibid.
30 After the failure of a merger with Rosneft planned for October 2004, the state increased its stake in Gazprom to more than 50 percent by creating a special-purpose holding, Rosneftegaz, which held state shares in Rosneft to be used as collateral for the state's purchase of an additional 10.74 percent of Gazprom's shares. See William Tompson, "Back to the Future: Thoughts on the Political Economy of Expanded State Ownership in Russia," *Le Cahiers Russie*, no. 6 (2008): 1–18.
31 Calculated from Table 3.1 in this chapter.
32 Technically, during most of the Soviet period gas exports were managed not by Gazprom itself, but by Soyuzgazexport, which in 1991 was incorporated into Gazprom but largely retained a separate corporate culture and personnel.
33 While Gazprom has enjoyed a de facto monopoly on exports since the Soviet period, its monopoly was given a legal status in 2006 when a law was passed giving Gazprom's arm Gazprom Export a legal monopoly on exports. Article 3 of the law confers this monopoly on the owner of the USGS transit network; that is, as of 2008 Gazprom and Gazprom Export. Stern, "The Russian Gas Balance to 2015," 91, footnote 80. However, 2010 reports that independent gas producer Novatek, thanks to its well-connected co-owner Gennadiy Timchenko, may have received permission to independently export some LNG from future production points to the fact that the rules may be changing, at least concerning LNG and those with the right connections. See Irina Reznik, "Chelovek nedeli: Gennadiy Timchenko," *Vedomosti*, 28 June 2010.
34 See Heinrich, "Under the Kremlin's Thumb," 1547.
35 See Stern, "The Russian Gas Balance to 2015," 65.
36 In 2006, gas production by oil companies amounted to 55.5 bcm, about 15.7 percent of Russian production. From Table 2 in Heinrich, "Under the Kremlin's Thumb," 1546.
37 While on paper the level of access by non-Gazprom producers to Gazprom's pipelines grew steadily from the late 1990s (37 bcm in 1997) to the mid-2000s (ca. 114.3 bcm in 2008), a closer look reveals these numbers as showing not so much a real de-monopolization of the market, but access by either intermediary companies (such as Eural Trans Gas and RosUkrEnergo, suspected of having had special ties with the Gazprom leadership at some point or another) importing gas from Turkmenistan to Ukraine, or

non-Gazprom producers with whom the company had reached long-term agreements (LUKoil and Novatek). IEA, *Optimizing*, 32.

38 On sales to companies associated with Gazprom, see R. Ahrend and W. Tompson, "Unnatural Monopoly: The Endless Wait for Gas Sector Reform in Russia." *Europe-Asia Studies* 57, no. 6 (2005): 801–21, here 803–4.

39 Calculated from gas production figures in Table 1 in Heinrich, "Under the Kremlin's Thumb," 1545. Gas flaring refers to the practice of burning-off at the well and into the open air surplus gas otherwise not considered economically feasible to use or transport; it is also used for safety purposes. According to official Russian statistics, 2004 loses due to gas flaring amounted to 15 bcm of gas; IEA and a number of Russian and Western experts estimate the number to be much higher, up to 60 bcm per year (IEA, *Optimizing*, 17, 21). As late as 2010, there was no federal legislation limiting the flaring of associated gas, with regulations on the issue only set at the regional level or in the production licenses issued jointly by the Ministry of Natural Resources and regional authorities; fines for above-limit flaring have been low. See ibid., 147, 154, and J. DeLay, "Moscow Considers a Move on Gas Flaring," *NewsBase, FSU Oil & Gas Monitor*, no. 21, 30 May 2007, cited in Heinrich, "Under the Kremlin's Thumb," 1565.

40 In the early 2000s, Gazprom started paying lip service to the idea of allowing new players into the market, but it is widely suspected that this was related to individual attempts at asset stripping involving Itera. Interested in supporting the move to unregulated prices for domestic industrial gas consumers as a means to increase domestic gas prices and in reducing its domestic sales to be able to concentrate on more profitable exports, in 2006 Gazprom supported the creation of a gas exchange (the Mezhregiongas [MRG] exchange), whose aim was to help move towards unregulated prices for domestic industrial gas consumers. However, as of 2007, the exchange accounted for only about 2 percent of gas sold in Russia, and was dominated by Gazprom "in terms of volumes, access to information and trading rules." Stern, "The Russian Gas Balance to 2015," 72.

41 The term "intermediary companies" can be used to denote a variety of types of companies, especially in the gas area – including domestic gas distribution companies with intermediary functions (for example Ukraine's United Energy Systems [UES] in the mid-1990s), gas trade companies with access to their own gas resources in Russia (Itera until 2001), as well as transit intermediaries (Eural Trans Gas) and companies dealing with a single (Dujotekana in Lithuania) or multiple suppliers (RosUkrEnergo in Ukraine since 2006). Our discussion here focuses mostly on Itera, the most clear and best-known example.

42 The first intermediary company was arguably Itera, established in 1994.

43 Similarly, it has been argued that the easing out of Itera from Gazprom's markets a few years later was a way for Gazprom to regain profits, especially after these CIS markets started to recover. Katja Yafimava, *Post-Soviet Russian-Belarussian Relationships: The Role of Gas Transit Pipelines* (Stuttgart: Ibidem-Verlag, 2007) makes the last argument in the case of Belarus.

44 Stern, *The Future of Russian Gas*, 69 (Table 2.2).

45 See Jerome Guillet, "Gazprom's got West Europeans Over a Barrel," *The Wall Street Journal*, 8 November 2002, and Hermitage Capital Management, "How Should Gazprom Be Managed in Russia's National Interests and the Interests of its Shareholders?" (Moscow, June 2005), 4, cited in Global Witness, "It's a Gas – Funny Business in Turkmen-Ukraine Gas Trade" (April 2006), available at http://www.globalwitness.org/sites/default/files/library/its_a_gas_april_2006_lowres.pdf (accessed 15 February 2013), 35.

46 For a nuanced and possibly more positive assessment of intermediary companies' role in securing a gradual, soft-landing transition from heavily subsidized to market gas prices, see Andrei Konoplyanik, "Russia-Ukraine Gas Trade: From Political to Market-Based Pricing and Prices," presentation at the conference "Reassessing Post-Soviet Energy Politics: Ukraine, Russia, and the Battle for Gas, from Central Asia to the European Union," Harvard University, 7–8 March 2008, available in streaming video at http://www.youtube.com/watch?v=U8ngolw-f74 (accessed 24 February 2013).

47 See Konstantin Levin, "Viakhireva rezhut po polam," *Kommersant-Dengi* 2000, no. 4 (January 2000): 15.

48 It has been argued that intermediary companies and the associated corruption opportunities were part of a Russian strategy to weaken Ukrainian resolve to deal with its energy dependency on Russia. See Margarita M. Balmaceda, "Energy Business and Foreign Policies in Belarus and Ukraine," presentation at the conference "Economic Interests and Foreign Policy Choices: the Case of Slavic Triangle," University of Toronto, 26–27 January 2006, and Paul D'Anieri, "Ukrainian-Russian Relations: Beyond the Gas," presentation at the conference "The Ukrainian-Russian Gas Crisis and its Fallout: Domestic and International Implications," Harvard University, 5–6 February 2006. Streaming video available at http://www.huri.harvard.edu/events/event-archive/102-gas-crisis-conference-2006.html (accessed 24 February 2013).

49 Erika Weinthal and Pauline Jones Loung, "The Paradox of Energy Sector Reform," in *The State after Communism: Governance in the New Russia*, eds. Timothy Colton and Stephen Hanson (Lanham: Rowman & Littlefield, 2006), 225–60, here 235.

50 As most likely happened in during the January 2006 negotiations in-
volving Ukraine's Naftohaz, Gazprom, and the intermediary company
RosUkrEnergo. See Oleksander Chalii (former Ukrainian Minister of
European Integration) in Radio Free Europe program for Ukraine, *Vichirna
Svoboda*, 8 January 2009, heard on www.radiosvoboda.org.

51 On the intentional creation of artificial scarcities as a means of rent-seeking, see James M. Buchanan, "Rent-seeking and Profit-seeking," in *Toward
a General Theory of the Rent-Seeking Society*, eds. J.M. Buchanan, R.D. Tollison, and G. Tullock (Texas: Texas A & M University Press, 1980).

52 The use of Central Asian gas to fulfill Gazprom export commitments
increased significantly after 2000, to 59.7 bcm in 2007. By 2008, Gazprom
had in place contracts with Turkmenistan, Kazakhstan, and Uzbekistan
amounting to about 70–100 bcm per year by the early 2010s. Stern, "The
Russian Gas Balance to 2015," 70.

53 Exports to the Asia-Pacific Region and LNG exports involved a different
logic and a different type of calculations. See Bradshaw, "A New Energy
Age in Pacific Russia."

54 While the 2008 Gazprom agreement with Turkmenistan was done largely
in an attempt to prevent the latter from selling those volumes to the EU-
supported Nabucco gas pipeline project and the Chinese market, it also
implied significant economic costs, in particular a significant reduction in
Gazprom's arbitrage gains in reselling CA gas in Europe at higher prices
than originally paid. Stern, "The Russian Gas Balance to 2015," 75. See also
Andrew Kramer, "Gazprom Caught in a Trap of its Own," *International
Herald Tribune*, 15 May 2009.

55 Here it is interesting to note comments by the Gazprom management,
especially in the early 2000s, to the effect that states such as Ukraine
should rely less on Gazprom gas and import more from Turkmenistan, and
the question of whether such comments may be related to the profits made
by various intermediaries, possibly related to the Gazprom management.

56 For examples of this situation in the case of Ukraine, see chapter 4 and
Balmaceda, *Energy Dependency*, 92 ff. and 112.

57 On Viakhirev and Luzhkov, see V. Paniushin and M. Zygar, *Gazprom: Novoe
russkoe oruzhie* (Moscow: Zakharov, 2008).

58 As of 2010, only four members of Gazprom's seventeen-member management board had a gas-industry background. See http://www.gazprom.
ru/management/board/ (accessed 10 May 2010).

59 See also Vladimir Milov, Leonard L. Coburn, and Igor Danchenko, "Russia's Energy Policy, 1992–2005," *Eurasian Geography and Economics* 47, no. 3
(2006).

60 It has been argued that this lobby's interest specifically in building pipe-lines is related to rent-seeking considerations, as non-transparent financial flows are easier to maintain in that area. On the pipeline lobby, see also *Neftegazovaia Vertikal*, no. 12 (2005), 80.

61 In particular, for much of the 2000s Gazprom enjoyed a preferential tax treatment vis-á-vis oil companies. On preferential tax treatment regarding the Natural Resource Extraction Tax (NDPI), see Elena Mazneva, "Pomo-gla pogoda. Pochemu Putin zashchitil 'Gazprom' ot rosta NDPI," *Vedo-mosti*, 11 July 2007.

62 In 2004, this amounted to two bcm, equivalent to 27.5 percent of Russia's total final gas consumption (TFC). IEA, *Optimizing*, 36. TFC is defined as the sum of consumption by the different end-use sectors (industry, trans-port, other); that is, amounts that were not used in transformation into heat and power or in the energy sector itself or were lost in distribution. For a definition, see http://www.iea.org/glossary/glossary_T.asp.

63 Ibid., 19. In 2002, "Gazprom had to reduce the throughput of the system to 60 bcm less than its rated operational capacity." Ibid.

64 For 1996 data on the percentage of state ownership in each of Russia's eleven vertically integrated companies, see International Energy Agency, *Russian Energy Survey 2002* (Paris: IEA, 2002), 69 (Table 4.3).

65 Most analysts see these declines as an undesired outcome resulting from structural issues and tax disincentives; Gaddy and Ickes, on the other hand, see them as the intended result of a conscious depletion rates man-agement policy by the Russian state aimed at preventing over-production and over-reliance on oil rents. Clifford C. Gaddy and Barry W. Ickes, "Rus-sia's Declining Oil Production: Managing Price Risk and Rent Addiction," *Eurasian Geography and Economics* 50, no. 1 (2009): 1–13. See also Gaddy and Ickes, "Resource Rents" and (for a perspective focusing on "hidden" rents) E. Guvrich, "Neftegazovaia Renta v Rossiiskoi Ekonomike," *Voprosy Ekonomiki* 11 (2010): 4–24.

66 See David Lane, ed., *The Political Economy of Russian Oil* (Oxford: Rowman and Littlefield, 1999). World prices nearly tripled during this period. The previous period, 1995 to 1998, had been a difficult one for Russian oil companies due to weak domestic demand and the over-valuation of the Russian currency, which led to reduced export profits once these were converted back into rubles.

67 Gaddy and Ickes, "Russia's Declining Oil Production," 2.

68 See Figure 2 in Valeriy Kryukov and Arild Moe, "Russia's Oil Industry: Risk Aversion in a Risk-Prone Environment," *Eurasian Geography and Eco-nomics* 47, no. 3 (2007): 341–57, here 344.

69 Indeed, as noted by Gustafson, this Soviet legacy has led to a subop-
timal fit between upstream and downstream assets in specific companies.
However, given Russian regulations, "Russian companies cling to what
they have, partly because of the difficulty of transferring licenses, as
well as (in some cases) because of the relationships that go back to Soviet
times." Thane Gustafson, *Wheels of Fortune: The Battle for Oil and Power in
Russia* (Cambridge, MA: Belknap Press of Harvard University Press,
2012), 476.

70 Some export shipments took place outside the Transneft pipeline system,
for example by rail. Although starting in the early 2000s oil companies
started to develop plans to build their own pipelines (most prominent
among which were Yukos' proposal to build a pipeline to China in the
early 2000s, and the plan by LUKoil, Yukos, Surgutneftegas, TNK-BP, and
Sibneft to build a pipeline from West Siberia to Murmansk that would
have facilitated exports to the United States), these did not progress far, as
the state did not want to lose an important lever (Transneft's monopoly on
oil pipelines) of control over oil companies.

71 Other means of state control and state pressure over individual oil companies included the amount of oil that the government receives as part of
Production-Sharing Agreement (PSA) arrangements involving Russian oil
companies (*gosdol*), the granting (or not) of licenses and other privileges in
privatization and other investment opportunities, as well as other, ad hoc
measures, such the intentional overzealous tax review of specific companies, as in the case of Yukos, 2003–2004.

72 While Russia's oil production grew significantly in the early 2000s,
Transneft's pipeline capacity did not, and actually was reduced with the
termination of pipeline shipments to Latvia's Ventspils in 2004. Subsequent initiatives, such as the development of the Baltic Pipeline System in
Russia's Baltic coast, have sought to address export capacity issues as well
as perceived over-dependence on transit states.

73 IEA, *Russian Energy Survey 2002*, 93, footnote 50.

74 On whether political or just economic interests played the central role in
these decisions, see Yakov Pappe, *Oligarkhi* (Moscow: Vysshaia Shkola
Ekonomiki, 2000). Oil companies received additional export quotas for
a variety of reasons: in one case, an oil company received an additional
quota to be able to afford reconstruction after damage sustained in an
earthquake, another because it supplied oil to hardship-stricken Ka-
mchatka, another because it operated in Dagestan, in the border with
war-ridden Chechnia. These examples show that the system of additional

export quotas was often used not only or not so much to regulate exports, but as a way to deal with a variety of domestic concerns.

75 Yukos overtook LUKoil, the 1990s Russian oil industry leader, in oil production just before Khodorkovskii's arrest.

76 Technically, this took place through a series of sales to totally – or partially – state-owned companies to cover Yukos' unpaid taxes.

77 In 2005, Rosneft had signed a confidential agreement with Western creditor banks to assume Yukos' debt in the event the company was forced into liquidation, which made Rosneft a creditor in Yukos' bankruptcy filing. See Andrew E. Kramer, "Lithuanians Are Given a Taste of How Russia Plays the Oil Game," *New York Times*, 28 October 2006.

78 Heinrich, "Under the Kremlin's Thumb," 1542. See also the previous discussion of post-2001 divisions within Gazprom.

79 See Vladimir Milov, "Russian Energy Policy in a Broader Context," presentation at the American Enterprise Institute, Washington, DC, 16 March 2006, power-point presentation available at http://www.energypolicy.ru/files/March16-2006.ppt (accessed 25 June 2006). See also Vladimir Milov, *Russia and the West: The Energy Factor* (Washington, DC: CSIS, 2008) and P. Vahtra, K. Liuhto, and K. Lorenz, "Privatization of Re-nationalisation in Russia," *Journal of East-European Management Studies* 12, no. 4 (2007): 287–93. For a review of Russian discussions on a possible Putin interest in Gazprom, Surgutneftegaz, and oil trader Gunvor, see Adrian Blomfield, "'$40bn Putin is Now Europe's Richest Man.'" *The Daily Telegraph*, 21 December 2007.

80 See Andrei Yakovlev, "The Evolution of Business-State Interaction in Russia: from State Capture to Business Capture?," *Europe-Asia Studies* 58, no. 7 (2006).

81 Sagers, "Russia's Energy Policy," 513, quoted in Clifford G. Gaddy and Barry W. Ickes, "Russia after the World Financial Crisis," *Eurasian Geography and Economics* 51, no. 3 (2010): 281–311. See also Clifford G. Gaddy and Barry W. Ickes "Resource Rents and the Russian Economy," *Eurasian Geography and Economics* 46, no. 8 (2006): 559–83, and the Appendix to Gaddy and Ickes, "Russia after the World Financial Crisis." Gaddy and Ickes define informal taxes as nominally voluntary but de facto mandatory contributions needed to be made by a business in order to survive. Gaddy and Ickes, "Resource Rents," 561. See also Clifford C. Gaddy and Barry W. Ickes, *Russia's Virtual Economy* (Washington, DC: Brookings Institution, 2002).

82 Kryukov and Moe, "Russia's Oil Industry," 353.

83 See Alexeev and Conrad, "The Russian Oil Tax Regime," 109. Oil export
taxes were abolished in 1996 at the urging of the IMF, but were reinstated
in 1999 as a means to appropriate some of the profits made by exporters
in the wake of the 1998 economic crises, when the devaluation of the ruble
reduced dollar production costs and increased the profitability of oil and
gas exports. In 2002, oil export taxes started to be calculated according to a
formula that increased them as world oil prices increased. See IEA, *Russian
Energy Survey 2002*, 78, and Shinichiro Tabata, "Russian Revenues from Oil
and Gas Exports: Flow and Taxation," *Eurasian Geography and Economics* 43,
no. 8 (2002): 610–27, here 617.

84 The hope of no export duties was an original source of support for the CIS
Customs Union; similarly, whether oil and gas deliveries will be duty-free
has been one of the major issues of debate concerning the Russia-Belarus-
Kazakhstan Customs Union that entered into force on 1 July 2010.

85 The taxation of Russian oil (and gas) exports to former Soviet states has
been subject to a variety of complex and changing regulations involving
country-of-origin or country-of-destination application of VAT, export, and
excise taxes. For a background on the issue and its impact on Ukraine, see
Clinton R. Shiells, "Optimal Taxation of Energy Trade: the Case of Russia
and Ukraine," 2–6 (available at http://www.etsg.org/ETSG2005/papers/
shiells.pdf (accessed 28 June 2006), and Clinton R. Shiells, "VAT Design
and Energy Trade: The Case of Russia and Ukraine," *IMF Staff Papers*
52, no. 1 (2005): 103–19. While it is impossible to fully trace the changing regulations here, it is worth noting that the very complexity of these
regulations facilitated their manipulation for both tax-evasion and political
purposes. See also Tabata, "Russian Revenues," 625–6.

86 On 1 January 2010, in the midst of worsening relations, Russia introduced
export duties on crude oil deliveries to Belarus.

87 Similarly, the dramatic decrease in world oil prices since 2008 and reduction in the gap between domestic and world prices reduced the possible
profits that could be accrued by Russian companies through refining
and reexporting operations. As will be discussed in chapter 5, in the case
of Belarus, changes in the distribution of tax and duties between Russia
and Belarus after 2007 further reduced Russian companies' incentives in
this area.

88 There were repeated changes in this area due to changing Russian regulations and membership in various customs agreements, but, for most of the
period under consideration, supplies to Belarus were considered equivalent to domestic supplies, while supplies to other post-Soviet republics
were not.

4. Ukraine

1 Repeated cut-offs took place after Ukraine relinquished on a zero option agreement that would have erased its mounting gas debt vis-à-vis Gazprom in exchange for giving Russia full control of the Black Sea Fleet. A weaker version of the arrangement was approved in 1997.

2 *Source*: International Energy Agency (IEA), *Key World Energy Statistics 2007* and *Key World Energy Statistics 2008*, available at http://www.iea.org (accessed 16 April 2009). Belarus' level of dependency for this period was 85.40 percent (2005), and 86.29 percent (2006), and Lithuania's 56.68 percent (2005) and 62.88 percent (2006). As per international practice, the calculation does not include imported nuclear fuels needed for nuclear energy production.

3 Fuel cells and nuclear fuel are almost exclusively imported from Russia, which also provides 85 percent of the nuclear power plant equipment. In the mid-2000s, Ukrainian government sources calculated imported uranium as being equivalent to a further 11.7 percent of Ukraine's energy consumption. See *Enerhetychna Stratehiia Ukrainy na period do 2030 roku*, Kyiv, Ministerstvo Palyva ta Enerkhetyky, March 2006, Section II, 14, available at http://mpe.kmu.gov.ua/control/uk/archive/docview;jsessionid=3C2134C B829F6B49B827B34128BA604F?typeId=36172&sortType=4&page=0 (Accessed 3 June 2006). See also Christian von Hirschhausen and Volkhart Vincentz, "Energy Policy and Structural Reform," in *Eastern European Economics* 38, no. 1 (January-February 2000), 63.

4 This calculation is based on the assumption that ca. 70 percent of Gazprom's profits come from exports to WE, and that ca. 80 percent of those exports transit through Ukraine. The 70 percent figure is from Jonathan Stern, declarations at the "Commons Defence Select Committee evidence session on UK relations with Russia," 17 March 2009, as reported in http://www. epolitix.com/latestnews/article-detail/newsarticle/committee-briefing-uk-relations-with-russia/ (accessed 17 April 2009).

5 International Energy Agency (IEA), *Ukraine Energy Policy Review 2006*, (Paris: OECD/IEA, 2006), 205.

6 Ibid, 204.

7 IEA, *Ukraine 2006*, 208, 210, citing NAK Naftohaz at www.naftogas.ua.

8 In the mid-2000s, Ukraine had a refining capacity of about 55 million tons per year, a form of the country's oversized energy infrastructure inherited from the Soviet period. EIA, *Country Analysis Brief: Ukraine*, available at http://www.eia.doe.gov/cabs/Ukraine/NaturalGas.html (accessed 14 July 2010).

9 Data on imports from 2008. International Energy Agency, *Key World Energy Statistics 2009*, 13. Data on consumption (2007) from the EIA.

10 As was, for example the case with Lithuania in the mid-1990s. See chapter 6 below.

11 IEA, *Ukraine 2006*, 20.

12 Data from Jonathan Stern, Simon Pirani, and Katja Yafimava, *The April 2010 Russo-Ukrainian Gas Agreement and its Implications for Europe*, NG42 (Oxford: Oxford Institute for Energy Studies, 2009), available at http://www.oxfordenergy.org/wpcms/wp-content/uploads/2011/05/NG_42.pdf (accessed 16 February, 2012. The 2011 data are from IEA, Ukraine 2012, 107.

13 As of the mid-2000s both of Ukraine's major refineries, Kremenchuk and Lisichansk, accounting for 78.8 percent (2006) of total refining, were owned in full or majority by Russian oil companies. Mykhailo Honchar (ed.), *Naftohazovyi sektor Ukrainy: prozorist' funktsionuvannia ta dokhodiv* (Kyiv: Anna-T, 2008), 85–6.

14 Oleh Havrylyshyn, *Divergent Paths in Post-Communist Transformation* (Basingstoke, Hampshire: Palgrave Macmillan, 2006), 239. See also chapter eight, "Future Prospects for Captured States."

15 See Anders Aslund, *How Ukraine Became a Market Economy* (Washington, DC: Peterson Institute for International Economics, 2009), 151–74.

16 After a slowdown in 2005, growth rebounded to 7.3 percent in 2006, 7.6 percent in 2007 and peaked at an annualized (y/y) value of 11 percent in August 2008. World Bank, *Ukrainian Economic Update*, December 2008, 1.

17 On sectoral interests during the 1994-1999 period, see Tor Bukkvoll, "Defining a Ukrainian Foreign Policy Identity: Business Interests and Geopolitics in the Formulation of Ukrainian Foreign Policy 1994-1999," in *Ukrainian Foreign and Security Policy*, Jennifer D. P. Moroney et. al (Westport: Praeger, 2002): 131–53.

18 V. Dubrovskyi, W. Graves, Y. Holovakha, O. Haran', R. Pavlenko, and J. Szymer, et. al. "The Reform in a Captured State: Lessons from the Ukrainian Case," first draft, Understanding Reform Project (Kyiv: Mimeo, 2003), 60.

19 By party of power in the Ukrainian case it is understood the former top nomenklatura supporting the current president (in this case, Kuchma) despite not being organized as a single political organization but active in a number of parties. See Taras Kuzio, *Ukraine: Perestroika to Independence* (London: Macmillan, 2000), 21–2, 154.

20 While these groups are commonly referred to as clans, the term "Business-Administrative Groups" better captures their essence and role joining economic and administrative resources. See also Vladimir Dubrovskyi et. al. "Reform Driving Forces in a Captured State," first draft (CASE Ukraine, 2004), 67.

21 In the Rada, these groupings became best known through their public faces, oligarchs-turned-politicians: Andrii Derkach and Serhii Tyhypko of the Dnipropetrovsk BAG (Working Ukraine Party), Viktor Yanukovych and Rinat Akhmetov of the Donetsk BAG (Party of Regions), and Viktor Medvedchuk, Hryhorii Surkis and Leonid Kravchuk of the Kyiv BAG (Social Democratic Party of Ukraine (United), SDPU [o]).

22 For example, in the late 1990s the Dnipropetrovsk BAG had important interests in gas distribution, coal mining, and metallurgy, the Donetsk BAG in metallurgy, electricity (oblenerhos), and gas distribution, and the Kyiv BAG in electricity, petroleum products, and coal mining.

23 For example the Channel Five TV channel inaugurated in 2003.

24 As noted by van Zon, "privatization tenders were formulated in such a way that only a specific clan had the chance to win and to get state property on the cheap." Hans van Zon, "Political Culture and Neo-Patrimonialism under Kuchma," *Problems of Post-Communism* 52, no. 5 (September–October 2005): 12–22, here 14.

25 See Steven Levitsky and Lucan A. Way, "The Rise of Competitive Authoritarianism," *Journal of Democracy* 13, no. 2 (April 2002): 51–63, especially 52.

26 Dubrovskyi et al, "The Reform in a Captured State," 92.

27 See Paul D'Anieri, "Leonid Kuchma and the Personalization of the Ukrainian Presidency," *Problems of Post-Communism* 50, no. 5 (September-October 2003), 60.

28 On Kuchma's strong informal powers, see ibid. For a strong argument of 1995–2005 Ukraine as a presidential system, see D'Anieri, *Understanding Ukrainian Politics*, 35–36. Others have categorized the Ukrainian system under Kuchma as semi-presidentialist emphasizing the president and prime minister as a dual executive. Oleh Protsyk, "Troubled Semi-Presidentialism: Stability and the Constitutional System in Ukraine," *Europe-Asia Studies* Vol. 55 No. 7 (2003), pp. 1077–95, here 1077.

29 Tor Bukkvoll, "Private Interests, Public Policy: Ukraine and the Common Economic Space Agreements," *Problems of Post-Communism* 51, no. 5 (September-October 2004): 11–22, here 13.

30 See Kimitaka Matsuzato, "From Communism Boss Politics to Post-Communism Caciquismo – the Meso-Elites and Meso-Governments in

Post-Communist Countries," *Communist and Post-Communist Studies* 34, no. 2 (2001), 189.

31 See Keith A. Darden, "Blackmail as a Tool of State Domination: Ukraine Under Kuchma," *Eastern European Constitutional Review* 10, nos. 2/3 (spring/summer 2001): 67–71.

32 This was due to a number of factors, having to do, first and foremost, with the nature of the party system, in particular the fact that parties were most frequently created around one particular person and not a shared ideology, or even artificially created (or taken over) by BAGs for their own purposes (As happened, for example, with the Kyiv clan's and Hryhorii Surkis' 1996 takeover of the SDPU[o].) See Iurii Aksenov (Yurii Aks'onov) and Igor' Guzhva, "Deti gaza i stali," *Ekspert*, October 11, 2004, reprinted in Energobiznes, *TEK i Pressa. Ezhednevnyi obzor*, 14 October 2004. *TEK i Pressa. Ezhednevnyi obzor* is listed in the ISI portal under the English name "Fuel and Energetical Complex - Monitoring of the Ukrainian Press" and is listed as FEC-MUP in subsequent entries.

33 Dubrovskyi (Dubrovs'kyi), "The Reform in a Captured State," 74.

34 In the system in place until 2005, once elected to the Rada, each MP could choose to join a number of factions and could change factions at will.

35 De facto, however, parliamentary immunity was not absolute – in a number of occasions it was lifted by Rada vote. I thank Lucan Way for this insight.

36 Geir Flikke, "Pacts, Parties and Elite Struggle: Ukraine's Troubled Post-Orange Transition," *Europe-Asia Studies* 60, no. 3 (May 2008), 375–96, here 375, 387.

37 See Alla Yer'omenko (Alla Eromenko), "Shalom Hazavat, slov'iany," *Dzerkalo Tyzhnia*, no. 1/580, 14 January 2006, "Ukrainskie deti Gazproma," *Korrespondent*, May 6, 2006 (reprinted in FEC-MUP, 10 May 2006, via ISI), Iuliia Mostova (Iuliia Mostovaia), "Hazova Firtashka," *Dzerkalo Tyzhnia*, no. 17/596, 29 April–12 May 2006, available at www. zn.kiev.ua/ie/show/596/53328/ (accessed 15 May 2006, via ISI), and Andrzej Szeptycki, "Oligarchic Groups and Ukrainian Foreign Policy," *Polish Quarterly of International Affairs* no. 2 (2008): 43–68.

38 On reduced incentives for cooperation between parties, see Paul D'Anieri, *Understanding Ukrainian Politics*, 153–73 and 174–91. For a succinct description of changes in Ukrainian electoral legislation, see Erik S. Herron, "State Institutions, Political Context and Parliamentary Election Legislation in Ukraine, 2000–2006," *Journal of Communist Studies and Transition Politics* 23, no. 1 (March 2007): 57–76, here 58–9. While some expected that the change from a single mandate district to a full proportional representation

system (effective the 2006 parliamentary elections) would change the situation, this failed to produce the desired results.

39 A low point was reached in late April 2009, when 401 (out of a 450 total) Rada deputies supported a proposal to move forward the presidential elections, against Yushchenko's wishes.

40 I thank Volodymyr Kulyk for this insight.

41 For example, it has been noted that as of 2007 more than half of independent gas producing companies were controlled by Verkhovna Rada deputies. Anna Tsarenko, "Overview of Gas Market in Ukraine," *Case Ukraine Working Paper* WP 2 (2007), 5, 14, available at www.case-ukraine.com.ua.

42 In gas, 63 percent of imports came from Russia and ca. 37 percent from Turkmenistan. In crude oil, nearly 100 percent of net imports came from Russia. Calculated on the basis of data in International Energy Agency, *Energy Policies of Ukraine. 1996 Survey* (Paris: OECD/IEA, 1996), 144 (for gas), 125, 127 (Table 29) (for oil), and 186. Oil imports data is from 1992 (no data is available for the origin of oil imports in 1991).

43 Calculated by the author on the basis of information in IEA, *Ukraine Energy Policy Review 2006*, 127, 186.

44 According to estimates from Krasnov and Brada the average cost of gas imports from Russia to Ukraine jumped from $9.30/ tcm in 1992 to $49.80 in 1993. Average prices for oil imports from Russia increased from $42.20/ tcm to $80.00/tcm in 1993. Krasnov and Brada, "Implicit subsidies," Table 1, 830.

45 In 1991, Ukraine paid $0.25/tcm of natural gas. Calculated from IEA, *Energy Policies of Ukraine* (1996), 150.

46 Andreas Wittkowsky, "The Ukrainian Disease: Rent-seeking, the Debt Economy, and Chances to Harden Budget Constraints" (Berlin: German Development Institute, 2000), 4.

47 See IEA, *Energy Policies of Ukraine* (1996), 154–5.

48 The share of nuclear-generated electricity increased significantly, from ca. 27 percent in 1991 to ca. 50 percent in the mid-2000s. Calculated from IEA (1999), 52, and IEA, *Ukraine Energy Policy Review 2006*, 289.

49 IEA, *Ukraine Energy Policy Review 2006*, 270. As of 2005, Ukraine possessed four NPPs, including fifteen working reactors. Ibid, 289–90.

50 IEA, *Ukraine Energy Policy Review 2006*, 296.

51 As part of the 1997 Black Sea Fleet agreements on the division of the Fleet on a fifty percent-fifty percent basis, Ukraine received, in exchange for a twenty-year contract leasing Black Sea Fleet bases in Crimea to Russia at a reduced rate, a $526 million relief on its debt to Gazprom, plus a further $200 million debt relief in connection with the 1992 transfer of nuclear

weapons to Russia; a subsequent agreement gave Russia an additional share in the fleet in exchange for additional energy debt relief, bringing the Russian total to 81.5 percent of the Black Sea Fleet. See Alyson J.K. Balies, Oleksii Melnyk, and Ian Anthony, "Relics of Cold War: Europe's Challenge, Ukraine's Experience," *SIPRI Policy Paper*, no. 6 (Stockholm, November 2003): 39, available at http://books.sipri.org/files/PP/SIPRIPP06.pdf (accessed 18 February 2013) and Mikhail A. Molchanov, *Political Culture and National Identity in Russian-Ukrainian Relations* (College Station: Texas A&M University Press, 2002): 232–3.

52 However, most oil purchases between refineries located in Ukraine and their mother companies in Russia were made at intra-corporate prices, usually lower-than-market prices. Honchar, *Naftohazovyi sektor*, 85–86.

53 In reality, the deal was more complicated than a simple gas for transit barter, as, in addition to payments in the form of gas (nominally valued at $50/tcm to compensate for transit nominally valued at $1.09/100 km), some part of the transit was paid in cash and in advance, and some was used to offset Ukraine's gas debts from the 1990s. See Energy Charter Secretariat, *Gas Transit Tariffs in Selected Energy Charter Countries* (Brussels, 2006), available at http://www.encharter.org/index.php?id=127 (accessed 24 February 2009), 61.

54 IEA, *Ukraine Energy Policy Review 2006*, 219.

55 Between 2000 and 2005, Ukraine charged Russian-affiliated companies ca. $1.80/ tcm for gas storage, raised to $6.60 in 2005 and reduced to $2.25 in the January 2006 agreements (while the Czech Republic and Germany were charging ca. $87 and $110, respectively in 2006). Ferdinand Pavel and Anna Chukhai, "Gas Storage Tariffs Along the Route to EU Market," (Kyiv: IER 2006), available at http://www.ier.kiev.ua (accessed 24 February 2009) and IEA *Ukraine Energy Policy Review 2006*, 213. Ukraine's 2005 transit charge of $1.09/tcm/100 km was lower than the fee charged by all other European states with the exception of Belarus. See Energy Charter Secretariat, *Gas Transit Tariffs*, 63–4.

56 IEA *Ukraine Energy Policy Review 2006*, 154. As noted by the IEA, between 1995 and 2005, "the implied price of this gas was USD 80 per 1 000 m3, although most public sources quote the price of USD 50 per 1 000 m3 (the lower price factored in a lower price formula for the gas transit and storage fees)." IEA, *Ukraine Energy Policy Review 2006*, 169.

57 Officially, these users would be supplied with domestically produced gas and gas supplied in exchange for transit services, while industrial users, paying higher prices, would be supplied with imported gas.

58 Until the end of 1994 there were no significant end-user price increases for gas and other energy sources, despite of the fact that import prices for Ukraine had increased, significantly in the case of oil.

59 See IEA, *Energy Policies of Ukraine* (1996), 46 and 53.

60 *Gaz i neft´. Energeticheskii biulleten´*, 15 March 2000 (via ISI).

61 Article 7 of the 1999 gas supply agreement between Gazprom and Ukraine explicitly banned the reexport of Russian gas. See Ganna Liuta, "Kazhdoi vetvi vlasti – po gazotreideru," *Zerkalo Nedeli*, no. 48/218, 5–11 December 1998.

62 For examples see Balmaceda, *Energy Dependency*, 103–4.

63 The *New York Times* estimated that Lazarenko personally netted around $200 million a year in oil and gas deals. Raymond Bonner, "Ukraine Staggers in the Path to the Free Market," *The New York Times*, 9 April 1997. See also Jerome Guillet, "Gazprom's got West Europeans Over a Barrel," *The Wall Street Journal*, 8 November 2002. Lazarenko is accused of stealing and laundering over $100 million in energy-related corruption deals during his tenure as PM of Ukraine in 1996–1997; these came from multiple multi-million dollar bribes received from regional gas companies as conditions for granting them distribution rights in their respective regions. He was tried and convicted in Switzerland (in absentia) on money laundering charges and in the United States (where he was arrested in February 1999) of money-laundering, wire fraud, and interstate transportation of stolen property. After Lazarenko's 1999 arrest his second-in-command at IESU, Tymoshenko quickly distanced herself from him to form her own political movement, Bat'kivshchyna (Fatherland).

64 Bills of exchange (also known in English as offset arrangements) formalized a barter-like chain of exchange, where, for example, a gas distributor would supply gas to a company and would be paid partially in bills of exchange, which it in turn could use to partially cancel its tax liabilities vis-á-vis the state. On bills of exchange operations, see Iurii Savka, "Vzaiemozalik iak sposib zhyttia," *Enerhetychna Polityka Ukrainy*, no. 6 (2000): 30–4.

65 V. Khmurych and T. Tkachenko, "Opportunities for Corruption in the Ukrainian Gas Market," Eurasia Foundation (1999), available at www.eurasia.org/programs/eerc/Kyiv/papers/khtk.htm www.eurasia.org/programs/eerc/ (accessed 1 May 2004).

66 Kostiantyn Hryhoryshyn, at the time deputy director of the Ukrainian state-owned electrical company Enerhorynok, described such schemes as follows: "At the same time that Russia was agreed to sell Europe gas as

Dollars 60 per 1,000 cubic meters, Ukraine for some reason agreed to buy it for Dollars 80, even though transport to Europe is far more expensive than transport to Ukraine. (. . .) the reason was that you could charge Dollars 80 cash in Ukraine, and pay Russia with, say, Dollars 40 worth of barter goods which you would value at Dollars 80, and the difference would find its way somewhere else." Kostiantyn Hryhoryshyn, interview with Charles Clover, "Sharp Whiff on Corruption Threatens Ukraine Sell-off," *Financial Times*, 20 October 2000, 9. See also Aslund, *How Ukraine Became a Market Economy*, 135.

67 Ukrainian companies involved in barter with Turkmenistan regularly overcharged heavily for the products being bartered, or sneaked into the barter agreements overpriced but little-needed products, of which rain boots bartered in the mid-1990s to chronically draught-prone Turkmenistan became the best-known example.

68 See Jan Adams, "Russia's Gas Diplomacy," *Problems of Post-Communism* (May/June 2002), 17–18, and *Gaz i neft´. Energeticheskii biulleten´*, 15 June 2001 (via ISI). Differentiating stolen gas from gas drawn from a pipeline above contract levels, and paid at especially agreed prices, an item present in most if not all Ukrainian gas contracts with Gazprom, is especially difficult given the lack of gas meters on the Ukrainian side of the border, as well as wide statistical discrepancies concerning transit gas, even within Ukrainian official statistical sources. For a discussion of these statistical discrepancies, see Pirani's explanatory note following Table 3.1 in "Ukraine: a Gas Dependent State," 99.

69 According to estimates, even without an absolute reduction in transit through Ukraine, the commissioning of even only the first line of Nord-Stream would reduce Ukraine's share in Russian gas exports from 73.22 percent in 2008 to 65.64 percent in 2012. See Graph 3, "Ukrainischer Anteil an Transitpipelines für russisches Erdgas," and Table 1, "Gazproms Exportrouten (in Mrd. m3)," in *UkraineAnalysen* 50 (2009), 10. In addition to the first two lines commissioned in 2011–2012, two further lines are under discussion. (Data refers to Ukraine's share in gas export pipelines volume *capacity*, not in terms of *actual transit*, which can be different.) Completion of the proposed South Stream pipeline (ca. 31 bcm/year) would further reduce Ukraine's role in Russia's gas export.

70 See for example Andreas Wittkowsky, "The Ukrainian Disease: Rent-seeking, the Debt Economy, and Chances to Harden Budget Constraints" (Berlin: German Development Institute, 2000), 7, where he refers to gas siphoning as a strategy used by Ukraine to deal with sharply rising prices in the early and mid 1990s.

71 Ukraine's top energy experts, as well as a number of policy-makers, have been largely unanimous in their assessment of the question. See for example Oleksandr Moroz (leader of Ukraine's Socialist Party) quoted in *Gaz i neft´. Energeticheskii biulleten´*, 13 February 2002 (via ISI), Volodymyr Saprykin, interview in Radio Svoboda Ukrainian service *Priamyi Efir*, 12 April 2005 17:00 UTC, text available at www.radiosvoboda.org/article/2005/04/69d7a9c5-6fdb-489e-9075-c4ed57a3c7bb9.html (accessed 14 April 2005), Dmytro Vydrin (Director, European Institute of Integration and Development, Kyiv) quoted in "Gazovyi kontsortsium. Otsenki ekspertov," *Gaz i neft´. Energeticheskii biulleten´*, 16 July 2002 (via ISI), and Dmytro Vydrin, interview in *Nezavisimaia Gazeta*, 16 November 2000.

72 Surprisingly (and perhaps suspiciously), as of 2012 (i.e., after two major gas crises with Russia directly or indirectly involving disputes on disappeared gas) there were no gas metering stations on the Ukrainian side of the border with Russia, with all measurement of import flows taking place on the Russian side. See IEA, *Ukraine 2012*, 104.

73 Dubrovskyi et al, "The Reform in a Captured State," 26. See also "Antologiia 'Bizonov,'" *NefteRynok*, 25 March 2001 (via ISI). For more details on the battle of interests around EFIs, see Balmaceda, *Energy Dependency*, 107–108, and 183–184 (footnote 59).

74 For details see Honchar, *Naftohazoviy sektor Ukrainy*, 21, and Balmaceda *Energy Dependency*, 10.

75 For example, both Oleksandr Volkov and Viktor Pinchuk of the Dnipropetrovsk BAG gave significant monetary support to Kuchma's 1999 reelection campaign, "and to compensate the first [Volkov] it was necessary [to give him control over] several newspapers and TV channels, and to compensate the second [Pinchuk] [it was necessary to give him control over] several metallurgical complexes and oil and gas companies." "Starye pesni o glavnom," *Gaz i neft´. Energeticheskii biulleten´*, 23 December 1999 (via ISI).

76 See Petr Burkovskii, "Rozhdennaia evoliutsiei," *Kompan'on*, no. 14/374, 16–22 April (2004): 45–47, here 46, and author's interviews with energy analysts, Kyiv, July 2004.

77 See for example "Starye pesni o glavnom," *Gaz i neft´. Energeticheskii biulleten´*, 23 December 1999 (via ISI), Kost´ Bondarenko, "Igra po-krupnomu," *Delovaia Nedelia*, no. 22/182, 10–16 June 2004, 3, and "Russia & the 2004 Presidential Elections," *Global Security.org*, available at http://www.globalsecurity.org/military/world/ukraine/election-2004-r.htm (accessed 23 January 2007).

78 Commenting in 2002, Volodymyr Dubrovskyi of CASE Ukraine argued that, of the $1.5 to 2 billion that should accrue to the state yearly from gas transit fees, the state received only a small portion not exceeding twenty percent. Volodymyr Dubrovskyi (CASE Ukraine), quoted in "Gazovyi konsortsium. Otsenki ekspertov," *Gaz i neft´. Energeticheskii biulleten´*, 16 July 2002 (via ISI).

79 Global Witness, "It's a Gas."

80 Although its creators intended NAK Naftohaz to control most of the oil sector, including refineries, significant opposition in the Rada against this possibility in 1997–1998 meant the company was never able to add oil refineries to its holdings. See Alla Eremenko (Alla Yer´omenko), "'Naftohaz Ukrainy': Kratkaia istoriia v sobytiiakh i litsakh," *Zerkalo Nedeli* 2003, no. 19/444, 24–30 May 2003), and *NefteRynok*, 2 April 2002 (via ISI).

81 See Vitalii Kniazhanskii, "Comrade Reverse," *The Day* (Kyiv), 16 March 2004, 3; originally published in Ukrainian in *Den´* 12 March 2004, 4.

82 See, among others, Petr Vlasov, "Bednye Liudi: Bor´ba za kontrol' nad gazovym rynkom – vazhneishii element vnutripoliticheskoi zhizni Ukrainy," *Ekspert*, 31 May, 1999, pp. 22–24, and Oles´ Tyshchuk and Kost´ Bondarenko, "Geometriia ot Bakaia," *Gaz i neft´. Energeticheskii biulleten´*, 15 June 2001 (via ISI).

83 Thus, it has been argued that Tymoshenko brought to office a desire to settle accounts with rival gas oligarchs Hryhorii Surkis and Ihor Bakai, her main opponents from her period as head of IESU after Lazarenko's departure; both were widely considered as bearing the main responsibility for IESU's loss of is trading license and subsequent closing in 1998. Balmaceda, *Energy Dependency*, 55. See also Vlad Trifonov, "Delo Yulii Timoshenko otpravilos´ na dorabotku," *Kommersant*, 3 February 2005, reprinted in FEC-MUP, 3 February 2005 (via ISI).

84 The $1.8 billion figure from Tymoshenko's is from Dubrovskyi, et al, "The Reform Driving Forces," 84. Aslund quotes Tymoshenko as arguing the forgone rents amounted to $4 billion: $2 billion in gas rents, $1.8 billion in electricity rents, and $0.2 billion oil rents. Aslund, *How Ukraine Became a Market Economy*, 139. None of these sources explain the specific source of these rents.

85 See Balmaceda, *Energy Dependency*, 72.

86 Yuliia Tymoshenko, as quoted in *Gaz i neft´. Energeticheskii biulleten´*, 17 January 2001 (via ISI).

87 Heiko Pleines, "The Political Economy of Coal Industry Restructuring in Ukraine," *KICES Working Papers* 1 (2004), 29.

88 *Source*: Naftohaz Ukrainy, quoted in World Bank, "Ukraine: Challenges Facing the Gas Sector" (September 2003), 10, available
at http://siteresources.worldbank.org/INTECAREGTOPEN-
ERGY/34004325-1112025344408/20772948/ukrainegassector.pdf (accessed
18 February 2013).

89 I thank Andrzej Szeptycki for bringing this point to my attention.

90 The connection between gas, coal mining, and steel production has to do
with the energy-intensive nature of metallurgical production, and with
the fact that, together with iron ore and electricity (usually produced from
natural gas), coke, usually produced from coal, is one of the major inputs
going into metallurgical production. Metallurgical magnates sought new
ways to secure cheap energy for their production plants, for example by
seeking to obtain coal at extremely low prices, even when this made coal
mines economically unviable. Some of the ways in which such low prices
could be forced were "by loaning to undercapitalized mines money to purchase mining equipment at exorbitant prices" and, when they could not
repay, forcing them to choose between creditor-initiated bankruptcy and
"selling those magnates coal" at especially low prices. Pleines, "The Political Economy," 17. See also John A. Gould and Yaroslav Hetman, "Market
Democracy Unleashed? Business Elites and the Crisis of Competitive Authoritarianism in Ukraine," *Business and Politics* 10, no. 2 (2008): 1–33, here
13. See also IEA, *Ukraine Energy Policy Review 2006*, 46.

91 See Aslund, "The *Ancien Régime*: Kuchma and the Oligarchs," in *Revolution in Orange: The Origins of Ukraine's Democratic Breakthrough*, ed. Anders
Aslund and Michael McFaul (Washington, DC: Carnegie Endowment,
2006), 9–28, here 14, and Aslund, *How Ukraine Became*, 149.

92 See Balmaceda, *Energy Dependency*, 56–57 and 163, footnote 68.

93 On the differences in economic interests between Buniak and Marchuk,
concerning the extension of the pipeline to Poland, see Balmaceda, *Energy
Dependency*, 93, footnote 69.

94 See Iurii Shcherbak, "Vybor Tseli," *Stolichnye Novosti*, 22–27 February 2000,
quoted in Tor Bukkvoll, "Defining a Ukrainian Foreign Policy Identity:
Business Interests and Geopolitics in the Formulation of Ukrainian Foreign
Policy 1994–1999," in *Ukrainian Foreign and Security Policy: Theoretical and
Comparative Perspectives*, Jennifer D. P. Moroney et al., (Westport: Praeger,
2002): 147 and Balmaceda, *Energy Dependency*, 93, and 175–76, footnote 65.

95 The fact that official Moscow was looking for much more than an inexpensive way to bring Russian oil to Western markets – and namely seeking to
torpedo the Odesa-Brody project – is shown by Transneft's 2003 rejection

of a less expensive proposal that would have allowed the same oil intended for transit through a reversed Odesa-Brody pipeline to be transported by the already existing Transdniester Pipeline System to Odesa.

96 In 2003, TNK joined British Petroleum as TNK-BP.

97 See Elena Dem'ianenko, "Po proektu Odesa-Brody naiden kompromis," *Delovaia Nedelia-FT* (Kyiv), 28 January 2004 (via ISI).

98 See Vitalii Kniazhanskii, "Truba bez nefti," *Den´* (Russian-language edition), 30 June 2004, p. 5, Garik Churilov, "Ianukovich v Moskve 'pridumal,' kak napolnit´ nefteprovod 'Odesa-Brody'," obkom.net.ua, 5 July 2004, reprinted in FEC-MUP, 6 July 2004 (via ISI), Tat'iana Vysotskaia and Iurii Lukashin, "Mozhet, po krugu. Ukraina ofitsial'no podderzhala i revers, i avers 'Odesa-Brody,'" *Ekonomicheskie Izvestiia*, no. 26, 9 July 2004, reprinted in FEC-MUP, 6 July 2004 (via ISI), and Vitalii Kniazhanskii, "Rasshifrovka signala,' *Den´* (Russian-language edition), 14 July, 2004, 1.

99 See "Russia & the 2004 Presidential Elections," Global Security.org, available at http://www.globalsecurity.org/military/world/ukraine/ election-2004-r.htm (accessed 23 January 2007).

100 Ukraine's permanent abandonment of the original Odesa-Brody project would mean losing an important possible source of energy diversification for Ukraine, Poland, Slovakia, the Czech Republic, and Germany. It would also have important ecological implications for the Southern European region, as oil transit through the pipeline (instead of by tanker) would have reduced transit through the ecologically sensitive Bosphorus straits.

101 After the reversal, only a fraction of the pipeline's capacity of 14 million tons per year was used, with the respectively reduced revenue. In 2005, only 5.8 million tons of oil were shipped via the pipeline, in contrast with the promised 9 million tons; in 2006, only 3.42 million tons. Transit increased again in 2007 (to 9 Mt), but only after a 50 percent reduction in transit fees at the insistence of the pipeline's offshore operator, Skilton Ltd. Honchar, *Naftohazovyi sektor Ukrainy*, 98, 101. Reverse shipments ended in 2007.

102 For a discussion of some of the continuities between Itera and Eural Trans Gas, see Roman Kupchinsky, "The Unexpected Guest: RosUkrEnergo" (paper presented at the conference on "The Ukrainian-Russian Gas Crisis and Its Fallout: Domestic and International Implications," Harvard University, 5–6 February 2006, available at http://www.huri.harvard.edu/ events/event-archive/102-gas-crisis-conference-2006.html (accessed 23 February 2013).

103 See Catherine Belton, "Suspicions Raised by Gas Giant's New Deal," *The St. Petersburg Times*, 28 February 2003, available at http://www.sptimes. ru/index.php?action_id=2&story_id=9440 (accessed 28 June 2006), as well as additional materials from *Jane's Intelligence Digest*, Radio Free Europe/Radio Liberty, and the early March 2003 Moscow press.

104 See Global Witness, "It's a Gas."

105 See Belton, "Suspicions Raised," and Oleksandr Ivchenko (head of NAK Naftohaz in 2005), cited in Oksana Liven´, "Kreditnaia dobycha," *Energobiznes*, 19 September 2005 (via ISI), accessed 21 October 2005.

106 Pirani, "Ukraine: a Gas Dependent State," in *Russian and CIS Gas Markets and their Impact on Europe*, ed. S. Pirani (Oxford: Oxford University Press for the Oxford Institute of Energy Studies, 2009), 97.

107 See "A teper´ – revoliutsiia," *Vlast´ deneg*, 12 March 2005.

108 During this period Turkmenistan often overbooked, concluding multiple sale contracts for the same sale volumes.

109 See Table 4.1. Belarus and Russia figures are for 2004-2005. IEA, *Ukraine Energy Policy Review 2006*, 183.

110 IEA, *Ukraine Energy Policy Review 2006*, 45.

111 On 17–18 February 2005, armed individuals (presumably members of the police or other state security forces) occupied the offices of the Ivano-Frankiivsk and Poltava oblenerhos, where a property conflict between Hryhory Surkis, one of the most powerful businessmen of the Kuchma entourage, and at-the-time Yushchenko supporter Kostiantyn Hryho-ryshin had been simmering for years. Hryhoryshin, emboldened by Sur-kis' defeat in the Orange Revolution, was seeking to reestablish control over five Ukrainian oblenerhos.

112 See Turchinov's press conference, 15 September 2005, as transcribed by the *Ukrains'ka Pravda* website, available at www.pravda.com.ua/ru/ news/2005/9/15/32610.htm (accessed 18 February 2013).

113 Calculated from information in Jonathan Stern, "Natural Gas Security Problems in Europe: The Russian-Ukrainian Crisis of 2006," *Asia-Pacific Review* 13 No. 1 (2006) pp. 32–59, here p. 44. No European costumers were directly affected. Ibid.

114 The last major agreement based on this model was August 2004 Long-term Contract between Gazprom and Naftohaz of Ukraine. IEA, *Ukraine Energy Policy Review 2006*, 218.

115 On transit fees see footnote 55 above.

116 The price demanded by Gazprom was suddenly reduced to $95 (2006 price as per the agreements of 4 January 2006) once RosUkrEnergo entered the picture as an intermediary.

117 See Pirani, "Ukraine: a Gas Dependent State," 100.

118 Oleksander Chalii, in Radio Free Europe program for Ukraine, *Vechirnia Svoboda*, 8 January 2009, heard on www.radiosvoboda.org.

119 Balmaceda, *Energy Dependency*, 140. Milov argues Gazprom's generous support of RosUkrEnergo during this period included giving the company $1.25 billion in profits from gas trade with Turkmenistan it could have received itself. See Vladimir Milov and Boris Nemtsov, *Ekspertnyi doklad. Putin i Gazprom* (Moscow: Novaia Gazeta, 2008).

120 IEA, *Ukraine Energy Policy Review 2006*, 218.

121 It has been argued that several ministers – according to some, even PM Iurii Yekhanurov himself – were largely kept out of the negotiations. Iuliia Mostovaia (Iuliia Mostova), "Eto po-vashemu- Van Gog, a po-nashemu-Gogen," *Zerkalo Nedeli*, no. 3/582, 28 January–3 February 2006.

122 Rada deputy Vira Ul'ianchenko, cited in Mostovaia, "Eto po-vashemu-Van Gog."

123 See "Ukrainskie deti Gazproma." Criminal responsibility can only be ascertained by a court of law, however.

124 Mostovaia, "Hazova Firtashka."

125 *Ukrains'ka Pravda*, "Khto stane nastupnym holovoiu 'Naftohazu Ukrainy'?" Available at http://www.pravda.com.ua/news/2006/5/17/41816.htm (accessed 26 May 2006), Tyshchuk, "Sovinaia bolezn'," Iuliia Mostovaia, "Osada Zamknutogo kruga," *Zerkalo Nedeli*, no. 19/598, 20–26 May 2006, available at www.zerkalonedeli.com/ie/show/598/53426/ (accessed 1 June 2006), and Vitalii Haiduk, interview with Iuliia Mostova, in *Dzerkalo Tyzhnia*, no. 41/620, 28 October-3 November 2006, available at http://www.zn.kiev.ua/ie/show/620/54930/ (accessed 27 January 2007).

126 The agreements were leaked and published in the *Ukrains'ka Pravda* website, 5 January 2006. Available at http://www.pravda.com.ua/articles/4b1a9a608c9b1/ (accessed 15 July 2009).

127 Pirani, "Ukraine: A Gas Dependent State," 101.

128 Despite Yushchenko's attempt to portray the prices set in the agreements as a bargain, in reality, Russian gas (as opposed to the cocktail of gases sold for $95/ tcm) would still cost Ukraine $230/tcm, the price originally demanded by Gazprom. Given the fact that most of the gas delivered to Ukraine in the first six months of 2006 was officially coming from CA, what this meant was not Russian gas at a reduced price of $95/tcm, but CA gas at much higher prices than those contracted directly between Ukraine and Turkmenistan, at that time $65/tcm. Pirani et al., argue the price formula was likely based on a net forward (production costs plus a

predetermined percentage of profit) calculation of Turkmenistan prices . See Stern et al., *The Russo-Ukrainian Gas Dispute*, 9.

129 Storage fees Ukraine charged Russia and Russian-affiliated companies had been increased from ca. $1.80/tcm (2004) to $6.60 in 2005, and were reduced to $2.25 in the January 2006 agreements.

130 As discussed in chapter 1, while geographical diversification refers to importing energy from several countries and/or geographical areas, contractual diversification refers to developing a variety of contractual relationships both in terms of companies and of types of contracts (short-term, long-term, etc.) even when the energy originates from a single country.

131 See Table 3 in US Department of Energy, Energy Information Administration, Country Analyses Briefs, Ukraine, available at http://www.eia.doe. gov/emeu/cabs/Ukraine/Full.html (accessed 15 April 2009).

132 According to that source, in 2007 Ukraine imported, 35.5 (36.5 in 2006) bcm of gas from Turkmenistan, 2.8 (2.8) from Uzbekistan, 7.7 (6.5) from Kazakhstan, and 4.6 (9.1) from Russia. Pirani, "Ukraine: a Gas Dependent State," 99 (Table 3.1). Taking into account Pirani's nuanced discussion of the lack of coherence between various Ukrainian statistical sources on its gas trade in a detailed note following this table, such statistics must be taken with a grain of salt, however.

133 One cannot exclude a degree of official Ukrainian manipulation and instrumental securitization of the alleged geographical diversification element for public relations reasons. For example, in October 2006, then Minister of Fuel and Energy Yurii Boiko proudly announced that in 2007 Ukraine would not import Russian gas.

134 As noted by former head of Ukrtransnafta Oleksandr Todiichuk: if the price for Ukraine was to be significantly higher, then, "it should, at least psychologically, be a different gas." Oleksandr Todiichuk, in Radio Svoboda program for Russia, *Itogi Nedeli*, 10 January 2009, transcript available at http://www.svobodanews.ru/Transcr ipt/2009/01/10/20090110152009547.html (accessed 12 January 2009).

135 See Leonid Gusak, "Kto 'krishuet' RosUkrEnergo," *2000*, no. 52/444, 26 December 2008, available at http://news2000.org.ua/a/61114 (accessed 8 January 2009).

136 See Iurii Shkoliarenko, "Kartochnye igry s 'Gazpromom'," *proUA*, 20 March 2008, in FEC-MUP, 20 March 2008 (via ISI).

137 For example, in November 2006 UkrHazEnerho stopped gas supplies to sixteen competing factories, largely belonging to the Privat Group. See Oles' Tyschuk, "Treider-reider," *Infobank Oil and Gas Monitor*, 25 November 2006 (via ISI).

138 Mikhail Koremchin, quoted in Svetlana Dolinchuk, "Potrebnost' v posred-
     nikakh otpala," *Ekonomicheskie Izvestiia*, 12 March 2008, in FEC-MUP
     12 March 2008 (via ISI). See also Petra Opitz and Christian von Hirschhau-
     sen, "Ukraine as a Gas Bridge to Europe, "Working Paper No. 3, Institute
     for Economic Research and Policy Consulting, October 2000, 4.
139 For additional details, see Myroslav Demydenko, "Ukraine, Vanco En-
     ergy, and the Russian Mob," *Eurasian Daily Monitor 5*, no. 177, 16 Septem-
     ber 2008 (available at http://www.jamestown.org, accessed 17 September
     2008).
140 Following a dispute over managerial control of the company, in 2007 Tat-
     neft ceased crude oil supplies to the Kremenchuk refinery, leading to its
     greatly reduced operations. See "Key Ukrainian Refinery Announces Oil
     Supply Agreement with Azerbaijan's SOCAR," *HIS Global Insight*, 9 Octo-
     ber 2010, available at www.ihsglobalinsight.com/SDA/SDADetail17731.
     htm (accessed 15 July 2010).
141 Gazprom threatened that if Ukraine did not pay its gas debt, it would
     start reducing supplies to Ukraine on 3 March. On 3 March 2008 Gaz-
     prom reduced gas supplies by 25 percent, on 4 March by an additional 25
     percent.
142 Tymoshenko argued Gazprom and the Russian side had insisted on keep-
     ing RosUkrEnergo on. See also Roman Olarchyk, "Ukraine Premier Fails
     to Oust Gas Group," *Financial Times*, 11 April 2008. Similarly, despite the
     decision to eliminate UkrHazEnergo from the Ukrainian market effec-
     tive 1 March 2008, de facto the process dragged itself for many months
     as a result of a series of lawsuits from both sides (NAK Naftohaz and
     UkrhazEnergo) on ownership rights over UkrHazEnergo gas stored in
     underground storage facilities. See "Naftohaz khochet podelit' gazovoe
     nasledstvo Ukrhaz-energo," *Gaz i Neft'. Analiticheskii biulleten'* (cited in
     translation as *Infobank Oil & Gas Monitor*), 25 September 2008 (via ISI).
     Such ownership issues led to RosUkrEnergo suing NAK Naftohaz at the
     Stockholm Arbitration Court, a process it won in June 2010.
143 A Memorandum of Understanding ("Memorandum mezhdu pravitel'stvom
     Rossiiskoi Federatsii i Kabinetom Ministrov Ukrainy o sotrudnichestve v
     gazovoi sfere") of October 2008, despite having no legal validity, was
     widely cited by PM Tymosheko as proof of her success on this issue.
144 For an explanation of where these two numbers come from, see Iurii Feo-
     fantov, "Rynok Gaza: Dolg platezham opasen," *Gaz i Neft'. Analiticheskii
     biulleten/*, 25 November 2008 (via ISI).
145 Ibid.
146 Gusak, "Kto 'krishuet' RosUkrEnergo."
147 See Balmaceda, *Energy Dependency*, 56–7 and 163, footnote 68.

148 Leaving aside politically motivated accusations, Ukraine's energy transit system was, throughout the period covered in this book, in dire need of modernization. Pipeline gas pumping units are in particularly bad condition, which means increasing amounts of gas are needed to pump gas through the pipelines (technical gas). In 2001, almost 10 percent of Ukraine's yearly gas consumption was used for this purpose.

149 As the conflict deepened and supplies to several EU states were interrupted, the EU started to play a more active role in its resolution. After the end of the conflict, the EU unveiled new initiatives to strengthen the reliability of Ukraine's gas transit system, for example through a 23 March 2009 declaration of principle reached with the Ukrainian government on EU help for Ukraine's raising of ca. $3.5 billion needed for the modernization of its gas transit system.

150 Alan Riley, "Corruption in Kiev and an E.U. Trade Pact," *The New York Times*, 4 October 2011, available at http://www.nytimes.com/2011/10/05/opinion/05iht-edriley05.html (accessed 16 October 2011).

151 For a detailed analysis of the agreements, see Stern et al., *Russo-Ukrainian Gas Dispute*, 26–30. The agreements were leaked to *Ukrainsksa Pravda* and published there on 22 January 2009, available at http://www.pravda.com.ua/articles/4b1aa351db178/ and http://www.pravda.com.ua/articles/4b1aa355cac8c/ (accessed 10 July 2010).

152 At the time of the January 2009 crisis, Russia accused Ukraine of stealing 63.5 mcm of Gazprom's transit gas, but such accusations were not confirmed by international observers especially deployed to monitor possible siphoning of gas from the export pipeline.

153 In November 2009, an addenda to the earlier contracts waived take-or-pay clauses for 2009 in recognition of Ukraine's weaker gas demand as a result of the world economic crisis; gas supply volumes for 2010 were also reduced from 52 to 33.75 bcm.

154 On the connection between the danger of bankruptcy and Gazprom's taking away of clients from NAK, commented Volodymyr Saprykyn: "We got an European market contract for the supply of gas to Ukraine. But inside the country we really do not have a market." Volodymyr Saprykyn, cited in Tetiana Iarmoshuk, "Naftohaz mozhe vlizty u borhy pered 'Gazpromom'," *Radio Svoboda* (Ukrainian program), 19 February 2009, available at www.radiosvoboda.org (accessed 19 February 2009).

155 See the discussion on transit fees in footnote 55 above.

156 In 2011, Tymoshenko would be officially accused of abusing her powers as PM by ordering NAK Naftohaz to sign an agreement with Russia in

April 2009 seen by the Yanukovich camp as disadvantageous for Ukraine. After a trial highly criticized by the EU and the United States as selective justice and politically motivated, she was sentenced to seven years in jail and a fine of ca. $190 million. See "EU Says Tymoshenko Sentence Could Hit Ukraine Ties," *Kyiv Post*, 11 October 2011, available at http://www.kyivpost.com/news/nation/detail/114538/#ixzz1btUuxhAA (accessed 25 October 2011). In January 2013 she was formally charged with commissioning the 1996 murder of Donetsk gas businessman and MP Yevhen Scherban as part of the battle for the control of the gas market, during her tenure as second-in-command at IESU. See Katya Gorchiskaya, "Prosecutors tie Tymoshenko to Lawmaker's 1996 Murder," *The Kyiv Post*, 25 January 2013, available at http://www.kyivpost.com/content/politics/prosecutors-tie-tymoshenko-to-lawmakers-1996-murder-319321.html (accessed 18 February 2013).

157 After a suit in which many argued the Yanukovich government installed in February 2010 had not defended its interests proactively, RosUkrEnergo won the process in June 2010, after which the Court ordered NAK Naftohaz to return 11 bcm of natural gas to RosUkrEnergo, in addition to 1.1 bcm of natural gas in lieu of penalties.

158 von Hirschhausen and Vincentz, "Energy Policy and Structural Reform," 64. If in 1990, the energy sector, metallurgy, and chemicals accounted for 25 percent of the gross industrial output, by 1995, their share had grown to 53 percent. Conversely, the share of "relatively energy-efficient industries (engineering, light industry and the food industry)" fell from 60 percent to 34 percent from 1991 to 1995. IEA, *Ukraine Energy Policy Review 2006*, 118.

159 The IEA, *Ukraine Energy Policy Review 2006*, 118, using Purchasing Power Parity (PPP) GDP data, reports a 30 percent increase in energy intensity between 1991 and 1995, and gradual declines since then. Other sources (using different units of GDP measurement) report a somewhat larger increase over a slightly longer period. IEA, *Ukraine Energy Policy Review 2006*, 118.

160 In 2004 alone, Ukraine's metal exports grew by 10 percent in terms of volume, and by ca. 60 percent in price, part of a trend that continued until mid-2008. *Source*: Metaly Ukrainy, available at <http://www.business.dp.ua/me/data/0801.htm> (accessed 15 June 2006).

161 von Hirschhausen and Vincentz, "Energy Policy and Structural Reform," 65.

162 These included the Law on Energy Conservation (1994), the Comprehensive National Program on Energy Conservation (1996), and the 1999 presidential decree on energy savings in the public administration sector.

163 Source: UNDP 2007/2008 Human Development Report, available at http://hdrstats.undp.org/countries/data_sheets/cty_ds_UKR.html (accessed 4 April 2009) and IEA, *Key World Energy Statistics 2009*. Between 1995 and 2004 Ukraine improved its energy efficiency by over 40 percent, reversing the setbacks of the mid-1990s. See Figure 4.1 in IEA, *Ukraine Energy Policy Review 2006*, 118. If Ukraine's improvements in energy intensity were not especially impressive, total energy use and imports decreased significantly between independence and 2007 (and even more so since then). If in 1991 Ukraine's total energy supply (TPES) was 250.6 Mtoe, by 2010 it had declined to 130.5. 2010 figure from IEA, *Energy Policies Beyond IEA Countries*, 21.

164 Calculated from Table 3.7 in Pirani, "Ukraine: a Gas Dependent State," 117. Total gas consumption went down by a much more moderate 3.3 percent between 2005 and 2006. Ibid.

165 See Pirani, "Ukraine: a Gas Dependent State," 118–120.

166 Calculated from IEA, *Key World Energy Statistics 2008*.

167 All 2007 data for this section calculated from IEA, *2007 Energy Balance for Ukraine*, available at http://www.iea.org/stats/balancetable.asp?COUNTRY_CODE=UA (accessed 15 July 2010).

168 "Gas Data," available at http://www.iea.org/Textbase/stats/gasdata.asp?COUNTRY_CODE=Select&Submit=Submit (accessed 3 April 2009).

169 See Volodymyr Saprykin, "Restructuring Ukraine's Coal Industry: Key Problems and Priority Measures," *National Security and Defence*, no. 11 (2004): 2–9.

170 In April 2008, Ukraine signed an agreement with Westinghouse Electric to buy nuclear fuel for one if its NPPs, and started to receive this fuel in 2011.

171 Although the last reactor in the Chernobyl complex was shut-down in 2000, in defiance of tacit Chernobyl-related agreements with the European Bank for Reconstruction and Development, Ukraine put into operation two new nuclear power plants in 2004, the Khmelnytskyi Unit no. 2 and the Rivne Unit no. 4.

172 See "Kuda postavit′ pristavku 'ėks'," *NefteRynok*, 25 December 2000 (via ISI).

173 Pirani, "Ukraine: a Gas Dependent State," 108.

174 The *Enerhetychna Stratehiia Ukrainy na period do 2030 roku* (2006) estimates gas reserves at 1024 bcm, sufficient to sustain the current yearly production up to 2062.

175 Ukraine's level of energy losses (measured in terms of the difference between the TPES and final consumption) is one of the highest in the world, with TPES exceeding consumption by ca. 67 percent in 2006 – a much higher percentage than in the EU (where TPES exceeds final energy consumption by 41 percent), or even Russia (50 percent). See World Bank, "Ukraine: the Impact of Higher Natural Oil and Gas Prices," December 2005, available at <http://web.worldbank.org/WBSITE/EXTERNAL/COUNTRIES/ECAEXT/UKRAINEEXTN/0,,contentMDK:20774978~pagePK:141137~piPK:141127~theSitePK:328533,00.html>, 4 (accessed 1 June 2006), and IEA Energy Statistics, Energy Balances for Ukraine, available at http://www.iea.org/Textbase/stats/balancetable.asp?COUNTRY_CODE=UA (accessed 27 March 2009).

176 Iurii Aks'onov (Iurii Aksenov), "Mrii ta real'nist' dyversyfikatsii hazozabezpechennia Ukrainy," *Enerhetychna Polityka Ukrainy* 2000, no. 6 (December 2000): 14–23, here 21.

177 As noted above, following a dispute on control over the company, Tatneft had ceased crude oil supplies to the refinery in 2007.

178 Igor Petrov, "Sozdanie strategicheskikh zapasov nefteproduktov ne provalilo, a vsego lish' otsrochilo na god," *Delovaia Stolitsa*, no. 47, 22 November 2004.

179 See IEA, *Ukraine 2012*, 147. In 2007, the goal to develop a system of strategic oil reserves was announced once more, but few official details of its intended implementation were provided.

180 Gas import prices paid by Ukraine per tcm increased from $95 in 2006 to $130 in 2007 to $179.50 in 2008.

181 We have no evidence, however, that the inclusion of intermediary companies in the 2006 agreements was first and foremost the result of a specific attempt by the Ukrainian side to moderate the effects of price increases. Rather, available evidence points to the 4 January 2006 agreements as a much more direct and crude attempt to simply maintain access to rent-seeking despite changed conditions, while restoring supplies as soon as possible.

182 The text of the Strategy, *Enerhetychna Stratehiia Ukrainy na period do 2030 roku*, Kyiv, Ministerstvo Palyva ta Enerhetyky, 2006, is available at the Ministry of Fuel and Energy's Website, <www.mpe.kmu.gov.ua/control/uk/archive/docview?typeId=36172> (accessed 5 May 2006).

183 Such inaccuracies and inconsistencies included counting oil production by Ukrainian companies abroad as domestic production, or planning for Ukraine to reduce emissions, while at the same time calling for an increased use of coal. On the document's coal policy see Sergei Ermilov [former minister of Fuel and Energy], "Zametki k programme Partii Ekologicheskogo Spaseniia "EKO+25%," (paid political advertising) *Zerkalo Nedeli*, no. 584 (11–18 February 2006), available at <http://www.zerkalo-nedeli.com/nn/show/584/52569/> (accessed 1 March 2006). For additional comments on the Strategy, see *Energeticheskaia Polityka Ukrainy* 2006. no. 3 (March 2006).

184 The International Energy Agency referred to the projections contained in the document as "based not on economic analysis, but on policy goals" and "government aspirations" more than "real projections." IEA, *Ukraine Energy Policy Review 2006*, 81.

185 Thus, for example, institutions such as the National Energy Regulatory Commission remained highly politicized and did not provide nearly the same level of publicly accessible reports as its Lithuanian or other EU counterparts. See "Starye pesni o glavnom," *Infobank Oil and Gas Monitor* (Lviv), 23 December 1999 (via ISI), "Regulatori Capture, abo zakhoplennia organu regulovannia grupami inteeresiv" (interview with Iuryi Kiashko), *Dzerkalo Tyzhnia*, no. 8/587, 4–10 March 2006, and Marko Grabovskii, "PRIVAT brosaet perchatku," *Infobank Oil & Gas Monitor*, 25 March 2008 (via ISI).

186 In addition, the work of organizations such as the Nomos Research Center (through its project and publications on Oil and Gas Revenue Transparency) has been crucial in bringing to light the details of what they call the black box of gas business and starting a public debate on the effects of lack of transparency in the sector. See Honchar, *Naftohazovyi sektor Ukrainy*.

187 IEA, *Ukraine 2012*, 106.

188 For a comparison of Naftohaz gas import prices and average German border prices from 2006 to 2012, see Figure 7.4 in IEA, *Ukraine 2012*, 107.

189 "Ukraine Cuts Gas Transit 19.1% in 2012," *Kyiv Post*, 18 January 2012, available at http://www.kyivpost.com/content/business/ukraine-cuts-gas-transit-191-in-2012-319038.html (accessed 9 February 2013).

190 See IEA, *Ukraine 2012*, 133 and 142.

191 Ministry of Energy and Coal Industry of Ukraine, "Statistichnaia informatsiia," available at http://mpe.kmu.gov.ua/fuel/control/uk/publish/article?art_id=231058&cat_id=35081 (accessed 18 February 2013).

192 From 30.5 bcm in 2008 to 18.4 bcm in 2009. IEA, *Ukraine 2012*, 102.

193 IEA, *Ukraine 2012*, 19.

194 IEA, *Ukraine 2012*, 125; see also Figure 7.9 in ibid.

195 Ibid. Refers to residential users using less than 2,500 cubic meters of gas per year.

196 See IEA, *Ukraine 2012*, 125–6.

197 Ibid., 140.

198 Ibid., 81.

199 Ratio for Ukraine calculated on the basis of its 2005 domestic gas consumption.

200 See footnote 55 above.

201 "Ukraine Cuts Gas Transit 19.1% in 2012," *Kyiv Post*, 18 January 2012, available at http://www.kyivpost.com/content/business/ukraine-cuts-gas-transit-191-in-2012-319038.html (accessed 9 February 2013).

202 There is good reason to believe that such sharing of corrupt rents also took place with actors in Ukraine's other major gas supplier, Turkmenistan. See Global Witness, "It's a Gas."

203 See Bakai's quotation in *The Warsaw Voice*, 8 April 2001, available at www.warsaw.voice/pl/v650/News12.html (accessed 25 April 2003). Given the large role played by gas imports from Turkmenistan in the acquisition of energy rents, the statement should be amended to read "all political fortunes in Ukraine were made on the basis of Russian *and Turkmen* hydrocarbons."

204 See Babanin, Dubrovskyi, and Ivashchenko, *Ukraine: The Lost Decade*, 50.

5. Belarus

1 Belarus' domestic oil production has remained relatively stable (with a slight downward trend) since 1996. Belarus also possesses small brown coal reserves (in 2008 estimated at 0.5 billion tones), but these are located at great depths, making their exploitation difficult and expensive. See *Eurasian Chemical Market*, 30 January 2008, available at http://chemmarket.info/?mod=news&lang=en&nid=6457 (accessed 15 July 2011).

2 Data for 2007. Institut Privatizatsii i Menedzhmenta (thereafter IPM), "Rost tsen na gas: novye vyzovy dlia belorusskoi ekonomiki," 7 (Minsk, 2007), available at http://www.research.by/pdf/wp2007r03.pdf (accessed 3 October 2009). This is higher than in many gas-rich countries, including Russia.

3 The overall resource intensity (including energy intensity) of Belarus' products is ca. 4-5 times higher than that in highly developed countries. Leonid Zlotnikov, "Zhestkaia posadka," *Belorusy i Rynok*, 17 November 2008.

4 As of 2006, Belarus' two underground gas storage facilities had a total capacity of ca. 660 million cubic meters, a small fraction of the recommended
6.6 bcm (30 percent of current yearly gas consumption). Tatiana Manenok
(Tatsiana Manenak), "Tol'ko po rinochnoi stoimosti," *Belorusy i Rynok*, no.
5/690, 6 February 2006. Belarus' concept of energy security, published in
2005, calls for an increase in underground gas storage capacities by 5 bcm
by 2020. See also Beltransgas's official website at: http://www.btg.by/
proizvodstvo/hranenie/.

5 Source: Valeriia Kostiugova, "Perspektivy uchastia Belarusi v ekspluatatsii
nefteprovoda Odessa-Brody," Belarusian Institute for Strategic Studies,
BISS SA 4/2008-EG (April 2008): 3, available at http://www.belinstitute.
eu/images/stories/documents/odessabrody.pdf (accessed 24 October
2008).

6 Data for 2007 from IPM, *Monitoring Infrastrukturi Belarusi 2008*, 33. Of all
countries through which the Yamal pipeline crosses, Belarus is the only
one where the pipeline itself belongs to Gazprom, and where it has a long-
term lease for the land under it.

7 See George Sanford, "Nation, State and Independence in Belarus,"
Contemporary Politics 3, no. 3 (1997): 225–45, and David R. Marples and
Uladzimir Padhol, "The Opposition in Belarus: History, Potential and
Perspectives," in *Independent Belarus: Domestic Determinants, Regional
Dynamics and Implications for the West*, eds. Margarita M. Balmaceda,
James Clem, and Lisbeth Tarlow (Cambridge, MA: HURI/Davis Center
for Russian Studies, distributed by Harvard University Press, 2002):
55–76, here 60.

8 Leonid Zlotnikov, "Possibilities for the Development of a Private Economic
Sector and a Middle Class as a Source of Political Change in Belarus," in
Independent Belarus, eds. Balmaceda et. al., 122–161, here 125–6.

9 Belarus had been heavily russified during the Soviet period and many
resisted what they saw as the forced reintroduction of the Belarusian language in education and administration.

10 Leonid Zlotnikov, "Etapi Transformatsii Ekonomiki Belarusi: Problemy i
dostizheniia," in *Predprinimatel'stvo. BSPN. Biznis-sreda*, eds. L. K. Zlotnikov,
T.A. Bykova, G.P. Badei and Zh.K. Badei (Minsk: BSPN, 2005), 39.

11 World Bank, "Belarus at a Glance," available at http://devdata.worldbank.
org/AAG/blr_aag.pdf (accessed 31 October 2008).

12 Data for 2008 from IPM, *Ezhemesiachnii obzor ekonomiki Belarusi*, no. 9/72,
September 2008, 1, available at http://www.research.by/analytics/
bmer/ (accessed 20 February 2013). On the growth of real wages see
also World Bank, "Country Economic Memorandum on Belarus," World
Bank Report, no. 32346-BY, May 2005 (executive summary available at

http://siteresources.worldbank.org/INTBELARUS/Resources/CEM_
Ex_Sum.doc).

13 Praneviciute has argued that in the case of Belarus economic well-being
(and ever-improving economic conditions) was so important as to become
part of a Soviet Belarus' (and the Lukashenka regime's) foundational
myth. See Jovita Praneviciute, "Security and Identity in Belarus: How
Securitization of National Identity Defines Foreign Influence," paper presented at the 2008 Convention of the Association for the Study of Nationalities, Columbia University, New York, 10–12 April 2008.

14 In 2007, in addition to the 12.4 percent of enterprises considered loss-
making (*ubytochnye predpriatiia*) according to official data, many more
depended on state subsidies to pay wages and salaries. Leonid Zlotnikov,
"Igra v tseitnote."

15 On some of the effects of inexpensive energy in Belarus, see Elena Rakova,
"Energeticheskii sektor Belarusi: povyshaia effectivnost'," Working Paper
WP/10/04, Institut Privatizatsii i Menedzmenta, Minsk, 2010 (available at
www.research.by) (accessed 9 September 2010), 8–11.

16 On military cooperation see John R. Pilloni, "The Belarusian-Russian Joint
Defense Agreement," *The Journal of Slavic Military Studies* 22, no. 4 (October
2009): 543–48, and Ruth Deyermond, "The State of the Union: Military Success, Economic and Political Failure in the Russia-Belarus Union," *Europe-
Asia Studies* 56, no.8 (December 2004): 1191–205.

17 See Article 3 of the 2008 Civil Code.

18 See Margarita M. Balmaceda, "Understanding Repression in Belarus," in
The Worst of the Worst: Rogue and Repressive States in the World Order, ed.
Robert Rotberg (Washington, DC: Brookings Institution, 2007): 193–222.

19 Independent polls conducted in 2002–2004 yielded a 29 percent to 37
percent support for Lukashenka. See Andrei Sannikov, "The Accidental
Dictator," *SAIS Review*, January 25 (2005): 75–88, here 83, and materials
from the Institute of Social and Political Research (NISEPI), available at
www.iiseps.by.

20 Stepan Sukhovenko, "Oligarkhi Lukashenko ili na chom razrabativaiut
samye bogatye liudi Belarusi?," 24 July 2004, originally published in Batke.
net, (accessed 24 June 2008), reprinted in http://forum.delta.by/view-
topic.php?t=1925&highlight=&sid=2096e5d040eec864071491d651d24c9f.

21 In this sense, it is hard to characterize Belarusian clans as BAGs as in the
case of Ukraine. This is so because the term BAGs assumes these groups
also have administrative power in addition to economic power (see Balmaceda, *Energy Dependency*, 17), while similar groups in Belarus lacked
that power.

22 See Belarusian Institute of Strategic Studies, "Privatization in Belarus: Legislative Framework and Real Practices," BISS Working Paper BISS SA 1/2008-PRIV, available at http://www.belinstitute.eu/images/stories/documents/priv1en.pdf (accessed 11 December 2008), 4.

23 As noted by Belarus' Institute of Privatization and Management, "Despite the fact that Beltransgas is a publicly held company, all of its financial data is kept secret, leading to lack of transparency not only in the company but the whole sector." IPM, *Monitoring Infrastrukturi Belarusi 2008*, 35, footnote 49.

24 On the Borovskoi case, see Sergei Panchenko, "Podkovernye shagi ili bor'ba s korruptsiei," 30 May 2007. Available at http://www.dw-world.de/dw/article/0,2144,2569596,00.html, (accessed 8 August 2007).

25 Astrid Sahm and Kirsten Westphal, "Power and the Yamal Pipeline," in *Independent Belarus*, eds. Balmaceda et. al., 270–301, here 272.

26 Alex Danilovich, *Russian-Belarusian Integration: Playing Games Behind the Kremlin Walls* (Aldershot England: Ashgate, 2006), 62.

27 A naval communications unit in Vileika and a radar station in Hantsevichi (Gantsevichi). As discussed in chapter 4, Ukraine signed a similar agreement in 1996. In contrast with that case, however, in Belarus there was little organized opposition to the treaty.

28 See Concept of National Security of Belarus (*Kontsepsiia national'noi bezopasnosti Respubliki Belarus)*, available at: http://www.mod.mil.by/koncep.html (accessed 10 November 2008).

29 Vadim Dubnov, in RFE/RL (Radio Svobody) program for Belarus, *Pratskii Akzent* ("Klubok belaruskai zamezhnai palitiki: Raseia, Europa, 'tretsi s'vet,'"), 10 October 2006, transcript available at http://www.svaboda.org/PrintView.aspx?Id=774535.

30 See Margarita M. Balmaceda, "Myth and Reality in the Belarusian-Russian Relationship: What the West Should Know," *Problems of Post-Communism* 46 (May/June 1999): 3–14.

31 See Yurii Drakokhrust and Dmitri Furman, "Belarus and Russia: the Game of Virtual Integration," in *Independent Belarus*, eds. Balmaceda et. al., 232–55.

32 Some of this increase was the result of the substitution of oil by gas, as oil imports decreased from 37 million tons in 1990 to 20 million tons in 2006 (with the steepest decline from 1991 to 1992 and stabilization after that).

33 For an unofficial English translation of the document, see http://cis-legislation.com/document.fwx?rgn=7286 (accessed 20 Febraury 2013).

34 Elena Novozhilova and Vadim Sekhovich, "Gazavat' po-gazpromovskii," *Belorusskaia Delovaia Gazeta*, 6 November 2002.

35 See Andrew Ryder, "Economy," in *Eastern Europe, Russia and Central Asia 2004* (London: Europa Publications, 2003), 147, and Iaroslav Romanchuk (Yaraslau Ramanchuk), "Nado chashche vstrechat'sia: Putina i Lukashenko vnov potianulo drug k drugu," *Belorusskaia Gazeta*, 20 January 2003.

36 Olga Tomashevskaia, "Legkaia pobeda," *Belarususskaia Delovaia Gazeta*, 13 November 2002.

37 From Beltransgas' official website, available at http://www.btg.by (accessed 10 June 2010).

38 Aleksei Urban and Aleksei Nikolskii, "Bez pridannogo. Gotovit'sia Belarus otdat' 'Beltransgas'," *Vedomosti*, 25 November 2002.

39 It has been argued that, in addition to Russian pressure, the late 2002 decisions by the EU and the United States to refuse visas to Lukashenka and other Belarusian leaders played a role. Fearing he might end in total isolation may have moved Lukashenka to seek better relations with Russia.

40 Tikhon Klishevich, "Istoriia bor'ba za 'Beltransgas,'" Deutsche Welle radio service to Belarus, 29 November 2006, transcript available at www.dw-world.de, (accessed 5 August 2007).

41 Druzhba starts in Russia and later divides into northern (Belarus) and southern (Ukrainian) branches, of which the northern one has a larger capacity. The setup of the pipeline, which divides in Mozyr between its two branches, makes it relatively easy to redirect transit flows to react to transit fees and other conditions, allowing pipeline operator Transneft to play Belarus and Ukraine against each other. Throughout the 1990s and 2000s, Russia used the possibility of transiting oil through Belarus as safeguard against Ukraine's perceived or real demands for excessively high transit tariffs from Russia.

42 *Transport i sviaz' Respubliki Belarus* (Minsk, Ministry of Statistics and Analysis, various years).

43 A September 1999 decree by Russia's minister of Fuel and Energy Viktor Kalyuzhny made Russian crude oil deliveries to refineries in Belarus equivalent to deliveries to Russian ones. Interfax, Daily Financial Report, 21 September 1999, FBIS-SOV-1999-0921.

44 Author's interview with independent economist, Minsk, 18 November 2008.

45 Vadim Sekhovich, "Belorusskaia promyshlennost': v novyi god s novymi khvorami," *Belorusskaia Delovaia Gazeta*, 29 December 1997.

46 See Andrei Liakhovich, "Palitichnii kantekst napiaredadni vybarou i referendum," in *Nainoushaya gistorya belaruskaga parlamentaryzmu* (Minsk: Analitichnii Grudok, 2005), available online at http://kamunikat.fontel.net/www/knizki/palityka/parlamentaryzm/index.htm (accessed 20 June 2008) and Feduta, *Lukashenko*, 591. It has also been argued that as a

condition for Russia's recognizing the results of the 2001 elections, LUKoil was promised a controlling package of shares in the Naftan refinery at a price much lower than the company's market price. Author's interviews, Minsk, 17 November 2008. For related information see Marina Zagorskaia, Vadim Sekhovich, Aleksandr Starikevich. *Belarus'. 1991–2006. Itogi.* (Minsk: Avtorskii kollektiv, 2008), 144–70.

47 As nearly all electricity in Belarus is generated through gas, this section includes electricity as well. The section is based on chapter 3 of Margarita M. Balmaceda, *Living the High Life in Minsk: Russian Energy Rents, Domestic Populism and Belarus' Impending Crisis* (Budapest: Central European University Press, forthcoming 2013).

48 See IPM, "Rost tsen na gas," 7.

49 Ibid.

50 Data for 1992 calculated from Graph 1, K. von Hirschausen and I. Rumi-antseva, "Ekonomicheskie aspekty razvitiia atomnoi energetiki v Belarusi," in IPM, *Energetika Belarusi: puti razvitii* (Minsk, IPM, 2006), 85–122, here 92 (on the basis of IEA data). Data for 2005 from F. Pavel and E. Rakova, "Improving Energy Efficiency in the Belarusian Economy – an Economic Agenda," GET Policy Paper (Minsk, 2005). This made this proportion higher than in gas-rich Russia itself (ca. 45 percent in 2005).

51 By December 2003, for example, gas prices charged residential end-consumers amounted to 150 percent of the import prices paid by Belarus. IPM, "Rost tsen na gas," 14.

52 IPM, *Monitoring Infrastructury Belarusi 2008*, 34. Although the list was not made public, interviews with experts revealed that companies usually offered such preferences were electricity producer Belenergo, some petrochemical companies, cement producers, wood processing plants, and selected light industries.

53 For example, Lukashenka's 2004 declaration that household energy prices could not be increased by more than 2 percent per month, even when import prices were rising faster than that. See Sergei Zhbanov, "S novym gazom," *Belorusskaia Gazeta*, no. 2/470, 17 January 2005.

54 As of 2002, the retail price of the most common gasoline grades (A-92 and A-95) was nearly 40 percent higher than in Russia and Ukraine. Yaroslav Romanchuk, "Degradatsiia monopolista. Kak 'Belneftekhim' tianet na dno belorusskuiu ekonomiku," 7 April 2002, in http://liberty-belarus.info/content/view/449/46/ (accessed 15 July 2008).

55 See "Gorkii nefteklapan."

56 In February 2002, the Cabinet of Ministers mandated oil refineries to support agricultural work by selling a percentage (6 percent of diesel

and 1.5 percent of A-75 gasoline) of their production at prices set by the Belneftekhim, at that time 30 percent lower than market prices. "Gorkii nefteklapan."

57 According to the IMF, the subsidy effect of low gas prices amounted to 11.5 percent of GDP in 2000, and to 6.1 percent in 2005. IMF, "Republic of Belarus: Selected Issues," Country Report No. 05/217 (Washington, DC, 2005). See also IPM, "Rost tsen na gas," 16.

58 IPM, "Rost tsen na gas," 8, footnote 4.

59 See Irina Selivanova, "Ekonomicheskaia Integratsiia Rossii i Belorussii i ee vlianie v razvitie narodnogo khoziaistva Belorusi," in *Belorussiia i Rossiia: Obshestva i Gosudarstva*, D.E. Furman (Moscow, 1998), 324. By 2005, the role of barter-like transactions had been reduced to less than 5 percent. IPM, "Rost tsen na gaz," 8 (footnote 4), 10.

60 Vadim Sekhovich, "Gazovaia otrasl'," in Zagorkaia et al., *Belarus'. 1991– 2006. Itogi)* 48–60, here 53. See also Dashkevich, *Energeticheskaia Zavisimost' Belarusi*. In 1998, it was estimated that by buying from Belarus instead of from cheaper suppliers, Russia was de facto subsidizing the Belarusian economy by a further US $200–$300 million a year. Leonid Zlotnikov, "Vyzhivanie ili integratsiia?," *Pro et Contra* (Spring 1998): 84.

61 See Kostiugova, "Perspektivy uchastia Belarusi."

62 Source: Data for 2000 from Ministry of statistics and analysis of the Republic of Belarus, http://belstat.gov.by/, as quoted in Kostiugova, "Perspektivy uchastia Belarusi," 2. Data for 2006 from Ministry of statistics and analysis of the Republic of Belarus, *Foreign trade of the Republic of Belarus. Statistical abstracts*, various years.

63 Tatiana Manenok, "Valiutnye donory slabeiut," *Nashe Mnenie*, 27 November 2008, available at www.nmnby.org/pub/0811/27j.html (accessed 11 December 2008).

64 Article 28 of the December 1999 Treaty on the Creation of a Union State (*Dogovor o sozdanii Soiuznogo gosudarstva*) restates the same point, i.e., that both sides will apply the same import and export duties.

65 See Vadim Sekhovich "Neftianaia i neftepererabativaiuschaia otrasl'" in *Belarus'. 1991–2006. Itogi*, Marina Zagorskaia, Vadim Sekhovich, Aleksandr Starikevich (Minsk: Avtorskii kollektiv, 2008), 144–70, here 151.

66 Tatiana Manenok, "Benzinovyi signal," *Belorusy i Rynok*, no. 43/678, 8 November 2005.

67 Tatsiana Manenak (Tatiana Manenok) comments in RFE/RL (Radio Svabody) program for Belarus, *Ekzpertiza Svobodi*, ("Kryzys z pastaukami raseiskoga gazu u Belarus"), 4 November 2002, transcript available at

http://archive.svaboda.org/programs/bel-rus/2002/11/20021104175816. asp, (accessed 25 April 2008). On the un-sanctioned siphoning of gas from the pipeline, see also Tatiana Manenok, "Poslednii argument," *Belorusskii Rynok*, no.7/591, 23 February 2004.

68 Selivanova, "Ekonomicheskaia Integratsiia," 326.

69 See for example Andrei Suzdaltsev, interview in DW-World, 1 January 2007 (accessed 1 February 2007), transcript available at http://www.dw-world.org/dw/article/0,2144,2296562,00.html. For additional information on corrupt trade deals organized by the Presidential Administration or individual actors within it, see, among others, Mikhail Zygar' and Iurii Svirko, "Chlena semi sdali organam," *Kommersant*, 13 February 2004, available at http://www.kommersant.ru/doc.aspx?fromsearch=02166f53-83e8-4205-b1c5-f31f6ccc266f&docsid=449515 (accessed 8 November 2008), and Aleksandr Barnatovich, "Biznes Vlasti," *Belorusskaia Delovaia Gazeta*, 26 October 2004, available at http://bdg.press.net.by/2004/10/2004_10_2 6.1474/1474_7_1.shtml.

70 See Feduta, *Lukashenko*, 418–19 and 458.

71 In some cases, the connection between support for some of these special projects and the acquisition of business privileges has been especially clear. In a June 2007 interview, Yuri Chizh (Iurii Chizh), one of Belarus' richest businessmen, described how he received quotas for oil trade from a very high-level leader by proposing to direct the resulting profits to supporting Belarus' Dinamo soccer club. Iurii Chizh, interview in *Forbes* (Russian Edition) ca. 24 July 2008, cited and partial selections reproduced in http://allminsk.biz/content/view/1772/ (accessed 12 August 2008).

72 Sekhovich, "Neftianaia i neftepererabativaiuschaia otrasl'," 159.

73 See Feduta, *Lukashenko*, 418–19, and comments by Leonid Sinitsyn, former Vice-PM in the first Lukashenka period, quoted in ibid, 414.

74 Leonid Zaiko and Yaroslav Romanchuk, *Belarus' na razlome* (Belgorod, Russia: Belgorodskaia poligrafiia, 2008), 142. While official statistics spoke of greatly increasing monthly salaries and standards of living, it must be kept in mind that some of these results may have been related to the artificially high value of the Belarusian ruble (BRB) vis-á-vis the dollar. (As noted by Zlotnikov, such results are based on an artificially high value of the Belarusian ruble vis-á-vis the dollar resulting from the large influx of dollars from record oil products exports in the mid-2000s. Leonid Zlotnikov, in RFE/RL (Radio Svabody) program for Belarus *Ekzpertiza Svobody* ("Tsi vyratue dyrektyva No. 3 belaruskuiu ekanomiki?,") 18 June 2007, transcript available at http://www.svaboda.org/content/Transcript/758987.html). See

also Elena Rakova, "Kakaia energeticheskaia politika nuzhna Belarusi?" 6 July 2005, Nashe Mnenie website, available at http://www.nmnby.org/pub/030705/energy.html (accessed 15 December 2008). Morevoer, materials from the UNDP's Human Development Report showed a stagnation of Belarus' growing standards of living during this period. In fact, despite the much higher GDP growth in Belarus since the mid-nineties, its Human Development Index values did not jump far beyond those of Russia and Ukraine. For more information on Human Development rankings, see http://hdr.undp.org/en/countries/.

75 In 1998, 65 percent of Belarus' exports went to Russia, significantly more than in 1992 (42 percent). *Source: Official Statistics of the Countries of the Commonwealth of Independent States.*

76 Between 1999 and 2004, Itera and (to a much lesser extent) other independent suppliers such as TransNafta and Sibur provided from 23.94 percent (2001) to 38.55 percent (2004) of total gas supplies received by Belarus. Itera stopped supplying gas to Belarus in 2004. Calculated from Tables 2.2 (58–59) and 4.1 (106) in Yafimava, *Post-Soviet Russian-Belarussian Relationships.* It is interesting to note, however, that as long as Belarus was having difficulties paying for gas in cash, in order to minimize losses due to payments arrears, Gazprom allowed independent companies to supply about a third of the Belarusian market, but that once payment discipline increased around 2003 and Belarus started to pay predominantly in cash, Gazprom moved to gain more direct control of the market. See Chapter 3 for some alternative explanations for this development.

77 While oil supplies to Lithuania were temporarily suspended in the Spring of 1991, that event has a different meaning, as it took place before the dissolution of the USSR.

78 If in 1999, nearly 50 percent of Belarusian exports went to Russia, by 2005 this had been reduced to 35 percent and, by 2010, to 32 percent. Source: Leonid Zaiko, "Russia and Belarus: Between Wishing and Reality," *Russia in Global Affairs*, no. 1 (January–March 2006), available at http://eng.globalaffairs.ru/numbers/14/1003.html (accessed 4 December 2008) and IPM, *Ezhemesiachnii obzor ekonomiki Belarusi*, various issues.

79 Leonid Zlotnikov, "Podtsepili 'gollandskuiu bolezn," *Beloruskii Rynok*, 17/652, 2 May 2005.

80 Author's interviews, Minsk, 19 November 2008.

81 Tatiana Manenok, "Valiutnye donory."

82 See Drakokhrust and Furman, "Belarus and Russia," 255.

83 See Andrei Liakhovich, "Palitichni kantekst."

84 Tatiana Manenok, "Podarok s raschetom," *Belorusskii Rynok*, no. 15/650, 18 April 2005.
85 See Tatiana Manenok, "Kto ostalsia na trube," *Belorusy i Rynok*, no. 36/671, 19 September 2005.
86 Klishevich, "Istoriia bor'ba za 'Beltransgas.'"
87 These provisions included the inalienability of Gazprom's shares while the deal was being completed, the commitment not to impose a state controlling share in the company, as well as the commitment to increase the markup (nadtsenka) paid by Belarusian end users in order to increase Beltransgas' profitability. IPM, *Ezhemesiachnii obzor ekonomiki Belarusi*, no. 6/57, June 2007, 2, available at http://research.by/rus/bmer/.
88 IPM, *Ezhemesiachnii obzor ekonomiki Belarusi*, no. 1/52, January 2007, 2, available at http://research.by/rus/bmer/.
89 IPM, *Ezhemesiachnii obzor ekonomiki Belarusi*, no. 4/67, April 2008, 2, available at http://research.by/rus/bmer/. See also Tatiana Manenok, "Starye problemy dlia novogo pravitel'stvo," *Belorusy i Rynok*, no. 12/796, 24 March 2008. See also Sergei Zhbanov, "Bachili vochi, sho kupovali," *Belgazeta*, no. 13/634, 31 March 2008, available at http://www.belgazeta.by/20080331.13/020060671 (accessed 15 June 2008).
90 IPM, *Monitoring Infrastrukturi Belarusi 2008*, 35.
91 As quoted by the Associate Press Worldstream, 19 February 2004.
92 Aleksander Lukashenka, in *Nashi Novosti*, ONT (TV news), 19 February 2004 quoted in Feduta, *Lukashenko*, 635.
93 The new rules prescribed the application of VAT on a country of destination as opposed to on a country of production, basis. Although the 18 percent VAT now accrued to the Belarusian side, such change de facto increased by 18 percent prices paid by Belarusian consumers, which led the Belarussian government to request compensation, either in the form of reduced pre-VAT prices or other compensation. See IPM, "Rost tsen na gas," 9–10 (Footnote 10). See also Chloë Bruce, "Friction or Fiction? The Gas Factor in Russian-Belarusian Relations," *Chatham House Briefing Paper* REP BP 05/01 (May 2005), available at http://www.riia.org/pdf/research/rep/BP0501gas.pdf, 18 (accessed 20 September 2005).
94 *Novaia Gazeta*, no. 75, 2 October 2006, available at http://www.novayagazeta.ru/data/2006/75/09.html.
95 Yaroslav Romanchuk, quoted in DW Programme to Belarus, 26 December 2006, heard on www.dw-world.de (accessed 27 December 2006).
96 See for example Katja Yafimava, *Post-Soviet Russian-Belarussian Relationships: The Role of Gas Transit Pipelines* (Stuttgart: Ibidem-Verlag, 2007).

97 The agreement also included important clauses such as a single contract covering both gas prices and transit fees.

98 IPM, *Ezhemesiachnii obzor ekonomiki Belarusi*, no. 1/52, January 2007, 2, available at http://www.research.by/analytics/bmer/ (accessed 20 February 2013).. The calculation was as follows: to European prices was deducted the difference in transportation expenses and 30 percent duties, and this amount was further multiplied by the corresponding coefficient. Tatiana Manenok, "Torg za lgoty," *Belorusy i Rynok*, no. 4/890, 25 January 2010, available at http://belmarket.by/ru/62/65/4780 (accessed 28 January 2010)

99 The difference in transportation costs corresponds to the cost of transit from Belarus to Poland. Calculated at $1.75/1,000cm per 100 km, a transit length of 525 km via Belarus costs $9.19. Thus, 67 percent of $330.81 ($340 – $9.19) would be $221.64. Belarusan economist Leonid Zlotnikov confirmed: "In 2008 this price formula was not applied" and estimates the agreement-based price would have been ca. $200–$220/1000 cm. Leonid Zlotnikov, Deutsche Welle program for Belarus, *Belorusskaia Khronika*, December 17, 2007, heard on http://www.research.by/analytics/bmer/ (accessed 20 February 2013).

100 See comments by Aliaksandr Chubrik in RFE/RL (Radio Svabody) Program for Belarus, *Ekspertiza Svobody* ("Privatyzatsya Belarusi – use na prodazh raseitsam?"), 20 May 2008, transcript available at http://www. svaboda.org/content/Transcript/1116684.html.

101 A small crisis erupted in late July 2007 as Belarus delayed paying back these amounts and Gazrom threatened to reduce gas supplies by 45 percent by 3 August 2008 should payments not be made by then. Payments were made at the last moment.

102 Intended as the first installment of a $2 billion loan.

103 Calculated by the author on the basis of Table 11 (based on data from the Ministry of Energy) in IPM, "Rost tsen na gas," 24.

104 Calculated by the author on the basis of Table 11 in IPM, "Rost tsen na gas," 24.

105 Energosoft database, available at http://energosoft.info/news2004.html.

106 *Postanovlenie Soveta Ministrov Respubliki Belarus No. 1680*, December 2004, available at http://pravo.by/webnpa/text_txt.asp?RN=c20401680 (accessed 9 November 2008), and *Gosudarstvennaia kompleksnaia programma modernizatsii osnovnykh proizvodstvennykh fondov Belorusskoi energeticheskoi sistemy, energosberezheniia i uvelicheniia doli ispol'zovaniia v respublike sobstvennykh Toplivo-energeticheskikh resursov na period do 2011 goda*

(Ukaz No. 575 from 15 November 2007), available at http://energosoft. info/news2004.html.

107 In the "Direktiva No. 3 Prezidenta Respubliki Belarus ot 14 iulia 2007 g.," available at http://www.government.by/index?page=rus_gdoc_prog211 22007_5&mode=printable&lang=ru (accessed 11 December 2008).

108 "Direktiva No. 3 Prezidenta Respubliki Belarus ot 14 iulia 2007 g."

109 See the official announcement, "Glava gosudarstva v tselom odobril proekt kontseptsii energeticheskoi nezavisimosti Belarusi do 2020 goda," available at www.president.gov.by/press34523.html#doc (accessed 16 December 2008).

110 Full title: *Gosudarstvennaia kompleksnaia programma modernizatsii osnovnykh proizvodstvennykh fondov Belorusskoi energeticheskoi sistemy, energosberezheniia i uvelicheniia doli ispol'zovaniia v respublike sobstvennykh toplivo-energeticheskikh resursov na period do 2011 goda.*

111 Tatiana Manenok. "Bezopasnost' v range prioriteta." *Belorusy i Rynok*, no. 34/769, 10–17 September 2007.

112 Andrei Alekhnovich, "V Belarusi ustanovleni limiti na potreblenie elektroenergii dlia promyshlennykh predpriatii," Deutsche Welle program for Belarus, *Belorusskaia Khronika*, 17 September 2008, transcript available at http://www.dw-world.de/dw/article/0,2144,3650767,00.html (accessed 25 September 2008).

113 See Andrei Alekhnovich, "Energeticheskaia Strategiia Belorusi: smelye plany i surovaia realnost'," available at http://www.dw-world.de/dw/article/0,,5956254,00.html (accessed 3 September 2010). The text of the document, Postanovlenie Soveta Ministrov 5/32338, "Strategiia razvitiia energeticheskogo potentsiala Belarusi do 2020 goda," is available at http://www.pravo.by/webnpa/text.asp?RN=C21001180#3аг_Утв_1 (accessed 15 September 2011).

114 In 1998, a commission at the Belarusian Academy of Sciences had concluded that nuclear energy should be part of the Belarusian energy supply basket, but, given the low price of Russian oil and gas at the time, there was little urgency to act, and a seven-year moratorium on the issue was adopted. Aleksander Voitovich, in "Nakanune iadernogo vozrozhdeniia," a debate organized by the Belarusian Institute for Strategic Studies, Minsk, 29 February 2008 (materials published in Nasha Niva, www.nn.by).

115 Sovet Bezopasnosti Respubliki Belarus, *Postanovlenie Sovbeza No. 1"O razvitii atomnoi energetyki v Respublike Belarus'*," 31 January 2008. See also David Marples, "The Energy Dilemma of Belarus: The Nuclear Power

Option," *Eurasian Geography and Economics* 49, no. 2, March–April 2008.

116 Interview with Jekaterina Tkaschenko, Deutschlandfunk, 10 December 2008, audio file available at http://www.dradio.de/aod/html/?broadcas t=196841&page=3& (accessed 13 December 2008).

117 See Tatiana Manenok, "Bezopasnost' v range prioriteta," *Belorusy i Rynok*, no. 34/769, 10 September 2007.

118 See various articles in the leading official newspapers *Belarus Segodnia* and *Respublika*, May 2008.

119 On some of the tensions in negotiations with Russia on the nature and extent of Russian financing and ownership of the NPP, see David Marples, "Surge in Nuclear Power Projects Imperils Belarusian Program," *Eurasia Daily Monitor* 7, no. 150, 4 August 2010.

120 Kirill Koktysh, interview in Nashe Mnenie website, 13 November 2006, available at http://www.nmnby.org/pub/0612/13d.html (accessed 10 August 2007).

121 See Pontis Foundation, "The Regime Change(s): Survey of Current Trends and Development in Belarus Summer 2007," available at http:// www.nadaciapontis.sk/tmp/asset_cache/link/0000017223/Pontis%20 Survey%20The%20Regime%20Change(s).pdf. That year, Belarus' GDP grew ca. 10 percent, exports 24.5 percent, inflation was the lowest since independence, personal income grew, and purchases of consumer goods increased significantly. Valer Karbalevich (Valerii Karbalevich), in RFE/ RL (Radio Svobody) program for Belarus, *Pratskii Akzent*, "Iakiia prychiny ekanamichnaga rostu?," 29 November 2006, transcript available at http://www.svaboda.org/content/Transcript/777228.html.

122 See Tatiana Manenok, "Mificheskii dolg," *Belorusy i Rynok*, no. 15/650, 18 April 2005. There was little legal basis for applying 2004 regulations concerning a state controlling share in MNPZ Plus, however.

123 Andrei Belousov, Deputy Minister for Economic Development of the Russian Federation, cited by Tatiana Manenok, "Starye problemy."

124 Leonid Zlotnikov, "Podtsepili 'gollandskuiu bolezn'."

125 IMF, "Rapid growth in Belarus: puzzle or not?," June 2005, available at http://www.imf.org/external/pubs/ft/scr/2005/cr05217.pdf, 9.

126 Calculated by Leonid Zlotnikov on the basis of *Foreign trade of the Republic of Belarus. Statistical abstracts. Ministry of statistics and analysis of the Republic of Belarus* (Minsk: yearly), *Rossiia v tsifrakh 2008. Ofitsial'noe izdanie Federalnoi sluzhby gosudasrtvennoi statistiki* (Moscow, 2008) and (for data on the first half of 2008) the statistical compendium *Sotsialno-ekonomicheskoe polozhenie Rossii* nos. 1–7 (2008).

127 IPM, *Ezhemesiachnii obzor ekonomiki Belarusi*, no. 4/55, April 2007, 2, available at http://www.research.by/analytics/bmer/ (accessed 20 February 2013). Data on refinery profitability from IPM, "Rost tsen na gas."

128 Tatiana Manenok, "Nestabil'naia neftianka," *Belorusy i Rynok*, no. 30/765, 13 August 2007, http://www.br.minsk.by/index.php?article=30803 (accessed 29 August 2007).

129 IPM, *Ezhemesiachnii obzor ekonomiki Belarusi*, no. 2/53, February 2007, 2, available at http://www.research.by/analytics/bmer/ (accessed 20 February 2013).

130 See Tatiana Manenok, "Po shchadiashchei stavki," *Belorusy i Rynok*, no. 3/787, 21 January 2008.

131 See Kostiugova, "Perspektivy uchastiia Belarusi," 11, and Tatiana Manenok, "Druzhbu ne pochiniat," *Belarusi i Rynok*, no. 46/781, 3 December 2007, available at http://www.belmarket.by/index.php?article=31605&year=2007 (accessed 24 April 2008). Thus, 2007 export duties for oil going to Belarus were reduced from $180 to $53 per ton.

132 Tatiana Manenok, "Nevygodnyi eksport," *Belorusy i Rynok*, no. 8/743, 26 February 2007, available at http://www.br.minsk.by/index.php?article=29634&year=2007 (accessed 15 May 2007).

133 Calculated on the basis of Tables 3.1 and 3.2 in Rakova "Energeticheskii sektor," 10–11.

134 See comments by Yaraslau Ramanchuk (Yaroslav Romanchuk) in RFE/RL (Radio Svabody) Program for Belarus, *Ekspertiza Svobody* ("Tsana na gaz – geta tsena palitychnai liaial'ns'tsi") 13 February 2008, transcript available at http://www.svaboda.org/content/Transcript/977620.html (accessed 8 July 2008).

135 In July of 2010, the Russian TV broadcasted a three-part documentary, *Krestny Batka*, accusing Lukashenka, among other wrong-doing, of being responsible for the disappearance and presumed death of several political opponents.

136 Although imports of Venezuelan oil via Ventspils (Latvia) were also planned, in November 2010 the Latvian company LatRosTrans (34 percent owned by Russia's Transneft) closed this possibility by rendering the Ventspils-Polotsk part of the Druzhba pipeline unusable by emptying the technological oil located in the pipeline, preventing its further use in a Belarus-bound direction. See also Vladimir Socor, "Belarus Warns It May Cancel Its Subsidies To Russia," *Eurasia Daily Monitor 4*, no. 17, Wednesday, 24 January 2007, available at http://www.jamestown.org/edm/article.php?article_id=2371830 (accessed 13 July 2007).

137 Manenok, citing the official Belarusian Statistics office, quotes a price of
$656/t for the Venezuelan oil. See Tatiana Manenok, "Aprobatsia sever-
nogo tranzita," *Belorusy i Rynok*, no. 28/914, 26 July 2010, available at
http://belmarket.by/ru/86/65/6680 (accessed 28 July 2010).

138 Tatiana Manenok, "Podstegnet neftianoi stimul," *Belorusy i Rynok*, no.
20/804, 19 May 2008, available at http://www.br.minsk.by/index.
php?article=32808 (accessed 15 June 2008). Additional details in Kostiugova, "Perspektivy uchastiia Belarusi," 2.

139 "Energeticheskaia bezopasnost' Respubliki Belarus na 2005–2010 gg. i
na period do 2020 g.," discussed in Tatiana Manekok, "Deshevogo gaza
nuzhno vse bol'she," *Belorusskii Rynok*, no. 51/635, 27 December 2004,
available at http://www.br.minsk.by/index.php?article=23797 (accessed
7 February 2009).

140 IPM, *Ezhemesiachnii obzor ekonomiki Belarusi*, no. 4/55, April 2007, 1–2,
available at http://www.research.by/analytics/bmer/ (accessed 20
February 2013). Azerbaijan proved a reliable ally in another respect:
when $186 million were urgently needed in June 2010 to face a Gazprom
ultimatum on overdue gas payments, President Haydar Aliyev promptly
loaned the necessary funds.

141 See comments by Sviatlana Kalinkina, in RFE/RL (Radio Svobody)
program for Belarus *Ekzpertiza Svobody* ("Povinen zastat'sia albo Sheiman
albo Viktar Lukahshenka"), 12 September 2007, transcript available at
http://www.svaboda.org/content/Transcript/761925.html (accessed 3
July 2008).

142 See ibid.

143 IPM, *Ezhemesiachnii obzor ekonomiki Belarusi*, no. 8/59, August 2007, 4,
available at http://www.research.by/analytics/bmer/ (accessed 20 February 2013). Data on subsidies to oil suppliers from IPM, *Ezhemesiachnii
obzor ekonomiki Belarusi*, no. 3/66, March 2008, 2, available at http://www.
research.by/analytics/bmer/ (accessed 20 February 2013).

144 Tatiana Manenok, "Potoki s politicheskoi logistikoi," *Belorusy i Rynok*,
no. 15/799, 14 April 2008, available at http://www.br.minsk.by/index.
php?article=32589 (accessed June 16, 2008).

145 Sokrat Research: *Belarus: country report 2008*, available at http://investory.
com.ua/community/diary/1208/sokrat_daily__december_11__2008/
(accessed 11 December 2008).

146 A number of Belarusian economists such as Zlotnikov argued that some
of the negative economic tendencies observable in 2007 were not the result of the oil-and-gas shock, whose effects were only beginning to be felt,
but of broader negative tendencies accumulating since 2005, in particular

Belarus' growing deficit in its trade with Russia. See Zlotnikov, "Igra v tseitnote."

147 Tatiana Manenok, "Izbiratel'nyi dokhod," *Belorusy i Rynok*, no. 4/788, 28 January 2008, available at http://www.belmarket.by/index.php?article=31998 (accessed 5 May 2008).

148 In July 2008, a state resolution confirmed a list of 519 state and 147 joint-stock companies that would be – at least theoretically – open for privatization between 2008 and 2011. IPM, *Ezhemesiachnii obzor ekonomiki Belarusi*, no. 8/71, August 2008, 2, 4, available at http://www.research.by/analytics/bmer/ (accessed 20 February 2013). The list included several energy companies, among them the Druzhba oil pipeline. Tatiana Manenok, "Obstoiatel'stva prizhali," *Belorusy i Rynok*, no. 36/820, 8 September 2008. ·

149 Given Lukashenka's distrust of Russian capital, such modest opening of the door to other (i.e., non-Russian) investors must have appeared as a good option from his perspective.

150 Valerii Karbalevich, "Miagkaia adaptatsiia," *Svobodnye Novosti Plus*, 9 January 2008.

151 Zlotnikov calculates a yearly oil subsidy of ca. $4 billion–$5 billion and a gas subsidy of ca. $5 billion–$6 billion, for a total of ca. $9.5 billion. Zlotnikov, "Zhestkaia posadka." This would be equivalent to 22.2 percent of Belarus' nominal GDP of $44.8 billion in 2007. GDP figures from IPM, *Ezhemesiachnii obzor ekonomiki Belarusi*, no. 2/65, February 2008, p. 2, 4, available at http://www.research.by/analytics/bmer/ (accessed 20 February 2013).

152 A 2007 paper by the World Bank noted, "Belarus has made good progress in reducing energy intensity in the past decade. Energy efficiency has been a top priority for the Belarus government since the mid-1990s. This has brought tangible results, with the energy intensity factor reduced from 0.76 to 0.45 in 2004." World Bank, "Belarus: Addressing Challenges Facing the Energy Sector" (June 2006), available at www.siteresources.worldbank.org/BELARUSEXTN/Resources/BelarusEnergyReview_July2006-full.pdf, 13.

153 See also Rakova, "Kakaia energeticheskaia politika."

154 Reference to the report of Belarus' PM Sergei Sidorskii for January–February 2008, in Aleksandr Krugleevskii, "Febral'. Dostat' chernila i . . .," *Ezhednevnik*, no. 376, 17 March 2008.

155 See Sergei Tkachev and Vladimir Timoshpolskii, "Strategiia razvitiia natsional'noi energetiki," *Nauka i innovatsiia*, no. 11/57, 2007, 25 (available at http://innosfera.org/energy_strategy).

156 IPM, "Rost tsen na gas," 7.

157 See World Bank. "Belarus Energy Sector 1995." *Report No. 12804-BY.* Available at http://www-wds.worldbank.org/external/default/WD-SContentServer/WDSP/IB/1995/04/21/000009265_3961008003331/Rendered/INDEX/multi_page.txt (accessed 8 November 2008), 9.

158 Aleksandr Voitovich, quoted in Marina Mazurkevich, "Drova, torf, veter i solntse," 4 February 2007, available at: http://www.dw-world.de/dw/article/0,2144,2337240,00.html (accessed 10 March 2007).

159 "Direktiva No. 3 Prezidenta Respubliki Belarus ot 14 iulia 2007 g."

160 See Olga Miksha, "Snova v obkhod Belarusi," *Belorusskii Rynok*, no. 23/440, 14 June 2004.

161 Kostiugova, "Perspektivy uchastiia Belarusi."

162 The Baltic Pipeline System-2 (BPS-2), commissioned in 2012 and planned to run from the Unecha junction in the Druzhba pipeline inside Russia to the Russian Baltic Sea terminal of Ust-Luga, would divert significant oil volumes away from the Belarusian portion of the Druzhba pipeline.

163 Technically, the change was about subjecting to full export duties all oil not used domestically in Belarus; under the new system, nearly two-thirds of oil supplies were subjected to duties compared to only about one-third in 2009.

164 At issue was the division of oil products export rents, as Russian oil producers saw the new trade conditions as particularly beneficial to Belarus. Under these new conditions, Russia would no longer charge oil export duties on any oil exported to Belarus (as compared to the previous year, where only oil intended for domestic use was supplied duty-free), in exchange for Belarus handing to Russia all export duties levied on the resulting oil products. As the latter duties were significantly lower per unit than those levied on crude oil, this meant significant savings for Belarus and increased profits for (non-tolling) refining operations by Belarusian refineries. Wanting to share in this new source of rents, Russian oil producers insisted that a "price premium" of around $45 per ton be paid to the Russian companies above and beyond the base price, increasing Belarus' oil imports bill. All of Belarus' economic indicators showed a sharp dip on January 2011, evidencing the economy's deep dependency on the oil trade conditions offered by Russia.

165 Calculated on the basis of gas imports expenditures data from Table 5.6 in this book, and nominal GDP in US$ from IPM, *BMER* 3/114, March 2012, 5.

166 IPM *BMER* 3/114, March 2012, 3.

167 Based on data for the first eleven months of 2012. See Tatiana Manenok, "Belarusi balans nuzhnee, chem Rossii," *Belorusy i Rynok* no. 3/1036, 21 January 2013.

168 See Ivashkevich, "Belarus' i neft': po trope kontrabandistov," 1.

169 IPM, *BMER* 6/117, June 2012, 1, data on budget loses from Manenok, "Belarusi balans nuzhnee."

170 The takeover of Beltransgaz in 2011 was conditioned on Gazprom committing to ship 43 bcm per year via Belarus during the period 2012–14, "with unknown volumes after that." IEA, *Ukraine 2012*, 114–15.

171 This is not invalidated by the fact that, at times, Belarusian opposition figures sought – and received – direct or indirect (as in the case of Russian media campaigns against Lukashenka, as in July of 2010) support from Moscow. The fact remains, however, that these figures lacked control of important energy policy levers that could be used in the rent-seeking and value-added chains of Russian energy players.

172 The announcement was made by Lukashenka after his meeting with Russian president Dmitry Medvedev on 9 December 2010, but the details remained murky.

173 Interview with Dmitrii Lukashev of the investment group Aton, "Iskliuchenie iz pravila – Belarus'," *Belgazeta*, no. 14/482, 11 April 2005.

174 In May 2005, then-President Putin made clear that the trend of energy companies setting their export prices to former Soviet republics according to market principles was indeed a firm trend but had one exception – Belarus, "because with her we are trying to find the way to build a union state," that is, because of political considerations. Declarations by Vladimir Putin, cited in Tatiana Manenok, "Politicheskii barter," *Belorusskii Rynok*, no. 20/655, 23 May 2005.

6. Lithuania

1 In 1992, Lithuania's parliament, the Seimas, passed a constitutional act explicitly barring entry in the CIS or other alliances in territory of the CIS. Terry D. Clark and Jovita Pranevičiūte, "Perspectives on Communist Successor Parties: The Case of Lithuania," *Communist and Post-Communist Studies* 41, no. 4 (2008), 260.

2 European Commission, Directorate of Energy and Transport. "A European Strategy for Sustainable, Competitive and Secure Energy: Green Paper." EU, European Commission: 2006, 6. As of 2010, the only connection was a low-capacity (350 mW) electricity cable between Estonia and Finland, built in 2007.

3 In 2007, Lithuania imported 3.62 bcm of gas, while Latvia 2.4 bcm, and Estonia 1.47 bcm. Source: Energy Information Administration, "Total Dry Natural Gas Imports," available at http://tonto.eia.doe.gov/cfapps/ipdbproject/IEDIndex3.cfm?tid=3&pid=26&aid=3 (accessed 15 May 2009).

4 Clark and Praneviciute, "Perspectives," 455. In the run up to the 1990 parliamentary elections, reformist elements within the LCP, led by Brazauskas, renamed the party Lithuanian Democratic Labour Party (LDLP); conservatives left and formed their own party, the LCP (CPSU).

5 Corina Herron Linden, "Power and Uneven Globalization: Coalitions and Energy Trade Dependence in the Newly Independent States of Europe," (Ph.D. dissertation, Political Science, University of Washington, 2000), 189.

6 Following the 2000 parliamentary elections, the LDLP merged with the old Lithuanian Social Democratic Party to form the new LSDP.

7 Authors such as Sedelius further define the Lithuanian system (together with, Bulgaria, Moldova, Poland, Romania, as well as Ukraine after 2006) as a premier-presidential system, where "a popularly elected president shares executive power with the Prime Minister and her government." Thomas Sedelius, *The Tug-of War between Presidents and Prime Ministers. Semi-presidentialism in Central and Eastern Europe* (Orebro, Sweden: Orebro Studies in Political Science 15, 2006, Doctoral Dissertation), 16.

8 Several landmark decisions of the Constitutional Court have also affected the scope of presidential competencies. See Kimitaka Matsuzato and Liutaras Gudžinskas, "An Eternally Unfinished Parliamentary Regime: Semi-presidentialism as a Prism to view Lithuanian Politics," *Acta Slavica Iaponica,* 23 (2006): 146–70, here 166.

9 Tomas Klepšys, personal communication, 28 April 2007.

10 We are referring to the Labour Party and the Liberal Democratic Party's entrance into the political scene in the 2002-2004 period, to the impeachment of President Paksas in 2004, and to the resignation and criminal prosecution of Labour Party leader Viktor Uspaskich, who fled the country in 2006.

11 This trend was clearly seen in the strong showing of new players (New Union/Social Liberals and Lithuanian Liberal Union and in 2004, the Labour Party) in the 2000 and 2004 Seimas elections. See Darius Žeruolis and Algimantas Jankauskas, "Understanding Politics in Lithuania," *Demstar Research Report 18, 2004* (available at http://www.demstar.dk/papers/UnderstandingLithuania.pdf, accessed 7 February 2007), 12–13.

12 After the June 2006 dissolution of the coalition between the LSDP, the New Union and the Labour and Peasant Parties, a minority coalition government (led by PM Gediminas Kirkilas) of LSDP, the Civil Democracy Party, the Liberal Centre Party and Peasant Party formed, with the Conservative Party (Homeland Union) de facto supporting the coalition as a loyal opposition.

13 Matsuzato and Gudžinskas, "An Eternally Unfinished Parliamentary Regime," 146, 170.

14 Indeed, an oligarchic system of the type seen in Ukraine never developed in the Baltics, neither in Lithuania nor its northern neighbours. Mel Huang, "Wannabe Oligarchs: Tycoons & Influence in the Baltic States," Conflict Studies Research Center, May 2002, available at http://www.defac.ac.uk/colleges/csrc/document-listings/cee// (accessed 5 April 2007), 9.

15 EIU Riskwire Lithuania, 24 November 2008, (via ISI, accessed 14 March 2009). See also Clark and Praneviciute, "Perspectives on Communist Successor Parties," 259.

16 See Republic of Lithuania, *Law on Energy* (1995), available in English at http://www.litlex.lt/Litlex/Eng/Frames/Laws/Documents/376.HTM (accessed 1 August 2007). The law has been modified almost yearly since then, but the role of the Seimas has remained largely unchanged.

17 The formal reason for the Ministry's dissolution was the "massive debt it has allowed to accumulate." Sabonis-Chafee, *Power Politics*, 87.

18 If electricity generated from Russian nuclear fuel is accounted for as an import, the country's real level of energy dependency in 1990 was about 97.3 percent. Data from Vlacovas Miškinis, Lithuanian Energy Institute (LEI).

19 Other instances of energy blockades or near-blockades from Russia in the immediate post-independence years included the fact that in the Fall of 1991, Lithuania received from Russia only "between 40 and 50 per cent [*sic*] of the fuel promised," forcing the country to introduce rationing of gasoline, heat, and hot water, and the June 1993 brief suspension of all gas supplies by main supplier Gazprom, arguably because of unpaid debts. See Thomas Lane, *Lithuania: Stepping Westward* (London: Routledge, 2001), 172, and Sabonis-Chafee, *Power Politics*, 83.

20 See Clark and Praneviciute, "Perspectives on Communist Successor Parties," 259, 262.

21 Gas supplies from Russia decreased from 3.4 bcm in 1992 to 1.8 bcm in 1993. Calculated from Energy Information Administration, at http://www.eia.doe.gov/pub/international/iealf/table43.xls.
Lithuania's TPES dropped from 16.Mtoe to 8.01 Mtoe from 1991 to 1994. Source: AB Lietuvos Dujos, *Annual Report 2000*, as presented in Figure 4.9 in International Atomic Energy Agency, *Energy supply options for Lithuania: a detailed multi-sector integrated energy demand, supply and environmental analysis.* (Vienna: IAEA, 2004), 68. (Data provided here is a numerical rendering of information presented in graph form.)

22 In 1991, Lithuania's GDP decreased by 5.7 percent and in 1992 by 21.3 percent.

23 World Bank, *Lithuania Energy Sector Review,* Report 11867-LT (Washington, DC: 1994), 29–30.

24 This is not to say that in the Lithuanian case gas prices immediately reached average European levels.

25 See Stern, "Soviet and Russian Gas," 157, and Sabonis-Chafee, *Power Politics,* 124.

26 See World Bank, *Lithuania,* iv.

27 Lietuvos Energija was unbundled only in 2002 and partially privatized in 2003.

28 Ignalina's closest city, Visaginas (formerly Sniečkus) was one of the few cities in Lithuania with a very high concentration (47 percent) of ethnic Russian population. See Linden, *Power and Uneven Globalization,* 179.

29 In early 1992, the average salary of Ignalina NPP workers was higher than that of the Minister of Energy. *Nucleonics Week,* 25 February 1992, cited in Sabonis-Chafee, *Power Politics,* 111.

30 Saulius Kutas and Jurgis Vilemas, "Legacy of the Past and Future Energy Policy in Lithuania," paper prepared for the World Energy Council, 2005, available at http://www.worldenergy.org/wec-geis/publications/default/tech_papers/17th_congress/1_4_31.asp?mode=print&x=59&y=5 (accessed 20 February 2007), 9. As of 2007, Lithuania's total installed electricity-generating capacity exceeded its needs by more than two times. See *National Energy Strategy of Lithuania,* 2007 (Vilnius, 2007), 19, and NC-CPE, "Annual Report on Electricity and Natural Gas Markets in Lithuania, prepared for the European Commission," (2008), Available at www.Energy-Regulators.eu (accessed 21 May 2009).

31 In 2004, for example, Ignalina exported nearly half of the electricity it produced. NCCPE, "Summary of the Annual Report to The European Commission, 2005" (2004), available at http://www.regula.lt (accessed 21 May 2007), 4. Between 1999 and 2009, the bulk of Lithuania's electricity exports went to Belarus and smaller amounts to Latvia and Russia.

32 Pumped storage facilities store electricity by using it to move water to a higher-elevation reservoir, later using this water to generate electricity by creating an induced hydroelectric process.

33 Because of these limitations, Ignalina often had no choice but to sell its excess electricity to Belarus. Chronic payment problems with Belarus complicated the process of Lietuvos Energia's (Ignalina's mother company) privatization. "Country Briefing Lithuania economy: Some progress with utilities privatization," *Economist Intelligence Unit –Country Economic News,* 4 October 2001 (via ISI, accessed 20 March 2007). See also Olga Miksha, "Atomnyi Triumvirat," *Belgazeta,* 13 March 2006, available at

http://www.belgazeta.by/20060313.10/040121511 (accessed 10 November 2006), and *National Energy Strategy of Lithuania 2007* (Vilnius, 2007), 8.

34 Thus in 1993, for example, the year of the deepest reduction in gas supplies from Russia, Lithuania responded by decreasing the share of fossil fuels in electricity generation from 19.4 percent to 9.2 percent (and from 41 percent in 1991), and increasing the share of nuclear power to a record 88 percent. (Dalia Streimikiene, "Lithuania," in IAEA/UN DESA, *Energy Indicators for Sustainable Development: Country Studies on Brazil, Cuba, Lithuania, Mexico, Russian Federation, Slovakia and Thailand* (2005), available at http://www.un.org/esa/sustdev/publications/energy_indicators/index.htm (accessed 17 July 2007), 129–92, here 169.)

35 Sabonis-Chafee, *Power Politics*, 133. See also Jane I. Dawson, *Eco-nationalism: Anti-nuclear Activism and National Identity in Russia, Lithuania and Ukraine* (Durham: Duke University Press, 1996), 34–63.

36 In 2001, 5.1 million tons of oil were loaded through Butinge, increasing to 10.7 million tons in 2003, before declining to 5.9 million tons in 2006; Russian oil exports via Butinge ceased altogether in July 2006. Oil loading data from Tomas Janeliūnas, "Energy Security of Lithuania and the Impact of the Nord Stream Project," power-point presentation available at http://www.tspmi.vu.lt/files/mokslkonfer/Janeliūnas_energy%20security%20of%20lithuania%20and%20impact%20of%20nord%20stream%20project.ppt (accessed 16 May 2009).

37 Some questioned the rationale of such a large investment given give the fact that an oil imports facility was already available not far from the border in Ventspils, Latvia.

38 Sabonis-Chafee, *Power Politics*, 128.

39 Joanna Hyndle and Miryna Kutysz, "Lithuania, Latvia and Estonia's Aspirations to Integrate with NATO and the EU in the Context of these Countries' Relations with Russia," *OSW Studies*, January 2002, available at http://osw.waw.pl/en/epub/eprace/04/02.htm (accessed 3 May 2007).

40 Sabonis-Chafee, *Power Politics*, 128.

41 Ibid, 129.

42 As in February 2004, when Gazprom's suspension of gas shipments to and through Belarus led to a stoppage of supplies.

43 For example by requiring, in 1996, "all government industries to pay their energy bills, and prepare budgets demonstrating allocations for energy costs." *Verslo Zinios*, 4 July 1996, cited in Sabonis-Chafee, *Power Politics*, 116.

44 Sabonis-Chafee, *Power Politics*, 124. Although at a reduced level, debt issues continued to be a problem in relations with Gazprom through the late 1990s.

45 A version of Stasiukynas' reform plan as negotiated with the World Bank in 1994 can be found in World Bank, *Lithuania Energy*, Annex 5.1 (no page number). See also Sabonis-Chafee, *Power Politics*, 86, 119.

46 Originally created in 1995 as the State Price Regulation Commission of Energy Resources and reestablished as an independent state agency in 1997 under the name of National Control Commission for Prices and Energy (NCCPE).

47 Incukalns' capacity is equivalent to nearly 50 percent of both countries' combined yearly gas consumption. Despite an agreement dating to 2000, until 2005 Lithuania was unable to use the facility, as the lack of gas metering stations in the Lithuanian-Latvian border hindered gas exchanges between both systems. This project was completed in 2005, making it possible for Lithuania to draw small amounts (up to 0.5 bcm per year) in case of need. IAEA, *Energy supply options*, 66.

48 Zeyno Baran, "Lithuanian Energy Security: Prospects and Choices," Hudson Institute, 2006, available at http://www.hudson.org/files/publications/LithuanianEnergySecurityDecember06.pdf (accessed 21 February 2007) 1, 29. In addition, a clause in the contract with Gazprom banning the resale of gas means the connection may only be used in emergency cases, not as part of regular commercial supply. NCCPE, "Annual Report to the European Commission. Summary," (2004), available at http://www.regula.lt (accessed 21 May 2007), 9. Since 2007, LD has been accumulating its own contingency gas reserve at Incukalns.

49 The gas pipeline connection to Suwałki in Poland would have connected to a planned (but not materialized as of 2012) pipeline linking Poland to Norway.

50 Railway traffic between Kaliningrad and the rest of Russia must go through Lithuania.

51 The original gas pipeline linking Vilnius and Kaliningrad was commissioned in 1986, and, until the late 1990s had a capacity of about 0.5 bcm per year. From 2001 to 2008, gas transit volumes to Kaliningrad through Lithuania increased from 0.52 to 1.257 bcm. World Bank, *Lithuania Energy*, 14, 90, Annex 9.2 (no page number), Tomas Janeliūnas and Arunas Molis, "Energy Security of Lithuania: Challenges and Perspectives," *Lithuanian Political Science Yearbook 2005*, ed. Algimantas Jankauskas (Vilnius, 2007), 22, NCCPE, "Annual Report on Electricity and Natural Gas Markets in Lithuania prepared for the European Commission," (2006), available at http://www.regula.lt (accessed 21 May 2009), 51, and LD, *Annual Report 2008*, 24.

52 Gintaras Denafas, "Regional and Local Environmental Impact caused by Closing of Ignalina Nuclear Power Plant in Lithuania" (no date provided, presumably 2003), available at http://www.statvoks.no/synergy/INPP_lt.doc (accessed 21 May 2009).

53 Janeliūnas and Molis, "Energy Security of Lithuania," 21.

54 Ibid, 22.

55 See Vladimir Skripov and Aleksei Grivach, "Litovskii gazovyi put', "Gazprom" i Vilnius zhdut ustupok drug ot druga," *Vremia Novostei*, 8 August 2002. In 1998, Gazprom itself had proposed the building of an additional gas pipeline to Kaliningrad. See *RFE/RL Newsline*, 21 September 1998.

56 See also Žygimantas Vaičiūnas, "Towards Energy Independence," *Lithuania in the World* 16, no. 1 (2008).

57 The company had been reorganized from a state-owned company to a special purpose joint stock company in 1995.

58 Some have questioned the technical rationale of the EU's requirement to close the Ignalina NPP and similar nuclear power plants in Slovakia and Bulgaria as a condition for EU admission, seeing it as a sign of imperialist arrogance.

59 *Lietuvos Energetika 2007*, 4, available at http://www.lei.lt/_img/_up/File/atvir/leidiniai/Lietuvos_energetika-2007.pdf. For a detailed discussion of energy supply options for Lithuania after the closing of Ignalina's second block, see IAEA, *Energy supply options*.

60 Few public figures addressed the issue publicly until 2010. President Grybauskaite was one of the first politicians to do so openly: "The interests surrounding the plant had tied Lithuania to Russia and did not allow us to develop alternative energy resources or to connect the electricity network to the Western one." Interview with Ausra Leka, weekly magazine *Veidas*, 1 January 2010, translated in "Lithuanian president interviewed on Russia ties, economy, energy," *BBC Monitoring*, 1 January 2010 (via ISI, accessed 30 June 2010).

61 Tomas Janeliūnas, "Lithuania's Energy Strategy and Its Implications on Regional Cooperation," in *Energy: Pulling the Baltic Region Together or Apart?*, eds. Andris Spruds and Toms Rostoks (Riga: Zinatne, 2009) 190–222, here 203–4.

62 Thus the famous declaration attributed to LUKoil CEO Vagit Alekperov in the late 1990s "Mazeikiu Nafta is ours, and we will buy it back for one dollar." In addition to its historical ties, LUKoil had an immediate interest in MN, as its location made it a very convenient starting point for supplying both WE markets and some Russian regions.

63 This slogan is best known in its Russian-language form: "Ne dopustit' Ivana k trube!"

64 The refinery's director was murdered in 2000. In addition, MN's finances were negatively affected by the high cost of the Butinge project, which was largely financed by the refinery.

65 Quoted in in Peter Zashev, "Russian Investments in Lithuania," Electronic Publications of the Pan-European Institute 10/2004, Turku School of Economics and Business Administration, available at www.tukkk.fi/pei (accessed 30 March 2007), 13.

66 The Economist Intelligence Unit, *Lithuania: Energy Provision*, 1 September 2002 (via ISI, accessed 15 March 2007) and Lane, *Lithuania*, 184.

67 It has been argued that Vaizga was created with the specific goal to "funnel funds to political groups in Latvia and Lithuania"; the company was also considered "the second-largest financial contributor" in the 2000 elections. In addition, Brazauskas found itself under fire due to his wife's lucrative business deal involving the privatization of a state-run hotel, where she bought part of the building from Vaizga. See "Constitutional Watch: Lithuania," *East European Constitutional Review* 10, no. 1 (2001), Vincent Giedraitis, "Multi-Dependency in the Post-Socialist Period: the case of Lithuania," (Ph.D. dissertation, Sociology, University of California-Riverside, 2006), 194, and "Business Interests in Lithuania's Parliamentary Elections," *The Jamestown Monitor* 6, no. 187 (9 October 2000), available at www.james town.org (accessed 20 March 2007).

68 Valdas Vasiliauskas, "Slaptoji Rolando Pakso misija," *Ekstra*, 2 February 2004. Republished in Delfi.lt, 2 May 2004, http://www.delfi.lt/archive/article.php?id=3663899 (accessed 17 June 2007). Paksas is believed to have had close contacts with LUKoil Baltija. See also Matsuzato and Gudžinskas, "An Eternally Unfinished Parliamentary Regime," 162.

69 Paksas resigned as he believed the large commitment to Williams (such as the taking over some of MN's debt obligations) would push Lithuania's deficit to a dangerous level. After his resignation from the Conservative Party, Paksas was appointed by President Adamkus as advisor on energy affairs.

70 LUKoil established a de facto on-and-off blockade of the refinery, interrupting oil supplies at least nine times in the 1998–1999 period, allegedly for technical reasons. It also sought to block MN's attempts to receive oil from other sources, as was the case in 1999, when it tried to prevent a Kazakh company from selling oil to MN, threatening Russia would hinder the oil's transit to Lithuania. Giedraitis, "Multi-Dependency," 193. See also Huang, "Wannabe Oligarchs," and Ian Lilly, "Geopolitics and Economic Fragility,"

paper presented at the New Zealand European Union Centres Network Conference, Auckland, 9–10 November 2006 (available at http://www.euc network.org.nz/activities/conference/conference_auckland_06/docs/ililly. pdf, accessed 3 February 2007). In 2004, Russia also sent a former energy minister, Victor Kaluzhny as ambassador to Latvia to try to convince the country to boycott oil shipments to Lithuania. Keith C. Smith, "Russian Energy Politics in the Baltics, Poland and Ukraine: A New Stealth Imperialism?" (Washington, Center for Strategic and International Studies, 2004), 43.

71 See Reuters, "Lithuania's Prime Minister Quits over Oil Deal," 28 October 1999 (via ISA, accessed 15 March 2007) and The Economist Intelligence Unit, "Lithuania: Energy Provision," 1 September 2002 (via ISI, accessed 15 March 2007). See also Vladimir Skripov, "Ivan idet." *Ekspert Severo-Zapad*, 22 February 2004, cited in Zashev, "Russian Investments." For Vytautas Landsbergis' (at the time, 1996 to 2000, Speaker of the Seimas) perspective on the issue, see his book *LUKoil prieš Williams* (Vilnius: Tėvynės Sąjunga, 2004).

72 This was the first of two resignations by Paksas. Having returned to the office of PM in 2000, he resigns again in June 2001, presumably because of his opposition to a greater role of Yukos in MN.

73 Jurgis Vilemas, cited in Pavyk et al, "Diktatura chernogo zolota, *Baltiiskii Kurs*, no. 4/17 (2000), available at http://www.baltkurs.com/russian/ arhiv/17/03politekonomija.htm, accessed 20.3.2007."

74 The conflict with Paulauskas should not be underestimated as a second important reason for Paksas' 2001 resignation.

75 AB Mazeikiu Nafta website, available at http://www.nafta.lt/en/content. php?pid=47 (accessed 27 June 2007).

76 In order to create a package attractive to possible investors, the Lithuanian state decides to also sell the 30.6 percent of shares belonging to it.

77 A Lithuanian government inquiry unveiled in May 2007 established that the fire had been accidental.

78 In particular, the stoppage of oil supplies by pipeline was a potentially effective way to hinder the sale, as the contract with PKN Orlen included an escape clause that could be used "if the market value of the refinery dropped significantly before the sale closed." Andrew E. Kramer, "Lithuanians Are Given a Taste of How Russia Plays the Oil Game," *New York Times*, 8 October 2006.

79 "Litva budet davit' na Rossiiu vmeste s ES," *Litovskii Kurier*, no. 11/629, March 2007. Very small, test volumes of Venezuelan oil were also received.

80 Source: MN's consolidated financial statements for the 2005–2007 period and results for 2008 and 2009, available at the company's website at http://www.nafta.lt (accessed 9 May 2009).

81 "Privatization becoming energized," *The Baltic Times*, 26 January 2000 (via ISI, accessed 15 March 2007).

82 Among politicians supporting this initiative were first and foremost Paulauskas of the Social Liberal Party, and among energy-related businessmen, Bronislovas Lubys, one of Lithuania's richest men, head of the Lithuanian Industrialists' Confederation and CEO of the fertilizer company Achema, the country's largest gas user, as well as others associated with the close-to-Gazprom Stella Vitae intermediary gas company, such as Bosas.

83 See Antanas Bosas, declarations to Baltic News Service, cited in *The Baltic Times*, 21 June 2001 (via ISI, accessed 22 March 2007).

84 In contrast with the cases of Estonia and Latvia, however, in the Lithuanian case the decision on the modalities of privatization took much longer.

85 The remaining 8 percent of shares had been previously privatized.

86 In addition, clear regulations were put in place limiting which investors could bid for the strategic investor shares.

87 Paksas' Liberal Union receiving 17.25 percent and Paulauskas' New Union 19.64 percent.

88 See Matsuzato and Gudžinskas, "An Eternally Unfinished Parliamentary Regime," 162–65.

89 Virgilijus Savickas, "Lithuanian privatization sets coalition at odds," *The Baltic Times*, 21 June 2001 (via ISI, accessed 20 March 2007).

90 Itera toyed with the idea of putting in a bid, but withdrew its application. See "Itera weighs in ahead of Lithuanian gas privatization," *The Baltic Times*, 13 September 2001 (via ISI, accessed 22 March 2007).

91 "Nakanuni vstuplenia Baltii v ES obostriaetsia borba za kontrol nad gazovym khoziaistvom regiona," available at Rosinvest, http://www.rosinvest.com/dir/analysis/74/84/, (original source, no date provided, presumed 2003), (accessed 14 March 2007).

92 See "Khot shersti klok," *Vedomosti*, no. 228, 10 December 2001 (via ISI, accessed 19 March 2007) and Zhanna Skripova, "Stranam Baltii smeniat postavschika gaza," *Biznes i Baltiia*, 31 October 2001 (via ISI, accessed 15 March 2007).

93 Although both purchased an equal number of shares, Gazprom was able to negotiate a lower price than that paid by strategic investor EON/Ruhrgas (100 million Litas as opposed to 116 million Litas).

94 See commentary by Valdas Vasiliauskas, "New Politics Mark 2," translated in "Lithuanian commentary sees Gazprom interests dividing the country," BBC Monitoring (via ISI, accessed 15 March 2007).

95 Not counting the gas sold directly by Gazprom to Achema (25.9 percent of total Gazprom exports to Lithuania in 2005) and the Kaunas Combined Heat and Power Plant (9.7 percent). NCCPE, "Annual Report," (2006), 62.

96 As noted by the NCCPE in 2006, "many eligible customers would like to change their gas supply undertaking and purchase cheaper gas from Lietuvos Dujos AB, but their option possibilities are limited" given the fact that they can choose from only two gas suppliers – LD and Dujotekana, "both of which purchased gas from the sole external supplier." NCCPE, "Annual Report on Electricity," (2006), 64.

97 In the period 1997–2001 oil prices paid by Lithuania amounted to, in average, 92.6 percent of the price of Brent crude oil, with the difference largely explained by lower transportation costs. IAEA, *Energy supply options*, 78. The actual price difference is even smaller, considering that Lithuania imported mainly Urals oil, usually about 3 percent cheaper than Brent.

98 Lilly, "Geopolitics," 2.

99 Price converted to US$ from data in Litas provided in IAEA, *Energy supply options*, 78.

100 Article 31 of the 2003 Gas Directive (2003/55/EC). Technically, the debate centred on "whether regulation of natural gas to eligible customers is required when there is no competition," in other words, where a single supplier controls the market. NCCPE, "Annual Report to the European Commission. Summary," (2004), available at http://www.regula.lt/en/publications/report-to-the-european-commission/report.summ.EU2004.doc (accessed 21 May 2007), 4. While other countries highly dependent on a single gas supplier, Latvia and Finland, asked for a derogation in the Directive's implementation, Lithuania did not. I thank Vidamantas Jankauskas for this observation.

101 Continuing the trend of strong showings by populist leaders, the Labour Party emerged as the biggest winner of Seimas elections of October 2004, while Brazauskas' Social Democrats and Paulauskas' New Union-Social Liberals lost seats. After a failed attempt to build a coalition with the Homeland Union, the Social Democrats found it easier to go into a coalition with Uspaskich, who becomes Minister of Economics in the new coalition. Yet there was conflict between Brazauskas and Uspaskich from the very beginning. The Economist Intelligence Unit, "Country Briefing: Lithuania politics: See-saw politics, May 13, 2005" (via ISI, accessed 21 March 2007).

102 Officially, Borisov contributed 1.2 million Litas (US$ 300,000) to Paksas' campaign; under-the-table support may have been much larger. See,

among others, Radio Free Europe/Radio Liberty Newsline, various issues. Lithuanian analysts Raimundas Lopata and Audrius Matonis, however, see the case not only or not so much as an example of an improper relationship between an individual politician and an individual sponsor, but as a Russian intelligence operation, with Paksas' electoral success attributed largely to the work of Kremlin-sponsored political consulting companies. Although Lopata and Matonis do not find any connections between Paksas and Russian energy companies, they note that those political consulting services could have been paid by Paksas' Russian supporters (possibly energy companies) with business interests in Lithuania. See Raimondas Lopata and Audrius Matonis, *Prezidento suktukas* (Vilnius: Versus Aureus, 2004), 43 and 47, and Tomas Klepšys, "Background paper on Rolandas Paksas: Impeachment and Russian Energy Companies," unpublished paper, 2 July 2007, 3.

103   See LNK and Baltic News Service, "R. Paksą rėmė Rusijos energetikos kompanijos?," Delfi.lt, 26 November 2003, http://www.delfi.lt/archive/article.php?id=3241569 (accessed 17 June 2007), and LNK, "News," 26 November 2003, republished in Tv.lt, available at http://new.tv.lt/mconsole.asp?id=01DB6DEB-0AA0-48B3-8181-23A69FFFC376','TVMConsole',' width=641,height=512 (accessed 17 June 2007), cited in Klepšys, 3, Lopata and Matonis, *Prezidento suktukas*, 43 and 47 and Klepšys, "Background paper," 3. The source of the original information on LUKoil's and RAO's alleged contributions has not been verified, and some believe it may have been ordered by LUKoil's rival Yukos. See Vasiliauskas, "Slaptoji Rolando."

104   Lopata and Matonis, *Prezidento suktukas*, 39, quoted in Klepšys, 3.

105   See Aleksandr Shakhov, "V Litve naschitali 30 tolstosumov," *Biznes i Baltiia*, 19 April 2005 (via ISI, accessed 15 March 2007).

106   See Antanas Petraitis, "Dolgaia doroga k khramu," in website www.sedmitza.ru, Available at www.sedmitza.ru/index.html?sid=470&did=18023 (accessed 3 May 2007).

107   Petraitis, "Dolgaia doroga."

108   By 2009, in addition to selling gas through LD and Dujekatana, Gazprom sold gas directly to only two enterprises, both closely associated with it formally or informally: chemical fertilizer producer Achema and the Kaunas Combined Heat and Power Plant owned by a Gazprom-controlled consortium.

109   Zhanna Skripova, "V Litve 'zachistili' detei Rema Viakhireva," *Biznes i Baltiia*, 3 December 2001 (via East View Universal Databases CIS and Baltic Periodicals [thereafter EVUD CISBP], accessed 15 March 2007), referring to report on *Lietuvos Rytas*, no date provided. In addition to Stella Vitae and

Vikonda, there was IteraLit associated with Achemas' Lubys, although
the company lost significant business after the establishment of another
Gazprom-related intermediary, Itera Lietuva, by Antanas Bosas in 1999.
According to one commentator, Itera Lietuva was specifically created by
Antanas Bosas to oust Bronislovas Lubys from the profitable gas business.
"Rivalry runs high in Lithuanian gas business," *The Baltic Times*, 12 Janu-
ary 2000 (via ISI, accessed 21 March 2007). See also Vasiliauskas, "New
Politics Mark 2."

110 See also Margarita M. Balmaceda, "Corruption, Intermediary Companies,
and Energy Security: Lessons of Lithuania for the Broader Central-East
European Region," *Problems of Post-Communism* 55, no. 4 (July/August
2008): 16–28.

111 See Galina Molochkova, "Zapakhlo gazom. Tseni na gaz v Latvii mogut vyrasti," *Biznes i Baltiia*, 14 June 2000 (via EVUD CISBP, accessed 21
March 2007) and "Gazprom poboretsia za Lietuvos dujos," *Kommersant*,
24 October 2002 (via ISI, accessed 15 March 2007).

112 Audrius Baciulis, "Valstybės nesaugumo departamentas" (State Insecurity Department), *Veidas*, 7 December 2006, translated as "Lithuanian
commentary reports on ad hoc security committee findings," *BBC Monitoring* (available via ISI, accessed 15 March 2007). The coming to public
light of the Uspaskich corruption scandal was preceded by a worsening
of relations between Uspaskich and Artūras Paulauskas. In 2005, in the
midst of a complex political situation, Paulauskas, at that time Seimas
speaker, started to press for an investigation into black accounts involving Uspaskich to which Uspaskich, at that time minister of Economics,
responded by seeking to initiate Paulauskas' removal as Seimas speaker.
Saulius Stoma, "Arbatėlė su išdaviku, arba kaip susigrąžinti Uspaskichą
per tris dienas. Rašytojo komentaras, Žinių radijas," 17 November 2007,
available at www.delfi.lt. Translated by BBC Monitoring, 17 November
2007 (via ISI, accessed 15 March 2007).

113 As the accusations get increasingly serious, Uspaskich flees to Russia in
September 2006 and becomes a fugitive before returning to Lithuania
in 2007, upon which he was immediately arrested and released soon
afterwards.

114 *Verslo Zinios*, 22 January 2007, translated in "Lithuanian daily criticizes
Seimas for indecision on natural gas act amendment," BBC Monitoring,
22 January 2007 (via ISI, accessed 15 March 2007). By 2006, Dujotekana's
profits margins had declined to 17 percent.

115 Stoma, "Arbatėlė su išdaviku."

116 Ibid.

117 Ištrauka iš Nacionalinio saugumo ir gynybos komiteto atlikto "Valstybės saugumo departamento veiklos parlamentinio tyrimo" 2006 m. spalio 20 d. 11 posėdžio stenogramos. Extract from 11th session stenograph (20 October 2006), available at http://www.lrt.lt/news.php?strid=5082&id=3687465 (accessed 20 April 2007). A note of caution concerning these materials should be raised, however. Despite the great interest of the materials, the nearly 180 pages of testimony published in March 2007, and the 400 pages published in April 2007 are only a fraction of the total 1500 pages of the committee's sessions' transcripts, and many personal names have been removed. It is also not clear why exactly these pages were chosen for publication, and whether they are representative of the whole file. In addition, the materials were released by Algimantas Matulevicius, head of the Seimas commission and known for his long-standing feud with the VSD, without proper authorization. The first set of transcripts made public contains mainly transcriptions of testimony given by VSD employees, the second set declarations by VSD head Arvydas Pocius, his deputies Darius Jurgelevicius, Dainius Dabasinskas, and Andrius Tekorius, former VSD Director Mecys Laurinkus, relatives of Vytautas Pociūnas, other former and current VSD staff, and Conservative Party Seimas MPs Jurgis Razma and Andrius Kubilius. See Jurga Tvaskienė and Stasys Gudavičius, "Kaunas Found Itself in Scope of Interest," translated in "Lithuania declassifies 400 pages of state security materials," BBC Monitoring Lithuania (via ISI, accessed 21 May 2007).

118 The Lithuanian official investigation stated that he died as a result of an accident and mentioned no foul play. "Seim Litvy kopaet pod shefa gosbezopasnosti," *Kommersant*, available at http://www.kommersant.ru/doc.html?docId=727433 (accessed 14 March 2007).

119 "Seim Litvy kopaet pod shefa gosbezopasnosti."

120 Author's interview with economics journalist, Vilnius, 31 March 2007. See also Kestutis Maciunis' declarations in Rokas M. Tracevskis, "Secret Agent's death is under re-investigation," *The Baltic Times*, 13 January 2010 (accessed 30 June 2010). New allegations surfaced in early 2010 about Pociūnas' role in investigating corruption within Lithuania's Ministry of Foreign Affairs. Ibid.

121 "Gazprom poboretsia za Lietuvos dujos," *Kommersant*, 24 October 2002 (via ISI, accessed 15 March 2007.) The restructuring took place immediately after Gazprom head's Aleksei Miller's visit to Lithuania.

122 Svetlana Novolodskaya, "'Itere' zakrili zadvizhku," *Vedomosti*, 6 November 2002 (via ISI).

123 Daniel Treisman has referred to this process as the "rise of the Silovarchs." See Daniel Treisman, "Putin's Silovarchs," *Orbis* 51, no. 1 (2007): 141–53.

124 See Vasiliauskas, "New Politics Mark 2."

125 Vasiliauskas, "New Politics Mark 2."

126 Yakunin was widely believed to be a (former) high KGB officer. See Treisman, "Putin's Silovarchs." The security services connection hypothesis is also supported by the fact that at some point before Fall 2006 former KGB employee and Russian citizen Piotras Vojeika owned 49 percent of Dujotekana's shares. See interview with Rimantas Stonys, were the moderator referred to such versions. TV show Savaite, LTV, no date provided, reported by Lietuvos Rytas Internet version 13 November 2006, 0413 GMT, translated by BBC Monitoring, 13 November 2006 (via ISI, accessed 15 March 2006). By mid-2002 the company was owned, in addition to Gazprom (with over 50 percent control), by the Industrial Finance Corporation of Western Lithuania controlled by Bosas and Stonys. Lithuanian law protects the confidentiality of shareholder information, and little is known about Dujotekana's later ownership structure.

127 Personal names were removed from the parliamentary investigation transcripts made public.

128 See *Veidas*, various issues March–May 2007.

129 Kauno termofikacijos elektrinė, known in English as the Kaunas Combined Heat and Power Plant, is one of Lithuania's two major power plants.

130 See Oleg Sheremetinsky, "Obzor SMI Litvi za 31 iulia–6 avgusta 2006 goda," citing *Kauno diena*, available at www.regnum.ru/news/683836.html (via ISI, accessed 15 March 2007). The Kaunas CHP was especially significant because of its being one of the only two enterprises purchasing gas directly (and at discounted prices) from Gazprom.

131 Some Lithuanian commentators went farther, arguing, in a somewhat far-fetched manner, that "[a]ll of the most important events in our country [in 2005–2007] were merely the result of fighting between two Gazprom groups," that associated with the Yeltsyn-era groups and represented in Lithuania by Uspaskich, and that associated with new close-to-Putin personal interests and represented in Lithuania by Dujotekana's Stonys. Stoma, "Arbatėlė su išdaviku."

132 See Gediminas Stanisauskas: "In the Mud of Secret Interests," *Kauno Diena*, 18 September 2006, translated by BBC Monitoring Europe: Political, 20 September 2006 (via ISI, accessed 15 March 2007).

133 Miriam Elder, "Gazprom, LUKoil to Buy Oil Assets, *The Moscow Times,* 17 November 2006 (via ISI, accessed 19 April 2007.) Elder writes: "Each senior figure had his own camp, and Ryazanov's lost."

134 Author's consultations with energy and national security analysts, Vilnius, March 2007. See also various materials in *Kauno Diena,* July 2006.

135 According to extracts from parliamentary investigation stenographs, Albinas Januška, former Secretary of the Ministry of Foreign Affairs, was asked by Stonys to organize VSD support in the Kaunas conflict, and Januška used his connections at the VSD to send VSD agents to the plant during an attempted takeover by the Dujotekana group. Parliamentary investigation on State Security Department's actions carried out by Committee for National Security and Defence material. See Nacionalinio saugumo ir gynybos komiteto atlikto, op. cit.

136 Unattributed editorial, "Up to Our Ears in Democracy," *Verslo Zinios,* 22 March 2007, translated in "Lithuanian daily says state security scandal 'disgrace' for country," *BBC Monitoring,* 22 March 2007 (via ISI, accessed 2 May 2007).

137 In 2005, for example, Dujotekana's profit margin was 24 euros per tcm of gas. Considering it sold 0.517 bcm of gas that year, this amounts to 12.4 million euros in margin. The year 2005 was a weak one for Dujotekana, which in 2002 and 2004 sold over 1 bcm of gas. Information provided by Dujotekana, as reported in "Lithuania's Dujotekana Gas Importer Posts 46 Pct Drop in Fy Profit," BNS Daily Business News, 9 February 2006 (via ISI, accessed 15 March 2007), and Gediminas Stanisauskas, "In the Mud."

138 Darius Kuolis (Director, Civil Society Institute), "Moving towards Putin-Style Governance," *Verslo Zinios,* 6 April 2007, translated in "Lithuania moving towards 'Putin-style governance,' – pundit," *BBC Monitoring,* 6 April 2007 (via ISI, accessed 6 April 2007).

139 For example, as in summer 2006 MN's sale to Orlen was being negotiated, and it was believed Russia might interrupt oil shipments by pipeline as a way to hinder the sale, "the refinery immediately retooled for tanker oil, a decision that proved prescient; the first shipment arrived a week before the pipeline was shut." Andrew E. Kramer, "Lithuanians Are Given a Taste of How Russia Plays the Oil Game," *New York Times,* 28 October 2006.

140 Gas import prices reached a record $515 per tcm for a short period in August 2008. Rasa Laukaitytė, "Lietuva už dujas jau moka brangiau

nei „Gazprom" žada parduoti Europai," 2 October 2008, http://www.
delfi.lt/news/economy/energetics/article.php?id=18742907, cited in
Janeliūnas, "Lithuania's Energy Strategy," 198. Gas import prices are
revised monthly based on fuel oil price in the international market and
remain confidential. Hansabank/Swedbank, "Lietuvos Dujos," *The Baltic
Region*, 7 October 2008, available at http://www.swedbank.lt/lt/
previews/get/495/rss (accessed 13 May 2009).

141 The Nord Stream pipeline envisions a branch to Kaliningrad. In addition,
the Russian proposal to build an additional nuclear power plant in Kaliningrad would reduce the area's dependence on both Lithuanian electricity
and Lithuanian gas transit services.

142 *Lietuvos Energetika 2007*, 4, available at http://www.lei.lt/_img/_up/
File/atvir/leidiniai/Lietuvos_energetika-2007.pdf. Until the closing of
Ignalina's first bloc in 2004, nuclear power provided about 37 percent of
Lithuania's TPES. Streimikiene, "Lithuania," 168–9. After the closing of
Ignalina's first unit in 2004, Lithuania's energy dependency increased
from 46.06 percent (2004) to 60.12 percent (2007) Calculated from IEA, *Key
World Energy Statistics* (Paris, various years).

143 Previous versions of the National Energy Strategy, although also setting
important goals, did not so much emphasize energy *diversification* as a
goal in itself, but first and foremost the *security* of energy supply. English
versions of the 1999, 2002, and 2007 National Energy Strategies can be
found at the Ministry of Economy website, at http://www.ukmin.lt/en/
energy/general/ (accessed 28 April 2009).

144 *National Energy Strategy of Lithuania 2007* (Vilnius, 2007), 9.

145 For a discussion of problems hindering implementation of the official
strategy, see Janeliūnas, "Lithuania's Energy Strategy," 207–8.

146 The 2007 Strategy called specifically for the preparation of feasibility
studies on building an interconnection between Polish and Lithuanian
gas pipelines and on and the possible building of an LNG terminal in
Lithuania or elsewhere in the Baltic region, as well as for the building of
connections with Swedish and Polish electricity grids by 2012. Lithuanian
Energy Institute, *National Energy Strategy* (Kaunas, Lithuania, 2003) [com-
mented edition of Lithuania's Energy Strategy, 2002], 12–13 and 25.

147 Concerns were also raised about the composition of the management
company assigned to the project, and about the fact that some shares
in the company had been provided to the fertilizer company Achema,
Gazprom's largest direct gas consumer in Lithuania, without a tender. I
thank Vidamantas Jankauskas for this insight. In 2010, it was announced

that the LNG terminal would be built within two years. See Rokas M. Tracevskis, "From the Grybauskaite vs. Putin Match," *The Baltic Times* 17 February 2010 (accessed 30 June 2010).

148 The Lithuania-Sweden electricity link project received its final green light in March 2010, and was expected to be completed by 2015. *Lithuanian Energy Quarterly* 2010, Q2, 1, 3.

149 Draft National Energy Strategy (2007), as discussed in Egle Markeviciene, "No electricity and no natural gas for making electricity," *Verslo Zinios*, 5 January 2007, translated in "Analysis predicts Lithuania, region to experience electricity shortage in 2010," *BBC Monitoring*, 5 January 2007 (via ISI, accessed 15 March 2007).

150 Draft National Energy Strategy (2007), as discussed in Markeviciene, "No electricity."

151 Of those who participated in the referendum, nearly 89 percent supported extending Ignalina's period of service.

152 In this scheme, popularly known as the "three-headed dragon," three companies (the Western Distribution Network [VST], the Eastern Distribution Network [RST], and the Lietuvos Energija high-voltage national transmission grid) would merge to create a single National Investor (the Lithuanian Electricity Organization or LEO Lt.) for the project. Controversy arose as to how the value of VST's contribution would be assessed, how shares in the new entity would be divided, and whether the creation of such a national company would create a new and undesirable monopolization in the energy area, violating EU unbundling regulations. See Raimondas Kuodis, cited in TBT Staff, "Report: State to take 60 percent in merged utility," *The Baltic News*, 18 April 2007 (via ISI, accessed 9 May 2007) and Žygimantas Vaičiūnas, "Towards Energy Independence."

153 With the exception of small projects such as the granting Lithuania emergency-use access to gas in Latvia's Incukalns underground gas storage facility.

154 Energy Ministry Press Release, 3 December 2010, available at http://www.enmin.lt/en/news/detail.php?ID=1138 (accessed 10 December 2010).

155 Ausra Iterauliskyte, advisor to President Adamkus, head of Law Department, cited in Larisa Kostrub, "Prezident ne budet vetirovat' Zakon o prirodnom gaze," *ELTA Lithuanian Newswire*, 13 April 2007 (via ISI, accessed 17 April 2007). See paragraph 8 of Article 25 of the EU Directive 2003/55EC, discussed in *National Energy Strategy of Lithuania 2007*, 26. LD's main co-owners Gazprom and Ruhrgas, on the contrary, argued the new law was not in agreement with the directive. "Germany's E. on

Ruhrgas slams New Lithuania's Natgas Legislation - Daily," BNS, 18 May 2007, citing Lietuvos Rytas (via ISI, accessed 21 May 2007).

156 The NCCPE, led by its 2002-2007 chairman Vidmantas Jankauskas, played an important role in these discussions. Yet after the NCCPE passed a new methodology for gas price calculations based on the new Gas Law, Dujotekana sued it in the Administrative Court, which required a six-month postponement of the application of the new methodology. During this period, Dujotekana was able to continue selling gas at a high, unregulated margin. I thank Vidamantas Jankauskas for this insight.

157 The unbundling of national gas companies was also an EU requirement related to the Union's third package of legislative proposals for electricity and gas markets of September 2008. On that basis, in May of 2010 Lithuania passed an amendment to its Law on Natural Gas mandating the separation of gas supply from gas transmission through high-pressure gas pipelines. See http://www.enmin.lt/en/news/detail.php?ID=872 (accessed 30 June 2010).

158 For an alternative explanation of this "blocking," see Žygimantas Pavilionis, "Lithuanian Position Regarding the EU Mandate on Negotiations with Russia: Seeking a New Quality of EU-Russian Relations," *Lithuanian Foreign Policy Review*, no. 21 (2008): 174–81.

159 Measured in terms of total energy consumption, it went from 16.96 Mtoe TPES in 1991 to 6.93 Mtoe in 2010. The 1991 data is from Streimikiene, "Lithuania," 141. The 2010 data is from International Energy Agency, *Key World Energy Statistics* 2012 (Paris, 2012).

160 Calculated from information in Streimikiene, "Lithuania," 154.

161 In 2002, Lithuania's per capita Total Final Consumption (TFC) was only 41.6 percent of the 1990 level, significantly lower even than the other Baltic states Latvia (47 percent) and Estonia (47 percent), as well as Belarus (58 percent). While TFC was decreasing in all CEE states up to 2000, Lithuania's decrease was the largest until 2005, losing to Estonia after that. Data from Vlacovas Miškinis, LEI. See also Figure 4 in Romualdas Juknys, Vaclovas Miškinis, and Renata Dagiliute, "New Eastern EU Member States: Decoupling of Environmental Impact from Fast Economy Growth," *Environmental Research, Engineering and Management*, no. 4/34 (2005): 68–76, here 71.

162 See Jurgis Vilemas, "Renewables in Lithuania: Reasons for Slowness in the Past and Future Expectations," presentation at the Conference "Renewable Energy: Development and Sustainability," Vilnius, 10 June 2008, power-point available at http://www.lsta.lt/files/seminarai/080610_radison%20SAS/5_Vilemas.ppt (accessed 27 April 2009).

163 Calculated at purchase power parity (PPP) prices, Lithuania's energy intensity (the amount of energy necessary to produce a set amount of GDP) more than halved between 1991 and 2007. Juknys, Miškinis, et al., "New Eastern EU," 72. Calculated at market prices, the amount of energy needed to produce $US1,000 of GDP, calculated in terms of 1995 US dollars, went from about 0.44 tons of energy equivalent (toe) in 1992 to about 0.29 in 2001. Calculated from Anil Markandya, Suzette Pedroso, and Dalia Streimikiene. "Energy Efficiency in Transition Economies: Is There Convergence Towards the EU Average?" (May 2004). FEEM Working Paper No. 89.04. Available at SSRN: http://ssrn.com/abstract=556237 (accessed 12 July 2007), 8.

164 Calculated from European Commission, *EU Energy in Figures 2009* (available at http://ec.europa.eu/energy/publications/doc/statistics/part_2_energy_pocket_book_2009.pdf, accessed 30 May 2009), Tables 2.6.1 and 2.6.15. For important caveats about limits to the comparative use of energy intensity indicators for the CEE countries, see Vaclovas Miškinis, Jurgis Vilemas, and Inga Konstantinavičiūtė, "Analysis of Energy Consumption and Energy Intensity Indicators in Central and Eastern European Countries," *Energy Studies Review* 14, no. 2 (2006): 171–88.

165 IAEA, *Energy supply options for Lithuania*, 39.

166 Until 1997, there were also important differences between prices charged different gas users. If in January 1993 the price paid by households for gas for heating was only 5.2 percent of that charged industries, by 1996 industrial and residential electricity prices had largely equalized, and by 2000 residential gas prices were higher than those charged industrial consumers. Dalia Streimikiene, "Removing/Restructuring Energy Subsidies in Lithuania," paper presented at the UN-ECE/OECD Workshop on Enhancing the Environment by Reforming Energy Prices, Prühonice, Czech Republic, June 2000, available at http://www.env.cz/www/zamest.nsf/0/ddf10194ec514cc2c12568f00035398d?OpenDocument, 3 (accessed 13 July 2007) and Christian Von Hirschhausen and Thomas W. Waelde, "The End of Transition: An Institutional Interpretation of Energy Sector Reform in Eastern Europe and the CIS," *MOCT-MOST: Economic Policy in Transitional Economies* 11, no. 1 (2001): 93–110, citing IEA data.

167 See Streimikiene, "Lithuania," 158, and Streimikiene, "Removing/Restructuring Energy Subsidies in Lithuania," 2.

168 Kutas and Vilemas, "Legacy of the Past," 2–3.

169 See Streimikiene, "Lithuania," 157-66 and 187. As Lithuanian incomes continued to grow in the 2000s, the affordability of household energy increased.

170 Between 1992 and 2007 Lithuania's industrial sector diminished its role in the economy from about 42 percent of the country's gross value added to 25.9 percent. The commercial sector, on the other hand, increased its role in gross value added formation from 22 percent in 1990 to 48 percent in 2007. The 1990 data is from Streimikiene, "Lithuania," 153.

171 If in 1990 renewable resources comprised 2 percent of the TPES, by 2008 that amounted to 11.4 percent, an impressive increase but still behind EU levels. Streimikiene, "Lithuania," 168. The 2008 data is from Paulius Koverovas, "Renewable Energy in Lithuania," 2008, available at www. laiea,.lt/users/userfiless/file/Presentation_renew.

172 The EU's 2009 Directive on the Promotion of the Use of Energy from Renewable Sources (2009/28/EC, OJ L 140/16, 5 June 2009) set the target for Lithuania to generate 23 percent of its total primary energy balance from renewable sources by 2020.

173 Seimas of the Republic of Lithuania, Law on "The Basics of National Security of Lithuania," passed on 19 December 1996, available at http://www3.lrs.lt/pls/inter3/dokpaieska.showdoc_e?p_id=39790&p_query=&p_tr2= (accessed 1 August 2007). See also National Security Strategy, approved by the Parliament of the Republic of Lithuania, 28 May 2002, available at www.kam.lt (accessed 30 July 2007), 5, 18, and 2005 update (available at http://www3.lrs.lt/pls/inter3/dokpaieska. showdoc_l?p_id=262943), 4, 6, 14, 20).

174 *National Energy Strategy of Lithuania 2007* (Vilnius, 2007).

175 See J. Augutis, V. Matuziene, and R. Krikstolaitis, "Analysis of Energy Disturbances and Energy Security of Supply in Lithuania," paper presented at the PSAM9 Conference, Hong Kong, 18–23 May 2008, available at http://psam9.zapto.org/psam9/Presentations/Parallel_Session/B_Harbour_II/Tue_4-6/B6_1520-1650/Analysis_of_Energy_Supply_Disturbances_and_Energy_Security.pdf (accessed 10 May 2009), slide 8.

176 In 2004, 4.4 percent of electricity was Orimulsion-generated. NCCPE, "Annual Report to the European Commision" (2004), 4. The importation of Orimulsion fell significantly after that, reaching 1,500 tons in 2007 (compared to 9.3 million tons of Russian oil) and ceased in 2008. However, in 2008 there was a commercial demonstration of a comparable fuel: Multiphase Superfine Atomized Residue Synthetic Fuel Oil (made of a liquid hydrocarbon with water and proprietary additives) developed in Canada and manufactured by MN. I thank Vaclovas Miškinis for this observation.

177 *National Energy Strategy of Lithuania 2007*, 26. It must noted, however, that, as of 2012, the largest Lithuanian crude user, the MN refinery, is fitted to

process high-sulphur Russian oil and not lighter sorts, significantly limiting its ability to diversify supplies.

178 *National Energy Strategy of Lithuania* 2007, 8. Although the *National Energy Strategy* does not mention Dujotekana, it is clear that this passage refers to the company.

179 After the closing of the first Ignalina nuclear unit in late 2004, Lithuania's level of energy imports dependency started to grow – to 55.58 percent in 2005 and 59.96 percent in 2006.

180 Ignalina provided about 32 percent of Lithuania's TPES at the time of its closing. Ministry of Energy of the Republic of Lithuania, "Energy Independence" (brochure), 1.

181 Streimikiene, "Lithuania," 168–69. In 1995, 87.4 percent (in 1993, 88 percent) of electricity generated in Lithuania came from nuclear power plants, a very high percentage in international comparison. See Streimikiene, "Lithuania," 169. Even after the closing of Ignalina's first bloc in 2004, Lithuania's 64.4 percent (2007) role of nuclear power in electricity generation was second only to France's 76.9 percent. Source: Table on Nuclear Share Figures, 1996–2007, World Nuclear Association, available at http://www.world-nuclear.org/info/nshare.html (accessed 28 April 2009). Data for 2003 from Vlacovas Miškinis, LEI.

182 Electricity exports declined sharply in the early 1990s, going from 11.7 TWh in 1990 to 2.7 TWh in 1993. Data from Streimikiene, "Lithuania," 133.

183 Lithuanian Energy Institute, *National Energy Strategy*, 10. The rationale for including energy generated by NPP as domestic production regardless of whether the nuclear fuel used is imported is that there is a low level of day-to-day dependence on nuclear fuel supplies, and that large nuclear fuel inventories can be maintained. Ibid, 7. Data for 2006 from Vlacovas Miškinis, LEI.

184 Data for 1990 from Vlacovas Miškinis, LEI.

185 The most obvious contrast is with Belarus, where no separate energy regulatory authority exists, and even basic information on differentiated electricity tariffs is not publicly available. In Ukraine, a National Energy Regulatory Commission was established in 1994, but its independence from political control or external influence has been questioned at times; in addition, it does not provide nearly the same level of publicly accessible reports as its Lithuanian or other EU counterparts.

186 See Transparency International Lietuvos Skyrius, "Lietuvos verslininkai bijo žiniasklaidos ir laiko ją neskaidria," (31 May 2007), available at http://www.transparency.lt/new/index.php?option=com_content&

task=view&id=10826&Itemid=24 (accessed 30 July 2007) and Artūras Racas, interview in "Facing Media Corruption in Lithuania," *The Baltic Times*, 13 June 2007, available at http://www.baltictimes.com/news/articles/18062/ (accessed 30 July 2007).

187 Republic of Lithuania, *National Energy Independence Strategy of the Republic of Lithuania* (Vilnius: Ministry of Energy, 2012).

188 A second option was to retain ownership but transfer management of the network to an independent entity; a third option would allow the gas producer/supplier to continue owning and managing the pipeline, but allowing other companies access on the basis of set criteria.

189 As noted by Janeliūnas, the success in implementing reforms in the immediate post-independence period may be related to their relative low cost and to the still fresh memories of the Soviet oil blockade in 1990. Tomas Janeliūnas, personal communication, 16 June 2009.

190 See Sabonis-Chaffee, *Power Politics*, 76–133.

191 Lithuania in particular may have been especially attractive due to the fact that – at least up to 2003 – it had a more liberal legislation than Estonia or Latvia, legislation that gave intermediary companies broader rights than those given them in Latvia and Estonia, for example the right to build their own, independent gas pipelines, as was the case with the construction, in 2003, of a 25-km-long gas pipeline from Belarus to Druskininai, built by the Latvian branch of Itera. "Nakanune vstuplenia Baltii v ES obostriaetsia bor'ba za kontrol' nad gazovym khoziaistvom regiona," (available at Rosinvest, http://www.rosinvest.com/dir/analysis/74/84/ original source, date not provided, presumed 2003. accessed 14 March 2007). On the Druskininai pipeline, see Vladimir Skripov, "Kupi rynok," *Ekspert Severo-Zapad* 2004, no. 2, 2 February 2004, (via ISI, accessed 15 March 2007).

192 "Konservatori podgotovili proekt strategii sderzhivania Rossii," ELTA, 9 May 2007 (via ISI, accessed 10 May 2007). Although in absolute terms Russian investments in Lithuania were quite small (in 2004, when measured in terms of cumulative investments, Russia occupied the seventh place, behind Estonia), they nevertheless remained very significant, especially because of their concentration in strategic sectors of the economy, especially energy and energy transit. In addition, many investments from Cyprus may be in reality from Russian offshore companies. Zashev, "Russian Investments," 2, 11.

193 Whereas in the other Baltic States, relations over the Russian-speaking minority have been tense, this has not been an issue in Lithuania; Lithuania was also the first of the three states (and until Latvia ratified its

border treaty with Russia in May of 2007, the only) to, in 1999, sign and ratify a border demarcation treaty with Russia.

194 The Baltic Energy Ring aims at integrating Lithuania, Latvia, Estonia, Finland, Sweden and Poland in a single electricity and gas grid.

195 For a representative view see the declarations of former President Vytautas Landsbergis at a meeting with EU Commission President José Manuel Barroso: "In Lithuania we do not feel we are an EU member state when it comes to energy. We remain an insecure post-Soviet exclave or an enclave in the EU, still a part of Russia's energy system." Quoted in EU-Russia Centre, "Landsbergis to Barroso: We do not feel an EU member state when it comes to energy," 18 December 2008, available at http://www. eu-russiacentre.org/news/landsbergis-barroso-feel-eu-member-state-energy.html (accessed 28 April 2009).

196 It should be noted, however, that, at least up to 2007, Lithuania had not moved to paying full Western European-level prices for its gas imports from Russia.

197 As noted by a Lithuanian analyst, once the active relationship stops, "they may be rich, but they no longer have power . . . they are creatures of Moscow." Author's consultation with economics journalist, Vilnius, 23 March 2007.

198 Thus, for example, Clark and Versekaite have argued that the way the Paksas impeachment crisis was managed and ultimately resolved actually shows, not so much the weakness of the Lithuanian political system, but its resilience and capacity for self-healing. See Terry D. Clark and Egle Verseckaite, "PaksasGate: Lithuania Impeaches a President," *Problems of Post-Communism* 52, no. 3 (May–June 2005): 16–24, here 23.

7. Conclusion

1 Leo Tolstoy, *Anna Karenina* (Ware, Herdtfordshire: Wordsworth, 1995), 1. The point here is that while none of our three cases was fully able to break away from energy dependency until at least 2010, the dynamics at play worked in different ways, through different policies, and with different effects in each of them.

2 The year 2007 is the last one for which official information is available. The important trends started in 2010 (such as the importation of Venezuelan oil by Belarus), although potentially very important in the medium term, are not likely to significantly affect Belarus' 2010 level of energy dependence, as they are unlikely to exceed 1 percent of its TPES.

3 In the case of Ukraine, despite the seemingly similar situation involving the closing of the Chernobyl NPP in late 2000, the impact was not

noticeable as its two remaining reactors represented only a fraction of the country's nuclear capacity; the actual production of the nuclear sector as a whole did not decrease the year following the final decommissioning of Chernobyl. For 1993–2004 time series data on nuclear production, see IEA, *Ukraine Energy Policy Review* 2006, 349.

4 It should be noted, however, that Lithuania did not start paying full Western European-level prices for its gas imports from Russia until the 2007–2008 period.

5 Although Lithuania is a transit country for Russian gas supplies to Kaliningrad and until mid-2006 – when Russia stopped oil shipments via the Druzhba pipeline – it also played an important role in the indirect transit of Russian oil through its refining and subsequent reexport to WE, due to its location relative to the main European oil and gas transportation networks, its role in the transit of Russian oil and gas was always much more limited than that played by Ukraine or Belarus.

6 Ukraine and Lithuania also benefitted from such prices, but, as seen from Tables 1.6, 4.3 and 5.3, to a lesser extent than Belarus.

7 Similarly, as discussed in chapter 4, the stealing of gas from transit pipelines must be seen as often involving not only unilateral action on the part of an energy-poor transit state, but collusion of private interests-within-the-corporation on both sides of the border.

8 Although later on specifically energy rents would lose relative importance relative to those that could be made in the metallurgical sector, as discussed in chapter 4, both kinds of rents were closely related, and much of the initial gas profits were invested by Ukrainian oligarchs in the metallurgical sector.

9 Since 2010, Lithuania has been paying gas prices higher than the European reference price (border price in Germany, see Table 1.6). This was also true for Ukraine during the first quarter of 2010, when it was paying $305/tcm as the European reference price (German border) for gas was $273. The $305 price was effective before a new agreement with Russia extending the Russia's lease of the Sevastopol Naval Base in exchange for a reduction in gas prices entered into force in April 2010. In 2012, Ukraine's gas import prices once again exceeded the European reference price.

10 As noted in chapter 1, if throughout the period under study long-term (ca. 20–30 years) contracts were the rule in Gazprom exports to WE, the usual arrangement in sales to CIS countries was yearly contracts, often subject to political volatility and negotiated at the very end of the previous year or – as happened repeatedly in the case of Belarus – after the start of the new year.

11 The Trojan horse analogy is taken from Valdas Vasiliauskas: "Trojan Gas," commentary in Lithuanian Television, Vilnius, in Lithuanian translated by BBC Monitoring, 16 January 2006.

12 In some cases of domestically produced oil and gas, the maintenance of low prices was related to profitable insider deals. Thus, for example, oil and coal trade sweetheart deals in Ukraine – as opposed to public sale through auctions – often led to their sale at prices too low to make domestic production profitable. During her time as First vice PM for energy issues in 2000–2001, Tymoshenko sought to eliminate such deals and replace them with auctions as a way to procure higher prices. See Balmaceda, *Energy Dependency*, 55, 69.

13 In fact, when intermediary companies were discussed at all by public officials, low prices as an ultimate goal of energy policy was used as a main justification of their existence.

14 The CIS can hardly be considered such an institution, as it did not, or only to a very limited extent, provide for effective institutions to deal with these transitional issues.

15 Russian policies towards Estonia (such as the boycott of Estonian goods, the closing of the Narva bridge to truck traffic, and computer hacker attacks on Estonian government websites in May 2007 as response to Estonia's move of a memorial to the Red Army) provide further examples of this pattern.

16 That this is by no means an easy process is shown by the power of EU-state energy companies to define the future of key strategic import initiatives, such as the alternative Nabucco and South Stream gas pipelines.

17 As of early 2013, of the three countries discussed in this book, only Belarus seemed not to have taken any measures to take advantage of the unconventional gas revolution.

18 Thane Gustafson, "Wheel of Fortune: The Battle for Oil and Power in Russia," Davis Center for Russian and Eurasian Studies, 15 February 2013.

Bibliography

Abdelal, Rawi. *National Purpose in the World Economy: Post Soviet States in Comparative Perspective*. Ithaca, NY: Cornell University Press, 2001.

——. "The Profits of Power: Commercial *Realpolitik* in Europe and Eurasia." *Harvard Business School Working Papers* 11–028. Available at http://hbswk. hbs.edu/item/6505.html (accessed 1 December 2010).

Adams, Jan. "Russia's Gas Diplomacy." *Problems of Post-Communism* 49, no. 3 (2002): 14–22 .

Adamson, David M. "Soviet Gas and European Security." *Energy Policy* 13, no. 1 (1985): 13–26. http://dx.doi.org/10.1016/0301-4215(85)90077-1.

Ahrend, R., and W. Tompson. "Unnatural Monopoly: The Endless Wait for Gas Sector Reform in Russia." *Europe-Asia Studies* 57, no. 6 (2005): 801–21. http://dx.doi.org/10.1080/1080/09668130500199376.

Aksenov, Iurii, and Igor´ Guzhva. "Deti gaza i stali." *Ekspert*, 11 October 2004. Reprinted in FEC-MUP, 14 October 2004 (via ISI).

Aks'onov, Iurii. "Mrii ta real'nist´ dyversyfikatsii hazozabezpechennia Ukrainy." *Enerhetychna Polityka Ukrainy* 2000, no. 6 (2000): 14–23.

Alekhnovich, Andrei. "V Belarusi ustanovleni limiti na potreblenie elektroenergii dlia promyshlennykh predpriatii."Deutsche Welle program for Belarus, *Belorusskaia Khronika*, 17 September 2008. Transcript available at http://www.dw-world.de/dw/article/0,2144,3650767,00.html (accessed 25 September 2008).

——. Deutsche Welle program for Belarus, *Belorusskaia Khronika*, 20 March 2007. Available at http://www.dw-world.de/dw/article/0,2144,2397689,00.html (accessed 7 August 2007).

Alexandrova, Lyudmila "Russia wants Belarus to make up its mind." *ITAR-TASS*, 2 December 2008. Available at http://www.itar-tass.com/eng/level2.html?NewsID=13334991 (accessed 11 December 2008).

Alexeev, M., and R. Conrad. "The Russian Oil Tax Regime: A Comparative Perspective." *Eurasian Geography and Economics* 50, no. 1 (2009): 93–114. http://dx.doi.org/10.2747/1539-7216.50.1.93.

Ames, Barry. *The Deadlock of Democracy in Brazil.* Ann Arbor: University of Michigan Press, 2001.

Amineh, Mehdi Parvizi. *Globalisation, Geopolitics & Energy Security in Central Eurasia and the Caspian.* The Hague: Clingendael International Energy Programme, 2003.

Andreikėnas, A., D. Bui, J. Danaitienė, A. Galinis, N. Golovanova, A. Jalal, F. Juškas, I. Konstantinavičiūtė, V. Krušinskas, V. Linkevičius, et al. *Energy Supply Options for Lithuania: A Detailed Multi-sector Integrated Energy Demand, Supply and Environmental Analysis.* Vienna: IAEA, 2004.

"Antologiia 'Bizonov.'" *NefteRynok*, 25 March 2001 (via ISI).

Aslund, Anders. "The Ancien Régime: Kuchma and the Oligarchs." In *Revolution in Orange: The Origins of Ukraine's Democratic Breakthrough*, ed. Anders Aslund and Michael McFaul, 9–28. Washington, DC: Carnegie Endowment, 2006.

———. *How Ukraine Became a Market Economy.* Washington, DC: Peterson Institute for International Economics, 2009.

Aslund, Anders, Peter Boone, and Simon Johnson. "Escaping the Under-Reform Trap." *IMF Staff Papers*, no. 48 (2001).

Associate Press Worldstream. 19 February 2004.

"A teper´ – revoliutsiia." *Vlast´ deneg*, 12 March 2005.

Augutis, J., V. Matuziene, and R. Krikstolaitis. "Analysis of Energy Disturbances and Energy Security of Supply in Lithuania." Paper presented at the PSAM9 Conference. Hong Kong, 18–23 May 2008. Available at http://psam9.zapto.org/psam9/Presentations/Parallel_Session/B_Harbour_II/Tue_4-6/B6_1520-1650/Analysis_of_Energy_Supply_Disturbances_and_Energy_Security.pdf (accessed 10 May 2009).

Austvik, Ole Gunnar, and Marina Tsygankova. "Petroleum Strategies in Norway and Russia." First draft of article in *Osteuropa*, September 2004. German version available at *Osteuropa* 54, nos. 9–10 (2004).

Auty, Richard M., and Alan H. Gelb. "Political Economy of Resource-Abundant States." In *Resource Abundance and Economic Development*, ed. R. M. Auty. Oxford: Oxford University Press, 2001.

Babanin, Olexander, Vladimir Dubrovskyi, and Oleksii Ivaschenko. *Ukraine: The Lost Decade and the Coming Boom.* Kyiv: CASE Ukraine, 2002.

Baciulis, Audrius. "Valstybės nesaugumo departamentas." State Insecurity Department, *Veidas*, 7 December 2006. Translated as "Lithuanian Commentary Reports on ad hoc Security Committee Findings." *BBC Monitoring* (via ISI, accessed 15 March 2007).

Balies, Alyson J.K., Oleksii Melnyk, and Ian Anthony. "Relics of Cold War: Europe's Challenge, Ukraine's Experience." *SIPRI Policy Paper*, no. 6 (2003). Available at http://editors.sipri.se/pubs/RAPPORT_RELICSOFCOLD-WAR.pdf (accessed 5 May 2006).

Balmaceda, Margarita M. "Belarus as a Transit Route: Domestic and Foreign Policy Implications." In *Independent Belarus: Domestic Determinants, Regional Dynamics and Implications for the West*, ed. Margarita M. Balmaceda, James Clem, and Lisbeth Tarlow, 162–96. Cambridge, MA: HURI/Davis Center for Russian Studies, distributed by Harvard University Press, 2002.

———. "Corruption, Intermediary Companies, and Energy Security: Lithuania's Lessons for Central and Eastern Europe." *Problems of Post-Communism* 55, no. 4 (2008): 16–28. http://dx.doi.org/10.2753/PPC1075-8216550402.

———. "Der Weg in die Abhängigkeit: Ostmitteleuropa am Energietropf der UdSSR." Special issue on *Europa Unter Spannung: Energiepolitik Zwischen Ost und West. Osteuropa* 54, nos. 9–10 (September–October 2004): 162–79.

———. "Energy Business and Foreign Policies in Belarus and Ukraine." Presentation at the conference on "Economic Interests and Foreign Policy Choices: The Case of the Slavic Triangle," University of Toronto, 26–27 January 2006.

———. *Energy Dependency, Politics and Corruption in the Former Soviet Union: Russia's Power, Oligarchs' Profits and Ukraine's Missing Energy Policy, 1995–2006.* London: Routledge, 2008.

———. *Living the High Life in Minsk: Russian Energy Rents, Domestic Populism and Belarus' Impending Crisis* (Budapest: Central European University Press, forthcoming 2013).

———. "Myth and Reality in the Belarusian-Russian Relationship: What the West Should Know." *Problems of Post-Communism* 46, no. 3 (1999): 3–14.

———. "Russian Energy Companies in the New Eastern Europe: The Cases of Ukraine and Belarus." In *Russian Business Power: The Role of Russian Business in Foreign and Security Policy*, ed. Andreas Wenger, Jeronim Perovic, and Robert W. Orttung, 67–87. London: RoutledgeCurzon, 2006.

———. "Understanding Repression in Belarus." In *The Worst of the Worst: Rogue and Repressive States in the World Order*, ed. Robert Rotberg, 193–222. Washington, DC: Brookings Institution, 2007.

Baran, Zeyno. "Lithuanian Energy Security: Prospects and Choices." Hudson Institute, 2006. Available at http://www.hudson.org/files/publications/LithuanianEnergySecurityDecember06.pdf (accessed 21 February 2007).

Beblawy, Hazem, and Giacomo Luciani, eds. *The Rentier State*. London: Croom Helm, 1987.

Bekker, Aleksandr. "Polufinal. Rossiia i Ukraina pochti dogovorilis'." *Vedomosti*, 20 November 2000.

Belarusian Institute of Strategic Studies. "Privatization in Belarus: Legislative Framework and Real Practices." *BISS Working Paper* BISS SA 1/2008-PRIV. Available at http://www.belinstitute.eu/images/stories/documents/priv1en.pdf (accessed 12 December 2008).

Belarus Today, 9 November 2002. Available at belarustoday.info/news/news.php?id=13372&lang=eng (accessed 15 May 2004).

Belton, Catherine. "Suspicions Raised by Gas Giant's New Deal." *The St. Petersburg Times*, 28 February 2003.

Beltransgas's official website. Available at http://www.btg.by.

Best, Ulrich. "Die anderen Räume des Sozialismus. Internationale Baustellen in der Sowjetunion und ihre Erinnerung." In Kakanien Revisited, http://www.kakanien.ac.at/beitr/emerg/UBest1/ (accessed 21 August 2011).

BISS Trends, no. 2, January–March 2010.

Blokhin, A. In Tatiana Manenok, "Premeri ne dogovorilis'." *Belorusskii Rynok*, no. 16/600, 28 April 2004.

Blomfield, Adrian. "$40bn Putin Is 'Now Europe's Richest Man.'" *The Daily Telegraph*, 21 December 2007.

Bondarenko, Kost'. "Igra po-krupnomu." *Delovaia Nedelia*, no. 22/182, 10–16 June 2004.

———. "Khto i chym volodiie v Ukraini." *L´vivs'ka Hazeta*, 17 July 2003.

———. "V nemetskom plenu." *Gaz i neft´. Energeticheskii biulleten´*, 22 August 2001 (via ISI).

Bonner, Raymond. "Ukraine Staggers in the Path to the Free Market." *The New York Times*, 9 April 1997.

Bosas, Antanas. Declarations to Baltic News Service, cited in *The Baltic Times*, 21 June 2001 (via ISI, accessed 22 March 2007).

Bradshaw, Michael. "A New Energy Age in Pacific Russia: Lessons from the Sakhalin Oil and Gas Projects." *Eurasian Geography and Economics* 51, no. 3 (2010): 330–59. http://dx.doi.org/10.2747/1539-7216.51.3.330.

Brower, Derek. "NE: Gazprom Is Winning its Caucasian Chess Game with EU." *Business New Europe*, 15 December 2006. Available at http://derekbrower.wordpress.com/2007/01/06/hello-world/ (accessed 15 May 2007).

Bruce, Chloë. "Friction or Fiction? The Gas Factor in Russian-Belarusian Relations." *Chatham House Briefing Paper* REP BP 05/01 (May 2005). Available at http://www.riia.org/pdf/research/rep/BP0501gas.pdf (accessed 20 September 2005).

Buchanan, James M. "Rent-seeking and Profit-seeking." *Toward a Theory of the Rent-Seeking Society* 3 (1980): 15.

Bugajski, Janusz. *Cold Peace: Russia's New Imperialism*. Westport, CT: Praeger, 2005.

Bukkvoll, Tor. "Defining a Ukrainian Foreign Policy Identity: Business Interests and Geopolitics in the Formulation of Ukrainian Foreign Policy 1994–1999." In *Ukrainian Foreign and Security Policy: Theoretical and Comparative Perspectives*, ed. Jennifer D.P. Moroney, Taras Kuzio, and Mikhail Molchanov, 131–53. Westport, CT: Praeger, 2002.

———. "Private Interests, Public Policy: Ukraine and the Common Economic Space Agreement." *Problems of Post-Communism* 51, no. 5 (2004): 11–22.

Burkovskii, Pëtr. "Rozhdennaia evoliutsiei." *Kompan'on*, no. 14/374, 16–22 April 2004.

"Business Interests in Lithuania's Parliamentary Elections." *The Jamestown Monitor* 6, no. 187 (2000). Available at www.jamestown.org (accessed 20 March 2007).

Buzan, Barry, and Ole Wæver. *Regions and Powers: The Structure of International Security*. Cambridge: Cambridge University Press, 2003. http://dx.doi.org/10.1017/CBO9780511491252.

Buzan, Barry, Ole Wæver, and Japp de Wilde. *Security: A New Framework for Analysis*. Boulder, CO: Lynne Rienner Publishers, 1998.

Chalii, Oleksander. In Radio Free Europe program for Ukraine, *Vechirnia Svoboda*, 8 January 2009. Heard on www.radiosvoboda.org.

Chiz, Iurii. Interview in *Forbes* (Russian edition), 24 July 2008. Cited and partial selections reproduced in http://allminsk.biz/content/view/1772/ (accessed 12 August 2008).

Chubrik, Aliaksandr. In RFE/RL (Radio Svabody) Program for Belarus, *Ekspertiza Svobody* ("Privatyzatsiia Belarusi – use na prodazh raseitsam?"), 20 May 2008. Transcript available at http://www.svaboda.org/content/Transcript/1116684.html.

Churilov, Garik. "Ianukovich v Moskve 'pridumal,' kak napolnit´ nefteprovod 'Odesa-Brody." obkom.net.ua, 5 July 2004. Reprinted in FEC-MUP, 6 July 2004 (via ISI).

Clark, Terry D., and Jovita Pranevičiūte. "Perspectives on Communist Successor Parties: The Case of Lithuania." *Communist and Post-Communist Studies* 41, no. 4 (2008): 443–64. http://dx.doi.org/10.1016/j.postcomstud.2008.09.003.

Clark, Terry D., and Egle Verseckaite. "PaksasGate: Lithuania Impeaches a President." *Problems of Post-Communism* 52, no. 3 (2005): 16–24.

Closson, Stacy. "Networks of Profit in Georgia's Autonomous Regions: Challenges to Statebuilding." *Journal of Intervention and Statebuilding* 4, no. 2 (2010): 179–204. http://dx.doi.org/10.1080/17502970903533694.

———. "State Weakness in Perspective: Strong Politico-Economic Networks in Georgia's Energy Sector." *Europe-Asia Studies* 61, no. 5 (2009): 759–78. http://dx.doi.org/10.1080/09668130902904910.

"Constitutional Watch: Lithuania." *East European Constitutional Review* 10, no. 1 (2001).

D'Anieri, Paul. *Economic Interdependence in Ukrainian-Russian Relations.* Albany, NY: SUNY Press, 1999.

———. "Leonid Kuchma and the Personalization of the Ukrainian Presidency." *Problems of Post-Communism* 50, no. 5 (2003): 58–65.

———. *Understanding Ukrainian Politics: Power, Politics, and Institutional Design.* Armonk, NY: M.E. Sharpe, 2007.

———. "Ukrainian-Russian Relations: Beyond the Gas." Presentation at the conference on "The Ukrainian-Russian Gas Crisis and its Fallout: Domestic and International Implications." Harvard University, 5–6 February 2006. Streaming video available at http://www.huri.harvard.edu/events/event-archive/102-gas-crisis-conference-2006.html (accessed 24 February 2013).

Danilovich, Alex. *Russian-Belarusian Integration: Playing Games Behind the Kremlin Walls.* Aldershot, England: Ashgate, 2006.

Darden, Keith A. "Blackmail as a Tool of State Domination: Ukraine Under Kuchma." *Eastern European Constitutional Review* 10, no. 2/3 (2001): 67–71.

———. *Economic Liberalism and its Rivals: The Formation of International Institutions among the Post-Soviet States.* Cambridge: Cambridge University Press, 2009.

Dashkevich, Valerii F. *Energeticheskaia Zavisimost' Belarusi: posledstviia dlia ekonomiki i obshestva.* Minsk: Lovginov/ Fond imeni Fridrikha Eberta, 2005.

Davis, Mark, Dejan Ostojic, Olga Pindyyuk, and Ruslan Piontkivsky. "Ukraine: The Impact of Higher Natural Oil and Gas Prices." *World Bank,* December 2005. Available at http://documents.worldbank.org/curated/en/2005/12/7386006/ukraine-impact-higher-natural-gas-oil-prices (accessed 4 February 2013).

Davydova, Milana. "Zavedomo Ubytochnoe Slianie: Ob"edinennuiu neftianuiu kompaniiu zhdet nesladkaia zhizn' za schet dotatsii." *Nezavisimaia Gazeta,* 9 February 1999.

Dawson, Jane I. *Eco-nationalism: Anti-nuclear Activism and National Identity in Russia, Lithuania and Ukraine.* Durham, NC: Duke University Press, 1996.

DeLay, J. "Moscow Considers a Move on Gas Flaring." *NewsBase, FSU Oil & Gas Monitor,* no. 21, 30 May 2007.

Dem'ianenko, Elena. "Po proektu Odesa-Brody naiden kompromis." *Delovaia Nedelia FT* (Kyiv), 28 January 2004.

Dempsey, Judy. "Gazprom Wins Belarus Victory." *International Herald Tribune,* 29 December 2005.

———. "Russia Extends Energy Spree, Buying Serbian Oil Monopoly." *The New York Times,* 23 January 2008.

Demydenko, Myroslav. "Ukraine, Vanco Energy, and the Russian Mob." *Eurasian Daily Monitor* 5, no. 177, 16 September 2008. Available at http://www.jamestown.org (accessed 17 September 2008).

Denafas, Gintaras. "Regional and Local Environmental Impact caused by Closing of Ignalina Nuclear Power Plant in Lithuania." (No date provided, presumably 2003.) Available at http://www.statvoks.no/synergy/INPP_lt.doc (accessed 21 May 2009).

Deyermond, R. "The State of the Union: Military Success, Economic and Political Failure in the Russia-Belarus Union." *Europe-Asia Studies* 56, no. 8 (2004): 1191–1205. http://dx.doi.org/10.1080/1465342042000308910.

Dienes, Leslie. "Energy, Minerals, and Economic Policy." In *The Ukrainian Economy*, ed. I.S. Koropeckyi. Cambridge, MA: Harvard Ukrainian Research Institute, 1992.

Dienes, Leslie, Istvan Dobozi, and Marian Radetzki. *Energy and Economic Reform in the Former Soviet Union*. New York: St. Martin's Press, 1994. http://dx.doi.org/10.1057/9780230377158.

Dienes, Leslie, and Theodore Shabad. *The Soviet Energy System: Resource Use and Policies*. Washington, DC: V.H. Winston & Sons, 1979.

"Direktiva No. 3 Prezidenta Respubliki Belarus ot 14 iulia 2007 g." Available at http://www.government.by/index?page=rus_gdoc_prog21122007_5&mode=printable&lang=ru (accessed 11 December 2008).

Dixon, Sarah. *Organisational Transformation in the Russian Oil Industry*. Cheltelham, UK: Edward Elgar, 2008.

"Dlia chago Raman Abramovich priletau u Mensk?" *Nasha Niva*, no. 37/539, 11 October 2007.

Drakokhrust, Yurii, and Dmitri Furman. "Belarus and Russia." In *Independent Belarus: Domestic Determinants, Regional Dynamics and Implications for the West*, ed. Margarita M. Balmaceda, James Clem, and Lisbeth Tarlow, 232–55. Cambridge MA: HURI/Davis Center for Russian Studies, distributed by Harvard University Press, 2002.

Dubnov, Vadim. In RFE/RL (Radio Svobody) program for Belarus, *Pratskii Akzent* ("Klubok belaruskai zamezhnai palitiki: Raseia, Europa, 'tretsi s'vet,'") 10 October 2006. Transcript available at http://www.svaboda.org/PrintView.aspx?Id=774535.

Dubrovskyi, V., W. Graves, Y. Golovakha, O. Haran´, R. Pavlenko, and J. Szymer. "The Reform in a Captured State: Lessons from the Ukrainian Case." First draft, *Understanding Reform Project*. Kyiv: Mimeo, 2003.

Dunning, Thad. *Crude Democracy: Natural Resource Wealth and Political Regimes*. Cambridge: Cambridge University Press, 2008.

Ebel, Robert E., and Rajan Menon. *Energy and Conflict in Central Asia and the Caucasus*. Oxford: Rowman & Littlefield, 2001.

Economist Intelligence Unit. "Country Briefing: Lithuania Politics: See-saw Politics," 13 May 2005 (via ISI, accessed 21 March 2007).

———. *Country Economic News*, 4 October 2001 (via ISI, accessed 20 March 2007).

———, "Lithuania: Energy Provision." 1 September 2002 (via ISI, accessed 15 March 2007).

———. *Riskwire Lithuania*, 24 November 2008 (via ISI, accessed 14 March 2009).

Elder, Miriam. "Gazprom, Lukoil to Buy Oil Assets." *The Moscow Times*, 17 November 2006 (via ISI, accessed 19 April 2007).

Energeticheskaia Strategiia Rossii na period do 2020 goda. Moscow, September 2003. Full text in Russian available at http://www.gazprom.ru/articles/article4951.shtml (accessed 21 June 2006).

Energosoft database. Available at http://energosoft.info/news2004.html.

Energy Charter Secretariat. *Gas Transit Tariffs in Selected Energy Charter Countries*. Brussels: 2006. Available at http://www.encharter.org/index.php?id=127 (accessed 24 February 2009).

———. *Putting a Price on Energy: International Pricing Mechanisms for Oil and Gas*. Brussels: Energy Charter Secretariat, 2007.

Enerhetychna Stratehiia Ukrainy na period do 2030 roku. Kyiv: Ministerstvo Palyva ta Enerhetyky, 2006. Available at the Ministry of Fuel and Energy's website, www.mpe.kmu.gov.ua/control/uk/archive/docview?typeId=36172 (accessed 5 May 2006).

Eremenko, Alla. "Cherchez Le Petrol." *Zerkalo Nedeli*, no. 6/534, 19–25 February 2005. Available at www.zerkalo-nedeli.com/ie/print/49288 (accessed 5 May 2006).

———. "'Naftohaz Ukrainy': Kratkaia Istoriia v Sobytiiakh i litsakh." *Zerkalo Nedeli*, no. 19/444, 24–30 May 2003.

Ermilov, Sergei. "Zametki k programme Partii Ekologicheskogo Spaseniia 'EKO+25%.'" *Zerkalo Nedeli*, no. 584, 11–18 February 2006. Available at http://www.zerkalo-nedeli.com/nn/show/584/52569/ (accessed 1 March 2006).

Esping-Anderson, Costa. *Politics Against Markets: the Social Democratic Road to Power*. Princeton, NJ: Princeton University Press, 1985.

Estrada, Javier, Arild Moe, and Kare Dahl Martinsen. *The Development of European Gas Markets*. Chichester, UK: John Wiley & Sons, 1995.

Eurasian Chemical Market, 30 January 2008. Available at http://chemmarket.info/?mod=news&lang=en&nid=6457 (accessed 20 January 2010).

Europa Publications, ed. *Eastern Europe, Russia and Central Asia 2004*. London: Routledge, 2003.

European Commission. *EU Energy in Figures 2009*. Available at http://ec.europa.eu/energy/publications/doc/statistics/part_2_energy_pocket_book_2009.pdf (accessed 30 May 2009).

——. *Green Paper: A European Strategy for Sustainable, Competitive and Secure Energy*. 8 March 2006. Available at http://eur-lex.europa.eu/LexUriServ/LexUriServ.do?uri=COM:2006:0105:FIN:EN:HTML (accessed May 23, 2013).

——. *Second Strategic Energy Review – Securing our Energy Future*. EU, European Commission, 2008.

——. *Towards a European Strategy for the Security of Energy Supply: Green Paper*. Luxemburg: European Communities, 2001.

EU-Russia Centre. "Landsbergis to Barroso: We Do Not Feel an EU Member State When it Comes to Energy." 18 December 2008. Available at http://www.eu-russiacentre.org/news/landsbergis-barroso-feel-eu-member-state-energy.html (accessed 28 April 2009).

"EU Says Tymoshenko Sentence Could Hit Ukraine Ties." *Kyiv Post*, 11 October 2011. Available at http://www.kyivpost.com/news/nation/detail/114538/#ixzz1btUuxhAA (accessed 25 October 2011).

Feduta, Aleksandr. *Lukashenko: Politicheskaia Biografiia*. Moscow: Referendum, 2005.

Feofantov, Iurii. "Rynok Gaza: Dolg platezham opasen." *Gaz i Neft'. Analiticheskii biulleten'*, 25 November 2008 (via ISI).

Finon, D., and C. Locatelli. "Russian and European Gas Interdependence: Could Contractual Trade Channel Geopolitics?" *Energy Policy* 36, no. 1 (2008): 423–42. http://dx.doi.org/10.1016/j.enpol.2007.08.038.

Fish, M. Steven. "The Executive Deception: Superpresidentialism and the Degradation of Russian Politics." In *Building the Russian State: Institutional Crisis and the Quest for Democratic Governance*, ed. Valerie Sperling, 177–92. Boulder, CO: Westview, 2000.

Flikke, G. "Pacts, Parties and Elite Struggle: Ukraine's Troubled Post-Orange Transition." *Europe-Asia Studies* 60, no. 3 (2008): 375–96. http://dx.doi.org/10.1080/09668130801947986.

Fortescue, Stephen. *Russia's Oil Barons and Metal Magnates: Oligarchs and the State in Transition*. Basingstoke, Hampshire: Palgrave Macmillan, 2007.

Frieden, A., and R. Rogowski. "The Impact of the International Economy on National Policies: An Analytical Overview." In *Internationalization and Domestic Politics*, ed. R.O. Keohane and H.V. Milner. Cambridge: Cambridge University Press, 1996.

Gaddy, Clifford C., and Barry W. Ickes. "Resource Rents and the Russian Economy." *Eurasian Geography and Economics* 46, no. 8 (2005): 559–83. http://dx.doi.org/10.2747/1538-7216.46.8.559.

——. "Russia's Declining Oil Production: Managing Price Risk and Rent Addiction." *Eurasian Geography and Economics* 50, no. 1 (2009): 1–13. http://dx.doi.org/10.2747/1539-7216.50.1.1.

——. *Russia's Virtual Economy.* Washington, DC: Brookings Institution, 2002.

Gas Matters, November 2002.

Gaz i neft´. Energeticheskii biulleten´, 15 March 2000 (via ISI).

"Gazovyi konsortsium. Otsenki ėkspertov." *Gaz i neft´. Ėnergeticheskii biulleten´*, 16 July 2002 (via ISI).

"Gazprom and Beltransgas Ink Gas Supply and Transit Contract for 2006." Available at Gazprom's website, http://www.gazprom.ru/eng/news/2005/12/18593.shtml (accessed 15 March 2006).

"Gazprom poboretsia za Lietuvos dujos." *Kommersant,* 24 October 2002 (via ISI, accessed 15 March 2007).

"Gazproms Exportrouten (in Mrd. m3)." In *UkraineAnalysen* no. 50 (2009).

"Gazpromu pridetsia podozhdat'." *Vedomosti,* 28 May 2008.

"Germany's Eon Ruhrgas slams New Lithuania's Natgas Legislation- Daily." *BNS,* 18 May 2007. Citing *Lietuvos Rytas* (via ISI, accessed 21 May 2007).

Giedraitis, Vincent Roland. "Multi-Dependency in the Post-Socialist Period: The Case of Lithuania." Ph.D. dissertation, Sociology, University of California-Riverside, 2006.

"Glava gosudarstva v tselom odobril proekt kontseptsii energeticheskoi nezavisimosti Belarusi do 2020 goda." Available at www.president.gov.by/press34523.html#doc (accessed 16 December 2008).

Global Witness. "It's a Gas – Funny Business in Turkmen-Ukraine Gas Trade" (April 2006). Available at http://www.globalwitness.org/sites/default/files/library/its_a_gas_april_2006_lowres.pdf (accessed 15 February 2013).

Goldman, Marshall. *Petro-state: Putin, Power, and the New Russia.* Oxford: Oxford University Press, 2008.

Golobud, Bogdan. "Ne vse zoloto, chto blestit." *Gaz i neft´. Energeticheskii biulleten´*, 22 August 2001 (via ISI).

Gorchinskaya, Katya. "Prosecutors tie Tymoshenko to Lawmaker's 1996 Murder." *Kyiv Post,* 25 January 2013. Available at http://www.kyivpost.com/content/politics/prosecutors-tie-tymoshenko-to-lawmakers-1996-murder-319321.html (accessed 18 February 2013).

"Gorkii nefteklapan." *Oil Market Weekly (Nefterynok),* 18 March 2002 (via ISI).

"Gosudarstvennaia kompleksnaia programma modernizatsii osnovnykh proizvodstvennykh fondov Belorusskoi energeticheskoi sistemy, energosberezheniia i uvelicheniia doli ispol'zovaniia v respublike sobstvennykh toplivo-energeticheskikh resursov na period do 2011 goda." *Ukaz* no. 575, 15 November 2007. Available at http://energosoft.info/news2004.html.

Gould, John A., and Yaroslav Hetman. "Market Democracy Unleashed? Business Elites and the Crisis of Competitive Authoritarianism in Ukraine." *Business and Politics* 10, no. 2 (2008): 1–33. http://dx.doi.org/10.2202/1469-3569.1236.

Government of Lithuania. *National Energy Strategy*. Vilnius: Ministry of Economy, 2002. Other years available at http://www.ukmin.lt/en/energy/general/ (accessed 28 April 2009).

Government of Ukraine. *Updated Energy Strategy of Ukraine for the Period till 2030*, June 2012, Kyiv. Available at http://mpe.kmu.gov.ua/fuel/doccatalog/document?id=50508 (accessed 18 February 2013).

Gowa, Joanne. *Allies, Adversaries, and International Trade*. Princeton, NJ: Princeton University Press, 1994.

Grabher, Gerner, and David Stark. "Organizing Diversity: Evolutionary Theory, Network Analysis and Post-socialism." In *Theorising Transition: the Political Economy of Post-communist Transformations*, ed. John Pickles and Adrian Smith, 54–75. London: Routledge, 1998.

Grabovskii, Marko. "PRIVAT brosaet perchatku." *Infobank Oil & Gas Monitor*, 25 March 2008 (via ISI).

Grib, Natalia. "Ivan Bambiza otkroet cello . . . Prezidentu." *Belorusskaia Gazeta*, no. 21/438, 31 May 2004.

Grigas, Agnia. *The Politics of Energy and Memory between the Baltic States and Russia*. Aldershot, England: Ashgate, 2013.

Grivach, Aleksandr. "Minsk nachal platit'." *Vremia Novostei*, 11 November 2002.

Guillet, Jerome. "Gazprom's got West Europeans Over a Barrel." *The Wall Street Journal*, 8 November 2002.

Guvrich, E. "Neftegazovaia Renta v Rossiiskoi Ekonomike." *Voprosy Ekonomiki* 11 (2010): 4–24.

Gusak, Leonid. "Kto 'krishuet' RosUkrEnergo." *2000*, no. 52/444, 26 December 2008. Available at http://news2000.org.ua/a/61114 (accessed 8 January 2009).

Gustafson, Thane. *Crisis Amid Plenty: The Politics of Soviet Energy under Brezhnev and Gorbachev*. Princeton, NJ: Princeton University Press, 1989.

———. *Wheel of Fortune: The Battle for Oil and Power in Russia*. Cambridge, MA: Belknap Press of Harvard University Press, 2012.

Haiduk, Vitalii. Interview with Iuliia Mostova in *Dzerkalo Tyzhnia*, no. 41/620, 28 October – 3 November 2006. Available at http://www.zn.kiev.ua/ie/show/620/54930/ (accessed 27 January 2007).

Hardt, John P. "Soviet Energy Policy in Eastern Europe." In *Soviet Policy in Eastern Europe*, ed. Sarah M. Terry. New Haven, CT: Yale University Press, 1984.

Havrylyshyn, Oleh. *Divergent Paths in Post-Communist Transformation*. Basingstoke, Hampshire: Palgrave Macmillan, 2006.

————. Participation in conference on "The Ukrainian-Russian Gas Crisis and its Fallout: Domestic and International Implications." Harvard University, 5–6 February 2006.

"Hazova uhoda Tymoshenko-Putina. Povnii tekst." *Ukrains'ka Pravda*, 22 January 2009. Available at http://www.pravda.com.ua/articles/4b1aa351db178/.

Heinrich, Andreas. "Under the Kremlin's Thumb: Does Increased State Control in the Russian Gas Sector Endanger European Energy Security?" *Europe-Asia Studies* 60, no. 9 (2008): 1539–74. http://dx.doi.org/10.1080/09668130802362292.

Hellman, Joel S. "Winners Take All: The Politics of Partial Reform in Postcommunist Transitions." *World Politics* 50, no. 2 (1998): 203–34. http://dx.doi.org/10.1017/S0043887100008091.

Hellman, Joel S., and Mark Schankerman. "Intervention, Corruption and Capture – The Nexus between Enterprises and the State." *Economics of Transition* 8, no. 3 (2000): 545–76. http://dx.doi.org/10.1111/1468-0351.00055.

Helmke, G., and S. Levitsky. "Informal Institutions and Comparative Politics: A Research Agenda." *Perspectives on Politics* 2, no. 4 (2004): 725–40. http://dx.doi.org/10.1017/S1537592704040472.

Heritage Foundation and Wall Street Journal. "2008 Index of Economic Freedom." Available at www.heritage.org/research/features/index/countries.cfm.

Hermitage Capital Managenent. "How Should Gazprom Be Managed in Russia's National Interests and the Interests of its Shareholders?" Moscow, June 2005. Cited in *Global Witness*: "It's a Gas – Funny Business in Turkmen-Ukraine Gas Trade" (April 2006). Available at http://www.globalwitness.org/sites/default/files/library/its_a_gas_april_2006_lowres.pdf (accessed 15 February 2013).

Herron, E. "State Institutions, Political Context and Parliamentary Election Legislation in Ukraine, 2000–2006." *Journal of Communist Studies and Transition Politics* 23, no. 1 (2007): 57–76. http://dx.doi.org/10.1080/13523270701194961.

Hewett, Ed. *Energy, Economics and Foreign Policy*. Washington, DC: Brookings, 1983.

Hirschhausen, Christian, and Anne Neumann. "Long-Term Contracts and Asset Specificity Revisited: An Empirical Analysis of Producer-Importer Relations in the Natural Gas Industry." *Review of Industrial Organization* 32, no. 2 (2008): 131–43. http://dx.doi.org/10.1007/s11151-008-9165-0.

Hirschman, Albert O. *State Power and the Structure of Foreign Trade*. Berkeley: University of California Press, 1980 (original work published 1945).

Hoff, Karla, and Joseph E. Stiglitz. "After the Big Bang? Obstacles to the Emergence of the Rule of Law in Post-communist Societies." *World Bank Policy Research Working Paper* no. 2934 (December 2002).

———. "The Creation of the Rule of Law and the Legitimacy of Property Rights: Political and Economic Consequences of a Corrupt Privatization." *NBER Working Paper* no. 11772 (November 2005).

Honchar, Mykhailo, ed. *Naftohazovyi sektor Ukrainy: prozorist' funktsionuvannia ta dokhodiv*. Kyiv: Anna-T, 2008.

Horn, Manfred. "Energy Demand Until 2010 in Ukraine." *Energy Policy* 27, no. 12 (1999): 713–26. http://dx.doi.org/10.1016/S0301-4215(99)00061-0.

Hryhoryshyn, Kostiantyn. Interview with Charles Clover: "Sharp Whiff on Corruption Threatens Ukraine Sell-off." *Financial Times*, 20 October 2000.

Huang, Mel. "Wannabe Oligarchs: Tycoons and Influence in the Baltic States." Conflict Studies Research Center, May 2002. Available at http://www.defac.ac.uk/colleges/csrc/document-listings/cee// (accessed 5 April 2007).

Humphreys, Macartan, Jeffrey D. Sachs, and Joseph E. Stiglitz, eds. *Escaping the Resource Curse*. New York: Columbia University Press, 2007.

Hutchcroft, Paul. "Booty Capitalism: Business-Government Relations in the Philippines." In *Business and Government in Industrializing Asia*, ed. Andrew McIntyre. Ithaca, NY: Cornell University Press, 1994.

Hyndle, Joanna, and Miryna Kutysz. "Lithuania, Latvia and Estonia's Aspirations to Integrate with NATO and the EU in the Context of These Countries' Relations with Russia." *OSW Studies*, January 2002. Available at http://osw.waw.pl/en/epub/eprace/04/02.htm (accessed 3 May 2007).

International Energy Agency. *Energeticheskaia Politika Rossii. Obzor 2002*. Paris: OECD/IEA, 2002.

International Energy Agency. *2007 Energy Balance for Ukraine*. Available at http://www.iea.org/stats/balancetable.asp?COUNTRY_CODE=UA (accessed 15 July 2010).

———. *Energy Policies Beyond IEA Countries: Ukraine Energy Policy Review 2012*. Paris: OECD/IEA, 2012.

———. *Energy Policies of the Russian Federation*. 1995 Survey. Paris: OECD/IEA, 1995.

———. *Energy Policies of Ukraine. 1996 Survey*. Paris: OECD/IEA, 1996.

————. *Energy Statistics of Non-OECD Countries.* Paris: OECD/IEA, various years.

————IEA. *Key World Energy Statistics.* Paris: IEA, various years. Available at http://www.iea.org.

————. *Oil Supply Security. The Emergency Response Potential of IEA Countries in 2000.* Paris: OECD/IEA, 2001.

————. *Optimizing Russian Natural Gas.* Paris: OECD/IEA, 2006.

————. *Russian Electricity Reform.* Paris: OECD/IEA, 2005.

————. *Russian Energy Survey 2002.* Paris: OECD/IEA, 2002.

————. *Ukraine Energy Policy Review 2006.* Paris: OECD/IEA, 2006.

International Monetary Fund. "Republic of Belarus: Selected Issues." In *Country Report,* no. 05/217, ed. Balázs Horváth, Veronica Bacalu, Milan Cuc, and Brenda González-Hermosillo. Washington, DC: International Monetary Fund, 2005.

————. "Rapid Growth in Belarus: Puzzle or Not?" June 2005. Available at http://www.imf.org/external/pubs/ft/scr/2005/cr05217.pdf.

Interfax. *Daily Financial Report,* 21 September 1999, FBIS-SOV-1999–0921.

International Atomic Energy Agency. *Energy Supply Options for Lithuania: A Detailed Multi-sector Integrated Energy Demand, Supply and Environmental Analysis.* Vienna: IAEA, 2004.

International Gas Report, no. 448, 26 April 2002.

Institut Privatizatsii i Menedzhmenta. *Ezhemesiachnii obzor ekonomiki Belarusi,* various issues. Available at http://www.research.by/analytics/bmer/.

————. *Monitoring Infrastrukturi Belarusi 2010.* Minsk: IPM , various years 2010. Available at http://www.research.by/analytics/bim/ (accessed 25 February 2013).

————. "Rost tsen na gas: novye vyzovy dlia belorusskoi ekonomiki." Minsk, 2007. Available at http://www.research.by/pdf/wp2007r03.pdf (accessed 3 October 2009).

Ishiyama, John T., and Ryan Kennedy. "Superpresidentialism and Political Party Development in Russia, Ukraine, Armenia and Kyrgyzstan." *Europe-Asia Studies* 53, no. 8 (2001): 1177–91. http://dx.doi.org/10.1080/09668130120093183.

"Iskliuchenie iz pravila – Belarus." *Belgazeta,* no. 14/482, 11 April 2005.

"Istochnik rosta i zavisimosti." *Belorusskii Rynok,* no. 12/647, 28 March 2005.

"Itera Weighs in ahead of Lithuanian Gas Privatization." *The Baltic Times,* 13 September 2001 (via ISI, accessed 22 March 2007).

Janeliunas, Tomas. "Energy Security of Lithuania and the Impact of the Nord Stream Project." Power-point presentation. Available at http://www.tspmi.

vu.lt/files/mokslkonfer/janeliunas_energy%20security%20of%20lithuania%
20and%20impact%20of%20nord%20stream%20project.ppt (accessed 16 May
2009).

———. "Energy Security of Lithuania: Challenges and Perspectives." *Lithuanian Political Science Yearbook 2005*, ed. Algimantas Jankauskas. Vilnius,
2007.

———. "Lithuania's Energy Straregy and Its Implications on Regional Cooperation." In *Energy: Pulling the Baltic Region Together or Apart?* ed. Andris
Spruds and Toms Rostoks, 190–222. Riga: Zinatne, 2009.

Janeliunas, Tomas, and Arunas Molis. "Energy Security of Lithuania: Challenges and Perspectives." *Research Journal of International Studies* 5 (May
2006): 10–34.

Johnston, M. "The Political Consequences of Corruption – A Reassessment." *Comparative Politics* 18, no. 4 (1986): 459–77. http://dx.doi.
org/10.2307/421694.

Juknys, Romualdas, Vaclovas Miškinis, and Renata Dagiliute. "New Eastern
EU Member States: Decoupling of Environmental Impact from Fast Economy Growth." *Environmental Research, Engineering and Management* 2005, no.
4/34: 68–76.

Kalinkina, Svetlana. In *RFE/RL* (Radio Svobody) program for Belarus, *Ekzpertiza Svobody* ("Povinen zastat'sia albo Sheiman albo Viktar Lukahshenka"),
12 September 2007. Transcript available at http://www.svaboda.org/con-
tent/Transcript/761925.html (accessed 3 July 2008).

Kalinovskaia, Tat'iana. "Dlia latanie dyr." *Belorusy i Rynok*, no. 49/784,
24 December 2007. Available at http://www.belmarket.by/index.
php?article=31775&year=2007 (accessed 15 February 2008).

Kang, D.C. "Transaction Costs and Crony Capitalism in East Asia." *Comparative Politics* 35, no. 4 (2003): 439–58. http://dx.doi.org/10.2307/4150189.

Karbalevich, Valerii. "Belorusskie Novosti." January 2008. Cited in Aleksandr
Mishin. "Luchshe v Venezuele." *Ezhednevnik*, 18 January 2008.

———. "Miagkaia adaptatsiia." *Svobodnye Novosti Plus*, 9 January 2008.

Karbalevich, Valer (Valerii Karbalevich). In RFE/RL (Radio Svobody) program
for Belarus, *Pratskii Akzent* ("Iakiia prychyny ekanamichnaga rostu?"), 29
November 2006. Transcript available at http://www.svaboda.org/
content/Transcript/777228.html.

Karp, Ihor. "Problems of Ukraine's Energy Sector and Ways of their
Resolution." *National Security and Defense*, no. 2 (2001).

"Key Ukrainian Refinery Announces Oil Supply Agreement with Azerbaijan's
SOCAR." *HIS Global Insight*, 9 October 2010. Available at www.ihsglobal
insight.com/SDA/SDADetail17731.htm (accessed 15 July 2010).

Khalip, Irina. "Lukashenko prigrozil Rossii razryvom otnoshenii." *Novaia Gazeta*, no. 75, 2 October 2006. Available at http://www.novayagazeta.ru/data/2006/75/09.html.

Khmurych, V., and T. Tkachenko. "Opportunities for Corruption in the Ukrainian Gas Market." Eurasia Foundation (1999). Available at www. eurasia. org/programs/eerc/Kyiv/papers/khtk.htm www.eurasia.org/programs/eerc/ (accessed 1 May 2004).

"Khot' shersti klok." *Vedomosti*, no. 228, 12 October 2001 (via ISI, accessed 19 March 2007).

"Khto stane nastupnym holovoiu 'Naftohazu Ukrainy'?" *Ukrains'ka Pravda*, 17 May 2006. Available at http://www.pravda.com.ua/news/2006/5/17/41816.htm (accessed 26 May 2006).

Kingstone, Peter R. "Privatizing Telebrás: Brazilian Political Institutions and Policy Performance." *Comparative Politics* 36, no. 1 (2003): 21–40. http://dx.doi.org/10.2307/4150158.

Kirshner, Jonathan. "The Political Economy of Realism." In *Unipolar Politics: Realism and State Strategies after the Cold War*, ed. Ethan B. Kapstein and Michael Mastanduno. New York: Columbia University Press, 1999.

Klapp, Merrie Gilbert. *The Sovereign Entrepreneur: Oil Policies in Advanced and Less Developed Capitalist Countries*. Ithaca, NY: Cornell University Press, 1987.

Klepšys, Tomas. "Background Paper on Rolandas Paksas: Impeachment and Russian Energy Companies." Unpublished paper, 2 July 2007.

Klishevich, Tikhon. "Istoriia bor'ba za 'Beltransgas'," 29 November 2006. Available at www.dw-world.de (accessed 5 August 2007).

Kniazhanskii , Vitalii. "Comrade Reverse." *The Day* (Kyiv), 16 March 2004. Originally published in Ukrainian in *Den'*, 12 March 2004.

———. "Truba bez nefti." *Den'* (Russian-language edition), 30 June 2004.

———. "Rasshifrovka signala." *Den'* (Russian-language edition), 14 July 2004.

Koktysh, Kirill. Interview in *Nashe Mnenie*, 13 November 2006. Available at http://www.nmnby.org/pub/0612/13d.html (accessed 10 August 2007).

Konoplyanik, Andrei. "Russia-Ukraine Gas Trade: From Political to Market-Based Pricing and Prices." Presentation at the conference "Reassessing Post-Soviet Energy Politics: Ukraine, Russia, and the Battle for Gas, from Central Asia to the European Union." Harvard University, 7–8 March 2008. Streaming video available at http://www.youtube.com/watch?v=U8ngolw-f74 (accessed 24 February 2013).

"Konservatori podgotovili proekt strategii sderzhivaniia Rossii." *ELTA*, 9 May 2007 (via ISI, accessed 10 May 2007).

"Kontrakt pro tranzyt rosiiskoho hazu + dodatkova uhoda pro avans 'Gaz-promu'," *Ukrains'ka Pravda*, 22 January 2006. Available at http://www.pravda.com.ua/articles/4b1aa355cac8c/ (accessed 10 July 2010).

Kontseptsiia natsional'noi bezopasnosti Respubliki Belarus'. Minsk, 2001. Available at http://www.mod.mil.by/koncep.html (accessed 10 November 2008).

Koremchin, Mikhail. Quoted in Svetlana Dolinchuk. "Potrebnost' v posredni-kakh otpala." *Ekonomicheskie Izvestiia*, 12 March 2008. In FEC-MUP, March 12, 2008 (via ISI).

Kostiugova, Valeriia. "Perspektivy uchastiia Belarusi v ekspluatatsii neft-eprovoda Odessa-Brody." *Belarusian Institute for Strategic Studies*, BISS SA 4/2008-EG (2008). Available at http://www.belinstitute.eu/images/stories/documents/odessabrody.pdf (accessed 24 October 2008).

Kostrub, Larisa. "Prezident ne budet vetirovat' Zakon o prirodnom gaze." *ELTA Lithuanian Newswire*, 13 April 2007 (via ISI, accessed 17 April 2007).

Kotkin, Stephen. *Armaggedon Averted*. New York: Oxford University Press, 2001.

Koverovas, Paulius. "Renewable Energy in Lithuania." 2008. Available at www.laiea.lt/users/userfiless/file/Presentation_renew.

Kramer, Andrew. "Gazprom Caught in a Trap of its Own." *International Herald Tribune*, 15 May 2009.

———. "Lithuanians Are Given a Taste of How Russia Plays the Oil Game." *The New York Times*, 28 October 2006.

Kramer, John M. *The Energy Gap in Eastern Europe*. Lexington, MA: Lexington Books, 1990.

Krasner, Stephen. "State Power and the Structure of International Trade" and "Oil is the Exception." In *International Political Economy: Perspectives on Global Power and Wealth*, ed. Jeffry A. Frieden and David A. Lake. New York: Bedford/St. Martin's Press, 2000. http://dx.doi.org/10.2307/2009974.

Krasnov, Gregory V., and Josef C. Brada. "Implicit Subsidies in Russian-Ukrainian Energy Trade." *Europe-Asia Studies* 49, no. 5 (1997): 825–43. http://dx.doi.org/10.1080/09668139708412475.

Krueger, Anne. "The Political Economy of Rent-Seeking Society." *American Economic Review* 64, no. 3 (1974): 291–303.

Krugleevskii, Aleksandr. "Febral'. Dostat' chernila i . . ." *Ezhednevnik*, no. 376, 17 March 2008.

Kryukov, Valeriy, and Arild Moe. "Russia's Oil Industry: Risk Aversion in a Risk-Prone Environment." *Eurasian Geography and Economics* 48, no. 3 (2007): 341–57. http://dx.doi.org/10.2747/1538-7216.48.3.341.

Kubicek, Paul. *Unbroken Ties: The State, Interest Associations and Corporatism in Post-Soviet Ukraine*. Ann Arbor: University of Michigan Press, 2000.

"Kuda postavit' pristavku 'ėks'." *NefteRynok*, 25 December 2000 (via ISI).

Kuodis, Raimondas. Cited in *TBT Staff*, "Report: State to Take 60 Percent in Merged Utility." *The Baltic News*, 18 April 2007 (via ISI, accessed 9 May 2007).

Kuolis, Darius. "Moving towards Putin-Style Governance." *Verslo Zinios*, 6 April 2007. Translated in "Lithuania Moving Towards 'Putin-Style Governance' – Pundit." *BBC Monitoring*, 6 April 2007 (via ISI, accessed 6 April 2007).

Kupchinsky, Roman. "Naftohaz Ukrainy: A Study in State-Sponsored Corruption" (Parts I and II). *Radio Liberty/Radio Free Europe Corruption Watch* 3, no. 25. Available at www.rferl.org/corruptionwatch/archives.asp and www.uanews.tv/archives/rferl/cct/cct037.htm (accessed 25 August 2003).

———. "The Unexpected Guest: RosUkrEnergo." Paper presented at the conference on "The Ukrainian-Russian Gas Crisis and Its Fallout: Domestic and International Implications." Harvard University, 5–6 February 2006. Available at http://www.huri.harvard.edu/events/event-archive/102-gas-crisis-conference-2006.html (accessed 23 February 2013).

Kutas, Saulius, and Jurgis Vilemas. "Legacy of the Past and Future Energy Policy in Lithuania." Paper prepared for the World Energy Council, 2005. Available at http://www.worldenergy.org/wec-geis/publications/default/tech_papers/17th_congress/1_4_31.asp?mode=print&x=59&y=5 (accessed 20 February 2007).

Kuzio, Taras. *Ukraine: Perestroika to Independence*. London: Macmillan, 2000.

Kuzio, Taras, and Andrew Wilson. *Ukraine: Perestroika to Independence*. London: Macmillan, 1997.

Landsbergis, Vytautas. *LUKoil prieš Williams*. Vilnius: Tėvynės Sąjunga, 2004.

Lane, David, ed. *The Political Economy of Russian Oil*. Oxford: Rowman and Littlefield, 1999.

Lane, Thomas. *Lithuania: Stepping Westward*. London: Routledge, 2001. http://dx.doi.org/10.4324/9780203402740.

Laukaitytė, Rasa. "Lietuva už dujas jau moka brangiau nei „Gazprom" žada parduoti Europai." 2 October 2008. Available at http://www.delfi.lt/news/economy/energetics/article.php?id=18742907 (accessed 15 December 2008).

Lavigne, Marie. *International Political Economy and Socialism*. Cambridge: Cambridge University Press, 1991.

Levin, Konstantin. "Viakhireva rezhut po polam." *Kommersant-Den'gi*, no. 4, January 2000.

Levitsky, S., and L.A. Way. "The Rise of Competitive Authoritarianism." *Journal of Democracy* 13, no. 2 (2002): 51–65. http://dx.doi.org/10.1353/jod.2002.0026.

Liakhovich, Andrei. "Palitichnii kantekst napiaredadni vybarou i referendum." In *Nainoushaia gistoria belaruskaga parlamentaryzmu*. Minsk: Analitichnii Grudok, 2005. Available at http://kamunikat.fontel.net/www/knizki/palityka/parlamentaryzm/index.htm (accessed 20 June 2008).

"Lietuvos Dujos." *The Baltic Region*, 7 October 2008. Available at http://www.swedbank.lt/lt/previews/get/495/rss (accessed 13 May 2009).

Lietuvos Energetika 2007. Available at http://www.lei.lt/_img/_up/File/atvir/leidiniai/Lietuvos_energetika-2007.pdf.

Lietuvos Rytas. Internet version, 13 November 2006, 0413 GMT. Translated by *BBC Monitoring*, 13 November 2006 (via ISI, accessed 15 March 2006).

Lilly, Ian. "Geopolitics and Economic Fragility." Paper presented at the *New Zealand European Union Centres Network Conference*, Auckland, 9–10 November 2006. Available at http://www.eucnetwork.org.nz/activities/conference/conference_auckland_06/docs/ililly.pdf (accessed 3 February 2007).

Linden, Corina Herron. *Power and Uneven Globalization: Coalitions and Energy Trade Dependence in the Newly Independent States of Europe*. Ph.D. dissertation, Political Science, University of Washington, 2000.

Lithuanian Energy Institute. *National Energy Strategy*. Kaunas, Lithuania: Lithuanian Energy Institute, 2003.

"Lithuanian President Interviewed on Russia Ties, Economy, Energy." *BBC Monitoring*, 1 January 2010 (via ISI, accessed 30 June 2010).

"Lithuania's Dujotekana Gas Importer Posts 46 Pct Drop in Fy Profit." *BNS Daily Busines News*, 9 February 2006 (via ISI, accessed 15 March 2007).

"Litva budet davit' na Rossiiu v meste s ES." *Litovskii Kurier*, no. 11/629, March 2007.

"Litva obnaruzhila energeticheskuiu ugrozu s Vostoka." *Biznes i Baltiia*, 22 April 2005 (via ISI, accessed 15 March 2007).

Liuta, Ganna. "Kazhdoi vetvi vlasti – po gazotreideru." *Zerkalo Nedeli*, no. 48/218, 5–11 December 1998.

Liven´, Oksana. "Kreditnaia dobycha." *Energobiznes*, 19 September 2005.

LNK. "News." 26 November 2003. Republished in Tv.lt. Available at http://new.tv.lt/mconsole.asp?id=01DB6DEB-0AA0-48B3-8181-23A69FFFC376','T VMConsole','width=641,height=512 (accessed 17 June 2007).

LNK and Baltic News Service. "R. Paksą rėmė Rusijos energetikos kompanijos?" *Delfi.lt*, 26 November 2003. Available at http://www.delfi.lt/archive/article.php?id=3241569 (accessed 17 June 2007).

Lo, Shiu-hing. "Bureaucratic Corruption and its Control in Macao." *Asian Journal of Public Administration* 15, no. 1 (1993): 32–58.

Locatelli, Catherine. "The Russian Oil Industry between Public and Private Governance: Obstacles to International Oil Companies' Investment Strategies." *Energy Policy* 34, no. 9 (2006): 1075–85.

Lopata, Raimondas, and Audrius Matonis. *Prezidento suktukas.* Vilnius: Versus Aureus, 2004.

Lucas, Edward. *A New Cold War: Putin's Russia and the Threat to the West.* London: Palgrave Macmillan, 2008.

Luong, Pauline Jones, and Erika Weinthal. "Prelude to the Resource Curse: Explaining Oil and Gas Development Strategies in the Soviet Successor States and Beyond." *Comparative Political Studies* 34, no. 4 (2001): 367–99. http://dx.doi.org/10.1177/0010414001034004002.

———. "Rethinking the Resource Curse: Ownership Structure, Institutional Capacity, and Domestic Constraints." *Annual Review of Political Science* 9, no. 1 (2006): 241–63. http://dx.doi.org/10.1146/annurev.polisci.9.062404.170436.

Mahdavy, Hossein. "The Pattern and Problems of Economic Development in Rentier States: The Case of Iran." In *Studies in the Economic History of the Middle East,* ed. M. A. Cook, 428–67. Oxford: Oxford University Press, 1970.

Mainwaring, Scott. *Rethinking Party Systems in the Third Wave of Democratization.* Stanford, CA: Stanford University Press, 1999.

Manenok, Tatiana. "Belarusi balans nuzhnee, chem Rossii." *Belorusy i Rynok,* no. 3/1036, 21 January 2013.

———. "Benzinovyi signal." *Belorusy i Rynok,* no. 43/678, 8 November 2005.

———. "Bezopasnost' v range prioriteta." *Belorusy i Rynok,* no. 34/769, 10 September 2007.

———. Comments in *RFE/RL* (Radio Svabody) program for Belarus, *Ekzpertiza Svobodi* ("Kryzys z pastaukami raseiskaga gazu u Belarus"), 4 November 2002. Transcript available at http://archive.svaboda.org/programs/bel-rus/2002/11/20021104175816.asp (accessed 25 April 2008).

———. "Deshevogo gaza nuzhno vse bol'she." *Belorusskii Rynok,* no. 51/635, 27 December 2004. Available at http://www.br.minsk.by/index.php?article=23797 (accessed 7 February 2009).

———. "Druzhbu ne pochiniat." *Belorusy i Rynok,* no. 46/781, 3 December 2007. Available at http://www.belmarket.by/index.php?article=31605&year=2007 (accessed 24 April 2008).

———. "Energobezopasnost' poka nedostizhima." *Belorusy i Rynok,* no. 34/669, 5 September 2005.

———. "Izbiraatel'nyi dokhod." *Belorusy i Rynok,* no. 4/788, 28 January 2008. Available at http://www.belmarket.by/index.php?article=31998 (accessed 5 May 2008).

————. "Kto ostalsia na trube." *Belorusy i Rynok*, no. 36/671, 19 September 2005.

————. "Mificheskii dolg." *Belorusskii Rynok*, no. 15/650, 18 April 2005.

————. "Nestabil'naia neftianka." *Belorusy i Rynok*, no. 30/765, 13 August 2007. Available at http://www.br.minsk.by/index.php?article=30803 (accessed 29 August 2007).

————. "Nevygodnyi eksport." *Belorusy i Rynok*, no. 8/743, 26 February 2007. Available at http://www.br.minsk.by/index.php?article=29634&year=2007 (accessed 15 May 2007).

————. "Obstoiatel'stva prizhali." *Belorusy i Rynok*, no. 36/820, 8 September 2008.

———— "Podarok s raschetom." *Belorusskii Rynok*, no. 15/650, 18 April 2005.

————. "Podstegnet neftianoi stimul." *Belorusy i Rynok*, no. 20/804. 19 May 2008. Available at http://www.br.minsk.by/index.php?article=32808 (accessed 15 June 2008).

————. "Politicheskii barter." *Belorusskii Rynok*, no. 20/655, 23 May 2005.

————. "Po shchadiashchei stavki." *Belorusy i Rynok*, no. 3/787, 21 January 2008.

————. "Poslednii argument." *Belorusskii Rynok*, no. 7/591, 23 February 2004.

————. "Potoki s politicheskoi logistikoi." *Belorusy i Rynok*, no. 15/799, 14 April 2008. Available at http://www.br.minsk.by/index.php?article=32589 (accessed 16 June 2008).

————. "Spor ischerpan." *Belorusskii Rynok*, no. 42/626, 25 October 2004.

————. "Starye problemy dlia novogo pravitel'stvo." *Belorusy i Rynok*, no. 12/796, 24 March 2008.

————. "Tol'ko po rinochnoi stoimosti." *Belorusy i Rynok*, no. 5/690, 6 February 2006.

————. "Torg za l'goty." *Belorusy i Rynok*, no. 4/890, 25 January 2010. Available at http://belmarket.by/ru/62/65/4780 (accessed 28 January 2010).

————. "Valiutnaia blagodat'." *Belorusy i Rynok*, no. 13/197, 31 March 2008. Available at http://www.belmarket.by/index.php?article=32499.

————. "Valiutnye donory slabeiut." *Nashe Mnenie*, 27 November 2008. Available at http://www.nmnby.org/pub/0811/27j.html (accessed 11 December 2008).

————. "Valiutnyi ruchei." *Belorusy i Rynok*, no. 1/785, 8 January 2008. Available at http://www.belmarket.by/index.php?article=31801 (accessed 5 May 2008).

————. "Vtoraia otlkliuchka.' *Belorusskii Rynok*, no. 6/590, 16 February 2004. Available at http://www.br.minsk.by/index.php?article=20999&year=2004 (accessed 15 March 2008).

———. "Zolotaia Aktsia vvedena v chastnom predpriiatie." *Belorusskii Rynok*, no. 19/654, 16 May 2005.

Markandya, Anil, Suzette Pedroso, and Dalia Streimikiene. "Energy Efficiency in Transition Economies: Is There Convergence Towards the EU Average?" *FEEM Working Paper*, no. 89 (2004). Available at http://ssrn.com/abstract=556237 (accessed 12 July 2007).

Markeviciene, Egle. "No Electricity and No Natural Gas for Making Electricity." *Verslo Zinios*, 5 January 2007. Translated in "Analysis Predicts Lithuania, Region to Experience Electricity Shortage in 2010." *BBC Monitoring*, 5 January 2007 (via ISI, accessed 15 March 2007).

Marples, D.R. "The Energy Dilemma of Belarus: The Nuclear Power Option." *Eurasian Geography and Economics* 49, no. 2 (2008): 215–27. http://dx.doi.org/10.2747/1539-7216.49.2.215.

Marples, David. "Lukashenka Removes KGB Chief." *Eurasia Daily Monitor* 4, no. 140, 19 July 2007. Available at http://www.jamestown.org/edm/article.php?article_id=2372302 (accessed 9 August 2007).

———. "Surge in Nuclear Power Projects Imperils Belarusian Program." *Eurasia Daily Monitor* 7, no. 150, 4 August 2010.

Marples, David R., and Uladzimir Padhol. "The Opposition in Belarus: History, Potential and Perspectives." In *Independent Belarus: Domestic Determinants, Regional Dynamics and Implications for the West*, eds. Margarita M. Balmaceda, James Clem, and Lisbeth Tarlow, 55–76. Cambridge, MA: HURI/Davis Center for Russian Studies, distributed by Harvard University Press, 2002.

Marrese, Michael. "CMEA: Effective but Cumbersome Political Economy." *International Organization* 40, no. 2 (1986): 287–327.

Martinovich, Viktor. "Aleksandr Fadeev: Ne budet nikakogo akta." *Belgazeta*, no. 24/492, 20 June 2005.

Matlary, Haaland Janne. *Energy Policies in the European Union*. New York: St. Martin's Press, 1997.

Matsuzato, Kimitaka. "From Communist Boss Politics to Post-Communist Caciquismo – The Meso-Elite and Meso-Governments in Post-Communist Countries." *Communist and Post-Communist Studies* 34, no. 2 (2001): 175–201. http://dx.doi.org/10.1016/S0967-067X(01)00007-1.

Matsuzatu, Kimitaka, and Liutaras Gudžinskas. "An Eternally Unfinished Parliamentary Regime: Semi-presidentialism as a Prism to View Lithuanian Politics." *Acta Slavica Iaponica*, 23 (2006): 146–70.

Matyas, Aleksandr. "Analiz osobennostei, faktorov i istochnikov ekonomicheskogo rosta v Respublike Belarus." Published in *Nashe Mnenie* (2005). Available at nmnorg.by (Accessed 13 June 2008).

Mazeikiu Nafta. Available at http://www.nafta.lt (accessed 9 May 2009).

Mazneva, Elena. "Pomogla pogoda. Pochemu Putin zashchitil 'Gazprom' ot rosta NDPI." *Vedomosti*, 11 July 2007.

Mazurkevich, Marina. "Drova, torf, veter i solntse." 4 February 2007. Available at http://www.dw-world.de/dw/article/0,2144,2337240,00.html (accessed 10 March 2007).

McGillivray, Fiona. *Privileging Industry: The Comparative Politics of Trade and Industrial Policy*. Princeton, NJ: Princeton University Press, 2004.

Metaly Ukrainy. Available at http://www.business.dp.ua/me/data/0801.htm (accessed 15 June 2006).

Miksha, Olga. "Atomnyi Triumvirat." *Belgazeta*, 13 March 2006. Available at http://www.belgazeta.by/20060313.10/040121511 (accessed 10 November 2006).

———. "Snova v obkhod Belarusi." *Belorusskii Rynok*, no. 23/440, 14 June 2004.

Milner, Helen. *Resisting Protectionism: Global Industries and the Politics of International Trade*. Princeton, NJ: Princeton University Press, 1988.

Milov, Vladimir. *Russia and the West: The Energy Factor*. Washington, DC: CSIS, 2008.

———. "Russian Energy Policy in a Broader Context." Presentation at the American Enterprise Institute, Washington, DC, 16 March 2006. Available at http://www.energypolicy.ru/files/March16-2006.ppt (accessed 25 June 2006).

Milov, Vladimir, Leonard L. Coburn, and Igor Danchenko. "Russia's Energy Policy, 1992–2005." *Eurasian Geography and Economics* 47, no. 3 (2006).

Milov, Vladimir, and Boris Nemtsov. *Ekspertnyi doklad. Putin i Gazrom*. Moscow: Novaia Gazeta, 2008.

Ministry of Energy and Coal Industry of Ukraine. "Statistichnaia informatsiia." Available at http://mpe.kmu.gov.ua/fuel/control/uk/publish/article?art_id=231058&cat_id=35081 (accessed 18 February 2013).

Miškinis, Vaclovas, Jurgis Vilemas, and Inga Konstantinavičiūtė. "Analysis of Energy Consumption and Energy Intensity Indicators in Central and Eastern European Countries." *Energy Studies Review* 14, no. 2 (2006): 171–88.

Mitrova, Tatiana. "Natural Gas in Transition: Systemic Reform Issues." In *Russian and CIS Gas Markets and their Impact on Europe*, ed. Simon Pirani. Oxford: Oxford University Press for the Oxford Energy Institute, 2009.

Molchanov, Mikhail A. *Political Culture and National Identity in Russian-Ukrainian Relations*. College Station, TX: Texas A&M University Press, 2002.

Molochkova, Galina. "Zapakhlo gazom. Tseni na gaz v Latvii mogut vyrasti." *Biznes i Baltiia*, 14 June 2000 (via EVUD CISBP, accessed 21 March 2007).

Montias, J.M. "Background and Origins of the Rumanian Dispute with COM-ECON." *Soviet Studies* 16, no. 2 (1964): 125–51.

Moroney, Jennifer D.P., Taras Kuzio, and Michail Molchanov, eds. *Ukrainian Foreign and Security Policy: Theoretical and Comparative Perspectives.* Westport, CT: Praeger, 2002.

Moroz, Oleksandr. Quoted in *Gaz i neft'. Energeticheskii biulleten'*, 13 February 2002 (via ISI).

Mostovaia, Iuliia. "Eto po-vashemu- Van Gog, a po-nashemu- Gogen." *Zerkalo Nedeli*, no. 3/582, 28 January – 3 February 2006.

———. "Hazova Firtashka." *Dzerkalo Tyzhnia*, no. 17/596, 29 April – 12 May 2006. Available at www.zn.kiev.ua/ie/show/596/53328/ (accessed 15 May 2006).

———. "Osada Zamknutogo kruga." *Zerkalo Nedeli*, no. 19/598, 20–26 May 2006. Available at www.zerkalo-nedeli.com/ie/show/598/53426/ (accessed 1 June 2006).

———. "Protivogaz – odin na vsekh . . ." *Zerkalo Nedeli*, no. 49/577, 17–23 December 2005.

Murillo, Victoria. *Political Competition, Partisanship and Policy Making in Latin American Public Utilities.* Cambridge: Cambridge University Press, 2009.

"Naftohaz khochet podelit' gazovoe nasledstvo Ukrhaz-energo." *Gaz i Neft'. Analiticheskii biulleten'.* Cited in translation as *Infobank Oil & Gas Monitor*, 25 September 2008 (via ISI).

Naftohaz, N.A.K. Available at www.naftogas.ua (accessed 15 March 2008).

"Nakanune vstupleniia Baltii v ES obostriaetsia bor'ba za kontrol' nad gazovym khoziaistvom regiona." Available at http://www.rosinvest.com/dir/analysis/74/84/ (original source, no date provided, presumably 2003) (accessed 14 March 2007).

National Agency for Energy Regulation (ANRE). Available at www.anre.md (accessed 15 July 2010).

National Energy Strategy of Lithuania, 2007. Vilnius, 2007.

National Security Strategy of Lithuania. Approved by the Parliament of the Republic of Lithuania, 28 May 2002. Available at www.kam.lt (accessed 30 July 2007). 2005 update available at http://www3.lrs.lt/pls/inter3/dokpaieska.showdoc_l?p_id=262943.

National Control Commission for Prices and Energy (Lithuania). "Annual Report on Electricity and Natural Gas Markets in Lithuania Prepared for the European Commission." 2006. Available at http://www.regula.lt (accessed 21 May 2009).

———. "Annual Report on Electricity and Natural Gas Markets in Lithuania Prepared for the European Commission." 2008. Available at www.Energy-Regulators.eu (accessed 21 May 2009).

———. "Annual Report to The European Commission. Summary." 2004. Available at http://www.regula.lt (accessed 21 May 2007).

———. "Summary of the Annual Report to The European Commission, 2005." 2005. Available at http://www.regula.lt (accessed 21 May 2007).

Neftegazovaia Vertikal 12, 2005.

NefteRynok, 8 July 2001 (via ISI).

NefteRynok, 2 April 2002 (via ISI).

North, Douglass C. "A Transaction Cost Theory of Politics." *Journal of Theoretical Politics* 2, no. 4 (1990): 355–67. http://dx.doi.org/10.1177/095169289000 2004001.

———. "Government and the Cost of Exchange in History." *Journal of Economic History* 44, no. 2 (1984): 255–64. http://dx.doi.org/10.1017/S0022050700031855.

Novolodskaia, Svetlana. "'Itere' zakryli zadvizhku." *Vedomosti*, 6 November 2002 (via ISI).

Novozhilova, Elena. "Fradkov podtalkivaet ekonomicheskie reformy v Belarusi?." *Narodnaia Volia*, no. 103–4, 29 June 2007. Available at http://naviny.by/rubrics/economic/2007/06/20/ic_articles_113_151527/ (accessed 15 June 2008).

Novozhilova, Elena, and Vadim Sekhovich. "Gazavat' po-gazpromovskii." *Belorusskaia Delovaia Gazeta*, 6 November 2002.

Nygren, Bertil. "Putin's use of Natural Gas to Reintegrate the CIS Region." *Problems of Post-Communism* 55, no. 4 (2008): 3–15. http://dx.doi.org/10.2753/PPC1075-8216550401.

Olarchyk, Roman. "Ukraine Premier Fails to Oust Gas Group." *Financial Times*, 11 April 2008.

Olson, Mancur. *Power and Prosperity*. New York: Basic Books, 2000.

Omonbude, Ekpen J. "The Transit Oil and Gas Pipeline and the Role of Bargaining: A Non-Technical Discussion." *Energy Policy* 35, no. 12 (2007): 6188–94. http://dx.doi.org/10.1016/j.enpol.2007.06.001.

Opitz, Petra, and Christian von Hirschhausen. "Ukraine as a Gas Bridge to Europe." Working Paper No. 3. Institute for Economic Research and Policy Consulting, October 2000.

Orban, Anita. *Power, Energy and the New Russian Imperialism*. Westport, CT: Praeger, 2008.

Panchenko, Sergei. "Podkovernye shagi ili bor'ba s korruptsiei." 30 May 2007. Available at http://www.dw-world.de/dw/article/0,2144,2569596,00.html (accessed 8 August 2007).

Paniushin, V., and M. Zygar. *Gazprom: Novoe russkoe oruzhie.* Moscow: Zakharov, 2008.

Pappe, Yakov. *Oligarkhi.* Moskow: Vysshaia Shkola Ekonomiki, 2000.

———. "Otraslevye lobby v pravitel'stve Rossii (1992–1996)." *Pro et Contra* (Fall 1996): 61–78.

Pavel, Ferdinand, and Anna Chukhai. *Gas Storage Tariffs Along the Route to EU Market.* Kyiv: IER, 2006. Available at http://www.ier.kiev.ua (accessed 24 February 2009).

Pavel, F., and E. Rakova. *Improving Energy Efficiency in the Belarusian Economy – An Economic Agenda.* Minsk: GET Policy Paper, 2005.

Pavel, Ferdinand, and Inna Yuzefovych. "How to Deal with 'European Prices' in Ukraine." *GAG/IERPC Policy Paper Series* PP/06 (October 2008). Available at www.kiev.ier.ua (accessed 15 November 2009).

Pavilionis, Žygimantas. "Lithuanian Position Regarding the EU Mandate on Negotiations with Russia: Seeking a New Quality of EU-Russian Relations." *Lithuanian Foreign Policy Review,* no. 21 (2008): 174–81.

Pavuk, Olga, Damuskas Zhidrunas, and Tat'ana Merkulova. "Diktatura chernogo zolota," *Baltiiskii Kurs,* no. 4/17 (2000), available at http://www.balt-kurs.com/russian/arhiv/17/03politekonomija.htm, (accessed 20.3.2007).

Petraitis, Antanas. "Dolgaia doroga k khramu." Available at www.sedmitza.ru/index.html?sid=470&did=18023 (accessed 3 May 2007).

Petrov, Igor. "Sozdanie strategicheskikh zapasov nefteproduktov ne provalilo, a vsego lish' otsrochilo na god." *Delovaia Stolitsa,* no. 47, 22 November 2004.

Pilloni, John R. "The Belarusian-Russian Joint Defense Agreement." *Journal of Slavic Military Studies* 22, no. 4 (October 2009): 543–48. http://dx.doi.org/10.1080/13518040903355778.

Pirani, Simon. "Ukraine: A Gas Dependent State." In *Russian and CIS Gas Markets and Their Impact on Europe,* ed. Simon Pirani. Oxford: Oxford University Press for the Oxford Institute for Energy Studies, 2009.

"PKN Orlen Fed up with Lithuanian Partners." *News2biz Energy and Environment,* no. 170, February 2010.

Pleines, Heiko. "The Political Economy of Coal Industry Restructuring in Ukraine." *KICES Working Papers* 1 (2004).

Polach, J.G. "The Develpoment of Energy in East Europe." In *Economic Development in Countries of Eastern Europe,* ed. John P. Hardt. Washington, DC: US Government Printing Office, 1970.

Polterovich, Viktor M. "Institutional Traps." In *The New Russia,* ed. Lawrence R. Klein and Marshall I. Pomer. Stanford, CA: Stanford University Press, 2000.

Polokhalo, Volodymyr. *The Political Analysis of Post-Communism.* Kyiv, 1995.

Pontis Foundation. "The Regime Change(s): Survey of Current Trends and Development in Belarus. Summer 2007." Available at http://www.

nadaciapontis.sk/tmp/asset_cache/link/0000017223/Pontis%20Survey%20
The%20Regime%20Change(s).pdf.
Postanovlenie Soveta Ministrov Respubliki Belarus' No. 1680, December 2004.
Available at http://pravo.by/webnpa/text_txt.asp?RN=c20401680 (accessed 9 November 2008).
Praneviciute, Jovita. "Security and Identity in Belarus: How Securitization of National Identity Defines Foreign Influence." Paper presented at the 2008 Convention of the Association for the Study of Nationalities, Columbia University, New York, 10–12 April 2008.
"Privatization Becoming Energized." *The Baltic Times*, 26 January 2000 (via ISI, accessed 15 March 2007).
Protsyk, Oleh. "Troubled Semi-Presidentialism: Stability of the Constitutional System and Cabinet in Ukraine." *Europe-Asia Studies* 55, no. 7 (2003): 1077–95. http://dx.doi.org/10.1080/0966813032000130693.
Przeworski, Adam, Susan Stokes, and Bernard Manin, eds. *Democracy, Accountability and Representation*. Cambridge: Cambridge University Press, 1999. http://dx.doi.org/10.1017/CBO9781139175104.
"Q&A." *Financial Times*, 9 January 2009.
Racas, Arturas. Interview in "Facing Media Corruption in Lithuania." *The Baltic Times*, 13 June 2007. Available at http://www.baltictimes.com/news/articles/18062/ (accessed 30 July 2007).
Radio Free Europe/Radio Liberty (RFE/RL) Newsline 3, no. 86, Part II, 4 May 1999. Available at http://www.rferl.org/archive/en-newsline/latest/683/683.html (accessed 28 May 2009).
Rakova, Elena. "Energeticheskii sektor Belarusi: povyshaia effektivnost'." Working Paper, 10/04, Institut Privatizatsii i Menedzmenta, Minsk, 2010. Available at www.research.by (downloaded 9 September 2010).
–––. "Kakaia energeticheskaia politika nuzhna Belarusi?" Nashe Mnenie website, 6 July 2005. Available at http://www.nmnby.org/pub/030705/energy.html (accessed 15 December 2008).
–––. "Reformy administrativnymi metodami." *Nashe Mnenie*, 14 March 2007. Available at http://www.nmnby.org/pub/0703/14m.html) (accessed 15 December 2008).
Rakova, E., I. Tochitskaia, and G. Shimnovich. "Rost tsen na gaz: novye vygody dlia belorusskoi ekonomiki," 2007. Available at www.research.by (downloaded 24 November 2007).
"Ravnenie na Belarus'." *Oil Market Weekly*, 9 September 2002 (via ISI).
"Regulatori Capture, abo zakhoplennia organu regulovannia grupami interesiv." Interview with Iuryi Kiashko. *Dzerkalo Tyzhnia*, no. 8/587, 4–10 March 2006.
Reisinger, William M. *Energy and the Soviet Bloc: Alliance Politics After Stalin*. Ithaca, NY: Cornell University Press, 1992.

Republic of Belarus. "Osnovy gosudarstvennoi politiki regional'nogo razvitiia do 2015." Cited in translation as "Grundsätzen zur staatlichen Raumplanungspolitik der Republik Belarus bis 2015." Cited in Jaŭhen Šyrokaŭ, "Mit dem Wind: Energiewirtschaft und nachhaltige Entwicklung." *Osteuropa* 54, no. 2 (2004): 84–95.

Republic of Belarus. Ministry of Statistics and Analysis. Available at http://belstat.gov.by/.

Republic of Lithuania. *Law on Energy* (1995). Available in English at http://www.litlex.lt/Litlex/Eng/Frames/Laws/Documents/376.HTM (accessed 1 August 2007).

Republic of Lithuania. *National Energy Independence Strategy of the Republic of Lithuania*. Vilnius: Ministry of Energy, 2012.

Reuters. "Lithuania's Prime Minister Quits over Oil Deal." 28 October 1999 (via ISA, accessed 15 March 2007).

Reznik, Irina. "Chelovek nedeli: Gennadyi Timchenko." *Vedomosti*, 28 June 2010.

———. "Rem Viakhirev vybiraet gazodollary." *Kommersant*, 6 October 2000.

RFE/RL Armenian service. Available at http://www.azatutyun.am/content/article/2005637.html.

RFE/RL Newsline, 21 September 1998.

Riley, Alan. "Corruption in Kiev and an E.U. Trade Pact," *The New York Times*, 4 October 2011. Available at http://www.nytimes.com/2011/10/05/opinion/05iht-edriley05.html?_r=1 (accessed 25 February 2013).

Rinkevičius, Leonardas. "Lithuania: Environmental Awareness and National Independence." In *Public Participation and Sustainable Development: Comparing European Experiences*, ed. A. Jamison and P. Ostby, Pesto Papers 1. Aalborg: Aalborg Universitetsforlag, 1997.

———. "Shaping of the Public Policy Culture in Lithuania: Sociological Exploration of Change in Environmental Policy and Public Participation." *Sociologija. Mintis ir Veiksmas*, no. 1 (2006): 113–27.

"Rivalry Runs High in Lithuanian Gas Business." *The Baltic Times*, 12 January 2000 (via ISI, accessed 21 March 2007).

Roberts, Andrew Lawrence. *Politics of Social Policy Reform in Eastern Europe*. Ph.D. dissertation, Princeton University, 2003.

Romanchuk, Iaroslav. "Degradatsiia monopolista. Kak 'Belneftekhim' tianet na dno belorusskuiu ekonomiku." 7 April 2002. Available at http://liberty-belarus.info/content/view/449/46/ (accessed 15 July 2008).

———. "God ubaiukivaiushchego rosta." *Belgazeta*, no. 1, 7 January 2008. Available at http://www.belgazeta.by/20080107.1/040040241.

———. In RFE/RL (Radio Svabody) Program for Belarus, *Ekspertiza Svobody* ("Tsana na gaz - geta tsana palitychnai liaial'nas'tsi"),

13 February 2008. Transcript available at http://www.svaboda.org/content/Transcript/977620.html (accessed 8 July 2008).

———. "Kormiaschie Belarusi." *Belgazeta*, no. 39/609, 1 October 2007. Available at http://www.belgazeta.by/20071001.39/040150241 (accessed 15 November 2007).

———. "MVF rasskryvaet sekret." *Belgazeta*, no. 17/497, 11 July 2005.

———. "Nado chashche vstrechat'sia: Putina i Lukashenko vnov potianulo drug k drugu." *Belorusskaia Gazeta*, 20 January 2003.

———. "Polozha ruku na esko." *Belgazeta*, no. 41, 15 October 2007. Available at http://www.belgazeta.by/20071015.41/040250241 (accessed 30 November 2007).

———. Quoted in Deutsche Welle Programme to Belarus, 26 December 2006. Available at www.dw-world.de (accessed 27 December 2006).

———. "V strane sluchilsia bum." *Belorusskaia Gazeta*, no. 8/486, 9 May 2005.

Romanova, Liudmila. "Budet' li Gazprom renatsionalizirovan?" *Nezavisimaia Gazeta*, 6 November 1999.

RosBiznesKonsulting. "Rossiia nachala postavki gaza v Moldaviiu po evropeiskim tsenam," 1 January 2011. Available at http://top.rbc.ru/economics/01/01/2011/523960.shtml (accessed 7 May 2011).

Ross, Michael L. *The Oil Curse: How Petroleum Wealth Shapes the Development of Nations*. Princeton, NJ: Princeton University Press, 2012.

———. *Timber Booms and Institutional Breakdown in Southeast Asia*. New York: Cambridge University Press, 2001. http://dx.doi.org/10.1017/CBO9780511510359.

Rossiia v tsifrakh 2008. Ofitsial'noe izdanie Federal'noi sluzhby gosuddarstvennoi statistiki. Moscow, 2008.

Russel, Jeremy. *The Energy Factor in Soviet Foreign Policy*. Lexington, MA: Saxon House/Lexington Books, 1976.

"Russia and the 2004 Presidential Elections." Global Security.org. Available at <http://www.globalsecurity.org/military/world/ukraine/election-2004-r.htm> (accessed 23 January 2007).

Russian Petroleum Investor, November 1996.

Rutland, Peter. "Russia as an Energy Superpower." *New Political Economy* 13, no. 2 (2008): 203–10. http://dx.doi.org/10.1080/13563460802018547.

Ryder, Andrew. "Economy." In *Eastern Europe, Russia and Central Asia 2004*, ed. Europa Publications. London: Routledge, 2003.

Sabonis-Chafee, Theresa. *Power Politics: National Energy Policies and the Nuclear Newly Independent States of Armenia, Lithuania and Ukraine*. Ph.D. dissertation, Political Science, Emory University, 1999.

Sagers, M.J. "Comments on the Flow and Taxation of Oil-Gas Export Revenues in Russia." *Eurasian Geography and Economics* 43, no. 8 (2002): 628–31. http://dx.doi.org/10.2747/1538-7216.43.8.628.

Sahm, Astrid, and Kirsten Westphal. "Power and the Yamal Pipeline." In *Independent Belarus: Domestic Determinants, Regional Dynamics and Implications for the West*, ed. Margarita M. Balmaceda, James Clem, and Lisbeth Tarlow, 270–301. Cambridge, MA: Ukrainian Research Institute and Davis Center for Russian Studies, Harvard University: Distributed by Harvard University Press, 2002.

Sanford, George. "Nation, State and Independence in Belarus." *Contemporary Politics* 3, no. 3 (1997): 225–45. http://dx.doi.org/10.1080/1356977970 8449928.

Sannikov, Andrei. "The Accidental Dictator," *SAIS Review*, January 25 (2005): 75–88.

Saprykyn, Volodymyr. Cited in Tetiana Yarmoshuk: "Naftohaz mozhe vlizty u borhy pered 'Gazpromom." *Radio Svoboda* (Ukrainian program), 19 February 2009. Available at www.radiosvoboda.org (accessed 19 February 2009).

———. Interview in Radio Svoboda Ukrainian service *"Priamyi Efir,"* 12 April 2005 17:00 UTC. Available at www.radiosvoboda.org/article/2005/04/69d7a9c5-6fdb-489e-9075-c4ed57a3c7bb9.html (accessed 14 April 2005).

———. "Restructuring Ukraine's Coal Industry: Key Problems and Priority Measures." *National Security and Defence*, no. 11 (2004): 2–9.

Savelev, Vitalii. Quoted in *RFE/RL* (Radio Svabody) program for Belarus ("Gazpram zaiavlae, shto, pastavliaiuchy gaz u Belarus, zaimaetsia dabrachynnasciu"), 14 September 2002. Transcript reprinted at http://www.ucpb.org/?lang=bel&open=206 (accessed 15 December 2002).

Savickas, Virgilijus. "Lithuanian Privatization Sets Coalition at Odds." *The Baltic Times*, 21 June 2001 (via ISI, accessed 20 March 2007).

Savka, Iurii. "Vzaiemozalik iak sposib zhyttia." *Enerhetychna Polityka Ukrainy*, no. 6 (2000): 30–34.

Sedelius, Thomas. *The Tug-of-War between Presidents and Prime Ministers. Semi-presidentialism in Central and Eastern Europe.* Orebro, Sweden: Orebro Studies in Political Science 15, 2006, Ph.D. dissertation.

Segura, Edilberto. "Energy: Current Problems and Long-term Strategy." In *The EU & Ukraine: Neighbours, Friends, Partners?* ed. Ann Lewis. London: Kogan Page, 2002.

"Seim Litvy kopaet pod shefa gosbezopasnosti." *Kommersant*. Available at http://www.kommersant.ru/doc.html?docId=727433 (accessed 14 March 2007).

Seimas of the Republic of Lithuania. Law on "The Basics of National Security of Lithuania." Passed on 19 December 1996. Available at

http://www3.lrs.lt/pls/inter3/dokpaieska.showdoc_e?p_id=39790&
p_query=&p_tr2= (accessed 1 August 2007).

———. "Nacionalinio saugumo ir gynybos komiteto atlikto, Valstybės saugumo departamento veiklos parlamentinio tyrimo, 2006 m. spalio 20 d.,
11 posėdžio stenogramos ištrauka." Parliamentary investigation on State
Security department's actions carried out by Committee for National Security and Defence material, extract from 11th session stenograph, 20 October
2006. Available at http://www.lrt.lt/news.php?strid=5082&id=3687465
(accessed 20 April 2007).

Sekhovich, Vadim. "'Belorusskaia promyshlennost': v novyi god s novymi
khvorami." Belorusskaia Delovaia Gazeta, 29 December 1997.

———. "1991–2006. Itogi. Gazovaia otrasl'," 30 October 2006. Available at
http://www.gazetaby.com/index.php?&sn_nid=3380&sn_cat=34 (accessed
15 August 2008).

Selivanova, Irina. "Ekonomicheskaia Integratsiia Rossii i Belorussii i ee vlianie
v razvitie narodnogo khoziaistva Belorusi." In Belorussiia i Rossiia: Obshestva
i Gosudarstva, ed. D.E. Furman. Moscow: Prava Cheloveka, 1998.

Shakhov, Aleksandr. "V Litve naschitali 30 tolstosumov." Biznes i Baltiia, 19
April 2005 (via ISI, accessed 3 March 2007).

Sheremetinskii, Oleg. "Obzor SMI Litvi za 31 iulia-6 avgusta 2006 goda." Citing Kauno diena. Available at www.regnum.ru/news/683836.html (via ISI,
accessed 15 March 2007).

Shiells , Clinton R. "Optimal Taxation of Energy Trade: The Case of Russia and
Ukraine." Available at http://www.etsg.org/ETSG2005/papers/shiells.pdf
(accessed 28 June 2006).

———. "VAT Design and Energy Trade: The Case of Russia and Ukraine."
IMF Staff Papers 52, no. 1 (2005): 103–19.

Shkoliarenko, Iurii. "Kartochnye igry s 'Gazpromom'." proUA, 20 March 2008.
Reprinted in FEC-MUP, March 20, 2008.

Shleifer, A., and R. Vishny. The Grabbing Hand: Government Pathologies and their
Cures. Cambridge, MA: Harvard University Press, 1998.

Siriprachai, Somboom. "Rent-Seeking Activities in Developing Countries: A
Survey of Recent Issues." Available at ftp://econ.tu.ac.th/class/archan/
SOMBOON/my%20discussion%20Papers.

Skripov, Vladimir. "Ivan idet." Ekspert Severo-Zapad, no. 7, 23 February 2004.

———. "Kupi rynok." Ekspert Severo-Zapad, no. 4, 2 February 2004 (via ISI,
accessed 15 March 2007).

Skripov, Vladimir, and Aleksei Grivach. "Litovskii gazovyi put'. 'Gazprom' i
Vilnius zhdut ustupok drug ot druga." Vremia Novostei, 8 August 2002.

Skripova, Zhanna. "Gazprom traditsii ne meniaet." *Biznes i Baltiia*, 23 August 2001 (via ISI, accessed 15 March 2007).

———. "Stranam Baltii smeniat postavshchika gaza." *Biznes i Baltiia*, 31 October 2001 (via ISI, accessed 15 March 2007).

———. "V Litve 'zachistili' detei Rema Viakhireva." *Biznes i Baltiia*, 3 December 2001 (via EVUD CISBP, accessed 15 March 2007).

Smith, Benjamin. *Hard Times in the Lands of Plenty: Oil Politics in Iran and Indonesia*. Ithaca, NY: Cornell University Press, 2007.

Smith, Keith. *Russia and European Energy Security: Divide and Dominate*. Washington, DC: CSIS, 2008.

Smith, Keith C. "Russian Energy Politics in the Baltics, Poland and Ukraine: A New Stealth Imperialism?" Washington, DC: CSIS Report, 2004.

Snyder, Richard. "Does Lootable Wealth Breed Disorder? A Political Economy of Extraction Framework." *Comparative Political Studies* 39, no. 8 (2006): 943–68. http://dx.doi.org/10.1177/0010414006288724.

Socor, Vladimir. "Belarus Warns It May Cancel Its Subsidies to Russia." *Eurasia Daily Monitor* 4, no. 17, 24 January 2007. Available at http://www.jamestown.org/edm/article.php?article_id=2371830 (accessed 13 July 2007).

Sokrat Research. *Belarus: Country Report 2008*. Available at http://investory.com.ua/community/diary/1208/sokrat_daily__december_11__2008/ (accessed 11 December 2008).

Sonin, Konstantin. "Why the Rich May Favor Poor Protection of Property Rights." William Davison Institute Working Papers Series (University of Michigan), no. 544 (December 2002). Available at http://deepblue.lib.umich.edu/bitstream/2027.42/39929/2/wp544.pdf (accessed 20 February 2013).

Sotsial'no-ekonomicheskoe polozhenie Rossii, nos. 1–7 (2008).

Sovet Bezopasnosti Respubliki Belarus'. "Postanovlenie Sovbeza No.1 'O razvitii atomnoi energetiki v Respublike Belarus'." 31 January 2008.

Stanisauskas, Gediminas. "In the Mud of Secret Interests." *Kauno Diena*, 18 September 2006. Translated by *BBC Monitoring Europe: Political*, 20 September 2006 (via ISI, accessed 15 March 2007).

"Starye pesni o glavnom." *Infobank Oil and Gas Monitor* (Lviv), 23 December 1999 (via ISI).

Statistical Review of World Energy, June 2010.

Stern, Jonathan P. Declarations at the "Commons Defence Select Committee Evidence Session on UK Relations with Russia." 17 March 2009. Available at http://www.epolitix.com/latestnews/article-detail/newsarticle/committee-briefing-uk-relations-with-russia/ (accessed 17 April 2009).

———. *The Future of Russian Gas*. Oxford: Oxford University Press, 2005.

———. "Natural Gas Security Problems in Europe: The Russian-Ukrainian Crisis of 2006." *Asia-Pacific Review* 13, no. 1 (2006): 32–59. http://dx.doi.org/10.1080/13439000600697522.

———. "The Russian Gas Balance to 2015: Difficult Years Ahead." In *Russian and CIS Gas Markets and Their Impact on Europe*, ed. S. Pirani. Oxford: Oxford University Press for the Oxford Institute of Energy Studies, 2009.

———. "Soviet and Russian Gas: The Origins and Evolution of Gazprom's Export Strategy." In *Gas to Europe: The Strategies of Four Major Suppliers*, ed. Robert Mabro and Ian Wybrew-Bond. Oxford: Oxford University Press/ Oxford Institute of Energy Studies, 1999.

Stern, Jonathan, Simon Pirani, and Katja Yafimava. *The April 2010 Russo-Ukrainian Gas Agreement and its Implications for Europe*. Working Paper NG42. Oxford: Oxford Institute for Energy Studies, 2010. Available at http://www.oxfordenergy.org/wpcms/wp-content/uploads/2011/05/NG_42.pdf (accessed 18 February 2013).

———. *The Russo-Ukrainian Gas Dispute of January 2009: A Comprehensive Assessment*. Working Paper NG42. Oxford: Oxford Institute for Energy Studies, 2009. Available at www.oxfordenergy.org/pdfs/NG27.pdf (accessed 1 June 2010).

Stevens, Paul. *Transit Troubles: Pipelines as a Source of Conflict*. London: Chatham House, 2009.

Stoma, Saulius. "Arbatėlė su išdaviku, arba kaip susigrąžinti Uspaskichą per tris dienas. Rašytojo komentaras, Žinių radijas." 17 November 2007. Available at www.delfi.lt. Translated by *BBC Monitoring*, 17 November 2007 (via ISI, accessed 15 March 2007).

Streimikiene, Dalia. "Lithuania." In *Energy Indicators for Sustainable Development: Country Studies on Brazil, Cuba, Lithuania, Mexico, Russian Federation, Slovakia and Thailand*, ed. IAEA/ UN DESA, 129–92, 2005. Available at http://www.un.org/esa/sustdev/publications/energy_indicators/index.htm (accessed 17 July 2007).

———. "Removing/Restructuring Energy Subsidies in Lithuania." Paper presented at the UN-ECE/OECD Workshop on Enhancing the Environment by Reforming Energy Prices, Průhonice, Czech Republic, June 2000. Available at http://www.env.cz/www/zamest.nsf/0/ddf10194ec514cc2c12568f00035398d?OpenDocument (accessed 13 July 2007).

Stulberg, Adam N. *Well-Oiled Diplomacy: Strategic Manipulation and Russia's Energy Statecraft in Eurasia*. Albany: State University of New York, 2007.

Sukhovenko, Stepan. "Oligarkhi Lukashenko ili na chom razrabativaiut samye bogatye liudi Belarusi?" 24 July 2004. Originally published in *Batke*.

net (accessed 24 June 2008), reprinted in http://forum.delta.by/viewtopic.
php?t=1925&highlight=&sid=2096e5d040eec864071491d651d24c9f
(accessed 15 January 2009).

Suzdaltsev, Andrei. Interview in DW-World, 1 January 2007, Transcript available at http://www.dw-world.org/dw/article/0,2144,2296562,00.html
(accessed 1 February 2007).

Szeptycki, Andrzej. "Oligarchic Groups and Ukrainian Foreign Policy." *Polish Quarterly of International Affairs* no. 2 (2008): 43–68.

Tabata, Shinichiro. "Observations on the Influence of High Oil Prices on Russia's GDP Growth." *EGE* 47, no. 1 (2006).

Tabata, S. "Russian Revenues from Oil and Gas Exports: Flow and Taxation." *Eurasian Geography and Economics* 43, no. 8 (2002): 610–27. http://dx.doi.org/10.2747/1538-7216.43.8.610.

"Table on Nuclear Share Figures. 1996–2007." *World Nuclear Association.* Available at http://www.world-nuclear.org/info/nshare.html (accessed 28 April 2009).

Taghiyev, Elgun A. "Measuring Presidential Power in Post-Soviet Countries." *CEU Political Science Journal* 3 (2006): 11–21.

Tarr, D.G., and P.D. Thomson. "The Merits of Dual Pricing of Russian Natural Gas." *World Economy* 27, no. 8 (2004): 1173–94. http://dx.doi.org/10.1111/j.1467-9701.2004.00651.x.

"Tekst uhody mizh 'Naftohazom' i 'Hazpromom,'" *Ukrains'ka Pravda,* 5 January 2006. Available at http://www.pravda.com.ua/articles/4b1a9a608c9b1/ (accessed 15 July 2009).

Titenkov, Ivan. "Lukashenko nuzhno proiti cherez nezavisimuiu komissiiu." *Belorusskii chas,* 25 May 2001. Available at http://www.charter97.org/bel/news/2001/05/25/16 (accessed 21 August 2008).

Tkachev, Sergei, and Vladimir Timoshpolskii. "Strategiia razvitiia natsional'noi energetiki." *Nauka i innovatsiia,* no. 11/57, (2007): 16–25. Available at http://innosfera.org/energy_strategy.

Tkaschenko, Jekaterina. Interview in *Deutschlandfunk,* 10 December 2008, 06:16. Available at http://www.dradio.de/aod/html/?broadcast=196841&page=3& (accessed 13 December 2008).

Todiichuk, Oleksandr. "Interview in Oil Market Weekly." *Nefterynok,* 30 October 2001 (via ISI).

———. Radio Svoboda program for Russia, *Itogi Nedeli,* 10 January 2009. Available at http://www.svobodanews.ru/Transcript/2009/01/10/20090110152009547.html (accessed 12 January 2009).

Tomashevskaia, Olga. "Legkaia pobeda." *Belorusskaia Delovaia Gazeta,* 13 November 2002.

Tompson, William. "Back to the Future: Thoughts on the Political Economy of Expanded State Ownership in Russia." *Le Cahiers Russie*, no. 6 (2008): 1–18.

Tracevskis, Rokas M. "From the Grybauskaite vs. Putin Match." *The Baltic Times*, 17 February 2010 (accessed 30 June 2010).

———. "Secret Agent's Death Is under Re-investigation." *The Baltic Times*, 13 January 2010 (accessed 30 June 2010).

Transparency International Corruption Perceptions Index 2004. Available at http://www.transparency.md/Docs/2004_indicele_perceperii_cor_en.pdf (accessed 15 May 2005).

Transparency International Corruption Perceptions Index 2006. Available at http://www.transparency.lt/new/images/tils_cpi_2006.pdf.

Transparency International Lietuvos Skyrius. "Lietuvos verslininkai bijo žiniasklaidos ir laiko ją neskaidria." 31 May 2007. Available at http://www.transparency.lt/new/index.php?option=com_content&task=view&id=10826&Itemid=24 (accessed 30 July 2007).

Treisman, Daniel. "Putin's Silovarchs." *Orbis* 51, no. 1 (2007): 141–53. http://dx.doi.org/10.1016/j.orbis.2006.10.013.

Trifonov, Vlad. "Delo Yulii Timoshenko otpravilos´ na dorabotku." *Kommersant*, 3 February 2005. Reprinted in FEC-MUP, 3 February 2005 (via ISI).

Tsarenko, Anna. "Overview of Gas Market in Ukraine." *Case Ukraine Working Paper* WP 2 (2007).

Tsentar Politichnai Adukatsii. "Sostoianie i obozrimye perspektivy belorussko-rossiiskikh otnoshenii." In *Zbornik analitichikh dakladau*, 56–72. Minsk: Tsentar Vydavetskikh Initsiatiu, 2007.

Tsokolenko, Sergei. "Gde nachinaetsia neft´, tam zakanchivaiutsia natsional'nye interesy?" *Zerkalo Nedeli*, no. 19/292, 13–19 March 2000.

Tsygankov, Andrei P. *Pathways after Empire: National Identity and Foreign Economic Policy in the Post-Soviet World*. Lanham, MD: Rowman and Littlefield, 2001.

Turchinov, Aleksandr. Declarations at press conference, 15 September 2005. Transcribed by the *Ukrains'ka Pravda* website. Available at http://www.pravda.com.ua/ru/news/2005/9/15/32610.htm (accessed 1 October 2005).

Tvaskiene, Jurga, and Stasys Gudavicius. "Kaunas Found Itself in Scope of Interest." Translated in "Lithuania Declassifies 400 Pages of State Security Materials." *BBC Monitoring Lithuania* (via ISI, accessed 21 May 2007).

Tyschuk, Oles'. "Treider-reider." *Infobank Oil and Gas Monitor*, 25 November 2006 (via ISI).

———. "Sovinaia bolezn'." *Zerkalo Nedeli*, no. 19/598, 20–26 May 2006. Available at www.zerkalo-nedeli.com/ie/show/598/53426/ (accessed 1 June 2006).

Tyshchuk, Oles', and Kost´ Bondarenko. "Geometriia ot Bakaia." *Gaz i neft´. Energeticheskii biulleten´*, 15 June 2001 (via ISI).

"Ukraine and Its Neighbors." Conference in Kennan Institute, Washington, DC, May 2000.

"Ukraine Cuts Gas Transit 19.1% in 2012." *Kyiv Post*, 18 January 2012. Available at http://www.kyivpost.com/content/business/ukraine-cuts-gas-transit-191-in-2012-319038.html (accessed 9 February 2013).

"Ukrainischer Anteil an Transitpipelines für russisches Erdgas." In *Russland Analysen*, no. 50.

"Ukrainskie deti Gazproma." *Korrespondent*, 6 May 2006. Reprinted in FEC-MUP, 10 May 2006 (via ISI).

United Nations Development Program. *2007/2008 Human Development Report.* Available at http://hdrstats.undp.org/countries/data_sheets/cty_ds_UKR.html (accessed 4 April 2009).

"Up to Our Ears in Democracy." *Verslo Zinios*, 22 March 2007. Translated in "Lithuanian Daily Says State Security Scandal 'Disgrace' for Country." *BBC Monitoring*, 22 March 2007 (via ISI, accessed 2 May 2007).

Urban, Aleksei, and Aleksei Nikolskii. "Bez pridannogo. Gotovit'sia Belarus' otdat' 'Beltransgas'." *Vedomosti*, 25 November 2002.

Ürge-Vorsatz, D., G. Miladinova, and L. Paizs. "Energy in Transition: From the Iron Curtain to the European Union." *Energy Policy* 34, no. 15 (2006): 2279–97. http://dx.doi.org/10.1016/j.enpol.2005.03.007.

U.S. Department of Energy, Energy Information Administration. Available at http://www.eia.doe.gov (accessed 15 July 2010).

Vahtra, P., K. Liuhto, and K. Lorenz. "Privatization of Re-nationalisation in Russia." *Journal of East-European Management Studies* 12, no. 4 (2007): 287–93.

Vaičiūnas, Žygimantas. "Towards Energy Independence." *Lithuania in the World* 16, no. 1 (2008).

Van Zon, Hans. "Political Culture and Neo-Patrimonialism under Kuchma." *Problems of Post-Communism* 52, no. 5 (2005): 12–22.

Vasiliauskas, Valdas. "New Politics Mark 2." Translated in "Lithuanian Commentary Sees Gazpron Interests Dividing the Country." *BBC Monitoring* (via ISI, accessed 15 March 2007).

———. "Slaptoji Rolando Pakso misija." *Ekstra*, 2 February 2004. Republished in Delfi.lt, 5 February 2004. Available at http://www.delfi.lt/archive/article.php?id=3663899 (accessed 17 June 2007).

———. "Trojan Gas." Commentary in Lithuanian Television, Vilnius, in Lithuanian 1013 gmt, 16 January 2006. Translated by *BBC Monitoring* (via ISI, accessed 15 March 2007).

Vernon, Raymond. *Sovereignty at Bay: The Multinational Spread of US Enterprises.* New York: Basic Books, 1971.

Verslo Zinios. 22 January 2007. Translated in "Lithuanian Daily Criticizes Seimas for Indecision on Natural Gas Act Amendment." *BBC Monitoring,* 22 January 2007 (via ISI, accessed 15 March 2007).

Vienna Institute of Comparative Economic Studies. *COMECON Data 1989.* New York: Greenwood Press, 1990.

Vilemas, Jurgis. "Renewables in Lithuania: Reasons for Slowness in the Past and Future Expectations." Presentation at the Conference "Renewable Energy: Development and Sustainability," Vilnius, 10 June 2008. Available at http://www.lsta.lt/files/seminarai/080610_radison%20SAS/5_Vilemas.ppt (accessed 27 April 2009).

Vlasov, Pëtr. "Bednye Liudi: Bor'ba za kontrol nad gazovym rynkom – vazhneishii element vnutripoliticheskoi zhizni Ukrainy." *Ekspert,* 31 May 1999.

Voitovich, Aleksander. In "Nakanune iadernogo vozrozhdeniia." Debate organized by the Belarusian Institute for Strategic Studies, Minsk, 29 February 2008. Materials published in Nasha Niva. Available at www.nn.by.

von Hirschhausen, Christian, and Hella Engerer. "Post-Soviet Gas Sector Restructuring in the CIS: A Political Economy Approach." *Energy Policy* 26, no. 15 (1998): 1113–23. http://dx.doi.org/10.1016/S0301-4215(98)00062-7.

von Hirschhausen, Christian, Berit Meinhart, and Ferdinand Pavel. "Transporting Russian Gas to Western Europe – A Simulation Analysis." *Energy Journal* 26, no. 2 (2005): 49–68. http://dx.doi.org/10.5547/ISSN0195-6574-EJ-Vol26-No2-3.

von Hirschausen, K., and I. Rumiantseva. "Economicheskie aspekty razvitiia atomnoi energetiki v Belarusi." In *Energetika Belarusi: puti razvitii,* ed. IPM, 85–122. Minsk: IPM, 2006.

von Hirschhausen, Christian, and V. Vincentz. "Energy Policy and Structural Reform." *Eastern European Economics* 38, no. 1 (2000): 51–70.

Vydrin, Dmytro. Interview in *Nezavisimaia Gazeta,* 16 November 2000.

———. Quoted in "Gazovyi kontsortsium. Otsenki ékspertov." *Gaz i neft'. Energeticheskii biulleten',* 16 July 2002 (via ISI).

Vysotskaia, Tat'iana, and Iurii Lukashin. "Mozhet, po krugu. Ukraina ofitsial'no podderzhala i revers, i avers 'Odesa-Brody.'" *Ekonomicheskie Izvestiia,* no. 26, 9 July 2004. Reprinted in FEC-MUP, 6 July 2004 (via ISI).

Warsaw Voice, 8 April 2001. Available at www.warsaw.voice/pl/v650/News12.html (accessed 25 April 2003).

Weinthal, Erika, and Pauline Jones Loung. "The Paradox of Energy Sector Reform." In *The State after Communism: Governance in the New Russia,* ed. Timothy Colton and Stephen Hanson, 225–60. Lanham: Rowman & Littlefield, 2006.

Wilson, Andrew. *Ukraine's Orange Revolution.* New Haven, CT: Yale University Press, 2005.

Wilson, David. *The Demand for Energy in the Soviet Union.* Totowa, NJ: Rowman and Allanheld, 1983.

Wintrobe, Ronald. "The Tinpot and the Totalitarian: An Economic Theory of Dictatorship." *American Political Science Review* 84, no. 3 (1990): 849–72. http://dx.doi.org/10.2307/1962769.

Wittkowsky, Andreas. *The Ukrainian Disease: Rent-seeking, the Debt Economy, and Chances to Harden Budget Constraints.* Berlin: German Development Institute, 2000.

World Bank. *Anticorruption in Transition: A Contribution to the Policy Debate.* Washington, DC: World Bank, 2000.

———. "Belarus: Addressing Challenges Facing the Energy Sector." June 2006. Available at www.siteresources.worldbank.org/BELARUSEXTN/Resources/BelarusEnergyReview_July2006-full.pdf.

———. "Belarus at a Glance." Available at http://devdata.worldbank.org/AAG/blr_aag.pdf (accessed 31 October 2008).

———. "Belarus Energy Sector 1995." *Report No. 12804-BY.* Available at http://www-wds.worldbank.org/external/default/WDSContentServer/WDSP/IB/1995/04/21/000009265_3961008003331/Rendered/INDEX/multi_page.txt (accessed 8 November 2008).

———. "Country Economic Memorandum on Belarus." *World Bank Report,* no. 32346-BY, May 2005. Available at http://siteresources.worldbank.org/INTBELARUS/Resources/CEM_Ex_Sum.doc.

———. "Lithuania Energy Sector Review." *Report 11867-LT.* Washington, DC: 1994.

———. "Paying Taxes 2008." Available at http://www.doingbusiness.org/documents/Paying_Taxes_2008.pdf.

———. "Ukraine: Challenges Facing the Gas Sector." September 2003. Available at www.siteresources.worldbank.org/INTECAREGTOPENENERGY/112205344408/20772948/ukrainegassector.pdf (accessed 2 June 2006).

———. *Ukrainian Economic Update,* December 2008.

World Development Index Online. Available at http://ddp-ext.worldbank.org/ext/DDPQQ/report.do?method=showReport (accessed 15 May 2008).

Yadukha, Viktor. "Bol'shoi gazovyi sekret." *Segodnia,* 20 November 2000.

Yafimava, Katja. *Post-Soviet Russian-Belarussian Relationships: The Role of Gas Transit Pipelines.* Stuttgart: Ibidem-Verlag, 2007.

Yakovlev, A. "The Evolution of Business – State Interaction in Russia: From State Capture to Business Capture?" *Europe-Asia Studies* 58, no. 7 (2006): 1033–56. http://dx.doi.org/10.1080/09668130600926256.

Yates, Douglas A. *The Rentier State in Africa: Oil Rent Dependency and Neocolonialism in the Republic of Gabon.* Trenton, Asmara: Africa World Press, 1996.

Yegorov, Yuri, and Franz Wirl. "Ukrainian Gas Transit Game." *ZfE Zeitschrift für Energiewirschaft* 33, no. 2 (2009): 147–55. http://dx.doi.org/10.1007/s12398-009-0017-x.

Yer'omenko, Alla. "Shalom Hazavat, slov'iany." *Dzerkalo Tyzhnia* No. 1/580, 14 January 2006.

Zagorskaia, Marina, Vadim Sekhovich, and Aleksandr Starikevich. *Belarus'. 1991–2006. Itogi.* Minsk: Avtorskii kollektiv, 2008.

Zaiko, Leonid. "Russia and Belarus: Between Wishing and Reality." *Russia in Global Affairs*, no. 1, January–March 2006. Available at http://eng.globalaffairs.ru/numbers/14/1003.html (accessed 4 December 2008).

Zaiko, Leonid, and Iaroslav Romanchuk. *Belarus' na razlome.* Belgorod, Russia: Belgorodskaia poligrafiia, 2008.

Zashev, Peter. "Russian Investments in Lithuania." Electronic Publications of the Pan-European Institute 10/2004, Turku School of Economics and Business Administration. Available at www.tukkk.fi/pei (accessed 30 March 2007).

Žeruolis, Darius, and Algimantas Jankauskas. "Understanding Politics in Lithuania." *Demstar Research Report 18, 2004.* Available at http://www.demstar.dk/papers/UnderstandingLithuania.pdf (accessed 7 February 2007).

Zhbanov, Sergei. "Bachili vochi, sho kupovaly." *Belgazeta*, no. 13/634, 31 March 2008. Available at http://www.belgazeta.by/20080331.13/020060671 (accessed 15 June 2008).

———. "Nazlo 'Gazpromu.'" *Belgazeta*, no. 39. 1 October 2007. Available at http://www.belgazeta.by/20071001.39/040120421/ (accessed 10 November 2007).

———. "S novym gazom." *Belorusskaia Gazeta*, no. 2/470, 17 January 2005.

———. "Zolotuiu aktsiiu spisali v util'." *Belgazeta*, no. 10/631, 10 March 2008. Available at http://www.belgazeta.by/20080310.10/010020421 (accessed 13 June 2008).

Zisk, Kimberly Marten. *Weapons, Culture and Self-Interest: Soviet Defense Managers in the New Russia.* New York: Columbia University Press, 1997.

Zlotnikov, Leonid. "Deutsche Welle program for Belarus." *Belorusskaia Khronika*, 17 December 2007. Available at http://www.dw-world.de (accessed 17 December 2008).

———. "Etapi Transformatsii Ekonomiki Belarusi: Problemy i dostizheniia." In *Predprinimatel'stvo. BSPN. Biznis-sreda*, ed. L. K. Zlotnikov, T. A. Bykova, G. P. Badei, and Zh. K.Bade. Minsk: BSPN, 2005.

———. "Igra v tseitnote." *Belorusy i Rynok*, no. 39/774, 15 October 2007.

———. In RFE/RL (Radio Svabody) program for Belarus *Ekzpertiza Svobody* ("Chi vyratue dyrektyva #3 belaruskuiu ekanomiku?"), June 18, 2007. Available at http://www.svaboda.org/content/Transcript/758987.html.

———. "Podtsepili 'gollandskuiu bolezn." *Beloruskii Rynok,* no. 17/652, 2 May 2005.

———. "Possibilities for the Development of a Private Economic Sector and a Middle Class as a Source of Political Change in Belarus." In *Independent Belarus: Domestic Determinants, Regional Dynamics and Implications for the West,* ed. Margarita M. Balmaceda, James I. Clem, and Lisbeth L. Tarlow, 22–61. Cambridge MA: HURI/Davis Center for Russian Studies, distributed by Harvard University Press, 2002.

———. "Vyzhivanie ili integratsiia?" *Pro et Contra,* Spring 1998.

———. "Zhestkaia posadka." *Belorusy i Rynok,* 17 November 2008.

Zygar', Mikhail, and Iurii Svirko. "Chlena semi sdali organam." *Kommersant,* 13 February 2004. Available at http://www.kommersant.ru/doc. aspx?fromsearch=02166f53-83e8-4205-b1c5-f31f6ccc266f&docsid=449515 (accessed 8 November 2008).

Index

Studies in Comparative Political Economy and Public Policy